rise

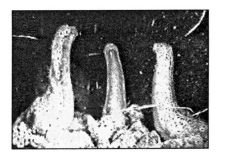

　　　浮 け 海 鼠 仏 法 流 布 の 世 な る ぞ よ 　 一 茶

The three spawning sea cucumbers are not the variety Japanese call *namako* that are haiku'ed in this book. The photo was found on the internet, in "Palau Country Map"→ "Sea Cucumber" and would seem to come from "Palau Paradise of the Pacific," apparently part of the Reader's Digest's *The Living Eden,* which seems to have been aired on PBS, but someone neglected to properly credit the photo. If you are the cameraman or cinematographer who took it, *please write me* and I will gladly give credit where it is due!

The cover photo of sea cucumber ossicles (details, skipped) is by Dr. Mike Reich, Center of Geosciences, University of Göttingen, Germany. (The original, like all of Mike's photos has exquisite grey tones I have ruined.)

"Surviving by eating the sand one lives upon is like realizing the dream of living in a gingerbread house. The sea slug,[1] by staying still and learning to live on so little, has turned this world into its paradise.[2] " – Motokawa Tatsuo [3]

---

1. *Sea Slug and Gingerbread* I chose to translate "slug," rather than "cucumber," for the sake of metaphorical accuracy and "gingerbread" over "sweets" for idiomatic affect.

2. *Stay Still Philosophy: Another Exemplar* The closest English language relation to the professor's sea slug, and to more metaphysical sea slugs we shall meet in haiku, is Richard Lovelace's *Snail,* likewise an exemplar of the *still-is-beautiful* philosophy: "but now I must (analyz'd king) / thy economic virtues sing; / thou great stay'd husband still within, / thou, thee, that's thine dost discipline . . . " and a creator of paradise on earth: ". . and when the trees grow nak'd and old, / thou clothest them with cloth of gold, / which from thy bowels thou dost spin, / and draw from the rich mines within."

3. *Motokawa Tatsuo* Tokyo Institute of Technology professor Motokawa Tatsuo, interviewed in the "Chi no Boken" (intellectual adventure) column of the *Nihon Keizai Shinbun* (Japan's equivalent of the *Wall Street Journal)* June 15, 1997.

浮け海鼠仏法流布の世なるぞよ　一茶

"Rise, Ye Sea Slugs!"

a theme from IN PRAISE OF OLDE HAIKU, with many more poems and fine elaboration

by

robin d. gill

道可道
非常道

paraverse press

paraverse press
publisher from this book on
key biscayne
florida for now (depending
on many things)
but easy to reach at
paraverse.org
©
2003
paraverse
press

we would be delighted
if the library of congress would catalog our books
but we have done our best and here is
the publisher's cataloging-in-publication (pcpd) data:

Rise, Ye Sea Slugs: a Theme from In Praise of Olde Haiku,
with Many More Poems and Fine Elaboration – compiled, translated
introduced and essayed by robin d. gill,
with the original japanese for all poems, bibliographical references and index.
p. cm
IPOOH
ISBN# 0-9742618-0-7 (pbk)

1. Haiku – Translation from Japanese into English
2. Natural History – Sea Cucumber – literature
3. Japanese Poetry – 17th – 21st c. – haiku, senryû, tanka, kyôka
4. English Poetry – Translations from Japanese and original
5. Literary Criticism – translation and interpretation
6. *Apostichopus japonicus* (*namako*)
7. Ethnology – Japanese
8. Metaphor in Poetry
9. Food – symbolism
10. Ambiguity
11. ___?

First edition (10-2003), printed by *Lightningsource* in the United States & United Kingdom.
If you order a copy from a bookstore, note it is distributed by *Ingram* or *Baker & Taylor*.
If you prefer ordering on-line, Amazon and B&N should have it listed by December, 2003.
If you would like to make a large order, visit paraverse.org for direct orders information.

<u>the translations in this book</u>

Unless otherwise noted, all translations are mine and done directly from the Japanese original. Almost all of the haiku have never before been translated into any language.   – r.d. gill

初英訳千句也.

海 鼠 海 鼠 汝 成 佛 し て 何 の ほ と け 醒 雪

namako namako nanji jôbutsu shite nan no hotoke – seisetsu[1] (1871-1917)
(sea cucumber (x2), thou become-buddha[die]-do, what corpse/buddha/saved?)

sea-slug, sea-slug,
what kind of buddha
will you turn into?

trans. r.h. blyth [2]

1. *Japanese Names* Haiku poets have traditionally used a single name comprised of two Chinese characters. Seisetsu, for example, is "sober" + "snow," and the more famous Issa, whose poem supplied the title, is "one" + "tea." In the mid-twentieth century, most poets began to use their full name. In this book, all Japanese names will be given in their correct order, family first, given or pen name next. For pre-modern poets, only the pen name will be given.
2. *Translation R.H. Blyth* Blyth may have begun the tradition of translating *holothurian* as "sea-slug" rather than "sea cucumber." I have centered his translation and uncapitalized the first words of each line because Japanese neither capitalize nor break the haiku into lines (they are almost always a single unparsed line in print, though haiku in ink paintings are often broken into two or three lines). I also add a word-for-word translation, a sort of gloss, under the Romanized Japanese. The reason for this apparent weirdness is explained in the Foreword, and a Key is provided in the Appendix.

目次 TABLE OF CONTENTS

<u>preface</u>

holothurian culture in japan – by namako hakase   11

<u>foreword</u>

I   why sea slug?   15   II   which sea slug?   21   III   what is haiku?   30
IV   how translation?   31   V   when verbatim?   33   VI   *apologia*   35

<u>text</u>

the _____ sea slug   36

ch. 1   the frozen together (solid, collective, reified, dead/alive)   39
ch. 2   the featureless (neither head nor tail, fin nor scale, lots of nots)   49
ch 3   the protean (shrinking/stretching, form-fitting/losing, self-eviscerating)   65
ch. 4   the do-nothing (ancient, still-to-be, unmoving, taoist)   79
ch 5   the agnostic (un/patriotic, rational, moderate, confucian)   97
ch 6   the mystic (true-believer, or zen buddhist)   103
ch 7   the scatological (ikkyû's fundamental)   113
ch 8   the helpless (trusting, drifting, easy-going, fatalist)   121
ch 9   the meek (shy, weak, victimized, body-armoring, hiding)   131
ch 10   the ugly (disgustingly odd, embarrassing, yet homely and blessed, gross)   155
ch 11   the lubricious (shell-loving, sexy yet impotent, squirting)   167
ch 12   the just-so (the silenced, dewy, rock, whale poop, star and wave-born)   189
ch 13   the tasty (gourmet, novelty, ozone and moon-scented, trans-substantialist)   201
ch 14   the slippery (slimy, hard to pinch and hard to pin down)   213
ch 15   the chewy (hard, grounded yet transporting, self-reflective, cathartic)   223
ch 16   the drinking (manly, solitary, gut-slurping and drunken)   237
ch 17   the silent (close-mouthed, macho, up-tight, precious)   247
ch 18   the melancholy (dark and heavy, *nimia solitudo*)   257
ch 19   the stuporous (sleepy, mumbling, snoring)   275
ch 20   the nebulous (overcast, placid)   287
ch 21   the cold (and deep)   297

<u>sundry sea slugs:</u>   313 (then, find the following, in order!) the poem-bag, laughing, molten, seducing, dragon-palace, cobbler, flying, playing, monster, exorcist, catfish, spam, burped, kept, stone, meaningless, dream, witch's tit, canary, sewage engineer, sick, "it", omniscient, A.I. porno, Japanese porno, moral, non/cartesian, assertive, seeing, getting and giving, new world, place-name, ridiculous prose, *memento mori*, tanzanian-chinese, english haiku, toefl, cotton-gut, parade, ridiculous poetic, bislamic, renku'ed, beloved, r/lace-lover's, urban myth, mistaken, medicinal 1, med. 2, bitten bottle, double-cold, chinese cuisine, chinese poetry, gigged, boats, measured, seasonal, spring, hokkaido, christian, ancestral, don, charmed, imagist wall, panoramic, bethlehemite, run-down, ole-boy, new year's, analyzed, unchewed, female, objective, avant-garde, nightmare, imaginary, known revelation, unknown revelation, reciped, global, unsolved, exploding, waiting, wondrous.

<u>maxim for sea slugs:</u> a *haibun* by shikô   440
<u>postscript</u>: the serendipitous sea slug   443
<u>key:</u> to pronouncing romanization   445, & comprehending verbatim gloss   446;
<u>acknowledgement</u> 448, *fie! fie!* 450; bibliography: **annot. bib.** 451; 日本人読者へ 455, 海鼠句募集 456, 欄外注情報 457, 正誤表情報 459, index source acronyms/ abbrev. 460, by **poem** (alphabet.) 464, by **poet** 472; too much monkey business 475, **blurbs** 478

ローマ字化ＡＢＣ順 全句引、全俳人引は、書末にある。本文には、和文のまま。

blab
from the
author/publisher
to the reader

This book is my first
to be published in english and
my first as a publisher. I apologize for
major faults in the *design* of the early chapters
and imperfections in the *structure* of the whole!
Thanks to the impenetrable opacity of ms-word,
this author-editor was robbed of so much time
better spent on the *aesthetics* and *content*
that he was forced to compromise on both.
As the proofing proceeded from chapter
to chapter, i/he learned to overcome *some*
of the software's *unforgivable shortcomings*
(which are listed on the paraverse.org website,
for we who write need to do something about
software that ignores the needs of creators);
but, i fear, some irregularities remain,
both because time has run out and because,
in some cases, i am not sure *what* looks best.
Suggestions regarding the design are welcome
and will be taken into consideration
in preparing the 2nd edition

paraverse press
was founded in 2003
to foster creativity in nonfiction,
writing, entirely free from world-making,
that *ought to* be far more interesting than fiction,
which is constrained by the need to be "convincing."
Yet, *truly* creative, i.e., literary, nonfiction is hard to find.
Almost everything that calls itself such today is mere journalism.
No flair for fancy words or clever plotting can belie this deplorable fact.
The publisher and author of the lead-off title for paraverse press, robin d. gill,
as might be expected of one who spent his entire adult life writing in Japanese alone,
is by no means an accomplished writer of English. Most journalists and novelists can write circles
around him. If his books, nevertheless, entertain bright people (see the blurbs), it is only
because he plays with something such readers value above all else: ***ideas.***

With the software available today, our publishers should be
offering us far more diverse, multilingual books;
but that potential is far from fulfilled,

This book includes almost a thousand Japanese haiku *in the original,* yet is inexpensively priced.
With your support, I hope it will be only the first of many. As they say in Japan,

よろしくお願いします

You are cordially invited to visit ***www.paraverse.org*** to participate, or just to find out more.

preface
by
Namako Hakase[1]

holothurian culture in japan

Visiting the West, one is struck by the absence of the sea cucumber. It is not that the *holothurian*[2] itself is absent. With 1,400 odd species[3] found around the globe, sea cucumbers are cosmopolitan. (ed. note: The popular and poetically necessary term "sea slug," used in this book, is misleading, for the scientist and skin-diver's "sea slug" is the *nudibranch*,[4] a shell-less mollusk with colorful tentacle-like projections on its back.). Nor is there a lack of scientific interest in this plain-looking relative of the sea urchin and starfish. The sea cucumber's unique physiology – how it quickly hardens or softens itself, how it throws away organs and later re-grows them, how it survives without a brain – fascinates Occidental researchers, as it does ours, in Japan. Its various medicinal uses are achieving worldwide attention and, with some species endangered from over-fishing and poaching, non-Japanese marine biologists, ecologists and diving enthusiasts are doing much to help publicize and protect and grow this creeping vacuum-cleaner so vital to the health of the sea floor. No, what is missing outside of Japan is not information nor concern for the sea cucumber, it is something more subtle, something we Japanese take for granted: the traditional sea cucumber, the *holothurian* as culture.

In Japan, one never knows when or where one is going to run into a sea cucumber (*namako*). There is, of course, our culinary culture, boasting various *namako* delicacies; but the *namako* provides us with far more food for our head than for our belly. *Holothurians* pop up in science fiction under guises such as the "sea-cucumber starman" (*namako-hoseijin*), in pop music songs such as the recent "sea cucumber who slept-in" (*neboke-namako*), in midi files (short animation) where they dance, snore and otherwise show off, in web-page names such as "sea cucumber soliloquy" (*namako-no-hitorigoto,* an exceptionally boring diary) or "sea cucumber shrine" (*namako-jingu,* a fortune-teller's web-page), in the martial arts as the "sea cucumber sword-guard" (*namako-tsuba*) of Miyamoto Musashi or simply the "sea cucumber" (*namako*) once used to restrain criminals (ed. note: It is vernacular for the *sodegarami,* or "sleeve-grabber."), in the marital arts as the "sea cucumber ring"(*namako-wa*), a tickler, in architecture as raised grout "sea cucumber walls" (*namako-kabe),* "sea cucumber roof tiles" (*namakogawara*),"sea cucumber (corrugated) iron sheet" (*namako-ita*) and swollen rounded "sea cucumber (door) frames"(*namakobuchi*), in foundries as "sea cucumber (pig) iron" (*namakosen*), in dress as bumpy "sea cucumber weave" (*namako ori*) and stylish sea cucumber tie-dye (*namako shibori*), in pottery as the complex purplish-gray sea cucumber glaze (*namakogusuri*) for expensive "sea cucumber hand-warming-pots" (*namako-hibachi*) or "sea cucumber-handled [pots]" (*namakode*), in folk events, such as occasional reenactments of ancient tribute-bearing delegations or the annual "sea cucumber drag" (*namako-hiki*), where a sea cucumber doll is dragged around by children on the day the Big New Year gods are sent off,[5] or even as a mascot for a low entropy-creating ecological lifestyle. (ed. note: To get a gut-feeling of why this book uses the scientifically incorrect "slug," compare the sound of "sea *slug* starman," "the sea *slug* who slept in," or "sea *slug* soliloquy" with the cacophonous "cucumber" versions of the same, above!)

The high level of holothurian consciousness in Japan is further reflected in the quality and quantity of the poems translated in this book and in the contemporary publishing world, where mass-market paperbacks largely or wholly about sea cucumbers boasting titles that translate as *The Sea Cucumber's Eye, The Sea Cucumber and the Sea Urchin, The Dolphin, Sea Cucumber and Sea People,* and *Sea Cucumber Reader* are not only printed but reprinted, this in marked contrast to the situation in the English language world, where the only "books" on our subject are pamphlets about fishery issues (the exception is a novel named for, but not primarily about *namako* – by a Japanese-American – and a book of poetry called *The Sea Cucumber,* but containing only a single line about them!).[6] If we add Japanese books new and old which use a trait of the *namako* as an allegory but do not concern the sea cucumber itself, such as the early twentieth century *Droll Haiku: The Sea Cucumber's Tongue,* mid-twentieth century science essay *The Sea Cucumber's Bones,* and a popular author's recent best seller *The Sea Cucumber Watching the Moon*, the gap is even more obvious.

Perhaps, the difference in the degree of familiarity of the *namako* in our respective cultures is best summed up by the fact that in the English-speaking world and, doubtless, the rest of the West, the sea cucumber is often described as "looking like a cucumber," whereas, in Japan, to the contrary, the *kiuri,* or cucumber, has been described as "a warty thing like a *namako.* Some of the stunted ones are the spitting image of it."[7] Were it not for the fact that our *kiuri* (cucumber) are generally far too sleek and elongated to resemble said holothurian, the vegetable would probably be called a "land *namako*!"

The first appearance the *namako* makes in our culture was by no means a felicitous one.[8] In the *Kojiki,* or *Records of Ancient Matters* (712 AD), when the gods round up all the fish, fat and thin and ask them if they are ready to serve the children of the gods, that is to say, the Japanese, only the *Namako* remained mum. Amanouzume-no-mikoto – the same goddess with the presence of mind to powder her face and do the world's first striptease to make all the gods laugh and entice the sun goddess Amaterasu-Ômikami out of the cave – angrily pulled out her dagger and saying, "so that mouth of yours renders no reply," rendered *Namako*'s mouth. (One must look at a live sea cucumber's mouth to fully appreciate the punishment: there are no lips, no tongue, only what appears to be a horribly lacerated orifice[9]). Just so, the *Record* concludes, "it remains cut out and the *namako* is silent."[10]

Thus chastened, for almost a millennium the Japanese sea cucumber held its silence.[11] You cannot find any mention of it in old poetic forms such as *waka* or *renga.* It took the emergence of the *hokku* (the first verse in traditional linked-verse) as an independent short poem, that is to say, the development of what we now call "haiku," to finally give the *namako* back its voice. With the publication of this book by the American writer and translator Robin D. Gill, *a.k.a.* "keigu," [12] the Japanese sea cucumber will make itself heard around the world. And, translated back into Japanese, which it surely will be, a new generation of readers will, many for the first time, hear the voice of the traditional sea cucumber, the *namako* of old Edo's poets, a confused and melancholy but always witty character, who sometimes has great trouble making himself heard over the electronic din of today's popular culture.

0. *A Note on Notes* These are the first and last notes in this book to be placed at the end of a chapter. I believe notes worth reading should, as far as possible, be *on the same page as the text*, even if it is harder to edit and, according to publishers, harder to sell such a book because notes are (wrongly) assumed to be boring. Readers and reviewers who share my dislike for having to search for end-notes and appreciate what Paraverse Press is doing are encouraged to speak up!
1. *Namako Hakase* Professor, or, Doctor Sea Slug, is my invention.
2. *Holothurian?* This word is the vernacularization of the scientific genus term *Holothuroidea* and, as such, is *not* properly italicized. I do so once or twice because most readers, like me until recently, will encounter it for the first time. Likewise for *nudibranch!*

3. *Holothurian Numbers* Books published in the early 1960's claim there are about 500 species. By the 1990's, the figure had climbed over 1,000. Today, over 1400 living species have been described, and this, according to Alexander Kerr, "is probably a great underestimate, since from our ongoing work, we have found dozens of large (and colorful) cukes on coral reefs that are undescribed and many more that have been unfairly lumped under the name of others. This lumping is partly due to the fact that sea cukes, especially tropical forms, were mostly described from preserved material. Preserved cukes often look alike, yellowed blobs of collagen, and so taxonomists relied instead on the often fantastic shape of the microscopic ossicles in their tissues. Unfortunately, ossicles are not always enough to differentiate species." (corres.)

4. *"Nudibranch" and "Holothurian," or a Note on Nomenclature* Although scientific terminology (in the broad sense, for I include its vernacularization) is intended to avoid confusion by standardization, in the English-speaking world, it is itself partly responsible for popular confusion about what is what, for laymen are generally ignorant of the meaning of the Greek and Latin roots. The word "holothurian" is so opaque that only a classics scholar would stand the slightest chance of guessing what it meant. In Japan, even scientists call the *namako* (etymology given later in the text) simply *namako* and the *nudibranch* ("bare-lungs"), or sea slug proper – as opposed to the sea slug improper, the sea cucumber – "sea-cow" (*umi-ushi*), so anyone can grasp its scientific identification, to wit, a "soft-body+move-thing(animal)-class," as it is much more transparent than our *mollusca,* which only conjures up the image of a shell, unless we happen to remember the root *moll* (as in the novel *Moll Flanders*) means something soft. This is not to say difficult terms are always bad. We enjoy not knowing and knowing we know when others do not. Here are some lines from Kingsley's *Water Babies* that illustrate what we might call *delightful opacity* using none other than *our* new word that I, at least, did not know before writing this essay:

> He [the know-it-all professor] felt the net very heavy; and lifted it out quickly, with Tom all entangled in the meshes.
> *"Dear me!"* he cried. *"What a large pink Holothurian; with hands, too! It must be connected with Synapta."*
> And he took him out.
> *"It has actually eyes!"* he cried. *"Why, it must be a Cephalopod! This is most extraordinary!"*
> *"No, I ain't!"* cried Tom, as loud as he could; for he did not like to be called bad names.
> *"It is a water-baby!"* cried Ellie; and, of course, it was.

Note the capitalization of the two vernacularized terms. Kingsley would seem to do it in lieu of italics. Neither are proper, but laymen are reassured by them, for we don't like to see unknown words appear as if we knew them. The professor's pink holothurian may not be a purple cow, for I googled my way to a report by a Japanese back from an inspection of a nuclear power plant a hundred kilometers from a place in China that translates as "Blue Island," in which he mentions eating small pink sea cucumbers and shows a photo of them in a plastic bucket. Of course, he may be wrong about their identity. (As regards to the identity of the landmark, OM writes, "Blue Island, of course, is Tsindao as in beer.")

5. *Big and Small New Years?* In Japan, there are many New Years. The Big New Year begins on the first and ends on the 14th or 15th, when the Little New Year, also called the Woman's New Year, begins. In the past, when the year began in early spring and the calendar included the moon as well as the sun, the Small New Year fell on the full moon. Old-fashioned farmers still think this New Year the more portentous of the two. Sea-cucumber dragging (*namakohiki*) will be explained later in the text.

6. *Namako Books* See the annotated bibliography. Although the *Sea Cucumber Handbook* (*namako dokuhon*) has several dozen haiku in it, most are modern and none are explained. RISE is the first book to collect and examine the metaphorical sea cucumber of the port. Namako Hakase does not mention the largest book written entirely about the *namako,* the 191 pg *Japanese Sea Cucumber* by V.S. Levin (Arakawa's *Handbook* is 120 pgs, and Tsurumi's *The Sea Cucumber's Eye* (NNM), though almost 700 pages, largely concerns the history of the trepang trade and its participants rather than the Japanese sea cucumber), published in Russian by the USSR Academy of Sciences (Far East Center. Institute of Marine Biology, Science Council for Biosphere Problems, Vladivostok: 1982). I have not seen this book, but Vladivostok holothurian specialist Igor Dolmatov assures me it has no haiku. A book on nearby nations by Japan's top author of books on Chinese culture, Nakano Miyoko (『辺境の風景』) includes a chapter *"Destroyers and Namako: New Vladivostok Tale."*

7. *Cucumber Metaphor* The cucumber described as *namako*-like is cited from the Kyoshi-edited Sanseido *Shinsaijiki*'s (new haiku theme almanac) July themes. Kyoshi is the father of modern haiku. Needless to say, there were more poems about *sea* cucumbers than *land* cucumbers in the world of haiku when he wrote. I say "were" because, today, *land* cucumbers are so popular I suspect that is no longer the case. A nice point lies hidden between Namako Hakase's lines: *to be a metaphor is to be familiar.* A line from a Japanese childhood memory found floating on the internet, "The drowned rat resembled a *namako*," does not tell us much about the rat (we can imagine its body without the help of metaphor!) sunken in the neighborhood stream, but it tells us a lot about the holothurian's primary position in Japan.

8. *First Appearance* There are at least a half dozen records of cured *namako* on 8th century tribute tablets dating back to close to the *Kojiki.* This suggests that ancient Japanese nobility already ate – or offered to the gods – a lot of *namako,* so they had good reason to find it did something wrong to justify its sacrifice. Some Japanese offer a less kind interpretation. One internet page, taking issue with the *namako's* alleged crime, noted that the

Kojiki was made with Imperial approval, and after exclaiming "what a self-centered hypocritical Yamato Court!" (. . .*yamato chôtei-mo katte-na mono-de aru*), prayed for the wronged *namako* to rest in peace! Another internet page makes far more serious charges, namely, the drowning of the god of Ise, Sarutahiko (monkey-man, once a proboscis fishing-monkey?) held under by a huge shellfish when he was on the sea bottom trying to convince the sea slug to cooperate and the fury of his bossy goddess wife, Uzume (same as above) who pulverized the shell (*just so*, it is no longer found near Japan) and took away the sea slug's potential to speak (in the manner described in the text) is an allegory for a far more horrific cultural tragedy of conquerors and conquered, disguised as an innocuous creation-story. Personally, I find the standard just-so story taken at face-value interesting enough, for it shows a culture stereotypically depicted as doing things "with" or "following" nature, possessing gods (serving the emperor and the people) who request other animals to obey them. Well, at least, the Japanese Gods *ask.* Or, *do they?* If the *namako* was punished for remaining mum, one can't help wondering about the unwritten fate of animals that actually might have replied "No way!"

9. *Lacerated Mouth* The original Japanese is ambiguous on the *what* and *why* of the dagger's cut. All expert commentary I've seen suggests a punishing laceration, as reflected by the ugliness of the shrunken up tentacles lining it. It is not always interpreted in that way. A web site offering fishing stories by the captain of the Shionagi-maru (operating out of Hamanako) naively explains that when the goddess looked "she couldn't see a mouth, so she pulled out her dagger and gave it a mouth by cutting one straight line (*hitosuji no kireme no irekuchi o tsukutte yatta*). That talk is in the *Kojiki*." In other words, some Japanese who have not read the *Kojiki* closely assume it was a kind cut! (Don't ridicule the captain, I have read the same elsewhere.)

10. *A Millennium of Silence?* A reader objected that a millennium was far too short, for the event took place centuries before Jimu Tenô, the first unified Emperor of Yamato (Japan) who, as every school boy or girl learns, began to reign in 660 BC. Like Christian calculations of Old Testament lives and reigns, Japanese dynasties are generally inflated. The 660 BC figure found googling was always from official (?) sites, while the thinking sites vary, depending on the average length of the reign used for calculating. None of the latter give BC figures. The earliest is 80 AD and the latest 379 AD, with the average between 200 and 300 AD. I don't know where that puts the heinous laceration of *namako's* mouth, but why not call it Point 0?

11. *Silent Sea Slug* Remarkably, a similar Dark Ages of the sea cucumber occurred in the West. Aristotle and others described some varieties, but "after the time of Pliny there is no mention of holothurians until the end of the Middle Ages. Only in the mid-16th century [when they appear in haiku!] are they again mentioned as scientific inquiry develops." (A. Kerr, corres.)

12. *Keigu is Me* "Keigu" is the most common term for closing letters and translates word for word as "respect[ful]-tool." I substitute another *gu,* "fool," for "tool," and hope to be known as one who respects foolishness, or *"Your Respectful Fool."*

The two characters 敬具 become 敬愚!

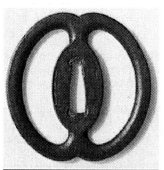

this is the *namako* sword guard
of the great swordsman, artist,
strategist and moralist,
miyamoto musashi
(died 1645)

foreword

ut palata, sic judicia

The foreword has five sections. Readers may read or ignore any of them according to their interests and intellectual capacity. Please bear in mind the fact that the details which bore you may well be a treat for someone else and vice versa.

I

why "sea slug?"

俳 諧 の 上 手 を 志 す 海 鼠　　 未 知
haikai no jôzu o kokorozasu namako – loser [1] (1995)
(*haikai's* skillful/better[obj] aspire/s sea cucumber/s[subj])

#2

sea slugs:
for the betterment
of *haikai*

My twenty-book selection of Edo era poetry, *In Praise of Olde Haiku*, [2] has only two hundred themes. The *namako*, or "sea slug" – patience, biologists, an explanation for the wrong name is in the next paragraph! – is one of them, despite the fact that it barely makes the top five-hundred themes included in Japanese *saijiki, or* haiku almanacs.[3] Why, then, include it? And why expand it further in this spin-off? Because sea slug offers a unique challenge. *Namako* is not only a winter theme. It is a three-dimensional litmus test. To some poets it is food. To some it is a grotesque creature. To others it is chaos embodied. Unlike most of the main haiku themes, the sea slug is freshly invented, for it did not grace classical Japanese poetry. This may owe something to its low cultural visibility over the *waka*-writing centuries (900-1500), something that changed in the Tokugawa era (1603-1867) when the dried slug (*trepang*) became the mainstay of Japan's trade with China.[1→] But the general consensus is that this "mere blob of fleshy matter" (Blyth: Hv4)) did not appeal to the *haute culture* of the *waka* and *renga* poets because it was, in a word, *gross*. For the same reason, it offered *haikai* poets (who

1. *Loser* This haiku was one of "640 *hahdo ejji no rakusen haiku* 1995-2001" which is to say, one of 640 haiku that failed to make the *Hard Edge* magazine (?) cut between the years of 1995-2001. I do not know anything more about the medium, the poem, or its author, but I suspect the editor thought the poet denigrated himself as a *namako* (this sea slug / only seeks to improve / at *haikai*), whereas I think it a *meta-haiku* (a haiku about haiku), where the poet read many namako poems and was impressed enough to pen this recognition of the sea slug's contribution toward developing haiku.. The rare use of *haikai* – poets today do not think of themselves as doing *haikai* – rather than "haiku," supports my reading.

2. *In Praise Of Olde Haiku* Check the progress of the IPOOH project at my site, paraverse.org). My selection and comments are designed to bring out the largely neglected wit in the dense multi-layered haiku of the Edo era, something that becomes possible only by digging up and sorting out the lines of development of poetic trope for each theme.
3. *Saijiki* Most major publishers have haiku almanacs called *saijiki,* which list tens of thousands of themes, called "season-terms" (*kigo*), each of which is followed by a paragraph of definition and a selection of haiku (anywhere from one to thirty or so) in chronological order. Readers unfamiliar with *saijiki* are advised to do an internet search., for much is now available in English.

wrote what came to be called haiku as well as poems that were far too risque for the current canon) a good chance to prove how different they were, to show off their a-lyrical stuff. Finally, it offers *me* a chance to prove to readers not fluent in Japanese, that even a subject this foreign to their literary tradition – "the winter *kigo* [seasonal word/theme] 'sea slugs' does not resonate for us," writes one American haiku association [2] – may be interesting.

In this book, the holothurian is not a cuke as science would have it, but a slug. Exacting readers may find me like Humpty Dumpty, who smugly informed Alice that when he used a word, it meant what *he* meant it to mean. Unlike Humpty, I am happy to explain. The word "sea slug" is both good and bad for our subject. It is *good* because "slug" suggests something *sluggish*, which the holothurian certainly is. It may lack those tremulous "horns" with eyes on them and lack the proper descent from a soft-bodied animal, but it is clearly even more sluggish (slow) than most scientifically correct slugs (mollusks), land or sea.[3] It is *bad,* however, because it drives true sea slugologists – and other nudibranch lovers – completely bananas.[4] This is because, with sea cucumber/slug confusion already endemic, they are already on edge. (How would *you* like to waste half your time responding to inquiries about the wrong animal on *your* web site? [↪])

#3 下

←**1. Namako's Changing Fortunes** If I read the painstakingly researched yet boldly speculative Tsurumi Yoshiyuki's *Namako no Manako* correctly, dried sea slug was one of a select number of tribute items, or offerings, traditionally sent to the Imperial family and Shrines but, by the ninth or tenth century, it lost this honored position, partly because Japanese Buddhist sensitivities preferred vegetable offerings and partly because the migrant sea-folk who harvested the slug lost their close relationship with the Court. He notes that abalone, which was harvested from the side of sea-rocks (boulders are connected with mountains and have a noble character) by women with sacred (Shinto) affiliation – whose boats had implements proving them part of the Imperial Navy – continued to remain in favor, where *namako*, living on the sand (literally "low-down") and harvested by marginal males may have had an image problem. Someone should do a doctorate about these two tribute items!
2. Haiku Association I quote from the minutes (2001 May 27) of the North Georgia Haiku Association, publisher of the delightful internet magazine *"Pinecone."* The previous sentence: "The group discussed the impossibility of always using traditional Japanese *kigo* in American poetry"
3. Sea Slug Moves Some nudibranches are as slow as their name suggests. Most, however, get around. They "crawl about the fronds of algae, swim, foot upward, with a gentle and undulating motion, or, when caught between tides, may be seen clinging to the under surface of rocks." (Augusta Foote Arnold: *The Sea-beach at Ebb-tide*) On the other hand, the fastest move our holothurian can make is to change shape. Our *Stichopus japonicus* can occasionally use this ability to move in caterpillar-like waves, but it averages only about 100-200 cm per hour.
4. Sea Slug on Sea Cuke An Ambrose Bierce-like dictionary googled off the web defines the *umiushi*

(lit. "seacow" = sea slug proper) as follows: *SEA SLUG: A mollusc [soft-body-animal] that never approaches a holothurian for fear of being confused for a sea cucumber and eaten by man.* (lr) So the sea slug itself seconds the scientist's concern. The nudibranch's real defense is that it does not taste good. From the West, we have the testimony of Steinbeck who witnessed an impromptu tasting by Ed Ricketts: "Once in a tide pool we were discussing the interesting fact that nudibranchs, although beautiful and brightly colored and tasty-looking and soft and unweaponed, are never eaten by other animals which should have found them irresistible. He reached under water and picked up a lovely orange-colored nudibranch and put it in his mouth. And instantly he made a horrible face and spat and retched, but had found out why fishes let these living titbits completely alone." (LSC) From the East, we have the word of none other than the Shôwa Emperor (Hirohito's posthumous title), a serious marine biologist, who, shortly after World War II, had his cook prepare an *umiushi*, saying "if we can eat sea cucumber, why not sea slug?" Although the Emperor was a consummate diplomat – an unkind historian calls him disingenuous – who rarely admitted to disliking *anything,* when asked, he was said to rub his head and say "to tell the truth, it was pretty bad." Apparently, the sea-hare (techibranch), (closer to the nudibranch than holothurian) is eatable if one knows how to prepare it, as some French, Italians and Koreans supposedly do. Speaking of the Emperor, there is a haiku about him eating *namako*: "this god man / increasingly taboo / eats sea slug" (*tabuh to nariyuku kami no hito namako tabu* – tazumi michio (1993) タブー となりゆく神の人海鼠噛む　田住満夫) – the pun on "taboo" and *tabu* (eat) is a poor groan, but I'll grant that it did make me reflect upon the homophony of "god" and "chew" (*kami*) in Japanese. **#3.**

I happen to have grown up calling the only *Holothurian* I knew a "sea cucumber." This term was popular where I grew up (Key Biscayne) and informally used by marine scientists, at least for the species in question, which was probably *Pentacta frondosa* (the "fronds" – tentacles that come out when it feeds – suitable for our coconut-tree-covered island). Pliny the Elder records the name *cucumis marinus* (cucumber/gourd [of the] sea) in his *History of Animals*; and both early modern natural philosophers such as Rondelet in his *Summa Zoologica* (c.1550) and European vernacular terms seem to follow suit.[2] Considering how slowly the *Holothurian* moves, and the fact it is generally sleeping in the sand or on sea grass when we see it – at which time it usually holds a very cucumber-like shape – the vegetable metaphor is not inappropriate. Nevertheless, it is "sea slug" who rules *this* book, for the metaphorical reason already given, because one syllable fits into haiku better than three, and because, "wrong" or not, enough English speakers are familiar with it to justify its use.

There are several reasons (aside from the obvious one of custom) why so many English speakers may prefer sea *slug* to sea *cucumber*. First, the English cucumber – or, at least, what I have seen – unlike the knobby vegetable found in America, is so sleek, thin, and streamlined that the metaphor seems a less-than-perfect fit for the warty *namako*.[3] Second, because even granting some likeness, the conservative palate of the United Kingdom (and its inheritors elsewhere) may not be emotionally prepared to admit it. As a character in Rita Hogan's novel *West Dreams East* puts it, "The only dish I take exception to is, of course, one of the greatest delicacies of Chinese Cuisine. It is euphemistically called 'Sea *Cucumber*,' but the more appropriate and deserving translation would be 'Sea *Slug*.'" That

1. *http://www.seaslugforum.net/seacusec.htm* I must confess it is entertaining to see Bill Rudman, sea slug expert ("sea-cucumbers, although 'sluggy' are not really my area of expertise"), getting letter after letter about sea slugs that turn out to be cukes and doing his gracious best to answer. In some cases, the writers are not naive for, superficially, it can be hard to tell the difference between the two, but most letters prove that laymen do not live in the same word-world as experts. There is no such informal forum for sea cucumbers, though there is an extraordinary on-line industry magazine, *The Beche-de-Mere Bulletin,* edited by Professor Chantal Conand of the Université de La Réunion, and an equally extraordinary and even more beautiful on-line magazine for the larger phylum. People interested in the aesthetic presentation of science might well visit *The Virtual Echinoderm Newsletter* website (ed.: Cynthia Ahearn, Design: Susan Hottenrott) that includes the sea cucumber.

2. *Cucumis Exceptions* The actual history is more complex, for the term was not necessarily applied to all sea cucumbers and there were many *other* names, popular and scientific, for the class, genus or species including: "biscuit of the sea" (*pagnotella di mare* – only for *Stichopus regalis*) by Neapolitans, the "sea sack" (*sjoe punge*) by a Swedish researcher, "sea sausage" (*so polser*) by Danes, "squirting worm" (*Spritzwuermer*), "leather skin" (*Lederhaeuter*), "star worm," (*Sternwuermer*), "cylinder/roller beam" (*Walzenstrahler*), "leather beam" (*Lederstrahler*), "sea roller" (*Seewalzen*), "sea cucumber/gherkin" (*Seegurken*), "trembling bladder" (Zitterblase – for a mediterranean species),

"sea-ghost" or "witches' foot" (*Seegespenst* or *Hexenfuss* – for the *Psolus phantapus*) by Germans, "tube/ulcers" (Fistulidae), "bumpy-worm[?]" (Cirrhi-Vermigrada) and "hide-skins" (Scytodermata) by Englishmen and "flowering-lard" (*le fleurilarde*) by a Frenchman (for a *cucumarie* once named *Hydra corolliflora*). For the names in context, see Ludwig H. 1889-1892. *Echinodermen. Die Seewalzen.* In: Bronn HG (ed.) *Bronn's Klassen und Ordnungen des Their-Reichs.* Band II. Abteilung 3. Buch 1. Leipzig. Unpublished translation by Alexander M. Kerr.

3. *Cucumberology* A Swedish friend was puzzled by the English "sea slug". He thought all Europeans call the holothurian a "sea cucumber." It would seem to be true that a "slug" equivalent is not found outside of English. But, there are counties where sea "cucumber" is not used either. Perhaps it has something to do with the historical distribution of warty versus sleek *land* cucumber. Sea cucumber may also have more white-collar support, while blue-collar workers prefer more pithier "sea slug." In Australia, for example, fishermen call holothurians "sea slug" (S. Uthicke, corresp.), while divers (who tend to be more highly educated) call them "sea cucumber" (Dhugal corres.) This may hold true in parts of the USA as well. Finally, the "sea cucumber" has a problem "sea slug" (as a totally wrong outsider term) lacks. It is not universally accepted. The holothurian*s* of the Far East are often called by the Malay word *trepang* (*tripang*). I had thought it should be applied to dried sea cucumber alone, but Russian scientists use it for the Japanese sea cucumber.

is to say, she would prefer to keep the *ugh!* in the slug.[1] And, third, because the English became familiar with the holothurian largely through the French, whose *lingua franca* internationalized the Portuguese sea-farer's *bicho do mar* as *beche de mer* and this "worm" (according to some Englishings) of the sea turned into a "slug" by translation, i.e., while crossing the Channel.[2]

Regardless, the sluggish English shall not have their way with *all* the translations, for poetry demands occasional use of the scientist's preferred term to take advantage of one of *our* finest similes: *as cool as a cucumber.* With the original poetry so often lost in translation, we must, wherever the opportunity presents, take advantage of what is found only in the recipient language to create something equally good. Moreover, the longer "cucumber" is occasionally useful to fill out an excessively short haiku. More commonly, the opposite is true. Following the lead of Japanese, which tends to abbreviate pronunciation (but not the characters) of *namako* down to a mere *ko* (eg.: *konowata*: slug guts, *konoko*: slug roe (gametes)), "sea slug" will, itself, occasionally be cut down to an even more ambiguous and unscientific "slug" when it seems to me that even the one syllable "sea" would hurt the sound of the poem. In other words, to have consistently readable haiku, consistency in nomenclature will be axed, or, considering the habitat of our charge, deep-sixed.

The Japanese do not share our confusion. While Terashima Ryoan's encyclopedia *Wakan Sansaizue* (1712) introduces nearly a dozen names or descriptions used mostly by Chinese, which translate as "sea-youth," "earth-meat," "painted-pipes," "large leech," "bumpy cocoons," "sand-spurs" (the bumps in some species stick out like spines), and "livestock entrails," they remained academic; Japanese have continued to use one common word, *namako,* often cut down to *ko* when modified.

1. *The* Ugh! *in the Slug* The description of the food in question leaves no doubt about the character's feelings with respect to it:

> I shove a piece of the slimy, primeval,
> dank glob into my mouth . .

As we shall see, her description to this point sounds remarkably Japanese, yet her reaction to the primeval experience is completely opposite, for the passage continues:

> . . and force a smile and appreciation to
> the eagerly awaiting Chinese hosts.

Many, if not most Japanese would appreciate the food for the reasons – slick mouthfeel, embodiment of ancient things – she is disgusted by it! Her cucumber-as-a-euphemism idea is charming, but the opposite use of "slug" rather than "cucumber" in order to disgust – as a cacophonism – is probably much more common: eg., from the "Anatomy" section of a *"How To Japanese"* site (www.twics.com): "Non-Japanese, lacking the necessary imprinting, may need hyperactive imaginations to derive the same degree of pleasure from the nape of the female neck as the Japanese do. But, like sea *slugs*, fermented beans and other delicacies for which an appreciation is somehow acquired, the neck is no exception." (*italics* mine) Learning to like sea *cucumbers* would not seem so outlandish. On the other hand, the *ugh* factor is not

necessarily a turn-off. West Coast Americans revel in their *land* slugs. Not only the damp and dark North of Gary Larson's cartoons, but the generally sunny South California -- *"Do you know that the UC Santa Cruz' mascot is a banana slug?"* (OM) *No, I didn't!* – boasts a remarkably slug-positive attitude.

2. *Bêche-de-mer* Actually, the "worm" began to morph before it hypothetically crossed the channel. While the Portuguese phrase did indeed mean "worm of the sea," the French adaptation kept the sound at the expense of the meaning, for, according to one etymology, *bêche* in French means "spade" – a small garden trowel with edges curled up is about the right size – and *bêcher* means "to dig in," which is, of course, what a sea cucumber does; while another claims the meaning is "grub" (no "a" or "to" to indicate which). No matter, the French term is usually Englished as if it *were* what it *was!* So saying, the Portuguese etymology itself is confusing, for the "worm" (*bicho*), itself, would seem to be derived from *bestulus,* a diminuitive of the Latin "beast" (*bestia*). So, who can say if we are talking about a worm, a beastie or a scoop? I asked Chantal Conand, editor of the *Beche de Mer Bulletin* if French cuisine incorporated the *beche*: "No, French generally do not eat [it] (I have a personal test to know if people will like it: people who like veal head like it; my test has been 100% successful!)" (corresp.) She also writes most French do not use the term *beche de mer,* or a "sea cucumber" equivalent, but call them *holothuries.*

Namako has two obvious etymologies, the phonetic one being "raw-child," [1] and the visual one – *i.e.* the meaning of the Chinese characters – "sea-mouse/rat." [2]

君 知 る や 生 海 鼠 は 海 の 鼠 な り　紅 緑

kimi shiru ya namako wa umi no nezumi nari – kôroku (1873-1949)

(you [i]know!/: seaslug[live/raw*[2]-sea-mouse/rat], ocean's mouse/rat is)

4

i know you

namako, the rat

of the ocean

This is worthless chop logic.[3] By the same brush, we might write any number of things such as, "i know you / hippopotamus, the horse / of the river"[in Japanese, our Latinate "water-horse" is a "river-horse."]! After all, in this era of new haiku, there is no reason to favor the sea slug alone. (Frog-on-a-hill: *Droll Haiku: The Sea Slug's Tongue* (*kokkei haiku namako no shita,* 1918) kkhk)

Some people, perhaps influenced by the sound, write it with the three characters, "raw/live-sea-rat/mouse," as in the above haiku, or "sea-mouse/rat-child." More rarely, four characters – one more than the syllabets they loosely represent! – "raw-sea-mouse-child," are used. If these are not, strictly speaking, correct, neither are they wrong, for written Japanese is tolerant – free! – in ways modern English is not. The actual derivation of the literally childish suffix *ko* would seem to be "roe" and other delicacies ending in the same (OJD).   While only foreign readers of Japanese tend to get hung up on the literal meanings of characters,[4] Japanese may be unconsciously affected by the diminutive

5 下

1. *Live/Raw* The same Chinese character may mean "living" or "raw." Not commonly used to write *namako* ("sea rat./mouse" is enough), today, it is often mispronounced *"namanamako."* Sound and etymology favors "raw," but I have noticed the extra character is often used to emphasize the fact the sea slug is alive.

2. *Rat/Mouse* English has no equivalent for the Sino-japanese "rat/mouse" character. Unless we don't mind the squirrel and ground-chuck joining in, "rodent" won't work. Rather than continue with "rat/mouse" in my transliterations, I will sometimes go with one and sometimes the other, depending upon whether the poem favors the "gross" (i.e., rat) side or the "cute" (i.e., mouse) side.

3. *Worthless Chop Logic* The poem introduced by the anonymous Frog-on-the-hill (Oka no Kaeru) is indeed, to directly English, "fart-logic." In RISE, I introduce a good number of bad haiku, for they, too, are part of the Japanese haiku experience, which is not properly conveyed in books that only translate the best poetry.

4. *Literal Characters* Foreigners are literal-minded because they *see* writing and *hear* speech rather than simply using them. A Japanese who was not an American (raised in the USA) would not write: "I came at last to *namako,* a word that in the Japanese combination of characters means both 'sea cucumber' and 'raw child,' a symbol for the simplicity and vulnerability that I feel is at the root of the Japanese and perhaps all psyches." (from the jacket of Linda Watanabe McFerrin: NAMAKO *sea cucumber* (nsc)). Only the foreigner notices neatly wrapped packages of "roasted-female-children" on sale in the fish-shop's of Tokyo or likewise labeled on fancy pet food.   Japanese – with the possible exception of hypersensitive feminists – do not think about how *yaki-kônago* (roasted inch-long fish properly called *ikanago,* i.e., "a sand eel," "launce," or "lance.") are labeled. In Japanese, there are scores, if not hundreds of common words written in uncommon ways. Some, like "five-month (June) fly" (*urusai*), for a "nuisance" make metamorphic sense and some, such as this "roasted-woman-child," are chosen for the sound-match and neglect the meaning of the characters. (Written Japanese is heaven for the pun-lover and hell for others. Luckily, I am the former.) There are exceptions. I found one haiku contradicting my claim that Japanese are not conscious of *namako's* characters: "those letters, shape / i dislike sea slug / without tasting it!" (*moji katachi namako wa kuwazu kirai kana* --- itô kitajo 1993 文字容海鼠は食わず嫌ひかな　伊藤きた女). And, I would not doubt that the Japanese, like all of us, become literal-minded in their dreams. (Because McFerrin introduced the "raw child" *namako* in a trance-like episode, it would, as it turns out, work well in Japanese, too.)

sense of *ko,* a suffix we might describe as the *ling* in "duckling," or the *y* in "ducky").[1] And, what is diminutive is *kawaii,* "cute." For better or worse, cuteness goes far in modern Japan. Perhaps, this *ko* is one reason why Japanese are far more *sea-cucumber-conscious* and *sea-cucumber-positive* than their consumption [2] and its looks [3] warrant. While there is not a tremendous difference in the number of Google hits found for "sea cucumber" and *namako* – 25,300 for the former, and 20,500 (in the *hiragana* syllabary) +22,000 (in the *katakana* syllabary) +4,100 (in the Chinese characters) for the latter – the English hits are almost all about the biological, environmental (90% the same Galapagos poaching), medical creature or cuisine in the Far East, where the Japanese (with their comparatively smaller internet presence) hits take me to any number of businesses incorporating *namako* in their name or product, literature, cute cartoons, sea cucumber philosophies of life, as well as the expected biology and cuisine. Namako Hakase's preface does not exaggerate.

1. *More 'Ko' Etymology* A less likely, once common etymology derives *namako* from *numekori,* meaning "slippery-hard." Yanagida Kunio (1875 - 1962) father, patron saint and, sometimes even called *god* of modern Japanese folklore studies, favored "raw+*ko,*" with the *ko* meaning the thing itself, the sea slug (not "child" or snacks other than the *namako*), and this pretty well settled it. While "ko" has also referred to other small delicacies for centuries, according to Wayne Farris (pmjs listing), our creature had the patent on the "*ko*" (let us skip details on sound and writing!) in pre-Heian tax tablets. Perhaps it was a more important food when Japanese with Southern roots were ascendant and was relegated to the side when continental culture and taste gained stock. If we grant this, the *Kojiki* myth might be putting the *ko* in its place in more ways than one. (Not too likely, for North China has strong claims, too.) The character used for "ko" (子) is, in other contexts, often pronounced "shi," which is close to the current Chinese "zi" for the same. After introducing elementary particles in Chinese (electron=dianzi=spark-seed, proton= zhizi= primal-seed, etc), Douglas R. Hofstadter opines:

> Note that the final constituent in these names is always *zi,* which is the character we saw earlier inside the word for "chopsticks." I called it "thing" there, while here I've rendered it as "seed." But the fact of the matter is that it is a tremendous oversimplification – dare I say "grotesque betrayal"? – to render *zi* by "seed", by "thing", or by any other single English noun, since off of that very high-frequency and densely-laden character dangles a phenomenally complex of meanings, including "honored master", "person", "son", "fledgling", "sprout", "seed", "egg", "kernel", "bead", and "coin". This *zi* is, by the way, the same "tse" as ends the names of ancient and

venerated philosphers such as Laotse and Chuangtse ("Old Honored Master" and "Serious Honored Master"). What a zoo of meanings has *zi.* (*Le Ton beau de Marot:* (I apologize for dropping the tonal marks)1997)

This, then, is the character that would follow the character for "raw" if *namako* were ever actually written that way, which it is not. (But, note, that the character in question does not seem at all weird in Japanese or Chinese. By itself, it does NOT mean "seed" or "egg" or any of the things mentioned above. Though it is a noun and can mean "child" by itself, it functions more as a suffix. (Would you be shocked at "er" meaning (?) "mast*er*" and "kill*er*" and "lov*er*"?) Could the fact that *ko/shi/zi/tse* can indeed serve as a noun (meaning "child") by itself make it seem stranger than it really is?

2. *Sea Cucumber Consumption* Japanese probably eat far less sea cucumber per capita than other more Southeast Asians with more Chinese and Chinese cuisine. I have found no international statistics on consumption fine enough to prove this impression based upon trade figures showing the lion's share of the sea cucumber (*trepang*) market does not involve Japan. I could not find any sea cucumber poems from these nations, though I suspect they must exist and would welcome them for the next edition!)

3. *Sea Cucumber Looks* There are glamorous sea cucumbers, beautifully colored and lit up like the proverbial Christmas tree. Like the Christmas tree, they must be seen in the dark. Seen with the tentacles which ring the mouth fully extended, *most* sea cucumber look presentable, some even beautiful, for these delicate appendages become fronds or lacy fans or the ribbons women dance with, while the plain body becomes a trunk, a mere backdrop →

II
which sea slug?

Personally, I find details taxing. But, I have had many friends and readers whose first interest is knowing exactly what the subject is. So, for them and others like them, I trace the *namako* to its twig on the scientific classification tree proceeding in the same logical order by which Orientals, Serbs and Joyce's Stephen Daedelus write their addresses, from the broad to the precise – this is called *nesting* – contrary to our addresses, which illogically force the poor postal clerk to work his or her way up from the bottom of the letter, though no written language in the world is written or read in that direction. While narrowing down life, I occasionally peek ahead or behind in the history of the species (phylogeny), discuss individual development (ontogeny), and include taxonomically dubious categories to make things more comprehensible and entertaining for the lay reader, at the cost, I fear, of irritating the scientist, who will note logical glitches and, worse yet, sins against parsimony. Ancient readers should not mourn the occasionally missing taxonomic category. Our understanding of life has outgrown "King Phillip Crosses Ocean For Gold Specie" or "Keep Pussy Cat Out For Goodness Sake!" (kingdom/phylum/class/order/ family/genus/species). Today, the tree of life, I am told, has too many limbs, sticks and stems to call things anything other than what they are called.[1] The abundant metaphor and occasional teleology is, needless to say, facetious, though not, I hope, complete nonsense.

→ for the spectacle. (The *Cucumaria pallida* tentacles resemble the high voltage electrical display surrounding Tesla on the famous photograph – actually, a double exposure – on the cover of Margaret Cheney's TESLA: MAN BEYOND TIME!) Unfortunately, the sea cucumber of this book is no cheesecake. It only has tiny tentacles like the hairs on the head of a vacuum-cleaner and even these are not seen for it only sucks dirt, not water like Cucumaria varieties. The Japanese adore it *despite* its ugliness. Their cartoons of *namako* do not turn them into pretty varieties, but use anthropomorphic adornment such as bowties or ribbons to make them seem cute. Meanwhile, the sea slug proper (*umiushi*) has become popular enough to challenge the sea cucumber in Japan, for divers around the world photo their diverse beauty which, unlike the *namako* that tends to wear its inner beauty on its sleeve at night, can usually be seen in color and by day. There is even a diver-supported website featuring a *"nudi of the day!"* (Personally, I am most attracted to the more subtle markings and purple panic juice of the third contestant in this beauty contest, the *sea slug's* close relation, the *sea hare,* whose euphonious Japanese name, *amefurashi,* is written either "rain-faller" or "rain-tiger.") And the *nudi* is no airhead. "She" has a brain with 20,000 very large neurons which (with some help of Nobel prize winner Eric Kandel) has taught us a lot about how our 10,000,000,000 small neurons work, and, most importantly, that the brain can physically change to cope with outside stimulus (neuronal plasticity) – suggesting that talk therapy can change brain function. As a simple model of intelligence, we now have "CyberSlug v1.0.8b" (*"Harness the power of the sea slug brain on your computer!"*) written by Mikhail Voloshin, a student in the Neuroscience Program at the University of Illinois at Urbana-Champaign, with Dr. Rhanor Gillette of the Department of Molecular and Integrative Physiology (Found in Ben Tarr: "Mindless Machines" from http://www.colorado. edu/pwr/occasions/AI.html.). So, nudibranch lovers, please do not begrudge my borrowing your name for this book. Your pretty *and* bright sea slug's place in the world is secure.

1. *Missing Categories* Why? "This is because in the intensely branched tree of life, taxonomic names have only been attached to some branches, often before zoologists even recognized that life was a branching process. Since then, we've resolved and labeled other important branches, hence the extra names, but no longer place as much emphasis on regimented levels, since taxonomic levels, order, family, etc., don't always correspond to anything real in nature, e.g., some orders are older than some classes, etc. Even more damning is that some taxonomic names don't even correspond to all members of a particular branch." (A. Kerr)

Bio (life): Usually defined as something that grows, reproduces, adapts and evolves by itself; but, considering the fact that if the Sun stopped shining, we the proudly autonomous would freeze to death as surely as artificial life (it does all that same stuff) that has the plug pulled on its computer world would kick the bucket, one wonders about the validity of such definitions.

Aerobes (air- ites): Life that needs oxygen to live, as opposed to those that not only don't need it, but find it poisonous despite having created it themselves. Now we aerobes are trying our best to return the favor – as H. Odum put it, "to complete the carbon cycle" by digging up all the fossil fuel and returning it to the atmosphere – by restoring the earth to its first and rightful owners, the descendents of whom still hold on to life inside of sulfurous hot-springs, underwater volcanic ducts and, perhaps, within us. [1]

Eukaryota (true-nut-critters): The Greek for "nut" or "kernal" was adopted to refer to the nucleus of a cell. To be a "true-nut" is to have one's insides partitioned by tissue so that genes and digestive juices don't just float about promiscuously, as is true for the prokaryota, that may or may not proceed us (there is some debate here). Eukaryota are not only single cells full of covered things (organels). They are any life with such compartmentalized cells. Coconut trees, sea cucumbers and humans are all Eukaryotes, we just wear more layers of covering. (Should we call the Japanese women of the Heian era who wore twelve or so layers of colored fabric, Super-Eukaryota? The more specialized functions permitted by such organ-ization are not to be sneezed at but with each bounty gained, we drift further from the "high and fast" direct exchange with the environment enjoyed by simpler life forms. Should we speak of adaptation-as-alienation?

Protozoa (first-animals) Until the 1970's, even single cells were classified as animal or plant, but animals are now considered to have evolved independently, perhaps from multi-cellular Eukaryotes rather than from a common stock of single-celled ones, so the protozoa are no longer considered the first animals. Though none deny these "little beasties," as a certain geochemist calls them, do many things considered animal, even their name is suspect, for they are now thought to belong to a number of unrelated kingdoms. But even if the protozoa were still with us – it might even be argued animals are overgrown colonies of them – we would not be with them. Humans and sea cucumbers are biotic, aerobic and eukaryotic, but we cannot nest within protozoa, for we are not single-celled.

Metazoa (overall-animals):   The hyperactive part of eukaryotic life that, lacking the ability to synthesize energy from primary stuff like sunlight, minerals and water alone (in this respect we are like another Eukaryotic kingdom, fungae) depends on fancy, highly organic/organized food and, with some notable exceptions is incapable of staying put, something reflected by the Sino-Japanese term, "moving-thing", but not by the Western "animal," (except turned into animation) which means "breath." By ecological grouping, animals are said to be "superfluous consumers" – supply-side economics does not hold in the greater picture of life – as opposed to being "producers" or "decomposers" (although, it is the author's belief that this schemata is unfair to animals such as the sea cucumber, who, we will see, leave their habitat cleaner than when they find it!).   Many animals use that extra energy to pile on unneeded chrome and fins that make them the biological equivalent of 1950's cars.[1→] But, the lack of a single design team in nature – we have the desires of the creatures themselves, the environmental constraints, accidents, and so forth all putting in their two bits – means that correctly understood, all animals are camels (apparently designed by committee). Or, that is how

---

1. *What Happened to the Anaerobes?*   "We do not know the total biomass in underground biomes (SLiMEs: subsurface lithautotrophic microbial ecosystems). Some people estimate it to be much larger than all our well known organisms taken together, because it extends so far down below the earth's surface where we just live on the outer skin. In addition, many survive in low oxygen conditions (e.g., sediment in Long Island Sound), and some (have been argued) survived as parasites in guts of ruminants or indeed evolved into forms that can tolerate (if not like) oxygen." (ET – corresp.)

it seems, at any rate, to the author, who encounters oddity wherever he happens to look.

Radiata (radiating-critters): While Plato's spherical hermaphrodites go too far, all animals radiate enough roundness to claim loose allegiance with this group - which is why I can leave it in my nesting scheme and also why modern parsimony makes it obsolete (for not excluding enough information) for proper taxonomy. Radiality provides extraordinary resistance to pressure at minimal material cost, unbeatable simplicity of design – which can facilitate the apparent complexity of abundant detail [2] – and strength (which may explain why the echinoderms (below) to whom our charge belongs, were smart enough to regain some of their radiality after a strongly bilateral period). There are, however, certain kinds of complexity – not just skewed or distorted, but kinds of irregularity that defy the worlds within worlds of fractal geometry – that the relatively unrestricted play of radial design can not come up with.

Bilateria (two-sided-critters): Something, perhaps the advantage of experiencing less friction when moving with respect to the surrounding medium (or when standing in place within a strong current) combined with the need to know which was front and which back in order to make choices led some creatures to drop the original default, i.e. spherical symmetry, for more limited tubular, conical, football and discus-like forms. Because equal ends would be inefficient for various ergonomic reasons, we more or less simultaneously got front and back, heads and tails. To my (uninformed) mind, this was, and is, accomplished not so much by adding on ends, as restricting the full play of radiality about the middle, so the free ends, like pens limited by meter and rhyme, end up with otherwise highly unlikely creative solutions. I imagine the limits represented by bilateral development as the starting point for the design-upon-design – rhyme-upon-rhyme – serial ingenuity (please, scientific reader, don't ask me to relate the ontogenetic and phylogenetic aspects of my abstractions!) that leads to the Rube Goldberg-type contraptions called "higher animals."

Deuterostomia (second-mouth critters): The original gut – phylo- and ontogenetically speaking – was a dead-end street, not extending from a hole opened up from the outside as Taoist creation myth might have it, but enfolded, as an old tennis ball indented until one side touches the other making a pocket. Eventually, a channel opened through the bottom of this invagination letting stuff flow clean through the animal. Most animals are *"protostomes"* (original/first mouths), whose aboral opening develops *after* the oral one in the age-old manner. But with us "deuteros" – chordates (vertebrates and near-vertebrates) and echinoderms (so the sea cucumber is still with us, or we with it!) – this process is literally bassackwards. The aboral opening, i.e. the anus, develops first and the mouth opens later. [3] I

1. *Under the Chrome and Fins* Evolution can be read in two ways, as a flowering of diversity, a triumphant expansion of possibility, or as a brutal weeding process, where tremendously diverse basic forms are crowded out and eclipsed by a limited number of success stories. Both readings are, I think, equally true, yet neither seems sufficient to describe the world of micro-organisms. At Dirtland (part of a website with the fine name Microbe Zoo), we learn that "some scientists estimate that each gram of soil may contain 10,000 species of micro-organisms! That's more biodiversity . . . than all the different types of mammals in the entire world." That's nothing! The first line from a bio of the first lady of the prokaryota reads: "Lynn Margulis = She personally represents 250 million extant species of nonhuman mute microorganisms and their larger descendents (the protoctists)." (lr) Nice number! Everyone in the USA could sponsor their own microbe.

2. *Abundant Detail* The prime example of profuse radial development would be the Caribbean Giant Basket Starfish (*Astrophyton muricatum*), photos of which can be found on the internet, as can the famous drawings by Haeckel.

3. *Oral-Aboral Order* If our tubing has grown from the anus to mouth, science would seem to contradict the psychologically persuasive Taoist myth, where the anus is the last hole to be opened. I cannot help but think of the geological analogy of the river, where the Ainu of Japan put the "head" and source of a river's growth at the entrance to the sea, while Japanese and Westerners put it up the mountain at the narrow end.

chuckle to read biologists mention "the *fate* of the blastopore (the original opening)" as mouth or anus, and that "we don't know how this happened since there are no intermediate fossils but it certainly was *a significant change!*" But one of my science advisors pooh-poohs: *"I don't think that these statements were meant to be humorous. The term 'fate' is a standard technical one . . ."*

Invertebrates (without-back-bones): Because this term "is a semantic blanket that covers most of the animal kind [97% not only of species, but of the radical (phylum level) diversity] and reveals nothing of the varied shapes that have been thrust under it" (Buchsbaum and Milne) – which is to say it excludes little information – taxonomy does not find it useful anymore and generally skips to the next category, the phylum *Echinodermata*. It doesn't take a biologist to see the term itself is misleading, for the existence of *in*vertebrates presumes the prior existence of – or majority of – *vertebrates*, which is to put the cart before the horse. Moreover, as the inverts far outnumber the bassackwards, I am making a mess of my nesting by including them here (Since the mouth-first/anus-first split precedes the vertebrate/invertebrate one, taxing, even if uncalled for, requires this order), but do so because the term is contextually significant: it is *as an invertebrate*, that the echinoderm's bassackwardness is appreciated, for the combination is unique. It is why Buschbaum and Milne (and others) claimed that these "sluggish creatures, lacking a head, losing their two-sided symmetry, and possessing the most feeble kind of nervous system," i.e., the echinoderm, was the "stock [from which] man and the vertebrates appear to have come."(TLA) Though zoologists are less certain about our paternity today – the *Hemichordata* (acorn worms and what-not) phylum, not the echinoderm, is the current front-runner in the running for our closest mutual ancestor – the *idea* of an ancestral sea cucumber has survived in some semi-scientific circles (viz fn) and is not too far off the mark when you consider that the echinoderm *is* our closest invertebrate relative.

Echinodermata (spike/hedgehog-skin critters): A very successful phylum dating back at least to the early Cambrium (before the first fish), and boasting some six thousand plus species of sea urchin, sea star, sea cucumber, sea lily, sea biscuit and sand-dollar sharing an underlying pentaradial (five-sided) symmetry around a mouth centrally situated with most (some sea urchins have their mouths out-of-whack), a dermal endoskeleton (it doesn't cover the skin but is or – as it is mesodermally derived – becomes the skin) of calcium carbonate with protruding spikes in some classes (if not all echinoderms show their spikes, well, not all mammals display their breasts), a water-vascular system and patented hydraulic control system possessed by all, with tiny tube-feet utilizing this in various manners. The big question (to me, at any rate) is why pentaradial. What advantage can sides not perfectly parallel bring? [1] Since "almost none of their actions resembles the activities of other kinds of animals," (Buchsbaum and Milne), any number of names might have been given to the phylum.

1. *Pentaradial or Pentameral Advantage* So what is particularly good about five? I came up with eight guesses in minutes, all of which my experts found of dubious merit. Here are a few, so you may laugh too. 1) If the proto-echinoderm were square or hexagonal, masses of them would fit together like a puzzle and lock themselves in, whereas pentagonality (pentagons can only fit on a sphere) would ensure breathing space. 2) When any tip of a pentagon directly points at something, the back side is perpendicular to it (This is true for a triangle, too, but its angles are too sharp for most life) and such might prove uniquely stable in certain seafloor conditions, e.g., it would be easy to stabilize in a strong current or, pushed from behind, would go straight (this later benefit not found among the hexagonal). 5) A pentagon turned on its side with three corners on top and two below is pretty close to your basic house-shape and would be ideal for living in a place where things fell (even under water) from above. (Later thoughts: *No doubt, the real answer lies within.* The nature of the corner-to-corner trusses. A triangle only ties on the perimeter. Squares also crisscross through their center. Hexagons do likewise, with three lines. With the pentagon's odd number of corners, a single truss from each corner cannot cross, but only meet in the center, where each strikes the apex of a triangle formed by two others. This may create a type of stability (or spring) not found in the simpler structures and, in three dimensions (to my mind), leads inevitably to an axis or central shaft.)

Holothuroidea (wholly-lewd/gross/polyp-critters):   Used for the entire class of sea cucumbers sometimes described as naked thick-skinned sea urchins stretched out and lying on their side, this term may be traced back to Aristotle's *holothourion* which, according to the nineteenth century German zoologist Ludwig, textual comparison suggests might have been meant for another sea creature of similar aspect (LHE). [1] The father of naturalists presumably adopted the root from the vernacular term *thouris*, which included the connotations of "vulgar" and "unseemly" probably because of its resemblance to a penis [2] (IBID). Perhaps, that is why Japanese science let this term alone and just call the class *namako* (sea cucumber) rather than translating the etymological meaning as is done for most terms. Besides the suggestive shape of the typical sea cucumber – not, strictly speaking, true for the entire class, because some sub-classes are vermiform, spherical, lopsided-boomerang (one side a fin/wing), bagpipe and so forth – the holothurian boasts walls of connective tissue capable of of wondrous extension and contraction, hardening and softening that have replaced the hard exoskeleton and spikes protecting other echinoderms (excluding the crinoid (flowerlike crown) sea lilly, which I find stranger than the holothurian, for it usually passes for a plant!). Enough said for now. More holothurian characteristics will be elaborated in the course of this book.

Aspidochirotacea (shielded-hands): This name suggests the shape of this subclass's tentacles, which, partially extended with branches sheathed, looks like a hand with gloves on. Buchsbaum and Milne describe the representative organ in action: "something in common can be seen between a child solemnly licking its fingers to clean them of jam, and a big sea cucumber in its normal method of feeding . . .spreads its tentacles over the sea bottom and rubs them around, gathering food particles in the mucus coating. Then, one at a time, the animal thrusts a loaded tentacle into its mouth, closes fleshy lips around it, and pulls out the tentacle all clean and ready for reloading."

Aspidochirotida (shield-hands): One may think of *tida* (a classifier more specific than *tacea* but otherwise adding no information) as "tide" – though it isn't – to remember the name of this order living in relatively shallow water. Luckily its "hands" only open underwater, so *aspidochirotacea* are never confused for drowning people.

Stichopodidae (prickly-feet): We can observe pointed little feet. Of course, this is true for many if not most sea cucumbers, but these guys own the name. Sometimes, they form three neat rows on the bottom forming a sole of sorts and two less obvious on top, and other times, they are prosaically scattered on the ventrum side, too.   There is also a tendency toward relatively elongated papillae (warts, if you think them ugly or, nipples if you like them). They are all shallow cold-water bottom-feeders (i.e., swallow sand and other detritus, rather than sucking stuff out of the water), most have the ability to do some caterpillar-like movement, and many can melt to the point of dissolution, as well as harden their tissue. These behavioral traits, the scientist says, are out of place in a discussion of

1. ***Holothuroidea as a Term*** A perfect name would describe an objective trait, true for all members of the class described and for no members of other classes. This is, however, practically impossible. To my mind, Aristotle's holothourion (wholly-lewd) is a bit too subjective. Since gourds are found in almost as many shapes as sea cucumber, Pliny's cucumis (cucumiform = cylindrical)/gourdlike would have been preferable. But it is too late. As the United States of America (a description substituting "States" for "Colonies") can no longer be called Columbia, the name it was once supposed to adopt, because it is taken, *cucu* already belongs to the genus *Cucumaria* and cannot be adopted by

the whole class. Besides, to tell the truth, I have come to like the sound of "holothurian" --- if a centurion commands a century, the holothurian sounds like it should command the whole damn thing --- and find its vulgar etymology a welcome poke at things proper and politically correct.
2. ***The Penis Alone?***   The holothurian is obviously phallic. But is it *only* phallic? Since Aristotle thought of the vagina as the penis turned inside out and vice versa   – i.e. male and female parts as inverse rather than essentially different (see Thomas Laqueur: *Making Sex*) – I like to fantasize that he saw tubular forms as hermaphrodite, living reifications of Plato's original all-in-one sex. ～～

taxonomic features, but I will leave them, for behavior, together with other factors, is a useful aid for identification when no obvious single trait distinguishes these prickly-feet from all other shield-hands, or even from some holothurians with shield-hands in different sub-classes. The lack of clear-cut difference doesn't bother the scientist, for he or she doesn't take things at face-value, anyway, and has the means to peep (pardon the verb, I can't help recall Erasmus Darwin's playfully polygamist stamens and polyandrous pistils [1]) deeper within at things missed by the layman. To wit: the prickly-feet is ultimately distinguished from other holothurians by the shape of the plates forming the calcareous ring,[2] a structure encircling the mouth of all holothurians (the longitudinal muscles extending the length of the body attach to it) and the particular form and distribution of the miniscule crystals of calcium carbonate called ossicles, which will be discussed later! And this is, of course, a matter of degrees of shape and numerical averages. Japanese scientists tend to call this category *Manamako-ka,* or "true-namako family," which is to say sea cucumber that approach their idea of *namako-ness.*

Apostichopus (separate[i.e., different]-prickly-feet), also **Stichopus**: The old genus name *Stichopus* suggested that said sea cucumber is a middle-of-the-road *Stichopod* possessing all of the most typical family qualities. The new name *Apostichopus,* proposed by the Chinese researcher Liao in 1980, largely on the basis of differences found between the *Stichopus japonicus* and the *Stichopus chloronotus,* that has largely replaced *Stichopus* in China, Russia and, increasingly, Japan, suggests this *Stichopus* is separate from other *Stichopodidae*. The nature of holothurians is such that it is hard to tell where species or even groups of species (genus) begin and end. Like any continuum, the divisions are bound to be somewhat arbitrary (which does not make them meaningless, anymore than the keys on a piano are meaningless, though other scales are possible). I do not know the details of the difference and since this book is more poetry than science, I shall just let it go at that and only point out that in a googled article by Prof. V. S. Levin Kamchatka of the Institute of Fishery and Oceanography, it is explained that a very pronounced morphological and chemical similarity between S. japonicus and P. californicus was "established by us," and that this corroborated Liao's more limited data supporting this monotypic genus (that, so far, only includes what follows below).) Be that as it may, Japanese scientists do not pay much attention to the name as they tend to use the vernacular *manamako-zoku,* or "true-namako sub-family" for a designation.

Apostichopus japonicus (japanese prickly-feet), also **Stichopus japonicus**: (A quick google search shows only 154 hits for the former versus 480 hits for the latter, but the majority of the former hits are for serious science sites, where the majority of the latter concern over-the-counter medicine made from sea cucumber.) This species, if indeed it is one species – there is debate as to whether some sub-species, generally called "variety" or "forms," deserve species-hood – takes us to the *manamako* or true-*namako*, itself. I fear that any species-specific attributes that might be found in the substantial (untranslated) Chinese and Russian writing on the Japanese sea cucumber might be too technical for me and most readers.   Yet, this species *is* the star of the book; I feel obliged to come up with more

The Loves of the Plants In the introduction to his 1,746 line versification of Linnaean botany, Charles Darwin's Grandfather, Erasmus, had his readers imagine they were walking into a Camera Obscura to view his "Inchanted Garden." He calls the pistils "goddesses," "virgins," "syrens," "belles," etc; and the stamens, "males," "swains," "youths," "beauxs," and so forth.   No minor stuff, this. Darwin, an M.D. (and an extraordinarily kind man) was the leading poet and scientist-inventor of his time and deserves to be *far* more well-known today (See Desmond King-Hele's *Erasmus Darwin: A Life of Unequalled Achievement*).
Calcareous Plates "Why do men, sitting at the microscope, examine the calcareous plates of a sea-cucumber, and, finding a new arrangement and number, feel an exaltation and give the new species a name, and write about it possessively? It would be good to know the impulse truly, not to be confused by the 'services to science' platitudes or the other little mazes into which we entice our minds so that they will not know what we are doing." (LSC) Talk about coincidence, this is the penultimate sentence of the first paragraph of Steinbeck's introduction to *The Log from the Sea of Cortez,* a book I got translated into Japanese about ten years ago (when mention of those plates made no impression whatsoever on me).

information, though it is hardly of a taxonomic sort. We might note, for example, that despite the adjective *japonicus*, this sea cucumber can be found in the coastal water around Russia, China, and much of the Yellow Sea ("West Sea" to Koreans, this shallow water gulf is shared by China and Korea), as well as Japan, where it is generally referred to by scientists and poets alike as *namako*, unless in a parched form, when it is called *iriko* domestically but "trepang" in international settings. Unlike most sea-cucumbers – including some species cured as trepang – almost every part of it may be eaten raw or fermented. This suggests that a low level of toxicity (mostly meaning *saponin*) is one of its outstanding traits. It is popularly – by locals and scientists alike – divided into the following three varieties:

The **aonamako** (*aoko* in some parts), or "blue sea cucumber," generally lives in and on sand and mud in shallow water, where it absorbs organic matter from the same, but moves further out if it grows large enough. As far as I know, it doesn't stretch its tentacles out and lick its fingers as might be expected from a shield-hand class holothurian (But we primates don't get much mileage from our tailbone either, so who's complaining!) Eaten raw, pickled [1] or stewed, it is favored in the Kanto (Tokyo) area and in Hiroshima for being relatively soft. The color *ao* is usually translated as "blue" for it modifies the sea and the sky, but it also means "green" and "pale" (not outlandish if you recall Homer's wine-colored sea). More precisely, the *aonamako* is described as dark blue-green on top and yellow-to-blue on the bottom.

The **akanamako** (*akako* in some parts), or "red sea cucumber," [2] lives in boulder reefs and rocky sand about 15 feet down, where it eats sand, seaweed, shellfish detritus, etc.. Because it has a smaller population and is preferred for its flavor by what is the largest *namako* market (80%) in Japan, i.e., Kansai (Osaka, Nagoya, Kobe), the *akanamako* tends to cost about three times more than its softer blue counterpart. It is not bright red but stippled bluish-green and hempen orange (or rusty brown) on top with an orangish bottom (sometimes with dark lines, judging from photos), holds less water and demonstrates greater changeability (shrinkage/expansion) than its shallow water counterpart. The taxonomic relationship between the red and blue *namako* is debated. [3]

The **kuronamako** (*kuroko* in some parts), or "black sea cucumber," is found on scummy (?) ["floating mud"] nutrient-rich seabed, strongly affected by runoff from land. It dissolves

1. In a Pickle about Pickled The *pickled sea cucumber*, or *su-namako,* who will play a big role in this book is no more pickled than a sautéed green is deep-fried. The Japanese vinegar is much milder and the time for the "pickling" is closer to that of a short marinade – one could almost say "dressed sea slug" – but "marinated" won't do for it is two syllables longer (the "sea" would not fit in the first or third line) and suggests (to English speakers) oil and a mix of ingredients too complex for our dish. "Vinegared" is only one syllable longer than "pickled" and it is the most accurate translation, but it is also a phonetic and visual disaster, despite the pleasant "vine" hidden within. So, misleading or not, like Peter Piper, *pickled* is my pick.

2. Red Sea Cucumber The Japanese *aka-namako* should not be confused with different species of *Holothurian* called trepang eaten by the Chinese, which often appear to be red. Mark Vaile MP addressing the Australia-China Trade Investment Summit (7 Sept 99): "The humble sea slug was actually Australia's first processed food export. Fishermen [from Sulewesi, Indonesia)] spent several months [in North Australia] collecting and processing the trepang using a particular species of mangrove for dyeing the trepang red." Chinese call the mangrove "vermillion-tree." Their merchants bought the auspicious red slugs from the fishermen in Sulewesi and "re-exported" them back to China.

3. Red vs Blue Given the large number of differences between these types of *namako,* some argue that they deserve to be considered a different sub-species if not a different species altogether. Differences between blue and red *namako* include: little crude fat *vs.* a lot of crude fat, no gelatin membrane on eggs *vs.* gelatin membrane on eggs, simple and limited number of ossicles *vs.* complex ones, short papillae-feet *vs.* long and thin ones, a short and thick *vs.* long and thin polian vesicle, liking low salt *vs* liking high salt. . . (From ndh: 1990, and the web) Too little is known about the big question of sex and reproduction to settle this.

rapidly when exposed to air, the gonads (*konowata,* a delicacy) are dark – where the best tasting ones are light – and is considered low fare. In the past, this *kuronamako* was ignored, but with the falling productivity of the red and blue *namako,* it has become a viable fishery and as of 1990 came to comprise 40% of the total catch (much frozen for export?)

Cucumaria japonica (gourd/cuke-[of]sea): belongs to a different family of sea cucumber (*Cucumariae*) that, as suspension-feeders (also called "plankton-eaters"), use their longer oral tentacles in a more finger-licking manner (as described in *Aspidochirotacea,* above, rather than sucking up sludge in a vacuum-cleaner-like manner as per the three "true sea cucumber" (*manamako*) and is rarely called *namako* today, for its species has a different popular name:

> The **kinko,** usually written "gold-sea-mouse" or "gold-old," live just offshore on muddy-bottomed seabed 50-150 feet down. They range in color from light yellow – popularly reflecting the gold found in the mountains – to grey, vermillion and wisteria purple (so some are called *fujiko,* where *fuji* is "wisteria"). As they are usually cured, they are mistakenly equated with *iriko* (*iri* meaning "dried/parched"), or cured sea cucumber, by many. They were haiku'ed in the seventeenth century as *kinko, iriko* and some rarer names, or simply, *namako.* Because haiku poets did not actually observe/eat them, in this book, they are a marginal presence and only appear in force among the Sundry Sea Slug section, in "The Ecological Sea Slug" and "Place Pun Sea Slugs."

Holothuria atra (completely-lewd-black): Until recently called *Halodeima atra,* or "salt-monster black" (black brine-monster), *H. atra* belongs to a family of sea cucumber on the equivalent taxonomic level with *Stichopodidae,* and *Cucumariae,* above. In 1943, Yamauchi described it as "a true black color probably unexampled in the animal world," though it may sometimes wear coral detritus and appear white. Like the above-mentioned black *S. japonicus,* it was popularly called *kuronamako,* or "black sea cucumber." In Japan, it was used for stunning fish (details later) but generally not eaten. One of the main species comprising the international trepang trade, it was cured and exported to East Asia from South Japan. It may appear in some export-related haiku as *iriko* and is commonly depicted housing a fish in its coelomic cavity ungracious enough to nibble on its lungs.[1]

Halodeima lubrica (slimy-salt-monster): Commonly found in the surf in South Japan, this reddish navy-blue or blackish-blue family is known for being extremely slippery to handle. Known only by local names such as *ômushi* ("big-bug"), *gorô* ("lazy-guy?") and so forth, it was cooked and cut up for porgy – does "sea bream" sound better? – bait. Perhaps there are haikus in local dialect.

Questionable holothurians: A number of sea cucumber names appearing more often in literature than in haiku are problematic. I give only the most common one here for it has aspects relating to markings and identification.

---

1. *Fish-Boarder* This fish, or its relative, receives three paragraphs in the fourth part of the 1871 *Harper's New Monthly Magazine's* article "Along the Florida Reef." Some choice sentences: "As the trepang begins to stretch up his mouth toward the air, a fish's head is seen bobbing up and down, peering into the external world from the interior. Now, 'a joke is a joke;' and we first thought someone had perpetrated a joke on us. On various and numerous investigations, this species of fish is found living *within* the intestine or stomach of the trepang! Is it not unaccountable that a fish, well formed and perfect in all its parts, should be placed in such a position [depending on 'the kindly offices' of a 'lower' creature] for life? A hanger-on he certainly is." The author/s guessed that either the doubling intestine had no secretion in the latter half or the fish is protected by "an extra secretion of mucus" of its own and concludes that this "apparently absurd situation . . . affords another instance of the presence of a Guiding Hand in this wondrous world." As a matter of fact, the fish avoids the sandy bms by puncturing the cloaca to live between it and the body wall of the sea cucumber. The sand is bound by a mucus coating, so it does not leak into the cavity. (A. K. corresp) *torako, torago* – (tiger-sea-cucumber). This name is not as common now as it was in the Edo era when it was sometimes written in Chinese characters as "tiger-sea-mouse" or glossed as a pronunciation for the more usual "sea-mouse." Some red sea cucumbers (once, perhaps, more plentiful?) show tiger-like stripes and are called *torako*, but the literature cited in OJD and the locations where it appears in haiku (*geographical sea slugs*), suggests it was more commonly used for *kinko*. It is also the most common name for the *namako* – of whatever species – used to exorcise moles: presumably, a tiger would be taken more seriously than a mouse.

Haiku almost never specify the variety of sea cucumber referred to. I suspect this is probably not because the poetic form is too short, nor because the poets didn't know, but because they didn't want to divide and thereby damage a more valuable entity: the *idea* of the creature called *namako*. Thoreau once marveled at the man curious enough to pursue the identity of various crying bugs. He, for his part, preferred to let them remain unseen in their dens and continue to enjoy the wonder of not-knowing. With the apparently amorphous sea cucumber embodying this very state of mind and the haiku poet working in a tradition that deeply respected original naivety, how could they feel other than Thoreau? But I may be wrong.[1] The lack of identification may be due to nothing more than the fact that – unless we are taxonomically inclined – wherever we may be, the sea cucumbers we know are simply "sea cucumbers."

So saying, the *Holothuroidea* class has been blessed with too many wondrous names, both scientific and popular, too ignore. What is more curious than those of the genus to which the sea-cucumber which is not a proper *namako*, the *kinko* belongs, the *Cucumaria*.[2] The *maria* are obviously "sea-things" (*mar+ia*) and *cucu*, "cucumiform," (or, wrongly, "cuculate," "hooded"), but I imagine a cuckoo, a virgin and, with the species *Cucumaria curata*, a curate, as well. *Hello, Boccaccio!* The popular name for *C. curata* is better yet: the Black Brooding Sea Cucumber. That, as you will soon see, happens to be a short description of the most powerful metaphors found in Japanese *namako* haiku! Then, there is the long thin *Holothuria impatiens,* a variety easily irritated into shooting out its Cuvierian tubules.[3] In Japanese, it is called *uma-no-mara*, or "horse's dong."[1→] What do you know! A different variety I grew up, possibly *Pentacta frondosa*, is called "donkey's dong," although most I have seen are closer to human dimensions. More poetic yet are the Swedish (?) *Holothureia forskali,* "cotton spinner," because of the white thread protruding from its anus (those Cuverian tubules, again) – in the Nggela tongue more romantically yet, such *pou* (holothurians) are modified by *luluhi*, mother's milk! – the long polka-dotted *Bohadschia argus,* after the hundred-eyed watchdog, called the snake-eyed sea cucumber (*ja-no-me namako*) in Japanese, and, finally, the genus with five tooth-like bone-plates guarding the aboral opening, which boasts the wonderful name *Actinopyga*, or "star-buttocks."[2→]

 # 6

1. *I may be wrong*. As a matter of fact, I *was* wrong. The reason colored *namako* are not found in haiku is not so poetic. Until recently, the terms may not have existed outside of dialect! They are not listed in my ten volume OJD (1975), whereas the red, blue and black catfish (*namazu*) all get *their* own listings! The first red sea slug I find, by Matsumoto Seiki = "peeking in the tub / i'd buy a red sea slug / if there were one" (*akanamako naraba kaubeshi oke nozoku* (net) 赤海鼠ならば買ふべし桶覗く　松本正氣), is dated 1942. While I have found a few more red sea slug haiku on the net, I have yet to find a one in print. I found no blue sea slug haiku, until a poet I knew spoofed one (cf. "Talking Sea Slugs."). And, at last moment, a few more colored sea slug barely slipped under the wire.

2. *Cuckoo Maria* Other *Cucumaria* include *C. fisheri fisheri, C. frondosa, C. lubrica, C. miniata, C. mirabilis, C. pallida, C. piperata, C. sinorbis, C. stephensoni and C. vegae.* Cuckoo Maria of the fish fish, of the palm trees, lubricated, miniature, miraculous and pallid with longing . . .

3. *H. impatiens* A photograph of *Holothuria impatiens* in Buchsbaum and Milne ( ) shows it emitting "bluish white, opalescent, and very sticky threads" resembling maiden-hair spaghetti – *somen* in Japanese – [Cuverian tubules] longer than its body, which is only 4-5x its width. A Japanese photograph of the same shows a relaxed creature at least 20x longer than its width and truly resembling what its Japanese name suggests, the part of a stallion, extended.

III
what is haiku?

Most educated occidentals have heard something about haiku, and there are excellent haiku poets, publications and general interest in many languages, as may be gathered from William Higginson's *Haiku World: An International Almanac*, which "includes over 1,000 poems originally written in 25 languages by 600 poets from some 50 countries." But judging from the appalling amount of "haiku" that bear no resemblance to haiku in the North American mass media and the love-poems that all too often pass for haiku in Spanish (I can't speak for other Western languages/cultures), haiku is in danger of losing its soul as it gains in popularity. In Vanatu, formerly the New Hebrides, a hodgepodge of English, Spanish, French, and local tongues – spoken by people engaged in the production and trade of trepang (dried sea cucumber) – is called by the localization of the French term for sea cucumber, *bêche-de-mer* ("worm of the sea;" pron.: beach-du-mar): *Bislama.*[1] Call it sea slug pidgin. If haiku is

→ **1. Donkey's Dong** The best proof of this metaphor is in the pudding. According to the Ming Dynasty Chinese book 食物本草 (plants-real-herbs), "Today, people from the North [of China] make fake dishes of this [tasty and valuable] sea slug out of donkey penises." In the first paragraph of his *Namako no Dokuhon,* Arakawa Kôman writes further that "there are quintessentially Chinese true stories that seem made-up about diplomatic disputes and wars caused because of this [fraud]." (No source of these stories is given.) Perhaps, I should add that one of the many old Chinese names for sea cucumber was "man-child," i.e. the male member. As we see in the *Holothuroidea* paragraph above and will explore further in "Lubricious Sea Slugs," this resemblance was even more central to the natural history of the sea cucumber in the West.

→ **2. Anus with a Bite as Well as a Bark?** An actively defensive *anus dentatus* is an atractive concept, but not necessarily true: "The idea that these anal teeth protect *Actinopyga* from pearlfish is speculation and has never been tested. Indeed, some *Actinopyga* house pearlfish, while some cukes lacking teeth do not." (AK: corres.) Apparently, the sea cucumber does pucker up when the fish tries to return – finding the spot with its sharp-pointed tail and wriggling in backwards! – after going out, "but eventually the need for oxygen [cukes breath through the anus] becomes too great" and the "rear end" opens (Buchsbaum and Milne). To paraphrase Darwin, in a world where wedges will be driven into all spaces, nothing is completely inviolable. Who would think that a moray eel was unable to defend its mouth? Yet, the cornet fish shoves its bone-covered snout right in – perhaps to take gut content and, perhaps bits of the gut itself right from one of the world's most ferocious mouths (and we are not talking symbiosis, it injures the moray)! To return to our subject, the fish does not

really live in the *anus,* but passes through a hole in the cloacus to live within the body cavity (AK corres). Steinbeck, in *The Log of the Sea of Cortez,* mentions finding what he and Ricketts thought a new species of Pearlfish which he hoped to name *Proctophilus Winchellii,* presumably in honor(?) of the dirt-dishing father of sleaze journalism. Years later, a proctophobic National Geographic photograph caption failed to mention even the end of the sea cucumber used by the fish, euphemizing: "Backing into its garage, a pearlfish parks inside a sea cucumber." (W.A. Stark II:"Marvels of a Coral Realm." Nov. 1966)

1. Bislama One abecedarian claims Bislama comes from "Beach La-mar." Where the "La" comes from we are not told. Bislama may be properly capitalized because it has been adopted as the national language of Vanatu. Here is an example passage from Jack London's *Jerry of the Islands*: "'Sati,' Van Horn read. 'Last monsoon begin about this time, him fella Sati get 'm sick belly belong him too much; bime by him fella Sati finish altogether,' he translated into beche-de-mer the written information: Died of dysentery July 4th, 1901." Tsurumi Yoshiyuki identifies Bislama more broadly with Melanesia and writes in a poetic vein:

> Through the sea slug on the sea floor, a common tongue was born to the people who worked there together: *namakogo* (seaslugese? Viz "Talking Sea Slug" in "Sundry Sea Slugs") In order not to conflate the sea slug *bislama* with the language *bislama,* the latter is also written B&M. (NNM:1993)

Q = So what could we call a country music ditty in Melanesia?   A = *C&W in B&M.*

not to lose its distinct character and, likewise, turn into an amorphous disappointment, we must make an effort to define and keep alive the spirit of traditional haiku.[1] So, I hope all readers who *think* they know haiku, but are not fluent in Japanese, pay careful attention to the next paragraph.

In Japanese, a haiku is a one-line poem touching upon seasonal phenomena, natural or cultural of about seventeen syllabets (my term for uniformly short syllables that can be written with a single letter of a phonetic syllabary). Aseasonal haiku do exist, *but only as exceptions included with a body of properly seasoned work.*[2] Japanese do not separate their written words, but do recognize that syllabets usually sound best clumped in fives and sevens. While 5-7-5 is the most common pattern, I doubt if it is found in even half of the haiku, for one also finds 12-5, 7-5-5, 5-5-7, 5-12 and others which, together, comprise a majority. There is, as everyone notices, no end-rhyme *per se,* but there is *much more* internal rhyme than is generally recognized, and most good poems have a crisp snap, or failing that, a sound suitable to the subject. *It is not enough to simply count syllabets.* While Japanese do not recognize beat — they usually claim all their syllabets are equally stressed and equal in length (both things patently absurd) — I *do.* I have found, independently of Blyth, who discovered it long before me, that Japanese haiku, even when the syllabet count exceeds the ideal (in old haiku, six and eight count clumps are fairly common) — usually have seven beats.[3]

IV
how translation?

In English, I find seven beats produces snappy poems of length roughly similar to the original. I generally use a three-line translation, not because it is correct — who can say what is correct given the facts as I gave them above — or current, but because it looks good when centered. Unlike English,

1. *Amorphous Disappointment.* On second reading, I realized this is terribly unfair to pidgin tongues, for they are very creative and satisfying in their own way (Peter Farb, in *Word Play,* is convincing here.). I apologize, but leave the sentence, for it is *also* true that there is something precious about vertically deep culture and language, as typified by written Japanese in general and haiku in particular. It, not pidgin, is endangered as globalization acts, in a sense, as a powerful pidginizing force.

2. *Aseasonal Haiku* Returning to the semitropics, I have found the seasonal requirement difficult. It is not so much that there are less seasonal changes, but that they are often too subtle to share with others in a form as brief as haiku, where many of the best poems exist in a symbiotic or parasitic relationship with other poems on the same theme. I find that including something about the time of day makes a poem *seem* more haiku, even if it wouldn't help placement in a haiku almanac. Without the connection to some kind of time, or flow outside the writer, haiku risks becoming too narcissistic. If a haiku is too unconnected to evoke a response in most readers, it should be embedded in a *haibun* narrative.

3. *Beats, Not Syllables!* Reading Hofstadter's *Le Ton beau de Marot* (1997), I see a word may not be sufficient even for the wise. *Look.* I agree that

sticking to form is a stimulus to the imagination and, myself, love rhyme (and have published essays in defense of rhyme) for that reason. But you are mistaken if you think of haiku as forming "a symmetric 5-7-5 pattern." Bashô's *furuike ya / kawazu tobikomu / mizu no oto,* which you give for the example — it *is* the most famous haiku ever written, not "what he [Sato] says must be the most famous haiku ever written" — is, in fact, a good example of an asymmetrical 5-12 split, for the *ya* cuts the first part (the old pond) from frog and verb *tobikomu* (jump-in) which modifies, i.e. links to the *mizu-no-oto* (water-sound) in the original. The poem has eight beats, one more than usual in the first part of the poem, which gives the old pond a strong presence. (the "ya" is not too strong, though, so we might say 7 beats plus a hint of one more). Many old haiku had six syllabets in the first or last part, so eight beats were not uncommon. But no Japanese has ever come close to the plodding thirteen or fourteen beats (!) of Hofstadter's "We won't hiccough back, / won't spring through time toward the past. / It's phony, it's dead." (from *"Once Upon a Time Alone"* in IBID) A phonetic atrocity such as this belies the sub-title of Hofstadter's book, *In Praise of the Music of Language!* Content aside, the "formal constraint" of a haiku is, first and foremost, to *sound* right.

where a single horizontal line has no thingness,[1] a single line haiku, written vertically in Japanese, looks like an objéct, a work of art suitable for hanging. This enjoyable visual experience is what I would reproduce in English.[2] When possible, I use an AAB rhyme scheme, with Emily Dickinson vowel rhymes rather than full rhymes when possible, for I feel this best approximates the internal rhyme of the original. Less often, I use what is almost *de rigor* in Brazil, ABA. But I don't hold myself to rhyme, because traditional haiku is not that consistent, and no rhyme – or, at least, nothing obvious – often works. In this case, the translation usually needs something else: extreme brevity (the beat compressed into few syllables), a good punch line, wording that is astonishingly apt . . .

瓦とも石ともさては海鼠かな　來山

kawara to mo ishi to mo sate wa namako kana – raizan (1653-1716)
(tile-neither stone-neither, well, then, sea slug!/?/ó)

7

natural rorschach

neither tile
nor stone: what, then
a sea slug?

小石にも魚にもならず海鼠哉　子規

koishi ni mo sakana ni mo narazu namako kana – shiki (1867-1902)
(small-stones-as-even, fish-as-even, be/become-not seaslug!/?/ó)

8

it doesn't seem
a small stone or a fish
the sea cucumber

contrary [3]→

it won't be
a stone or a fish,
the sea slug

何の実の沈んで動く生海鼠哉　尾風

nan no mi no shizunde ugoku namako kana – bifû? (1768)
(what seed's sunken/sinking moves/moving sea slug/s !/?/ó)

#9

instant evolution

some seeds
that sunk now move?
sea cucumbers

---

1. *Single Line Haiku* The only successful one I have seen in English was Ginsburg's mosquito blown over the swamp, for the subject's horizontal movement fit the form.

2. *Visual Experience of Poetry* Because of the beauty of the brush stroke and, even with printed poems, the large number of double readings dependent on visual discrimination, Japanese poetry is not so oppressively aural as ours; but, please do not think my care for poems as visual objects extends to the graphic art of Occidental (here, I include the Near East, for it is West to the Japanese) "pattern-poems," which I find akin to the childish titillation of topiary art.

As a quick perusal of this book will show, I make more than one translation of many poems. This is not just laziness or a failure of nerve (something unforgivable, for the selection and translation of haiku is a test of editing ability). Multiple translation is often the only way to translate all the faces of a poly-faceted poem in a witty, which is to say, brief manner, when trying to squeeze all the information into one poem would kill it, and not including that information – and this is, regretfully, almost standard with haiku translation today – would constitute negligence with respect to the intent of the original. Multiple translation is also fun. The playful polymath Douglas F. Hofstadter built a huge book around a score or more translations of a single poem, *Le Ton beau de Marot.* There is much more to this art of *paraversing*, as I call it, [1] but I will not waste words on something the reader will soon discover anyway. Let me just say that Titles, likewise, are added to supply information otherwise lost; although I must confess to playing with them when my wit so wills. I do not think it irresponsible for it is obvious. Using "Rorschach" to title a seventeenth century haiku fools no-one.

> *What we are engaged in when we do poetry is error, the willful creation of error, the deliberate break and complication of mistakes out of which may arise unexpectedness.*" (Anne Carson: "Essay on What I Think About Most" in *Men in the Off Hours*)

Anne Carson's words are a far more accurate description of *my* translation than her own poetry. Error played a central role in the writing of this book. Occasionally , I do something that may sorely test the patience of all who would be happier to get it right from the start – the academic 5% of my readership who are most likely to review the book – namely*, I leave my mistranslation/s in place and take my time revealing the process of correcting it.* I do this for several reasons. First, because the metamorphosis of a poem, like that of anything first viewed as one thing that changes into something else – as with Raizan's and Bifû's haiku, above, describing their perception – is part of its attraction and brings a touch of narrative, mystery to the book. Second, because poems so gained are often too pleasing to abort merely because they are wrong. With the best, I felt very lucky to have misread the original! (For this reason, I now do at least one translation of all poems before asking questions to someone who might know more than me). And, third, because I think the problems of translation between exotic tongues is itself fascinating and mistakes often tend to be instructive. There is something to be said from the point of view of professional writing or scholarship for cleaning up one's act and revealing only the well-polished final result. But, I do not think of myself as a writer or as a scholar. I am only someone who has many interesting things to share. In my opinion, nothing beats *show and tell.*

V

when verbatim?

Japanese grammar is largely topsy-turvy to ours. The verbs are at the end, after the objects with their *post*positions rather than prepositions. More troublesome for the translator, haiku are often written in something we might call "Japanese-style," which I first noticed in the oldest collection of Japanese

→ **3. "Contrary" Sea Slug?** As we shall see later, *contrariness* is one trait associated with the sea slug and the sea slug-eater. On the other hand, the sea slug is also a synonym for spinelessness and meek acceptance of fate. Titles sometimes help to bring out the metaphor between-the-lines.
1. Paraversing I fully define and demonstrate types of paraversing at my new website, www.paraverse.org.

Readers interested in wordplay that creates something of lasting worth – if you think poems are worthwhile, that is – rather than simply killing time (creating crosswords and acrostics, etc., the pleasure of which ends when they are solved) – are invited to participate in the paraversing part of my website, which, you will find, is not limited to Japanese or translated poetry.

poetry, the *Manyôshû*, where *the entire poem is but the modification of a single noun*, the subject, that comes last.[1]   Were this sort of modification limited to a short adjectival phrase, English could do quite well, for it has the ability, not found in Romance languages, to modify front and back. Unfortunately, there is more to it. Take this extremely simple contemporary haiku:

古びたる船板に置く海鼠かな　草城

furubitaru funaita ni oku namako kana – hino sôjô   (1901-1956*)*
(aging[weather-beaten] deck-on place/put sea slug/s!/?/ó)

#10

placed on
the weathered deck
a sea slug!

∼

sea slugs
put on
the old deck

Unlike Japanese, English cannot place the sea slug directly after the active verb. Instead, it must use a passive verb and turn the modifying phrase into a dependent clause as in the first translation, in which case the poem weakens, or put the sea slug up front as in the second translation, thereby losing the greater dramatic effect of leaving the sea slug/s for last. Other problems far less important than this destructive difference of syntax include the lack of number (sea "slug" or sea "slugs") and specific persons (in this case, we could get away without knowing whether it was first or third person, but this is often impossible).   In a word, translation as most people think of it, based on their understanding of cognate tongues, is *impossible* between languages as mutually exotic as English and Japanese. Perhaps we should not even speak of "translation" but deconstruction followed by "re-creation."[2]

This is where verbatim glossing, that is to say, rendering the original into English word for word, as ridiculous and confusing as our widely differing syntax's make it, comes in handy. By studying it, the reader who does not know Japanese can *feel* why the phrase "an accurate and precise translation" does not rightly apply to exotic tongues (even if such is written down in publishing contracts). I know that this verbatim translation sometimes looks as indigestible as dried sea slug, but slow down and you will discover its use.   For, together with the real translations and my explanations, this ugly device is intended to show interested readers something other books of translated poetry generally do not: *what*

1. *Japanese Style*   Many of these Japanese-style trains of modification, which might also be called *plot-less poems,* say only "[i] love [you] *so* much," with the "so" part comprising 90% of the poem, itself a problem to translate because in English we cannot love someone "as much as there are countless grains of sand on the beach," or, "as intensely as the waves that never stop bashing into the rocky shore are myriad." We do not think that countable things (even if infinite in number) can serve as a simile for emotional extent. My books in Japan/ese have emphasized similarities between our respective languages, but writing for English speakers, I feel it important to emphasize the reverse, for most readers have virtually no experience with an exotic tongue.

2. *Translation, Recreation and Compensation* Because

of the extraordinary nature of translation between exotic tongues, the brain-power expended in doing a good job – trying to keep close to the meaning of the original without completely losing its style – is greater than that expended to ferry poems across smaller gulfs. This is indirectly acknowledged by the Japanese when they pay translators royalties as high as that paid to authors, include a translator's afterword and translator's biography (sometimes longer than that of the author) and place the name prominently on the cover (in many cases equal in size to the author). In the USA, this is generally not the case. Though it requires more years of study to make a good translator of an exotic tongue than to make a medical specialist or lawyer, translators don't earn a fraction of their income. They should, at least, receive more nominal reward.

is really going on.   This allows me to enjoy more liberty to play with the translation, all the while secure in knowing I am not misleading my readers.

One caveat – the verbatim gloss (the funny-looking hyphenated/slashed English) *itself* misleads in the sense that the lack of equivalent grammatical devices in the two languages might seem to suggest that Japanese is crude and even weird, when it is neither. Indeed, Japanese may well have a larger vocabulary (The claim on English vocabulary made by English scholars and Guinness Book to the contrary), and *surely* boasts a greater variety of styles than English. The paradox of translating between exotic tongues is that *closeness can take us apart.*[1] The closer the verbatim gloss gets to the Japanese syntax, the rougher the English, where it is a fact that the original Japanese is as smooth or smoother than my translations that follow. Likewise, for details such as "slug/s." Obviously, Japanese is not expressed in slashes; but is there a simpler way to show that the original (like the English pronoun "you") has no number? The hyphenated postpositions look outlandish, where they are as normal in Japanese as our prepositions; but, I think that showing them in their original place gives the non-Japanese reader a better sense of the original structure than shifting them before the nouns or adjectives would. (For more details on how to get the most out of the word-for-word gloss, see the Verbatim Gloss Key in the *Appendix*.)

VI

apologia

I leave the history of haiku and its poets to others. Here, I only concern myself with the history of haiku on my subject. And even that will be loose and incidental to this book, because my approach of choice is thematic, which is to say analytical, rather than chronological, though I do my best to establish priority by dating as I go. If I occasionally criticize others, or, by adding information they neglected, appear to put them on the spot, it is not because I do not appreciate their work. It is because I have an ax to grind, a very important ax that could help remake the modern idea of haiku. In a word, years of reading old collections has brought me to the realization that *most old haiku are multi-layered.*[2] They are not the simple snapshot of nature they might seem to one ignorant of the allegorical possibilities, allusions and poetic conceit. Furthermore, in my opinion, this complexity, this artfulness, is not a *minus* (as many if not most Japanese scholars, who deprecate it as "Chinese" and "artificial," might think) but a *plus*. It is why, on the whole – with many exceptions being my rule – I prefer pre-twentieth century haiku to post-twentieth-century haiku. There is simply so much more to chew! (And, for the first edition, I apologize for the uneven design and lack of a full index.)

1. *Close Translation*   In Japan, there is a school of thought which seriously believes that close translation reflects the mind-set of the foreigner. A translator of this school carries all of the pronouns found in the English original into Japanese, ignoring the fact that pronouns carry much more weight in Japanese (where they tend to be used in what linguists call a "marked case" and stand-out phonetically because of the syntax), with the result of making English speakers come across as pushy louts.   The reverse side of this is the "honorable tea" and "honorable mother" and so forth of early twentieth century Japanese-English translation, which makes Japanese seem absurdly polite because English has no equivalent of the "o" placed other (i.e. used where we might use the possessive pronoun).   Translating between exotic tongues is a damned-if-you-do   and   damned-if-you-don't proposition. If you don't try to carry across things without equivalents on the other side of the exotic divide, you lose the difference, the newness, the information; but if you do carry it across, this difference, newness, information turns into gobbledygook or worse, ends up creating misunderstanding.   See my   *Orientalism & Occidentalism*: Is Mistranslation of Culture Inevitable? (also from Paraverse Press, 2003?)
2. *Layered Haiku* The meaning of my assertion will become clear over the course of the first few chapters, so let me just say here that thanks to the mix of Chinese characters and Japanese phonetics, the density of old haiku can compare with that of Joycean phrases typified by the title of one of his novels: *"Finnegan's Wake."*

<u>text</u>
<u>the . . . . sea slug</u>[1]

Each chapter of RISE, YE SEA SLUGS! focuses on a different type of sea cucumber, not a different biological species, but a different semiological species. In biology, the line between species is not always solid. Even with DNA called in to arbitrate, arbitrary lines, i.e. definitions, have to be made. The same thing is true with respect to organizing a poetic typology.

直線を知らぬ存ぜぬ海鼠かな　マツク・ヒデ

chokusen o shiranu zonzenu namako kana --- matsuku hide (contemp)
(straight-line/s[obj], know/ing-not, knowing/existing-not, seaslug/s[subj] !/?/ó)

#11

allogical animal

straight lines
are beyond the ken
of a sea slug

Moreover, I had to do this work completely *de novo,* with no Linnaean system, indeed no prior system at all, to assist me.[2] My *modus operandi* was simple. I collected every old haiku and *senryu* on the sea cucumber I could – and tried to divide them thematically. I wavered back and forth as I made new finds. It was something like playing cards, where a new draw might make you decide to go for a full-house rather than a straight. In the end, I had a good hand.[3] As the Table of Content shows, I managed to invent no less than twenty-one semiological species – metaphorical groupings, if you prefer – and, as the text will show, many more sub-species, scores of which have been compiled into a large extra chapter of Sundry Slugs.

oh, sea slug!
not knowing not living
straight lines

If the range of individual difference for a given trait in a species can be listed in serial or drawn as a simple distribution curve, even a complex graph of overlapping curves – or for that matter, a tree[1] → –

1. *"Sea Slug" from Now On!* Beginning with chapter 1, the sea cucumber will generally answer to the name "sea slug" both in the translations and in my commentary, for it is hard to use one word *in* a poem and another *outside* of it! Since the sea slug proper, the *Nudibranch,* will make no more appearances in this book, no harm should come from borrowing its name. No more apologies or explanations shall be made.

2. *Prior Systems* Actually, there is *one* prior system, Shiki's 12 volume *Bunrui Haiku Zenshu,* or "categorized haiku anthology;" but it is phenomenological, rather than semiological. To wit, his sub-categories of "sea slug" poems are (poems including elements that are: 1)"meteorological, biological, geographical;" 2) "implements;" 3) "costume and corpus;" and 4) "exclude corpus, etc.," to which he adds a category with only one poem, 5) "big sea slug," two more with only two poems each 6) "sea slug seller" and 7) "sea slug chopping"[a dish], and, finally, 8) "sea slug guts." Shiki, known as the father of modern haiku, but, in my opinion, the last great old-style haiku poet, wrote more sea slug poems than any poet up to his time, but his taxonomy was of no help to me! (The anthology, itself, however, is a great data bank!)

3. *Good but Not Perfect Hand* I would be lying by omission not to say that my hand could have been better yet had I known at the start what I do now. I might have pulled off a Royal Flush; created a more inclusive, multi-tiered system of metaphor that managed to fit more of the Sundry Sea Slugs. I ended up swallowing far more modern sea slug haiku than I had time to digest and restructure.

cannot show the convoluted relationship of many species, sub-species and their various traits. That is to say, my chapters and the haiku within them not only overlap each other, but do so in ways that defy proper narrative. The overall relationship can only be grasped at a glance by three-dimensional modeling, or the next best thing, overlapping Venn diagrams, a sample of which, I plan to offer (below) in the best tradition of Laurence Sterne.[2] Arranging such material in a serial narrative was, to borrow holothurian expert and curator Philip Lambert's fine pun, truly a taxing problem![3] I hope that even if the ride is occasionally bumpy, good readers from every ilk of life will still find themselves transported by my sea slug serenade.

tristam sandy

straight lines
are beyond sea slug's
wildest dreams

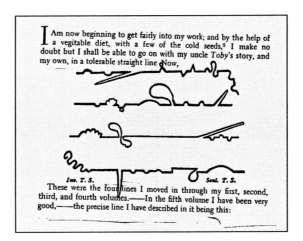

←1. *Tree Diagrams* [new] If the tree is modeled in three dimensions and limbs are allowed to loop back and fuse with themselves or other limbs, a tree might work. Indeed, the ideal tree of life is now such an animal.

2. **Laurence Sterne** As we shall later see, in Japan, *Tristam Shandy* has a specific holothurian connection. I managed to find some of Sterne's strange squiggly plot lines penned for his exuberant mid-eighteenth century book in my unpublished book about the mind-life of a cat who thinks too much: *Han-chan's Dream*. Had Sterne known about Venn diagrams, he might have tried them, too. He also would have forgiven me for not actually doing those diagrams. They will be in the 2nd edit..

3. *Philip Lambert* The curator of Invertebrate Zoology at the Royal B.C. Museum. His poetic article "Taxing Problems" will be cited later.

this is a reproduction of an illustration of a trepang
(as the soviet scientists call the sea cucumber that japanese call namako)
published in Arakawa Kohman's Namako Dokuhon (ndh), but originally from Levin, V.S. 1982:
Japanese Sea Cucumber (USSR Academy of Sciences, Far East Center, Institute of Marine Biology,
Science Council for Biosphere Problem, 192p. Vladivostok).
as you can see, it does not look very cucumbery
there is no need to translate the details
for biologists will know and
others will not care
to know
+
note
however
the external spike-like things
for they are played upon in a number of haiku

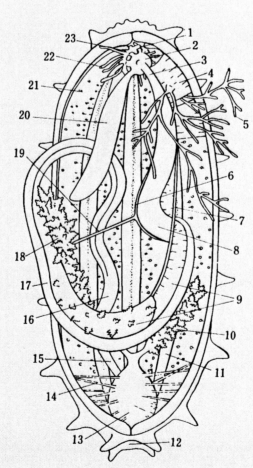

図6. マナマコの体制模式図. 内部構造を示す(レービン,1982)
1.石灰管, 2.環状水管系, 3.食道, 4.腸間膜, 5.生殖巣, 6.腹血管, 7.背血管, 8.腸第
1部, 9.腸間膜(血管網, 奇網, 怪網), 10.呼吸樹(水肺), 11.縦走筋(輻筋), 12.肛門,
13.総排泄腔, 14.総排泄腔索引筋, 15.後腸, 16.腸第3部, 17.腸第2部, 18.呼吸樹,
19.横血管, 20.ポーリ氏嚢, 21.瓶嚢, 22.口縁触手, 23.石灰管(囲食道骨片)

1
the frozen together sea slug

The sea slug is not so catholic a winter phenomenon as coldness, snow, dead trees or iced-over lakes. It just so happens that in most of the main island of Japan, and more importantly in Kanto, the region including the "water-gate" city of Edo (Tokyo), capital of Tokugawa (1603-1867) Japan and the cradle of haiku, as well as in the secondary cradle of haiku of Kansai (especially the sea near Osaka), they are caught, prepared and eaten in the winter, both because that is when they are visible and in their prime and because catching them was generally forbidden in other seasons for reasons we would now call "ecological." Had Hokkaido – the northern island – been the capital of Japan, the *kigo* (seasonal term for haiku) "winter sea slug" wouldn't fly, for the situation is reversed there, and the slugging season doesn't begin until the summer! This point was made by the man who wrote the largest book on sea slugs ever written, Tsurumi Yoshiyuki, who further observed,

> I can't remember where I heard it, but Kuramoto Satoi criticized the NHK weather broadcast saying "the typhoon has made it to remote Hokkaido" as "Tokyo ethnocentrism." The same thing might be said about the selection of *kigo.* (nnm)

The Japanese Public Broadcast Service (NHK) is supposed to have a national perspective, but it is hard for the poor weatherman to pretend he is nowhere in particular. In the case of haiku almanacs, the *saijiki* maker wouldn't even want to pretend, for locality rather than universality is what almanacs are all about. Still, there is a strong tendency to create "Japanese," rather than regional almanacs. There might well be *saijiki* made in Hokkaido where the sea slug is a summer theme, as there are maps in Australia which set the "land down under" on top of the world where it and, for that matter, all of us belong; [1] but I have yet to read a haiku almanac that didn't put the *namako* in the winter – indeed there were few Japanese in Hokkaido over the period when most of the poems in this book were written – or begin its sea slug listing with the following, very wintry poem by the *okina,* or old gentleman, as haiku's most revered master came to be called (and depicted) despite his dying at age 50.[2]   Far be it for me to break so hallowed a tradition.

生 き な か ら 一 つ に 氷 る 生 海 鼠 哉　 芭 蕉

ikinagara hitotsu ni kôru namako kana – basho (1693)
(living-while, one-in [together] freeze sea slugs!/?/ô)

#12

sea-slugs
– alive –
but frozen into one

trans. blyth (hh1) [1] →

1. Hokkaido Haiku In 1980, I wrote a Japanese molecular biologist in Australia suggesting that Australians could use an upside-down map. He responded by sending me one that was already on sale. This experience taught me that locals can look out for themselves. Hence, I suspect there are Hokkaido *saijiki* with sea slug poems incorporating summer phenomena, though the Northerners share the mainland (*hondo*) food culture to the extent that sea slug is a winter food there, too. See "Hokkaido Sea Slugs" in the Sundry Sea Slugs appendum.

2. Bashô Ogina I have an illustrated book of haiku for Japanese children, which shows Matsuo Bashô walking with his famous gnarled cane. He looks at least 70. Another in Robert Hass's *The Essential Haiku* has him seated, looking a toothless 90 if he is a day! It would be interesting to poll the Japanese on his age at death.

still alive
they are frozen in one lump
sea slugs

trans. ueda (mb) [2]

a solid catch

still alive
sea slugs freezing
together

rigor im/mortis

frozen
together: living
sea slugs

So the original sea slug of the haiku world was taken, rather than witnessed, in the wild. I first imagined Bashô saw sea slugs pulled up by long poles fitted with rake-like scoops, and thrown together to freeze by cold-fingered fishermen; but chances are he saw them in a pail on land. I have never come across an allegorical reading of this poem, but, considering that most of Bashô's poems alluded to his social circumstance – greeting, farewell, praise, censure, description – we might *also* dare to imagine our poet sleeping together with other travelers in a very cold inn.

芭蕉の句屹立しくる海鼠かな　宇佐美魚目
bashô no ku kitsuritsushikuru namako kana – usami gyomoku (1936)
(bashô's haiku looming-stands seaslug/s!/?/ŏ)

#13

bashô's *ku*
looms up before us
sea slugs

This modern poet with a pen name that translates as "fish-eye" apparently means to excuse his difficulty with writing sea slug haiku on Bashô's famous haiku, or *ku*, to use the more economic Japanese term. Do not imagine our sea slugs rising yet; the looming alludes to a *namakokabe*, or "sea slug wall." The bulging grout on this wall does resemble a mass of slug, so the allusion isn't bad but, luckily for this book, most poets were not psyched-out by Bashô's sea slug/s. If anything, the sea slug would seem to be a lightning rod for inane poems, so much so that one contemporary poet writes:

真面目さが取り柄の海鼠踏まないで　みよこ
majimesa ga torie no namako fumanai de – miyoko (contemp)
(seriousness-is-handle=worth/value's seaslug tread-not [please])

#14

just don't tread
on the seriously cool
sea cucumbers

1. *Blyth Translation Format* The punctuation of Blyth's original translation is "Sea-slugs; / Alive, – / But frozen into one." The period is in the poem and the first and third verses are indented. I suppose the visual ugliness of such an arrangement might be considered appropriate here, but the same ugly parsing is found for beautiful subjects and the holothurian is, at least, symmetrical.

2. *Ueda Translation* I only removed one colon here. The added "lump" is a good word and a good vowel-rhyme with "slug." Without the unneeded "they are," this would be a fine translation.

> just take care
> not to step on slugs good for
> being earnest

I am not sure that Miyoko (a self-effacing soul) herself knows how good her poem is. I do know that I cannot do it justice, because, in English, *worthiness* is not expressed as a "handle" and even if it were would not pun on the very sea sluggish problem of getting a grip.   The poet herself has written a very light sea slug verse, as we will see, so I take this poem to be a reminder to herself as well as to others that the serious sea slug poem deserves attention. It makes me reflect: I hope *my* introduction of a variety of haiku of the likes that I dare say have never been translated does not distract the reader from the serious poems!

かたまつてあはれ凍てつく海鼠かな　鬼城
katamatte aware ite tsuku namako kana – kijô (1864-1938)
(lumped/grouped/hardened pitiful/beautiful, frozen-stick seaslug!/?/ǿ)

#15

> sea slugs
> pathetic together
> frozen fast

> *still life*

> sea slugs
> pathetically frozen
> in a knot

> *in a fix*

> how pathetic
> those huddled sea slugs
> freezing together

> *ice-slug*

> how touching
> in a lump! *namako*
> frozen fast

That this is a commentary on Bashô's poem is obvious. What it *means* is not. Did Kijô think the solitary sea slug – depicted as a hermit sage in Shikô's *Maxim* (1712: see appendum) – particularly suffered from being thrown together with its fellows?

#15

悲しみの形のままに海鼠凍て　鷹羽狩行
kanashimi no katachi no mama ni namako ite – shugyô (contemp)
(sadness/despair/grief's shape's as-is seaslug/s freezing/frozen)

> a sea slug
> frozen in the shape
> of sadness

We have seen the collective sadness of the sea slugs. Here, imagine a singular slug frozen while shrunken up. Unlike the previous haiku, where I may have helped things along, this "shape of sadness/despair/grief" is clearly the trans-specific body language which Darwin elaborated in *The Expression of the Emotions of Man and Animals.* [1]

解もやらず氷もやらずなまこかな　素丸

toke mo yarazu kôri mo yarazu namako kana – somaru (1712-95)

(thaw-too done-not, ice too done-not sea slug!/?/ó/the/behold)

#17

the sea slug
neither thawed out
nor put on ice

observation

neither thaws
nor turns to ice
sea slugs

We usually thaw fish out or put them on ice, but, the sea slug takes care of itself, going to market *as is*, that is, in the condition described by Bashô – or, that, at least, was what I *thought* the poem described until K.S. informed me that the grammar, properly understood, describes how the subject *is* (reading two) and not how it is *done to* (reading one). As such, the poem would seem to be a fine observation of the ability of sea slugs to live close to zero and would more properly belong to a slightly different metaphorical grouping, *The Cold Sea Slug.*

一塊のままに海鼠の売られけり　徳田千鶴子

ikkai no mama ni namako no urarekeri – tokuda chizuko (2001)

(one-lump's as-is seaslug's sold[+finality])

#18

sea slugs
sold as is
in a lump

Two hundred years later, the *Frozen Sea Slugs* are still here! I do not think that temperature is the whole story here. By being sold frozen together, sea slugs are giving up their clear-cut individual nature to become part of an undifferentiated *lumpen*, a mass. I think the description may well be of a box of frozen imported sea slug, though that would not be the case for the next two older poems.

賣りウリてひとつ凍へる海鼠かな　來爾

uri urite hitotsu kogoeru namako kana – raiu (1772)

(selling, selling one freezes/ing sea slug tis!/?/ó)

#19

sold off
one by one, now one
frozen sea slug

---

1. ***Trans-specific Body Language***   In his running commentaries on Darwin's book, Paul Ekman writes: "The American primatologist Sue Parker remarked that using the term 'analogous' . . . to describe the similarities between human and nonhuman primates, modern biologists would describe those that are due to common ancestry as 'homologous' or as 'shared derived' characters." I would go further. While sea slugs may not share most of the gamut of emotions we associate with specific behavior such as squirming or shrinking, the behavior is none-the-less *homologous* rather than analogous in my opinion – *viz.,* shrinking-up and tensing when uncomfortable, swooning and softening when overcome . . .I think Darwin would agree that the pathetic fallacy is itself partly false.

生きのまま海鼠凍れり桶の底　児玉小秋
iki no mama namako kôreri oke no soko – kodama koshû (2001)
(living as/while-is seaslug/s frozen tub/s' bottom)

#20

still alive
sea slugs frozen
to the bottom of the tub

As Meisetsu (1848-1926) comments about Raiu's poem, the condition of being frozen to the bottom of a tub – not specified in the poem, but possible (why I added the contemporary take) – is in itself "a naturally sea-sluggish feeling" (msbs).   I imagine the salesman walking around from dawn to dusk's end, when he himself begins to chill to the bone, like his sole remaining charge.

#21

海鼠ゐる桶の上水氷りけり　蔦月
namako iru oke no uwamizu kôrikeri – chôtsuki (1932)
(seaslug/s-is/are-tub's top-water freeze[finality])

sea slug tub
the water on top
frozen over

Though the sea slugs are not frozen and this haiku probably should have been saved for the "cold sea slugs" of the last chapter, I found this a delightful new twist on the slugs+freezing motif. The water on top freezes because of the ambient temperature, but the original, with its "tub [where] sea slugs are" – economical in Japanese syntax, but too clumsy to translate into an English haiku – makes it seem as if the presence of the sea slugs has chilled the water to that degree. [1]

#22

凩に生きて届きし海鼠かな　露月
kogarashi ni ikite todokishi namako kana – rogetsu (1872-1928)
([cold winter]gale-in alive/living arrive/delivered seaslug/s !/?/ó)

sea slugs
arriving in a gale
still alive

∼

delivered
in a gale, a live
sea slug

The winds of the winter gale are colder than snow and cut to the bone, but the sea slug, colder yet – perhaps frozen as in Bashô's poem – are alive when they are brought to the poet's home by someone who, likewise, obviously survived. The second reading assumes Rogetsu's sea slug was singular and brought by a friend.

1. *Frozen Water and Sea Slugs* If the water described by Chôtsuki is fresh water, something interesting may happen: Because the sea slug's body fluid is isotonic with its environment – it sucks in water which serves as its blood through perforations in its body – and its body presumes the water around it will be within its required range of salinity, for physiochemical reasons beyond me, they may expand until they pop if left in fresh water! However, if the water had some salt in it, but not as much as that of the sea, the ice would take out water while leaving salt (a process called "brine rejection") and, thereby, prevent the sea slug from expanding and keep it healthy! If, however, the salt level was too high already because of evaporation, the ice would turn the sea slug into ham. Or so I imagine by extrapolating upon what little I know. (Comments from those who *know* are welcome.)

俎板に這ふかとみゆる海鼠かな　太祇

manaita ni hau ka to miyuru namako kana – taigi (1709-72)
(cutting board-on creep-perhaps appears: sea slug!/?/ó)

looking like
it'll creep on the cutting board
a sea cucumber

#23, #24

俎板の氷をぬめるなまこかな　太祇

manaita no kôri o numeru namako kana – taigi
(cutting board-on ice[obj] slides/slips/slimy sea-slug!/?/ó)

slip-sliding
on an icy cutting board
a sea slug

The comatose creature ends up on a cutting board, itself freezing, something not uncommon in the poorly heated Japanese house (I have woken up to find water frozen in a glass by my bed).   For the first poem, "sea *cucumber*" was used because the nominal contradiction of animal motion and vegetable nature is amusing, while "sea *slug*" fits the second poem better.   Call it an opportunistic translation.   Now, combining Taigi's cutting board haiku, which almost bring the sea slug back to life, with Bashô's poem, we get:

いざ斬れば殺生可否の氷海鼠　敬愚

iza kireba sesshô kahi no itenamako – keigu
(in-the-event cut[=cut down]-if, kill[life]-ok/not frozen seaslug)

***that* is the question**

so is it killing
or not killing? to carve
a frozen sea slug

#25, #26

海鼠切る何処から何処まで命か　敬愚

namako kiru doko kara doko made inochi ka – keigu
(seaslug cuts/cutting, where-from, where-to life?)

cutting sea slug
so where is the start
and end of life

～

who can tell
when life is lost, dicing
sea cucumber

1. *Slugs on the Block*   A modern poem on our sea slug's namesake: "the trail of / a passing slug left on / the cutting board" (*namekuji-no tôrishi-ato-no manaita-ni* – kuritsu fukuko).   Another describes the trail: "the slug creeps / leaving behind a charm / or a curse" (*namekujira haite jûbun-o nokosu-goto* – tsuyu-hisashiku mezasu kaori onna).   For the latter, I turned the word for magical writing that could in the original be for good or bad into the wit of the poem.   Perhaps, a more responsible translation would be: "slug creeps on / its writing left behind / for a spell."   When I was in Japan, every Spring I was amazed by the writing left by a slug or snail on wild *daikon* (Japanese huge radish) leaves; it was so similar to the *hiragana* handwriting of the classical female poets. As we shall see later, the sea cucumber also leaves something behind in its trail!

命まだあるかあらんか海鼠斬る 敬愚
inochi mada aru ka aran ka namako kiru – keigu
(life still is or is-not, seaslug cut[=cut down])

#27

ahimsa

whether life
is still there or not
i cut the slug

In the first poem, Keigu plays on the ambiguity of the Japanese word *sesshô* (kill-life[let-live]), which can mean "taking life" in the sense of violating what we call (using the Indian term) *ahimsa,* or "killing, rather than letting live." At the time, he wrote the poem, he thought that the imperfectly frozen creatures may have been alive due to their low metabolism and a unique anti-freeze system.[1]

海鼠酢に漬ける殺生いたしけり 高沢良一
namako su ni tsukeru sesshô itashikeri – takasawa yoshikazu (2003)
(seaslug vinegar-in put/pickle kill-life[buddhist term] doing[+humble and polite verb])

#28

putting up slug
in vinegar i dare to
take a life

Since English lacks a way to make "to do" (here, to "do" or "carry-out" the killing) seem humble and polite, as if it were – and, in a sense, it is – an honor. The best I could do was add the "dare to." Needless to say, no frozen sea slug is involved, but Takasawa's haiku (first read after Keigu wrote the above series) is a good example of the way that the sea slug, by moving little, paradoxically makes us think of life and death more than active fish do. The haiku is also faultless in its realism for, as we shall see in a later chapter, the tissue of the sea slug was long-lived and the pieces being put into the vinegar would, therefore, be alive, in a sense. But to return to the whole slug, sometimes, they doubtless did revive on the cutting board. A young contemporary of Taigi has the slug clearly moving itself.

俎にあくれは動く生海鼠哉 一草
manaita ni agureba ugoku namako kana – issô (1732-1820)
([carving]board-on raised/placed-if/when moves seaslug!/?/ó/'tis)

#29

placed upon
the cutting block, it moves
a sea slug

～

hoh, the slug
moves just before
it is carved

As we shall find out, sea slugs can move, though they tend to sleep by day. They may be awakened, but I imagine this occurring at night. The second reading makes what *might be* the idea explicit.

1. Sea Slug Antifreeze Somewhere, I read – or some night I dreamed? – that sea cucumbers have layers of tissue which work in interesting ways to resist the cold, but all of the biologists I subsequently questioned tell me that frozen sea cucumbers do not revive. This is disappointing because there are "higher" forms of life that can do this, and I would prefer to think it a primitive property we lost.

凍りあふて何を夢みる海鼠かな　青々

kôriôte nani o yumemiru namako kana – seisei (1869-1937)

(frozen-together, what dreams see seaslug/s!/?/ŏ/'tis)

#30

frozen together,
what dreams do they see,
the sea-slugs?

trans. r. h. blyth (hoh2)

frozen together,
what are they dreaming?
sea slugs

trans. addiss+yamamoto (ahm)

frozen together
what do sea slugs
dream about

The "are" of the second translation (Aldiss+Yamamoto) beats Blyth and my "do," for it pulls us closer to the sea slugs. Seisei, whose name translates "blue-blue," asks a wonderful question: *Why?* I don't know. Maybe he saw the sea slugs as cocoons and thought of the dreaming butterfly. Or, maybe he is only fusing elements from two of Bashô's poems. The obvious one we have just seen. The other is Bashô's far more famous octopus, dreaming briefly under the summer moon in his octopus pot. The octopus will be pulled up, perhaps the very next dawn. The dreams of these sea slugs are likewise doomed to a rude awakening.[1]

雪の夜の夢見るものに海鼠かな　高橋睦郎

yuki no yo no yumemiru mono ni namako kana – takahashi mutsurô (contemp)

(snow's night's dreaming/ed thing-as/in[include] sea slug/s !/?/ŏ)

#31

a snowy night
my dreams include
a sea slug

〜

a freezing bed
my dreams are full
of sea slugs

1. *Sea Slug Dreams* I wouldn't be surprised if Octopae did dream – and there is some indication they do -- for they are more intelligent than many land animals that dream. If sea slugs and other *Echinoderms* dream, however, it would probably have to be in/as the dream of a higher form of life, for they have no brain to speak of. There is sweet coincidence here in the fact that the only mammal claimed not to dream is also of the *Echi-* ilk, i.e., the egg-bearing echidna -- "spiked ant eater" in English, and "spiked mole" in Japanese – of Australia (Tasmania) and New Guinea. Since the echidna also boasts a larger frontal lobe than any other animal – including man! – this apparent trait was much extrapolated upon by people interested in the evolution of intelligence. Recent research has shown that the echidna *does* dream, and dreams a lot, but only when its body cools below 28C. While the echidna's body temperature may drop to 6C, the dreaming stops at about 15C, so, *sob!* we have no frozen dreams. (Viz: the work of Stuart Nicol et al of the University of Tasmania)

Depending on how the poem is translated, we can read this contemporary poem as a statement of fact or a play on Seisei's dreaming sea slugs: "Dreaming sea slugs, indeed! I *did* dream sea slugs!" With respect to the sea slug poem that started this, Bashô's, one further reading made in 1935 shows the greater room for such play allowed by Japanese:

> The sea slug frozen together with the vessel. The phrase "while alive/living"(*iki-nagara*) skillfully suggests the sluggish nature of the sea slug. (Ebara Taizo: *Haiku Senjaku*)

I made Ebara's sea slug singular because my Japanese correspondent wrote that, unlike Ebara, he (as I and most readers) saw many sea slugs frozen to each other. But singular or plural, stuck to the vessel, each other, or both, Ebara makes a good point: Bashô described a particularity to capture a generality, to define. His frozen sea-slug/s is an extension, or clarification of what we might call "sea-sluggishness." With this in mind, Seisei's dreaming sea slugs bring to (my) mind a Swedish claim that their (the Swedes) calm and cold exterior belie a passionate interior life beyond the comprehension of more outgoing people.

#31(2) oops!

寒なまこにもぬくもりのありにけり　早乙女健

kannamako ni mo nukumori no arinikeri – saotome ken (1997)
(cold-sea slug-in-too warmth is/has [finality])

even cold
sea slug has some
warmth in it

cold sea slugs
but i can still feel
some warmth

Since *kan* can refer to the coldest two-weeks of the year and/or to food or drink served chilled, one cannot tell if the poem refers to a cold living or prepared sea slug – in the latter case, the warmth would come from the energy expended chewing.

#32

(s) 人の目にどう映ろうと海鼠生き　太田とねり

hito no me ni dô utsurô to namako iki – ôda toneri (c2000)
(people's eyes-in however reflect, sea slug/s live/s)

no matter
how men see them
sea slugs live

This poem was found in a *senryu* site, so it's possible the subject is a lazy or even unconscious person; but if we assume the other possibility, that the sea slug is the subject, we are led to an interesting anomaly. As a rule, men err on the side of life, because it is safer to mistake a snake for a vine than a vine for a snake, or a rock for a bear than a bear for a rock. The survival value of betting – or erring – on the side of caution is such that we may well have an inbred tendency toward zoomorphism. In *Faces in the Clouds: a new theory of religion,* Stewart Elliot Guthrie developed this into a hypothesis of why so men naturally came to believe in God. But, for some reason, with the holothurian, the tendency is to go the other way, to turn this animal into an inanimate object such as a cucumber or even a lifeless one, such as a stick. This is why Basho's haiku about sea slugs frozen together en masse was so astute. It calls our attention to the fact that no matter that we *know* they live, we must work not to literally mortify sea slugs.[1]

1. *Mortify or Reify* Perhaps because it is unnatural, we have no words to denote the opposite vector of *zoomorphize*, i.e., the Cartesian fallacy of treating life as if it were dead. So, I pretend that *mortify,* means "to make dead." *Reify* might have been better, but only academics would know its meaning and that is complicated by the fact not only people but concepts may be *reified=thingified* and, in the case of the latter, the vector is not opposite of zoomorphize, but different altogether.

生 き て 居 る 海 鼠 と 見 れ ば 面 白 し 　麥 人

ikiteiru namako to mireba omoshiroshi – bakujin (1876-1965)

(living seaslug see/view-if/when interesting)

#33

the sea slug
interesting when you
think it's alive

perspective

seen as alive
the sea cucumber is
a lot of fun!

This fine haiku seems ecologically enlightened.   Then, again, to suggest we regard the sea slug as alive is to suggest its apparent lifelessness.   And, there is a possibility the reference is to the challenge of catching slippery dead sea slugs (a theme we will see before long) .

海 底 に 一 存 在 の 海 鼠 哉 　松 本 正 氣

unazoko ni hito sonzai no namako kana – matsumoto seiki (1942)

(sea-bottom/floor-on one-existence-seaslug!/?/ó/ˈtis)

#34

its world

a sea slug
on the bottom of the sea
truly exists

place

a *namako*
on the seabed has
a presence

on the seabed
a *ding an sich* called
sea cucumber

beneath it all

on the bottom
a singular being
the sea slug

it goes deep

there's reality
on the floor of the sea
eg. *namako*

Now, it may be that the poet [1] has recognized how a sea slug in its element has a far more impressive presence than one in a fish-shop or the chafing dish.   But it is more likely that he finds its thingness – being nondescript, *namako* makes a far better *thing* than something with particulars messing with its generality – a fine excuse to pull philosophy down to solid ground, no, lower, to the very bottom of the sea.   The Japanese, after their allies, the Germans, were big on existentialism at the time this poem was written.   While I *did* use the word "being" in one translation, the sea slug need not be alive to serve as proxy for existential reality.   Like Bashô's sea slugs, frozen in a lump, *namako's* life remains a question, as, ultimately, does ours.

1. *Matsumoto and This Haiku* A haiku, theoretically speaking, is itself supposed to be a thing that stands on its own, but a few words, no matter how skillfully chosen, cannot rule out enough possibilities to stand unquestioned. Only a longer poem offers the additional information needed to tell whether it stands for something other than what it purports to be.   Knowing nothing about this poet's circumstances, I cannot say for sure that we do not have here a nod to a friend thrown in jail for being less than patriotic or to another in a submarine, or a sort of victimization mentality, where the oppressed individual (or nation) remonstrates that even us sea slugs have a life! I hope to gain more information about this poet/haiku before the next edition. 再版までに、松本正氣とこ の、海鼠の存在句について、もっと知りたいので す！専門家諸氏、よろしくお願いします。

2
<u>the featureless sea slug</u>

> "This is a sea cucumber," I [10-year-old Ellen] said. "It is an animal. Doesn't it look a lot like a vegetable, though? It's even named for a vegetable. It must be horrible to be so strange that nobody knows what you really are." Linda Watanabe McFerrin: **NAMAKO Sea Cucumber** (nsc)

The early descriptions of *Holothurian* found in Japanese – or, rather, Chinese, for most are by Chinese and written in Chinese characters alone – tell us less about what the *namako* is than what it is *not*.[1] "No head, no tail, no eyes, no skin-bone (shell or exoskeleton);" "no bones, no scales, no tail, no fin." In a word, *lots of nots*. But, contrary to expectation, the sea slug, like its closest relatives the sea urchin and starfish, boasts "five-rayed radial symmetry" of body.[2] Although it has five rows of feet running from mouth to anus, the sea slug has an up-side and a down-side: two rows of feet are atrophied on the top while bumps (papillae that look protective, but are probably sensory) are not on the bottom. Unlike its relatives, who have their mouths below and anuses above, the sea-slug is elongated horizontally – like a sea urchin stretched out on its side.[3] This elongation gives the sea slug something the round sea urchin and the circumscribed starfish do not have: ends and a new problem, for us, at any rate: telling which end is which![4]

#35 下記(left, below)

1. *What is Not.* Stating what something does *not* have suggests that normality is having it. As a bundle of negatives, the *have-not* sea cucumber is abnormal by definition. It's featurelessness is an anomoly in a world of "haves.". The above examples are from *Wakan Sanzue* (1712) and Ôshima Hiroshi's *Namako to Uni*: 1962. This negative tendency is even found in this line from an old folk-song: "the octopus has no bones, the sea slug has no eyes, and i'm just a child with no color (sex appeal)" ((f) *tako ni hone nashi namako ni me nashi watashi ya kodomo de iroke nashi* --- yasukibushi (ndh) 蛸に骨なし 海鼠に目無し 私や子供で色気無し　安来節). I cannot help thinking *that* is a very strange folk song. The marine metaphor is fine, but the lament that "I have no sex appeal for I am still a child" seems odd because one thinks of a lament as a song sung by an adult. Perhaps, young girls in fishing villages longed to get married . . .

2. *Bilateral Pentamary* With the question of *how* a 2-sided animal evolved into a 5-sided one still begging , it is hard to know *what* said animal is: "Is each arm of a seastar (and row of tubefeet on a cuke) the equivalent of a bilateral body or are echinoderms bilateral animals curled up around the oral-aboral axis?" (A. Kerr: corresp)

3. *A Stretched Urchin* The metaphor of the sea cucumber as a stretched urchin is pervasive. "If we could roll this sea urchin into a cylinder" writes the author of an 1871 Harper's article – and I have seen many such descriptions in both English and Japanese. It needs qualification: "Current research indicates that cukes are more than just sea urchins fallen over. Their tentacles are developmentally equivalent to the arms of starfish and the rows of tube-feet running from mouth to anus on sea urchins. Hence the long body of a cuke is a new invention, a part of the body that only exists around the anus of a sea urchin." (A. Kerr: corresp) *Echinodermata holosphincteridea* anyone?

4. *Telling Differences* Front-rear is less informative than up-down. Without clear indications of sidedness, one needs purposeful movement to differentiate the former – where all we need is gravity to distinguish the latter. And, even this is only valid so long as the subject does not back up. But, I speak as an advocate for the metaphor (formlessness) developed in this chapter. Though the *holothurian* is less obviously defined than the starfish with its fingers or the urchin with its spines (or patterned shell), we shall see it has features that stand out for the marine biologist: "Sea cucumbers are unique among echinoderms in giving up the radial pattern after acquiring it. They lie over on one side, and thereby gain anew a distinction between right and left, between upper and lower surfaces." (Buchsbaum and Milne: *The Lower Animals*).

尾 頭 の 心 も と な き 生 海 鼠 哉　　去 来

okashira-no kokoromotonaki namako kana – kyorai (1651-1704)

(tail-head's heart(hint/solution)-base/place/origin-none: sea slug 'tis!/?/ó)

#36

the sea-slug
which the head and which the tail
god only knows

trans. blyth[1] (h4)

which tail, which head
. . . nobody knows . . .
the sea-slug

trans. blyth (hh1)

Together with Basho's *frozen together*, this is the most famous of all sea slug haiku.[2] The word *okashira,* or "tail-head" is most commonly used to describe a fish that still has its head and tail (*okashira*-tsuki) but the sea slug . . . There is no "god" in the original. But, Blyth is right to use it,[3] because *kokoromotonaki* is an emphatic expression of perplexity for which there is no English equivalent (Idioms rarely translate. At least, not the good ones.) About the suitability of the Japanese phrase, Ebara Taizô wrote: "though one checked all possible modifiers, it would be absolutely impossible to find any words that could substitute for these." (HKST:1935). Indeed, the poem brings the phrase to life so well it serves as a usage example in the Japanese equivalent of the OED for *kokoromotonai.* And, the 20-vol. *Nihon Kokugo Daijiten* I call the OJD (Only Japanese Dictionary) also uses the poem as its example of *okashira* (tail-head). I do not know how many haiku have the honor of such a double citation. Had Kyorai written in English, his wit might have led him to this:

end-less

the sea slug
who can make heads
or tails of it

Since *kokoro* means heart/mind, it is hard for one who is not a native speaker of Japanese, not to see the phrase *kokoro-moto-naki* in the (doubtless misguided) literal sense – suggesting the difficulty of pinning down the source of the creature's consciousness – as well. To wit: it is –

1. *Blyth In Drag?* The Peter Pauper Press collection of haiku with no translator and no one claiming to be editor includes: "Now this good sea-slug / has both head / and tail . . . . . but god / knows which is which." (*Cherry Blossoms: Japanese haiku series III* Note: PPP translations were all parsed into four lines.) Is this not Blyth's sea-slug wearing heavy make-up? If some one wished to do a book on exceptionally bad styles of haiku translation, *NOW THIS GOOD SEA-SLUG* might make a fine title!

2. *Kyorai's Poem* This poem appears in Sarumino, dated 1689, where Bashô's poem is dated 1693. Still, all but one anthology I have seen put the poem *after* Bashô's, despite the fact that the selections are supposed to be in correct chronological order. The editors would seem to want us to believe that everything began with Bashô.

3. *Only Blyth Knows* Let me add, that, as unlikely as it might seem (or, at least seemed to me), the idiom "god only knows" *can* be found in a haiku by Sôin (1604-82): "god only knows / what day the mountain / cherry will bloom!" (*sakan hi wa kami zo shiruran yamazakura*). This rhetoric – actually "god/s know/s!" with an exclamatory (*zo*) followed by an emphatic chuckle (*ran*) is, however, rarely used in Japanese and this "god/s" is not our monolithic King of the Mountain, but a god of a particular mountain, i.e., a local tutelary deity, empowered, perhaps, by imported ideas of Agni, God of Fire (and blacksmiths) associated with esoteric Buddhism and Shinto. I do not know if Blyth knew Sôin's poem.

so hard to find
the head, tail and mind
of the sea-slug

Sôseki, who never missed a chance to introduce the sea slug in his work, paraphrased this well-known poem to describe *Tristam Shandy*, the eighteenth century novel whose non-linear plot-line is literally shown in our foreword.[1] I should add that, as befits a nation of sea slug lovers, most Japanese intellectuals know about Sterne's novel (there are two full translations available today), if you don't, let me only add that the author was constantly getting in front or behind himself.[2] A renegade poet adopted a sea slug metaphor, too, cleverly attributing the ambiguity to the lack of a clear-cut lead and summation, something Japanese uses body words for:

首尾を裁つ添削の文は海鼠かな　碧梧桐
shûbi o tatsu tensaku no bun wa namako kana – hekigotô (1872-1937)
(head/lead-tail/end cut/edited/corrected sentence/passage/writing-as-for, sea slug!/?/ǒ)

#37

after editing

head and tail
shaved off, my writing
is a sea slug

Even with the help of science, the sea slug is not easy to figure out. Diver Woodword, again: "being a 'back-to-front' sort of creature, it breathes through its anus as well as discharging waste from it." Water is sucked in and oxygen absorbed by one or two lung trees lining the anus. When the side that eats is not the side that breathes, then, who is to say which is the head?[1→] As a matter of fact, the sea slug's nervous system starts from a ring that lies around its mouth – that is to say its mind is literally circular![2→] (The goddess in the RECORD OF ANCIENT MATTERS really knew where to hurt poor *namako!*)

1. *Torisutamu, Shiyandei* Natsume Sôseki's essay on *Tristam Shandy* as a *namako*-like book was published in a magazine *Eko Bungaku* in Mar. 1897. This information came from Takeda Mitsuhiro's short essay "A Consideration on Natsume Sôseki's *I Am a Cat* (*wagahai wa neko de aru*) found on the net. Sôseki wrote:

Thackeray's Vanity Fair may not have a main character, but it does have an overall structure, a complex protean plot line that continues from start to finish; as for *Shandy*, not only does it lack a protagonist, but a plot and even a real beginning and end, like the sea slug of which you can't make head nor tails of [Sôseki's original follows the wording of Kyorai's haiku more closely!] ...

As Andô Fumihiko, who more recently expanded the ground in Iwanami's *Tosho* 4-2002 (and there is more at his Waseda University website), points out, Sôseki followed Laurence Sterne in *I Am a Cat*, about which he claimed the advantage of this style was that any piece of the book could be read perfectly well by itself. Hoh! *The holothurion as*

holograph! Like *Tristam Shandy*, much of *I Am a Cat* was published as a serial in a periodical, where readers would indeed benefit from this. I wonder if Sôseki knew that a piece of a sea slug can sometimes live by itself? [Still, Andô noted that Sôseki consciously sea-slugged the *style* of his sentences in *I Am...* more so than the plot.] Additionally, in "Things Recalled, Etc." (*omoidasu koto nado*) Sôseki described a dream concealing a terrifying reality with no apparent beginning or end as *okashiranaki,* or head and tailless.

2. *Tristam Shandy* This novel, published between 1760 and 1767 is more modern than 99% of the novels published today. Laurence Sterne would have loved to know that about seven centuries before him, a Japanese lady had already written a book with a chapter containing nothing and parenthetical musing – meta-commentary – similar to his! I refer to Murasaki Shikibu's *Tale of Genji*, usually considered the world's first honest-to-goodness novel. Speaking of *goodness,* in the case of both authors, theirs is so apparent that to read them is to love them. We have three major translations of *Tale of Genji* and the Japanese have two of *Tristam Shandy*.

北 へ む く あ た ま も 持 た ぬ 海 鼠 哉　　晩 得

kita e muku atama motanu namako kana –bantoku (d.1792) or ôemaru (1719-1805)

#38　　　　　　(north-to face head has/have-not seaslug/s!/?/ó/'tis)

a problematic corpse

no head
to place due north
the sea slug

In Japan, even today, corpses are supposed to lie with the head due North. We live people are not supposed to sleep that way. This is a Buddhist custom and I suspect Bantoku/Ôemaru's(different books credited different poets) sea slug may allude to a disgraced monk [1] who dares not face his god for reasons described in a later chapter.

ま な 板 の 心 も し ら す 海 鼠 哉　　三 惟

manaita no kokoro mo shirazu namako kana – sani? (1699)

#39　　　(cutting-board's heart/intent/design-even knowing-not [a/the] sea slug/s!/?/ó)

at odds with
cutting board logic
the sea slug

→ **1.** *Siding Sea Cukes* While my comments "who is to say . ." were rhetorical, I later read that our charge has stymied scientists because they could not place the mouth and excretory openings on either the front/belly or backside, as holothurian *dorsal* and *ventral* surfaces extend lengthwise and the openings are at each end. Accordingly, Arnold writes, "the terms *oral* (mouth-side) and *aboral* (side opposite the mouth) are generally used in describing these species." (IBID)

→ **2.** *Circular Mind?* The circum-oesophageal nerve ring is not the only ring-shaped organ in the holothurian. The intestine also does not go straight through, but describes one large loop. We all know of single-celled animals, well, here is *a single-loop animal.*   But, I should qualify the "mind." The circular nerve connecting the radial nerves is "mind" only in the broadest sense of the word. Where I loosely called it the *namako's* "brain," A. Kerr corrected me "it is not a brain, it is not even a ganglion." To a further question about where the brain might have formed had the mouth not gotten in the way, he responded in a more poetic vein: "There is neither a beginning nor an end. They've no need of a brain or central processing centre and i suspect, were they able, might pity the awkward and, to their 'minds,' unnecessary complexity of our own nervous system, with its attendant manifold increase in pathologies. For me, part of the attraction of inverts [invertebrates], particularly my totem the holothourion, is their utter strangeness." (corresp) A less poetic web-find: "Rather than having a centrally-oriented system with a controlling 'brain', there are a series of nerve networks extending into each of the various body regions. . . .This unique 'radial' nervous system allows the echinoderms unusual flexibility in behavior, as any portion of the body can serve as the 'head' as it experiences its environment." (ASV5af3_9rAC:science.kennesaw.edu/biophys/biodiversity/ animalia/ echinoderm.html). In other words, a uniformly rapid response would be possible. Note that "the epidermis of a sea cucumber may contain upwards of 7000 sensory nerve endings per square millimeter, or, put another way, a staggering 4,500,000 nerve endings per square inch. They receive and somehow process an immense amount of information. They simply don't do it with a brain. They are the seagoing equivalent of politicians; bottom-feeding and essentially brainless." (Ron Shimek: www.animalnetwork.com/ fish2/aqfm/2000/jan/ wb/ default. asp: orig *Aquarium Frontiers*?)

1. *Monks* The Jesuits who first visited Japan were horrified to discover the habits, rites and props employed by Buddhists was similar to their own, and thought it a trick played by the Devil to capture Japanese souls. They called Buddhist monks by the Japanese word *bonze* (a corruption of *bouzu*), for using "monk" would equate Buddhism with Christianity, and this was not welcome (I oversimplify, for the Iberians used the term "*religiosos*" to refer to men of any faith). Bonze was used in most European languages, including English, until the mid-twentieth century. Against my antiquarian feelings, I use "monk" for the sake of the reader and the vowel-rhyme with "slug." Occasionally, I let the "bonze" revive for the alliteration and to keep this archaic word alive.

chef's dilemma

knowing nothing
of the way of the board
these sea slugs

俎 の ど ち ら む い て も 海 鼠 か な   桂 信 子

manaita no dochira muite mo namako kana – katsura nobuko (1993)
(cutting-board's whichever/either-way facing-even sea-slug tis!/?/ŏ)   #40

on the block   on the block
a sea slug faces   pointing either way
right or left   a slug's a slug

This modern haiku may play off Ôemaru's old one, but it is not in the least a metaphor and would seem to be saying the same thing as the lesser known, pre-Ôemaru poem above it. Japanese generally place fish on the cutting board facing left.[1] It is hard to conform with this etiquette when the "fish" is a sea slug. Still I suspect that the poets speak for themselves and professional chefs can distinguish the head and tail side of the *namako*. As cutlery was once a high art practiced by men with the same degree of seriousness (and with the same serious degrees) as a martial art, my "way of the board" in the second reading of the old poem is justifiable.

海 鼠 切 る 頭 ら し き を 右 に 向 け 高 沢 良 一

namako kiru kashirarashiki o migi no muke – takasawa yoshikazu (2003)
(seaslug cuts head-like/resembling[thing/side][+obj] rightward faces)   #41

cutting a sea slug
with what looks like the head
facing the right

～

cutting a slug
the head-like side
faces right

1. *Generally Left-facing Fish* Far more than half of all sketches of animals (including humans) depict them/us looking left, perhaps because right-handed people draw silhouettes most easily when they face that way and all of us, right or left-handed get so used to seeing left-facing creatures that we prefer to encounter them that way. In Japan, fish on plates always face left. (Is this because Japanese cuisine is pretty as a picture? Or is it true for other cuisines as well?) With food preparation, however, the question is more complex. The fish almost always faces left when its head is cut off (the right-handed chef holds the head with his left hand) but may face leftward at times in the carving process (when the chef holds the tail). Once – until the 1950's (?) – it was not only *de rigor* to start the process with the fish facing left but to make certain ocean fish had their belly toward the chef and river fish had their back to the chef, but now this is not always known,

much less followed. At one time, it was also the case that whereas fish in most of Japan were opened from the belly (as is true in most of the world for it is easier to do), those in the warrior-dominated culture of Kanto (Edo) were supposedly always opened from the back so as not to do something approaching the practice of *harakiri,* because, it would be inauspicious according to some and disrespectful to the samurai (for allowing the fish to usurp their right) according to others. Some claim that the opening from the back reduces damage to small bones, and is not just a quirk of samurai culture. Today, this difference does not always hold, but it does with one fish. *Eels.* With eels, Kanto and Kansai (the Osaka/Nagoya/Kyoto), are still at odds. In the Eel capital Hamamatsu (on the border of these cultures), one can even chose which style to buy (another difference is that the Kansai style comes minus head and tail).

I was unable to elicit a comment from the poet about the significance, if any, of the direction. Perhaps, it doesn't really matter, for the "head-*like*" uncertainty, and something – the utter calmness of the poet? – make the poem.

海鼠切し板前にあつまるマナコ 敬愚

namako kishi itamae ni atsumaru manako – keigu

(seaslug[obj] cuts chef-on gather eyes[subj])

#42

> eyes gather
> upon the chef cutting
> a sea slug

なまこだと俎板に眼が多すぎる 敬愚

namako da to manaita ni me ga ôsugiru – keigu

(seaslug is and/when carving board-on eyes [are] too many)

#43

> when it's a sea slug
> there are just too many eyes
> on the cutting block

俎板の海鼠に眼集まりぬ 敬愚

manaita no namako ni manako atsumarinu – keigu

(cutting-board's seaslug-on eyes gather/assemble)

#44

> a sea slug
> the cutting board heavy
> with eyes

Keigu imagines that most people in Japan, whether or not they are conscious of the right/left conventions, might be curious about how a sea slug is attacked. Their attention is described in a manner meant to remind us of the sea slug's missing eyes, or haiku calling attention to them.

海鼠あり庖厨は妻の天下かな 碧梧桐

namako ari hôchû-wa tsuma-no tenka kana – hekigoto (1872-1937)

(seaslug/s is/are kitchen-as-for wife's heaven[ie she is god, her domain] 'tis!/?/ô)

#45

> a sea slug   a sea slug
> my wife is now god   makes my wife shôgun
> in the kitchen   of the kitchen

女神

> with sea slugs
> in the kitchen my wife
> thinks she's god

This poem does not directly concern the theme, unless we are to assume that the difficulty of cutting up the featureless creature is what elevates Hekigoto's wife. I suspect that Hekigoto loved to eat sea slug and his wife knew it and showed she knew he knew it; but I do not know enough about Hekigoto and his wife to settle on a single translation of this early twentieth century haiku, which balances the traditional kitchen of the old haiku where man was assumed to hold the knife and, come to think about it . . . it *was* a goddess who first poked a sea slug.

（鬼の居ぬ間の）こはごはと海鼠を刻む留守居かな　吉原霧坊

(oni no inu ma no) kowagowa to namako o kizamu rusui kana – yoshiwara mubô? (c 2000)

　　(devil's not in while // fearfully seaslug dicing absent-being 'tis!/?/ǒ)　　　　　#46

when the cat's out

alone at home
a man dicing sea slug
with trepidation

Since the poet is male and evidently not at home in the kitchen, I filled in the unspecified subject with "a man." A sea slug, with its tough lumps and sliminess would be the last thing for an unskilled carver to attack, but Mubô could not resist some silent manly drinking with the perfect accompaniment, sea slug. There is something endearing about the man's trepidation, as opposed to a woman's that might be easily explained in a Freudian manner.[1]

ひと呼吸置ゐて捌かる海鼠かな　金子邦朗

hitokokyû oite sabakaru namako kana – kaneko kunirô (2002)

　　(one-breath placing, tackle/manipulate/carve [the] seaslug!/?/ǒ)

　　　　　　　　　　　　　　　　　　　　　　　　　　　　　　　#47

after taking
a deep breath i cut
the sea slug

Is it the unfamiliarity? Is the sea slug still alive? Or is it the physical difficulty of the operation about which this next old haiku chuckles? To wit:

胴切にしを（も）せざりける生海鼠哉　太祇

dôgiri ni shi mo sezarikeru namazu kana – taigi (1709-72)

　　(torso-cut do, and do-must [+finality]: sea-slug 'tis!/?/ǒ)

　　　　　　　　　　　　　　　　　　　　　　　　　　　　　　　#48

the way of five rings?

a body-cut
the only way to do in
a sea slug

Percentage-wise, some haiku themes contain more hard-to-crack poems than others. I sometimes wonder if the sea slug's ambiguous nature encourages poets to write equally enigmatic poems.[2] If I

1. Freudian Equality While men are far more likely to suffer from penis envy (90% of men wishing for bigger ones and presumably jealous of the lucky 10%) than women, a man cutting a cuciform object evokes little if any phallic associations, while women (or, the women in poetry written by men?) do, presumably because penis and sea slug are equally external for them. In other words, a man does not confuse phallic objects for *it*.

2. Enigmatic Poems "Perhaps, if I could read it [*Genji*] better, I might be less keen to turn it into English and find out what it says" explains the latest translator of the *Tale of Genji*, Royall Tyler

(ls). Unlike *Genji*, which has dozens of modern translations, some with detailed notes, in Japanese, and a few in English as well, almost all the old haiku in this book lack modern translation or explanation – indeed, for some, this is the first book (in any language) to reprint them *in decades* – so that I know Royal Tyler's feeling all too well. In some cases, I have no idea what the poem means until I finish translating. In these cases, I check with my Japanese advisors in case my muse is wrong; but, sometimes, they, too, cannot say for sure. This simultaneously disappoints me and delights me, for it makes me feel like a pioneer.

have solved Taigi's poem, as I think I have, it is only because I happened to read and remember Lafcadio Hearn taking precisely the opposite tack in a mock lament about the difficulty of killing crabs where *you cannot for dem break de* back, *for dat dey be* all *back . . .* etc..[1]   Well, here, the sea slug, lacking other distinction, is *all* torso, so one *must* use one particular sword stroke called a torso cut on them.   This terrifying stroke was used to divide men in two with a single stroke across the midriff in order to prove the sharpness of one's sword (An example (literary, not graphic!) in the OJD has the bottom half of the body still standing on its two feet!).   It was also called a *wagiri,* or ring cut – especially apt for sea slugs – so I added that title punning on Miyamoto's well known book title.

.包 丁 の 入 れ 処 な き 海 鼠 か な　森 み つ 子

hôchô no iredokoronaki namako kana – mori mitsuko (1998)

#49   (knife's enter-place-not, sea slug!/?/ŏ/ 'tis)

sea slug
no place to start
my knife

My first response to this haiku was: *Can't you stick the tip in the mouth? Oh, so that's it! You don't want to act like that mean goddess . . .* But then I remembered that while fish don't require such stabbing to start, they do have a line demarking tail and body, gills, and centers to their back and an anus near the tail (rather than right at the end which one already knows is an end anyway).   A scientist might notice its pentameral bias, but to other people, the sea slug is undemarcated territory.   A fastidious cook would need to chart it and mark where to slice.

便 な さ や い づ れ 生 海 鼠 の 裏 表　太 祇

binnasa ya izure namako no uraomote – taigi (1709-72)

#50   (way-not (how sad!) eventually sea slug's bottom/inside-top/outside)

what a shame!
it turns out sea slugs
have two sides

the fallen sage

what a pity!
sea slugs end up
with two sides

Lacking a clear context, *ura-omote* is problematic, for we cannot tell if something is being turned inside out, turned over, or simply has two sides.   I am saving my first choice, "inside-out" for the next chapter.   In this reading, the sea slug's undifferentiated form changes, not in reality but idiomatically to one with two sides. As already noted, fish are carved and served head-pointing left, in Japan. Because of this, the left side is always the *omote-mi* (top) and the right the *ura-mi* (bottom).   To wit:

1. Lafcadio's Crab *How can you make for dem kill so you not dem boil? You not can break to dem de back, for dat dey not be only all back. You not can dem bleed until dey die, for dat dey not have blood. You not can stick dem troo de brain, for dat dey be same like you – dey not have of brain.* (I think I got it from Hearn's 1885 *Sketch Book,* reprinted as part of *Creole Sketches* in 1924). In my book, *Goyaku* *Tengoku* (mistranslation paradise: hakusuisha 1989), I used this short sketch to example something so dependent upon style – written in thick dialect – to defy meaningful translation by anyone but a genius of dialect who could re-create it.   Recently, I came across some one who claimed to disprove me on an internet site.   I fear the wretched translation only served to prove my point!

the featureless and therefore side-less sea slug seemed inherently safe, but served up, proved that it had ultimately been sided and carved.[1] The title of the second reading suggests Taigi may also have been alluding to the idiom of a sage's lacking an *omote* and *ura* – i.e. being completely on the up-and-up without ulterior motives. Since Shiko's *"Maxim for A Sea Cucumber"* (1712) depicted a sage slug, this is not completely off the wall.

尻 口 の と ゝ の は ぬ 世 に 海 鼠 哉　草 也

shirikuchi no totonowanu yo ni namako kana – sôya (1756)

(rear-mouth's (rear (and) mouth) un-matching/uncleaned world-in, sea slug 'tis!/?/ŏ)　　　　#51

in this world
of lies, only sea slug
boasts one mouth

If the poet thought the sea slug, unlike men, had but one orifice [2] the above might make sense. Despite the fact sea slug anuses suck in water for breathing, they are tight-assed on land. This is especially true for the "gold-sea-mouse"), *kinko*. Because it ate plankton from the sea water rather than sand, it had less to *pass* and, at least one early nineteenth century Japanese naturalist and his source even thought, it had *no* anus whatsoever. [3] Still, the reading is probably wrong. It is unlikely this mistake would have been made regarding the ordinary *namako* and the sea slug isn't supposed to talk, *period*, right?

kudos to sea slug!	behold the slug	duplicitous times!
in an age when men speak	while we speak from both	better to stay mum, be
with forked tongues	sides of our mouths	a sea cucumber

1. *Siding Fish.* The top, or outside would for most fish be the left side for, as explained earlier, a fish faces left. And we assume said fish is right-side up in front of us. But it is not so simple with less fishy fish; in Kansai (Osaka area), for example, eels are cut from the dorsal side and in Kanto (Tokyo area) from the ventral. Things are further complicated with the sea slug, for the most belly-like surface is the part not seen, and hence the *ura,* where the back is the part that is seen, the *omote.* This differs from the way the generic fish belly is visible on the left and right, and, like the anomalous flounder, is the opposite of the back=behind, belly=front metaphorical bias our bodies create for us. Factually speaking, the top and bottom of the Japanese sea slug are pretty obvious, so I am not confident about the above reading of Taigi's poem.

2. *Orifice or Hole?* My first draft had "hole," but PYG suggested "orifice." Orifice does indeed sound more appropriate here. At the same time, I wonder why astronomy can get away with its *black hole* and physics with its *worm hole*, while we cannot simply speak of animal holes. In most of the world's cultures, humans are known to have seven, eight or nine "holes," depending on the definition of what constitutes a hole. Basho described his body in "Learn from the Pine" as "made of a hundred bones and nine holes." (I think of women as decimal – and wonder if it has anything to do with the discovery of zero in India, where the female principle was more active – but in Japan the vagina and urinary tract are counted as one big ninth hole (*dai-kyu ana*). I have never found ten holes directly mentioned in any literature, but is it chance Li Yu's ( ) story of a woman without a vagina, which happily ends in perforation is his tenth in a series of erotic essays? And what was on Andrew Marvell's mind when he offered to help a woman "put on *perfection*, if it was not the decimal "0"? The Chinese character for "mouth" has the same connotation as "orifice." That is to say, they have an alternative, but in the context of body openings, generally chose the more basic, and hence, poetic word, "hole."

3. *Source of Assless Cucumaria Japonica* The researcher Bansui Ôtsukigentaku wrote a book called "Gold Sea Pearl(?)" (金海一珠 = 1810)] which included "Notes on the Gold Sea Slug" (き んこの記). He described the *kinko* as a bumpless *namako,* bred by the spirit of nearby Gold Flower Mountain according to the locals, "ear, eye, fin and boneless, with only a mouth and *no bottom-hole."* He mistook the feeding tentacles, described as resembling poppy flowers made of silk thread and extended only in good weather – for its genitals. (from Ôshima Hiroshi's *Namako to Uni* (sea cucumber and sea urchin): 1962, p 144-6). Ôshima also notes that just two years later Kurimoto Suiken?(栗本瑞見:栗氏千虫譜) corrected the errors .

At first, I did not grasp the fact the rear-mouth+verb was almost certainly idiom for *statements that make no sense* (because what comes before and after contradict each other).[1] In my ignorance, I wrote:

> If, instead, the poet noticed that the openings were placed at the respectively identical location front and back – *os*, Latin for mouth – the above [the first reading] might be the correct reading. Then, again, it might be this:

in this world
of things left undone:
sea slug's anus

> Might the poet have noticed the thread-like lungs hanging out of the sea slug's anus – why Cuvier called it a spinner – and/or the equally messy-looking mouth [2] and thought it a good image for the most common idiomatic rendering of the Japanese *shirikuchi* phrase, "something left unfinished," whether it meant contradictory unsettled claims, a woman impregnated but not married, or someone moving out and leaving the place in a mess? These nuances of "rear-mouth match-not/cleaned-not" (*shiriguchi no totonowanu*) simply cannot be Englished [3] in a single idiom, which would be the only safe way to translate a poem without understanding it. An angrier version:

in a world
of dirty assholes:
sea slugs!

Still, one ambiguity remains.   It is theoretically/grammatically possible that the sea slug is an example rather than foil for the times.

vis the sea-slug!
so our muddled world
has a mascot

If there was a recognized fad (eighteenth century Japan was nothing if it was not a *very* faddish time/place!) for eating sea slug at the time Sôya wrote, this figurative translation might do:

what better food
for our brave new world:
sea cucumber!

I've come across a few *senryu* boasting of the Edo era as a time when a man's balls could hang low – the connection of loose balls and being relaxed was formalized by countless *senryu* about an old advisor of Tokugawa Ieyasu (the man who pacified Japan for good) who felt the balls of the Shogun to see if he was indeed as calm as he looked in very difficult circumstances, and finding they did indeed hang low predicted all would be well, which it was. But, some Japanese had mixed feelings about something we might call the corruption of peace in the Tokugawa era that followed:

this *fubar* world![1]
i think i'll just lie low
like a sea slug

---

1. *Idiom* An OJD e.g. shows the "rear-mouth" was sometimes combined with "head-tail" (*shirikuchi shûbi tsuzumaranu*) and a negative verb to mean inconsistent/contradictatory in a bad way.

2. *Messy Mouth* In the fullest Edo era introduction to the sea cucumber, *Wakan-sansai-zue* (1712), the author Terashima Ryôan, perhaps influenced by the ancient myth, described the sea slug's mouth and eyes (holes for spawn?) as scars made by a dagger. We might say the oral cavity would appear to be crudely crafted, as opposed to the cleanly cut or chiseled appearance of the mouths of many fish.

2. *Englished* I highly appreciate English's ability to verb many nouns and noun many verbs. I believe the verb "to English", most famously used by Sir John Falstaff when he asserts that the (married) barmaid's body language "rightly Englished" means "I have got the hots for big John," (first quote Shakespeare's, the second, my modernized expression) *ought to be* standard English today, and, accordingly, will use it in this book without quotations, italics or other apology.

3. *FUBAR* This is far and away the most useful acronym to come out of the United States military. In case any readers are un/fortunate enough to have missed it: *Fucked Up Beyond All Recognition.*

The poet was not necessarily as cool as a sea cucumber, either. He may have been expressing his frustration, for sea slugs, because they squirmed without vocalizing, were identified with repressed emotion as we shall see in *The Melancholy Sea Slugs* chapter.

in a world
that makes no sense:
sea slug me

Me or not, the questions remain: is the sea slug a good example or a bad one, and is it representative or contrasting with the world? As the reader can see from the extremely divergent nature of the eight translations, I have absolutely no idea what this sea slug is to the poet. And it wasn't for lack of trying. No one I consulted was any help. I suppose I should have transferred the poem to the *Unsolved Sea Slugs* mini-chapter among the *Sundry Sea Slugs* at the end of the book, but its incomprehensibility somehow made it fit this chapter well enough.

海 に あ る も の と は 見 え ぬ 海 鼠 哉　谷 水
umi ni aru mono to wa mienu namako kana – kokusui? (1773)
(ocean-in-is-thing-as, look/appear-not: sea slug!/?/ǿ/the/'tis)   #52

underwater mystery

i thought it
something that didn't belong
a sea slug

It is hard for us to identify the ocean with the crystalline clarity that once was not a monopoly of far-off places. In such a world, where pollution was the exception rather than the rule, marine life that was sleek and shiny and had clear-cut features would seem appropriate where, today, by the same token, nothing would fit our murky sea better than the *namako*. This, then, is a poem describing the gross appearance of the sea slug. At the same time, we may take it as a subjective description of the process of seeing, where an individual sea slug was first mistaken for a stick, seed, rock or sandal.

白 波 の 物 と し も な き 生 海 鼠 哉　角 米
shiranami no mono to shi mo naki namako kana – kakubei (?)
(white-wave[white-cap]/srf's thing do-even-not, seaslug!/:/these/ǿ)   #53

they cannot be
creatures of the surf
these sea slugs

Here, the slug is not so much foreign to the clarity of the water as to the crisp white-caps the reader may find depicted in countless woodcuts. White-caps are slang=metaphor for the cool gamblers, the square-jawed romantic *shiranami* of *kabuki* plays. What could be more antithetical to the slug? If I had saved this poem for *The Ugly Sea Slug* chapter, I would have felt tempted to paraverse: "cool creatures / of the brine, what's this? / a lame sea slug!"

捨 て ゝ あ る も の と 思 へ は 生 海 鼠 哉　美 濃 南 甫
sutetearu mono to omoeba namako kana – mino nampo?(1793)
(throw-away thing-as think-if seaslug!/?/ǿ/the/'tis)   #54

i thought it
something thrown away:
a sea slug!

Even today, things that are thrown away generally have less form than things we keep. In Japan, in 1793, this was much more true, for in a land where even old umbrella ribs were collected for reusing and piss was traded for greens, little with any form to speak of found its way to a dust bin.

(t) ともかくもこの海鼠には形あり 猶まとまらぬ我の寂しさ　与謝野寛

tomokaku kono namako ni wa katachi ari nao matomaranu ware no sabishisa – yosano hiroshi (1873-1935)
(at-any-rate, this sea-slug-to-as-for, shape is still gather/form-not my loneliness)

#55

> nevertheless
> this sea slug here
> has a form:
> i can't say the same
> for my loneliness

This *tanka* by the husband of twentieth century Japan's most famous woman poet, Yosano Akiko (1878-1942)[1], provides a good riposte for our formless metaphor. As we shall see in the next chapter, the sea slug may not have a *fixed* form, but it is hardly formless. Yosano Hiroshi was himself a major literary figure when he founded the literary magazine Myojo (Venus), but his talent failed to keep pace with his genius wife's and, by the time this was written, sulked in bed all day (which probably makes him "this sea slug"), as the family – Akiko bore 11 children! – survived on his wife's good health and royalties.

古 湯 婆 形 海 鼠 に 似 申 す よ　子 規

furu tanpo katachi namako ni ni môsu yo – shiki (1867-1902)
(old hot-water bottle: shape, sea slug-to resemble [i'd] say)

#56

> *appearances can be deceiving*
>
> a resemblance
> to the sea slug: my old
> foot-warmer

> *sick-bed taxonomy*
>
> i give a class
> to my old foot-warmer:
> *holothurian*

Shiki, who spent much of his adult life as a bedridden invalid, had a close acquaintance with hot water-bottles.[1→]). His haiku gives a familiar form to the formlessness. If I am not mistaken, Japanese readers of Shiki's time would also remember the reputation of the sea slug as a *cold* creature and chuckle at the false likeness. To wit:

> *my old hot-water bottle*
>
> the likeness grows
> abandoned, it *is* as cool
> as a sea cucumber

1. *Yosano Akiko* She is known for putting her passion (love-affairs) into poetry and, not surprisingly – for powerful women are worshipped in our time – well-translated into English. Her best known book of poetry is *Midaregami,* (tangled/disheveled hair.)

If Shiki's use of the hot water bottle metaphor evokes associations that endear the sea slug to us, the poem is, strictly speaking, not a sea slug haiku. Neither is this, strictly speaking, a sea slug *senryu*:

冷凍で、溶かしたバナナ、ナマコかな　黄昏

reitô de tokashita banana namako kana – Tora (contemp)
(frozen, thawed banana, seaslug!/?/ó/'tis/am)

#57

thawing out
a banana seems
a sea slug!

year's end party

here's our sea slug
a frozen banana
thawed out

This was one of a number of *namako* netted for me by AQ and I was lucky enough to misread the website address for this poem as "bounennkai.html," which was actually that for another poem. Well, a *bônenkai* is the "forget-year-meeting,"i.e., the wildest party of the year, when everyone with any sense drinks him or herself silly to help wipe the slate clean for the year to come and, as it happens, adding it to the reading greatly improves the poem, so I leave it. Refrigerated bananas *do* keep well, but their skins turn black. Metaphor laughs at grammar. If such a banana can look like a sea slug, then the reverse is equally true. [2] →

徹頭徹尾せぬを身上海鼠かな　成瀬桜桃子

tettôtetsubi senu o shinjô namako kana – naruse ôtôshi (1993)
(thorough-head-thorough-tail do/have-not [sole]merit/asset seaslug!/?/ó/'tis/am)

#58

to a certain someone

not having it
all together is what saves
you sea slug

moderation

sea slug sea slug
you and me! we never
go whole hog

the sea slug
bless you for never
going all out!

luke warm/cold

sea slug nation
our only saving grace
is moderation

the uncut gem

the saving grace
for the sea slug is that
it is unfinished

I suspect an allusion (the poet, herself? the prime-minister? the national mentality?) here because it would be wrong to say the only good thing about the animal sea slug is its *lack of thoroughgoingness*

1. *Japanese Hot Water Bottles* I thought Shiki's poem meant that rubber or leather hot water "bottles" were already in use over a hundred years ago – one nineteenth century term for *holothurian* was *scytodermata,* or "leather/hide-skin" – but OM writes "Until the 1970's, Japanese hot water bottles were not made of rubber or leather. They were flat oval-shaped tin (like a flattened football) with wave-like indentations which truly resembled *namako*." (corresp) Hot water bottles inspire many good haiku some of which are introduced in IPOOH-winter-1. One of their attractions may be the fact that the literal reading of the Chinese characters is "warm-water-*auntie*"!

last reading is highly unlikely, for the poet could have written the same more clearly if she wished to). I suppose we could say that whomever is signified here, the signifier is the literary sea slug, the invention of generations of poets. Keigu, speaking for all who dislike exhaustive clarity, cannot help himself –

if black and white is not your bag . . .

oh, happy day!
the sea slug is grey
in every way!

The only problem is that a overly thorough celebration of the un-thorough leads quickly to contradiction. Be that as it may, Keigu cannot help continuing.

悪夢にて海鼠が浮かぶ凝屋哉　敬愚
akumu nite namako ga ukabu koriya kana – keigu
(bad-dream-as, seaslug/s float-up[appear]perfectionist!/?/ó/hoh)

#59

their nightmares
are sea-slug-ridden:
perfectionists

凝り性の 叫びたくなる 海鼠 哉　敬愚
korishô no sakebitakunaru namako kana – keigu
(perfectionist's scream-out-want-become seaslug!/?/ó/hoh)

#60

made to make
a perfectionist scream
the sea slug

凝 り 性 を 苛 め る た め に 海 鼠 あ り 敬 愚
korishô o ijimeru tame ni namako ari – keigu
(perfectionist[obj] bully purpose-for seaslug is)

#61

the sea slug
here just to bully
fussy people

小心にて海鼠を入れる器なき　　敬愚
shôshin nite namako o ireru utsuwa naki – keigu
(small-heart[scrupulous]-as-for, seaslug put-in vessel/breadth not)

#62

yon sea slug:
behold the nemesis
of small minds

← **2. *Metaphorical Direction and Truth***   Most Japanese know the story about Hideyoshi, the great warlord, or *shôgun,* who united Japan at the end of the seventeenth century and was popularly thought to resemble a monkey. When he called his trusted advisor and asked him if it was true that he resembled a monkey, the advisor, knowing of Hideyoshi's temper and not surprisingly wanting to keep his job and his head, did not simply reply that it was false, for Hideyoshi would not accept a bald lie. His studied reply was, "No, my Lord does not so much look like a monkey, as some monkeys may, indeed, resemble my Lord." A metaphor may seem to be an "if a=b, then b=a" proposition, but it is also about belonging to sets. The metaphor provider is more well-known than the recipient and serves as a large set within which the latter is subsumed. Saying monkeys resemble the leader or that hot water bottles, bananas or rats (as mentioned in the Foreword) resemble sea slugs, the status of the sea slug is enhanced even if it is not the subject of the poem.

animalis inconsisterius

oh, sea slug,
you are no hobgoblin
of little minds

This paroxysm of aphoristic haiku-making, was evoked by the *hobgoblin,*[1] or, rather the aphorism which is the only place I have encountered it. 'Consistency is the hobgoblin of small minds' quotes a skotos.net article, enlarging upon Emerson's more qualified statement by omitting the "foolish" before "consistency" to justify a more grandiose explanation: "It's a well-known quote that derides our attempts to make order from chaos." I don't mind the hyperbole, for it is a perfect description of our sea slug!

尾 頭 の 不 明 は 海 鼠 無 限 也　敬愚
okashira no fumei wa namako mugen nari – keigu
(tail-head unclear-as-for, seaslug no-limit/s[infinite] becomes/is)   #63

no clear head, no clear tail
sea slug is infinite in scale!

The philosophizing that the brainless sea slug seems to encourage, raises a question about haiku itself. Is it *haiku* to take advantage of a seasonal theme for this sort of straight philosophizing? In my opinion, it is fine so long as it remains a part of a larger body of season-centered work. In other words, I don't think a haiku *by itself* can be judged. But, I think one would find strong opinions on both sides of this. Since I have no place within the haiku world, it will be fun to see the reaction of the haiku establishment, to the extent that such *is*.

尾 も 鰭 も な く? 退 屈 な り 海 鼠　小谷ゆきを
o mo hire mo naku[te?] taikutsu nari namako --- kotani yukio (contemp)
(tail-even fin-even not, boring becomes/is seaslug)   #64

no tail or fins:
the monotonous life
of a sea slug!

boredom is   no fin or tail
a sea slug, *sans* fin   no wonder sea slugs
sans tail   look bored

Life as a Torso. This haiku puts a new tooth on the old saw of have-not sea slugs while it plays with the idiom "put tail and fin on" (*obire-o tsukeru*), meaning to liven up a story with details. The double *sans* in my last translation was suggested by the line describing the "second childishness and mere oblivion" of old age in *"As You Like It,"* to wit: *"Sans teeth, sans eye, sans taste, sans everything."* I do not know if the poem is about the life of a sea slug or that of the poet. Either way, it reflects a modern attitude which, contrary to the traditional exaltation of doing nothing, assumes excitement is desirable. The poem improves immensely when you reflect upon life without any protuberances to play with or look at. Imagine the disembodied brain of science fiction, minus the brain. Or, consider

1. *Hobgoblin* I think this word that sounds so good is not more widely used because it sounds the opposite of what it is. As a "goblin," we feel it should be antithetical or negative, where it is rather something positive, something we cannot help doing. Because of this, the aphorism is often recalled as "*in*consistency is the hobgoblin of small minds." Despite the change, the meaning, as it is understood by the person who made the mistake, does not change, for the hobgoblin's reading does.

whether or not a brain could have evolved without appendages to stimulate their owner. I am reminded of Eiseley's essay on why the handless dolphin would not build a civilization even if it were as bright as us. The haiku can be seen as hopelessly anthropocentric or a laudable trans-specific sympathy.

尾 も 鰭 も 持 た ぬ 海 鼠 の 潔 し 無 名

o mo hire mo motanu namako no isagiyoshi – anon (contemp)

#65   (tail-even fin-even have-not seaslug's gallantry/manliness)

no fin or tail
i'd call the sea slug
very clean-cut

no frivolous stuff   no fin no tail
like a tail or fins to mar   no frills at all, sea slug
the manly sea slug   man of men

spartan samurai

sea slugs are
a true gallant race
doing without
tail, fins and lace.

There is a *meta*-contradiction here. The blatantly philosophical bent of this poem is far from the accepted Japanese style, but the argument itself – that lack of frills is manly=good – is typical twentieth century Japanese thought that had its origin in the late nineteenth century's international contest to be manlier than thou. Orientalism in the early modern West put down the supposedly effeminate East exemplified by the ornate Byzantine civilization and Japanese, who had not a few stern and stark genes in their own culture, joined the race toward plain black, grey and khaki by tossing out their ornately decorated heroes of old and revaluing their literature, putting down intricately crafted poetry as feminine (or contrived or foreign=Chinese) while praising the simpler "manly" *Manyôshû*. To this day, neither Japan nor the West has managed to overcome this prejudice. I appreciate what the poet does for the sea slug with his totally new take on its featurelessness; but, unless he is being facetious, I cannot abide his (our) worldview.

多 す ぎ る 海 鼠 の 数 に 買 惑 ふ   高 沢 良 一

ôsugiru namako no kazu ni kaimayou – takasawa yoshikazu (2003)

#66   (many-over[too many] seaslugs' number-as buy-bewildered[can't make up mind])

so many sea slugs
i cannot make up my mind
over which to buy

If we have strayed from the narrow haiku path in examining so many philosophical poems, this is a *bona fide* haiku by anyone's book. It is a simple objective description of a personal experience. It is pretty easy to select the best fish from their shiny eyes and their glossy bright colors, but it would be no easy matter to select one sea slug out of a mass of nondescript bodies. One might feel better choosing from a smaller selection.   So this haiku speaks to me of the featureless sea slug though I am not certain Takasawa, who has written more *namako* haiku than any other poet living or dead, would agree, for he might notice fine features, differences most of us would overlook.

3
<u>the protean sea slug</u>

THE GREAT SEA CUCUMBER

what is the power
of the Great Sea Cucumber
that it changes
its shape, making
now an hourglass,
now a globe,
stretching itself into
a worm?
what is this animation
in the mud?

. . . .

Gene Baro (b 1924)

I love that phrase "animation in the mud," for it reminds me of the more recent animations made by shaping the same. But, let me not digress before I have even started a chapter. In this, the only English poem I have found completely dedicated to our charge, [1] formlessness is not only a lack of obvious body parts and demarcating features. Ultimately, it is found in not sticking with *any* form: *formlessness as change itself.* Edo era poets didn't miss the protean nature of the sea slug:

重ばこのすみまで届くなまこかな　大江丸(?)
jûbako no sumi made todoku namako kana – ôemaru? (1801)
(double-box's corners-to reaches: sea-slug!/?/ǿ/the)   #67

a fitting demise

all four corners
of the container filled
by the sea-slug

I cannot see why a live sea slug would be in such a box – a rectangular (occasionally circular) box or, rather, one of a tier of "lunch-boxes" [2] – rather than a tub or pail; but the power to take the form of

1. The Great Sea Cucumber   The centering and decapping are mine. I fear the rest of this poem, found in the BBC website's nature poetry selection, gives up the metaphorical ghost and simply describes (the objective school of modern haiku lovers might like this; I do not.) appearance, until we get to the last three lines which are fascinating, for they contradict our image of the the motionless sea cucumber: "One we kept alive in a vessel / of sea water / was always in motion." Either this was a diurnal species which "worked" whenever it was in the light or the poet a night-owl. The first part of the poem was put to music by a band called Deep Freeze Mice published by Octagonal Rabbit Music! **2. Boxes to Eat from** I have a problem with our term, lunch-box, for in Japan and China such boxes are often elegant and used not only in restaurants but even for Imperial feasts. Most *bento* or convenience boxes were compartmentalized rather than tiered. Fancy large ones had a dozen or even a score of compartments, which even a *namako* could not have filled and formed auspicious Chinese letters.

something else is a perk of formlessness. Haiku does not bother to ask *why* sea cucumber do what they do. Professor Motokawa Tatsuo does. Here is part of a multi-stanza poem A SONG OF CONNECTIVE TISSUE which he sent me:

> Stichopus on the sand feeding on sands
> Stiff becomes very stiff when touch my hands
> When sea cuke hides inside crevice in rocks
> Softens his body to fit and then locks [1]

An unrhymed, yet more colorful description of the same by Rob Toonen: "they goopify their bodies, pour themselves into the hole, and then solidify their skin to prevent extraction." ("Cucumber Defenses" by Rob Toonen "Posted to ReefKeepers emailing list, Wednesday 16th September 1998"(googled)). In the sea cucumber, science fiction is fact! There is one haiku showing that the sea slugs reside in rocks, though it doesn't say why:

底岩に幾つとまれる海鼠かな　島村元

sokoiwa ni ikutsu tomareru namako kana – shimamura hajime (1868-1926)

(bottom-boulder/s-in how-many stay/fixed seaslug!/?/ô)

#68

just how many
are staying in those rocks
yep, sea slugs

seabed flat

sea slugs
how many live in this
one boulder

But to return to the result of such a lifestyle: there are three versions of another haiku similar enough to Oemaru's haiku to be called a paraverse:

器（いれ）物の形になりたる海鼠哉　嵐夕

iremono no nari ni naritaru namako kana – ranyû (1699)

(container's shape becomes sea slug the/'tis!/?/ô)

#69

a fitting lifestyle

it becomes
the shape of its container:
the sea slug

1. *Japanese Rhymester* If the reader is tempted to snort at the Professor's English, I would ask how well he can write in Japanese and whether he knows that Japanese are not familiar with rhyme. A translation of Mother Goose (by the illustrator for a more famous earlier translation!) makes a valiant attempt to rhyme where rhyme is most important – in nonsense verse, for it supplies the reason --- but the results are mixed (I explain in EKN why this is true). So I was delighted to receive a rhyme from a non-rhyming culture. As I wrote a friend upon receiving *A Song of Connective Tissue*, "The end of the world must be near! A Japanese has written an end-rhyme (aabb)!" "Oh, my god!" ER replied, "Next, they'll be doing abab!") Since the professor prefaced the poem with the qualification "*words only*," I imagine he sang it at an international *echinodermata* conference! (Japanese readers may buy his CD's of "Singing Biology" (*utau seibutsugaku*))

.岡持の形にしたがふ海鼠哉　哲亜

okamochi no nari ni shitagau namako kana – (tetsua (1798)?)
(container's shape follows sea slug-the/!/?/ŏ)

#70

other-directed

the sea slug
its body imitates
the old tray

器物の形に寝て居る生海鼠哉　山李

iremono no nari ni neteiru namako kana – sani? (1774)
(container's shape-in sleeping sea slug 'tis!/?/ŏ)

#71

dreamtime

the sea slug
asleep takes the shape
of its container

Basho wrote an ethereal poem about moonlight squared off by architecture (*waga yado wa shikaku na kage o mado no tsuki*). The perfectly round Buddhist Law mercifully fitting the poet's more acute circumstance, if I remember one (since lost) explanation correctly. I think of the above haiku of a literally conformist sea slug as more earthy but equally good in a Taoist sort of way. Considering the shapes a sea slug takes over its lifetime, the negative term "formless" must be traded for something positive, say, *polyform*. After Whitman, *big sea slug me* contains multitudes! And, am I crazy to imagine what might be done *on purpose*? We could shape sea slugs into squares (as Japanese have done to watermelons and tomatoes), gingerbread men or, if the genes could be altered to allow greater size, dolphins! That is to say, the sea slugs could pretend to be the stuff of nanotechnology.[1] At the same time, I must admit feeling something *obscene* in the sea slug's utter plasticity, its body slovenly.

出してをけば自堕落に成海鼠哉　尺布

dashite okeba jidaraku ni naru namako kana – shakufu (1773)
(taken-out-left-if debauched/slatternly/slovenly become seaslug/s!/?/ŏ)

#72

taken out
of the tub, sea slugs
debauch

∼

taken out
how the sea slugs
discompose

The word meaning "debauched/ …" literally translates "self-damage-fall" but might be called simply "loose" in English. It is the opposite of being upright (holding the line) or, as OM adds, *uptight*.. When

1. *Nano!* Here, I am referring to nano's supposed ability to make any thing out of some thing. (There is a perfect sentence on metamorphic possibilities, of changing anything into steak, in E. Regis' *Nano!*), As a matter of fact, the Chinese are *already* turning sea slugs into all different things. But such sea slug toads (described in *Sundry Sea* Slugs) and whatnot are formed of jelly made from reconstituted trepang (dehydrated slug). The sea slug does not do it by him or herself.

sea slugs grow weak, they tend to lose their form. I have seen a dying or overheated sea slug stretched out, melted down to pancake thinness (see *Afterword*) and can appreciate the truth of the haiku as an observation.

手 に 取 れ ば ぶ て う ほ ふ な る 海 鼠 か な　虚 子

te ni toreba buchôhô [1] *naru namako kana* – kyoshi (1916)

(hand-in-taken disorderedly/awkward/unaccustomed/impolite-become sea-slug/s!/?/ô)

#73

> picked up
> sea slugs are
> awkward

> *loss of gravitas*

> picked up
> a sea slug looks out
> of its element

Sea slugs, like rocks, are supposed to lie on the ground but, unlike rocks, react when they are picked up. The adjective *buchôhô* forms the meat of the haiku. As the broad connotations given in the gloss suggest, it is an amusing word. Sometimes it is used to describe nondrinkers or nonsmokers, presumably because male etiquette requires both, but I think Kyoshi is describing the real thing.

混 沌 と と り ひ ろ け た る 海 鼠 哉　乙 桌

konton to torihirogetaru namako kana – otsutô? (1699)

(chaos-like taking?-spreads/ing sea slug!/?/ô/the)

#74

> *supernova*

> the sea slug
> expands and grows
> chaotically

In the original poem the uglier but more usual adverbal form of *konton* (chaos), *kontonteki ni,* is eschewed for the onomatopoetic form, *konton to.* Though no actual sound is implied, this psychological mimesis binds more closely to the verb than the other forms. While there is no mention of the sea slug's dying, I added the anachronistic metaphor of a spectacular dying star (which the reader is free to remove from the poem!) because I think it is. As Ball noted in his classic THINGS CHINESE (c1900), if man turns into a *stiff,* sea slugs, "become a shimy mass." [2]

(fs) 君 に よ り な ご む 心 は に ひ 藁 に 包 む 海 鼠 の し か と く る ご と　長 塚 節

kimi ni yori nagomu kokoro wa nii wara ni tsutsumu namako no shi ka tokuru goto – nagatsuka takashi (1901)

(you/darling/lord-by relax/eased heart-as-for new straw-in/by wrapped sea-slug's melting like)

#75

> my wild heart
> that you calmed down
> now melts like
> a sea slug wrapped up
> in fresh straw

---

1. *Buchôhô*: **a disorderly word**: Various printings of this poem spell *buchôhô* differently. As KS explained to me, "whether written *buteuhofu,* *buteuhafu, buteuhou* or *buteuhau,* it is read *buchyouhou, i.e., buchôhô.*"

2. *Shimy?* A typo for "slimy?" Or shimmering?

This *tanka*, perhaps the earliest to treat sea slug (though older and longer *namako* poems should be out there! [1]), shows how gloppiness may be turned into a simile that reminds us of good folk song lyrics. This next, contemporary haiku implies something akin to a meltdown without actually mentioning it.

慟哭の姉は海鼠の系譜です　美代子

dôkoku no ane wa namako no keifu desu – miyoko (contemp)
(wail/ing/lamentation's [older]sister-as-for, seaslug-geneology is)　　　　#76

my sister wails
and i see generations
of us sea slugs

~

my sobbing sister
the incarnation of our
sea slug family

~

my sister lying
in tears: we come from
sea slug lineage

~

elder sister
wails with grief, the grief
of a sea slug

~

dissolved in tears
my sister wails for all
us holothurians

The original was tossed my way when I kidded the poet for playing with *namako* poems in a haiku-related forum. I could immediately realize that while sea slugs do not wail, wailing grief involves collapse with its attendant blubbering, tear-soaked wetness and liquidized innards. But I was confused

←#77, #78

1. Longer Sea Slug Poems As a turn-of-the century haiku bluntly put it, "there are / sea slug haiku but no / sea slug songs" (*namako no ku aredo namako no uta wa nashi* – ryûka (1927) 海鼠の句あれど海鼠の歌はなし 柳家). Strictly speaking, songs (*uta*) here mean *waka* and possibly its successor *tanka*. Perhaps, "there are / sea slug ditties but / no sonnets" would better reflect the feeling of the haiku.　More generally, such "songs" include *kyôka* – literally "crazy-song" and other less well known types of traditional poetry. I have not made much effort to find such poems for this book, but all indications are that some do exist. Here is one *much* older crazy-verse found by CZ: "meeting a tart / we tumbled all around/ and got soaked; / not that i am / a miura sea slug!" (*yone ni aute tawarakorobi de nuresometa miuramisaki no namako naranedo* --- kuroda getsudôken (?) (1688-1703) 寄俵恋　よねにあふてたはらころびで ぬれそめた　三浦みさきのなまこならねど　黒田

月洞軒). The punning is dense: 1) *yone* is "night-sleep"(a variation on *yobai*, or "night-crawling" which was something like New England bundling but more liable to involve sex) , "pretty-whore" and "rice" which comes in a 2) taut sack, or *tawara,* which tumbling is idiomatic for continual getting up and falling down *and* 3) means "sea slug" for they were shipped in sacks, were said to resemble sacks and "sack" was used to indicate sea slug over the New Years, while 4) wetness, suggests "spilling rice"(*yone kobosu*), the New Year taboo word for "tears" and all this wet tumbling about suggests a sea slug caught in the Miura Misaki surf. *Yone* may also mean the poet's 88th birthday, in which case the tumbling was of a more maudlin variety with the wetness the first tears of the year; but, either way, the poem is not really about sea slugs, so, in a sense, it is not a sea slug song.　The "not that I am" rhetoric disavowing the metaphor is more common in far older *waka* collections.

at that *keifu* or "genealogy." I thought it might refer to a metaphorical haiku tradition, but that would imply Buson's thing-thinking (longing or love-sick) creature rather than the wailing or bitterly crying creature required by the verb. I begged a fuller explanation and received an English rendering (by someone near her): "my elder sister crying with sadness is seen like the genealogy of sea cucumber family." I was still unsure if we were talking about someone whose ontogeny traced the holothurian phylogeny (devolution of the echinoderm's hard spiked exterior), or a family of people who share some sea slug trait. As it turns out, it was the latter. Elder sister, who is not so old, lives a somewhat hermit-like existence (a sea slug metaphor so little known today I did not expect it) and the family had a close-to-the-ground history. This poem could have been saved for the *Melancholy Sea Slugs* later to come, but I felt it provided good balance for the *tanka* before it. After finishing the above, the poet reconsidered her wailing sea slug and said I might just dump it and replace it with something like, "my elder sister is just a cucumber in the sea of the tear;" but how could I do that after all this work?

方 円 に 従 ひ な ま こ 生 き て お り　増 田 原 子

hôen ni shitagai namako ikiteori – masuda harako (contemp)

(square-circle-in/to follow/obey, seaslug living-is)

the sea slug
lives in obediance
circlesquare

~

circle and square
the sea slug, like water
obeys the twain

This is a far cooler way to describe the sea slug's formlessness. There is a Chinese saying, known to Japanese, about water "obeying" – which is to say, adopting the shape of – vessels, square or round. "Square-circle," meaning either or both of those characteristics (I say "square," but rectangles are included in the original nuance) is a fine example of an un-Englishable word.

身 軽 な り 纏 う も の 無 し 海 鼠 か な　舞 姫

migaru nari matou mono nashi namako kana – maihime (contemp)

(body-light[/nimble/relieved]become/is cover/encumbering-thing-not, seaslug!/?/ó/the)

light of body
the sea slug is bound
by nothing

free soul

the lightness
of being unbound
a sea slug

The way one thing fits the shape of another can be seen as total freedom or as total servitude. This poem clearly takes it in the former, Taoist, sense. Not bound by the unyielding skin, scales or other coverings that force other animals to keep their shape much as a river in a concrete straight-jacket,, nor bound to a certain path or den or family ties, the sea slug is "light" of body and, psychologically speaking, light of spirit.

かりそめに腸のある海鼠かな　青愚

karisome ni harawata no aru namako kana – seisei+keigu

(temporary/tentatively/transiently-even guts/intestines has sea-slug!/?/ǿ/the)   #81

> it does have guts
> tentatively speaking
> the sea slug

Earlier poems saw the protean nature of the sea slug from without. This treats the metamorphosis *within*. To the sea slug, guts are easy come easy go. Keigu's paraverse was born of the misreading of an early modern description of the physical nature of our creature by Seisei (1869-1937), which we shall encounter among *Meek Sea Slugs*. Japanese "guts" are not merely an asexual synonym for balls but, rather, stand for something larger we might call the seat, if not the very substance, of the soul.

便なさやいづれ生海鼠の裏表　太祇

binnasa [tayorinasa?] ya izure namako no uraomote – taigi (1709-72)

(way-not (how sad!) [helplessness]eventually sea slug's bottom/inside-top/outside)   #50 (repeat)

> *cruel, cruel*
>
> what good to live
> in a world which guts
> the sea slug?
>
> *dog-eat-dog*
>
> life's hard
> no doubt! sea slugs end up
> inside-out!

The above, my first readings of Taigi's poem, allude to the way some sea slugs self-eviscerate –split their sides – as soon as they are boiled for curing or, before boiling (or cutting), eject their entrails through the anus, something they may be coached to do in order to obtain the ingredients for *konowata,* fermented sea cucumber guts.[1] A modern haiku describes the result of this sea slug milking where the "cows" are sacrificed:

このわたは小樽海鼠は中樽に　　鈴木真砂女

konowata wa kodaru namako wa chûdaru ni – suzuki masajo (1937)

(slug-gut-as-for small-tub, seaslug-as-for medium-tub, in)   #82

> sea slug guts
> in small tubs, sea slug
> in medium ones

1. *Enticing Entrails* There are several ways to make sea slugs spew their guts out of their anuses. First, the sea slug can be milked as one might a cow; second, one may use electric shock (Arakawa writes "the result is not worth the danger"); and, third, it may be chemically induced. In this case, the live sea slugs are placed in a holding tank for a half day to wait for their bowels to evacuate, then, divided in groups of several dozen each, placed in smaller tubs, after which the guts of one or two sea slugs are removed, crushed and the juice squeezed out and injected into the tub where the other slugs breathe it in and are stimulated to spew (This collective response is known to aquarium experts who advise buyers to acclimate the cukes – let them get used to a cupful of the water – in individual bowls lest they spill their guts). If the spewer is more or less 20 cm, it's "shell" (meaning the meat) is marketed, but if it is 15 cm or smaller, it is returned to the ocean to regrow its guts, a process taking about a month (Arakawa: ndh). Most slugs are not "milked," however, they are just sliced open.

このわたを泳がせてゐる海鼠かな 矢島渚男

konowata o oyogaseteiru namako kana – yajima nagisaô (contemp)

#83

(slug-guts[obj] swim-make seaslug!/?/ó/the)

> sea slugs
> their guts are made
> to swim

While a sea slug in the wild does shoot its guts out its anus in self defense, I doubt that such would be called "swimming them" even in jest, so the second haiku probably describes the way they are washed to remove all the sand. With respect to the first, I felt tempted to put the slugs into "big" tubs because "medium" was too large for the poem, but large tubs would be the holding vats. Such a business probably got its sea slugs directly from the sluggers, for to do otherwise was to risk losing the guts:

ふつふつと腸噴く海鼠糶られけり　大石悦子

futsufutsu to chô fuku namako serarekeri – ôishi etsuko (contemp)

#84

(plopping/bubbling guts emit/spout seaslug auctioned-off)

> spurting guts
> the sea slugs are
> auctioned off

I suppose the waste of good guts might be lamented by some Japanese readers of such a haiku. An English speaker – in this case, someone who "camped out at a little cove" in 1975 – might put it differently:

> We spent one low tide collecting enough sea cucumbers for a meal. What a disgusting creature that is. When threatened, the sea cucumber will regurgitate nearly it's entire body. It has no bones, just a bag of muscle full of potential puke. ("Northwest to Alaska Chapter Six" (The harbor was a much nicer place to live than a parking lot) by Peter S. Oleson: www.pcpros.net/~oleson/NW2AK6.html / (c)1996

To be fair, the author was no sissy ("They didn't taste bad, just a little on the rubbery side.") but the equation of guts and *puke*, reveals his modern Occidental colors. "Regurgitation" suggests the wrong hole, too, but such confusion is normal. It is rare that the 1 of 3 possibilities is specified. For example, who can say if the ejaculation referred to in Australian poet Martin Johnston's *"The Sea Cucumber"* [1] is of the anal or ventral variety? "We'd all had a bit too much that night when you brought out your painting," Johnston begins in this two page-long title poem *for Ray Crooke*, " . . and my father talked about waiting . . . / he was pressing every word-drop like the wine of a harvest not quite adequate, / to trickle in brilliant iridules across the stained table: / what sorts of eucalypt to plant . .," but

> None of this, you see, will really go into writing,
> it takes time to leech things into one's sac of words.
> The bloated sea-cucumber, when touched, spews up its entrails
> as though that were a defense; my father's old friend
> the gentle little poet Wen-Yi-tuo. who collected chess sets
> and carved ivory seals in his filthy one-room hut,
> is gutted one night and flung into the Yangtze.
> The dark river runs through your dusty pigments . . . (TSC)

1. *"The Sea Cucumber"* This book is one of only two unscientific books with sea cucumber in the title in English (the other being the novel cited in the chapter-head quotation). Unfortunately, only a single line of one poem touches upon our charge, though the repercussions go further . . .

"*As though* that were a defense?" Does the Australian poet doubt nature? Would he doubt a lizard who drops a tail or a crab who leaves a leg? [1] It *is* a defense, *and doubly so*. We shall discuss the toxicity of these sticky entrails that stop delicate predators and divert tougher customers later (pg __). Here, we shall only observe that while the latter eats the *hors de oevres* – or tries to lick or rub it off their face (especially the cuvier tube (lung-trees) which are the stickiest and most toxic part) – the *piece de resistance,* which is to say main dish, melts into a crevice. Although there are plenty of sea cucumbers in Australia,[2] I think Johnston may have been influenced by Aldous Huxley:

> He kissed her again, whispering her name several times: Doris, Doris, Doris. The scientific appellation of the sea-mouse he was thinking, as he kissed the throat she offered him, white and extended like the throat of a victim awaiting the sacrificial knife. The sea-mouse was a sausage with iridescent fur: very peculiar. Or was Doris the sea-cucumber, which turns itself inside out in moments of alarm? ("*The Gioconda Smile*")

Let us hope she doesn't puke on him or worse! I do not know if Huxley envisioned entrails spewing from the anus or bursting from the ventral part of the torso, or something more figurative: is a life turned inside out anything like one turned upside down? [3]

so helpless!
we end up sea slugs
inside-out

evisceration

life sucks!
we end up sea slugs
inside out!

In this reading, I assume Taigi – like Johnston – is more anxious about the vicissitudes of human life than that of sea slugs, so I added the hint of *seppuku* (*hara-kiri*), for when the belly was cut right the guts would spill out, and, if that wasn't enough, a brave warrior might reach in and pull them out (this, the original "gut's pose" [1 →] could, un/fortunately, be performed only once in a life-time), make a very clean breast=belly of it.   Dramas depicted this by having the self-killer pull out yard after yard of red ribbon! [2] Whether the poet knew it or not, the semblance is deep. Not only do many varieties, includ-

---

1. *Part Dropping Animals* I mention the lizard and the crab because these are the best known, part-sacrificers in the West, but Tsurumi Yoshiyuki introduces a closer example, the milk fish of Indonesia, the Philippines and Taiwan. He fails to say whether it "vomits" its guts out through the anus or the mouth, but notes that it was probably evolved against its nemesis, the sea snake and that because the semi-aquacultured fish spoiled quickly, the fisherman "milked" out the guts by making a rope "snake" dance in the pond before harvesting them. (nnm) No doubt, more such examples could be found. (If man shits in his pants, it might indicate that our nemesis was coprophilic or coprophobic?)

2. *Australian Sea Slugs* Australia may well have more varieties of sea cucumbers than any other single nation. Tsurumi Yoshiyuki (nnm) gives a list of names used for various species(?) found at the Great Barrier Reef in 1928: Deepwater black fish, Teat fish, Mama teat fish, Red fish, Small black fish, Prickly fish, Tigu fish, Sand fish, Lolly fish, Chalk fish. I suppose the tits come from the large papules on some sea cucumbers, but I can't help thinking of the ejaculated entrails as milk and wondering if a haiku on the galaxy might not be in order.

3. *Inside-Out and Upside-down Question* I suspect that the metaphor is not the same. I knew clothes were usually worn with the right and left lapel reversed for burial – hidari eri – and hoped, for the sake of an interesting interpretation of Taigi's haiku, that they might have been turned inside out, too. But, the only inside-out clothing to turn up so far was worn by sleeping lovers hoping to attract their lovers in the Heian era (Dalby, correspondence).

including our *namako,* fire their poisonous or sticky entrails – the poison coming from their lungs rather than cloaca – from their anus, but in extremely life-threatening situations, some sea slugs, evicerate themselves at the drop of a hat (sand falling on it is sometimes enough to trigger the response!).   In Laura Woodward's amusing mixed metaphor,

> its sides split open and it voluntarily disembowels itself, tossing most of its internal organs over-board. Whether this bizarre phenomenon – called evisceration – is a method of defense is debatable. [3] (*"Anyone for Cucumber Sand Creatures"* (British Whales and Dolphins? t.o.p. www.divernet.com/biolog/ cucu1097.htm)

This response to dangerously hot or anaerobic conditions allows the sea slug to lower its metabolism until the condition improves and it can afford to grow back its organs.* Since *seppuku* was performed as an act of defense – by killing oneself, a man could save the lives and fortune of other members of his family – the sea slug and the pre-modern Japanese would appear to have something in common.[3]

つかまれて六腑吐き出す海鼠かな五臓残して元の姿に　荻上紘一
tsukamarete rokufu hakidasu namako kana gozô nokoshite moto no sugata ni -- ogiue koichi
(caught six-entrails disgorge seaslug   five-viscera leaving original/well shape-in)

#85

caught, sea slug
spews out all six of
its entrails
but its five viscera
stay and it recovers

→**1. Gut's Pose** The *gatsu pohzu* was invented by a pro-wrestler, Guts Takahashi, who helped the Japanese cope with their physical inferiority complex in the decade after the Occupation by beating up foreign pro-wrestlers. His unique action was pumping his fist/s in the air. It didn't catch on internationally either because the world was not yet ready for such aggressive, egoistic mannerism, or because international pop culture was not interested in Japan. Later, fist-pumping would be born in black America, a culture which is closely emulated – or, ripped off? – by the rest of the developed world.

→**2. Dramatic Seppuku versus Reality** Considering the exaggerated attention given to *harakiri* in the Occident, a caveat: the practice was not that common, and true evisceration was very rare, for a nominal cut generally sufficed to bring down the second's sword on the neck. For the sea cucumber, too, there are less dramatic forms of self-gutting. Some species seasonally resorb their guts and internal organs when quiescent. The *Apostichopus japonicus* does this before estivation and its relatively close relative, the *Parastichopus californicus,* does this before its hibernation. A circular graph of the former shows Sept-Oct as "recovery phase" for activity and guts, Nov-May as "development/growth phase," (with Jan-Feb for "greatest-development" of guts), June-July as the "involution[absorption]/pre-estivation phase," mid-

July-August as the "complete involution/estivation phase." This only holds true for most of the *hondo,* or main island of Japan, not the Hokkaido fishery. (ndh)

3. Cuke Evisceration   I let the Japan-connection overrule common sense in permitting the *seppuku* metaphor to stand. Marine biologist Augusta Foote Arnold's metaphor is better: "They also turn themselves inside out, as it were, as if from *nausea,* when confined in water too stale for their uses." Specialists are still trying to figure out exactly *how* the *Holothurian* splits open. A few lines from an abstract for and by a scientist suggests that even if they figure it out, we laymen had best stick to our metaphors: "Time lapse electron microscopy suggests that the changes in the connective tissue start from the peritoneal side of the introvert and continue outward as a wave of tissue disruption. During evisceration the coelomic fluid is propelled anteriorly by contraction of the body wall muscles, thereby forcing eversion of the introvert and a reduction in its thickness. It is suggested that the change in the connective tissue of the introvert during evisceration is caused or mediated by an evisceration factor present in coelomic fluid." Maria Byrne (Dept. of Anatomy and Histology, University of Sydney. ULTRASTRUCTURE OF AUTOTOMY AND CATCH CONNECTIVE TISSUE REGIONS OF THE INTEGUMENT OF *EUPENTACTA QUINQUESEMITA* (HOLOTHUROIDEA) .

The original crazy-verse plays on the Chinese terminology in ways the translation cannot, for there is no way to show the nature of those terms. The six entrails are the large colon, small colon, gall-bladder, urinary bladder, stomach and three-spot/burn (三焦 a triad of points under the navel that regulate breath, digestion and excretion), whereas, the five viscera are the liver, lungs, heart, kidneys and spleen." I doubt that the actual split is a perfect parallel, but the poet is a mathematician, not a biologist and most Japanese do not know the respective contents of the 6 and the 5, other than a vague idea of the latter as more solid because it includes a character that might be translated as "organ." Morever, the five viscera can also stand for the body, itself. I think it is enough to guess that the existence of two systems works in a sort of back-up capacity, but let me drop the Chinese terms for a lighter translation:

> sea slugs
> spew out their guts
> when caught
> but catch their breath
> and come right back

Protean sea slugs are not and never were restricted to poetry. Here are a few lines I have crudely Englished from the free-verse poem "Spring and Carnage" (*haru to shura*) by the polymath fablist Miyazawa Kenji[1] (1896-1933) to show how the sea slug served the obscure need of an imagism:

> . . . and the sun went behind a cloud / i sat on a rock as my numbness left / a scrap of wood on the bottom seemed a caterpillar or sea slug / and, first of all, i can't see your body / could it really have dissolved? / or was everything from the outset / only a hazy pale blue dream?

I think it no accident that we find abundant images of the sea slug in the work of Shiki, Sôseki and Miyazawa, respectively, the top poet, novelist, and fabulist of turn-of-the-century and early twentieth century Japan. Did the sea slug, once silenced by the gods of their ancestors, rise up to become the psyche of a nation voiceless in the face of the military, economic, political, social, psychological and cultural threat from the West?

青と見れば紫光る海鼠かな　東洋城

ao to mireba murasaki hikaru namako kana – tôyôjô (1929)

(blue-as seen-if, purple shine/shining seaslug/s!/?/ó)

#86

> sea slugs
> called blue, shine
> purple
> ～
>
> blue at a glance
> but purple is the color
> sea slugs shine

1. *Miyazawa Kenji and Sea Slug* Besides this passage and the other about ozone (elsewhere), Miyazawa wrote ". . so cut me up. My head and trunk and tail will fall in the sea and become *namako*" (trans. ? *The Twin Stars*). Starfish would be more accurate (and fit the title in English), for they are the best regrowers of all, but they are called "people-hands" in Japanese, and it would be too weird for all parts of the body to turn into one. No, poetry demands the sea slug here, for its lack of form makes it the better candidate for such fragmentation and subsequent wholeness, added to which, it has, in Japan, as we shall see, the brooding image of one aggrieved. (Readers interested in Miyazawa's magical mixture of science+fable, city+country, and modern+traditional are advised to google.)

If I am not mistaken, this was written shortly after Shiki noted that white snow was not purely white and Kyoshi noted that white peony were not perfectly white. I am no fan of such poems for they seem to boast "aren't we careful objective observers!" By contrasting an overall impression – not just the type "blue sea slug" (*aonamako*) – with the sheen, this Tôyôjô's poem is just complex enough to work.

かたまりて色のみだれの海鼠かな　野村喜舟

katamarite iro no midare no namako kana – kisen (1934)

(clumped color/s mess-up/go-wild seaslug/s!/?/ó/do)

#87

in a lump
sea slug colors go
hog wild

~

the promiscuous
colors in a promiscuous
lump of sea slugs!

一口に海鼠の色の言ひ難し　山崎房子

hitoguchi ni namako no iro no iigatashi – yamazaki fusako (2001)

(one-mouth/word-in seaslug's color/s say-difficult)

#88

the sea slug:
no word can do justice
to its color!

~

"sea slug"
a color hard to fit
into a word

Some animals and plants have colors easy to describe. Not the *namako*. The red ones are not really red and the blue not really blue. They have purplish greys in them or somewhat orange browns with slight differences top and bottom . . . And like many denizens of the sea, the color does not stay put.

大臣の台詞のごとき海鼠かな　藤井三吉

daijin no serifu no gotoki namako kana – fujii sankichi (2001)

(prime-minister's line/speech-like sea-slug!/?/ó/'tis/the)

#89

the sea slug:
like something uttered by
a politician

~

oh, sea slug!
prime ministers speak
like you look!

This may have been inspired by late twentieth century concern that the ambiguity of the prime-minister's pronouncements handicapped Japan in a world run by people who did not mince their words – one prime-minister was said to string together whole sentences of nothing more substantial than *aaauuu's* and *uuuaaa's* (with but two vowels: well, I suppose could be digitized!) – it could apply to many if not most politicians throughout the world. OM reminds me that my metaphor may be a bit off. The reader may substitute "feel" for "look" in the last translation, or spell it out:

> really, sea slug!
> you are as slippery as
> our p.m.'s words

In that case, the poem might be better with the *Slippery Sea Slugs*. Be that as it may, I think the wit of the poem is in its bassackwards, normally, a politician would be described as a sea slug (or a mule, an ostrich, or swine at the trough, etc).

スフインクスの謎より深い海鼠哉　敬愚
sufinkusu no nazo yori fukai namako kana – keigu
(sphinx's riddle-more-than deep seaslug!/?/ŏ/'tis/the)　　　　　　　#90

> the sphinx riddle
> is childstuff compared
> to the sea slug

The holothurian's most incredible metamorphosis occurs before it reaches the eye of the poet. Compared to it, human development is as simple as pie. A glimpse at sketches of developmental phases shows a satchel turning into an ovoid with latitudinal divisions turning into a bagpipe into a piece of a branch with twigs and some leaves called a juvenal sea cucumber. Considering the remarkable variability of their adult forms, the other surprise is that these stages of development – if the word "stages" can be applied to such an alinear sequence! – are roughly shared by most (all???) holothurians.[1] Though not all echinoderm classes show such adult variance, they all are extremely creative (?) developers.[2] One developmental biologist has gone so far as to to use the "sequential chimerism" of echinoderm larva as as the exemplar for his hypothesis about the existence of interspecies – even interphylum – cross-fertilization, or borrowing ("horizontal transfer of genetic information")[3] So, the protean *namako* is no figment of the poet's imagination.

1. *More Protean Holothurians* Some sea slugs are, in a sense, far less stable(?) than the Japanese *namako*. An inedible *Holothurian* of a different order (Apoda=footless) has the sloppiest body of all. "*Synapta* grows to a length of eighteen inches or more, but is constantly breaking pieces off its posterior end by muscular contractions. When kept in confinement, it soon commences to constrict its body at various points, and after a few hours there is nothing left but a mass of fragments." (A.F.Arnold:IBID) A. Kerr writes that "some species, primarily *Stichopus*, use it [mutable connective tissues] to autotomise (break off) part of their body as it is being attacked. The cuke gets away (sometimes swimming vigorously) and the predator . . . halts and munches on the torn bit. This form of defense however works against cukes when they are picked up in hand: incredibly, the whole body of several *Stichopus* species melts into ooze and dribbles right through ones fingers. Some *Stichopus* are eaten in the Pacific, so to prevent them from self-destructing, Micronesian women bang them fiercely against a rock. This causes them to stiffen and keep their shape. I speculate that this beating mimics the pounding of the cuke taken by a one in the surf; melting in response to this would be quite maladaptive." (corresp) .

2. *Holothurian Variance* Kerr and Kim note that Holothuroids boast the most morphologically derived echinoderms, including pelagic species and spheroid, plated taxa *with mouth and anus adjacent at the end of a long, flexible stalk.*"(italics mine) The title of their paper that relates this diversity to a complex evolutionary history condenses the structural mystery of this "least studied class of extant echinoderms," to wit: *Bi-deca-bi-pentaradial symmetry*: A review of evolutionary and developmental trends in Holothuroidea (Echinodermata). *Journal of Experimental Zoology* (Developmental and Molecular Evolution) 285: 93-103 (1999)

3. *Sequential Chimerism* I condensed and reformatted the following from Scott F. Gilbert's summary of retired Embryology professor

(University of Liverpool) Donald Williamson's hypothesis that the Tree of Life has "anastomases, where branches from different trunks fuse together."

> The echinoderm larva and the echinoderm adult are separate entities. The larva does not "grow into" the adult. 2) The *tornaria* larva of hemichordates is almost identical to that of sea urchins, even though the adults have nothing in common. He proposes that the first echinoderm to have a larva obtained it from the hemichordate. 3) The larval forms sometimes are at odds with the adult form. The echinoderm adult is radial, while the echinoderm larva is bilateral. There is nothing in the fossil record to suggest that modern echinoderms had a bilateral ancestor. . .

Thus, Williamson concludes, "I hold that all the evidence is consistent with regarding the [echinoderm] phylum as having evolved from radially symmetrical, schizocoelous protostomes, with, in most cases, the later insertion of a bilaterally symmetrical, enterocoelous, deutero-stomatous, larval phase." Here is a particularly scintillating example of how things might work:

> "I suggest that the ophiopluteus larval form of brittle stars was derived from the echinopluteus of a sea urchin, which, in turn, was derived from a bipinnaria of a sea star, and this was derived from an auricularia larva of a sea cucumber, which was derived from the tornaria of an acorn worm, and each larval transfer was the result of a cross-fertilization." (The adult program from the acorn worm, etc., would be represented as junk DNA).

Gilbert qualifies: "Most biologists would probably contend that what Williamson sees as a problem is not an anomaly at all, but merely the expected consequences of shared phylogenies and convergent evolution. Moreover, the bilateral ancestor of echinoderms would not be expected to fossilize if it were like a soft-bodied larva." But, as he points out, Williamson makes it clear that he only posits a hypothesis and that he hopes "someone will pick up the gauntlet and check his hypothesis."

AK informs me that a recent article in the journal *Evolution* did pick up the gauntlet and the results were not favorable to Williamson's hypothesis. AK adds that he and colleagues have done numerous phylogenetic analyses using different echinoderm genes and have never found DNA sequences more closely allied with non-echinoderms.

0. *More Protean Yet* **(Extra Note)**   Though the Echinoderms are champion-class morphers for animals their size, if we scale down and do not restrict ourselves to animals, we find morphers whose antics beggar the imagination. Take the *Pfiesteria piscicida,* an algae that makes the news when it enjoys a major fish-kill. It has a "life cycle that includes *at least* 24 flagellated, amoeboid, and encysted stages or forms" (*italics* mine). A sketchy explanation: Flagellated stages of *Pfiesteria piscicida* feed on bacteria, algae, small animals in the water or sediment. A large school of fish nears. Their excreta triggers a reaction in the Pp's cells making them toxic to the fish whom they approach and stun. The flagellated Pp eat the fish alive, then turn into amoeboid stages to better eat the rotting remains and, if a storm crops up, these quickly grow protective coverings and sink out of the water column as dormant cyst stages. These changes, the North Carolina State University Aquatic Botany Laboratory site notes, occur *within hours*.

4
the do-nothing sea slug

眼なきこそ海鼠の眼句によく見えて　敬愚

menaki koso namako no me ku ni yoku miete – keigu
(eyeless especially seaslug's eyes haiku-in often see)

#91

因為 sea slug
has no eyes, the poets
write about them

It's true. If sea slugs had eyes they would seldom if ever be mentioned. In a world where eyes are the norm, eyelessness has a scarcity value. Strictly speaking, it is not true that our charge lacks eyes. Holothurian expert Alexander Kerr writes:

The eyes are rather simple, yet have lenses and so must focus some light onto the layer of photosensitive cells opposite; I rather suspect that they see about as well as a scallop, who has similar eyes. (corresp)[1]

In other words, like most sightless humans, *namako* are not totally blind, but legally blind. Be that as it may, the apparent eyelessness of the slug takes us up a tangle of metaphorical alleys too disparate to flow in a serial narrative. Needless to say, it would have fit well in the *Featureless Sea Slug*. But, there are many more. *Sleepiness* (shut-eye is no eye). *Agelessness* (pre-hole means pre-life/death). Related to these two, we have the more complex metaphor of *the myth of the beginnings* (pre-science wholeness) and *blessed ignorance*. I have tried to separate the Taoist, Confucian and Buddhist sea slugs that draw on these metaphors into separate chapters. But, these religions – or philosophies – are so closely intertwined that I sometimes had to call upon all of them to explain a single haiku. I fear these next few chapters will be as formless as our subject and beg the reader to bear with me.

そこ言（ママ＝こゝ＝爱）と見れと（ば²）目のなき海鼠哉　太祇

sokokoko to miredo(ba) menonaki namako kana – taigi (1709-72)
(there-here, looking but, eyes-[have] not seaslug!/?/ó/'tis/the)

#92

"here they are! no, there they are!"
but searching, it has no eyes
the sea slug.

trans. blyth

～

we looked here
and there and found no eyes:
the sea slug

1. Holothurian Eyes Because of the great interest shown by my Japanese acquaintances in this subject, I would like to learn more about the eyes in question for the next edition. E.g., do the eyes on the head clearly aid in navigation, while the ones on the back help regulate the daily cycle?

2. ~miredo, ~miredo Different books give different versions of poems which are sometimes the result of mistaken transcription and sometimes reflect multiple versions of the original.

~
looking here,
there: the sea slug's eyes
are nowhere!

While I often find mistakes in Blyth, he saved me on this one. My eyes were so closely focused on the sea slug and its subtle groping motions that I was blind to the poet's eyes. Here is the proof: my mistranslations!

paradox

the sea slug
looks about without
eyes to see!

all-seeing

eyeless
the sea slug looks
everywhere

radar

looking here
and there – sea slug
has no eyes

Blyth's translation was followed by: "the humour and the pathos of the sea-slug brings out its thusness, its sea-slug-ness." My mistranslations (grammatically possible, to be sure, but so unlikely compared to Blyth's reading that they are to all practical purposes wrong) were followed by:

> This haiku with no metaphor is the first I know on the eyelessness of sea slugs. I imagine this sea slug is in a tub of salt water, but it could be that same sea slug that was creeping on the cutting board in Taigi's other haiku. Actually, the sea slug *does* have rudimentary eyes – light-sensors – both on its head and its back; but for all practical and poetic purposes, the sea slug is as good as blind and lacks eyes capable of catching ours. The paradox mentioned in my first title is a false one, for without focused vision, one *must* cast one's awareness about like a radar even if only to move straight.

Aside from the last line, which is true but hardly relevant to the correct translation, it stands.

海底にまなこ忘れてきしなまこ　鳥居真理子
unazoko/kaitei ni manako wasurete kishi namako – torii mariko (2002)
(sea-bottom eyes forgot/forgetting comes/came seaslug)

#93

the sea slug
its eyes left behind
on the seabed

hi, sea slug!
did you forget to
bring your eyes?

forgetful sea slug
leaves his eyes behind
on the sea floor

What a sweet poem this is! I wonder if the poet, like me, read Kyorai's poem wrong (if only for a second) and thought of a sea slug blindly groping for its eyes . . . It also ought to be considered a *Just-so Sea Slug.* None of my readings matches the *manako/namako* rhyme in the original. A Japanese reader thinks *unazoko* is the reading for the first two Chinese characters, for the rhyme value. I think we have enough rhyme already and favor the more prosaic *kaitei.* (I hope to have the poet's opinion by the second edition! 鳥居さま、この俳句大好きでご連絡下さい！)

俎板にまだ眼の覚ぬ生海鼠哉　素丸

manaita ni mada me no samenu namako kana – somaru (1712-95)

(cutting-board-on still eyes' awake/conscious-not sea slug!/?/ó/the)　　#94

hundun

on the cutting board
a sea slug with its eyes
yet to open

ground zero

a sea slug
yet to come to
on the cutting board

"Eyes-wake/conscious" (*mezameru*) means *to wake up* or *come to*. If a blind man can say "*I see*" in English without meaning more than he understands something, a blind man wakes or comes to by metaphorically opening his eyes in Japanese. I do not know if the poet means the sea slug is "still comatose" from being frozen, or that the creature has yet to reincarnate high enough to evolve eyes. The title of my first translation suggests the poet thought of the Chinese myth of origin where Hundun, the holeless sack or gourd of potential being named "Chaos" was simultaneously brought to higher life and killed by having holes made for its/our senses. [1]

達磨忌や戸棚探れは生海鼠哉　子規

darumaki ya todana sagureba namako kana – shiki (1892)

(bodhidharuma-memorial=deathday: cupboard searching/feeling seaslug!/?/ó/'tis/a)　　#95

daruma day
reaching into the cupboard
a sea slug!

this sea slug
turns up in the cupboard
on daruma day!

There is no question that this is a fine match. The bodhidharuma is a buddhified hundun. The eyes of its representations – statues with rounded bottoms which allow it to be knocked over yet right itself [1] (a sort of self-organizing universe?) – are painted in (usually, the pupils of the eyes are added when something is achieved) rather than punched through, but the idea is the same. The question is whether Shiki simply caught the coincidence or actually bought the sea slug to surprise a friend with (or had a friend surprise him with it). I favored something deliberate here, but my Japanese experts voted for sheer coincidence. Another possibility, however, arose after I found the following old haiku:

1. Hundun The name for this god is the same as the two-character word meaning "chaos." The Chinese myth itself is very inchoate. The Zhuangzi (370-301) version has the Emperors of the Northern and Southern Seas treat Hundun, the Emperor of the Middle, to his holes to repay his hospitality to them. The fact the holes are modeled *after* those of man ruins the sequence. In later versions, Hundun conflates with Pangu(n), a giant manlike god whose body parts seed our world. This later myth in Chinese–>Japanese–> German–> English translation: "The Chinese feign, that the first Man, whom they also own for their first Governor, was called Puoncuus, and had his Original out of a confus'd Lump, as out of an Egg." (Kaempfer:1692) The most common metaphor is neither egg nor sea slug. It is a calabash. In some stories, 5 sense holes are opened, in most 7, and others 9 (Pangu(n) underwent 9 transformations). The last, the anus, proved fatal. A New Year's haiku showing the Japanese awareness of Taoist "holism" which prob. predates Somaru's poem: "the seven holes / are opened up eye first: / the first sun" (*nana ana ya me yori hirakete hi-no hajime* – 禾十束山(p23brhkz).

達磨忌や無キ物さがす箱戸棚　桃丸

 # 96

darumaki ya nakimono sagasu hako todana – tôgan (1790)
(daruma-memorial:/! not-thing[missing thing?] search boxes/cupboards)

daruma day
groping for something not
in the closet

daruma day

it turns out
i searched the cupboard
for *nothing*

daruma day

how i search
the shelves for something
no longer there

daruma day
searching the cupboard
i don't find

something

I imagine the "shelf-box" in question within the tiny anteroom-like entrance to a traditional Japanese house. rather than in the kitchen, though it may also be a "god-shelf" or even an open dresser in a closet. Shiki's sea slug – the sea slug being a bundle of *have-nots* – makes so perfect a response to this haiku that I suspect it may well be an imaginary poem doing just that.

人何ヲカ士閑の無為ナル貌　揚水

#97

hito nani o ka namako no nurarinaru katachi – yôsui (1683)
(people what!? earth-meat[seaslug]'s no/t-doing/behavior[slimyness/gloopiness] is face/form)

freedom

poor humanity!
behold the artless form
of the sea slug!

exemplar

think of man!
then behold the artless
sea slug's form

The short and emphatic rhetorical question ("people what!?") at the start of this early sea slug haiku would seem to be criticism of our species wandering far from the Way. The Chinese characters "nothing+behavior/doing" – a term identified with the inactive, or rather anti-forcing philosophy of Taoism – are phonetically marked to read *nurari,* or "slimy", something that apparently alludes to a watery manner of following the natural course, going with the flow by being the flow And the word for sea-slug, "earth-meat" is probably Chinese medicine-derived. I didn't catch this haiku until I had already translated and guessed about the Hundun allusions for the less plainly Taoist poems. It doesn't prove me right, but supports such an understanding.

かかる世にぬらりとしたる海鼠哉　無名氏

#98

kakaru yo ni nurari to shitaru namako kana – anon (1763)
(this [type of] world-in inactive/artless/gloopy is/does seaslug!/?/ó/the)

do-nothing in busyland

in this age
it would still be still
the sea slug

miracle

in this world
it manages to remain
sea sluggish

1. *Extending Rolly Polly* What bounds back is not pinned down. Escape = slippery = formless (daruma always robe-hidden), ergo: daruma = sea slug. A slippery daruma: "daruma day / fermented bean soup for / the first principle" (*daruma ki ya nattôjiru o daiichigi* – seisei HKDZ). Fermented beans are slimy and the soup murky and thus it is metaphorically appropriate. As is the sea slug.

The *kakaru* before the "world/age" is hard to translate for it means "this all too whatever world." I think it means that the Japanese were self conscious of the busy nature of the times.

いつ見ても濡身のまゝの海鼠哉　馬光

itsu mite mo nuremi no mama no namako kana – bakô (1768)
(when[ever] see, wet-body as-is seaslug!/?/ö/the)   #99

whenever	wet as ever
we look, still wet	whenever we see
sea slugs	sea slugs!

always
moist as ever
sea slug

This might be just an observation about the uncanny way a sea slug, like a healthy dog's nose always seems wet; but old haiku are rarely "just." Chances are there is a figurative reading: *sea-slug-as-wet-behind-the-ears forever*.[1] There is something Godly about such permanent moisture, especially when combined with the creature's hoary ancient form. Moisture was (today, these connotations are largely obsolete) a mark of blessedness, tranquility and vacillation. There is yet another connotation, which is still doing strong today, but that belongs with the chapter on *Lubricious Sea Slugs*!

天地の昔しも今も海鼠哉　馬卵

ametsuchi no mukashi mo ima mo namako kana – bakuran (1714~60)
(heaven-earth's ancient-even now-even, sea slug!/?/ö/'tis/the)   #100

today
as long ago
sea-slug

〜

the sea slug
long ago and now
the sea slug

Perhaps an allusion to the same Hundun myth. Unlike other things, the sea slug is as it was in the beginning, amen. Indeed, *namako* was not uncommonly written with Chinese characters for "na" (as in Nara, the old capital) "ma" as *man* (ten-thousand) and "ko" meaning "ancient" or simply abbreviated as "ancient" rather than its homophone "child." (子→古)

天地いまだ開き尽くさでなまこかな　嵩谷

ametsuchi[tenchi?] imada hirakitsukusa de namako kana – sûya (19c)
(heaven-earth still open-exhausts-not because, seaslug!/?/ö/lo!/the)   #101

sleeping potential

because heaven
and earth are not yet done
lo! sea slugs!

1. *Wet Sea Slug* That the sea slug is identified with wetness is clear from an exampled syllabary from a primary school in Fukuoka. The syllabet ぬ (*nu*) is defined as a *nurunuru shita namako,* or a slimy (*nurunuru*) sea slug. Other syllabets in the syllabary are more of the "'B' is Busy on 'C' is Cleaning Day" type thing. That the sea slug slipped into such pedagogy speaks of its high presence in Japan.

raw stuff

all creation
is not yet done:
sea slugs

This likewise undated haiku (prob. 19c) begins with the same "heaven-earth" of creation and creation stories, but it is probably pronounced *tenchi* rather than in the more lyrical *ametsuchi* because otherwise the poem would be too long. Perhaps *Namako* is in the syllabary because the poet wanted to bring out the "raw" quality of *nama* rather than allowing the characters to bring up a mouse/rat.

万物の成れるが中のなまこかな　蕗谷

banbutsu no nareru ga naka no namako kana – roya (19c)

#102   (ten-thousand[myriad]'s becoming among's seaslug!/?/ó/lo/the)

a sea slug
part of all the world's
becoming

atavism

while all creation
is becoming something
lo, the sea slug!

The syntax of this poem found in the same book as the last permits either of the above readings, but the second reading – a somewhat exaggerated translation – would seem most likely. Either way, I wish I knew more about the poet and precise date of this poem![1]

天地を我が産み顔の海鼠かな　子規

ametsuchi o waga umigao no namako kana – shiki (1867-1902)

#103   (heaven-earth, myself-bore-faced seaslug!/?/ó/'tis/the)

cosmic parenthood   **the sea slug**

the sea slug   a face that says
a face that says "i bore   the whole wide world
heaven and earth"   was *my* doing!

the original face

the sea slug
a countenance parent to
all creation

This poem by the prophet of modern haiku echoes the language and thought of the earlier poems but, I think, is much better for its warm humor (This, not the oft mentioned objective realism, is what makes me a Shiki fan). The Japanese use of "face" as "expression" doesn't work so well in English. The third poem attempts to translate the boastful nuance – "I did it!" – of "my face" in Japanese. And maybe, the sea slug really *did*. Chaos is as much a prerequisite for life as order. There is something to the French term *beche de mer,* or "worm of the sea." A sea slug can turn over (push through its body) hundreds of pounds of sediment per year. They function homeostatically. That is to say, their density

1. Dates, Please! Aside from knowing these last two haiku were taken from "a book of late Edo and early Meiji era haiku", I have found nothing on these poems or poets. I'd like to know if they predate the introduction of the theory of evolution or not. Japanese readers, please keep your eyes open!

increases dramatically around sewer outfalls and rainwater runoff accompanying land development.[1] By filtering out nutrients from this harmfully rich sediment, the sea slug helps keep the sea-bed with its fola[2] and fauna – land words which don't suffice when we consider the plant-like invertebrates of the sea – in good repair for the littoral ecology that ultimately supports the life we want on our planet.[3] How sad that the greatest documented poaching[4] of endangered sea slugs occurred on a land sacred to

1. *Children of Development?*   Until reading, of concentrations of sea cucumbers in polluted areas (corresp. A. K.), I assumed the great number of *namako* reported by Japanese tourists in, say, Guam, was proof pure and simple of the pristine environment. Now, I see the hotels they stayed in may have attracted the cuke! Like weeds, called opportunistic by humans who think they are being taken advantage of, these cuke are only trying to repair what man would claim to improve. Unlike weeds, the result of their labor, clean sand, is something all can appreciate. The only problem is that the cuke itself may be considered an eyesore and a footyuck, so resorts try to displace them (see letter to Bill Rudman's Seaslug Forum (Nov 6, 1998)). Resort managers and guests might well read *The Unsung Plight of the Sea Cucumber*, a lively page-long appeal including these words: "Even with our lowly appearance and less than attractive habits, we are an important link in tropical and temperate marine ecosystems around the world. We eat what other organisms leave behind, removing organic matter from the sand and generally cleaning up after many other more colorful sea creatures. I bet you didn't know that the white sand you are fond of wiggling your toes in when on vacation is, in part, thanks to us . ." (c Zegrahm Expeditions 2001)

2. *Sea Flora*   Not strangely, considering our zoocentrism, we always picture the walking fish; not the plant that, landing first, literally prepared the ground. Ecologically speaking, sea flora (and plant-like fauna such as coral, hydrozoa and sponges), is indispensable for more reasons than we know. Testing his patented device for detecting minute amounts of gases on a long marine voyage on the HMS Shackleton, James Lovelock, father of the modern concept of Gaia, discovered that coastal sea flora produces trace compounds that, however minute, are vital for the existence of life. He also theorizes that the critical salinity of the sea is maintained by coral's enormous engineering works which over the millennia corral the salt and (allowing the water to evaporate) sink it into the earth.. Coral is particularly sensitive to excessive nutrients, so, extending this logic, we may thank *namako* that our ocean is not the Dead Sea.

3. *Life We Want*   In a sense, all life may be equally old – as US culture is as old as Europe's because, ultimately, it includes it – and all life may well be equally valuable in the eye of an ecologist, as all souls are equal to a Buddhist.   But I am not ashamed to admit a strong bias in favor of highly intelligent and/or beautiful life creatures. To me, the loss of that one Mediterranean pygmy elephant species matters more than the loss of the dodo, which matters more than the loss of a certain mosquito. I would forever mourn the extinction of the *higurashi* cicada with its musical chime, but shed not a tear for the *tsukutsuku-boshi,* whose call sounds like woody woodpecker retching. The total mass of the anaerobic bacteria that live up to several miles underground may exceed that of all aerobic life combined, but I do not feel for it and would gladly suffer it to die if that could only bring back the pretty little sea horses to the sea-grass off my native Key Biscayne. Perhaps the sea cucumber is, as poets and scientists remind us, our honorable elder; but, like other creatures that do not naturally attract most of us, I fear it will not be respected until it is proven beautiful in the Aristotelian sense of the word as something *useful*.   (下記) **#104**

4. *Galapagos Disaster*   Despite years of strict measures taken to guard the pristine environment of the archipelago, since the 1990's, the *Pepineros,* or "Cukers(?)," have poached thousands of tons – millions of individual – of cuke, *Isostichopus fuchus.* Even after the government crackdown, the cuke remained in a pickle, as revealed by articles such as that translated from *El Comercio* on 3 April, 1999: "On 31 March, 17,500 sea cucumbers were confiscated in the airport on Isabela Island (Galapagos) . . " When Ecuadorian weekly "La Television," founder Freddy Ehlers, visited the processing camp on this island, there were "50,000 sea cucumbers drying on any given day." Galápagos National Park Chief Officer D. Bonilla noted the effect: "If you see areas where the water is in bad condition, it's because the sea cucumbers have been stolen" (Korey Capozza: econet highlights 1998, ASIAN MARKET DRIVES LATIN AMERICAN MARINE POACHING).   Holothurians do not multiply like mice; recovery may take 50 years or more. A. Kerr comments: "Actually, this is only the greatest cuke poaching event documented in the popular press; most have gone unheralded. Numerous islands in the pacific and elsewhere have been stripped of their cukes. I have been to places picked over during the Japanese occupation that are still devoid of the large, slow growing and commercially valuable species." (corresp) I have found one 2002 haiku mentioning poachers: "sea slug cries / tread by the bare feet / of a poacher (*mitsugyô no suashi ga funde namako naku* – zankuro 密漁の素足が踏んで海鼠鳴くざんくろ一)

the science of evolution, the Galapagos archipelago! And, how ironic, considering the fact that Darwin's major research work – ten years in the making – was on the *namako's* distant terrestrial cousin, the *beche de terre,* or earthworm, whose labor makes life on *land* possible! [1]

釣 針 の 智恵 に か ゝ ら ぬ 海 鼠 哉　也 有

tsuribari no chie ni kakaranu namako kana – yayû (1701-83)

(fishing hook's wisdom-by/to, not catch/bite sea slug!/?/ó/the)

#105

not too smart

(for its own good)

the sea slug
the wisdom of the hook
escapes it

below it all

the sea slug
too dumb to fall for
a smart hook

mismatch

a baited hook
is too clever to catch
that sea slug

real intelligence

the sea slug
too bright to fall for
hook and bait

Unless the last translation, suggested by one Japanese reader (whose name I withhold for I fear he/she might be wrong) is right, the "wisdom/knowledge" in this poem is something bad. It is the trickery of our world and the poem lauds *not knowing* and the benefit of inaction. This would make it the first *definitely* Taoist sea slug poem. For someone versed in Chinese classics – as all educated Japanese once were – the idea of Shiki's world-birthing sea slug "doing" something, i.e. *creating the world,* as per one of my readings of his "My Face" poem, and my further mention of wormlike "labor," may not fly. While *doing* nothing is not really the same as *being* good for nothing, both Yayû's sea slug that (I think) does not know enough to take the bait, and the next haiku, by Shiki, remind me of Zuangzi's (?) huge gnarled tree that, being useful for absolutely nothing, outlived its more popular relatives. (The useful may be good for *you*, Socrates, but it is not necessarily good for *it.*)

1. *Life Without Worms?* Darwin was not the first to discover the earthworm, just the first to really research it. Gilbert White, whose *Selbourne* is still the amateur naturalist's and nature essayist's bible, wrote "The earth without worms would soon become cold, hard-bound, and void of fermentation, and consequently sterile" and Aristotle had summed it up in the beginning: "Earthworms are the intestines of the soil." (found on Joseph Garofola's extraordinary website that combines garden interest with more good haiku links than found anywhere else!) It is questionable whether the same can be said for the sea cucumber in respect to the under-water 7/10th of the earth, for porosity does not much matter for sea plants, most of which take their nutrition from the water. Still, by swallowing "a large amount of sediment, extracting organic matter," a "large population of sea cucumbers in an area can turn over vast quantities of surface sediments and can greatly alter the physical and chemical composition of the sediment;"(*Ency. Britannica*). Sea cucumbers seem to serve in a homeostatic capacity, for they gather in great number under the rafts of oyster culture (M.T. corresp)) and by sewer outfalls in the tropics (A.K. corresp). By reducing the nutrient build-up they play an important role in protecting coral, the intelligent buildings of the underwater world.

無為にして海鼠一万八千歳　子規
mui ni shite namako ichiman hassen sai – shiki (1867-1902)
(no-doing/behavior, sea slug one ten-thousand eight-thousand years old)   #106

dolche far niente

idle
sea slug lives
for eons

longevity   *sage government*

staying put   doing nothing
the sea slug makes it   the sea slug rules
a long way   a million years

Behold the lily counsels the BIBLE. "No, behold the *sea slug!*" says Shiki, taking a less beautiful but more appropriate – for it has animal needs like us – example from the bottom of the sea. Inactivity was a central tenet, an honored method of practicing religion and government in Taoism. (My last, admittedly hyperbolic "rules" suggests yet another reading for Issa's poem: re. a do-nothing government! But, let us put Issa's poem to rest.) Shiki's poem may also have socio-political intent. Shiki knew as much about Darwin's theory as any of his educated peers abroad, and social Darwinism as expounded by Spencer had many advocates in Japan. While Shiki's poem might be considered a paraverse, or rehash of Yôsui's poem, it also makes a fine repartee to the one-sided attention given to the struggle for survival or "law of the jungle" in Meiji era Japan.[1]

Doing nothing at all
The sea-slug has lived
For eighteen thousand years.

– trans. Blyth

Blyth's translation of the poem is better than his comment that Shiki portrays "not its lack of form, but lack of youth." I did not specify the age in my translations, because the unit for *ten-thousand* (something English, which skips from a *thousand* to a *million*, lacks) is not just a number. It can mean a multitude. Where we will say "a million to one," the Japanese will say "a *man* (ten-thousand) to one." Two *man* was also used in this way, because 2 (*ni*) is dividing, i.e. increasing. "New Years Day / at this time, mankind is / two *man* years (old)" (*ganjitsu ya kono toki jinjû niman sai* – hzg) goes an old poem, perhaps by Ôemaru. Shiki probably chose "one" (*ichi*) *man* to fit his syllabic count and allude to the singularity of this ancient survivor. Likewise, *eight* is not just "eight". It means "all," where we might say "all around." It has a nuance of infinitude in Japanese which English can give it only by turning the Arabic numeral on its side. Transliterating another Shiki poem: "eight *man* hair-holes [pores], waterfall's breeze cools" (*hachi-man no keana ni taki no kaze suzushi*). When Shiki means to be specific, he is. A Meiji 26 (1894) New Year's poem gives the precise age of the state of Japan as 2,553 years old (*kigen nisen gohyaku gojûsan nen no haru* – szs) whereas his Meiji 29 (1897) New Year's poem (*nisen gohyaku . . .*) gives it as 2,556 years.

1. *Evolution in Japan*   In the Soviet Union, there was a tendency to read Darwin without Malthus (*Darwin without Malthus* the title of a fine book by Daniel Todes), but in Japan, not only did Spencer hold sway, but the term "natural selection" was and still is usually translated as "natural elimination" (*shizen-tôta*), which, it goes without saying, puts evolution's bad face forward. This understanding was popularly summed up as "powerful-meal-weak-meat"(*jaku-niku-kyô-shoku*), i.e. the weak/poor are (meant to be) meat for, i.e. the meal of, the strong/rich).

> In the state of Hundun, Heaven and Earth were like an egg. Pan Gu was born in their midst. After eighteen-thousand years, the heavens split from the firmament as Yang cleared and Yin became turbid. In its midst, Pan Gu in one day completed nine transformations . . . (from the Taiping Yulang version of the myth (Song Dynasty) as transl by Stephen Field)

After finding the above, I had half a mind to drop my previous paragraph, for the passage shows that Shiki was, in a sense, precise with his numbers. Eighteen-thousand years was the period required for the world as we know it diversify and take shape, which, of course, is what sea slug did not do. Blyth was right to keep the number, but wrong not to tell where it came from.[1]

「老子」　混沌をかりに名づけて海鼠かな　子規

"rôshi" konton o kari ni nazukete namako kana – shiki(1867-1902)
(laotze? chaos [obj.] if [for the hell of it] name-given, sea slug!/?/ó/'tis/the)

#107

taoist nomenclature	*laotze at the restaurant*
chaos	sea slug
if it had a name:	let me name you:
"sea slug"	"chaos"

This poem comes right out and identifies the sea slug with the prime element of Taoism, though separate prose, from a letter the bed-ridden Shiki wrote the novelist Sôseki, suggests the possibility of an esoteric Buddhist element as well:

> "Someone who is a formless chaos of a sea slug becomes a tathagata [*nyorai:* someone who has attained buddhahood], becomes me . . . (而して有にもあらず混沌たる海鼠の如き者が如来なり。我なり。) These days I've come to think that little separates a tathagata from me, for a tathagata is a monster a fiction without real existence. Because it is a fiction people may recognize a tathagata. [It can also be seen as a rainbow, a witch or a demon] And if a poet sees it, it is the muse of poetry . . ." (From a letter Shiki wrote Sôseki found on http://www.geocities. co.jp/Bookend-Soseki/7017/geodiary.html. 2003 年 02 月 02).

My second Englishing of the poem is how I would have liked Shiki to have done it (*konton to kari ni nazukenu namako kana*). I imagine him joking with friends over the name of a sea slug found alive in a tub of water [2→] at a restaurant. But, either way, it is a charmingly simple poem. We need add but one piece of information. Lao-tze's name translates as "old-teacher." The characters for sea-squirt are "old sea-mouse," which is to say, "old sea slug." [3→] And, the sea slug was thought to turn into a

---

1. Blyth and Numbers Blyth let the number go without comment here, but in his discussion of the commentary to koan 25 of the MUMONKAN, [[where the enlightened Kyouzan (814-890) dreams he preaches to Makaen (na), who? is "the representation of the sound of Mahayana" (Don't ask me, I'm only quoting!) – *the commentary:* "Now tell me, did Kyôzan preach or did he not? If he opens his mouth, he is lost; if he shuts it, he is lost. If he neither opens nor shuts it, he is a hundred and eight thousand miles away from reality."]] Blyth writes: "The rather odd number, by the way, 108,000, seems to be a kind of parody of the 100,000 miles away to the west where Paradise is according to the *Amida-kyou.*" Actually, the original does not seem "odd" like 108 thousand does, for it is 10 *man,* 8 *sen.* 10 has a feeling of repletion in the Sino-sphere. As noted, *man* and 8 connote more than mere numbers, and *sen* (thous.) is often combined with *man* to emphasize the enormity of the sum.

sea-squirt (*hoya* in Japanese).　Shortly before wrapping up this book I came across a much older naming haiku: "we should call / our shit "mountains" at this / snowy lodge" (*secchin o yama to nazukeshi ya yuki no yado* – 江戸赤塚氏資仲＝ 雪隠を山と名付しや雪の宿 　「俳諧洗濯」). Because the "snowy inn" can also mean the place the snow stays, another reading is possible: "i'll call my shit / a mountain for it puts up / the fresh snow."　The original puns on the polite name for shit "snow-pile," which is lost in my [c]rude translation.　Needless to say, it is not as good a poem as Shiki's sea slug "Chaos."　Neither, to my mind, is this:

老 子 虚 無 を 海 鼠 と 語 る 魚 の 棚 寺 田 寅 彦

rôshi kyomu o namako to kataru uo no tana – terada toruhiko (1878-1935)

(old-child[respectful suffix]=lao-tze nothingness/nihility[obj] seaslug-with discuss fish-shelf)　　　　#108

the fish shelf	the fish shelf
where laotze and sea slug	laotsu and sea slug
discuss nothing	discussing *mu*

The famous physicist Terada was close to famous novelist Sôseki and likewise famous Shiki. Together, they exhibited so much interest in the sea slug that one can imagine they might have thought of themselves as a Secret Sea Slug Society.　This poem reflects the Taoist roots of Zen.　If Taoism worshipped nothing whatsoever, Zen Buddhism talked up *nothing* so much that they could be said to worship it, Nothing.　*Mu* with a capital N.　Reading Terada's poem, I think of Gary Larson's cows discussing E=MC,[2] but have some trouble understanding how he envisions Lao-tze (or Lao-tsu, for the pronunciation varied in different eras). The *uo no tana* or fish-shelf (where fish are sold in a store) may suggest the *ningyô tana* or doll-shelf, a small gallery found in most houses (at least at certain times of year) that sometimes included Lao-tze.　My Japanese respondents are split on this poem. Half believe the poem has the poet discussing (in his head) the philosopher and nothing with the sea slug, but I go with the interpretation that has Terada imagine the ancient philosopher meeting a sea slug, back in those times when such an interaction might have been possible. (The confusion stems from the ambiguity of the telegraph-c=Chinese style of the first part of the haiku, where neither Lao-tze nor nothing/emptiness have any grammatical signs attached.)

年 寄 り か ど う か わ か ら ぬ 海 鼠 か な や ま ね

toshiyori ka dôka wakaranu namako kana – yamane (contemp)

(old/elder or not? know-not seaslug!/?/ó/the)　　　　#109

a sea slug
you cannot tell if one is
old or not

Does the sea slug look like a larva, an unformed juvenile? Or does the sea slug look like something old that has lost the smooth skin humans cannot help but associate with youth? The word used for age is usually used only for humans, so the poem could refer to an incapacitated human; but I prefer to think of it as purely anthropomorphic.

→2. *Live Sea Slug* I do not know how long a sea slug in a tub would live, but imagine the cold would make-up for the lack of oxygen. Until K.K. pointed out my anachronism, I imagined the sea slug in a salt-water fish tank, as they have in sushi restaurants now, not likely at this time when electricity was still very rare. Still, we should not underestimate the ability of pre-modern people to keep fish alive. Sixteenth century Portuguese reported salt water fish of many types making it alive into 'landlocked' China.

→3. *Old-Sea-Slug* The character "old" on front of a name does not insult it as a modern might think, but was a mark of respect.　We could also translate the sea-squirt's name as "venerable sea slug!" As a graduate of Georgetown University I am of that ilk: we are called *hoya,* for reasons which are periodically dug up and debated but never settled.

海 鼠 の 寿 命 誰 も が 知 ら ず 初 句 会 出 口 孤 城

[nama]ko no jumyo dare mo ga shirazu hatsukukai – deguchi kojô (2002)

(seaslug's lifespan someone-even knows-not [no one knows] first haiku-meet)

#110

no one can say	our first *kukai*
how long a sea slug lives	no one knows the lifespan
at the first *kukai*	of the sea slug

In one sense, it is appropriate *not* to know the age of a sea slug. In this fine poem, it makes us feel the ageless age of the New Year season and the first haiku meeting (or contest) of the year Considering the advanced age of the poet (in his 80's), there may be a hint of self-reference, too. The reality is not so impressive. Depending on temperature and nutrients, the Japanese sea slug grows about 6 centimeters in one year, 10-20 in two and 20-40 in four years and is thought to survive up to a decade or so.[1] This is not quite eighteen thousand, but it is unusual for something which spawns in volume. It sucks most of its food from sand, which means it gets by on very little. As recent experiments on rodents and surveys of armadillo living on islands with different food resources, etc. have shown (with implications for humans), other things equal, low caloric intake extends life. Professor Motokawa Tatsuô of TIT (Tokyo Institute of Technology = Tokyo Kogyo Daigaku), whose quote we saw at the start of the book, puts it like this:

> The sea slug is a form of life excelling in the preservation of energy, while modern man consumes vast amounts of energy, running about leading a lifestyle unsuited to our size. The crunch is approaching. The success or failure of an aged society depends whether we can learn from the sea slug. (*Nihon Keizai Shinbun* 97/6/15 *chi-no boken* column)

The sea slug's ecological value is not just that of a metaphor, but that of being a pioneer of a lifestyle Schumaker might have described as *slow is beautiful*. And, if Schumaker in SMALL IS BEAUTIFUL wrote of what he called a Buddhist economy, the last two poems nominate the sea slug as an exemplar of what we might call a Taoist economy.

二 千 年 ぽ つ ち と 嗤 ふ 海 鼠 か な　　加 藤 静 夫

nisen nen pocchi to warau namako kana – katô shizuo (contemp)

(two-thousand years only/just [as if to say] laughs/smiles seaslug!/?/ô/the)

#111

just two millennia
don't make me laugh
says *namako*

small time

2000 years
is that all! snorts
namako

1. *Long-lived Holothurians* Generally speaking, species that broadcast large volumes of young are short lived while those that have few are long-lived. The sea cucumber's combination of large volume and long life presumes a high mortality of the larvae. Some large tropical species apparently survive for two or three decades but it is harder to keep a tag on a sea cucumber, than, say a tortoise, so it is hard to tell (A.K., corresp). Arakawa writes of a patented method of branding juvenile sea cucumber with a 0.5mm nichrome wire attached to a high-tension electric device which "allows one to make any marking desired on the body," but he fails to say how long it will remain legible (A:NDH).

By latest estimate, *holothurians* have been around for 540 million years. Compare *that* to us primates. Shiki could not have imagined such a figure in the late 19th century, when the world itself was thought to be no more than thousands of years old, but it may well be that he was addressing the ancient and presumably unchanged nature of the species --- rather than the individual sea slug – for, like most Japanese intellectuals, he was well acquainted with Darwin's work.[1] Be that as it may, I think Katô's deflation of the 2K hullabaloo is marvelous. I imagine he is also thinking about the greater age of Buddhism, Chinese writing and other things more ancient than "our" Christian hubris.

海 底 に 考 古 学 あ り 海 鼠 突 く　持 永 真 理 子
unazoko/kaitei ni kôkogaku ari namako tsuku – mochinaga mariko (contemp)
(sea-bottom-on archeology [there] is, seaslug/s[obj] stick/gig)   #112

on the seabed
living archeology
i gig a slug

must be shiki's   ***iconoclasm***

gigging sea slug   ancient thought
archeology found   dwells on the sea-bed
on the seabed   the slugs i stab

what's ancient

on the sea-bed
gigging archeology
what's sea slug

In Japanese, "archeology," is written "ancient-idea-lore." This haiku sent me to the dictionary. In English, it turns out, "archeology" is, etymologically speaking, even more holothurian than the Japanese, for "archeo" not only comes from Greek meaning "old" or "ancient," but is now used by science for "primitive." So the sea slug is literally an "archeological animal" for it makes one think about the primitive!

鉱 物 に 腸 あ る 不 思 議 海 鼠 突 く　な む
kôbutsu ni chô aru fushigi namako tsuku – namu (2003)
(mineral-with/in intestine/bowels is, strange [thing] seaslug stab/gig)   #113

strange to find
a mineral with bowels
gigging sea slug

Mineral in Japanese is literally "mine-thing." It has a more primitive – almost chunky, definitely tangible – feeling than the English word, which is too euphonious for the exterior of the *namako*. While minerals are not completely alive, neither are they fully dead. They can be seeded, they reproduce and they grow. It *would* be strange to find guts rather than crystal in an oolite. But minerals themselves are strange.

1. *Darwin in Japan* According to Morse (*Japan Day By Day*), who was in Japan when Shiki was alive, almost all Japanese, unlike many die-hard Christian Americans, thought highly of science and had an open mind about Darwin's theory of evolution. It is amazing how little has changed; this is true even today. Unlike other Westerners who turned up their noses at Japan's recycling of human waste, Morse noted that this efficient system of resource management also prevented water pollution.

海 鼠 喰 ふ 私 も 進 化 し そ こ ね て　笠 間 圭 子
namako kuu watashi mo shinka shisokonete – kasama keiko (2001)

#114   (seaslug-eating i/me-too evolution do-failed)

i who eat
sea slug also failed
to evolve

こ の 貌 が 海 鼠 好 き と は 思 は れ ず　土 居 民 子
kono kao ga namakozuki to wa omowarezu – doi tamiko (2001)

#115   (this face [is a] seaslug-lover-as-for, think-would-not)

who would think
this face the face of
a sea slug lover

ミ ニ ス カ ー ト 酢 海 鼠 好 き と 申 し け り　数 長 藤 代
minisukahto sunamakozuki to môshikeri – kazunaga fujiyo (1997)

#116   ([the] miniskirt[ed girl] vinegared-seaslug-like/fan, says[+finality])

the miniskirt
says she likes
pickled [1] slug

As the Neanderthal was neither primitive nor dumb, neither is the holothurian less evolved than us [1] – we all share the same long, long history – but we get the point, things *look* primitive or modern, rough or elegant. [1→] Looks are not egalitarian because human taste is subjective. It is human. The first poet claims to be no sophisticate and identifies with her food, where the second we imagine is conscious of the discrepancy of her fine feminine features with her taste and the third, by a man, proves the rule by noting the exception. Perhaps, I should note that food is more strongly sex-typed in Japan than in the West. Young with-it girls go out for tiny portions of *pasuta* in brightly lit Italianesque restaurants, [2→] whereas the women in the above haiku eat food a caveman might have gathered. A male poet writes more confidently about his taste:

海 鼠 噛 む 時 流 に 合 わ ず 阿 ら ず　管 原 さ だ を
namako kamu jiryû ni awazu omonerazu – sugahara sadao (2001)

#117   (seaslug chew/ing time-flow[the times]-to meet/adjust/ing-not, fawn/ning-not)

my way   *timelessness*

chewing sea slug   chewing slug
neither with the times   neither with it nor
nor pleasing them   trying to be!

1. *Vinegared or Pickled Sea Slug* The person I sincerely think the best translator in the world writes me that "I really think *sunamako* should not be translated as pickled namako, as I have written to you with my last mail. It is vinegarized namako or vinegar-seasoned namako, not a pickle." Because of her concern, I added a note to the introduction, which readers who entertain similar doubt should read. But I kept my pickled slug for the same reason I turn the sea *cucumber* into a *slug*. The term poetic license implies that a poet must take liberties with language, but translation demands we either make up words and use them in strange ways or give up really translating.

Would this be the *namako* version of Merle Haggard's *Okie from Muskogee?* Would it be out of place to praise the poet's panache (though, the presumption is that he only speaks up in his poem)? Perhaps not, for we will find so many similar poems in *The Chewing Sea Slug,* that being contrary when chewing sea slug seems normal. There are no first-person slug-chewing poems with "'*yes* men' and trendy types. But, the poem does have a saving grace; the word "time-flow" is extremely well-chosen. It suggests the central contradiction in Taoism, which on the one hand encourages us to flow with the tide=times, while, on the other hand, holding that there is no singular tide=time to flow with, for timelessness is what it is all about.

生き方は変えられません海鼠喰う いっち

ikikata wa kaeraremasen namako kuu – icchi (contemp)

(lifestyle-as-for change-cannot seaslug[obj] [i/we] eat) #118

a way of life
is not negotiable
we eat sea slug

i cannot change
the way i live: i eat
sea cucumber

eating sea slug
i know my lifestyle
is permanent

you can't change
the way you live if you
are a slug-eater

→ **1. *Sea Slugs as Dumb and Smart*** A few usage examples of dumb sea cucumber: ". . .this outrageously awful book, crammed with egregious errors of fact, and stuffed to the gills with writing so awful that it would insult the intelligence of a sea cucumber." Richard Ellis, re MEG: *A Novel of Deep Terror*, by Steve Alten (Los Angeles Times Book Review, July 20, 1996). "Must now put some toys on the page. I feel lazy and uninspired. As a matter of fact, today I am lazy and uninspired. Someone has replaced my brain with a sea cucumber." (vM6YkoZBZAIC: barrystock.home. mindspring.com/Old_Diaries /10.html). "There's only two knobs. VERY easy to get some cool sounds. A retarded sea cucumber could use this. There's no manual with this guy, but who needs it? This thing is simple and fun to use." (a review submitted for a Danelectro DJ-15 Chicken Salad Vibrato (US$ 37.99) with an "ease of use 10" ranking.) I do not believe Japanese misuse the sea cucumber like this. Here is the best summation of sea cucumber intelligence I know of:

We vertebrates are centralized animals. We have a smart brain and our body is made of stupid materials. Sea cucumbers are made of smart materials and they have no brain.- Motokawa Tatsuo (corresp)

This reminded me of British biologist Edwin Ray Lankester's 1898 poem about the Centipede who "was happy quite" until she thought about what she was doing and ended up lying in a ditch "not knowing how to run." When I joked to M.T. that we would seem to have a case of "mind in matter", rather than "mind over matter," he replied with a quote about another echinoderm: "Once von Uexkull (also Uexhull) said, "dogs move their legs, but tube feet move sea urchins. Mind lies in periphery in echinoderms [paraversed: in echinoderms, mind is a peripheral matter]." (corres). Uexhull is well known for his idea of "mental models" animals have of their various worlds, a subject dear to Professor Motokawa.

→ **2. *Pasta Restaurants in Japan*** How sex-typed are Japanese restaurants? Many cake shops (serving coffee and tea) and pasta restaurants cater almost completely to women, whereas a place where *namako* is served is liable to be full of men. We are talking about ratios of 10, 20 or 30 to 1. As K.K. notes, the fact that women, until recently, didn't drink as much as men, and even today tend to drink wine (identified with modernity and *haute* culture) rather than *sake* (identified, as *nihonshu*) with a manly traditional Japan) has something to do with the sex-typed nature of *namako*, for it is not only a drinker's food, but clearly does not go with wine. I'd add that outdoor-loving women tend to join men for beer which is not ideal with *namako,* but can wash it down.

This haiku impresses me for two reasons. First, the use of completely colloquial, rather than poetic Japanese makes the statement much more powerful because it rings true. Second, it neither sobs nor boasts but simply tells us how it is. The slug-eater who wrote this poem could be considered a pitifully limited personality, a human ossified in his or her ways. Or, he or she could be considered enlightened for accepting whatever he or she is.   The poet and the poem may have no truck with Taoism, but the poem helps us to see that even if everything may change, change is not everything.

どっちみち生き恥さらす海鼠かな　野本京

dotchimichi ikihaji sarasu namako kana – nomoto kyô (1991)

#119

(any way [whatever happens] living-shame expose seaslug!/?/ó/the/'tis/i'm)

to be or not to be

recover or not
how shameful to live
like a sea slug

If Japanese, as part of the Sinosphere, revere old age and admire inactivity, one might argue they do so to balance an equally strong shame for living long and fear of depending on others as invalids. This shame partly derives from Buddhism, for clinging to life contradicts the ideal of being detached from the things of this world, partly from older native traditions which, to me at any rate, clearly valued youthful vigor and beauty over all things, and partly, perhaps from the militarism of the early 20th century. I would guess this haiku either speaks for an old husband who lies dying or is the self-portrait of a depressed widow, for her haiku collection is titled "whether or not i am."

ひと噛に千歳の思ひ海鼠哉　敬愚

hitokami ni chitose no omohi namako kana – keigu

#120

(one-bite/chew-with, thousand-years' thoughts-even, seaslug!/ó/the/'tis)

time on the table

eating sea slug
we gain/lose a century
with each bite!

the perennial food

in every chew
a 1000 years of thought
eating sea slug

There is a Taoist connection I overlooked, which is the only one mentioned in Tsurumi Yoshiyuki's enormous work, NAMAKO-NO ME (the sea cucumber's eye: 1993/2001), namely, that the popularity of the food in the Sinosphere is owed largely to the association of the sea cucumber – recall its namesake, ginseng – with longevity, the pursuit of which to the Taoist meant as much as the pursuit of gold by the alchemists in the Occident. But, I don't feel bad about the lacuna, for my focus has been on what makes *namako* itself Taoist rather than how it serves Taoist aspirations.   Tsurumi also raises

1. Nomoto Kyô She evidently came out of her sea slug life, for seven years later she haiku's picking young greens in a state of mutual love (sôô-no koi ari ware-no wakana-tsumi) and a year later of finding a man – no doubt the same one – who could reply to her *tanka* (uta kaesu otoko ari keri . . .).

the possibility of other Taoist associations that I find impossible to follow, partly because I am very poor with proper nouns (something one learns in school and I am mostly self-taught in Japanese) – and this is doubly true when China is involved -- partly because he wanders even more than I do, and partly because he comes to no solid conclusions.   I am intrigued by one assertion, that the ports associated with sea slug trade are the same ones associated with Jofuku myths. Jofuku is the Japanese pronunciation for a Chinese king did a Ponce de Leon, coming to Japan, where he expected to find a land without aging (as it was to the East, where the sun rose but never set) with 500 handsome/beautiful youth/maidens. If seeking longevity is a Taoist ideal . . . But, as far as I could see, the possibility of this correlation being the result of a third factor was not ruled out. So, for now, all we are left with are vague impressions.

夜窃かに生海鼠の桶を覗きけり　石井露月
yo hisoka ni namako no oke o nozoki keri – rogetsu (1872-1928)
(night quietly/secretly seaslug's/s' tub peeking/spying[+finality])

primordial peek

quietly peering
into the sea slug tub
late at night

garden tub

very quietly
i spy on the sea slugs
late at night

dark watch

i tiptoe to
the sea slug tub and
peek at night

Three poor translations, for one good original, I fear. I imagined sea slugs stirrring in the moon light, a man witnessing the secret life of the sea slug. KS imagines an utterly dark night, the primordial pitch black nothing. Either way, after our discussion of Taoist sea slugs, we feel the poet has opened the window upon an ancient world. The question is whether we would feel that way without the conceptual priming. The same question could be asked about the next haiku:

小額をよせて海鼠の桶のぞく　筌民伸
kobitai o yosete namako no oke nozoku --- uetani shin (contemp?)
(small-brow approach/gather/coming-close seaslug-tub peek/spy[into])

peering into
the sea slug tub
a tiny brow

the delicate brow
of a young boy close to
a sea slug tub

little children
brow to brow peer into
a sea slug tub

what's the secret?

little children
huddling over a tub
of sea slugs

I took great liberty with this poem, adding a boy to my first imagined girl, then pluralizing (i.e., assuming the "approach" to be between brows as well as between brow and tub), removing and changing verbs and replacing "small" with "delicate" and, with the help of an English verb unmatched in Japanese (huddle), removing the brows altogether. The mere addition of "small" to "brow" is not quite the same as the original meaning of *kobitai,* is a fine body-word denoting both the part of the brow at and close to the hairline and the movements made by this part of the forehead! Old people may have a *kobitai,* but most Japanese readers will imagine a child of either sex or a young woman, perhaps reflecting in the water. I do not know what they will think of the sea slug/s. To me, the poem presents a picture of sensitive budding humanity against the hoary ancient presence in the tub. I think this would be an ideal poem to have a group of, say, ten artists paint each according to his or her mind's eye.

~

5
the agnostic sea slug

鬼 も い や 菩 薩 も い や と な ま こ 哉　一 茶

oni mo iya bosatsu mo iya to namako kana – issa (1814)
(devil too, yuck! bodhisattva, too, yuck! [says/and] sea slug!/?/ó/the/behold)   #123

no black, no white, just grey!

phooey to saints
as well as to devils,
huh, sea slug?

Even with the literary *kana* pegged on, this is one of Issa's most colloquial haiku, and Issa was known for colloquialism. Simple words, but this *iya~iya,* or *Double Yuck!* (as in "no way!") haiku is hard to crack and my readings – or, rather, guesses – fill most of the next two chapters! If new information is found that makes a definitive reading possible, they will still serve to illustrate what is ambiguous about Japanese haiku and how easy it is for a translator to go wrong *in fact*, though arguably right!

confucianism

denial of hell
and heaven, too – the life
of a sea slug

self-sufficient

bad gods stink
good ones stink, too
sez sea slug

The Orientalist stereotype of Confucianism, shared by the Communist ideologues of Mao's generation, centers on "blind obedience" and "ancestor worship." This respect for elders and the dead suggested by the misleading phrases was indeed one factor that endeared Confucianism to paternalistic Japanese leaders, but it is far from the whole picture. To Japanese intellectuals in Issa's time, it was, rather, identified with rational (as opposed to national, emotional or religious) thinking and scholarship.

the original

beyond good
and bad, simply
sea slug

the grey way

ye who'd neither
sin nor saintly be
be a sea slug!

my way

the way of saints
and devils forsaken
a sea slug

moderation

damn devils!
saints, too! – give sea slug
its due!

religious advice

hate devils?
and saints? return
to the sea slug

principle of non-action

bad deeds suck
good deeds suck, too
right, sea slug?

The "*kana*" after the *namako* (sea slug) means "!" or "?" or "!?" or nothing in particular other than making it obvious what the subject is – in this case, sea slug/s.   I took advantage of that ambiguity, together with that in the "yuck/phooey" expression "*iya*",[1] to put a variety of *english* on my readings.

winter hibernation

up to no good
up to no bad, call me
mr sea slug!

Issa has many wintering-in (*fuyugomori,* when one sits at home hibernating) haiku about "neither lighting incense nor farting" – i.e., remaining too inert to perform good deeds or bad – so something we might call *the way of idleness* is one interpretation of the poem's agenda. Japanese grammar lets us know the sea slug is the subject, or conclusion of the sentence but leaves ambiguous the exact nature of its relationship to the rest of the poem. Is Issa's attitude affirmative and reflective – i.e., *I am, or would be, a sea-slug* – or, negative and critical – i.e., *No passion either way, you are nothing but a sea slug?*   Is Issa *identifying* with the sea slug, or *challenging* it? Issa expert Yaba Katsuyuki [2] (corresp) votes for the latter.   Since the traditional sea slug image in haiku is undeniably *wishy-washy,* and Issa was Buddhist, the poem may be a criticism of "uncommitted laymen and faithless commoners." By this reading, the sea slug is the antithesis of the true believer. *It believes in nothing.*

faithless folk

loving neither
saint nor devil: how odd
these sea slugs!

The only difficulty here is that another of Issa's Buddhist sea slug poems identifies it with a saintly character (*hotokesho*). But, to continue along Yaba's negative line, *why stop with Buddhism?*   Could Issa have been of the opinion of Professor Bloom, who holds it is better to have a spine of prejudice than to believe in nothing?

nihilism

neither hating
nor loving, they lie
like sea slugs

And, is it not possible that Issa's criticism was directed not at the commoners, but rather at the intellectuals, i.e., at the unabashed skepticism of the Japanese Confucians, the scholars, the agnostic

1. *Phooey, Yuck, Damn and Fuck* English lacks a single word to express the original *iya*. I rendered it as "yuck!" to reflect its somewhat infantile quality, but could not use it for translation, for we cannot write, say, *"Yuck the devil!"* "Fuck" is not quite right because it is far more shocking than the original and because *iya* is an expression girls use more than boys (who tend to use *dame!* a more aggressive "no!" that sometimes means "Don't!"), which isn't true for our four-letter word.) The "damn" is still too strong; "phooey to" is harmless enough, so I used it for the first translation, but with some others I give up the active syntax and found appropriate but less dramatic ways to say that "both the devil / and the saint turn off / the sea slug."

2. *Yaba Katsuyuki* Yaba was one of the five editors of Issa's Works (zenshû), published by Shinano Mainichi, and wrote the ISSA DAIJITEN (encyclopedia of issa), the definitive reference work of issa's life: chronology, friends, works in his library and recent finds not in the Shinano Mainichi collection. He co-authored (with Joy Norton) a book half in English: FIVE FEET OF SNOW: Issa's Haiku Life, also published by Shinano Mainichi.

buke (samurai class), described in convincing detail by the Russian Captain Golownin who was held captive in Japan during Issa's life-time?[1] This is *my* preferred negative reading.

the way of the scholars

no faith, no passion
for the narrow or the wide
!sea cucumbers!

That is to say, they believe in neither esoteric nor popular Buddhism. One Japanese correspondent criticized my understanding of areligiosity as common in the upper classes, by pointing out their strict observance of Shinto rites and ancestor worship. I must say, I am with Ricci in that I do not find this Religious with a capital R.[2] That, in fact, is why Confucian observances can coexist with these faiths, provided said faiths permit it. And the question is not how religiosity is defined but, rather, what Issa and other men of faith would make of a Confucian, such as, say, Ueda Akinari and what they thought of his calm rationalism.[3] I can well imagine a poet influenced by Norinaga's nationalism writing:

我 朝 の も の と は 見 え ぬ 海 鼠 哉　 一 茶 (sic) （竹 阿）
waga chô no mono to wa mienu namako kana – issa (sic) chikua (d.1790))
(my/our realm/country/era's thing/person-as-for appear-not seaslug/s!/?/ǿ/the)   #124

it hardly looks a thing	these sea slugs
of our country	they just don't seem
this sea slug!	*japanese*
trans. blyth (hh1)	trans. hass (eh)

I first noticed this poem in poet laureate Robert Hass's *The Essential Haiku* (which, like most books of poetry translated into English fails to supply even a romanization of the original) and thought it might

1. *Golownin's "Agnostic" Japanese* I use Huxley's later coinage because it more accurately reflects the mindset of the Japanese in question than any other. Golownin, in English translation, called it *atheistic* and *skeptical*, similar to that of the "free-thinkers" in Europe (GOLOWNIN: MEMOIRS OF A CAPTIVITY IN JAPAN, vol 3). He also noted that these same Japanese intellectuals who thought supernatural things so much poppycock, argued that religion was good for the masses and useful for governing (E.g.: "In a word, he considered every religion as a fraud, necessary for the good of the people." vol.3 pg.50) Since these Japanese did not push their disbelief upon others, whereas Occidental "atheism," includes a strong *crusading* element – ergo, it is the flip-side of Christianity (or, a *Christian* atheism) – I thought a different term was called for. Perhaps the "Grand Inquisitor" chapter of *Brothers Karamatzov* was partially inspired by Golownin.

2. *Ritual Observances vs Religion* Ricci convinced the Emperor of China to sign a document attesting to the fact that what the West crudely calls "ancestor worship" was no more than an extension of natural affection and, strictly speaking, not a matter of religion. The Vatican sabotaged its Asian mission by not accepting this. Paying homage to one's ancestors is religious in the etymological sense of binding one to something larger than the self, but falls under a category which might be summed up today as "spiritual but not religious."

3. *Calm Rationalism* The playwright Ueda Akinari tore apart Norinaga's boastful nationalistic claims about Japanese as speaking the only correct language and being the only true descendents of the gods using rational argument similar to that of Thomas Paine in the West. I would like very much to know what Issa thought of his argument and cannot help wondering whether the fire that burnt most(?) of his library toward the end of his life held the key for understanding the *nay*-saying sea slug poem. Issa's diary has the words "Buddhism, Confucianism, are all impure [dirty/muddied], Shinto only [is] pure [pristine/clear]" (*butsudo, jûdo, minna nigoreru mo, shinto hitori sumeri* – bunsei kucho bunsei 7-12), and in Issa-related jottings (*haikaidera shoryoku*), we find "Issa says how strange/wonderful it is that Confucianism and Buddhism are impure and only Shinto pure" (*Issa iu, jûdo, butsudo nigorite shinto no hitori sumu mo fushigi nari*). I would bet that Issa, though nationalist in his younger days, noted the first words by someone else (probably Norinaga) and his rhetoric is critical/facetious: strange=suspicious= prejudiced and untrue). But, it may also be read as support for the nationalist position: strange= wonderful=marvelous=something to celebrate. Either a smoking gun or more circumstantial evidence is needed. （お願いします、皆様！）

it might be a very loose translation of the *"Demons yuck! Saints yuck!"* haiku. But, locating the original in Blyth, knew it was a different poem altogether. Blyth called it (with two other haiku) an example of Issa's "strong patriotism, unique among haiku poets." Perhaps in faulty recollection of Blyth, Hass wrote, further, that the haiku was "Issa's response to a call for patriotic poems." Since Issa has indeed written many chauvinistic poems, this made sense to me: a real Japanese would not lay about like a sea slug while Russians sullied the north. [1] He would act, as befitted a self-consciously martial race. [2] At first, I added the title *"a call to arms"* to Hass' translation to solidify this reading, but after being introduced to the following words (Richard W Tillinghast replying to the Poetry Society of America's question as to whether he considered himself an American poet), retracted the title so readers could form their own impression and hold it at least until learning more,

> When I consider my own 'tradition,' I think primarily of poets who have written in English, mainly from the US and the British Isles. I think of Yeats, Hardy, Hopkins, Heaney, Hughes; of Lowell, John Crowe Ransom, Creeley, Bishop. For me, the tradition is in English, and it flows through the Anglo-Saxon poets, Chaucer, Shake--speare, and so on. It's not a fetish for me, as it was for William Carlos Williams, for example, to be 'American.' I don't think the imagination recognizes nationality. It's like that haiku by Issa, which mocks the idea of nationality:

These sea slugs, / they just don't seem / *Japanese.*

Evidently Hass's translation is already so famous in English that it is "*that* haiku!" But note, dear reader, the turn-about: our patriotic poem now mocks nationality altogether! [3] Actually, the original words are even more ambiguous than the translation, and not only can be read as patriotic or anti-patriotic but as *neither.*

out of it

poor sea slug!
so far from the taste
of our time

Since *chô* was not only a place but a time – "not a thing of this realm" depending on the context could be either – and Issa was known for writing poems from the perspective of a clod-hopper from sluggish Shinano, we may read the poem as contrasting the do-nothing colorless sea-slug with the crisp and cocky stylishness of Edo era culture, with its smart striped fashions, countless fads and explosive riots. That would clearly put the poet on the side of the sea slug:

namako* and *namake
(slug and sloth) [1→]

ah, sea slug!
we're so out of place
in our time

1. *Russian Problem* An immature Russian captain, upset with not being allowed to trade freely with Japan wreaked havoc among Japan's Northern provinces, which is to say Japanese trading outposts on Ainu inhabited areas. Because of this, the fine captain Golownin and four of his men suffered their three year-long captivity in a highly aroused Japan.
2. *A Martial Race* The Japanese prided themselves in being a fearless/brave people in contrast to the timid/cowardly Chinese whom they despised as early as the 16th c. (according to Jesuits and traders).
3. *No Nationality?*   If Japanese tend to exaggerate their uniqueness=difference with respect to the rest of the world (usually meaning the West), Americans, to the contrary, fail to recognize difference even as they talk about respecting it! Yillinghast's assumption that poets are *by nature* not particularly nationalistic – and his failure to credit the translator – are themselves blatant Americanisms (as in USA)!

Two things make this pleasant reading unlikely. First, the man most likely to write it, Issa, is probably not the author. In the pre-World War II Issa anthology Blyth relied upon, he was; but, now, specialists believe it and a number of other haiku appended to 29 year-old Issa's *Hanami no Ki* (blossom-viewing record) are almost certainly the work of his teacher, Chikua (d 1790). The poems were dropped from subsequent anthologies (isz2, p32-3, isdj, p488). Second, it is unlikely the poem is affirmative, for, as W. H. pointed out to me, it mimics a sentence in stanza 103 of Kenkô's *Tsurezuregusa*:

> *waga chô-no mono to mo mienu tadamori kana*
> (my/our realm/country/era's thing/person-as-for appear-not Tadamori tis/!/?!/?/ó/the)
> "What is it, like Tadamori, that doesn't seem to be Japanese?" (Donald Keene transl.)

Only change the name Tadamori to *namako* and drop the Chinese character *mono* for phonetic syllabary and, *voila!* we have the poem. Keene's translation differs from the haiku's translations because, it follows the context of the stanza. Tadamori, a physician and poet of Chinese descent, had just come into the room and the answer to the question/riddle was a *kara-heiji* or Chinese flask.[2] His name is homophonically identical to that of a member of the defeated Heike (Taira) clan (who was mocked as an Ise flask) so he is doubly estranged as ethnically foreign and a loser. As the others laughed, he "angrily stalked out." A contemporary internet essay entitled "The History of Bullying in Japanese Literature" (*ijime no nihon bungakushi*) cites this episode as a prime example of its theme. [3]

unjapanese
like that sea slug
misfits!

Since poems generally do not contradict the general drift of their models, chances are the poem denigrates someone other than the poet. Unfortunately, there is no hint of an object of criticism, of whom is being called a sea slug. Is it a *namako-bushi,* or "sea-slug samurai," a feeble (lit. soft-weak=*nanjaku*) fighter?[4] But this is unlikely without a preface noting a specific target for criticism.

➔**1. *Namako* and *Namake*** The former word, our creature, suggests the latter, "laziness;" and a *namakemono* is a lazy person or the animal "sloth," depending upon the context or characters by which it is written. Since the sloth, like the sea cucumber, is slow moving, it taxes the ecosystem far more lightly than we who stride, fly, swim, run or burrow in the fast lane. If the sea cuke cleans sand, the sloth recycles its shit by eating it! The two deserve a Blue Planet Award (the Japanese equivalent of the Nobel Prize given to those who have done good things for the ecology) for non-humans!

2. *Chinese Flask* Another older poem: "i, too, float / in a vermillion boat / the chinese flask" (*sohobune ni ware mo ukitaru karaheiji* – haikai nana-kashiwa shu?) underscores the fact the Star Festival was from China. Otherwise, I don't get it, but the combination of the Chinese flask and the boat may have helped Chikua come up with his sea slug.

3. *Ijime=Bullying* Perhaps because of World War II experiences (I cannot describe here), Japanese are more sensitive to bullying problems than Usanians. Extraordinary publicity is given to students who commit suicide to protest being bullied (whereas only murder is press in the USA), and accounts of bullying written by students are published in leading media. The *namako* in the *Record* is sometimes seen as the exemplar of the bullied. A character in a novel by Nobel Laureate Oe Kenzaburo (THE SEAMLESS UNIVERSE) identifies the sea slug, "who resisted in silence" with his autistic friend and sees the gods behavior as a prototype of human violence.   **#125, #126**

4. *Rare Sea Slug Samurai* The "sea-slug samurai" is less common than "boar-samurai" (*inoshishi-bushi*), impetuous fighters who charge into battle without thinking. But it is cited in OJD, where both *zappai* examples are coupled with the slug's nemesis, straw: "Sea-slug samurai / routed by a smart tactic / straw manikins"(*wara mokugû chibô ni yaburu namakobushi* – zappai setoribune (藁木偶の智謀に敗る海鼠武士　雑俳瀬とり舟)). Japanese have long made use of fake ramparts and fake soldiers. Commodore Perry was amused by such in the mid-nineteenth century. "A country that / will fall for a straw-sack=bribe! / sea-slug samurai" (*warazuto ni katamuku kuni ya namakobushi* – zappai uguisu-yado-ume?? (藁苞に傾く国やなまこ武士　雑俳鶯宿梅)) . Usually, it is an expensive courtesan that corrupts the ruler and brings down a country. Here, the criticized "country" does not necessarily mean the nation. Japan was full of "countries."

In a broad sense, the sea slug's proverbial muddled quality is at odds with the crisp and clear[1]– pristine, as opposed to primeval – quality associated with the ideal national character. So, perhaps, the sea slug is itself being denigrated as a "sea slug!" Still, there is another possibility →

> hardly fitting
> these modern times
> sea slug pots

An out-of-style teapot with a "sea-slug grip" (*namakode*) or an opaque greyish-purple "sea slug glaze" (*namako-gusuri*), which could be called simply "*namako*," would be more likely. Such a vessel would resonate with the TSUREZURE *waga-chô* riddle, with its Chinese flask. The "sea-slug type" (*namako-gata*) *hibachi* (brazier) whose rounded niches didn't fit the clean-cut rectangularity [2] of the warrior-like taste of the time would also be a possible reading.

平 成 の 天 子 の 日 な り 海 鼠 食 ふ 　 加 藤 静 夫

heisei no tenshi no hi nari namako kuu – katô shizuo (contemp)

#127   (heisei (1988~) era's heaven-child's[emperor's] day becoming/is seaslug eat)

banzai

> emperor's day
> of the era heisei
> i eat namako

Any mention of the Emperor not critical seems patriotic, though saying this grossly oversimplifies the complex feelings Japanese hold for the Emperor and Imperial family. As mentioned in the Foreword, the ex-Emperor, Hirohito (now, Emperor Shôwa, after the era that died with him) was a marine biologist, so it would be particularly fitting to eat *namako* on his Deathday. But, judging from another Katô poem, where *Namako* laughs at 2K, I would guess this poem celebrates the birthday of the Heisei Emperor, for what better *banzai!* (literally, "ten-thousand years," but meaning "long-lived") than this hoary creature? Katô may also be enjoying the contrast between the high metaphor (heaven-child) of the Emperor and the low position occupied by the sea slug. If the Emperor is "heaven's child" (*tenshi*), should we call the *namako* "earth-child" (*chishi*)? Together, they would span creation. [3]

envoi

よ く 見 れ ば 鬼 も 菩 薩 も 海 鼠 か な 　 自 然

yoku mireba oni mo bosatsu mo namako kana – jinen (contemp)

#128   (closely/carefully look-if devil/demon/s and saint/s sea-slug!/?/ô/are)

> looking closely   scrutinizing
> devils and saints seem   a sea slug, we see both
> *holothurian!*   demon and saint

This haiku was the only response to my request for an opinion on Issa's double "yuck" haiku from a old friend who has been a Buddhist monk for almost 20 years. I cannot tell if it is awful or brilliant!

1. *Clean-cut Japanese* I am thinking of Motoori Norinaga, who claimed all "dirtied" syllabets (*ga, za, da* etc., as opposed to *ka, sa, ta, etc.*) were unworthy of the clear original language of Japan. *Namako* would be on the foreign side of this "we= clean/clear" *versus* "they=dirty/obscure" contrast. Now that Japanese are more likely to identify themselves with deep obscurity and subtlety as opposed to the shallow clarity of the West, the sea slug is no longer an embarrassment but an emblem.

2. *Samurai Rectangularity* Issa says it all in his poem: "samurai town: / you even dash water / in a square way!" (*bushimachi ya shikaku-shimen ni mizu o maku*) . Water was dashed on the ground to keep dust down, cool off the street and, more rarely, to reflect the moon (see: IPOOH summer 1).

3. *Heaven's Child* I take no offense at "heaven-child," for few modern Japanese hold it *absolutely* true in the sense that all too many Christians and Muslim fundamentalists do *their* respective deities.

6
<u>the mystic sea slug</u>

菩 提 も と 樹 に あ ら ず 海 鼠 魚 に あ ら ず　子 規

bodai moto ki ni arazu namako uo ni arazu – shiki (1897)
(bodhi originally/basically tree-in/as not, seaslug fish-in/as is-not)

#129

the bodhi and the sea slug

bodhi at heart
is no tree, sea slug
is no fish

The *Bodhi* is the Tree of Enlightenment. The Chinese characters *bo+dai* (used mostly for their sound mimicking the Indian pronunciation for the tree) mean a fragrant herb or mat that is spread, and the word "tree" (jû) must be added to it in normal conversation in Japanese: ie. *bodaijû.* The characters for sea slug, unlike those for most sea-life, have no "fish" radical. The poem would seem to say that if this tree is no mere vegetable, then the sea slug is no mere animal. If the tree is the end of Buddhism, then the sea slug could be its beginning. All of this is very vague, but there are more specific Buddhist sea slugs coming. Issa's neither buddha-nor-devil poem may be one, albeit in an allusive way. Bodhisattva (being the Buddha's incarnation prior to apotheosis, when he chose to stay around to help others achieve satori) in Japanese could signify someone of Mahayana persuasion, where the "devil" on the other hand, could refer to a Theravada adept who hides out in the mountains practicing religious austerities:

the third way

no! to the wide road
no! to the narrow – yes!
to the sea slug

By this interpretation, Issa would neither give away all his possessions nor engage in self-mortification, but just sit still, calm and cool as a sea cucumber if you will. David Lanoue, who has an Issa site with about 1800 translated poems at latest count, writes with more precision

> I believe that this haiku might be a reflection of Issa's *Jodoshinshu* (New Pure Land) belief. According to Shinran, the sects founder, one who attempts salvation by being saintly is misguided. [1] Sinner or saint, all that matters is one's absolute faith in Amida's saving power [grace?] (*tada tanome* – "simply trust!"). So the sea slug is an exemplar for remaining *kono mama* – "just as I am" – a recurring theme in Issa. (personal corresp)

A year before the Bodhi and the Sea Slug, Shiki did what Issa did not. He specified the holothurian sect:

1. Shinran   As D. Lanoue was writing me, I was reading up on Shinran for a project unrelated to sea slugs. Shinran taught that morality was not a matter of rules but something acquired automatically when one gave oneself over to the Amida Buddha and that a wicked person had a better chance of being saved than a kind one, for he had to rely entirely on the mercy of Buddha rather than feeling inclined to trust the efficacy of his own conduct. If this is the case, low life – such as the *let-what-be-be* sea slug – would receive more respect in this sect than in others.

「日蓮宗四個格言」 念佛は海鼠真言は河豚にこそ　子規

"nichirenshû shikokakugen" nenbutsu wa namako shingon wa fugu ni koso – shiki (1896)

#130   (think-buddha/prayers/chanters-as-for, seaslug/s; true-word[sect]-as-for, blowfish-in/as indeed)

the amithabas
are sea slug, true-words
surely blowfish

The followers of the Pure Land sect need only repeat the merciful Buddha's name (Amidabutsu) over and over to be saved. So they are called, for short, the chanters=*nenbutsu*. My translation India'ed this as *amithabas*. This literally mumbling faith is as forgiving as a sea slug. The True Word (*shingon,* often translated Pure Word) sect, on the other hand, stresses instantaneous enlightenment given to those who believe and had caustic things to say about those who did not. Eating a (poisonous) blowfish took a leap of faith, for it could turn one into a *hotoke,* a word meaning "corpse" or "buddha" who was, after all, dead to the world. This sectarian identification was echoed in the famous first-person novel "*I Am A Cat,*" by Shiki's friend, Sôseki, shortly after the cat takes off his hat to the first person brave enough to eat these respective indelicate-looking delicacies.[1] Eating a sea slug, he writes, "awaited the return of Shinran (*shinran-no sairai-ni shite*)," the blowfish "the birth of Nichiren." (literally, it was his veritable alter ego: *no-bunshin nari*) But I may be too objective, in this case, *kind,* for Shiki's haiku is prefaced: "the Nichiren sect's *Four Dicta,*" and in mid-Meiji – about the time the poem was written – when Buddhist sects had to come together to cope with the strong neo-Shinto bias of the government, the *Dicta* became a matter of public controversy, for they condemned the followers of the four other major sects of Japanese Buddhism to various hells. So, Shiki's poem

#131

1. *The Sea Slug As Oyster* Sôseki's statement mentions both the sea slug and the blowfish, but the latter is usually forgotten. One finds the brave sea slug eater almost as common in Japanese as our brave oyster eater. (It is ridiculous if you recall that hunter-gatherers ate almost anything, but may be true from the point of view of the more recent farming culture). The last two usages I googled across: "*the first person to eat a sea slug was heroic, but the first girl to strip and be bound on the Yamanote line [exhibitionist photos inside a car of the downtown Tokyo train line?] was just as heroic.*"(midokutsu.com/essays/ami.htm) and " *the first person to light a leaf of burning-grass* [tobacco] *and try to suck in the smoke was braver than the man who first ate a sea slug.*" (from cocofree.com/tokage/dairy[sic]2001-02). Another site suggests that Swift's witticism would make better sense in Japanese were the sea slug to replace the oyster. It is an interesting question for translation. The high consciousness of the sea slug as an *ugly food* is shown by a *sankô-sakuhin* (example) of a senryu about *shokuyoku* (appetite/hunger) given in the "primary school pupil" section of the "child-raising *senryu* collection"(*kosodate senryu sakuhinshû*): "in the fall / we know why ancients / tried sea slug" (*inishie no namako tameshi mo wakaru aki* – anon. editor (contemp) いにしえの　なまこ試しも　わかる 秋　子育て川柳作品集). The gloss would be: fall in Japan is formally recognized as the season of high appetite, hence, you ravenous children will

understand what drove our ancestors to try such grotesque fare." Despite their reputation for fearless eating, some Chinese might agree with this idea. To wit: an example of "the systematic occurrence of *already* in matrix clauses whose contexts typically license negative polarity items (NPIs)" given by linguist Vivienne Fong is "You see the live sea cucumber, dare not eat already" for what means "If you see the live sea cucumber, you won't dare to eat it anymore." ("An aspectual typology in Optimality Theory" – www:uilots.let.uu.nl/ conferences/ Perspectives on_Aspect).

2. *The Context of Sôseki's Namako* Unfortunately, the religious connections were not spelled out. The cat proceeds to note that his master respected letters not for being clear, but for being hard to grasp. He is delighted by the sudden appearance of things like a sea slug (or a mouse, for the first character of *namako,* the "sea" was left blank) and *setsuna-guso* ("shit that comes out from distress," according to the OJD which cites another passage in the same book to the effect that gods are only artifacts made by people to relieve their sufffering, "only pieces of hardened shit of distress") so he just leaves the letter on his desk and meditates on it. The chapter ends on the observation that "the only thing certain is that "I/we no longer know what is what."" [proper English translation in second edition!] The passage I paraphrase is found in the self-introduction (jijo) of the 1905 ed. of I AM A CAT, quoted by Takeda Mitsuhiro, Ibid) might mean that Pure Land folk mumbling prayers are as soft and harmless as sea slugs, while Pure Word Nichiren zealots are as prickly and poisonous and full of hot air as swellfish.[1] The poem might also be a counter to a Nichiren-*namako* connection I have found but not cracked. The sect traditionally ate sea-slug rice cake [2] and Shiki may have thought that contradicted his concept of the gentle Taoist sea slug.

桶 底 に ね ん ぶ つ 称 え 海 鼠 待 つ   高 沢 良 一
okezoko ni nenbutsu tonae namako matsu – takasawa yoshikazu (2003)
(tub-bottom-in *nenbutsu*[prayer]chanting/vocalizing sea slug waits)   #132

just trust

. . . *na-mu-da-bu-na* . . .
in the bottom of the tub
a sea slug waits

Here, it is the action of chanting, or rather mumbling the sutra that amounts to the name of Buddha rather than the chanter that defies translation. While *nenbutsu* often is translated as "prayer," to do so here would betray the point of the poem. Prayers suggest an appeal for help where the *nenbutsu* is an expression of accepting one's fate, of leaving things up to the mercy of Buddha. To translate, I dropped the verb and provided a muddled version of the words of the *nenbutsu* to fit the tub and the slug. The contemporary poet is neither anthropomorphizing nor hallucinating, he is viewing the sea slug as passive in the manner of a good Buddhist (likewise the manner of a Taoist gentleman, but the Taoist would not need to chant at all, so this is a Buddhist Sea Slug poem) and symbolizing this through the *nenbutsu* which is neither heard nor, for that matter, *not* heard. Back to the older poems:

ろ う（msword の 馬鹿[3]: 字 な し）八 や 河 豚 と 海 鼠 は 従 弟 ど し   子 規 ？
rôhachi ya fugu to namako wa itoko doshi – shiki? (1867-1902)
(*rô*-eight[enlightenment12/8-holiday]: blowfish and seaslug-as-for cousins-together)   #133

buddha stew?

on *satori* day
sea slug and blowfish
kissing cousins

Having read Shiki's other poems and Sôseki's comments, I think the sea slug and blowfish in this century-old haiku refer to the respective sects celebrating the same holiday – largely by practicing meditation – the first eight days of the last month of the lunar calendar. On the eighth day of this month in ancient India, Shakamuni (or was it, Gautama?) "became-road," i.e. found the Way, or experienced enlightenment while sitting naked under a tree (as I recall anyway). I am not sure what the logic of this next contemporary poem is – let the sea slug enjoy its buddha-nature until the Enlightenment is over, then dig in?

#134

1. Blowfish More in *The Ugly Sea Slug* and in a book I hope to publish in 2004: *Swellfish Soup*.
2. Sea Slug Rice Cake Sea-slug sweet-rice cake (*namako-mochi*) was eaten on Nichiren's deathday (*death*days rather than birthdays were celebrated in Japan). The cake, which is generally rectangular, is oblong and has rounded edges on top, which gives it a sea-slug-like aspect.* An example of a Nichiren *namako* senryu: "on founder's day / though the house is straw / sea slug mochi" (*omeikô waraie mo soshi e namakomochi* – (Y-102) おめい講藁家も祖師へ海鼠餅　柳多留). Sea slugs, (as pointed out elsewhere) fear straw. *OM writes: "This reminded me of "bull-nosing" or, in case of *namakomochi*, "double bull-nosing," the edge of our granite counter tops. Do you know the expression?" I must say I do not, though I am familiar with real bull's noses, which are remarkably strong and exude grease!
3. Rouhachi character I couldn't find the character in Ms-Word's all too limited vocabulary.

十二月八日を過ぎし海鼠かな　　原田明
jûnigatsu yôka o sugishi namako kana – harada akira (contemp.)

#135
(twelfth-month eighth-day passing/after seaslug!/?/ó/the/it's)

after the eighth day
of the twelfth month
time for sea slug

paradoxical coincidence

december eighth
sea slug from the day after
we declared war

In old Japan, this would have been February, the coldest time of the year, but now it is December, cold enough that not even an adept would sit under a tree naked. O.M. reminds me of the fact which makes the second reading necessary, where I only thought of Rôhachi stew, a food fitting the season. I hoped to find it full of sea slug and blowfish; but a search found only vegetable matter such as tea, dried persimmon(?!) and kelp, speaking of which:

磯草を頭陀にかけたる海鼠哉　　道耳
isogusa o zuda ni kaketaru namako kana – dôji? (1790)

#136
(shore/rock/coral-grass/laver[+obj] dhûta-as wear sea-slug!/?/ó/behold)

littoral adept

a sea slug
with a bit of laver
for a *dhûta*

The Sanskrit word *dhûta* is confusing for it means the practice, the practitioner and (in Japanese, at least) the single sack dangling from the practitioner.[1] The austerities are practiced to rid the *dhûta* of desires for clothing-food and dwelling, something, which the sea slug seems quite accomplished at. A haiku by Shiki about a somewhat similar practice where people wander about praying in the coldest part of the year possibly suggests the holothurian order: "a freezing prayer / bumps right into / another prayer" (*kannebutsu kannebutsu ni yukiatarikeri*). The poem may include a light jab at what has come to be called "territoriality," for begging bonzes took their metaphysical protection money from neighborhoods which they monopolized. But *why* does this implicate the sea slug? Well, cross the *dhûta* sea slug with this next poem see for yourself:

水底のなまこ（海鼠¹→）にあたるなまこ（海鼠）かな　　買明
minasoko no namako ni ataru namako kana – baimei (1772)

#137, #138 (下)
(water-bottom's sea slug-into hits [another] sea slug!/?/ó/the/a/'tis)

small world isn't it!

on the sea-floor
a sea slug runs into
another sea slug

1. *Dhuta's Duty* Before I looked up *dhuta* in the dictionary, I knew it made the haiku more interesting than a modern poem which simply observes: "a sea slug / draped with a strip / of green laver" (*hitosuji no aomo matoeru namako kana* – okada kôyô (2000) ひとすちの青藻まとへる 海鼠かな　岡田耿陽). It is that deliberate thought-provoking perspective that I find more common in old haiku than new (with some exceptions). Since Bashô himself traveled with a *zuta=dhuta* famous for including more poem drafts than food, we could even identify the old poem's sea slug with a poet.

By copying the idea of this poem – this poem is in his Categorical Haiku compilation, so he probably knew of it – Shiki makes the identification without putting it into words. It is not purely parody, either. A free-verse haiku attests to the association on a deeper, natural level: "just as walking on the sea-bed / i go through the city streets / this early winter night" (*umi no soko o aruku yô ni hatsufuyu no yoru o yuku machinaka* – Ippekiro (1885-1946)). The muted sounds coming from the closed houses, the thickness of the cold air filling your lungs and the strong presence of the winter firmament above, combine to give one this strange feeling. Be that as it may, the haiku poet Meisetsu (1848-1926) has something to say about Baimei's poem:

> If you look at sea slugs on the sea floor, it is a fact that sea slug A and sea slug B may come into contact now and then, but this does not mean that the minds of the two have met. [In this poem] it is just like two objects, parties A and B, have bumped into each other. The poet is playfully bringing out the nature of something not clearly alive. (msbs).

I am tempted to stick with Baimei's poem, but there are more possible readings of Issa's double *no!* sea slug worth pursuing. If dearth of information makes the translation of ancient Sumerian?[?] and Chinese poetry something like fleshing out a skeleton, translating old (up to the mid-twentieth century) Japanese haiku is, rather, one of trimming and selecting from a bloated body of allusion, metaphor and allegory. Haiku may be short, but it draws on a long tradition, even when it pokes fun of it. The shortness of the poem can even make translation harder for lack of internal evidence prevents the ruling out of possibilities. In other words, we haven't even begun to plumb the depths of possibility for this poem. To wit, four more readings:

One. There were Bodhisattva dances (*bosatsu-no-mai*) and devil dances (*oni-odori*) in which the respective masks were worn.

non-dancer

> call me "sea slug"
> i won't do the devil
> nor the saint.

Two. A Bodhisatta was a synonym for a kind and giving person, the devil a loud, mean one (or, in a good sense, what one with a powerful character, now called "an attitude"). Issa might have either been expressing preferences in women, or complaining, for it was the year he married. Since, Kiku seems to have been, if anything, a hot-blooded woman, this interpretation is almost surely wrong.

← **1. *Ways of Writing*** Some anthologies give the *namako* in the poem in the soft hiragana syllabary. To me, that suggests Japanese sea slugs on a murky sea bottom, for the words are hard to tell apart. Others give the Chinese characters, which are easier to read, but might suggest two rats running across one another. But my favorite haiku db (data-base) always chooses the Chinese characters in such a case because they exclude more – true, a word is a word, but there are no breaks between written words in Japanese, so Chinese characters help create boundaries – where the merely phonetic script does not – and thereby make searching easier. **2. *When a Sea Slug Meets a Sea Slug*** Meisetsu gives a stimulating reading, but I, at least, wonder what happens when a *real* sea-slug meets a sea slug on the bottom of the sea. My holothurian expert:

> As far as i know they ignore one another. If they're feeding and begin crawling over another cuke, they just keep sweeping their tentacles, first over the bottom, then over the back of the interloper and back to the substrate on the other side. (AK corresp)

This, he points out, is not the rule for all echinoderms, for sea urchins may "aggregate for reasons other than a concentrated food source (some sea urchins) or have aggressive encounters (some sea-stars)." So, there would seem to be something to the metaphor of the solitary sea slug found in haiku.

sea cucumber bride

no prissy saint
no noisy shrew, give me
a cool one!

new bride

fearing both
saint and sinner: i got
a sea slug!

[#139a, #139b, below]

Three. If there were a marine animal identified with the bodhisattva, we might assume that some historical figure became a sea slug because he didn't want to become it or a devil-crab (*heike-gani* is also called *oni[devil]-gani*).[1] Why? The connection is an old haiku, which Issa surely know, about a defeated Heike general who dove into the ocean, and "not becoming a sea slug, sure enough, [he] became a *heike* crab" (*namako to mo nara de sasuga ni heike nari* (生海鼠ともならて流石に平家也　涼菟) or, *sasuga ni namako to mo nara de heikegani* – ryôto (1658-1717 hkks, brhkz) 愁（右上を「力」に）海鼠ともならて平家蟹). The "sure enough" is a hard-to-translate word *sasuga,* that means both "as we now know" – this crab that has a design *incredibly* like a general wearing a war helmet is so called, as we already know – and that the man did what was "befitting" a warrior.[2] If Issa's poem were along this line (highly unlikely, I'll admit) we might take advantage of English vocabulary to translate:

middling along

turning neither
angelfish, nor devilfish
the sea slug

reincarnation

no angelfish
nor devilfish for me
sez sea slug

Four. According to the OJD, Bodhisatta was argot for a female prostitute, a devil was the same for a male prostitute.* "Red" or "blue," a sea slug is subdued, i.e., relatively colorless, and the word "color"– "liking-color," "male-color," "female color," etc. – being synonymous with *sex* in Japan:

oh, my goodness!

no to the wide way
no to the narrow, is this
monk a sea slug?

#139 下(c = should be a diff. #)
1. Heike Crab "Mask crab" is the first translation in my dictionary, but I have seen a number of crabs with human faces which do not necessarily look so much like Japanese warriors, so I prefer not to use "Mask crab" to refer to these Japanese crabs.
2. Stabbing Crabs The *sasuga* also seems to pun on "stabbing" (*sasu*), for the name of the cove where the ancient battle took place was Sanuki-no-ura, and once a warrior has drawn (*nuki*) his sword, he should use it. The stabbing association is likewise responsible for one of the strangest paragraphs of

haibun (prose mixed with haiku) we know, where Shôzan tells of his friend Ryôto dreaming about being a sea slug stabbed (poked, pinched, bitten, hurt) by "hundreds of crabs" and presumably uses this to explain why the Heike chose as they did (hkks). A take-off has no stabbing puns: "on the seabed / the heike die out: / sea slugs," (*minasoko ni heike horobite namako kana* – ryôshô (1762-1832) 水底に平家ほろびて海鼠かな　寥松) which I think means either that the dead samurai-clan, or crabs he could not find (?) turn into sea slugs.

This use of this "wide way" and "narrow way" in poetry, referring to sex with women and with boys, respectively, goes back at least as far as the very colorful 15th century Zen abbot Ikkyû, whom we shall soon see.[1]

> One could awake her, the other couldn't;
> Both have their own freedom.
> There is a god-mask, and a devil-mask;
>   The failure was very interesting.
>
> (Blyth: MUMONKAN)

If the possibilities already given are not confusing enough, 42 of the MUMONKAN, or "no-gate-pass" book of Zen koans introduces another god and devil in the above lines that are, as Blyth writes, "more of a puzzle than a poem." (Zen Classics 4). A learned teacher of seven Buddhas tried to but failed to awaken a woman sleeping/meditating next to Buddha – to find out how she was allowed to be closer to the throne than he was – while a less great Boddhisattva succeeded in waking her. If she had remained sleeping perhaps she could have become Issa's sea slug . . . But, wait, there is more!

rise? not me!

"neither demon
nor saint can budge me"
says sea slug

I base this reading on the explanation written for me by Maruyama Kazuhiko [2] in an article entitled "Issa and the Sea Slug" (*Nagano:* no 219, 2001-5), where he notes the juxtaposition of demon and saint in the Buddhist doctrine that one could "have the face of a saint and a heart as black as the night," and hypothesizes that this poem may be the reverse side of the *uke namako* (rise, ye sea slugs!) poem. Namely, that "it speaks for the sea slug who, not trusting human motives, remains on the seabed." Putting oneself in the place of the sea slug, rather than turning the sea slug into a metaphor is a fine attitude worthy of Issa's champion; but I fear the likelihood of this bold reading being right is no higher than any number of my own.

~   ~   ~   ~   ~

After reading all *that,* the reader is now ready for my favorite reading of Issa's double "yuck!" poem. It is a new one, having nothing to do with Taoism or Buddhism.   To find it, we must return to the origin of *namakobiki*, a children's *namako*-doll dragging game. It turns out that the doll was originally a real sea slug and the farmer dragged it because moles were believed to hate the smell of sea slug![1] → I do not know if anyone has tested whether this was true or not; and I can't help suspecting that this custom *itself* may well be a corruption of an older one where a lingam was dragged over the ground to fertilize it (as per Frazer's *Golden Bough*). Regardless, it seems to have been thought important enough in some parts of Japan that when children weren't around, the old farmer himself dragged about the sea-slug doll or, more often, a mallet used for pounding straw that might be substituted (perhaps to threaten of pounding?). Regardless, it is called the same thing, "sea slug dragging."

1. *Ikkyû's Poetry* There are a couple translations of the body of his work, which includes poems about the male and female parts. The significance of his powerful end-rhyming Chinese and the true extent of his poetic wit (versus his wit in life, which is depicted in countless comic books!) have been overlooked in the Japanese anthologies I have seen. (Find him on my website: www.paraverse.org)

2. *Maruyama Kazuhiko* The leading editor of classic haiku collections in Japan, he selected and annotated the standard collection of Issa's haiku published by Japan's most prestigious classics publisher, Iwanami; and supervised the multi-volume collection of Issa's work published by the Mainichi Newspaper in Issa's home prefecture of Shinano.

Issa wrote this poem in the year he got married to a younger woman who was, if I am not mistaken, the real farmer in the family. I like to imagine Issa was asked to pull around a mallet and found the whole thing pretty funny. Neither prayers to the saints, nor charms invoking the power of protective demons – things, he, as a buddhist, had at least some faith in – work, but a mallet in the name of a sea slug is supposed to drive away the moles!   You gotta be kidding! My last (but hardly final) interpretation, then, is that this is a *namako-biki,* or "sea slug drag" poem. Here are five paraverses:

to all our moles

we've prayed and cursed
and you've just laughed, prepare
for the sea slug!

you asked for it

no! to god?
no! to the devil? mole,
meet sea slug!

mole-be-gone

saints don't work
demons don't work, let's see
if sea slugs do!

when religion fails

the moles say "no!"
to saint and demon, so –
sic 'em, sea slug!

1. *Why Moles Fear Sea Slug* The reason why moles hate sea slug is lost in ancient history; but that did not stop n/rationalist Hirata Atsune ( ) from coming up with one, in order to explain why the information provided by the *tengu* (mountain-goblin)-raised little monk Torakichi about how to exorcize demonic moles arising from broken or opened jars of placenta (the afterbirth was so buried) by dragging about a sea slug and singing exorcism songs made perfect sense even if it seemed outlandish. "There is no living creature," wrote Hirata in his Senkyô-ibun 仙境異聞, "that is absolutely bloodless, except the sea slug which has not a single drop of blood. For that reason, it is efficacious for removing bad blood and producing new. Now, since the mole-demons are born of bad blood (according to Torakichi, who even reports of finding many in a placental jar), might they not lose that blood upon meeting up with a sea slug?" According to Hirata, it was a fact that if a sea slug was buried at each corner of your garden, you "could dig in vain to find a mole." (Found in a fine encyclopedia of supernatural beings on the website www.home4.highway.ne.jp./ deadsoul/ma/mogura moti.html) This Hirata is in/famous for fusing Western learning (including logic) and hyper-nationalism to come up with things like: "Well, maybe the world is round and we cannot say Japan is the only place where the sun rises, but we are the head of the world, for the barbarians are the ones who move about like arms and legs [visiting isolated Japan], while the place called Amerika is the posterior, for its inhabitants are said to be behind the times." (a paragraph roughly recalled from De Barry ed. *Traditions of Japanese Literature* (Columbus University Press). My guess is that the identification of the dried sea slug with sacks of grain (*tawara*) and, with this, good-fortune and, most specifically, a bountiful harvest provided its original charm value and this became – to use an ugly Americanism – pro-active with the passage of time. A simpler modern Japanese hypothesis is purely philological: moles are called "field/plot-rat/ mice," while *namako* are called "sea-rat/mice," so . . .(LD corresp) . So what? The reasoning is not explicit, so we do not know whether the assumption is a sort of competitive exclusion of likes (both being rodent), the enmity of opposites (sea *vs* land rivalry), *it-takes-one-to-catch-one,* or some other logic I am not yet familiar with!

the alternative

mole won't go
for god or the devil, so
sea slug it is!

I might add that there is no contextual evidence for this interpretation in Issa's journal. The poem has nothing about moles and it is together with two of Issa's other sea slug haiku, "rise, sea slug!" with its explicit Buddhism and a visual haiku (viz the *honobono* poem in *The Sleepy Sea Slug*) both of which suggest a seaside, rather than farm setting; and all three are in an additional section of 11th month poems squeezed in a blank space after the 7th month poems, whereas, the sea slug drag, as detailed in my preface notes, took place in the middle of the 1st month.[1] Moreover, I haven't yet found any haiku about mole exorcism dating back more than a hundred years or so (which is why I relegate the body of *Mole Exorcizing Sea Slugs* to the "Sundry Sea Slug" section). In other words, the meaning of the poem – if, indeed, that *is* the meaning of the poem – could not have been deduced from the information in it, or, for that matter, its context. Then, again, who can say whether it *is* the meaning?

It is one thing to try to decipher poems from fragments – Sappho, and the guy whose name I always forget – but, is it any easier when you have the entire poem and it is this short?

達 磨 忌 や 宗 旨 代 々 不 信 心 太 祇
darumaki ya shûshi daidai fushinshin – taigi (1709-72)
(dharuma day: religious-principle generation-generation un-believing-heart)

dharuma day:
a doctrine of disbelief
for generations

There is no sea slug in this paradoxical – continuing belief in disbelief – poem, it suggests yet another reading of Issa's double phooey *namako*.

達 磨 忌 は 海 鼠 菩 薩 も 鬼 も 嫌   太 茶 子 敬
darumaki wa namako bosatsu mo oni mo iya – taigi+issa+shiki+keigu   #140
(dharuma-day-as-for, seaslug: saint and devil-too, yuck!)

devils are humbug
saints are too: sea slugs
for daruma day!

The ungraspable, holeless dharma ,[2] founder of Zen, as pointed out in *Do-nothing Sea Slugs*, is more or less one with the Taoist creation god, Pangun, and the sea slug. Unlike the Buddha whose thin manifestations are sometimes female, the dharma always has a beard in addition to a robe, but the main purpose of the beard would be to erase his neck (as the robe erases his limbs) and maintain his original form as a single torso.   This roundness is represented in the sweet-rice (*mochi*) cakes offered to the Daruma (usually represented by a sumie painting hung in the *tokonoma* art-nook): "daruma day

1. Seasonalizing Haiku   If the Shinano Mainichi Anthology of Issa's works had recognized this as the likely meaning of Issa's haiku, it should have been in the "Small New Year" section instead of in the winter animal section in "Sea Slug" proper. And it should have been annotated. This poem is a splendid example of why theme in individual haiku cannot be decided nominally (i.e., if it says "sea slug" throw it in with "sea slug") but must be figured out and assigned.
2. Daruma, Dharuma, Dharma, Bodhidharma. The spelling to the left is most Japanese. All are fine, no?

/ eating the round form / of the *mochi*" (達磨忌やその円相の餅くらひ　子英(1759) 靭随筆) and that might be called *namako mochi,* in which case, . . . What I didn't point out before is that Dharma, and the radical *"believe nothingism"* Zen he preached, was perfectly compatible with Confucianism as well.　Zen was the Confucian classics-reading samurai bureaucrats religion of choice, for it was perfectly compatible with, indeed demanded disbelief. The translation of the double-phooey poem titled *"confucianism"* could as well be titled *"zen."*　So most of the threads followed in the past three chapters all lead to the same place.

海 鼠 老 い て 無 門 の 關 を 守 り け り 　 鶯 子

namako oite mumon no kan o mamorikeri – ôshi (c 1900)

#141　　　　(seaslug ages, no/not-door/gate's pass/barrier/gate[obj] guards/keeps/treasures[finality])

growing old
sea slug still guards
the gateless pass

zen biology

and sea slug
grows old treasuring
the no-gate

According to Blyth, the MUMONKAN, or "gateless-pass/barrier"(1228 or1229) is the first of the great Zen "textbooks" a beginner should read and should be a "set book" in every university in every country.　It aims at enlightenment, "the cutting of the Gordian knot of emotional and intellectual attachments." The first of the 48 *koan*-centered stories collected by Mumon, whose name reflects his indebtedness to no/thing in particular, concerns a monk Jôshû's enigmatic reply to the question "whether or not dogs have the buddha-nature." It was simply "not" (*mu*). The commentary advises that Zen practice requires one to pass the barrier set up by the masters, which means first "cutting off the workings of the ordinary mind completely" (need-cramp-heart-road-severe), and that this barrier or pass is *Mu,* "the Gateless Barrier of the Zen sect."　Blyth wrote "When we truly know what the universe is asking us, we don't need to answer. This is the meaning of Emerson's Sphinx." . . . And, I presume,　our sea slug,　who guards the Gateless Gate by saying what he has said from time primeval

nothing

7
<u>the scatological sea slug</u>

一 休 の 糞 に な つ た る 海 鼠 哉　子規
ikkyû no fun ni nattaru namako kana – shiki (1897)
(ikkyû's shit to/into becomes/is seaslug!/?/ô/the/'tis)   #142

buddhism writ large

sea slug you
were bound to be
ikkyû's shit

～

ha, sea slug!
ikkyû's shit is what
becomes you

This haiku [1] would *surely* be well known had it been written by Issa, who was known to be scatological, rather than Shiki.[2] Ikkyû (1394-1481), the most popular Zen priest of the folk, was known for his countless pranks and unabashed celebration of sex, drink and "raw-stinking" (*namagusai*) animal food. Unattached, it would seem, you can eat the world yet remain outside it. The poem is presaged by this one on the fate of the first bonito of the year:

誰 人 の 糞 に な る ら ん 初 松 魚　子規
tarebito no fun ni naru ran hatsugatsuo – shiki (1894)
(who-person's shit-into become, hey[i wonder], first-bonito)

and whose shit
will you become, huh,
first bonito?

The answer, I think, is *a very rich man's*, for the first bonito went to the highest bidder. Ikkyû's shit also may play off a very well known older haiku by Basho's contemporary Ransetsu:

海 鼠 食 ふ は（く へ ば）穢 い（き）も の か お 僧 達　嵐雪
namako kuu wa kitanai[ki] mono ka ozôtachi – ransetsu (1690)
(sea-slug eat-as-for dirty thing? monks)   #143

hardly kosher

so my monks,
do you think it unclean
to eat sea slug?

1. *This Haiku's Translation*   More translations later in the chapter. Don't dare quote without reading on! 章の終わりに近い又別な英訳あるから「違うってば」と言わないで。ここは、謎を解けた前の英訳。
2. *Scatological Issa and Shiki*   Over 2% of Issa's poems (2000 haiku) in the Iwanami classics selection concern toilet matters. Perhaps a fifth of these are about shit or dung. I believe Shiki has just as many. In fact, he has far more about horse-shit than any poet in history. He even notes when dung is *not* on the road! (*bafun mo miezu shiwasu no nihonbashi* – m28 winter) You would not guess this from reading collections of his work, for he is reputably a clean poet, a real gentleman. Once a poet gets a reputation, editors ensure that it remains. That is why to favor entire works over selections.

stuck up

this sea slug
is it too beastly for
proper monks?

neither fish nor fowl

monks, say,
am i sly to dine
on sea slug?

Most animal products were thought to be spiritually defiling by Japanese Buddhist monks, but they, like Thai Buddhists, had a tendency to accept if not justify seafood.[1] Why, then, should the sea slug be singled out like this? Are we talking about religious scruples, or something deeper? My Japanese mentor, KS, points out the fact that one connotation of *kitanai* is "sly" – something like "dirty play" in English – hence, the third reading. Or is there, perhaps, something else here? I can't help thinking of Ikkyû's delightfully obnoxious character and translating:

hey, monks!
(why wrinkle up your noses?)

if it is zen
to eat shit – why not
eat sea slug?

While monks were supposed to eat humble pie,[2] I did not find evidence for coprophagous behavior, so this may be going too far. Yet, to read Blyth (case 21 in the MUMONKAN etc.), Zen catechism, or rather *koan,* was literally full of it. Even the Buddha – especially the Buddha – was defined as "a shit-wiping stick" (wooden spatulas, sticks and straddle poles were once thus used!).[3] So, keeping the title,

---

1. *Buddhist Food* Tibetan Buddhists believe it best to eat as few souls as possible, so they think it proper to eat beef or goat or pig – the larger the better, for many people can be fed at the cost of depriving one soul of its body. They think eating small fish, as the Japanese and Europeans (baby eels) do, the most sinful act of all, for scores of souls are lost to this world with every bite. Japanese Buddhists speak of the equality of souls but do not really believe it, for they think eating large land animals, especially domestic ones, a worse sin than eating fish. Presumably, this reflects the Shinto aversion for defiling blood, but this choice is not rationalized. Thais, however, do rationalize. Although a fish may be caught, it dies by itself and the person who buys something dead is not responsible for the death unless the food was ordered, etc..

2. *What Monks Ate* I have been reminded not to underestimate the quality of the diet of the monks, for thanks to a vegetarian gourmet tradition going back to China, lack of animal protein aside, they ate very high on the hog in times when many people had trouble filling their bellies.

3. *The Stick That Wasn't? And The Shit That Wasn't.* K.S. wrote me that Japanese scholars have long determined that the "old shit-stick" (*kanshiketsu*) on which Blyth lavished such zany affection in his explanation of case 21 of the MUMONKAN was really a "piece of old shit" (the last character meaning a hard chunk of something, i.e., *crap,* rather than a pole or a spatula). The scholars Blyth relied upon were wrong. That would be easy to fix in my translations. Indeed, it makes the "eat shit" one, above, even better. But, the problem goes deeper, for K.S. also argues (and shows supporting examples) that dirtiness and pollution *had nothing to do with this Zen shit*, for the term in question (*kan-shiketsu*) only meant *something worthless,* indeed, something like our English "that old shit!" So far, so good. But, I am still not convinced, as he is, that this *proves* Ransetsu's poem has nothing to do with shit, for the existence of places like Excrement Hell (also introduced by Blyth) suggest that shit was something more than merely worthless. Finally, K.S. argues that shit and allusions to it did not fit the haiku of that era. Here, too, I hope he will pardon me if I continue to wonder/wander!

hey, monks!
(where's your zen?)

if the buddha
is a shit-stick what's wrong
with sea slug?

There is irony here. If monks were not supposed to eat *living* things,[1] they were also not supposed to shy away from *ugly* things. If all is *maya,* the repulsive is as false as the beautiful. So, Ransetsu has them over a barrel. And he is goading them, since the sea slug tastes good: it is a barrel full of *temptation.* Speaking of which, I have one truly outrageous reading:

hey, monks!
(pity this old man)

is it dirty
then, to play with
a sea slug?

Judging from his poetry, Kikaku, whose collection Ransetsu's poem was in, belonged to the Ikkyû school of Zen, not at all afraid of sex and body functions. So this reading – which is to say that the monks ignored older men with their soft and less smooth genitals – is by no means out of *his* ken, but Ransetsu's poems were generally of a more delicate nature, so I will admit this is more than far-fetched! But to return to Shiki's haiku, there is a second, complementary reading allowed by the Japanese grammar:

revelation

Ikkyû's shit
must have looked like
a sea slug!
～
oh, sea slug
you are what became
"ikkyû's shit"

When it comes to assholes, Japanese and English see eye to eye. We say "tight ass;" they "[have] a small/narrow asshole." (*ketsu-no-ana-ga chiisai/semai*) The connotation, however, is broader in Japanese, for it further means narrow-minded, intolerant and timid. Moreover, it has an antonym: to "[have] a wide ass-hole" is to be broad-minded and bold, if not outrageous. The Japanese sea slug is thicker than the sea cucumber of Florida and that, then, would be just right for anything coming out of Ikkyû's anus. One wonders if Shiki came across a Japanese translation of Swift's "Irish Problem", where the shape of excrement indicates the tight or loose nature of the ethnicity from which it came!

> The cuke can react to stress by either becoming flaccid and goopy, or by ejecting all the water from its system and becoming a small, hard turd-like lump. (*"Cucumber Defenses"* Rob Toonen Posted to ReefKeepers emailing list, Wed. 16th September 1998)

1. *Living Things* In Japanese, and some other languages, there is a distinction made between things considered to have feeling and those without it that is reflected in the choice of the verb we call "to be." Depending upon whether one is an animal (defined as *yûjô,* "have-heart=emotion) or a plant (defined as *mûjô,* "no-heart=emotions"), *to be or not to be* is a different question. Since animal itself is "moving-thing" (*dobutsu*) in Japanese – rather than "breath-thing" as with us – the sea slug is barely animal in Japanese, but in the time of olde haiku, the term was not used.

Modern Japanese would not find much in common between a sea cucumber and a "turd" because decades of cartoons have standardized stools into something like a fat coiled snake. Be that as it may (with an apology to cacophobics), we are still not done with Shiki's poem. A more trenchant allegorical reading is also possible:

reincarnation

dirty monks
who would copy Ikkyû
now sea-slugs

To be someone's shit or, worse, not even measure up to it, is to say in Japanese that someone is unworthy of whomever they would emulate. Now it just so happens that reincarnating [1] limbless was a standard punishment for Japanese Buddhist sinners. And what is more limbless than a sea slug? Here is an old poem Shiki surely knew:

五 百 生 女 の 手 か ら な ま こ か な 大 江 丸?
gohyakushô [aru zô no] onna no te kara [tegara] namako kana – ôemaru? (1719-1805)
#144   (five-hundred-lives=monks [a certain monk/s]: woman's hand [deed]-from seaslug!/?/ô/the/'a)

enjoy your new life, bubba!

the bonze
reborn of women
a sea slug

stick to boys next time!

once monks
now, thanks to a woman
sea slugs

carnal knowledge

knowing women
the dead monk returns
a sea slug

their proper station

bad bonzes
turned by good women
into sea slugs

1. *Reincarnation and Karma* The belief that reincarnation is not a lottery but a form of what might be called "reward and punishment" (of infinitely finer gradation than the crude Heaven-or-Hell of Christianity) can be used to justify vegetarianism because we never know whose ex-soul we might eat, or a diet of *any type* because the food, or victim if you will, did something in its last life to *deserve* whatever treatment it gets. As the folksy philosopher Adam Fitz-Adam wrote for the 163rd issue of THE WORLD (Feb. 12, 1756) about the Pythagorean *doctrine of transmigration*,

"Never can the delicious repast of roasted lobsters excite my appetite, whilst the ideas of the tortures in which those innocent creatures have expired, present themselves to my imagination. But when I consider that they must have once probably been Spaniards at Mexico, or Dutchmen at Amboyna, I fall to, both with a good stomach and a good conscience, and please myself with the thoughts that I am thus offering up a sacrifice acceptable to the manes [sic? names?] of many millions of massacred Indians."

Can this explain why Japanese, despite Buddhism had little problems with cutting up live fish, including the most harmless of all, the sea slug?

theology recapitulates philology?

an octopus
turned into a sea slug
by a woman

"Five-hundred-lives-limb-less" was the punishment that the monks originally warned would fall on those who pushed *sake* on others (the Japanese penchant to do this was decried by Jesuits in the 16th century). In time, the first part of the phrase came to be an appellation for the monks, themselves. At the same time, the punishment of limbless reincarnation became popular for other sins, such as a woman seducing a monk or the vice versa. Ôemaru's poem improves when you know that women were denigrated for giving birth to all desire – i.e. life! – yet praised for giving birth to Buddha in order to fix the problem they started. But, there is more. The allusion is specific. In this poem, the *k* sound in *onna no te kara* "from woman's hand" may also be read as a "g" sound [1] *~tegara* "~ deed/achievement/boast." (Because *tegara* is usually written with two Chinese characters, and here it is not, I think it is the pun rather than an equal reading.) Ikkyû reportedly said that giving birth to Buddha was *onna no tegara* – the exact same words – so the pun was pregnant enough for good readers to catch it). The poem, then, suggests that, ultimately, woman, by giving birth to the Buddha, is responsible for both the proliferation of monks and their corruption. Since monks were called octopus (*tako*) for their shaven pates and one etymology derives it from a many-handed sea slug ([*nama*]*ko*), my last reading is not utterly fatuous. [2]

P.S.1 to the Scatological Sea Slug

I made a discovery that *ruined* my last allegorical reading of Ikkyû's shit-as-bad-monks (and any relation it may have had with Ransetsu's poem) only days after I wrote it, but rather than ruin the flow of the chapter, and to better allow the reader to *feel* with me why haiku cannot always be cracked from the inside out, I leave it unchanged. Here, then, is *the rest of the story*.

Years ago, I bought a book for Ikkyû's poems. I did not read his apocrypha, also in it, for I prefer poems to stories, which even short are usually too long for me, perhaps because they mushroom like those unwanted web-pages that are all but impossible to kill, that is, like *hydra*, in my ridiculously fertile mind, even as I read. Thinking that I had *better* check, at least, for clues about the significance of Ikkyû's shit, I did; and, as it turned out, there were not one but two stories that evoke Shiki's haiku!

The second story in the collection – several pages long in the original *Ikkyû Banashi* – reputedly took place when Ikkyû was a novice monk at age 12 or 13. The abbot ate a soup made from dried salmon stock, [3] while the novices had to settle with vegetarian fare. Ikkyû, already the wise guy, demanded to have some too. Following a few words of discipline for the upstart, the abbot said "hear!" and addressing a piece of salmon, said:

> Thou were, after all, like a dried tree. I'd like to help thee, but as thou won't revive to
> sport in the water, let a humble[foolish]-monk eat and buddhify thee! Amen!

1. G and K Up to the 20th century, Japanese often neglected to place the sonant mark – in Japanese, "muddy/clouding dots" (*nigori-ten*) – on their syllabets to indicate whether the consonant was to be "clouded" or not. This was a great aid to poetry!
2. The Tako and the Namako The *namako* was once called just *ko* (the *nama* for "raw" came later) and the *ta* in *tako* (octopus) is one pronunciation for "hand," so that the octopus is a "handed-sea-slug"

according to this derivation, the second oldest (but, unfortunately undated) given in the OJD
3. Salmon Stock That is to say the whole dried salmon was pounded to soften it and used to make something between a soup and a stew (*kara-shake-o atsumono to shite*). Since dried Salmon has a somewhat saintly quality – the Far East has a tradition of self-mummifying monks – it is an especially appropriate fish for a Buddhist story.

Little Ikkyû wrinkled up his brow and pondered. That night he snuck out and bought a live carp, and prepared a *miso* soup stock. As he posed with knife in hand, ready to chop off the fish's head, the abbot came in. Horrified, he offered stronger words than before and threatened the novice with a beating if he didn't come up with a good reason for his misconduct. Ikkyû said, he had an *indô* (last words addressed to a person's soul offering guidance for a smooth passage to the other world) for *his* fish, too:

> Thou were, after all, like green wood. I'd like to help thee, but thou'd only slip away [through the net of Buddhist law]. Rather than living to sport in the water, become thee a humble monk's shit! Amen!

The abbot admitted the novice's forthright "shit" beat his indirect "buddhify" and went about town telling this story of a miraculously enlightened novice.

Shiki's *Ikkyû's Shit* sea slug is not quite there yet. Now, the second story, #9 in the collection, which takes place after Ikkyû became in/famous for his exploits – among which the most outrageous was his unique method of *kaigen* "opening the eyes" of a idol (a rite performed by a Buddhist priest to bring the soul into a new religious statue) where he urinated in its face and got run out of town as a result!

Rumors had it that this "Living Buddha" Ikkyû was eating fish and later spitting them back into the ocean, alive. When the rumors reached Ikkyû's ears, he posted a sign offering to do it right before everyone's eyes. On the settled day, true to his nature, Ikkyû wolfed down a large platter of fish. But, claimed that under the scrutiny of so many eyes, for some reason, just couldn't convince his body to vomit them back up. I'll just have to shit them up instead, he said,[1] and sent the people home. Needless to say, not everyone was convinced but one who understood said,

> Would it really be a good thing if all the fish just eaten were alive and dancing in the water? It is said that "there are no miracles in the Right-Way [miracles are a trick of the evil way]." If people have, by praising Ikkyû's powers, really damned him, doesn't his action make sense?

The story honestly records that this did not satisfy all the crowd, but it sounds good to me! A footnote to the collection says that a story of a living Buddha (Boddhisattva) eating strips of raw fish and spitting them up whole and alive again is found in the ancient *Konjaku Monogatari* (now-olden tales), and that Ikkyû was credited with something more painful to imagine in another apocrypha, spitting up a live deer!

Knowing all this, the reader can make the connection to Shiki's haiku as well as I can. Two last readings based upon it. We might subtitle either one, *living coprolite*:

<table>
<tr><td align="center">***mystery solved***</td><td align="center">***ikkyû's shit***</td></tr>
<tr><td align="center">loh, the poor
sea slug, so *you* are
ikkyû's shit!</td><td align="center">so *this* is what
those fish became!
a sea slug</td></tr>
</table>

These readings show how I might have first translated Shiki's poem had I known the stories first. Keigu cannot help paraversing:

1. *Ikkyû and Mahomet*   Ikkyû's claim and subsequent restatement bears resemblance to the following episode well told by Francis Bacon:

"Mahomet made the people believe that he would call a hill to him, and from the top of it offer up his prayers for the observers of his land.. The people assembled: Mahomet called the hill to come to him again and again; and when the hill stood still, he was never a whit abashed, but said, If the hill will not come to Mahomet, Mahomet will go to the hill."   ("Of Boldness." *Essays*)

一休の魚とはこれか大海鼠　敬愚

ikkyû no uo to wa kore ka ônamako – keigu

(ikkyû's fish-as-for, this? large seaslug)   #145

miracle maker

ikkyû, is this,
then, your "fish?"
a big sea slug

– where direct mention of the "shit" is done away with, or this next, which keeps it and adds explanation:

魚とは見えぬ御糞なまこ也　敬愚

sakana to wa mienu onkuso namako nari – keigu

(fish-as[+emphasis] appear-not honorable-shit become/is)   #146

it hardly looks
like fish! Ikkyû shat
a namako!

I wish I had a way to make the "shit" honorable, or at least *polite* in English. But all of this – the idea at least – has already been done. A half year after reading the stories, I was delighted to find another Ikkyû+sea-slug haiku predating that of Shiki!

一休の買てゆかれし海鼠哉　花讃女

ikkyû no kôte yukareshi namako kana – kasanjo (1807-30)

(ikkyû's buy-went sea-slug !/?/ó/the/'tis)   #147

a sea slug is
what Ikkyû went out
and bought!

I think Kasanjo addresses the same apocrypha Shiki did. Shiki did not read her work, for if he did, it would be found in his *Categorized* anthology of haiku (brhz), so I doubt he played off her poem, which is the more subtle haiku for not mentioning the "s" word; yet, in a hard to explain way, more natural. Although few anthologies include her, [1] I feel that had Kasanjo only lived longer, she may well have become *the* representative poet of nineteenth century Japan, for she, like Shiki had an extraordinarily light touch with idea as well as image.

P.S.2 to the Scatological Sea Slug

肛門の彼方なるべし海鼠浄土　裕

kômon no kanata narubeshi namako-jôdo – yû (2003)

(anus's horizon/distance/overseas is-ought-to-be seaslug-pureland)   #148

on the farside of the anus, pureland of the sea slug	the pureland of the sea slug beyond my fundament	sea slug pureland beyond the horizon of the anusgate

1. *Kasanjo*   She is not included among the top dozen female haiku poets in *Josei Haiku no Sekai,* the standard Iwanami press book on the subject by Ueno Sachiko. Was too little known about her life?

I do not know Yû's background, but I suspect he may know of Ikkyû's stories and feel almost certain he knows of Issa's namako and the indirect Pureland connection there.   I cannot ask him because I have no more time (this goes to the printer in *days!*).   One thing must be pointed out about the *kômon*. It is a *far* more beautiful word than the banal "anus" or rude "ass-hole."   "Fundament" is not bad, but too obscure and my coinage "anusgate" is poor.   Lacking a good word for this central item, a good translation is impossible.   A poem like this (part of *"How's That! Kukai Battle"* on a Namu-hosted site) is supposed to be judged or appreciated on the basis of the poems before and after it.   So, let me add that the poem before it was this, by Furiko: *"a gate fire / lit before dark on / welcome day"* (Omukae = the day when the dead come to visit from paradise, a buddhist all-soul's day) and that was proceeded by Yû's *"burning chaff / smoldering out when / father wind."*   So we have an interesting sequence from sky to earth, fire to water . . .   .[1]

P.S.3 to the Scatological Sea Slug

For readers unfamiliar with the history of eccentrics or hagiographies in the West, this chapter may have been more exoticizing than I intended.   This haiku, a last minute find, will give me a chance to make amends.

生 臭 く 生 き て 海 鼠 を 好 ま れ し 梅 子

namagusaku ikite namako o konomareshi – umeko (contemp)
(raw-stinky/pungent/gamey-living seaslug liking-able)

#149

living with	living a life
the stink of life i now	that is earthy, relishing
like sea slug	the sea slug

The word *namagusai,* if used with respect to a Buddhist monk would mean that he stunk from eating animal food, which presumed he was complicit with the sin of taking life.   Today, it is commonly used to describe any food with a strong smell or a smell that does not appeal to the person who uses the word.   A person who is strongly conscious of beef-eating as a foreign practice but positive about all fish, might use the word to describe beef that most other people would not call *namagusai.*   On the other hand, a person who has no trouble with beef but finds some fish, such as bonito or sardine overwhelming, might use it to describe those fish.   I can not recall seeing it used in a metaphorical manner, such as in the poem.   A sea cucumber does not have a very powerful smell, but it does have something we might call a pungent *presence* and a savage mouthfeel (a concept we will develop later) that turns off prissy people.   I presume the poet, once a neat little girl who would not even think of eating something so repulsive, has, in her adulthood, discovered a less than tidy life, moved in with and gone drinking with a boyfriend, experienced life with a dog or cat, had outdoor sex, got married and learned to sniff diapers, or perhaps even moved to the country where the toilets do not flush and tend to stink.   But I could be wrong; earthiness and eating sea slug might just be a family tradition.

1. How It Continued   Because I only found this sequence in this morning and must keep moving if this book has a chance of being published before the International Echinoderm Conference in October, I cannot read it all carefully enough to tell what is going on, but here are a few *ku* that followed directly after the Fundamental Sea Slug Pure Land haiku:
String theory: / now, anus and mouth / are joined
＝ひも理論いま肛門と口つなぐ　裕
The anus of / a yam bug but out / comes cabbage!

＝芋虫の肛門を出るキャベツかな　裕
Like taking / a sea anemone for / a walk: the anus
＝肛門はいそぎんちゃくに似て連れ歩く　勝之
The syntax of the last haiku, by katsuyuki, was lost in translation, so we might as well lose it further:
What's an anus? it's a malacoderm we can walk!
As was the case with the *kômon,* the *isoginchaku,* or, "sea anemone" does not translate, for the name in Japanese is reef-*purse.* The type of purse is what we call a *drawstring.* The other word, *malacoderm,* means "soft-skin," and also does not work.

8
the helpless sea slug

Before the fins, *I felt like a sea cucumber in the water, at the mercy of the relentless waves.* With the fins, I felt like a dolphin, paddling gracefully and speedily thru the water. Well, maybe I wasn't *that* graceful, but they did make a huge difference. I caught some pretty tight waves, and finally experienced "riding the tube" (www.alumni. caltech.edu/~naturboy/ index2-sep.html (Sept. 6, 2000)) (*italics* mine)

In the above quote, a Californian (judging from the use of "like" elsewhere in his text and the place, (Sunset Beach) body-surfer has managed to come up – better yet, *identify* – with a common haiku image of our *namako*.

満 て 行 く 潮 に 連 る 身 海 鼠 哉　和 貢
michiteyuku shio ni tsureru mi namako kana – wakô (1759)
(rising-tide-with/by accompany/ing body seaslug!/?/ó/the/'tis)   #150

a body that
follows the rising tide
the sea slug

The same inaction that let the sea slug off the hook may become the cause of the sea slug's undoing. Another poem gently personifies the consequences of going with the tide, the terror of the beach-line so sublimely depicted by Loren Eiseley in *The Star Thrower*.

引 き 汐 の わ す れ て 行 き し な ま こ か な　蝶 夢
hikishio no wasurete yukishi namako kana --- chômu (1731-95)
(ebbtide's forgetting leaves, seaslug!/?/ó/the/'tis)   #151

orphan

left behind
by the ebb tide
a sea slug

careless mother nature

the ebb-tide
forgot something
a sea slug

My titles may seem too much, but, without it, English loses something. The three Chinese characters used in Chômu's haiku are "ocean-mouse-child." The first two are all meaning, but the third, the "child" (or diminutive) matches the pronunciation *ko*. This cute name may be why the Japanese language internet gives us cute sea slugs (my favorites have sea slugs dancing or lying under *futon* covers.) The zoomorphic "forget" – man is not the only animal that forgets – works together with the "child" to create a subtle pathos not found in the purely objective poem:

砂（沙）原に吹上けられし海参哉　如行

sunabara ni fukiagerareshi namako kana – nyogyô (1692)

(sand-field[beach]-on blown-up seaslug!/?/ó/the/'tis)

#152

blown up
upon the sand dunes
a sea slug

Not that this objectivity must be boring. When we consider the fact that the sea slug is not upon the wet part of the beach, but has been blown up high and dry, we should feel the power of the winter gale that must have done it and the helplessness of the victim in the process of mummification.

引潮の忘れてゆきし大海鼠　栗田せつ子

hikishio no wasurete yukishi ônamako – kurita setsuko (2001)

(ebb-tide's forgetting leaves, big seaslug)

#153

the ebb-tide
forgot something
a big sea slug

This haiku though almost identical to that of Chômu, may well have been independently created. It draws our attention to the image – especially if we have ever been surprised by a particularly large sea slug (as I have) – and brings a smile not found in the older haiku: *How could Mother Nature forget something so large?*

引汐に引き残されし海鼠哉　子規

hikishio ni hikinokosareshi namako kana – shiki (1895)

(pulling=falling-tide-by, pull=retreating-left/remaining seaslug!/?/ó/the/'tis)

#154

the retreating tide
pulls out with sea slug
left behind

In Japanese, "ebb-tide" and military (or corporate) retreats equally "pull" out. So the ostensibly objective poem may have a bit of play in it.

長汀に放り出されし海鼠ども　高沢良一

chôtei ni hôridasareshi namakodomo – takasawa yoshikazu (2001)

(long-shoreline/beach thrown out sea-slug[+polite plural form])

#155

a long beach
littered with the bodies
of sea slugs

～

a long shore
here and there the body
of a sea slug

So we have them left behind, forgotten, thrown up and now thrown out. Had the sea slugs been picked up in the morning when they were still alive, they might have been eaten, but they lie there and start to rot. As another haiku has pointed out, they look like something that has been thrown away to begin with. So, now, they are doubly trashed. The second reading, a paraverse, is my way of saying that the long beach may be enough to make the haiku. I added the body/bodies to make the dead sea slugs more poignant. This is done in the original by the suffix *domo,* a rather polite plural form usually reserved for humans.

時折五十メートル飛びぬ海鼠哉　敬愚

tokiori goju metoru tobinu namako kana – keigu
(time-to-time fifty meters flies seaslug!/?/ǿ/the/'tis)   #156

ticket home

a sea slug
sometimes gets to fly
fifty yards

There are many haiku about sea slugs, thus brought in by the tide of fate, but none about going the other way, so Keigu makes amends with this haiku that might be considered a cross of the stranded slug poems and Eiseley's *Star Thrower* – who threw starfish back out to sea – for throwing sea slugs is something he has often done. Unfortunately, most sea slugs are not rescued.

泡沫の泡や海鼠に積りけん　月巣

hômatsu no awa ya namako ni tsumoriken – gesô (1729-85)
(foam/spume-end's bubbles! sea-slug-on piles-up)   #157

frothy spume
builds up on the body
of a sea slug

English has no word that means specifically the frothy spume found on the tips of waves that flies off into the air to scatter on the beach and in the wind.[1] This *hômatsu,* like dew, is synonymous with ephemerality. This is to the sea slug, what dew is to the morning glory: a poetic condiment of mortality. Metaphor-wise, we have the evanescent upon the trusting/fatalistic.

流れ来て海鼠は塵に吸れけり　義延

nagarekite namako wa chiri ni suwarekeri – giki (1759)
(drifting-came seaslug-as-for debris/trash/dust-in/by sucked-up)   #158

karma

drifting in
sea slug's sucked up
by debris

This, my title suggests, may conversely suggest a sand-sucker because the tables have been turned and the sucker is sucked. The *chiri* is always a problem to translate for it strongly suggests the dust that all – chimney-sweepers, butterflies and cherry blossoms – must come to, yet can refer to many more things, including the flotsam and jetsam of a beach.

1. *"Frothy" Second Reading* Plovers (*chidori*) were thought to be born of this spume/froth (a myth depicted beautifully by Hokusai). Another translation of *chidori,* a zigzag, hints at the metaphorical usage of the word: someone walking about drunk. Since a sea-slug is a good metaphor for a passed-out drunk, I think this innocuous haiku would be a good one to write on a scene of drunken revelry, but admit it is too far out to leave in the main text as a second reading.

尾 鰭 ふ る 中 に 睡 れ る 生 海 鼠 哉　備 後

obire furu naka ni nemureru namako kana – bigo (1793)

#159   (tail-fin-shake among sleeping seaslug/s!/?/ó/the/'tis)

those sea slugs
sleep among quivering
tails and fins

While this may be a simple fact, a description of a sea slug, or sea slugs sharing a net or tub with fish, it makes them seem cool compared to their quivering brethren: a subjective reading without being so.

打 波 に 身 を ま か せ た る 海 鼠 哉　車 庸

utsunami ni mi o makasetaru namako kana – shayô (c1700)

#160   (striking-waves-to body leave-up-to seaslug!/?/ó/the)

a sea slug   the sea slug
giving itself up to   just lets the waves give
the breakers   it a pounding

no fins, no fight

sea slugs
let breakers have
their bodies

Facetious zoomorphism and anthropomorphism are fine; but I have mixed feelings here, for the same reason I do about descriptions of cherry blossoms falling "without attachment." People forget that *letting go* – proof of enlightenment in Buddhist catechism – is as much a conscious decision as *holding on*; yet poems about the latter are disparaged as artificial, while the former are overlooked.

こ ろ り ん と 渚 に 海 鼠 波 枕　高 沢 良 一

kororin to nagisa ni namako namimakura -- takasawa yoshikazu (2003)

#161   (*kororin* [mimesis for tumbling and bouncing about]-with beach-to/by seaslug wave-pillow)

beach scene

the sea slugs
tumble in to rest with waves
for their pillows

~

tumbling in
sea slugs with waves
for pillows

~

as
they bob
along the beach
sea slugs dream
on foamy billows
a bit beyond
my reach

There are three possible readings of this haiku. The sea slugs could have tumbled into the beach to rest in the shallow surf, be tumbling in, or be moving longitudinally down the beach (for there are many beaches with strong currents in Japan). Regardless, the "wave pillow" has connotations of the so-called "floating-life" of marginal drifters who have given up all hope of controlling their fate and just take it one day at a time.

死 な ん こ と 知 ら て 静 な 生 海 鼠 哉 子 皐

shinan koto shira de shizuka na namako kana – shikô (1793)

(die-not-fact know-not-from/because, quiet seaslug/s!/?/ó/the/'this)   #162

not knowing
it will die, how placid
this sea slug

So the sea slug embodies *ignorance is bliss?* This is true in one sense. If the sea slug "knew" of the danger, it would move – for they *do* move – but false in that its ignorance is not what keeps it so still. [1]

と う な り と 生 海 鼠 は 人 に 任 す 哉   星 高

dô nari to namako wa hito ni makasu [1] *kana* – seikô? (1820)

(however becomes, seaslug/s-as-for person/man/others-to/on depend/allow/s!/?/ó/the)   #163

and sea slug
is something you always
leave to others

~

come what come will
sea slugs leave it
up to man

I favor the first reading because I like the idea of the sea slug metaphor transfering to us, but O.M. goes for the second, the enlightened sea slug.[2] The grammar allows either. The "others," implies cooks at restaurants, wives or parents and reflects the difficulty of preparation, as we shall see in the "tasty sea slug." *Hito,* while ostensibly meaning "person," also can mean "others." Since English can use "people" that way, the last line of the second reading could be "to people" rather than "up to man," and there is the possibility it alludes to a type of person.

1. *Makasu, Makasetaru* Especially in haiku where long constructions won't fit, English phrases such as "left up to" or "leave up to" are no equivalent for a single verb like *makasu* that also includes a "counting on the other" connotation which we must expand to "leave in the hands of" or describe as "a delegation of responsibility." And even if English had a word, the positive connotations of letting others decide – the mark of a true gentleman and Eastern sage – would not necessarily go with it.

2. *Enlightened Sea Slug* I am happier with the enlightened=dying sea slug found in the final page of Sôseki's *I Am a Cat*, where the sea slug is alluded to but not mentioned. After sipping some beer for the first time in his life, the high cat feels like taking a walk in the light of the moon and ends up slipping into a large pot with the water level lowered just enough from the crow's bird-baths to keep the edge of the pot out of his reach. After a series of thrashing around and hopeless clawing on the sides of the pot, the cat achieves a sort of enlightenment in his final moments as he quits his vain struggle and "and trusting his forelegs and hind-legs, his head and tail to the power of nature [*shizen-no chikara-ni makasete*], chose not to resist." After which, "it got increasingly pleasant. He couldn't tell if he was feeling bad or good." He sinks down as he floats up, above it all, intoning the sutra *namuamidabutsu-namuamida . .* The mention of "head and tail" combined with the *makasete* (cf above) together make it clear that the title of Andô Fumibito's article ("Tosho" 4-2002: Iwanami) is correctly titled: "Tale of a Cat that Became a Sea Slug" (*namako ni natta neko-no hanashi.*)

煮て焼いて呉れろと海鼠たじろがず　高沢良一
nite yaite kureru to namako tajirogazu – takasawa yoshikazu (1997)
(boilied/ing, toasted/ing do-for[me]: seaslug shrink/blench-not)

#164

sure, boil me
roast me! you can't faze
a sea slug!

心配はご無用顔の海鼠とも　高沢良一
shinpai wa gomuyôkao no namako to mo – takasawa yoshikazu (1999)
(worry-as-for, unneeded faces, seaslug even)

#165

worry, why worry!
that is what is written on
a sea slug's face

don't worry
about me says the mug
on the sea slug

sea slug's face
seems to say now don't you
worry 'bout me!

Though sea slug ends up on the beach, in a tub, on the cutting board or stove, or even in your stomach, it really doesn't care, for the sea slug embodies equanimity, the ideal of the Taoist gentleman and the Zen priest, which among the inactive, at least, is part and parcel with fatalism. After reading the poem that *follows,* I must admit to wondering if Takasawa might not have been influenced by a haiku of Issa's which requests a captain not to take a leak upon the sea, for the moon was afloat – a poem I once translated into about 30 (!) paraverses ranging from: *"Boatman, don't you dare make water in the sea / . . . you'll dilute the moonlight's purity!"* to *"Cap'n, close your fuckin' fly! / – the moon is floating by!"*(I know, they had no flies) – and includes the same *muyô.* Chances are it's chance, but

海鼠に小便そんな愚行もしてみたく　高沢良一
namako ni shôben sonna guko mo shitemitaku – takasawa yoshikazu (2003)
(seaslug-on urinate/piss/pee that foolish-behavior-even do-try[like to try])

#166

a dumb act
i'd like to do: pissing
on a sea slug

In Japan, the frog is known for its equanimity – I have seen some large toad like frogs that fit that bill in Japan – and for being at home in wetness. So, to lecture someone who is thick-skinned is "to pee on the face of a frog." Perhaps for that reason, Issa has a good half dozen haiku combining frogs and pissing. Takasawa does not seem so interested in micturition as Issa, who, after all, did most of his al fresco, where there was more to describe. But the sea slug is known for both these batrachian traits, so Takasawa pretends to want to test out a new version of the idiom. The way the pissed upon just sits and takes it makes the poem fit this chapter, but let's look at another of Takasawa's word-influenced sea slug haiku.

俎の上の鯉否海鼠切る　高沢良一
manaita no ue no koi ie namako kiru – takasawa yoshikazu (2003)
(cutting-board-upon carp, not/no, seaslug cut)

#167

cutting a carp
on the cutting block, no,
it's a sea slug

Japanese has a proverb "like a carp on the cutting block" which means that some one has a fate that is settled, i.e., "as good as dead." The poet suggests that a carp is hardly so helpless – it might, after all, flap and fly off the board into a pond – as the sea slug he is about to cut. Now, let's see how the fatalistic bent of the sea slug expands to encompass those in contact with it.

小廻りをつづくるうちの海鼠舟　八木林之介

komawari o tsuzukuru uchi no namakobune – yagi rinnosuke (mod)
(small-circle making within's seaslug-boat)

#168

the slug boat
within the small circle
it describes

In close to shore, where waves flowing in and out of openings in the reef would constantly change the current and wind would ricochet off the headlands, an anchored boat would circle about rather than pulling in one direction. This suggests fatalism without explicit mention.

海 鼠 突 く 蜑 の 小 舟 は 波 ま か せ　林 大 馬

namako tsuku ama no kobune wa nami makase – hayashi taima (contemp)
(sea slug stabbing *ama* [diving-woman]'s small-boat-as-for, waves left-to)

#169

oceanic

the *ama* gigs
sea slugs, letting her boat
drift freely

calm bay

her tiny boat
drifts about while *ama*
gigs sea slugs

#170, #171 (下)

Here the drifting *ama* saves the corny conceit of a fatalistic – or enlightened – sea slug with the realistic parallel of a seemingly fatalistic *ama*, as does this one in a plainer manner: "the slug-gigger / does not fight / the current" (*namako-tsuki shio-no ugoki-ni sakarawazu* – ôtake kinya (1998) 海鼠突き潮の動きにさからはず　大竹欣哉). The *ama* in her white swimming wear is a romantic image of ageless Japan, but the image is changing: "her diving gear / all of it, all black! / sea-slug *ama*" (*sensuigi mina ga mina kuro namakoama* – ôta aa (2001) 潜水着みながみな黒海鼠海女　太田嗟). This would be a description of wetsuits, but, coincidentally, a legend of a Japanese man (Hachitaro) who established himself in the Noto peninsula when it was not settled by Japanese first recorded in but predating the Edo era, happens to have the wives of men diving for sea slugs off the Noto Peninsula (to process as skewered *kushiko* and sell to the Chinese) *veiling their heads with black scarves* – logical, considering the cold weather there, but not "Japanese." [1]

1.Not Japanese Tsurumi writes that burial mounds have revealed that they were neither Yamato people (Japanese), nor Ainu, though Ainu had lived there until the seventh century, but from Koguryo, perhaps part of those refugees who scattered throughout South Asia when their kingdom was demolished by the Han Chinese [?kara?] in 668AD. If the Koguryo were the first to boil and dry sea cucumber, it was a history the Chinese did not bother to record. (NAMAKO-NO MANAKO. pgs.404-6)

礁 の 間 に 長 き 舳 や 海 鼠 舟　楠 目 橙 黄 子

shô no ma ni nagaki hesaki ya namakobune – kusume tôkôshi (1932)
(reef/s' between/among/gap-in long bowsprit:/! seaslugboat)

#172

a long bowsprit
heads through the reef
a sea slug boat

~

between reefs
this long bowsprit
a slug boat

There is nothing here about fatalism, but there is something about a bowsprit that makes us feel it. Is it the way it hangs out in front like a leading shadow or the severity of its hard and straight lines? As the gloss shows, the original does not make it clear whether the boat is sitting there or moving, but I think it is moving because that is the image that moves me to think of the movies of a certain Swedish director. The bowsprit picks up on the phallic image of a sea slug even as it contradicts its sluggishness by being so pointed, purposeful, and unbending.

海 鼠 舟 舳 先 な き ご と さ ま よ へ る　山 本 俊 二

namakobune hesakinaki goto samayoeru – yamamoto shunji (1998)
(seaslug-boat/s, bowsprit-not as-if drift/s)

#173

drifting about
as if it had no bowsprit
a sea slug boat

な ま こ 舟 舳 先 を 風 に ま か せ け り　黒 田 桜 の 園

namakobune hesaki o kaze ni makasekeri – kuroda sakura no en (2001)
(seaslug-boat/s bowsprit[obj] wind-in/to left[to])

#174

sea slug boats
their bowsprits left
up to the wind

#175

Here, the boat is no longer captain of its soul and betraying its bowsprit, acts like a sea slug. I find this play with bowsprits a great improvement [1] on the oldest of the haiku I have found the clearly depicts *let-it-be* sea slugs reflected by boats: "not fighting / the wind-blown surf / the slug boat" (*namakobune fukururu shio/umi ni sakarawazu* – suzushika noburo (1932) 海鼠舟ふくるゝ潮にさからはず　野風呂).

海 鼠 舟 不 二 へ 舳 先 を 揃 へ け り　衣 川 砂 生

namakobune fûji e hesaki o soroekeri – kinukawa sunao?(1990)
(seaslug-boat fuji-at bowsprit align[+finality])

#176

sea slug boats
bow-sprits aligned
on mount fuji

1. *Great Improvement* If the poem is the first to allude to the resemblance of sea slug and slug boat, then it would have been a fine read at the time it was written. For that reason, my "improvement" does not mean to imply that the original was lacking, except in retrospect. If we read widely, we cannot help but be Whigs and we cannot help but know we are unfair.

At first glance, the powerful image of Fuji and pointing objects appears to offer a startling counterpoint to the last two bowsprit haiku and, perhaps bring out the less-ordered sea slug by way of unmentioned contrast.   But, on longer consideration, the haiku brings out something obvious yet all-too-often ignored (at least in my original field of study, international politics), namely that *to aim for the same thing, is not to point the same way.*   This is, of course, if we imagine the boats are not close together, so they do not appear to be pointing in the same way (if parallel means the same way), which is to say, if we imagine a panoramic view from the coast above, from an airplane or, better yet, from space as pictured in the head of the poet, who has a wind, or, rather a compass of winds, blowing down the mountain and off the land, which is not a straight coast but an island. So the bowsprits are all pointing into the wind.[1] Since the wind, like magnetism, is invisible, you may think of Fuji, the metaphorical central-pillar or navel of Japan as a loadstone and the slug boats in the haiku fall into the dependency metaphor, as they should.

べ た 凪 の 足 で 舵 取 る 海 鼠 舟　瀬 戸 石 葉
betanagi no ashi de kaji toru namakobune – seto sekiyô (1997)
(dead-calm's leg/s-with, tiller/rudder take/hold seaslug-boat)   #177

a dead calm
the slugger holds the tiller
with his feet

海 鼠 突 き 足 で 操 る 舟 自 在　大 内 逸 山
namakotsuki ashi de ayatsuru fune jizai – ôuchi itsuzan (2001)
(seaslug-gigger/ing feet-with/by operate/juggle boat freely)   #178

the slug gigger
steering the boat freely
with his feet

The foot is almost as good a gimmick as the bowsprit. It is a fact and it can not escape being meaningful. The sea slugger may be quite good with his feet, but by not holding the tiller with his hands, together with the sea slug, he rests in the greater hand of fate.

海 鼠 捕 る 海 鼠 の や う な 仕 種 し て　井 上 比 呂 夫
namako toru namako no yô na shigusa shite – inoue hirô (2001)
(seaslug-take/catcher seaslug-like movement/motion/mannerism does)   #179

sea-sluggers   sea-sluggers
make motions just   with the mannerism
like sea slugs   of sea slugs

you are what you hunt

a sea slugger
moving as if he were
a sea slug

1. *The Wind and the Sea Slug.*   In *The Sea Slug's Eye* (nnm), Tsurumi Yoshiyuki devotes over a dozen pages to the wind. He points out that the wind was big in Taoism because of the needs of the dry land where it developed (shades of YWH!) and, later, those wind gods fit the needs of sea-going people in the Sinosphere. The sea-oriented Shinto Shrine of Ise, long associated with the Imperial line, and Taoism (as one of the major threads of its faith) has major shrines devoted to the Wind, is also the shrine most associated with the sea slug (many ancient offerings).   While the Wind was on a few occasions called upon to protect the nation with the *kamikaze,* or "God-Wind," (most famously against the Mongol armada) the most common prayer and local rites were for wind NOT to blow. And, of all fishing people, the slugger was most dependent on just that.

Which is to say, I guess, that he mostly stays still and looks down, but occasionally lifts his head slightly. If you are what you eat, you are much more so what you hunt!

風 向 き が ガ ラ リ 変 れ り 海 鼠 突 高 沢 良 一

kazamuki ga garari kawareri namakotsuki – takasawa yoshikazu (1999)

#180   (wind-direction suddenly/lurching/180 degrees-changes seaslug-gigger)

the sea wind   a slug gigger
suddenly shifts on   the sea wind suddenly
a slug gigger   lurches about

The wind can do this, especially when you are near to a shore with hilly land, which is the case for most of Japan's coast. There is nothing explicit in this poem about fate or the sluggishness of the sluggers, but I think it possible that the poet does not stop with the gigger, but imagines what happens below the water as well. When the slugger is suddenly whipped about by the wind, fate smiles on the sea slug he was slowly homing in on, who remains untaken as the slugger's attention focuses on another.   The poem also made me reconsider my simplistic *calm vs windy* opposition.   Surely a moderate but steady wind (in terms of direction) would be better than a lighter one that wandered all over the compass.

海 士 か 子 よ 宿 も 定 め ぬ 生 海 鼠 哉   月 居

amagako wa yado mo sadamenu namakotori – getsukyo (1755-1824)

#181   (diver-child[woman/women]-as-for, lodging-even settled-not seaslug-taker/s)

these poor *ama*
with no fixed abode?
~ sea sluggers ~

The sea slug season varies according to the water temperature and the fluctuating fortunes of the fisheries, so the *namako* harvesters – prototypically diving women or men with poles – live the life of a migrant worker and, thus, like the sea slug itself, seem to be homeless wanderers in a world beyond their control.

～

9
the meek sea slug

"spineless, but not weak" – *The Weekly Invertebrate*

Looking at the sea slug react to our touch, we cannot help but feel it is a meek rather than proud creature. This puts it square in the majority, for very few animals push their weight around. The sea slug's meekness is only notable because it seems exceptionally defenseless.

手にとれはさすかに逃る海鼠哉　吟江
te ni toreba sasuga ni nigeru namako kana – ginkô (1775)
(hand-in take-if, sure-enough flees/ing seaslug!/?/ô/the)   #182

grab hold and
sure enough, it flees:
the sea slug

With a single word, *sasuga,* Japanese can indicate something that happens is what one might have expected all along: perhaps a sea slug can not buck its fate by swimming for it, or flopping off the beach, but Ginkô chortles, *Hoh! It lives after all, for it would escape my clutch!* The *namako* takes fate into its own hands by slipping from mine! There is a good chance this took place at the sea shore, for Ginkô also haiku'ed "reef smell" (*isokusa no nioi*).

なまこさへ逃るこころか手をすべる　梅室
namako sae nigeru kokoro ka te o suberu – baishitsu (1839)
(sea slug even, flee mind/will [has]? hand out-of slips)   #183

slipping my hand
so even sea slugs have
a mind to flee?

Issa's contemporary Baishitsu may be explaining Ginkô's older haiku which doesn't specify the method of escape, or, the similarity may be coincidence, for Japanese have many sayings to the effect that even the tiniest and weakest worm has a heart, its own tiny, but nonetheless undeniable portion of will-power, and together with it the desire to live. [1] Yet, at the same time, there is something ignoble about fleeing – a Taoist sage would not do it. Keigu ABA's this moral turpitude:

すべすべ は海鼠唯一の術となり　敬愚
sube sube wa namako yuitsu no sube to nari – keigu
(slippery-as-for seaslugs' just-one/only trick/art/skill becomes/is)   #184

the great escape

being slippery:
a sea slug's only form
of trickery!

1. *Weakest Worm Saying* O.M. reminded me of the best known saying: *issun no mushi nimo 5bu no* *tamashii* (Even an inch-long worm has half-inch mind). *Even a worm will turn.*

When I was a child, we used to catch a slimy tubular fish in Biscayne Bay (between Miami and Key Biscayne) that we hated because it was hard to *un*hook and dared take our bait despite being inedible. Too young to know what it meant, we called it what everyone did: a *slippery dick.* (When I finally did start to catch on, I think we were told that the reference was to a certain president) To tell the truth, some sea cucumbers do have other tricks up their sleeve. If some cockle shells start to dance[1] like Madam Butterfly when they smell a sea star coming,

> when normally glacially-paced cukes encounter a predatory *Tonna* gastropod, they
> too can trundle along, sometimes by using the back end as a lever. (A. Kerr)

Either because men don't look, feel or smell like *Tonna* gastropods, because sea slugs are always caught sleeping, the *Stichopus Japonicus* is particularly slow or divers just don't write haiku and *namako* can't purchase a hold for their "lever" on the cutting board, nothing like this has been reported for our charge . But we do have another diversionary movement:

酢なまこの震へて箸を逃げんとす　飯田君子
sunamako no furuete hashi o nigen to su – iida kimiko (1997)

#185   (vinegar-seaslug's quivering, chopsticks[obj] flee-does/tries)

pickled slug
quivers and would flee
my chopsticks

This poem strictly belongs with the *Slippery Sea Slugs* because the sea slug in question is really pieces of sea slug and the shaking or quivering which helps the "escape" is facetious – caused by the poet, intent to hold on to her *namako* – but it *seems* like it belongs here.

海鼠哉捕らへられたる顔もせず　鳴雪
namako kana toraeraretaru kao mo sezu – meisetsu (1848-1926)

#186   (seaslug/s!/?/ó/the/behold taken/captured/holdable face/s-even has/shows-not)

at home

these sea slugs
you would never know
they're captured

nonchalant prisoner

a sea slug
that looks like he
is still free

1. ***Active Seabed*** Until researching this book, I assumed the seabed was pretty much a place for sleeping, but now I know that shells can jump up and swim about hysterically, sea cucumbers can trundle along – some, while partly grown, can even "swim to the surface at night by a curious twitching movement of the body, suggesting a scizzors kick." (Buchsbaum and Milne) – and sea urchins can zoom about: "There's an urchin on Indo Pacific reefs, Jeez, forgot the name, that comes out at night and is very difficult to catch becuz it 'zooms' into crevices when a flashlight is shined on it." (A. Kerr: corresp = in reply to my question on the relative speeds of the cuke and the urchin). Some one should teach this stuff to the people who make screen-savers!

hard-to-get

the sea slug
its face is also
ungraspable

There is a gloopy nonsensical thing like a sea slug
which cannot be grasped inhabiting human beings,
too. (*Droll Haiku The Sea Slug's Tongue*:1918 kkhk)

Fish either look like they are as good as dead or in trouble, but these sea slugs are another thing. *Ignorance is bliss?* Yes, but if that were so, why so many shrinking sea slugs? Is this the relatively rare constitutionally bold, or should we say, thick-skinned, sea slug? Or, are they just more relaxed in tubs than on cutting boards? My anthropomorphic titles reflect the original's use of "face/faces," which in Japanese, as in English, strictly belong only to members of the primate family or cats who are washing them. I suspect that the correct meaning of the poem escaped my first two readings, and only is found in the third, which I wrote after reading the comments about the poem by Oka no Kaeru, or "Frog-on-a-Hill" in his Droll Haiku.

刺 の ご と き を 満 身 に 生 海 鼠　檜 紀 代
toge no gotoki o manshin ni namanamako – hinoki kiyo (1996)
(spike-like[things] entire-body-on raw/nude/live seaslug)   #187

original punk

its whole body
is covered with studs
a live sea slug

The original's "spike-like" suggests something that looks like spikes but is really less formidable. Forgive the studs, they're mine. Spikes protrude more on lively sea slugs than on tired or dead ones.

身 を 守 る 尖 と も み へ ぬ 海 鼠 哉　太 祇
mi o mamoru toge to mo mienu namako kana – taigi (1708-71)
(body/self[obj] protecting-spikes even see/appear-not seaslug!/?/ô/the/'tis)   #188

echinoderm punk

they sure don't
look like real protection
sea slug spikes

Because, of course, they are not. This haiku is so obvious it is ridiculous. The worthlessness of the spikes *as spikes* was probably more significant in Edo Japan than it is now, to us. *Namako,* or "sea slug," was common slang for a tool in use by the police descriptively called a "sleeve-grabber." The spikes on the last foot or so of this long pole were bent slightly down/inward so they would hook the clothing of a suspect or prisoner attempting to flee police custody.

お も む ろ に 角 を お さ め ぬ 大 海 鼠　蔓
omomuro ni tsuno o osamenu ônamako – tsuru (mod)
(slowly/deliberately horn/s put-away large seaslug)   #189

deliberately
it draws in its horns
a big sea slug

This is a very careful observation. Either the physiology of the bumps of the large sea slug is different, or our brainless sea slugs have learned not to over-react. [1] The "horns" are, of course, no more horns than those of the snail that could only scare hatters in MOTHER GOOSE. The proto sea slug may have had horns, but it left that defense to its close relative, the sea urchin. Do we feel for it because we too are the naked part of our family, the only primate stripped of its protective hair and shorn of its tail?

大海鼠つつけば疣が押し返す　小谷ゆきを
ônamako tsutsukeba ibô ga oshikaesu – kotani yukio (contemp)
(big-seaslug tap/poke-if/when bump/s/parapodium push-back)

#190

a big sea slug
tap its bumps and
they push back

Large Japanese sea slugs are particularly warty-looking or, to put it more euphoniously, well-spiked. Perhaps the tissue is a bit like corn starch, giving like liquid when pushed slowly, but solid when smartly poked. The *ibô* (parapodium/papule) may pun on the *bô* = "pole," the object used by Japanese idiom for poking around in places perhaps best not poked. How refreshing to find a poet playing with sea slugs. Kotani's sea slug haiku is exceptionally original yet classic in its humor.

苟も腸のある海鼠かな　青々
iyashikumo harawata no aru namako kana – seisei (1869-1937)
(even guts/intestines has sea-slug!/?/ó/the)

#191

even sea slugs
to their credit are not
empty within

～

actually
it takes guts to be
a sea slug

腸のありて骨なき海鼠かな　千束
harawata no arite honenaki namako kana – chitsuka (1927)
(guts have/having bone/s-not seaslug/s!/?/ó/the/behold)

#192

a heart, yes
but no backbone
the sea slug

anomaly

sea slugs
all guts yet
spineless

Guts in Japanese are not so much synonymous with courage as with sincerity: they are the seat of deep truth, what might be called our heart of hearts. So, the second readings of both poems, which translate

1. *Learning Sea Slugs* The particular characteristic of the large sea slug endears for it gives the sea slug a personality. It also raises a fine question: can the brainless sea slug learn, which is to say act differently on the basis of memory without so much as a ganglia in its head?

"guts" as "guts" is not so accurate as the first, which changes them to not being empty or simply a "heart." But there is a touch of guts in the English sense of the word in the Japanese *harawata,* too, for it is hard to be spineless yet full of whatever you would call it, within. Perhaps the poets mean a sea slug, or a sea slug person may have guts though you would never know it. This next older poem is more positive, for it tells what bonelessness permits:

骨 の な き 身 を ち ぢ め た る 海 鼠 哉 富 水

hone no naki mi o chijimetaru namako kana – fusui?(1773)

(bones-not body[obj] shrinking sea-slug!/?/ó/the/behold)   #193

lacking bones
it shrinks its body:
the sea slug

homo holothurian

spineless
we shrink up:
sea slugs

Slipperiness may be useful to reduce water resistance and thereby protect the sea slug from being uprooted by currents, and it certainly helps defend the pieces of the dead sea slug from klutzy would-be eaters, but it is not one of the sea slug's main defenses against being captured or eaten alive. The first would be poison. Even our tasty friend *Stichopus japonica* has somewhat poisonous lungs which it can, like the skunk, put in the face of a predator. [1] The second defense, only possible for the boneless is to shrink down into obscurity (the boney, like the blowfish, *must* puff up). The original haiku has neither pronoun nor number, so both objective and subjective readings are possible, simultaneously.

き ん 玉 の や う に 凍 て た る 海 鼠 哉 松 本 正 氣

kintama no yô ni itetaru namako kana – matsumoto seiki (1940)

(gold-gem[balls]-like frozen-up seaslug!/?/ó/the/behold)   #194

a sea slug
all frozen up like
a man's balls

1. *Poisonous Sea Slugs* The strength and amount of a poison in the holothurian varies greatly. I assume it repels some would-be predators. Oshima Hiroshi (NAMAKO TO UNI: 1962) reports that in Yaeyama Japan, pieces of the black *namako, Halodeima atra* were thrown into the sea and dead fish floated up, while the soup from the same *namako* boiled was used to stupefy fish in Japan and in the Pacific. A. Kerr qualifies: "to kill fish, one has to use an awful lot of cuke and spread it in a fairly enclosed area such as a octopus hole, cave, or a pool on the reef flat." Specifically, "it is most commonly used to get octopus out of their holes. One takes the most common species *Holothuria atra*, a black species ca. 20 cm long, and rubs its length vigorously in the opening of the octopus's lair. A wine colored liquid is expressed called holothurin [first isolated in the form of a colorless aciform (needle-like) crystal by the Japanese researcher YAMAUCHI Toshiko in 1955] that diffuses into the hole. Holothurin is a respiratory poison. The octopus soon emerges, but one must be careful for if it is inexpertly speared or grabbed now, it may retreat back into its hole and there suffocate." A.K. adds that a small blennioid fish that can crawl around on wet rocks "just come rocketing outa the pool upon application of crushed cuke, flopping all over the place. We pick them up and use them as bait for bigger fish over the reef in deep water." (corresp) Perhaps, this is a nominal case of competitive exclusion: the name blenny comes from the Gk "blénnos," i.e., "slime, mucus," a trait identified with the sea cucumber. It also gives rise to a new scenario for the first fish's departure from the sea . .

The frozen balls are, no doubt, figurative, but the metaphor fits, for cold sea slugs shrink from the ends: their phallic tubularity changes into the rounder and sadder. . . balls.[1] This is not a comfortable sea slug. As the poem was written in the Winter of 1940, it may well be a commentary on the desperate mindset of the Japanese, who attacked the World's greatest power out of desperation, knowing they had almost no chance of winning.

灯 の 海 鼠 尾 羽 打 ち 枯 れ し ご と 縮 む　石 塚 ま さ を

tomoshibi no namako oba uchikareshi goto chijimu -- ishizuka masao (1973)

#195   (lamplight's seaslug/s' tail-feathers crestfallen-like shrink)

a sea slug
shrinks in the lamplight
looking crestfallen

~

in the lamplight
sea slugs look crestfallen
when they shrink

The face of defense, especially when we know it will lose, is not happy. Neither translation does justice to he original. The term translated as "crest-fallen" is actually "tail-feathers." While there is a touch of humor in using a hawking term, knowing the affection the ancient poets had for their hawks, there is pathos too. [2]

桶 の 海 鼠 半 ば は 水 に な り に け り　　漁 壮

oke no namako nakaba wa mizu ni narinikeri – gyosô (1927)

#196   (tub's seaslug/s partly water becomes[+finality])

sea slugs
in a tray now
half water

~

the sea slug
in a tub, it's turned
half water

Since a tray full of sea slugs would not show more water when sea slugs were removed – indeed the water level might drop from loss of displacement – we may assume the sea slugs are not doing well and have ejected their guts and/or are otherwise shedding water as they shrink. Or, to use human metaphor, have bepissed themselves from fear.

1. *Sad Balls* If the penis is a jolly thing that gets to have fun, balls are, as someone wrote, luggage that must wait outside the gate and, worse, are easily injured and, let's face it, ugly. The mango-like balls on a bull have a smooth artistic look, but human balls with their sparsely haired turkey gobbler-like appearance are made to be concealed.   The Japanese artists in the Tokugawa era (1603-1867), however, greatly enlarge them and treat them as a sort of natural geography. See my upcoming book *Tanuki Balls.* The tanuki, a fox that looks like a raccoon and is usually translated ambiguously as a "raccoon dog," or wrongly as a "badger," (it is definitely in the canine family with feet as delicate as a fox's) was alleged to have supernatural balls that become practically anything, a mattress, a sail. a sack, an umbrella, a roof, a club, or weapon to asphyxiate a hunter. I see this as welcome balance.
2. *Hawks in Japanese Poetry* An idiom coming from hawking? Actually, the most touching animal poem in the MANYOSHÛ concerns a hawk. The affection of the poet for his bird moistens this reader's eyes.

腹たてて丸う成たる生海鼠哉 桃丸

hara tatete marû naritaru namako kana – tôgan (c1790)

(belly/gut-stands[get angry/upset] round becomes sea-slug!/?/ô/the)   #197

angry
sea slug turns
round

While a weakened sea slug may flatten against the seabed, thereby reducing its visibility, current-catching surface and its chance of being bitten, one that is picked up or prodded generally shrinks longitudinally. The original poem is very clever. It fuses the idiom "belly-stand," meaning to be angry, to the concept of the (non-standing) sea slug as all torso=stomach, while contradicting both the Sino-Japanese metaphorical convention of *roundness-as-peaceful* and the normal way people interpret the sea slug's reaction (fear/discomfort). The metaphor does not English, but we can still appreciate the bolt from the blue, an Angry Sea Slug! And, if we think about it, Tôgan's logic is not completely unfounded, for a round sea slug is also a hard sea slug:

腹立てて拳をつくる海鼠哉　敬丸

hara tatete kobushi o tsukuru namako kana – keigan (keigu+tôgan)

(belly-standing[angry] fist make/making seaslug!/?/ô/the/behold)   #198

angry
sea slug makes
a fist!

Lacking the play on traditional metaphor, this ad-hoc haiku doesn't cut the cheese, but it does convey one truth: whatever sea slug makes, it puts its whole body into it. When Keigu made a fist of Tôgan's ball he had not realized a woman describing an auction – imagine trays lifted up roughly enough that the sea slugs roll about and occasionally fall off – beat him to the punch with this *bonafide* haiku:

海鼠糶る拳のごとくころがるを 井阪月子

namako seru kobushi no gotoku korogaru o – izaka tsukiko (2001)

(seaslug auction(v) fist-like rolls-about!/oh/alas)   #199

sea slug auction
something like fists
rolling about

Whether the "fists" are made from fear or anger – neither of which really apply to an animal whose nerves do not care to come together and brainstorm – doing this, turning the whole body into a knuckle sandwich, is what stops small fish from tearing off pieces, or larger ones from chomping down and pulling it from crevices, etc. It is in fact, a much more sophisticated defense than fisticuffs, for shrinking to increase the density is not the only mechanism for the sea slug's remarkable hardening by which flesh one can easily poke a nail through by hand turns into one that requires the use of a hammer. [1]

---

1. *Instant Hardening* How do they do it? The plate-mail armor of sea slug's ancestors has not completely vanished, but has metamorphosed into a more subtle form of chain-mail comprised of calcite crystals, "ossicules" of calcium carbonate. Moreover, the sea slug "can alter, rapidly and reversibly, the stiffness of their 'collagenous' connective tissues, commonly referred to as 'mutable connective tissues' (MCTs)." As a child, I was astounded by the unwashable slime of the conch and remember (probably wrongly) that its chemical composition became the recipe for STP→

嬲 ら れ て 球 に な り た る 海 鼠 か な 福 本 鯨 洋

naburarete tama to naritaru namako kana – fukumoto geiyô (contemp)

#200   (manhandled/baited[1] ball/gem into becomes sea slug!/?/ǿ/the/behold)

game

sported with
it turns into a ball
the sea slug

This more recent haiku is almost as clever as Tôgan's. A ball protects itself by going wherever it's hit or kicked, so this sea slug's meek behavior associates nicely with the *Trusting Sea Slug* metaphor.   It

→ motor oil. But the *holothurian's* dynamic mechanism, possessed to a lesser degree by all echinoderms, is far more wondrous, and even readers with as little interest in understanding hard science as me, should enjoy the following excerpts from Margot Higgin's remarkably readable synopsis of findings announced in an article by Greg K. Szulgit and Robert E. Shadwick of the Scripps Institutioin of Oceanography published in the *Journal of Experimental Biology* which "examines the amazing properties of the connective tissues of the humble sea cucumber *Cucumaria frondosa"* (not our species, but close enough):

"Szulgit and Shadwick investigated the mechanism behind this mutability by subjecting slices of sea-cucumber skin to a battery of mechanical tests. They find that alterations in stiffness are caused by the linking and unlinking of long, elastic collagenous fibres running through the tissue, and not by changes in the viscosity of the fluid medium surrounding the fibres. . . . over the past few years, researchers found that simply by freezing and thawing the entire dermis (underlying skin) of this animal, they could cause the inner part of the dermis to stiffen, while the outer dermis became very compliant. Following this work, Szulgit and Shadwick produced extracts of each dermal layer and attached them to segments of sea-cucumber dermis in various settings and treatments: varying the amount of calcium, freeze-thawed against fresh tissue, and so on. In general, they find that inner dermis extract stiffens things, whereas outer dermis extract makes things go soft, irrespective of any other treatment. In other words, sea-cucumber dermis appears to contain two different substances that affect stiffness – it does not depend on calcium [as previously believed].

Mechanical tests on segments of dermis showed a very clear signal: as stiffness increases, elastic fibres in the tissue (collagen) contribute relatively more to this stiffness than viscous materials (the soft materials in which the collagen fibres are embedded). In other words, stiffness was accompanied by an increase in resilience. All this points to collagen fibres, and their structure, as determinants of stiffness. When force is applied to

the dermis – a few gentle taps will do – the elastic collagen fibres somehow link up, making a tough, resilient network that runs through the entire tissue, stiffening it." (Macmillan Magazines Ltd 2000 - NATURE NEWS SERVICE)

The seemingly incongruous combination of greater elasticity and stiffness is very useful, for, as Higgins writes – and many articles agree – the sea cucumber can "provide insights into the behavior of 'smart materials' in general." For example, University of New Mexico researchers "plan to harness" this capability to "develop novel synthetic materials with dynamically controlled stiffness," leading to "artificial skins" that may show up on plant floors as anything from protective clothing to packaging materials" DARPA ... (gyre.org Critters kindle military curiosity (cache) – Staff – InTech – May 01, 2001) To my amateur eye, the sea slug seems like a sort of cornstarch with the ability to hold a shape without a container, respond rapidly to more variables than touch alone, keep hard for more varying lengths of time after stimulus is ceased and lacking the Achilles' heel of corn starch – or silly putty, for that matter – fracturability if twisted or bent when hard. (If you find this incomprehensible because you have not played with corn starch, go out and buy some immediately!)

1. *Manhandled in Japanese*. The Chinese character I glossed as "manhandles/baited" and translated as "sported with" comprises two small male *characters* around a female *radical*, but I doubt that effects the reading.   Describing the dastardly character for *naburu* (manhandle) is hard, for radicals are what generally make up *complex characters*, yet there is no "male" radical. "Man" is made of *two* radicals, "field+strength". "Women," though they must put up with being baited by characters such as *naburu* (three women together make "noisy," one under a roof "contentment" or "cheap," etc.) at least have *a radical of their own.* Poor man, he must *do* something to exist: he is forced to be a "human-*doing*." Lucky woman can do *nothing*: she can just *be*.

also reminds us of Lewis Carroll's, or rather, Alice's hedgehog croquette balls. But would a hard sea slug do for a ball? Put into figures, sea slugs that can be easily perforated when relaxed can withhold up to 14,000 pounds per square inch when tensed.[1] That is far more resilient than cement stucco (3,000 pounds per square inch) and would theoretically [2] hold up to a shark bite (12,000 pounds per square inch) or a baseball bat (When ball and bat meet, this "surprisingly violent" collision generates forces "in excess of 8,000 pounds per square inch" writes someone who neglected to give figures for, say, bunt versus homerun force, so I do not know where exactly where the sea slug stands in this). Geiyo's sea-slug-as-ball makes sense in another way, too. As biologist Motokawa Tatsuo of the Tokyo Institute of Technology, points out, "most other animals are either locomotion-oriented with little mechanical protection or protection-oriented with no locomotory activities," whereas echinoderms incorporate both designs.[3] So, it is correct to combine the ball-like hardening with motion.

俎に縮みきつたる海鼠かな　荒川遊季
manaita ni chijimikittaru namako kana – arakawa yûki (1997)
(carving board-on shrunken-up[to full extent] sea slug!/?/ó/the/behold)   #201

on the cutting board
a sea slug shrunken until
it cannot shrink

if i had a hole

on the block
completely shrunken
a sea slug

This contemporary poem exchanges the superfluous spineless spine of Fusui's 1773 shrunken sea slug for the cutting board – English lacks a single word for it, so I humpty-dumptied "block" – and defies translation with the powerful helper-verb *kittaru,* which makes the shrinking for more active than the descriptive "shrunken until . . ." or "completely shrunken." Here, we face the real sea slug, about to meet its fate. Although the haiku has not a sign of explicit feeling in it,   I do not think a more piteous

1. *Pressure Withstanding Figure*   "I measured the stiffness of the dermis of *Actinopygia echinites*. It was 3MPa(mega Pascal), that is about 14,000 Ibs/inch^2."(MT corresp).   This is almost three times stronger than necessary to withstand a stiletto heel of 1/16th inch area bearing the full weight of a 300 Ib woman (i.e., 4,800Ibs./Inch^2) or one of 1/64th inch area bearing the weight of a 200 Ib woman (12,800 Ibs/Inch^2). This is not to say a sea slug would be safe on the sidewalks of Paris. The response of the sea cucumber is not merely physical, but a complex nervous one, involving "mechanicoreceptor-sensory nerve-motor, nerve-effector [secretory] cells," etc.. In other words, the heels of the first few women would pierce it before it could fully tense. In this respect, the cornstarch mentioned earlier has the advantage of the dead, for its mechanical reaction is immediate. Why did a response that takes seconds, or even minutes not doom the sea cucumber? Mermaids don't wear high heels and, "the sea cucumber is a quite large animal compared to the possible predatory fish. Predators have to attack many times because they cannot swallow a sea cuke. This seems to be one of the reasons the response is slow." (M.T. corresp)

2. *Theoretical Strength* Pressure related statistics are fun but, by themselves, mean little, because the actual ability to withstand force varies greatly depending upon the size of the area in contact in ways not directly correlated to the area. Material A might stop a needle that Material B could not stop at much lower pressure, yet be less able to resist a fist-sized impact. Material C might be able to resist high-speed impact better than Material D, which for its part could better resist slow-speed impact, etc..

3. *Protection+Movement= MAC* Motokawa did not find "mutable connective tissue" (see last note) sufficient to describe what connected the unique exoskeleton-like endoskeleton behind his favorite animal's ability to protect itself mechanically and to move around.   In an oral contribution to the Calacademy Echinoderm Conference (199_) he suggested a word of his coinage, "mechanically active connective tissue (MAC)" instead.

description of a sea slug possible than this sharply focused masterpiece! A fish about to be turned into sashimi, flops and quivers on the cutting board. Our meek subject simply shrinks.

庖 丁 の 切 れ 味 を 待 つ 海 鼠 か な 　川 崎 展 宏
hôchô no kireaji o matsu namako kana – kawasaki nobuhiro (contemp)
(knife's cut-taste/feeling[blade] waits/awaits seaslug[subj]!/?/ó/the/behold)

#202

> a sea slug
> waiting for the touch
> of a knife
>
> ~
>
> a sea slug
> awaits the blade
> of my knife

Though we know a sea slug does not wait to be chopped up (as we wait, counting down before surgery), we cannot help but feel for it, as described. Unlike the haiku before and after, I imagine Kawasaki's sea slug resting calmly in a tub. The Japanese *matsu* is less active than the English "*a/wait,*" so the poem does not make the sea slug more knowing than it really is.

庖 丁 の 刃 に ち ぢ み け り 寒 海 鼠 　坪 根 里 杏
hôchô no ha ni chijimikeri kannamako – tsubone rikyo? (contemp?)
(knife blade-at/by shrink/ing-up cold[est-season]seaslug)

#203

> the cold month
> a sea slug shrinks up at
> my knife's touch
>
> ~
>
> in mid-winter
> a sea slug shrinks at
> the knife's touch

包 丁 の 刃 当 て ゝ 縮 む 海 鼠 か な 　無 名
hôchô no ha atatete chijimu namako kana – anon (contemp)
(knife-blade touching/touched shrinks/ing seaslug!/?/ó/the)

#204

> the sea slug
> shrinks up at the touch
> of my knife

English's need for articles can be infuriating. Japanese writers are so fortunate not to have to choose between "*a*" or "*the*" or "*my*," leaving such distinctions to the mind of the reader! (Only aesthetics – sound – dictated which translation got which article above.) Which is harder to cut – mentally speaking – a creature that keeps moving and flays about its limbs, or one that puts its head between its legs, like the sea slug would, if it had them? Perhaps that depends on the personality of the cook. Which is the better haiku, the one where "cold" is brought into the picture to complicate the shrinking (is it temperature or fear?) or the one where it is not mentioned? Unless the poet, feeling sorry for his or her sea slug, picks it up and drives it back to the ocean to set it free, this is what comes next:

己が身に伏してもなまこ斬られけり　敬愚

ono ga mi ni fushitemo namako kirarekeri – keigu

([its]own body-in crouch/hide even seaslug cut/killed[+finality])   #205

chopped up
hiding within itself
the sea slug

ostrich

even hidden
within itself, sea slug
is carved up

hito-oni

the knife finds
a sea slug hiding deep
within itself

Sea slugs aren't evolved to face humans and their extrasomatic teeth of steel. But even if a knife can cut a frightened/angry/defensive hard sea slug, it might be kinder to catch a sea slug sleeping and cut it too quickly for it to catch on.   Here is a dark description of the scene Keigu plays with:

屈 託 の う ち に 切 ら れ し 海 鼠 か な　杉 山 望

kuttaku no uchi ni kirareshi namako kana – sugiyama nozomi (2001)

(despondency-within cut[passive] seaslug!/?/ó/the)   #206

truly miserable end

cut down
in its despondency
the sea slug

The shrunken condition of a sea slug translates into depression for a human. I assume this poem means the sea slug is cut up while looking miserable. From the same book of contemporary haiku, something more cheerful:

せ り 台 に 罪 あ る ご と く な ま こ 緊 る　林 薫 女

seridai ni tsumi aru gotoku namako shimuru – hayashi kunjo (1978)

(auction-block-on sin/crime has like/as-if, seaslug shrinks/tightens/tenses)   #207

auction block
sea slugs tighten up
looking guilty

on the auction block

tightening up
like a guilty party
the sea slug

精いっぱい縮みて海鼠糶られけり　戎谷久代

seiippai chijimite namako serarekeri – ebisudani hisayo (2001)

#208   (spirit/energy-full shrinking seaslug auctioned-off)

sea slugs shrinking
for all they are worth
are auctioned off

humbler than thou

doing their best
to shrink, sea slugs
up for auction

Two ridiculous haiku. The second is, too my mind, more original. Its humor is more tongue in cheek in the original, which depends mostly on *sei-ippai,* an expression describing someone doing their best to do something positive. It makes it seem the sea slug auction is the scene for some sort of shrinking competition, where most creatures up for auction would preen themselves and stick out their chest. Ah, but don't get me wrong, the same expression suggests sympathy felt by the poet for the sea slugs.

何 の 故 に 恐 縮 し た る 生 海 鼠 哉　漱 石

nan no yue ni kyôshukushitaru namako kana – sôseki (1867-1916)

#209   (what reason-for, timid/fearful/shrinking sea slug!/?/ó/the/'tis)

literal

what makes it
shrink up like that?
the sea slug

figurative

the sea slug:
why is it so easily
overwhelmed?

fanciful

what in the world
made the sea cucumber
a shrinking violet?

The expression *kyôshuku desuga* is used to excuse oneself as *feeling small,* from trespassing in matters in which another is more expert, being unduly flattered, butting in, and so forth. Sôseki cleverly uses the term in both the normal figurative sense of behaving in an obviously humble or fearful manner and the literal sense of shrinking. We have discussed literal shrinking enough already and we have seen some clever takes on it, but there is nothing like this *"why!"* Does the great novelist refer to trauma deriving from the maltreatment accorded the sea slug in the RECORD OF ANCIENT MATTERS? Or, is he, rather asking:

what makes me
feel so small, am i
a sea slug?

why are we
such sea slugs, always
feeling small?

Since Sôseki uses the sea slug to describe the mindset of the master of the cat – which is to say, himself – in *I Am a Cat* and as a metaphor of a wishy-washy attitude toward life in a speech to college students about "My Individualism" given in 1915, this identification is probable. A contemporary reply to Sôseki might be that this meekness is a habit that can and should be broken for it is bad not to be confident, courageous and even proud. I think we have enough such types around and would prefer to say that if meekness is in the sea slug's nature, bully for it!

凹 む 顔 見 た さ に 海 鼠 硬 直 す　高 沢 良 一
hekomu kao mitasa ni namako kôchokusu – takasawa yoshikazu (2003)
(concave/reclusive face see-desire-want/ing-from/by seaslug stiffens)　　　　#210

the sea slug
froze when i tried to see
its reclusive face

～

when i'd see
its self-effacing face
sea slug stiffens

The original poem is much more ambiguous than my translations. If I got it right, the poet was trying to get a good look at the "face" of the sea slug but was not getting much cooperation. I imagine he had to pick it up and may have put a fingertip to its mouth. I like the poem, for it is rare to find a sea slug touched for reasons that are not ulterior (for buying and/or culinary preparation). This next older poem depicts the mild-natured creature in a more fantastic manner:

蒟 蒻 の 角 む つ か し と 生 海 鼠 哉　左 次
konnyaku no kado muzukashi to namako kana – saji (1774?)
(devil's tongue's corners-difficult [cantankerous] [says/and] seaslug!/?/ô/the)　　　#211

a sea slug
thinks devil's tongue
too sharp

Konnyaku is a food of little nutrition of a consistency between jello and pig-knuckles made from a plant that translates as "devil's tongue." It is often served in tofu-like sharply edged blocks.[1] Since there are both sharply-cornered devil's tongue sweet-rice cakes (*konnyaku-mochi*) – not really sweet-rice, but devil's tongue shaped like it was – and round-edged sea-slug sweet-rice cakes[2] (*namako-mochi*) – not really sea slug, but *mochi* so shaped – I thought the poem meant either "not succeeding

Sharp-edged Konnyaku The clean-cut edges of the devil's tongue cake, if such is the right word for a hard jello-like texture, gave rise to a facetious insult as beloved by philologists as it is seldom used: " "Hit your head against a corner of *konnyaku* and die!" (*konnyaku no kadoni atama o buttsukete shine!*) I would be curious to know its first usage!
Sweet Rice Cakes English lacks words for rice, so what Japanese call *mochi* becomes "sweet rice." It is a round yet sharp-tipped rice, stickier and sweeter than *rissotto,* the plumpest of the regular rices. The "cake" is not textured like wheat or corn cake, but completely smooth and, toasted, eaten with soy-sauce and laver (without sugar), put in soup or stuffed with sweet bean paste – or, more recently, a large strawberry – and sold as a confectionary. *Mochi* "cakes" that require toasting are generally sold in sharp-edged rectangular blocks even today in the Kanto=Tokyo area, while they are usually round in other parts.

with making smartly cut rice cakes, I (or, the wife) made them rounded off," or, "the devil's tongue / being too damn rough [to make] / sea slug it is!" But, KS's explanation, that the mellow sea slug, taking the (similarly blubber-like) devil's tongue for a fellow creature,[1] finds a problem in its character as expressed by its rectangularity – common idiom for a hard heart, for being ornery and uptight in Japanese – is far more delightful than mine, so it *must* be right.[2]

蒟蒻 の 砂 を 呑 み 込 む 海 鼠 哉　 敬 愚

konnyaku no suna o nomikomu namako kana --- keigu

#212

(devil's-tongue's sand[obj] drink-in seaslug!/?/ó/the/behold)

food cycle

sand spit out
by the devil's tongue
feeds sea slug

#213, #214, #215, 下

1. *Konnyaku* and *Namako* Their blubber-like feeling is but one of reasons the sea slug and the devil's tongue are of one ilk. Both are of dull color. One twitches, one palpitates when jiggled. Both are remarkably slimy: devil's tongue in white sauce (*shiraae*) was one of several dishes considered good to eat for slipping into paradise. (OJD has a quote from a Joruri play. As it is short, I don't know if the dying person or a praying monk is advised to eat it, but a haiku found elsewhere confirms my impression for it associates *tororo* juice (a potato that grates into a slimy mass that was used for some *shirae*) with smoothly entering paradise (*gokuraku-ni sutto iki-keri tororo-shiru* – tôsen (d.1725)). Both are usually kept in a wooden tub (*oke*). Both are connected with ambiguity: a *devil's tongue Q&A* (*konnyaku-mondo*) is an unintelligible dialogue. Both are connected with ugliness: "like features on a devil's tongue" (*konnyaku-dama-ni me-hana tsuketa yô-na*). Both were synonyms for a coward: the devil's tongue was the more common insult, for its jello-like quaking is more obvious than sea slug's spinelessness, twitching and shrinking. Both were connected to the thick Japanese quilt (*futon*) for the shape they sometimes take: the devil's tongue was quilt in the argot of thieves. Both had sexual connotations and/or uses: slit devil's tongue was used for masturbation by men and, more rarely, as a pessary by women. Both were associated with sand: the devil's tongue was thought good to soak up and expel it from the belly and the balls. And both were served as *sashimi*:   I think that Rokuko's(?) "one sprig of plum / placed upon a plate / of sea slug" (*hachi no namako ume no hitoeda nosetekeri* 鉢 の 生海鼠梅 の 一 枝 乗せ て け り　 鹿 古) plays upon Basho's offering to dead Kyorai: "plum blossoms / and some *sashimi* of / devil's tongue" (*Kyoraishi-e tsukawasu //*

konnyaku-no sashimi-mo sukoshi ume-no hana). Kyorai, it so happens, wrote many sea slug poems.

2. *Witty or Wrong*   While there may well be uninteresting haiku, I always start translating with two assumptions: 1) if the poem is not witty, the reading is wrong and 2) the more satisfying the wit, the more likely the reading is correct. Here is a haiku that failed to make it: "the devil's tongue / gets no help / from sea slug" (*konnyaku ya namako no koto ni azukarazu* – seisei (1869-1937 蒟蒻や海 鼠 の 事 に 與 ら ず 青々). If there is wit, it is too ambiguous. The sea slug has only slightly more flavor than the equally neutral *konnyaku* so the poet feels they shouldn't be served together? A sort of competitive exclusion in the kitchen?   Is that enough? I hoped --- this translator is not neutral! – it might be read as an envoi to the poem where the sea slug is put off by the smartly cut *konnyaku,* to wit: "the devil's tongue / wants nothing to do with / the sea slug."   The latter being uncouth in form. But CS and CZ say "no way!" (a sea slug can have an opinion but the devil's tongue can not?). I felt tempted to make work for the English translation of *konnyaku*: "devil's tongue! / it can't gain purchase / on a sea slug!" but couldn't find any significance in it.   Then, when I found another Basho era poem: "the sea slug: / because of bonzes, cousin to / the devil's tongue" (*konnyaku no itoko wa sô de namako kana* – hakusetsu (b.1660) 蒟蒻の従弟は僧 で な ま こ 哉　 白 雪), KS hypothesized that bonzes may have called sea slug "devil's tongue" – as boar was once called "mountain-whale" because eating fish were thought less sinful than eating four-legged beasts – accordingly, the earlier poem could be read, " *'devil's tongue?'* / the sea slug is not / thrilled by it!" In that case, I think we might *also* read the poem in the main text as: "how hard to be / a square like devil's tongue!" / says sea slug." (KS thought that was stretching it too far.)

In one sense, devil's tongue and sea slug are symbiotic, for the former was popularly considered a way to rid our organs of excessive sand,[1] while the latter was and is known to devour sand. People ate it after doing their yearly soot-cleaning. A *senryu* points out what happened when Edo was covered with volcanic ash in 1707: "in houei 7 / devil's tongue showed / a price hike" (*houei yonen konnyaku no ne ga agari* – yanagitaru 149-27). But to return to the metaphor of the chapter, meekness:

己 が 身 に 角 を 埋 め 込 む 海 鼠 哉　敬 愚

onoga mi ni tsuno o umekomu namako kana – keigu
(my/own-body-in horn bury seaslug!/?/ô/the/behold)   #216

pacifish

ancient spikes
sleeping deep inside
the sea slug

Protected by smart material or not, the sea slug does not *seem* secure. The evolutionary choice to replace an exoskeleton with real spikes with a relatively smooth one – bits of calcium buried in bumps of muscle tissue called spicules – does seem a form of disarmament. Compare stepping on a sea cucumber to a sea urchin. The Japanese in the time of the old haiku poets went from being the best armed people in the world to one of the least well armed. They voluntarily gave up the gun.[2] In this, they follow the sea slug, for its ancestors were also more heavily armed.

闘 争 に 飽 き て 海 鼠 に 生 ま れ た る　正 木 ゆ う 子

tôsô ni akite namako ni umaretaru – masaki yûko (contemp)
(struggle/fighting-with tired/sick-of, seaslug/s-as born)   #217

tired out
from fighting sea slugs
are born

～

tired of fighting
i am a reborn
sea slug
now

1. ***Removing Sand with Devil's Tongue*** Folk wisdom has it that when men eat, they unwittingly swallow some sand which builds up in the belly and slowly finds its way to the balls from which it may be extracted only by konnyaku says folk wisdom (*konnyaku no sunabarai* and *konnyaku wa kintama no sunabarai*: OJD).   This may concern kidney stone, for small grains do come out of the urinary tract and/or *senki,* a sort of lumbago that inflamed the public imagination for one of the symptoms, swollen balls.   The official line is that the devil's tongue was to be eaten for the healing effect, but it just so happens that a piece of devil's tongue (the spring resembles that of whale-blubber) with a slit cut in it has, next to rolled up bedding, long been the most popular masturbatory device in Japan. Because of this, it is hard to tell if it really functions as a diuretic or got that reputation by someone misconstruing a euphemism for its use to relieve seminal buildup.

2. ***Giving up the Gun*** Within decades of learning how to make guns from the Portuguese in the mid-16th century,   Japanese had more guns than any European national state and were hundreds of years ahead of Europe in terms of the numbers of guns used in pitched battles. (See N. Perrine: *Giving Up the Gun*)   In the early 19th century Golownin warned that Japan could re-arm and quickly become a world power if it was not treated with respect by the West. His warning was ignored.

If the Japanese word for rebirth/reborn were shorter, I think it might have been in the haiku, and that is reflected in my second reading, which is, I think, the correct one.   But to return to the real sea slug:

海 鼠 ま た 此 巖 蔭 に 雌 伏 せ る   虚 子

namako mata kono iwakage ni shifukusuru – kyoshi 1874-1959)
(seaslug also this/these boulder/s-shade-in lie-low)

#218

> sea slugs
> also lie low
> by these boulders

> *laying low*
>
> the sea slugs
> also bide their time
> below boulders

Because sea slugs were strongly identified with sandy sea bottom – no doubt because of their greater visibility – Kyoshi's poem could be read as a mere correction of a stereotype, but the "lie low" connotation of *shifukusuru* (written with the Chinese characters "female+prone") suggests that Kyoshi is broadening the common description of sea slug meekness. Not only do they eat sand on the sea floor, but cower in the shadow of boulders. As in English, the poem also contains a touch of hope, for the word also has the connotation of biding one's time, as we have been for, at last(!), the title poem of this book:

浮 け 海 鼠 佛 法 流 風 の 世 な る ぞ よ   一 茶

uke namako buppôrufu no yo naru zo yo – issa (1814)
(float [up] sea-slug/s! buddha-law's flow-spread-world becomes!)

#219

> **it's yours to inherit**
>
> *rise, ye sea slugs!*
> *the day of judgment*
> *is nigh!*

The sea slug's meekness is Buddhist, but it is also evangelical: it belongs to the same ilk as the Christian meek who shall, God knows when, inherit the earth. That is what this best of Issa's sea-slug poems and one of the most dynamic haiku ever written by anyone suggests to me. I turned its first five syllabets into the title of this book because of this raw emotive power (Note that the beat of *uke namako*, like that of *open sesame!* is on the first and third of five syllabets/syllables.), rare in the world of haiku.* With this poem, Issa shows us how religious fervor does wonders for poetry – and I speak objectively as an agnostic – because it encourages the poet to speak directly to things.*

1. Uke Namako Style Style-wise, the closest poem to *uke namako,* I found is by Yayu: "go back monkey! / when your homeland hills / are brocade" (**kaere saru** kokyo-no yama mo nishiki toki). The feet are, however, on the first and fourth syllabets.

2. Religious Style   Issa often spoke directly to animals, even outside of a religious context, but I think it is the religious element that makes the imperative tense so good in this poem. I think religion likewise improves *nature essays*. It is especially valuable in English, which lacks the neutral exclamatory conjugations available to the Japanese and, for all its fine mimetic verbs, is nearly impossible to energize. After admitting that Annie Dillard filled Thoreau's shoes better than anyone else, Edward Abbey found one failing in her work: the over-use of the big G word. Funny, I loved *Tinker Creek* for the very same reason! Stylistically speaking, Annie Dillard did not call on our Lord in vain!

"Rise, ye sea slugs!" was written in the same year Issa haiku'ed that the world was undergoing some rapid change, or wished it so: *the world is changing by leaps and bounds! leaps and bounds! (yononaka wa dondodo naoru dondo kana)*. His leaps-and-bounds mimesis (*dondodo*) alludes to a Shinto ceremony held on the full moon's Small New Year, when the holiday decorations, first writings (some calligraphy expressing one's spirit for the year) and so forth were burnt in what was called the *dondo-yaki*, or "dondo roast.." [1] The implication of the poem would seem to be that he hopes that the old gets burnt up to bear a new world. Japanese Buddhists of the Jodo sect, some sub-sects of which had close Shinto connections, also had something like Christian culture's Millennial – or, should we call it "cargo cult?" – beliefs. These sometimes led to riots, mostly the sacking of grain wholesalers. Does Issa, then, mean that the lowly, the meek, and the ugly, that is to say, *sea slugs*, are about to inherit the earth? I cannot rightly say.

~   ~   ~   ~   ~   ~

As David Lanoue, who has written a book about Issa's faith, points out, "there is no "Last Judgment" in this [Shinran's] eschatological scheme." True, but as he kindly agreed, my translation does *bring the poem home* to the English/Christian reader. Here, is his culturally proper translation:

> floating sea slug
> buddha's law permeates
> this world!
>
> trans. david g lanoue

Lanoue writes that he takes Issa's "float, sea slug/s" to mean ""Keep on being yourself; keep up the good work; keep floating!" (corresp) Grammatically, this is problematic – all my Japanese advisors are strongly against it – but *perhaps* not utterly impossible interpretation.[2] But, if, for the sake of anomaly, *uke* is not read as an imperative, I would hypothesize an exclamatory:

> ***buddhism rules!***
>
> way to float,
> sea slug! the whole world
> is converted!

1. Dondo Coincidence? The songs sung by children dragging sea slugs to repel moles sometimes have the same emphatic mimesis as in the Shinto ceremony held on that same day. An example from Kyushu: *mogura ei **tonto**-kose tonari-no setchin mori kuyase* (hey, mole! get up with a start (*ton-to*)! eat up lots of the neighbor's shit!) An example given in my OJD: *mogura mochi uchi-ni ka namako-**don-no** otoori da* (mole owner, are you in? [or, is mole in his borrow?] don sea slug is now passing through!) Because of the lack of cloudy marks indicating pronunciation, it is hard to separate the written *dondo, tonto* and *don*. Orally, they are somewhat different, but over time such terms can become confused, like our *shoals/schools* of fish. CZ, who sent me the Kyushu ditty, also sent me one close to the OJD version, which in his English translation, reads: *"mole, mole, are you in your hole? mr. trepang gae to meet you! go out! go out!"* (The use of the South Asian term for *namako* and the Scottish "gae" reflects C.Z's eclectic mindset perfectly!) See *"The Exorcist Sea Slug"* in the Sundry Sea Slug section for more moles!

2. Perhaps Not Impossible. The diversity in the conjugation of Japanese verbs was tremendous – today, it is simpler, but still far beyond anything an English speaker can imagine – and, in some cases, makes it very hard to be absolutely certain. One takes the most likely reading that complements the poem. Unlikely readings are not wrong, but should always be noted. David G. Lanoue's Issa site has ample notes, so that his translations need not be swallowed whole. I hope the notes will soon come to include more alternative translations, as well.

Here, CZ boldly comments: "When a person dies and becomes-buddha (*jobutsu-suru*), it is called 'floating' (*ukabareru*)." Moreover, *uke* (float) is a homophone for *uke* (receive), as in the aphorism: "people receive with difficulty, Buddhist law is met with difficulty (*hitomi uke-gatashi, buppo ai-gatashi*)." This is used in the sense of "receiving the Buddhist law," that is to say accepting the mercy of Buddha and dying (literally translated, "die" is much more pleasant: "paradise-buddha-become do!") cheerfully. So, it would seem Issa's poem may include the nuance: "die in peace, sea slug!"

invitation to paradise

rise, sea slug!
die in buddha's world
as a buddha!

If we also credit Issa with being a typical Shinano man with a voracious appetite and having an Ikkyû-like (Rabelaisian?) humor there is a wee possibility of this being the "right" reading. I.e., he licks his lips and says, *Let me Buddhify thee!*

晩 酌 に 海 鼠 お だ ぶ つ す る 夕 べ 高 沢 良 一
banshaku ni namako odabutsu suru yûbe – takasawa yoshikazu (2003)
#220
(evening-drink-with/for seaslug honorable-buddha-do tonight)

drinking tonight
this evening we buddhify
a sea slug

~

drinking tonight
tonight we sacrifice
a sea slug

~

for nibblies
tonight i'll ruin
a good sea slug

As slang, "Buddhification" means to *kill, do-in, polish-off,* or, just to *ruin.* While the last reading, i.e. the poet being self-denigrative about his ability to prepare sea slug is the superficial significance of the poem, Takasawa writes that the term (and, by extension his use of it) reflects "the common *animism* of the Japanese" and of "*awaremi*" (corresp), something I'd describe as bitter-sweet compassion (for the sea slug in particular and the nature of life in general). My second reading, above, is more in the nature of a paraverse. I include it because the use of "sacrifice" makes the sea slug something special, which it is, but realize it is wrong because a sacrifice is killing something for a God, and that is a type of cruelty foreign to the Japanese, or rather to their Gods.

I was delighted to receive Takasawa's poem with its example of a contemporary Buddhification of a sea slug only days before the final deadline for this book; but, to return to Issa's poem, I fear the most likely reading is probably not Buddification. I stick with my original understanding, which, in more neutral language – minus the *ye* and *judgment* – is:

it's your time!

rise, sea slugs!
the gospel of buddha
fills this world

CZ's explanation ends with a gem: "The dark, depressing old era (when the gods lacerated the sea slug's mouth) is now over; forget those *Records of Ancient Matters (Kojiki)* ! [1] It is an age of Buddhism, so speak up!" If I may rephrase: *Buddha rules! So, Sea Slug, speak up now, or forever hold your peace!* Perhaps we may say that sea slug chose that *peace.*

聖 者 の 訃 海 鼠 の 耳 を 貫 け り   普 羅

seija no fu namako no mimi o tsuranukeri – fura (1883-1954)

(holy-person(saint)'s tiding[of death] seaslug's/s' ears pierce/s)   #221

when saints die
the tiding pierces the ears
of sea slugs

There are a number of Japanese sayings about how news about good or bad deeds reaches this and that obscure place or creature and the vice-versa about how the will-power of a tiny creature can stir the heavens. Strangely, the sea slug, the sea-floor denizen par excellence – i.e., literally, the lowest of the low [2] – is absent in these sayings. Fura corrects this with his epigram of a haiku. I would guess there is more to the haiku, but I prefer Issa's call to activity to this passivity. So, back to the title poem, which I will honor with a few more paraverses bringing out allusions possibly intended by the original.

浮 け 海 鼠 言 わ ぬ ・ が ・ 仏 の 神 無 月   敬 愚

uke namako iwanu [ga] hotoke no kannazuki – keigu

(rise seaslug/s say/speak-not [is] buddha/blessing/blissful godless-month)   #222

rise, ye sea slugs!
in the godless month your
silence is golden

～

rise up, sea slugs
the godless month belongs
to silent souls

～

rise up, sea slug
the godless month is yours
oh, silent buddha

1. *Records of Ancient Matters* For what it's worth. It just so happens that this very seventh-month of Bunka 11 when Issa's sea slug poems are entered in his journal, he had a copy of said book (the volume of the Age of Gods, which includes the sea slug) sent to his friend Buntora as a return-gift after receiving a sack of large eggplant from him. (See: Yaba Katsuyuki: ISSA DAIJITEN (taishukan: 1993) pg 90)

2. *Lowest of the Low* The holothurian is not the champion deep-liver – the smaller aerobes (oxygen-breathing life) that it feeds on have that honor, and it does not dig so deeply into the sea floor as sea worms, but it is *the* exemplar of bottom-dwelling in Japanese culture. And one sub-class -- granted, it is far from the cuciform creature imagined by poets – lives in a manner worthy of particular note, for it might be said to perpetually mimic the proverbial ostrich with some astonishing differences. The molpadidd lives "buried in the substratum, mouth down, with the tail projecting into the water for purposes of respiration" as "it feeds by ingesting quantities of mud." (Details decontexted from *Chitin in Echinoderms? Tentacle sheaths in the deep-sea holothurian Ceraplectana trachyderma (Holothuroidea: Molpadiida)* by AM Kerr and Pawson, D. L. 2001) [We noted another similarly buried, but with mouth up with anus, no?]

Here, I contrast the attempt to force speech on the sea slug by the ancient goddess and the esoteric Buddhist teaching of silence. In the first reading, where the *ga* ("is" in this context) is included, *blindness* rather than ignorance *is bliss*. I substitute silence, though in translation the bliss ends up *golden*. The second and third readings, using different connotations for *hotoke,* respectively, are based on a *ga*-less version, which veers from the idiom. Here the "speak-not" modifies the *hotoke* and suggests a certain image of Buddha, where he was said to impart his wisdom without speaking.

浮 け 海 鼠 御 神 が 留 守 に 笑 む 仏　　敬 愚

uke namako mikami ga rusu ni emu hotoke – keigu

#223   (rise seaskug/s, honorable-gods absence-in/during smiles buddha)

mum is the word

rise, ye sea slugs!
the old gods are all gone
and buddha smiles

If Issa was thinking along the lines CZ and I imagine, he should have added a caption to the effect that the haiku belonged to *kannazuki* (or *kaminazuki),* the first month of winter, when the Shinto gods caucus in Izumo, leaving the rest of the country godless. As a Mutamagawa senryu baldly put it: "The Godless Month / Buddha now assumes / The reign of the world." – Blyth trans. (*kaminazuki hotoke no miyo ni narinikeri*). Since Issa left many uncut gems (haiku that require contextualization to really be appreciated) in his journal, this godless interpretation is *possible*, especially when we consider the fact that he wrote *another* "Buddhist-law-flow-permeates" (*buppô-rufu*) poem four years earlier: "the leaves fall / and buddhist-law permeates / this place" (*ochiba shite buppôrufu no arike kana*　お ち 葉 し て 仏 法 流 布 の 在 所 [1] 哉). In old haiku, leaves falling and creating a mess were associated with the tenth month and the absence of the Shinto gods. The month was also marked by cold showers written with the Chinese characters meaning "time-rain." Until recently, this "time-rain" was one of the top ten or twenty haiku themes – there are a hundred times more poems about it than about the *namako!* – so I shall not even begin to delve into its mystique here, other than to say that its coldness and ability to show up at any time made it popular with Buddhists who believed it helped us see just how sorry a thing life without enlightenment is. I could not help coupling it with Issa's "Rise" poem:

[神 無 月] 浮 け 海 鼠 し ぐ れ 呑 ま せ ば 口 直　　敬 愚

[kannazuki] uke namako shigure nomaseba kuchinaoshi – keigu

#224   (god-less-month // rise seaslug/s, time-rain[cold drizzle] drink-if/when mouth-refresh[renewal])

the gods are gone

rise, ye sea slugs!
the cold rain now falling
is just your taste

with buddha's grace

rise, ye sea slugs,
let the cold rain help
repair your mouth!

1. *Arike*=在所 There is a possibility Issa used a mistaken character and really was thinking of 在家, pronounced *zaike* and meaning a *layman* rather than simply the place for something. In that case, the poem might read: *"the leaves fall / and buddhist law spreads out / to all laymen."* The link with the *Rise, Ye* poem would grow stronger with this reading, for the slug would be the ultimate layman.

Nevertheless, a Godless Month reading is not *very* probable, because sea slugs formally belong to the second month of Winter rather than the first. But it is not improbable, for we also know that they were sometimes marketed, not to mention haiku'ed by this time of the year. A collection edited by Somaru, whom Issa spent some time with as a young man, includes a lame but informative "ho, is it now / an early winter treat / the sea slug" (*hitofuyu no mono ni wa arata namako kana* – kadô (1790) 一 冬 の 物 に は 更 た 生 海 鼠 哉　歌童). The "first-winter" (*hitofuyu*) means the first of the three months of winter. Moreover, none other than Issa's employer and teacher Seibi left a haiku about the Tenth-Night, or *jûya,* a monthly prayer service of Issa's Pure Land faith that take place on the Tenth day of the Tenth Month (the Godless Month, first of the winter).　　　　　　　　　(#225 上)

「見 佛 聞 法」 海 鼠 さ へ 此 時 に あ ふ 十 夜 哉　成 美
[kenbutsumonbô] namako sae kono toki ni au jûya kana – seibi (1748-1816)
("see-shaka-hear-[buddhist]law" seaslug even, this time-at meet tenth-night!/?/ó/the/'tis)　　　　#226

prayer meeting

at this time
you even meet up with
sea slugs

[?]

even sea slugs
gather at this time
the tenth night

#227(下)

Seibi's contemporary Michihiko (1746-1819) went even further: "venders come round / with sea slug and whatnot / the following moon" (*namako nado urikuru ato no tsukimi kana*海 鼠 な ど う り 来 る 後 の 月 見 哉　道彦). The "following moon" means 9-13 (the Moon after the Harvest Moon) so we know sea slug – unless we are talking about some illusive metaphorical sea slug here – was occasionally marketed from the fall.[1] Not knowing how common this was, it is hard to tell if the "even" applies to the earliness of the date or the unexpected animal food appearing at a Buddhist meeting. The fact that tenth-night octopus (*jûya-dako,* small octopae) were caught and vended at that time – and monks were called *tako,* or octupae (probably because their shaved heads resembled the creature) – may have given the poem a twist of associative humor. The poem also makes me wonder whether Issa's sea slug/s might, *by any chance,* be about sea slugs for sale, perhaps in the person of the sea slug vendor, though I prefer interpreting Issa's "Rise, ye sea slugs!" as a self-exhortation, a wake-up call to the sleepy-head poet (and his wife?) to float up and out of his/their futon to attend an important local tenth-night meeting.

up and adam
a buddhist world waits
for you, sea slug

It would be especially suitable if it was raining on that day, for a proverb claimed one *must* go outside for two reasons: *to hear Buddha's law expounded* or *to see what the rain is doing to one's straw roof.* And that straw-roof could have set Issa to thinking about our charge. The poem, so Englished, can be read as an exhortation to spiritually lazy laymen to become religiously committed – as Yaba (corres)

1. Fall Sea Slug Since the thirteenth day of the third month of fall was ideally spent moon-viewing with a courtesan in the pleasure quarters, the sex-tool sea slug (see *Lubricious Sea Slugs*) may be alluded to in Michibiko's haiku, but sea slugs *also* had to have been available, for even allusions require reality.

hypothesizes, along the same line as his reading of the *yuck yuck* (*iya iya*) poem, in which case I might title the above poem **religious awakening** – but I *prefer* to imagine Issa as a self-castigator than as a preacher. Or – there is a longer shot yet: white-haired, one-tooth 52 year-old Issa might be celebrating his good fortune at finally gaining his home (half-a-house, at any rate), getting married – he married a woman about half his age that year and began marking down his refreshments (as Mark Twain called coitus) in his journal – and through this socialization "acquiring a human face" as one senryu put it (*nyôbô-o motte ninsô tsura-ni nari*). Could this have proven to the religious poet that he was indeed living in a merciful Buddhist world?

the ugly old poet

rise, ye sea slugs!
buddhist law must now prevail:
issa's got some tail!

Forgive the *tail*. With sea creatures involved, I couldn't help myself. Readers may replace "some tail" with "a wife/life." Regardless, it is not the meaning that makes Issa's poem great. It is the sound.

uke namako!

Except in the vague overall sense that there is something sublime about calling sea slugs to action. With the sea slug-dragging haiku (if that is how we read the double *yuck!* poem) only two lines=poems away from this one in Issa's journal, the pathos of the lowly creature he exhorts heightens. Think about it! Not only does the sea slug lie close to senseless on the sea-floor, but it (or its namesake) gets dragged all over the farm!

rise, ye sea slugs!

I think we could all say *amen* to this. What is hard to understand, however, is the extent to which these mild creatures were accepted as metaphors of identity in Issa's day. As we see elsewhere, because they were used to indicate spineless character and stuporous states individuals might be described as sea slugs, but is it possible for someone – like, Issa, for example -- to identify *themselves* with the sea slug? That, I do not know. And, the same thing could be said for sea *slugitude* as a national trait. As mentioned with respect to the nationalistic sea slug that turned out to be no such thing (pg__), despite the long seclusion, Japanese thought of themselves as great warriors, braver than any other people. In this respect, they were like the Europeans who roved about on the outside, respecting only people as courageous – suicidal when facing European guns – as they themselves. No, they were anything but sea slugs! But times have changed; Japanese have changed:

#228, #229 (下)

Straw and Sea Slugs Believe it or not, there were no less than three well-known associations. 1) Straw is the sea slug's nemesis: "Cutting a sea slug with straw" was supposedly easy, and meant, if I am not mistaken, something "like twisting the arm of a baby," while "binding a sea slug with straw" was thought to make them melt and idiomatically is used to describe someone made to shut up and give in;   2) Straw was used to strengthen the bulging grout in a brick construction called a "sea-slug wall." (*namakokabe*); 3) Cheap "sea slug collars" (*namako-eri*), which served in the same capacity as a scarf to keep the neck warm in the winter, were generally stuffed with straw: "sea-slug collar, melts/unstuffs also, night-hawk=whore's straw shack" (*namakoeri tokeru mo wara no yodaka koya* – yanagidaru (107) 海鼠衿と けるも藁の夜鷹小屋　柳多留). The "also" conversely alludes to the low-class street-walker's business of packing-in (*tsume-komi*) customers. They pack them in and unpack=unload them, too, in shacks with mud and straw walls, scattered straw on the floors (where *tatami,* would be normal) and straw, rather than cotton or silk-refuse, etc.. stuffed futon. I have come across one senryu combining these associations: "wall sea slugs, too / pull out straw stuck in them / and they crumble" (*kabe no namako mo wara sasu ga dete kuzuru* – yanagidaru (122-26, 123-61,125-11) 壁の海鼠もわら苆（す さ）が出て崩　柳多留).

秋 津 島 化 し 海 鼠 に な り に け り 　 圓 水
akitsushima bakeshi namako ni narinikeri – ensui (2000)
(dragonfly-island metamorphizes sea slug-to becomes [+finality])

#230

> metamorphosis
> the dragonfly isle turns
> into a *namako*

> ***apostichopus japonicus***

> this island
> once a dragonfly is
> now a sea slug

Akitsu was the name for the Nara area, the ancient capital of Japan. The etymologies are too confusing to sort out here, but it is sometimes written with the same characters as "dragonfly" and I think that was the allusion here. Japan was once thought to be shaped like a dragon-fly. This contemporary haiku suggests that Japan is now a dull, reactive nation rather than a quick hunter. *Meekness has, finally, been nationalized.*

This haiku, I thought, bears investigation. I failed to reach the poet, but two members of the Right Brain Haiku (migi-nô haiku) association commented about Ensui's haiku on-line:

> Come to think about it, the main island of Japan (Honshu) *does* look like a sea slug [with the increased sea zone, all the more so]. This makes me recall an SF novel by Komatsu Arimiya (zai-kyo?) I read long ago, where the Japanese archipelago was a sleeping dragon that wakes up and swims off. If it were a sea slug, then what?
> – Shunpo

> Considering many aspects of our history, a sea slug is far more credible and interesting. – Areiko

I like the poem a lot and because I like it, I think I would like to change the original slightly.[1] *Bakeshi* (化し) is an expression too active, too magical, too monstrous, too full of connotation. Even if we don't imagine someone waving a wand over the archipelago and transforming it in a moment, the pure power of the verb *bakeru*[2], used for ghost stories or writing turning into gibberish by faulty software, overwhelms the reader. The less in-your-face verb *kashite* (化して) would be *far* better. This little change turns the poem from an SF haiku into a true poetic masterpiece, in my opinion. To tell the truth, my second translation of the poem does just that and more. It states what *was*, what *is*, so we know things have changed, and that is enough.

1. *Improving Poems* One of the delights of the extremely short poem is that it allows you to think seriously about how to improve one without spending excessive time on it, as might be the case for, say, reworking a sonnet. A top haiku show on TV features a panel of experts and an invited poet who spend most of their time selecting and improving haiku sent in by the public. *No poem is pure idea.* It is words; and words can often be improved by others. By suggesting ways to improve a poem, I do not insult the poet but express my love for the poem that is worth my while.
2. *Bakeru* While I do not care for the verb *bakeru* in this haiku, I do like it very much. I particularly appreciate it because it is one of many Japanese words I know English lacks. In short, it combines the magic of *bewitch* with *transform* in the sense of *metamorphose*.

蜑 の 子 や 生 海 鼠 に す べ る 塩 干 潟　尚 白

kani no ko ya namako ni suberu shiohigata – shôhaku(1649-1722)

#231

(crab-child/ren: sea-slug-on slip low-tide pool)

a tide pool
a small crab slides on
a sea-slug

(un)still life

a tide pool
little crabs slipping
on sea slugs

This type of wonderfully attentive realism is rare in old haiku. Unless the reader is pathologically ticklish, the picture is delightful. Though walked on by tiny feet, Shôhaku's sea slug is no suffering Gulliver. The poem presents a masterful contrast – inert and "deep" creature *versus* skitterish and shallow one – and offers a pleasant alternative to Sôchô's dream as exaggerated by Shôzan, or was it Kyoroku? (old Japanese prose is not my *forte*) of, presumably larger, crabs viciously sticking it to the sea slugs. The sea slug in Shôhaku's poem is meek and presumably helpless, but it is no victim. It makes me think back to those *Trusting Sea Slugs*.   Were the sea slugs cast up on the shore really doomed? [1]   Is it not possible the tide returned in time to carry them to a tide pool, where the wee pointy toe-tips of tiny crabs [2] tickled them awake?

1. *Sea Slugs on Shore Revisited*   On the beach where I grew up, sea cucumbers that were washed in and got coated with rough coral sand, did not make it to the next tide, but in the case of a tidal flat where sea slugs that are not knocked around in sandy water or tossed up onto the beach, simply find themselves out of water when the tide falls, we may find a different picture entirely. Here is a scene from the southern tip of Espiritu Santo Island, as described by Steinbeck and Ricketts:

"As the tide dropped on the shallow beach, we saw literally millions of these cucumbers. They lay in clusters and piles between rocks and under the rocks, and as the tide went out and the tropical sun beat on the beach, many of them became quite dry without apparent injury. Most of these holothurians were from five to eight inches long, but there were great numbers of babies some not more than an inch in length . . ." (LSC)

I do not know if the *namako*, or *Apostichopus japonicus*, is so tough as these *Holothuria lubrica* in the Sea of Cortez.

2. *Little Crabs* Sometimes, "a single or a mated pair of small *Lissocarcinus orbicularis* commensal crabs are found among the tentacles or in the mouth, but can occur elsewhere on the body, including the anus" of some varieties of sea cucumber (Debbie & Stan Hauter in http://saltaquarium.about. com/ blcucumberfam_stichopodiae.htm.) I do not know whether they are ever found in the *namako*, but if they are, this may be them playing on the roof of their live dwelling.

10
<u>the ugly sea slug</u>

外見より中身が大事海鼠かな 未知
gaiken yori nakami ga daiji namako kana – anon (contemp)
(outside-looks-more-than content-the important seaslug!/?/ǿ/the/'tis)   #232

take sea slugs
what's inside counts more
than the outside

viz.

what's inside
counts more than looks:
the sea slug

This haiku is simple to the point of inanity. About all one can say in its favor is that it gives a new name to the old saw about beauty coming from the inside: *namako*. As such, it also confirms our natural feeling towards the sea slug: *You sure are ugly!*

かわいいぞ切断面のナマコかな 魚子ちゃん
kawaii zo setsudanmen no namako kana – uoko-chan
(cute/pretty[+emphatic] section seaslug!/?/ǿ/the/'tis)   #233

"as a picture"

a section
of sea slug really
is pretty!

Ugliness taken for granted makes prettiness worth mentioning. I do not know if the poet [1] is describing a latitudinal cross-section on a slide or a draftsman's rendition of a longitudinal cut. In the former case, the symmetry and colors might be attractive, while the tree-like lungs adorn the latter. Either way, a sea slug looks better *inside* than we do (although I doubt that was what the previous haiku had in mind!). Outside, however, the honest human eye, that is to say, one untainted by objectivism, misunderstood relativity, [2] or art school, the sea-slug is *ugly*. Even the man who never forgot to compliment the so-called "lower animals," who championed the stupendous work of worms and the surprizing intelligence of potatoes, Charles Darwin – at least as a young man on the Beagle – failed to find them beautiful. He was, to use the vocabulary of my youth, *grossed out* by "the slimy, disgusting *holothuriae*." [3]

---

1. *Uoko-chan* ~*chan* is a diminutive term of endearment). Uoko is one of a number of characters who appear in work by Nanchattei Ginryû 難茶亭銀柳 ginryuu@ bh.mbn.or.jp. sez AQ
2. *Relativity* Misunderstood. "Relativity" originally meant that facts differ depending on one's place in space-time. It did not mean everything is relative= beautiful/good in some vague way. Relatively speaking, humans are more likely to be attractive to other humans than, say, sea slugs and vice versa.
3. *Source* I forget the original source but recall that this came direct from a co-author of Darwin's 800 page biography, James Moore. As a big fan of Darwin, I certainly would not have made it up!

面目坊海中に入てなまこかな　大江丸

menbokubô watanaka ni irite namako kana – ôemaru? (1801)
(appearances[valuing] monk/man: ocean-in entered seaslug!/?/ô/the/'tis)

#234

whereabouts

that monk
so concerned about his looks
a sea slug now

a just-so story

sea slugs
the reincarnation
of vain monks

occidental version

narcissus, he
fell in: god turned him
into a sea slug

come-uppance

on the ocean floor
a man of parts no more
hey, sea slug!

poetic justice

mister dandy
you are now as cool as
a sea cucumber

Ugliness is another way the sea slug relates to Buddhism that has nothing to do with its inactivity, meekness or circumstantial relationship to punishment for sin. According to the *Kokin-choubunshu* ( ), even attachment to the appearance of being religious was a deeply sinful thing. So what should be done about a preacher whose vanity even extended to his own good looks? As a *senryu* put it, "not looking / in the mirror is decorous / for a monk (*kagami-o minai koto-wa so-no tashinami* [from my memory, imperfect]), whereas samurai were supposed to use the mirror. One wonders what the snooty diva Sei Shonagon (c.965-) would have thought about Oemaru's poetic punishment – she who wrote that a preacher "ought to be good looking" to hold our attention, while an ugly preacher who could not, "may well be a source of sin!" (item 21 in *The Pillow Book of Sei Shonagon* [1])

1. *THE PILLOW BOOK* This book of elegant and witty jottings deserves to be on all lists of *great books*, for even if the author is ridiculously full of herself, she teaches us how interesting the world would be, had we real opinions about things other than politics. Unfortunately, Shonagon neglected to give her opinion on the denizens of the sea, including our subject. Her honest feelings, negative and positive, about various "trees," "flowering trees," "shrubs," "insects" and "birds" should be required reading in our Cowardly New World which so fears that discrimination called *taste*. Were Professor Bloom and other know-it-alls' own taste not so incorrigibly Western, Sei Shonagon would be known by all thinking Americans. (I quoted Ivan Morris' translation which has fine notes but, regrettably, no index. Norton Classics should publish it, with the usual complement of entertaining criticism.) As K.K. notes, the fact Sei Shonagon was in Kyoto, far from the sea, helps excuse the lacuna. I would add that since the sea slug of her day was most strongly represented (domestically) by its fermented guts, a part of the male drinking culture, her sex was also against her.

There is yet another way the sea slug's appearance and/or behavior may tie into popular Buddhism. Issa may have been the first to make the connection explicit in haiku.

人 な ら（ば）仏 性 な る な ま こ 哉 　一 茶

hito naraba hotokeshô naru namako kana – issa (1810)

(human-if, buddhist-nature becomes seaslug/s!/?/ô/the) 　　　　　#235

ugly is beautiful

if human
it would be a saint
the sea slug

the natural

if they were people
they'd be buddhas!
sea slugs

trans. david lanoue

I added a title to D. Lanoue's version. To have a Buddha-nature was to be naive and merciful, a helpful soul who wouldn't hurt a fly. One cannot be certain that looks were the point, but I suspect Issa may well have felt with Ben Franklin (*Letter of Advice to a Young Man* (to prefer older women in his amours)) that when people lose their looks they study to be good. Issa's poem was not written in a complete vacuum. Here is something from the playful Osakan (Danrin) school of poetry which long predates Issa's poem and suggests a strange type of ugliness:

し ら ぬ か な 海 鼠 の 目 鼻 白 う る り 　松 律

shiranu kana namako no mehana shiroururi – shôritsu (1679)

(know-not, huh: sea slug's eyes-nose (features) [is the] *shiroururi*) 　　　　#236

enigma solved

don't you know?
a sea slug has the face
of a *shiroururi*

An abbot famed for eating mountains of potato and nothing but potato was the only one who really knew what a *shiroururi* was (item 60 in Kenko's ESSAYS IN IDLENESS 1330-1332).

> Once, when this abbot saw a certain priest, he dubbed him the *Shiroururi*. Someone asked what a *shiroururi* was. He replied, "I have no idea, but if such a thing existed, I am sure it would look like that priest's face." (trans. Keene)

The haiku guesses that the sea slug, lacking "eyes and nose," i.e. features to speak of, is the correct answer. I doubt it. *Shiroururi* suggests a shiro=white=blank=unknown *uri*=melon. Though the faces Japanese drew on melons were doubtless cute, a long (the white melon is tubular) featureless face was not, and the word became identified with a ghoulish imaginary creature – the artists of Edo seem to have spent half their time drawing monsters and ghosts and gremlins, etc But, still, the creepy, slimy-sounding word evidently led the poet to our faceless fish. The next poem in the same Danrin anthology:

目 も 鼻 も な き 世 な り け り 海 鼠 ず き　不 関

me mo hana mo naki yo narikeri namakozuki – fuseki (1679)

(eye/s-too-nose-too-not world becomes [+finality]: seaslug-lover)

#237

this season

the world
is now featureless:
slug-lovers

That is to say, when *Apostichopus japonicus* is in season, the whole world is sea slug to the sea-slug-lover. To paraverse: *the world / is now our oyster: / shell-fish season.* Since snow covers topographical features leaving the world blank, and Japanese words for eyes and nose, *me* and *hana*, respectively, are homophones for "buds" and "flowers," a sea slug works better than an oyster. The original invokes the Japanese idiom "to have no eyes for," i.e., to love something (for "love is blind") and the middle seven syllabets may echo an old *waka* about the Godless-Month and cold winter rain by Zenchunagon Teika, which begins by saying "the world has become guileless" (*itsuwarinonaki yo narikeri~*) – something suggestive of the sea slug trope we have already seen.[1]

献 立 に 目 鼻 は 付 て 海 鼠 哉　也 有

kondate ni mehana wa tsukete namako kana – yayû (1701-83)

(menu-on eyes-nose[features]-as-for put-on/added sea slug/s!/?/ó/the/'tis)

#238

on a menu
features are given
to sea slugs

~

on the menu
sea slugs get eyes
and a nose

I imagine this means in a picture, for the illustrated or even sculpted(!) menus have a long history in Japan. But, it may be from the name given to the dish, or the dish, itself, if it is a gelatin-like Chinese concoction (not likely in Japan). Regardless, it is an ironic improvement, for a Buddhist should prefer to eat what is *not* animal. It bears noting that, unlike in the West, where relatively prominent nose and eyes were pretty much taken for granted, in Japan, the presence or absence of features (eyes-nose) themselves was equated with beauty/ugliness. Shiki made the same interspecies looks connection in two poems. The first is a cruelly true depiction of human nature, more *senryu* than haiku:

海 鼠 眼 な し ふ く と の 面 憎 み け り　子 規

namako menashi fukuto no tsura o nikumikeri – shiki (m31) szs

(sea-slug eyes-not: blow-fish's face [she] hates/envies)

#239

blind jealousy

miss sea slug
lacking eyes, covets the mug
of a blow-fish

1. Guileless World Teika's *waka* in full: "it has become / a world without guile / the godless month / from whose true feelings   does the cold-rain start?" (*itsuwari no naki yo nari keri kaminazuki dare ga makoto yori shigure somekemu*). I do not yet know *why* the absence of the Gods brings such a world. Could Teika mean that without the gods to blame/credit, man in said month lives in a straightforward manner. This *waka* may be behind other Godless month sea slug haiku. お願い、誰か！

The blow-fish is another kettle of fish (I am saving it for another book!). Let us just say that it was synonymous with an ugly fat woman. No other explanation is needed for the poem other than pointing out that it will *shock* those people who think they know Shiki from standard selections of his poetry.[1] Likewise, for Shiki's second ugly sea slug poem, which, as is, hardly merits parsing: "chaste woman rock-into changes, bad=ugly woman sea-slug-into changes, hoh!" (*teijo ishi ni kasu akujo namako ni kasu ya ran* (貞女石に化す悪女海鼠に化すやらん 子規).[1] Developing the metaphors beyond the original, we can do a bit better:

#240

いい娘 石 に 悪女 な ま こ に 終 わ り が ち　子 敬
ii ko ishi-ni akujo namako-ni owari-gachi – shiki+keigu
(good/pretty woman rock-as, bad/ugly woman sea-slug-as ends-up/tends-to)

#241

women, beware!

chaste beauty
turns to stone, ugliness melts
into a sea slug

In Japan, the most famous ancient poetess, Ono-no-Komachi, was said to be hole-less: more than chaste. *Senryu* doubted that a holeless woman could write love songs, but supposedly she was a flawless beauty who was just too damn picky (After she died, a lonely old hag, her skull was found with saw grass growing through, *i.e.*, violating, her eye-socket.) In the Japanese language, good and beautiful, and bad and ugly were synonymous. Hence bad=ugly.[2] Issa, who was apparently a pretty ugly guy, did well to separate that connection (I refer to his *hotoke-sho* haiku). Shiki was even uglier, extraordinarily homely. Photos confirm that he did indeed have "a face like a snail looking up" as he himself put it (*dedemushi no kashira motageshi ni mo nitari*), but he unabashedly revered beauty.

> *"The sea slug is beautiful. It is the very embodiment of natural beauty."*

> It is certain that there are people who think the sea slug tastes good and some who highly value it as a gourmet food. . . I don't know what percent of people [i.e. Japanese] dare to call themselves "sea-slug-lovers," but it is no exaggeration to say they belong to a special race (*tokubetsu-na jinshu*). And when it comes to the authentic sea-slug-lovers who not only like the flavor but the *form* of the sea slug, there are, no doubt, 0.0-something percent of the population. Being tiny, this group

#242, # 243

1. The Real Shiki   Shiki wrote more haiku on women and beauty (or its lack) than any haiku poet I know of. Some day, I hope to do a selection of his poetry that reflects this. Here is another of his ugly and possibly (but unlikely) sea slug woman haiku: "eating blowfish / that night i dreamed of / an ugly woman" (*fugu kûte akujo o yume ni miru yo kana* – m28 szs). He probably means that the ugly face of the blowfish inspired the dream, but blowfish was also known to heat one up and a cold sea slug woman would be the perfect cure for that! Keigu would rewrite: "eating blowfish / i dream of a cool / sea slug girl" (*fugu kûte nagusamu yume ni namako kana* (河豚喰て慰む夢に海鼠哉 子敬). TK suggests a rewrite of the rewrite: "eating blowfish / i warm up a sea slug / in my dreams"(*fugu kûte yume ni namako o nagusamete* 河豚食うて夢に海鼠を慰みて 子敬天). *Nagusamu* means to relieve and implies a wet dream. In the first haiku, the

blowfish-eater is cooled by the *namako,* in the second he warms the *namako.*

2. Bad=Ugly, Good=Beautiful   The ancient Greeks and the Japanese until recently shared such a vocabulary. As measures of cultural merit, such equations are a double-edged sword, good for suggesting the existence of a deeply aesthetic culture, where appearance was deeper than "face-value;" but, as ugly Aristotle knew, false, if not immoral for being patently wrong with respect to individuals. Today, Japanese have a specific term for "an ugly" (*busu*), and "bad-woman" in the old sense of "ugly" is almost obsolete. As K.K. reminds me, *akujo* (bad-woman) now has connotations of *beauty*, for it is commonly used to mean *femme fatale,* whose looks are prerequisite for baiting victims. Meanwhile, the opposite equation, good=beautiful/ handsome (*ii*) is used more than ever, and for both sexes!

would be tightly bound and find themselves the raison d'être of the sea slug, the reason why god brought diversity to the world. But I who am writing this feel like I really don't know what the sea slug is for . . . (day esu? ace? 01/1/28: yoshida naohiro@geocities.co.jp)

As the above paragraph lifted off the internet so honestly states, it is *normal* for humans to think of a sea slug as ugly. Issa's Buddhist leanings may have helped him appreciate the sea slug's karma as a blessing in disguise. Popular Buddhism was a haven for the looks-impaired. Temples often helped to arrange marriages for ugly women, even assisting with the dowry needed to convince a poor man to take them. And Buddhism gave them spiritual support, as hinted at by this early *senryu*:

極楽へゆくと痘痕の諦めて　無名（川柳）

gokuraku-e yuku to abata-no akiramete   anon.

(paradise-to go: pock-mark's resigning)

a beautiful future

thinking she'll go
to paradise, pock-marked
resigns herself

In Japanese, the pock-marked person is simple called "pock/s" (*abata*). Miss Pocks resigns herself to not finding a husband after many matches. Popular Buddhism believed that suffering in this world assured one of recompense in the next. So did popular Christianity in the West (For evidence, read the extraordinary account of Mrs. Hutchinson's ordeal: how *grateful* she was for her *opportunity* to suffer by being kidnapped by the Amerindians, who, if I recall correctly, ended up suffering more punishment at the hands of this spunky Puritan than vice versa).

海鼠汝ふみつけるべき面もなし　柳原極堂

namako nanji fumitsukerubeki tsura mo nashi – gyokudô (1872-1957)

#244   (seaslug you tramp upon ought/can face-even not)

sea slug, you
don't even have a face
to rub in the ground

This post-war haiku – I say "haiku" for it was in a haiku almanac of food, otherwise it would be a *senryu* – suggests another advantage to having a face-value of zero. It reminds us of the *senryu* Blyth translates as "the bride is so soft, / the mother-in-law / can't get her teeth into her" (*yawaraka na yome wa shûto no ha ga tatazu*). The haiku was probably written against that most difficult adversary of all, the faceless enemy, perhaps a bureaucracy, or someone who evaded war-time responsibility. Not looks *per se* but a clear *identity* is what may be lacking here.

あばたなる妻持にけり海鼠突　冥々

abatanaru tsuma mochinikeri namakotsuki – meimei (1750-1824)

#245   (pock-mark-is wife has[+finality] seaslug-gigger)

the sea-slug gigger
himself stuck with a wife
who's pock-marked

Unlike the other poems on looks we have seen, this is modern in the sense it does not explain things. If the poet saw a relationship between the man's job and his wife's looks, he does not say what it is.

安々と海鼠のごとき子を産めり 漱石

yasu yasu to namako no gotoki ko o umeri – sôseki

(easily easily seaslug-like child/babe bears)

#246

birth tiding

easy as pie
she bore my child
a sea slug

My first reading – *splitting open / easy as a sea slug / baby born!* – of this haiku written by the novelist Natsume Sôseki [1] to announce the birth of his first daughter Fude (brush) on March 31, 1899 assumed his wife had a Caesarian and he knew about the terrifying ability of some sea slugs to split open. As it turns out, it was *not* a Caesarian, but was more like my second reading, *easy and cool / as a sea cucumber / she gave birth.* The original grammar, like the third reading, does not make clear what was *holothurian,* the birthing or the birthling. Easy birth [2] suggests a tiny premature baby bearing a marked resemblance to its near-homophonic, the red sea slug (*akanbo/akako*). But Sôseki did not specify a red sea cucumber (*akako*) and, as KS kindly reminded me, describing one's own family members in a humble way (e.g., my "pig-child," "my dumb-wife") is a Sino-Japanese cultural tradition. [3] Sôseki described the birth as easy *and* found the sea slug useful for an exceptionally creative act of family=self-effacement, aided by the fact that, to be honest, *most* new born babies are not a pretty sight! – so the poem, which was first placed in "protean sea slugs," will in the absence of convincing evidence [4], remain here with the other *Ugly Sea Slugs.*

1. *Natsume Sôseki* A close friend of Shiki and Kyoshi, Sôseki can be found on Japanese 1000 yen notes, as you can find Dickens on one of the most common English bank notes. Perhaps we in the USA should consider exchanging the heartless Trail of Tears supporter and Seminole butcher Jackson with a far more admirable man, Mark Twain!

2. *Easy Birth* In a notebook of material Issa gathered for his patron Seibi, we find something from *Kijinden,* an "eccentrics' biography," possibly improved by Issa : "nothing is so auspicious as a woman: she bears all buddhas, all darumas as easy as pie." (*onna hodo medeto mono wa mata mo nashi shaka ya daruma o hyoihyoi to umu*) – The *hyoi-hyoi to* might be more accurately explained as pop out one after another. The section of the biography had to be on the Zen monk Ikkyû, who says the same in the last half of his poem about a woman's private part. Sôseki was quite the eccentric himself and may well have read the same biography. One wonders if his wife agrees with his evaluation of the birth!

3. *Self Denigration* This hyperbolic modesty with respect to oneself and one's family is not only found in the Sinosphere. It is a cultural trait that is probably as wide-spread or more wide-spread than our aren't-we-proud-of-ourselves! speech strategy, and some cultures – the Inuit being the prime example – have taken it far further than the Japanese and Chinese.

4. *Evidence on this Poem* By evidence, I mean comments by Sôseki or reports by those who knew him specifically touching upon the poem or on the use of sea slug as a term of self (or family) effacement. I have seen one other translation in an article on "laughter in japanese haiku" in the new internet magazine *haijinx* (vol 1 issue 1, vernal equinox, 2001) by Nobuyuki Yuasa:

safely, quite safely,
she managed to bear a child,
soft as a sea slug

and think the soft (pliant) baby is as good a reading as mine, but I have mixed feelings about his explanation – "The image of the sea slug is so startling that the whole poem sounds a bit like a bad joke. However, it shows the 'metaphysical' quality of Sôseki's humour, which would not even spare his own daughter." OM writes: "I agree with Yuasa. I don't particularly think Soseki's description of his child as "ugly" as a namako at all. To me the 'namako-like' baby suggests the looks and feel of a helpless (with an armless, legless, wiggling appearance) small newborn. Maybe I am more sentimental, but I feel Sôseki's relief for his wife's easy childbirth and endearment for his newborn." Considering the fact that Sôseki and his close friends (Shiki, Terada, Kyoshi) were all deeply into *namako,* I would agree that it endears even as it, *ostensibly,* debases in the traditional manner. ~   ~   ~   ~

大悪人虚子に私淑の海鼠かな　水内慶太

daiakunin kyoshi ni shifuku no namako kana – mizuuchi keita (mod)

(big-bad-man kyoshi-to/with/by adoring/admiring/groveling seaslug!/?/ó/the/'tis)

#247

that bad man
kyoshi and the sea slugs
who adore him

that's what he is
a sycophant sea slug of
big bad kyoshi

so just call me
mister big bad kyoshi's
adoring sea slug

The sea slug here stands for something ugly, not in the physical sense but in the psychological. The manner in which the apprentice poets grovel before their master and swallow all of his poems – haiku-eaters, rather than toad-eaters – is not pretty to one who is independent-minded and would prefer that men had spines. Nonetheless, I do not care much for a haiku(?) used as an insult, and would prefer to say that the last reading is the correct one and the poet is defending his own support for Kyoshi, but all indications are that this poet came from (and inherited) a school of haiku that was at odds with Kyoshi's greater establishment, which is to say the first two readings are correct.

ひとの手を借り得ぬものの海鼠買ふ　石川桂郎

hito no te o karienu mono no namako kau – keirô (1909-1975)

(person/other's hand borrow-not thing-seaslug buy)

#248

something one
must buy for himself
a sea slug

the sea slug
something a man must
buy alone

The sea slug is so grotesque – or ugly, or suggestive – a thing to purchase that it is unfair to leave it up to another, which in this case, may mean the poet's wife (If I am correct that this poem was written in 1931, when Keirô was only 21, so I do not know if this is true). Such a reading puts the poem square into this chapter, though I must confess to other readings, the best of which is that the poet may love sea slug so much and respect its symbolism as a silent solitary eating experience (as we shall see later) so deeply that he thought aesthetics dictated that he buy his own.

摑み出す最も器量のよき海鼠　岡田久江

tsukamidasu mottomo kiryô no yoki namako – okada hisae (2001)

#248-2[oops!]　(grabbing-[reaching]out/up most looks/features/capability/dignity-good seaslug)

discrimination

i pick up
the best looking
sea slug

fish-monger

taking out
"the most attractive"
sea slug

While English has many verbs to translate *tsukami* (grabbing/gripping/clutching/ pinching/holding), it has none whatsoever for "to out" except for "leave." This forces us to use makeshift constructions such as "picking out," "taking out," "lifting up from," and so forth. It is a big gap and English should be ashamed of itself. But, to return to the subject, even the sea slug is not beyond the beauty contest whether it is selected by the buyer or the seller (I think it most likely that the poet says "give me the best-looking sea slug!" and the shop-keeper complies, in which case "the most attractive sea slug" is a chuckling description of what the shop-owner has been commissioned to do). As KS reminded me, the proper Buddhist stance being one of non-discrimination, there may be a touch of humor and self-criticism here. Imagine discrimination even in the world of the relatively featureless sea slug!

そっと触れちぢむ海鼠を買ひにけり　田中春江

sotto fure chijimu namako o kainikeri – tanaka harue (2001)

(softly touching shrinks-seaslug[obj] buy [+finality])　　#249

i buy the slug
that shrinks though
barely touched

With mussels or clams, I tap to make sure they still stir. Here, the poet wants to buy the freshest sea slug to eat, but something about the slug invites our sympathy, our pity more than a shell-fish, with its hard covering. The poet must have felt she was acting a bit sadistically in choosing the sea slug with the most life to kill, life that is expressed in the cowardly act of shrinking. Should we just say that the sensitive sea slug gets eaten?

押し戴くやうに海鼠を買ひにけり　川崎展宏

oshi itadaku yô ni namako o kainikeri – kawasaki nobuhiro (contemp)

(push-accept[accepting with hands held out]-manner-in seaslug buying[final])　　#250

hands held up
reverently when
buying sea slug

apotheosis

hands raised
high to accept a sea slug
just paid for

While the sea slug may be ugly, it is dear to its lovers; and this poet, or someone he observes, cups his hands over and in front of his head to receive his purchase in the polite or even reverent manner used to honor sacred or otherwise valuable objects and gifts received from superiors. How remarkable that the brainy octopus is not accorded such respect while our brainless creature is! Is this because the formlessness of the sea slug allows us to read more into it? Or is it because centuries of haiku and haibun have given the sea slug a special presence? I do not know if we can call this event an apotheosis, but we can say that like poor Captain Cook, the sea slug is honored . . . and eaten.

古妻も出刃も海鼠も仏かな　野村喜舟

furutsuma mo deba mo namako mo hotoke kana – kishû (1934)

(old-wife and jutting-blade[knife]=buck-tooth and seaslug, buddha/saint!/?/ó/a/'tis)　　#251

<table>
<tr><td>

blessed things

my old wife
her chopping knife and
the sea slug

</td><td>

saintly things

my old wife
her cleaver and sea slug
blessed be

</td></tr>
</table>

the trinity

blessed things
old wives, cleavers
and sea slugs

Kishû's poem is *warm.* Remember Tom T. Hall's *old dogs and children and watermelon wine*? Here, all three items are homely. The cleaver, far from a sleek sword, is homophonic with "buckteeth," synonymous with ugly country girls, while the *hotoke* (buddha/saint/corpse), figuratively "blessed," suggests ugliness, as noted earlier with respect to Issa's *hotoke, i.e.,* saintly sea slug.

な つ か し き は は の 作 り し 海 鼠 か な 未知

natsukashiki haha no tsukurishi namako kana – anon (1999)

#252   (familiar/nostalgic mother's made/making seaslug!/?/ó/this/'tis)

familiar flavor

heart-warming

mother's home-made

sea slug!

This contemporary, googled haiku solves the problem of looks, for touched by a mother, even the homely becomes homey. The first part of the poem was a problem to translate. In a book challenging antithetical stereotypes of the English and Japanese language in Japan (*Eigo wa Konna ni Nippongo:* 1989), I noted the lack of a way "to miss" in Japanese. Japanese can say they want something or are lonely, but they lack a single word to express the sensation of *missing.* English, on the other hand, lacks a word for *natsukashi, i.e.,* the pleasure felt at encountering something long familiar to us. I improvised with "heart-warming." Let me peg on another *natsukashiki* sea slug that is not at all ugly:

酢 海 鼠 や な つ か し き 世 に 遊 び を り 角 川 春 樹

sunamako ya natsukashiki yo ni asobiori – kadokawa haruki (contemp)

#253   (vinegar/pickled-seaslug:/! familiar/missed/dear world-in play/ing/am)

pickled sea slug!	pickled sea slug
free to play again in	how beautiful to be
a familiar world	back in the world

pickled sea slug

free at last in this world

i dearly missed

Kadokawa wrote this not long after being released from jail. In Japanese, as in English, "play" means degrees of freedom as well as doing fun activities. It is also an elegant way to simply express the state of being. *Homo incarceratus* is once again a *Homo ludens.* The pickled slug, as we see elsewhere, itself "plays" when the would-be eater tries to fish the chunks out from the liquid. The last reading gave up on trying to translate the *natsukashiki* and found "beautiful" instead.

故郷にて海鼠を食べる喜びあり 鯵川祥代

kokyô nite namako o taberu yorokobi ari – ajikawa yôyo? (contemp)

#254   (home-country-at seaslug[obj] eat/ing pleasure/joy is)

there is joy	what delight
in eating sea slug	eating sea slug here
back at home	at home, tonight

If Aristotle argued *the useful is beautiful,* here we might say that the *delightful* is too. This haiku from a haiku fest for university students reminds me of Issa's delight to celebrate New Years at home after decades away. By leaving home, home becomes special.

~   ~   ~   ~   ~

何 も か も な く し て 仏 様 に な り 一 弦

nanimokamo nakushite hotoke[-]sama ni nari – ichigen
(everything losing, buddha=corpse=departed appearance becomes)

> losing everything
> he became
> a buddha

trans. blyth

A final qualification for this chapter. Because of years of interest in *the accident of beauty* (I borrow a term from Oliver Wendell Holmes for differences in personal beauty and its effect on our lives is not, and never was, a myth, Naomi), I may have put undo emphasis on *facial* features, or the lack thereof, in my explanation of Issa's "buddha-nature" (*hotoke-sho*) sea-slug, the second poem in this chapter. More generally, the fact the sea slug has *nothing,* means it has everything, from the Buddhist point of view. The above *senryu* by Ichigen brought me to my senses. Blyth's explains: "While there's life there's hope, and while there's hope there's illusion, and while there's illusion, there's no Buddha. After all, the real Buddha is the dead man." Paraversing on this line of thought,

hard bargain

> losing everything
> the dead man has won
> his buddhahood

a good trade?

> bereft
> he becomes
> buddha

The original senryu is not so simple. The Japanese can be read as *hotoke-sama-ni naru,* or *hotoke sama-ni naru.* The first *hotoke-sama* is a polite way of refering to a buddhist figure or the deceased;" the second, with the *sama* by itself, turns the last five syllabets into an idiom *sama-ni naru,* meaning "looks right for" or "properly fits the role." I believe the second reading is the primary one, although I do allow Blyth's reading also.

the dead man

> stripped,
> he finally looks
> his part

Considering the black-humor angle common to old *senryu,* I suspect we are talking about a wealthy man's corpse prepared for cremation or an unfortunate murdered and stripped. (losing all / a stiff as naked / as buddha)? The Buddha is, after all, usually depicted or sculpted practically naked. *Having nothing* is not only a mark of the undeveloped primordial chaos of the beginning so dear to Taoism, but of the final reality so close to the heart of Buddhism. Having no limbs or teeth to hold something with, the sea slug practices total unattachment.[1] Naked of all decoration, the Japanese sea slug is totally unaffected. Hence, it is as good as enlightened by nature.

何 も な く そ れ も 知 ら ぬ が 海 鼠 哉　敬 愚

nanimo naku sore mo shiranu ga namako kana – keigu

#255   (thing-not[having nothing] that too know/s-not-is seaslug!/?/ŏ/the)

bliss is

having nothing
and not knowing it
the sea slug

This plays upon the saying "blindness/ignorance is bliss" by exchanging the sea slug, *namako,* for the bliss=buddha, *hotoke.* A version suggested by TK drops the pun:

何 も な い こ と さ へ 知 ら ぬ 海 鼠 哉　敬 天

nanimo nai koto sae shiranu namako kana – keigu+tenki

#256   (thing-not[having nothing] thing even know/s-not-seaslug!/?/ŏ/the)

the sea slug
has naught and does not
even know it

---

1. ***Unattachment*** and ***Attachment*** in the Sea   The *Holothurian* does not need to grab food to eat, but is content to sift sand because its slow life and tubular body require minimal calories. If it is the exemplar for living peacefully with little, its echinodermata (spiked-skin) phylum mate, the starfish is its antithesis.   This "carnivorous and voracious" creature is driven by its belly; indeed, its stomach even extends a way into its clutching arms. (A.F. Arnold: IBID). Its vernacular Japanese name *hitode* is perfect to express its character, for it means "person's-hand." But, pity the starfish, they don't choose to desire.   Most have to eat alot because they are skinny and feel perpetually starved. A. Kerr didn't let this get by:

As with most anthropocentric terms, "voracious" is meant by the author to describe a human observers likely response to witnessing predation by

starfish. Such statements are not meant to be taken literally; they eat as much as they can to maximize reproduction and expend as little energy as they possibly can get away with procuring food just like everybody else, including us.   A carnivorous lifestyle is only true of temperate starfish; most tropical species are detritivores, eating muck and sand like the holothurians. (A.K.corres)

It is nice to know we have gentle starfish out there. But, I stand by my moralizing. Ruth Benedict, known for *Patterns of Culture* and the relative view of culture, later admitted that she had personal favorites (societies with a high synergy between the individual and social good), and I make no bones about confessing a preference for gentle, low-energy life, if nothing else for the counter-example it provides for our insanely active culture.

11
the lubricious sea slug

わ だ つ み の 底 に 物 あ る 海 鼠 か な　樂 南
wadatsumi no soko ni mono aru namako kana – rakunan (mod?)
(sea/ocean's bottom-on/at thing/s is/are: seaslug!/?/ó/the/'a/tis/behold)   #257

on the bottom
of the sea private parts?
sea cucumber

The poem does not *have* to be read this way. Indeed, another reading of it will begin chapter 20, *The Melancholy Sea Slug*. The trick is in the "thing" (*mono*). In Japanese, it is and was common to speak of male and female *things*, where English speakers once would have spoken of "parts." The "private" is *too* obvious, but "parts" alone would not do and, in this chapter, I am trying to err on the side of outrageousness. I do have some circumstantial evidence that suggests the poem is risqué. In the 27th episode of the *Nise Monogatari*, a ribald parody of the *Ise Monogatari* (Ise, a place-name; *nise,* "fake"), there are a couple 5-7-5-7-7 poems about a man spying on a woman washing clothes in a tub. She complains of loneliness noting there was only her and her reflection, and the Funny Man[1] pipes up with "in the water / i see a [your] thing! / even a horse / whinnies at the sight / of a tub of beans!" (*minasoko ni mono ya miyuran uma sae mo mamedarai o ba nozokite zo naku*). The "water-bottom" (*minasoko*) for some strange reason, is where Japanese fancy they see reflections, but the word is the same that would be used for the place sea slugs rest. In this case, the "thing" is the woman's rather than the man's, but one thing suggests another, so this might have primed the haiku.

す り 鉢 に 恐 縮 し た る 海 鼠 か な　岡 田 潟 人
suribachi ni kyôshuku shitaru namako kana – okada shajin (mod?)
(mortar-in, fear-shrink[cower/abject/humble]-being/doing seaslug!/?/ó//a)   #258

mortification

in a mortar
making itself small
a sea slug

The poet's wife may have just happened to place a sea slug in a mortar for lack of a better place to keep it, but one suspects the modern poet found a sort of Freudian humor here. The suggestiveness of the sea slug is one thing equally noted in the East and the West. Aristotle's name *olothourion* contains the root *thourios* (*thouraios*), or "vulgar," which makes the *holothurian* the sort of thing that might *embarasar* (in romance languages *impregnate*) a woman. This metaphor was central to the Western concept of our charge:

1. *The Funny Man* Episodes of the ISE MONOGATARI or Tales of Ise often begin with "*mukashi, otoko. . .*" or, "long ago, a man . . ." and thus this man (whom we will meet) became called "*mukashi otoko*" or the *Long-ago Man.* In this parody, the episodes begin with "*okashi*" or "funny," so we may call the main character Funny Man. The humor of the poems is too pun-dependent to work in translation. Here, there are hints of a horse-sized thing of his own and beans, for their color and identification with the clitoris are a double-take to confirm the nature of the thing that was seen.

With the older authors (Belon, Aldrovandi, Jonstonus) the sea cucumbers were called: *genitale marinum, mentula marina, priapus marinus, pudendum,* what the Italians called *cazzo di mare* [or, *cazo marino*] and the Greeks *psolo* [or, *psoli nuncupat*], whose meanings are the same and in the sense described by Bohadsch:

> *aquam ejicit, corpusque instar ligni indurescit, quae indurescentia, aquae ejaculatio una cum cylindrica coporis forma ansam dedisse videtur, quod hoc genus veteres mentulam appellarent.* [1] (Ludwig H. 1889-1892. Echinodermen. Die Seewalzen. In: Bronn HG (ed.) Bronn's Klassen und Ordnungen des Their-Reichs. Band II. Abteilung 3. Buch 1. Leipzig. Unpublished translation by Alexander M. Kerr.)

As this might suggest, "sea slug" and "sea cucumber" were not the only vernacular English terms for holothurians. One term apparently shared in this classic culture. Ludwig's translator notes that

> The English pre-enlightenment were probably most familiar with cukes as fishermen, who pulled up many in their nets. These they called sea pudding; pudding an 18th c. term for penis, i think ultimately derived from pudendum. Hence, I wonder if pudding was ultimately derived from a term used during Roman times in the Isles. (AK corresp)

This is more than mere speculation.[2]   Isn't the kilt-clad Northern fringe of the United Kingdom still the stronghold for big blood sausages called "black pudding?" But, let us return to poetry and Japan.

(2) い つ 見 て も 濡 身 の ま ゝ の 海 鼠 哉　馬 光

itsu mite mo nuremi no mama no namako kana – bakô (1768)

#259 [also #99]   (when[ever] see, wet-body as-is seaslug!/?/ó/the)

> their bodies
> always look wet
> sea slugs
>
> ～
>
> lubricious
> wherever they are
> sea slugs

These sea slugs were first introduced as Taoists; but the fact that a *nuremi,* or "wet-body" was generally understood to mean one that was sweaty and otherwise wet from sex suggests a more lubricious reading as well.   There is even a near-miss in the "male-color-big-mirror[exemplar]" (danshoku ôkagami in ukiyosôshi in OJD = *nuremi*), to wit: "[his] wet body, as is [without drying] wrapped in his underwear . ." (*nuremi sono mama hadagi no shita ni makikomerare . .*). The poem, read this way, may be a second take on that spineless dandy from the *Tale of Ise.*

1. *Learn Latin!* I haven't learned Latin well enough to really read, but it doesn't take much to find flaccidity, instant erection, and ejaculation from a cylindrical body justifying the "dirty" name here! Perhaps the best venereal name of all is Columna's *pudendum regale* for a specimen resembling a *Stichopus regalis.* As regality, I imagine a large, purple or crowned cuke.

2. *Pudding:Pudenda* It is interesting that Latins do not call sausage "pudding", but reserve the word for what English call custard "pudding" (pudin), so we have both hard and soft puddings = pudenda. My Random House suggests that the Middle English *poding,* a kind of sausage, comes from the Old English *puden,* a wen or sore. *Yuck!* Better by far the pudendum, originally referring to something shameful or embarrassing. (Incidentally, *pudin* in Japan always means what Usanians call *flan.*)

廓 の 灯 た ぬ し む ご と く 海 鼠 売   後 藤 夜 半

kuruwa no hi tanushimu gotoku namakouri – gôtô yahan? (1932)

(pleasure-quarter[whore-houses] lamp/s enjoy-as-if, seaslug-seller)   #260

> he seems to love
> the gay quarter lights
> the sea slug man

> ***suspicious shadows***

> that slug vendor
> is he playing with the lights
> of the gay quarter

The first reading suggests that the sea slug vendor with his dark goods seeks out the brightest part of the city like a moth seeking light – though, it could logically be explained by the fact that this is where people eat a lot at night.   The verb *tanushimu,* however, strongly suggests the vendor is actually enjoying or having fun with the lights. I imagine either purposefully or accidentally made risque shadows, against walls and/or paper windows and doors.

な ま こ 売 つ ま ん で 見 せ て 嫌 が ら せ   武 玉 川

namakouri tsumande misete iyagarase – mutamagawa 13 (1759)

(sea-slug seller squeezing shows, harasses)   #261

> ***public display***

> a repulsive
> sea slug vender plays
> with them

> ***boys will be boys***

> disgusting!
> the vender squeezes
> a sea slug

> ***time on his hands***

> kidding women
> the sea slug man plays
> with his goods

> ***let him sell sea urchin!***

> the sea-slug man
> harasses young women
> squeezing them

This *senryu* could, or rather, should have been written in a collection of haiku, for the depiction is both seasonable and impeccably real. Not only could the man have laid hand on his phallic goods, simulating things we need not mention, but he could have actually squirted the customers.[1] ➔ In the words of Belon, the first person to note the similarity of the sea urchin, sea star and the sea cucumber: *Exangue maris purgamentum!* (Ludwig:Ibid)

はさみあげ 吾 の 危 ふきふなべりに なまこは 細き 潮吹 きにけり　御供平佶
hasamiage ware no ayauki funaberi ni namako wa hosoki shio fukinikeri (t) – mitomo heikichi (1983)
(squeezing-raising my imperiled boat-side [gunnel] from/on seaslug-as-for thin brine squirt[+finality])
#262

> leaning over
> the gunnel, squeezing
> as i raise it:
> a sea slug squirts out
> a thin line of brine

The *tanka* seems to be about an incidental happening. The poet did not *deliberately* squeeze the sea slug, but by saying he squeezed it objectively removes the more poetic possibility of the sea slug doing the equivalent of bepissing itself (to use the old English expression for what is now called "pissing in ones pants") in the face of a waterless world. I would like a more positive poem. As a child, Keigu liked nothing better than bringing up a sea cucumber and squirting someone with it. They made fine squirt guns, even if their ammunition was limited:

［わが 最初 の 水鉄炮］水切れて 海へ 投げ 返す 海鼠哉　敬愚
"waga saisho no mizudeppô" mizu kirete umi e nagekaesu namako kana – keigu
("my first water-gun" water cutting[runs-out] sea-to throw-return seaslug!/?/ó/the)
#263

> **his first pistol**
>
> when the sea slug
> runs out of water, the boy
> tosses it back

> **single-shot**
>
> out of water
> the sea slug is tossed
> back into it

1. Squirting Cukes Spoilers for a gross movie called "Jackass" include a vignette where "the guys go in the surf and hold sea-cucumbers to their groin and pretend to masturbate, making the sea cucumbers spew their innards out (abbrev.). The dive instructor is embarrassed he ever showed them a sea cucumber." (www.themoviespoiler.com/Spoilers jackass.[html]). This is a good illustration of the puerile West, but biologically speaking this spewing is meaningless. However, as it turns out, some species of the *land* cucumber also squirt and do so in a way that is literally connected to sex! The following quote from an Islamic site claiming this and other interesting natural phenomena prove that creation was supernatural:

> As Mediterranean squirting cucumbers begin to ripen, they begin to fill with a slimy juice. Some time later the pressure exerted by this liquid builds up to such an extent that the outer skin of the cucumber cannot resist it and bursts off its stalk. When this happens, the cucumber sprays the liquid inside it like the trail of a rocket being fired into the air. Behind the cucumber comes a trail of slime and with it, seeds. (www.harunyahya.com/plants04.php)

Wow! Later, I came across a Christian site (address lost) that claimed "Not evolution, but God gifted the lowly sea cucumber with the ability to disgorge its insides and then manufacture new ones at its leisure. We would like to know, if evolution made this startling feat possible for the sea cucumber, why do not all other animals in the same category, and higher, have the same ability? Obviously, such miracles in nature are the work of a Supreme intelligent Creator." If the Creationists didn't squirt/disgorge such dogma into the ears of children, and misread science, I would support them for the amusement such remarks provide! (continues →)

［水 鉄 炮］水 切 れ た 海 鼠 海 へ と 投 げ 返 す　敬 天
" mizudeppô" mizu kireta namako umi e to nagekaesu – keigu+tenki
("water-gun" water cutting[runs-out] sea-to throw-return seaslug!/?/ổ/the)   #264

the water pistol

out of water
a sea slug is heaved
out to sea

水 切 れ て 海 鼠 海 鼠 に 換 わ り け り　敬 愚
mizu kirete namako namako ni kawarikeri – keigu
(water-cuts[runs-out] seaslug-a seaslug-with exchanged)   #265

new pistol

out of water
one sea slug's dropped
for another

来 日 し 水 鉄 砲 食 ふ 海 鼠 か な　敬 愚
rainichi shi mizudeppô kuu namako kana – keigu
(come-japan do, water-gun/pistol eat: seaslug!/?/ổ/'tis)   #266

eatable side-arm

in japan
i eat a squirt-gun!
sea slug

種 子 島 海 鼠 を み れ ば 水 鉄 砲　敬 愚
tanegashima namako o mireba mizudeppô – keigu
(tanegashima[island where firearms arrived] seaslug see-when/if water-gun)   #267

tanegashima

where every sea slug
seems a gun!

水 鉄 炮 何 口 径 乃 海 鼠 哉　敬 愚
mizudeppô nani kôkei no namako kana – keigu
(water-gun: what caliber's seaslug!/?/ổ/'tis)   #268

big enough for a whale

the sea slug
i wonder what caliber
the gun!

→ *Squirting Them* Brenna Lorenz, writing of the "Critters of Guam," next to her daughter? Megaera's drawing "Freud with Sea Cucumber" or "Sometimes a balate is just a balate," says what was once true on Key Biscayne, too: "Every Guam kid knows what you can do with the little black balates. You can pick them up, hold them in front of your body in the appropriate location, and pretend to pee. Since the animal obligingly expels a squirt of water, the appearance is quite convincing." (http://www.heptune.com/galwall1.html). I imagined a family of artists and writers on vacation, but here is AK: "Brenna was a geology prof at University of Guam when I was a student there; she's a very funny lady." Which is to say, an ideal teacher! Though I found her website, I couldn't get a letter through (Write me, BL! I'm sure you can add something to the second ed. of this book!)

If the gun, itself is a phallic symbol, we have one metaphor covering another. Tanegashima, the island associated with the arrival of guns to Japan is hard to carry into English, while the pun on slug=bullet does not work in Japanese, where the slug must become the gun and the caliber refer to that of its mouth or anus.

ちんぽこじゃ！女子海鼠の水とばす 敬愚

chinpoko ja menoko/onago namako no mizu tobasu – keigu
(weewee/penis is! woman-child[girl] seaslug water fly-lets))

#269

my weewee!
laughs the girl squirting
a sea cucumber

This is one of those memories I only think I *may* have. The girl is one of my sisters. It is far more interesting having a girl do it than a boy, and the metaphor seems more wholesome when the protagonist, rather than the poet calls attention to it.

手に取ればまだ脈の有る海鼠哉　武玉川

te ni toreba mada myaku no aru namako kana – mutamagawa 16 (1771)
(hand-in taken-if, still pulse has sea-slug!/?/ó/the/'behold)

#270

gently held
it still throbs with life
the sea slug

soft but alive

taken in hand
the sea slug still
has a pulse

I felt tempted to title the first translation: ***nothing that a little viagra can't cure;*** but Japanese reader KK feels such an interpretation "far-fetched" because *myaku-ga aru* (having a pulse) is simply an idiom for being alive. I can not argue with that but I would suggest that the idiom is suggestive when a sea-slug is "taken in hand," for the sea slug, like the elephant's trunk was a euphemism for a penis that would not – to use a pornographer's term picked up from *The New Yorker* – turn to *wood* (eg. "We have *wood*!" = turn the camera back on!). Another *senryu*, not worth a full treatment, confirms this: "a sea slug collar / when the straw comes out / becomes flaccid" (*namako eri wara ga nukeru to gunnya to naru* – Y50, 64 海鼠衿わらがぬけるとぐにやと成　柳多留). The psychological mimesis, *gunnya*, which suggests something "limp/flaccid/ droopy/soft" makes the haiku a poem in Japanese. But there may be a "B" side to this sea slug with a pulse, for there is an off-chance the *senryu* was meant to be an apparently dirty, but actually innocent, envoi for the following poem, one of the funniest haiku written by one of the great haiku-masters: 上 **#271**

生海鼠にも鍼試むる書生哉　蕪村

namako ni mo hari kokoromuru shosei kana – buson (1715-1783)
(sea-slug-on even needles practice intern/apprentice/s!/?/ó/the/)

#272

intern doctors
even sea slugs serve for
needle practice

because it's patient

apprentices
practicing acupuncture
on a sea slug

One early twentieth century critic-poet (Hekigoto) wrote this haiku meant the apprentices were bored with their difficult Chinese-style book-study and ready for fun as shown by the playful feeling of the word *kokoromuru* (test/try out). Another critic-poet (Seisetsu) claims, rather, that such practice makes metaphysical sense as treatment for a creature with too little backbone to make up its mind, in accordance with a Chinese idiom (*chômon-no-isshin*=gate-stone-one-needle) that means a needle is just the thing for a block-head (bkk).

trying to cure
sea slug's sluggishness
needle interns

I can't help wondering, however, if there wasn't some slow-poke student with the nick-name of sea slug who had to be poked out of his stupor:

the apprentice,
a sea slug by nature,
gets needled

Accepting the idea of an actual sea slug, we may still wonder if this scene was witnessed by Buson or whether he came up with the idea himself. The sea slug is perfect for the intern.

guinea pig

a live sea slug
perfect to try out
acupuncture!

It would squirm for indication (of whatever), but couldn't thrash about breaking needles. It is a guinea pig confined within its own straight jacket. (It might also allude to a comatose person, but let's vanish that vile thought!) Qualms about animal rights aside, one *hopes* the interns followed Buson's advice, for, as the Japanese proverb noted, *it takes a hundred dead patients to make one good doctor.*

intern acupuncturist

needle practice
poking even lovesick
sea slugs

This reverses another Buson poem (*omou koto iwanu* ...), where a man presumably suffering from pent-up emotion is a sea slug, to make the sea slug human; though true, it is farce rather than metaphor.

苦 を は な れ て 動 く な ま こ 哉　 青 羅
kurushimi o hanarete ugoku namako kana – seira (1739-1791)
(pain/suffering-from removed, moves/moving seaslug!/?/ő/the)　　　　　　#273

the sea slug
moves at a remove
from suffering

Given a Cartesian reading, this haiku seem to sanction acupuncture practice – for without ganglia to perceive pain, can the sea slug be said to "feel?" [1] – but at the same time, it does away with the fiction of the emotionally pent-up sea slug who would apparently stand to benefit from the same. It is possible Seira refers to something else, such as the continuing death throes (?) [2] of pieces of sea slug or even the hard to catch slippery bits of pickled slug we shall encounter soon enough in *The Slippery Sea Slug*.

酢をさせば闇浮にかへる海鼠かな　大江丸

su o saseba enbu ni kaeru namako kana – ôemaru (1721-1805)

(vinegar pour/apply-if jambû[this world]-to returns seaslug!/?/ó/the)

#274

> pour vinegar
> and the sea slug returns
> to this world

> *jambû*

> dash sea slug
> with vinegar and he is
> back with us

The exotic Sanskrit-derived term (*Jambû*) I translated as "this world" also suggests a shiny golden glow and, homophonically, a writhing dance. I cannot tell if the actual subject of this poem is an entire live sea slug or pieces of sea slug. And, does the poet mean that dousing with vinegar hardens what was melting away – as dying sea slugs may do this – or that it actually makes the sea slug or its freshly cut pieces squirm? Then, the pieces may be merely bobbing in the liquid.

#275, 276, 277

1. Sea Slug Feelings If we grant that a tree falling in a forest though no one witnesses it is still a fact, then, what about the tensing, the writhing, the apparent pain witnessed in the sea slug that, granted has no brain to perceive it with? ("I believe your mistake is to assume that a brain is required to feel pain or conversely even that a hardwired and often beneficial recoil to a strong mechanical stimulus is perceived anything like what we know as pain, or indeed need be perceived at all." A.K.) Or, conversely, thinking of the sea slug with its extremely high number of nerves *as* a loosely knit brain of sorts – call it a body-brain – could we then say it can not, then, feel *itself?* Be that as it may, we need not worry for the sea slug today. A television program witnessed by KS showed intern acupuncturists content to practice on needling apples as they bobbed in water.

2. Sea Slug Death Throes It is possible to kill a fish by braining it; but how do you kill something without a brain? The answer would probably be, by degrees. Since S. japonicus, as detailed elsewhere, can live though cut in half, or even less, even small pieces should retain something we might call the life-force for long enough that one could easily eat it. I assume that vinegar would hasten the death of the pieces about which MT writes "I have experienced that the dermis of 1x1x7mm size showed a response to the neurotransmitter acetylcholine after it had been kept in sea water for 2 days." (corres) This lingering life-force inspired Keigu to write three *ku*: "cutting sea slug / life vanishes / ever so slowly" (*namako kiri isogazuni kieyuku inochi* 海鼠切り急がずに消えゆく命　敬愚), "diced sea slug / its soul is creeping slowly / down death's path" (*namako kiri tamashii wa hau shidenomichi* 海鼠斬り魂は這ふ死出の道　敬愚), and "dicing sea slug / its life not one to rush / across the styx" (*namako kiri inochi isogazu shidenomichi* 海鼠斬り命急がず死出の道　敬愚). The "death-leave-path"(*shidenomichi*) is translated differently in the last two poems. The Styx is not quite right for things Japanese, though it is better than, say, the road to Hades, whose meaning has been corrupted by Christians who turned the other world into Heaven or Hell. (The amount of life-force in various tissues is a fascinating one. Note the sea turtle, described by Steinbeck (LSC), whose "litle cubes of white meat responded to the touch" and whose heart kept pulsing for hours after death. In this respect, the turtle and sea cucumber no doubt out-perform the frog whose leg muscle twitches contributed so much to the development of science.)

ぶっとくて小心海鼠は酢で締める　みよこ

buttokute shôshin namako wa su de shimeru – miyoko (2003)
(*thick/wanton/male timid/chicken seaslug-as-for, vinegar-with brace/firm/congeal*)   #278

i toughen up
a thick-set meek slug
with vinegar

bracing him up

i vinegarize
this hunk of a cowardly
sea cucumber

～

i fix a hunky
lilly-livered sea slug
with vinegar

The vinegar effect is not hyperbolized here as with the stone-making haiku we shall see later. The wit is, rather, in the contradicting modifiers, and does not work well in English, where "thick" does not *also* mean large/bold/wanton, a somewhat daunting man's man of a man. "Hunk" bears a semblance to the Japanese, but it is a much shallower and slangy term.   I did not recognize the intensification of the more common *futoi/futokute* and, assuming the *buttokute* meant "tossing aside"(for that was all my dictionary gave me) first translated: *tossing aside / my trepidation, i firm up / the slug in vinegar* (or, again, *tossing sea slug / into the vinegar to fix / our timidity*), then, more loosely, *quake no more! / sea slug and i grow hard / in the vinegar!* Perhaps misreading my translation, a single male reader, AQ, wrote the Yamoyomo haiku forum that this poem might be read as a salacious one. If I may borrow a *mammoth* from Mark Twain[1] → and substitute his *cod* for our charge, we get:

trying vinegar
to brace up a mammoth
sea cucumber

AQ was right, the poem does indeed look like it might fit right into an anthology of eighteenth century *senryu*, except for one thing.   *Shimeru* means hardens=shrinks=braces (in a refreshing way, like aftershave). As far as I know, there are no male members so large that they *shrink* to harden! Though Miyoko-san, after (playfully) chastising men for getting off on such subjects, was good-natured enough to say, "interpret my poem as you please, (it only reflects on you)," I could not possibly do so, even if it did make sense, for *she wrote it.* A conceited *enka* (the type of song that started *karaoke*) singer once answered the question about how to define his genre by replying "If *I* sing it, it is *enka.*" If a haikuist with a pure mindset writes a poem, it is *not* senryu, even if we may choose to read it that way.   I apologize to Miyoko – and to Buson, if his ghost is reading – for playing fast and loose with their poems to beef up this chapter!

褌もかかぬ海鼠のうんごうんご（太平の代や代や）知恵海

fundoshi mo kakanu namako no ungo ungo ~ taihei no yoyo (s) – chiekai (1723)
(loin-cloth, too, wear-not seaslug's wriggling/squirminess // peaceful reigns/generations)   #279

not quite still life

the squirming
of a sea slug: it wears
no loin cloth!

picture of peace time

this squirming
of countless sea slugs
sans loincloth

In the Warring Era, men had to sleep with their loincloths pulled tight, ready to leap from bed and defend themselves. But now, we – I showed this collective assumption by adding "countless" to the translation – can relax, and someone walking by might even get a glimpse of our crotches as we sluggishly lie about. In tense times, our cocks shrink and out balls retreat, but now they all relax and slowly squirm, as is normal for napping men. The sea slug is a perfect match for this lazy mood, for the minute movements and expansion of the genitalia. Now, to return to the subject of this chapter:

蛸壺にまぎれ込たる大海鼠　柳多留

takotsubo ni magirekomitaru ônamako yanagidaru s31
#279-b (octopus-pot-into wandering-enter/ed big-seaslug)

it's wandered	it has managed
into an octopus pot	to find an octopus pot
a big sea slug!	a huge sea slug

This senryû has found a way to get a not-so-hard sea slug penis into an object that is synonymous with a vagina that has a very tight entrance but is relatively expansive inside. The following senryu is much more well-known – I have seen it in many books – but hard to comprehend.

あわび取 なまこのくくるこころよさ（ふみこみにけり x 2）末摘花 初

awabitori namako no kuguru kokoro yosa (*fumikomi-ni keri* " ") – suetsumuhana (1776)
#280　　(abalone-taking/er sea slug's/s' snaking [through/into] heart/mind-goodness (step right in! x2))

pathetic phallusy?	*possession*	*seabed saga*
how good it feels	when sea-squirt*	how she loves it
for a sea slug to slip	slips into an abalone	an abalone girl slipping
into an abalone	what a feeling!	through the slugs

This comes from a particularly pornographic *senryu* collection whose title Englishes as either "the tip-pinch-flower" or the "lipstick-blossom." While the grammar may be stretched to make the sea slug an active shell-cracker, such readings are dubious. It makes more sense to read *awabitori* as an abalone-diver – a woman[1] – as my right reading and all Japanese readings do. One old interpretation by Laugh-mountain cited in a Suetsumuhana round-table discussion (rinkô) imagines a Saga woman (known for loving sex and for sea slugging), who would start to feel turned on "merely by gripping a warty sea slug." Be that as it may, it is still hard to see what exactly is happening in the poem.

→ **1. Mark Twain's *Mammoth Cod Society*** I'm sure the interested reader can google down Twain's book. Let me just say Twain suffered from the opposite affliction of Montaigne (Fie! Fie! Microsoft! "Montaigne" the father of the modern essay and psychology is not in the MSWord spell-check! You need an education, Bill Gates!), though in the long run all sea slugs are the same.
1. *The Sea Squirt* I know this creature is in a different phylum, but since it is written "old-sea-rat" in Japanese and was thought to be what a namako turned into, I couldn't resist a squirt in the shell! In the famous work of travel literature *Tosa Nikki* (a woman's diary written by a man, c 934), a sea squirt (pronounced *hoya*) is called the mate of an *izushi,* a marinated   blue mussel (*igai*) so perfectly labial, that, in the words of the anonymous author of a splendid book of cultural cuntology (*Nyônin Manko* 女陰万考), "looks so like the real thing that it cannot serve as a euphemism."
2. *Female Divers* Depending on the item being taken and the location (cold water no doubt had to go with the best insulated sex) either sex dove, but women would have been more common on the coast as men tended to be out in boats. On TV all traditional divers are women, but I doubt if the division of labor was that clear.   In the *Sea Cucumber's* Eye (namako no manako), Tsurumi Yoshiyuki does, however, make it clear that namako=male, abalone=female-divers.   ~ ~

.abalone dreams

how delicious!
a sea slug slips through
a diver's crotch

A contemporary Japanese commentator writes "I suppose a sea slug slipping through the crotch touching the privates would feel good but, unfortunately, as a man I cannot imagine it." If the older commentator seems to have the diver weaving between coral rocks with the sea slugs mixed in with abalone, this man apparently takes the *kuguru* (slip through a tight channel) very literally, and imagines her dropping the sea slug she has picked up so that it accidentally brushes her inner thighs.[1]

take-home

the fun of it
an abalone girl ties up
a sea slug!

Another Japanese contemporary [2] found slipping hard to buy and wondered if the verb might not rather be *kukuru*, or "tie-up." Perhaps, it meant the diver dropped it into her bag with the shellfish and pulled the cord tight. Because the *senryu* is prefaced with *fumikominikeri* or "just step right in!" (x2), I think the "Seabed Saga" reading is most probable. But, considering the imagination of the (male) *senryu* reader, the effective reading of the poem might be translated as:

i'd like to be
a sea slug slipping into
an abalone girl

Be that as it may, the abalone is not a common shell-as-cunt in *senryu*. A monovalve, it was busy enough serving as a symbol of one-sided, unrequited love. And that, needless to say, tends to be Platonic. But miracles happen. Every once in a while an abalone can be had. As we see here, the soft sea slug is not the only sea slug image. A sea slug is also thick and bumpy, characteristics strongly associated with stimulating women in Japanese popular sexology. The sea slug may *look* ugly, but he *feels* good. The abalone is a meat-eating shell. And what does the biological shellfish have to offer the real sea slug in return? Though "he" is a famously indiscriminate sediment-feeder, he does have his preferences and is happiest eating "her" shit. [3] Moreover, the historical sea slug has every reason to

The Sexy Ama The *ama* has long frequented the erotic imagination of Japanese men, yet I can only find one softly erotic poem, this *tanka*: "the *ama* gathers up sea slugs, shrimp, sea urchin, shell-fish, sea-weed, hugging them to her soft skin" or, perhaps,"she gathers sea slug, shrimp, sea urchin and sea weed, but making love, how soft her skin!" (*namako ebi uni kai mogusa kakiatsume ama wa idaku mo sono yawahada ni (t)* – minami masatane (mod) なまこえびうにかひもぐさかきあつめ海女は抱くもその柔肌に　南正胤).

Commentators Galore All these commentators for one minor senryu! Actually, they are side by side in one book by a group of senryu enthusiasts who take turns explaining the senryu in the Suetsumuhana and commenting on each others interpretations (srsth). I was relieved to find that

they, like me, were not sure about a lot!   #281

Coprophilic Sea Slugs Though sea slugs are known to be indiscriminate feeders who suck in as many varieties of tiny life and baby life-forms as is found in the sediment around them, they are mobile and known to congregate beneath barrier rocks or platforms with oysters, blue mussels and other bivalves where, Arakawa Kôman (ndh) writes, all oyster cultivators agree, they "chose to eat their excrement." He also reports that baby sea cucumbers grow faster when raised together with abalones (which I would think safer for not being bivalve!), developing best of all when the abalone are fed on *arame* (*eisenia bicyclis*), *kajime* (?), and other *katsumo* (brown-kelp type) seaweeds. Dr. Arakawa's main publications include Scatological Studies of the Bivalvia (Academic Press).

want to achieve closure with the abalone. To sum up Tsurumi Yoshiyuki's findings, once the sea slug and abalone were equally important tribute items to the head Shinto Shrine (Ise Jingu) and to the Imperial Court, but before we get to the Tokugawa (1603-1856), our charge was no longer so honored. Tsurumi guesses that because abalone were taken from the rocks by female divers with some sort of a shrine maiden and Imperial Navy connection, they outclassed the sea slugs netted from sandy bottoms by males who were part of a sort of sea gypsy people. So, we can see a lot going on here, more, no doubt than the poet could have imagined. Or, was it? See this next haiku:

汲（酌む）汐に転び（け）入るへき生海鼠哉　利（梨?）雪

kumu shio ni korobi[ge]irubeki namako kana – risetsu (1698)
(scooping/ed brine-in fall/roll/cavort-enter-ought sea-slug tis!/?/ó/the/a)

#282

salty dog

it really should
sport in that ladle o' brine:
the sea slug!

an eyeful

hey, sea slugs!
bet you'd like to get into
a ladle of brine!

The titles are necessary if the reader is to stand a chance of guessing what the poem is about. It went right by me at first, for I did not recognize scooping brine meant women working at a sea-side salt plant and *that* meant a view – unobscured because underwear had yet to be adopted – of the soft country where any *namako* would love to be. It seems the poet vicariously supplies the eyes!

蜆子にも逢はで漂ふ生海鼠かな　蓼太

shijimi ni mo awa de tadayou namako kana – ryôta (1717-1787)
(*corbicula*[a tiny shellfish]-even-to meet-not-because drifting sea-slug tis!/?/ó/the/'tis)

#283

bachelor

not meeting up
with a pretty *corbicula*
sea slug drifts

The *corbicula* is about a tenth the size of a clam and tastes good in miso soup, or, rather, makes the soup taste good, for it not every one bothers with the tiny morsels. They also stand for a tiny vulva.[1] Here it would seem that we have an ugly old man having no luck in bedding little girls. But the poet is a *bonafide* haiku poet and so I would guess this alludes to that spineless lady's man of *The Tales of Ise*, whose courting does not bring success, or . . . – Wait, we'll see at the head of the next chapter.

1. **Shellfish and Vulva** One generally only comes across this metaphor in old poems or in the plentiful pornographic cartoons. But once, I saw it *in action*. At a forget-the-year party (*bonenkai*), I went to in 1979, a young salesman from the boondocks of Japan who got up during a risqué song and wagged a large-size beer bottle up and down in front of his crotch was immediately matched by an older secretary who lifted a couple tiny shells (either *shijimi* or the slightly bigger but still tiny *asari*) out of her soup and deftly clicked them like miniature castanets as if to say that if the salesman was built like a horse, well she was as tiny as this shellfish. *Touche.* We might add that "our" ancients had the same idea. We can even find the pairing of sea cucumber and clam: "Or perhaps you thought →

海 男 子 東 海 夫 人 は 危 な い ぞ 敬 愚
umidanshi tôkai fujin wa abunai zo – keigu
(ocean-youth[seaslug] eastsea-lady[blue-mussel]-as-for, dangerous!)　　　　#284

master sea slug,
beware the hard lips of
the blue mussel!

共 食 ひ か 東 海 婦 人 に 海 男 子 敬 愚
tomogui ka tôkai fujin ni umidanshi – keigu
(together/mutual-eat/ers? east-lady-with/and ocean-youth)　　　　#285

sea slug and blue mussel

young sea man
and his east sea lady:
who eats whom?

Keigu follows the Chinese tradition of pairing the phallic "sea-youth" [1] (sea slug) with the more clearly vulvic "east-sea-lady" (the mussel *Mytilus coruscus,* in Japanese, *igai,* which includes a blue variety.[2] Japanese sea-slug penis metaphors are much rarer among senryu and haiku than one familiar with the Japanese penchant to eroticize sea-life might expect.[3] This is not because sea slug *contracts*

→ that you had very cleverly discovered how to craft a claim that I had sought these two sea creatures, the seacock [cockfish] and angelfish [cuntfish] for magical charms. In fact, learn the Latin names for the things which I have severally named so you can accuse me anew based upon proper information . . .[deletion] . . You claim that the clam and sea cucumber can be taken from the sea for erotic purposes on account of the double entendre of their names: how much less could a stone from the same shore be related to the bladder, a pot to probate, a crab to cancer, algae to the ague." (Hoffman transl. "APOLOGIA APVLEII" ccat.sas.upenn.edu/jod/texts/ apuleius/6.hoffman. html.　The "cockfish" and "cuntfish" I placed in the brackets were found in another translation.)

1. *Sea Slug as Youth or "Man-ling"* The suggestive Chinese term is given new life by the occasional factoid such as this from a South African newspaper: "As the celebrity cult cuts its swathe it creates its own monsters, like the rumoured sale of celebrity body parts – someone even claimed to own Rasputin's penis, which turned out to be a sea cucumber – and there are still pieces of James Dean's smashed Porsche floating around." (Lin Sampson: "The 15-minute industry: Idols" 5 sept 2002Sunday Times www.suntimes.co.za/2002/06/ 16/ lifestyle/life01.asp) .

2. *East Sea Lady* According to an old source, "there are some black hairs near this mussel's mouth." So Japanese readers will not think Keigu is making this up:　「貽貝の異名。。。重訂本草綱目啓蒙四

二。。「淡菜（略）口に少し黒毛あり。故に東海婦人の名あり。猶海参を海男子。。と称するか如し」」（OJD）

3. *Erotic Sea-life.*　Keep an eye on my website, for I plan to publish a small book of erotic (and disgusting) sea life *senryu* to be titled *The Mullet in the Maid* (It includes most of the fifty-odd shellfish haiku written by an Edo era female poet).　While the sea slug was little eroticized in the past, today, one finds *namako*=penises in pornographic novels on the net.　And get this snippet of a written chat centering on the attractiveness of pretty young stars dated 2001/2/1 by one "Sage:" "On a New Year's Special Program (a major channel TV show), the shot of Kago (last name of an *aidoru*=idol=pretty young thing of either sex) squatting down when she had sea slugs thrown at her showed she looked beautiful from behind . . ." Japanese women tend to turn away and squat when feeling threatened, whether by a shower of slugs or a rampaging moose (I saw such an AP or UPI photo once).　Japanese television shows like to do revolting things to young women to provoke erotic? facial expression and justify? squirming crotch shots. They do more revolting and painful things to men, but I suspect it is a compensatory smoke-screen. The most popular television show of the latter sort made a big hit in England, where keeping a stiff upper lip in the face of torture is still admired, as, I suppose, it should be. It is not a marginal phenomenon either, for its director, Beat Takeshi is internationally famous for his humorous and earthy movies.

rather than expands to get hard – making it the functional opposite of a penis. Most people don't look for *functional* parallels so much as for *formal* ones: the reason the *sea slug* is not more phallacized in Japan is that it lacks a quality of penis-hood stressed by Japanese – but not by Westerners, Han Chinese or most African cultures – a large *glans*. In Japan, this makes the mushroom the most sexy object in nature, for it has a *kasa,* an umbrella-like, or hat-like overhang. The glans is also called a *kasa* and a broad glans is depicted in Japanese art and, to a lesser degree, chosen for Japanese pornography.   In other words, if the sea slug had a head, it would be *much* sexier to the Japanese. [1]

海 の 底 海 鼠 む つ つ り 恋 す ら む　未知
umi no soko namako muttsuri koisuramu – anon (contemp)
(ocean's bottom seaslug taciturn/glumly/sullenly lovemaking)

#286

> the seabed
> sea slugs making
> glum love
>
> ～
>
> on the sea floor
> sea slugs are making love
> in moody silence

This is the only attempt to depict how sea slugs do it that I have come across in haiku. It is better than nothing and precisely how one might imagine the stereotypical sea slug, our metaphor of loneliness. I suppose it might also describe the sad reality of some human's life, but the truth is that our charge enjoys a much more uplifting love life in its low-gravity underwater world than most of us know. In Keigu's words,

ぐ ん に ゃ と 言 わ れ し な ま こ 立 居 か な　敬愚
gunnya to iwareshi namako tachii kana – keigu
(flaccid, said [to be] sea slug standing-position!/?/ó/the/behold)

#287

> *the sexy holothurian*
>
> mr sea slug
> supposedly impotent
> does it standing

How little do most of us know of the sea slug behind closed doors! Until I saw three of them reared up like a pair of Loch ness monsters or cobras in a PBS documentary on Guam, I imagined them limply spawning or, at most, clinging promiscuously together in a ball like another muddy creature, the toad! Catherine Malaval writes:

1. *The Mushroom and the Cucumber* Observing that Chinese, or, at least the Han ethnicity, colloquially refer to *namako* as a "sea man-ling" or a "donkey-dong," Tsurumi Yoshiyuki, writes that while one Japanese (the Matsumae fief's lord) thought it good for curing gonorrhea, this sexualization isn't found in Japanese, for "the Japanese don't seem to have been so hypersensitive about sex" (nnm). If he had thought about the mushroom, Tsurumi would have had to come up with another explanation. I believe all cultures may be roughly divided into those which emphasize the size (generally breadth) of the glans and that of the shaft (generally length). I believe this difference, observable in the art of the respective cultures, affects our metaphorization of nature. Japan is a glans = mushroom culture, whereas most Chinese ethnicities, like most Europeans, are a cucumber=shaft culture. We should note, however, that the Japanese *ma-namako* is not so sleek as the typical Occidental sea cucumber (one Occidental website – "water-softeners. com's" "Water Dictionary" simplistically defines *holothurian* as "long and slender in shape!"). *Namako* is more like a chubby gherkin.

> Its method of reproduction is quite astonishing – both males and females, which are ordinarily content to lie flat, rear up like cobras and swing backwards and forwards while releasing their sexual cells. ("The Sea Slug Should Stay Under," Liberation 25/1/1994)

Apparently, *most* holothurian release their eggs and sperm like this. The sperm or eggs pour out from slits located on what would seem to resemble the back of the head, if the oral end can be so called.* Less realistically, a drawing in Arakawa's *Sea Cucumber Reader* (ndh) borrowed from Dmitriev (1955),* shows two sea slugs raised up straight and high as smokestacks, ejecting clouds of sexual matter as forcefully as if from an aerosol can! The "spray" particles join, so it looks like the pair is mating, though they are more likely part of a group spawn. Recent research by Jean-Francois Hamel and Anne Mercier shows that *Cucumaria frondosa* also secretes a biologically active mucus "to help maintain gametogenic synchrony among co-specifics." That, Englished, means these cold-blooded cucumbers even force one another to come into heat! Alexander Kerr describes *Stichopus horrens* and *Bohadschia argus* and Ron Shimek the *Cucumaria miniata*:

> Usually the males rear up first in early evening. It is quite a sight to swim along a reef above a forest of large rearing holothurians, the milky sperm spilling out of pores on their "heads." The sperm also contains a factor that soon has the females rearing and spilling their purple or orange eggs as well. The whole show takes about a couple of hours. (A. K: corresp)

> I have seen populations of the large temperate cuke, *Cucumaria miniata*, spawn so completely that within a few minutes the color of the water in the bay has changed from blue to green due to the addition of the vast number of green eggs. Fertilization occurs, and the larvae develop while floating in the water. (www.animalnetwork.com/fish2/aqfm/2000/jan/wb/default)

The amount of ejaculation is incredible. Imagine ten, twenty, thirty percent of the body weight of thousands of sea cucumbers! The 1999-2000 Encyclopedia Britannica thinks they raise and wave their bodies "presumably . . to prevent eggs and sperm from becoming entrapped in the sediment, but the main idea may be that spawning together will overwhelm the appetite of the predators. Since other sea-creatures also tend to spawn on the full moon, this "lunacy" may also be a trans-species strategy for maximizing larva survival.

Holothurian Reproduction There is more to marvel about. Some holothurian not *only* reproduce sexually but asexually to boot! If the winter conditions are good, , they pinch-off the upper third and divide! (*cold fission*, svp.) This is found among edible trepang (*S. chloronotus*) but not among the *S. Japonicus.** The former, in Motokawa Tatsuo's words, "responds to strong mechanical stimulus by 'melting', that is becoming quite soft as if it melts" whereas the latter does not. "The mechanical properties of the body wall of two species are different" (corresp). Though the *S. Japonicus*, i.e. our *namako*, doesn't divide on its own, experiments show that cut in half, about 40-50% of the "head" side and 70-80% of the "tail" side survive. The aboral side is the more vital, for the tip of the head by itself never survives, whereas the tip of the tail does almost as well as half a namako! (崔相:1963, in Arakawa: ndh). According to Dolmatov (corres), Chinese research carried out from 1955-7 found that even the middle section of a J. Stichopus "could regenerate their lost organs" (i.e. survive) though it took longer (about a year!) than the oral or aboral ends (Chzgan Fyn-in and U Boo-lin 1958 cited in Levin: 1982) The care of the young is also varied. Most let their brood fare for themselves, but some species use a brood pouch, others allow the young to develop in a body cavity, carry their young on their back, let them cling "to the smooth areas of the creeping sole" or even "have been seen holding plant material against its body helping to keep young in place. "(Buchsbaum and Milne), something that, if true, speaks persuasively for the power of instinct.

Dmitriev (1955) Because Dmitriev, A.F. "Underwater Observations on Behavior of Trepangs" (in the Russian popular journal Nature 1955, #6, pg 96) is not cited (only his name is given), the illustration was probably taken from a reproduction in Levin: 1982.

なまこ曳き夜立ちの身を捕る魔女丸　敬愚

namakobiki yodachi no mi o toru majô maru – keigu

#288

(seaslug-drag, night-stand/ing[=erection]'s body takes witch [+[fishing]boat title])

witch boat

like a succubus
the dragnet takes sea slugs
standing at night

Neither mating nor science explains the whole picture. A fisherman from 留萌(Liumeng?) told Tsurumi Yoshiyuki that it was best to drag for sea cucumbers at night when they stood up, rather than when they were lying down asleep during the day. *Uh huh,* thought Tsurumi, *night-standing* (*yodatsu*)! *No wonder they are not only eaten for longevity but for sexual stamina!* Association aside, the 'standing" here would probably include not just the occasional sex and the plankton feeding of some species (not true for *namako*) but simply the way sea cucumbers lift up the middle of their body a little to move. The Japanese version of the poem is better because of the existence of a title (*maru*) specific to boats (only large ships have their *SS* in English), and especially common for fishing boats.

骨無しも死なばカタキや海鼠の身　敬愚

honenashi mo shinaba kataki ya namako no mi – keigu

#289

(boneless, too dead-if/when raises hard[=revenge]:/! black-seaslug)

spineless alive
dead sea slugs may turn
as hard as nails

~

called spineless
he dies and makes things hard
sea cucumber

Cured sea slug, which is neglected by haiku for not being much eaten in Japan, is very hard. In Chinese, it is called sea-ginseng. The second character is the same "-*seng*" as that used in "ginseng." And, like ginseng, it was considered good for the libido.[1] My guess is that it is the sea slug's ability to temporarily harden itself, rather than rumors of "night-standing" mentioned by Tsurumi, that makes the association. The translation would have worked if the second line were "he dies with a hard-on," but, unfortunately, the sea slug softens when it dies and is only hardened by the right curing process.

1. Sea Slug Aphrodisiac? The character shared with ginseng in itself is not sexy (it originally meant a hairdo and now is a respectful way to write "visit." It was borrowed from ginseng because it shares its medicinal properties. In Korea in my 20's, I once had three wet-dreams in a single night (!) after drinking ginseng wine. So, I can't help feeling there might be a little something to these libido foods. At the same time, it would be remiss not to point out, with Tsurumi Yoshiyuki, that the Occidental "aphrodisiac" – a food that immediately makes one lascivious – is something completely foreign to the medical foods of the Sinosphere: "Sexual potency and sexual arousal are completely different concepts" (nnm). David Gilbert's 1998 novel *Remote Feed* offers a case in point. In the words of a reviewer (Audrey Ferber): "While Edmund naps and dreams of the 15-year-old girls he prefers as sexual partners, Miguel tempts Chester and Debbie with the local aphrodisiac, *beche de mer*. They lick the green, warty sea slug and their willingness 'to participate in the unknown, in the uncertain' brings passion back to their lives." Perhaps this is "a dazzling appearance by a sea cucumber" (http *Dr. Sige Gaas*://www. nytimes.com/books/ 98/12/06/ reviews/notable-fiction.html), but make no mistake about it, the "appearance" is Occidental with a vengeance.

乳 母 は 桶 の 海 鼠 を 見 て ま た 歩 い た 　 一 碧 樓

uba wa oke no namako o mite mata aruita – nakatsuka ippekiro (1885/7?-1946)

(wet-nurse-as-for bucket/tub's seaslug[obj] seeing/seen again walked)   #290

the wet nurse
stopped looking at a bucket of sea cucumbers
and walked again.

[trans.by _____?]

On the one hand, this poem by a poet famed for fusing the haiku and free-verse sensibilities – the above poem could have been snipped from a paragraph of prose – is seems a typical modern observation of what is and only what is. On the other hand , the wet nurse in Japan at the time this poem was written (today's Japan is a foreign country) cannot be separated from her stereotype: a sex-crazed woman with an enormous hairy twat,[1] overflowing with bodily juices. Parenthetically speaking, this poem is followed on the same internet page by:

a dog with a long flank is sad.
rapes blossom.

No, it is *not* what it seems. I don't need to see the original to know that the rape – words like *rapina*, *canolla*. etc. are used by our jittery supermarkets for what we used to call unabashedly "rape" – has begun to blossom and its cheerful bright yellow bloom apparently makes the dog appear to be gloomy.

料 亭 の 真 っ 赤 な ル ー ジ ュ 海 鼠 食 い 　 南 茶 手 栗 金 時

ryôtei no makkana ruhju namakogui – nanchatte kurikintoki? (c 2000)

(restaurant's extremely-red rouge, seaslug-eater)   #291

in a restaurant
brightly rouged lips
a sea slug eater

赤 海 鼠 マ ニ ュ キ ア の 指 に 失 神 す 　 平 出 雅 春

akanamako manukia no yubi ni shisshin su – hirade gashun? (contemp)

(red-seaslug manicured finger/s-by lose-consciousness-does)   #292

a red sea slug
faints at the touch of
pretty fingernails

1. *Stereotypical Wet Nurse* Wet nurses, or rather their stereotypes, abound in *senryu*. Most commonly, they terrify children who catch glimpses of the hairy-lipped monster lurking between their crotches, and engage in wild sex while on the job.

her suit

the wet-nurse
up front she's a perfect
seaweed crab

Reputedly large of member, they go to any length to satisfy themselves, even going so far as to introduce a child's leg into their "furry-shoes" (!) This worthless (but marine) *senryu* combines three old saws: 1) the crab claw was a metaphor for the labia; 2) the crab species in question is hairy as wet-nurse's snatches were reputed to be;   3) seaweed was standard trope for pubic hair. I don't know if such crabs have anything to do with sea slugs and hate to investigate lest I discover they do not! (The original Japanese will be in my forthcoming book, *The Mullet in the Maid.*.)

海 鼠 食 べ つ つ 花 び ら と な り し 舌　鳥 居 真 理 子

namako tabe tsutsu hanabira to narishi shita – torii mariko (contemp.)

#293

(seaslug eat while petals become: tongue)

eating sea slug
my tongue turns into
cherry petals

Sent to the *Catwalk Haiku Kurinikku* (Clinic) website, the first haiku elicited the following comment from "Doctor" Watanabe Junko: "This is one of those instances where *ignorance is bliss*." I think she means that if this is a metaphor, she doesn't want to know what it stands for. And that tells me that rightly or wrongly it belongs in this chapter, or perhaps inscribed on certain lithographs by George Groetz [?] which I will not describe. Her *"diagnosis and prescription"* was "Who could get a handle on this one! Someone, please lend me your knowledge!" She might have written the same about the second haiku, found elsewhere. Still, both are easy compared to the third haiku. I have no idea what it means but I know a good poem when I see one. The falling cherry petals I imagine may be rose.

生 海 鼠 の 輪　若 狭 呼 ぶ と き 掛 け る 袈 裟　大 花 笠

namako no wa wakkyô yobu toki kakeru kesa (s) – obanagasa (c1720)

#294

(seaslug's ring, young-spring=well priming time [is] worn surplice)

recommended surplice for ritual drawing of water in the spring

a sea squirt ring
just the thing to wear
for well-priming

Despite suggestive poems such as the last two, softness and headlessness prevents the sea slug from assuming a true dildo-like identity in the Japanese erosphere. Still, thanks to its bumps, the *namako* (the "squirt" was just for effect) is a synonym for the Japanese equivalent – or, rather equivalents, as Japanese were big on sex tools – for what the English and Americans call "a French tickler," though it only fit around the neck of the penis (just under the glans). I had to make the ridiculously long title to explain the clean allegory in the dirty *senryu* about an artificially improved penis exciting the *well* found at the foot of *mons veneris*. Such pornography is hardly haiku, but this next, by someone in a haiku-get-together run by the early modern haikuists, Kyoshi,[1] Hekigoto and Hyôtei is:

こ わ い と や 海 鼠 を 京 の 女 郎 だ ち　虚 桐 庵 句 会

kowai to ya namako o kyô no jôrôdachi – kyoshi et al (1894)

#295

([they are] frightening! sea-slugs [+obj] Kyoto's whores)

clams, you say?

the sea slug
is the scary one, say
Kyoto whores

Having read a haiku about Edo whores eating snake sushi by Issa, I first thought this was similar (the absent verb might be "eaten" rather than "feared") but then remembered there was a haiku (by whom I

---

1. *Kyoshi* A major effort to describe *"World Literature in the Twentieth Century"* by Seymour Lipset fails to mention Kyoshi, who, more than any one else created the broad-based haiku movement of the twentieth century. This is regrettable (as are many of Lipset's glib remarks about the Japanese in the same). Kyoshi is a name you should know. In *Kyoshi: A Haiku Master*, Susumu Takiguchi proposes adding Kyoshi to the top four (Basho, Buson, Issa, Shiki) poets of the haiku pantheon. I do not like Kyoshi's pedagogy re. proper haiku, but have not read enough Kyoshi to cast my vote.

can't recall) describing *clams* as frightful in Kyoto, because the old capital is far from the sea and food-poisoning is more likely than in Edo or Osaka. Since clam (*hamaguri*) was a vulgarism for the female part, Kyoshi *et al's* haiku is probably a riposte to an allusion merely incidental to the older haiku: *You men say* our *clams are terrifying? Well, we think* your *sea slugs are scary!* At the same time, the pliant sea slug is an appropriate theme for the stereotypically soft-natured Kyoto.

海 女 浮 か ぶ な ま こ 掴 み し 手 を あ げ て 下 村 梅 子
ama ukabu namako tsukamishi te o agete – shimomura umeko (contemp)
(female-diver floats-up sea-slug gripping hand/s raising)   #296

> an *ama* pops up
> with a sea cucumber
> in each hand
>
> ~
>
> up comes ama
> a sea slug clutched
> in each hand!
>
> ~
>
> amas surface
> clutching sea slugs
> in raised hands

I suspect that this is a tourist situation, for an *ama* would probably put her catch into a pouch before surfacing. This is a purely factual haiku, and a wonderful snapshot at that, but I cannot help remembering some off-color jokes about finding *them* growing wild, jokes that the poet, Japanese and female, would not know. More to the point, I also remember the expression for a man lucky enough to enjoy the company of two beautiful women as having "a flower in both hands" (*ryô te ni hana*) and like to imagine this as a bawdy female equivalent with a *"Tadah! I did it!"* added by the ama's coming up with her hands raised as if to show off her coup. But, forget this conceptualization. The contrast of her fleshy white hand/s and the warty slug/s is in itself mildly erotic.

酢 海 鼠 や ご く り と 動 く 喉 仏 K. H.
sunamako ya gokuri to ugoku nodobotoke – K.H. (2000)
(vinegar/pickled-sea-slug: gulp/gokuri-with move throat-buddha[adam's apple])   #297

> pickled sea slug
> i see the bobbing of
> his adam's apple

This powerful close-up of the body, on the other hand, is *very* erotic. In the original – far more effective than my translation – you can see and *hear* the movement of the bone as the man swallows the incompletely chewed sea slug, perhaps washed down with beer. The fact it caught the poet's attention suggests her lover or husband has an especially large Adam's apple. If she is feeling affectionate toward him, I imagine it would be a turn-on, whereas estrangement would make it a turn-off. Either way, the effect is strangely heightened by the food he eats, for the Adam's apple resembles the protuberances found on the Japanese sea slug itself and is equally tough, for it tends more than any other bone (except for teeth) to survive cremation. Resembling a sitting Buddha, it was often kept in a small urn placed in the family's home-altar box after the rest of the ashes were scattered. If the poet, like most women, outlives her husband, only his "throat buddha" will remain to keep her company.

喉 す ぐ る 酢 海 鼠 こ の む 年 と な り   谷 口 満 寿 子
nodosuguru sunamako konomu toshi to nari – taniguchi mitsuko (contemp)

#298   (throat-passing vinegar/pickled-sea-slug-liking age become)

ah, old enough
to like sea slug passing
down my throat!

Swallowing slug would seem to be a learned pleasure. [1] KS opines, "as she aged, the initially unfamiliar feeling became a pleasant one. This may have something to do with the amount of *sake* she has come to drink." Since old people cannot chew their sea slug down as far as young people, it is a good thing, too! I could not fit the "pickled" nor "i become (old enough)" into the translation of this poem that might be considered auto-erotic, in the broad sense of the term. Here is a man appreciating the same: "when fresh, cool blue sea slug slips *surusuru* [mimesis] down your throat, it refreshes/braces your stomach." (from a Japanese internet site called "Rosetta News"). The word used for refresh/brace (*sukitto-suru*) is the same mimesis Coca Cola chose for the Japanese version of "*the pause that refreshes*."

a morsel from "uniyufururupurin" by ushijima naomi

[Re: Kanton cuisine eaten in a hong kong restuarant]. It uses many dried foods, such as blowfish fins, abalone, bird[swallow] -nest soup, flower[fish]-bladder and sea-present [sea slug]. All high-class gourmet items. And, excluding the abalone, . . . all are tasteless. They all seem made expressly for the purpose of the mouthfeel [1→] (*shokkan*). The *purin* of the blowfish fin, the *niyun,* and somewhat hard *nettori* of the abalone, and the sea slug, with its *pururin, nettori* and *furufuru,* which I thought the acme of the *unyufururupuri* foods.

#299 （下）

1. *Swallowing Sea Slug* People who dispose of their gum by swallowing it should love pickled sea slug, for it is often swallowed.   One modern haiku suggests how it might best be done: "pickled slug / it passes my throat / as i nod" (*sunamako no hitounazuki ni nodo suguru* – izawa masae (1978) 酢海鼠の一うなづきに喉過ぐる　井沢正江). Nods – performed every few seconds by Japanese engaged in conversation to indicate they are listening (though their eyes might be closed, they are nodding *on* not *off*! – are often preceded by the chin being slightly raised, something Doctors recommend for swallowing large pills (HB). Here is an excerpt from the net-found journal of one Greg Raven relating "by far the most revolting meal" he ever had in Korea. " When I inquired what the gray puddle was, the young man's pronunciation of 'sea cucumber' at first sounded like 'sh– cucumber,' which, it turned out, was appropriate. Overcoming last-minute hesitations at being faced with the prospect of eating this raw . . . we decided that a bottle of beer would be prudent, and committed ourselves to a small order of the sad little creatures (still living on the block, presumably spared from knowledge of their impending fate by a mercifully primitive neural system). Sure enough, a plate appeared of chunks of what had been a barely respiring sea beast 60 seconds before, gutted, dabbed in sauce, and topped with toasted sesame seeds. . . .The silence was pregnant. Time seemed to hold its breath as we each focused on what was going on in our mouths. No eloquence could describe it sufficiently. The taste was not particularly threatening—mild and reminiscent of the sea. But the texture – ah, the texture! At first bite I thought of the crunchiness of squid, only much firmer. But as I chewed further, it was obvious this was unique in the world. I could chew away the crunchiness, like breaking down clenched muscle (which is exactly what it was), but no matter how persistently I chewed, the matter would not break apart. So after a minute or two I ended up with an elastic, soft, slimy blob of mucus that tasted of the sea. . . .Over the course of another beer and a series of suppressed gags (I had to pause to pick the tenacious slime from the back of my throat), we managed to finish a respectable amount of the plate, killing the taste afterward with some nasty green *mochi* [rice ball] that Ketty had picked out earlier. ("Travels of a Vagabond Globetrotter" Friday, September 13, 1996) [rights?????]) Compare this to the "refreshing" swallow in the text!

[Re: another Chinese smorgesboard]. It included abalone, not dry but *rizunarubaru* [reasonably] steamed, goose-paddles[feet], blossom-melon, hair-greens [lichen?] and sea-present [sea-slug]; and each of these had its own unique tooth-reply [1] . Among these, the one that stimulated my brain the most was the sea slug.

I stuffed my mouth with that *unyufurupurin,* and as I enjoyed the feeling of it on my front teeth and gum, I slowly masticated one mouthful. My tongue tumbled over the *nettori,* and as I felt my *pururin* tooth-reply (*hagotae*), I savored the quivering *furufuru* tongue-touch (*shita-zawari*). How can I explain this, this feeling of welcoming *namako-san* (mr sea slug?) with my whole mouth? Ah, aaah! Just to think about it now. Gluttonous, I wanted it in my mouth forever. Oh, what a happy time it was! Stop, time, forever! That's what I was crying in my heart the entire time! All the others were proceeding with their vegetables, and there I was, alone, slowly chewing mr sea slug.

The next day, still unable to forget that happy feeling (*mi-kaku*= taste-feel/sense), I went to a Chinese department store to find sea slug. . . . The sea slugs were, as always, crude-looking lumps. . . . There were "boar-hag-presents,"* "hag-presents," "white-stone-presents," some with no spines [a central part of the Japanese image of sea slugs], and I suddenly realized that a sea slug, too is not a matter of appearance. . . . It always gets me, how these rough, bumpy, hard lumps can become so delicate an *unyupuri.*

This article was published as part of a series on Asian cuisine in the magazine *Asahi Internet Easter* [something from the *East*, not the Christian festival!] found on Asahi.com. It is connected with *Asahi Shinbun,* the *New York Times* of Japan. That is to say, the article was not published in an obscure cooking journal, nor part of a Fellini-style gustatory erotica, but *mainstream reading.* Still, even Japanese readers will find the third paragraph uncomfortably close to the descriptions of an act not uncommonly found in the sex pages of evening "sports" newspapers! I have not found a haiku to match it. As far as I know, the reporter deserves credit for inventing compound mimesis to describe particular combinations of food (something the male writers of Edo did for the sounds of mictiration and sex). Note, however, that she is writing about the softer rehydrated and stewed or gelatinized Chinese sea slug. She would find different words to depict the sound-feel of the chewier uncooked *namako* of her own country.

古妻や馴れて海鼠を膳に上（の）ぼす　嶋田青峰
furutsuma ya narete namako o zen ni nobosu – seihô (1881-1944)
(old-wife: used-to sea slug table-on lay-out)   #300

> my old wife
> serving the sea slug
> familiarly

The Japanese editor's explanation was that this poem expresses the poet's deep affection for his old wife, who he remembers as a young bride who couldn't even touch a sea slug. Like most Japanese men, I find something attractive in the blushing reticence that colors the faces of young men and women – but mostly women – in old-fashioned rural societies around the world. So, in a subtle way, this is a *Sexy Sea Slug* poem, and a very good one which might be titled *pink memories.*

→**1. *Mouthfeel*** This *bona fide* though not widely known word was introduced to me by professional food-writer DA and is exhaustively described in the *Chewy Sea Slug* chapter.

1. *Tooth Reply* This is my ad-hoc neologism for the common Japanese term *hagotae* . It also translates as "mouthfeel" of which it would be an important part. It, too, is described in *The Chewy Sea Slug.*

海 鼠 腸 を す す る や 絹 を す す る ご と 尺 山 子

#301

konowata o susuru ya kinu o susuru goto – shakusanshi? (1973)
(seaslug gut slurp/ing! silk slurping like[similar])

throatfeel

sea slug guts
slurping them is like
slurping silk

Neither the Japanese term "tooth-reply" (*hagotae*) nor the new English "mouthfeel" will do for this. Here, we must invent a new term, the title. The reader might note that silk is not a totally fresh invention here, for it is standard trope for smoothness. (Note that smooth tofu is called "silk" and rough "cotton," even though the latter, which requires more squeezings of the soy beans is, in Japan, generally more expensive.)

海 鼠 腸 を す す り に 来 た り 帰 り 花 千 来

#302

konowata o susuri ni kitari kaeribana – senrai? chiko? (1699)
(seaslug-guts[+obj] [to] slurp, [he/she] comes-and-so-forth, return-blossom)

why not?

she comes to slurp
slug guts and in her winter
blooms once again

The *return-blossom* is a late fall or early winter phenomenon – a tree with a second bloom, not that rare for some types of cherry – identified with elderly energy. Not knowing anything about the poet, I can not pin down the details of this visceral haiku and can only say that I feel a greater eros in it.

～

Chapter End Note It was impossible of me to ascertain just how many sea slug found their way into *senryu*. Some books of *senryu* have spelling-based indexes but these only work if the poem begins with the sea slug, *senryu* experts are impossible to find and there are no searchable *senryu*-banks. I can only hope to interest amateur *senryu* fans in Japan to keep their eyes open. 本格的な川柳の online db はないから、「海鼠」が初句でなければ、つまり 50 音のインデックスになければ、ほとんど見付けられない。で、ここにない面白い川柳に出会えば、教えて下さい！第二版に加えます。　～～.

12
<u>the just-so sea slug</u>

Unless we count the Taoist Sea Slugs as *just-so stories* for indirectly equating *namako* with the bag-like god of the beginning, haiku falls short in this genre. I am not certain why. Poets often play upon old poems and allude to both legendary and historical happenings. Perhaps, the *just-so story* favors a longer narrative than a haiku can provide. We will see one exception from a 17th century kinko=gold –sea-slug series (the rest of which remain with the *Place-pun Sea Slugs* in the Sundry section) but, even then, the place name is explained by the slug rather than vice versa. There is, however, considerable *indirect* reference to the *Record of Ancient Matters* myth respecting the sea slug's silence.

口 つ ぐ む 海 鼠 質 せ ば 一 理 あ り　高 沢 良 一
kuchi tsugumu namako tadaseba ichiri ari -- takasawa yoshikazu (2003)
(mouth shut-up/clam/med-up seaslug investigate/judge-if, one[a kernal/point of]-truth is)   #303

> that sea slug
> who kept mum may have
> had a point

> *?no miranda?*

> the sea slug
> who held his tongue
> got a bum rap

> ~

> ancient sea slug
> there is something to be said
> for its silence

Clever paraversing could not make-up for the fact that English has no verb that by itself means "to clarify the rights and wrongs of some matter" as does *tadasu[tadaseba]*. Most of the other haiku about *Silent Sea Slugs*, as we shall see in the chapter by that name, are really about people – but Takasawa writes about the sea slug, or, rather, the mythological sea slug, itself.

海 鼠 裂 く 板 前 口 を と が ら せ て 忍 草
namako saku itamae kuchi o togarasete – shinobugusa (2000)
(seaslug-slice/open board-before[sushi-chef] mouth points/sharpens/purses)   #304

> the sushi chef
> splitting a sea slug
> purses his lips

The focus on the chef's lips – pursed lips small but full of folds suggesting a parallel, while their tightness is diametrically opposed to the rendered mouth of the sea slug – gentle evokes *Ancient Matters*. In the body language of English, lips pursed tightly so that they jut out in front suggest petulance and possibly pouting, but in Japanese, they also speak of repressed anger and silent discontent (expected of a *Just-so Sea Slug*). Yet, some people do this, as others open their mouths or stick out their tongue when intent upon some difficult task. As the sushi chef wears a debonair rolled-cloth headband, one is also reminded of the similarly attired droll figure, *hyottoko*, whose lips are absurdly pursed and drawn out like the stem end of a gourd.

懸 命 に 海 鼠 の 口 を 探 し け り　原 田 喬

kenmei ni namako no kuchi o sagashikeri – harada kyo? (modern)

#305

(desperately/assiduously/intently, seaslug's mouth[+obj] searching[+fin])

assiduously
searching the mouth of
the sea slug

pickled parts

trying hard
to find the mouth of
the sea slug

The grammar of this poem first gives us the poet trying to find the location of the mouth, but that is not really hard to find, so my first reading has him searching, presumably for damage caused by Amenouzumenomikoto with her dagger. That is, looking to confirm, or perhaps see what exactly is *just-so.* Then, recalling that someone wrote that the oral and aboral ends of the sea slug were particularly tasty, it occurred to me that this man may be trying to find the mouth – or part of it! – among chunks of pickled sea slug! The original does not mention pickled slug, so this is *very iffy,* but *if* it is true, the haiku becomes delightfully concrete as well as suggestive.

酢瓶 い く つ 最昔 八 岐 の 大 生 海 鼠　田 代 松 意

subin ikutsu mukashi yamata no ônamako – tashiro shôi? (mod)

#306

(vinegar bottle how-many? most-ancient eight-peak's (yamata=place) big seaslug)

yamata no orochi

how many bottles
would the father of all
sea slugs fill up

ancient ancestor

pickled slug
how many bottles
for the *orochi*

This is the only poem I know connecting the sea slug to a *Records of Ancient Matters* story other than that cruelly rendered mouth. The geo-historical name Yamata conjures up the mighty eight-headed and eight-tailed serpent that made the folk sacrifice their maidens until the God Susano, having been kicked out of the Izumo heights for his pranks (the last which made the Sun Goddess flee into the cave), had the parents of the last maiden alive help him make eight vats of powerful *sake* stored in separate places so each head would drink it simultaneously, after which Susano hacked apart the plastered serpent/s for good and, naturally got to marry the maiden, this Eve he saved from the serpent. The weak link here is in the serpent-sea-slug connection. About all I can say is that the snake connects to the dragon that connects with the sea and the sea with the sea slug. Perhaps, the poet is also thinking of the heroic "struggle" involved with eating pickled slug which will be elaborated upon in *Slippery Sea Slugs.* Or, he even intends to suggest the sea slug was born of the pieces of the Orochi. If the namako were a bit smoother (more like a continental cucumber) it *might* be thought of as a section of serpent. But, I fear I have over-explained a splendid light verse. Even if you don't know about Susano hacking up the Orochi, you feel like saying *"How many bottles, indeed!"* Or, at least, *I* do!

古往今来切って血の出ぬ海鼠かな　漱石
koôkonrai kitte chi no denu namako kana – sôseki (1867-1916)
(ancient-cut, blood's come-out-not seaslug!/?/ó/the/behold)　#307

cut since
antiquity, sea slugs
don't bleed

With a possible hint from Lamark or Darwin, Sôseki, the novelist with a sea slug fixation, explains why the sea slug is not so much cold-blooded as bloodless – considering the bloodiness of baby humans, it is amazing the same man could use the *namako* for a metaphor of easy birth and term of endearment/denigration for his baby, then turn around and write this! (or vice versa, I haven't checked the order). Presumably, his "ancient" alludes to what the Goddess did to the sea slug as reported in the *Records*. That is to say, Sôseki turns the just-so story of the sea slug's mouth into one about its bloodlessness – for only water (or what *appears* to be only water [1→]) comes out when it is cut.

滾々と水湧き出でぬ海鼠切る　百間
kônkôn to mizu wakiidenu namako kiru – hyakken (1878-1971)
(gush-gush water boils/pours-out seaslug cut)　#308

cutting open
a sea slug, water
gushes out

俎板の海鼠は汐を吐きにけり　長田粋子
manaita no namako wa shio o hakinikeri – nagata suiko (contemp?)
(carving board's seaslug-as-for, brine spew[+finality])　#309

the sea slug
on my carving board
spews brine

大海鼠掴めば水を吐きにけり　島倉みつる
ônamako tsukameba mizu o hakinikeri – shimakura mitsuru (1993)
(big seaslug grab-when water[obj] spew[+finality])　#310

when i grab
a large sea cucumber
it spews water

大海鼠水吐き出して捌かれぬ　田辺風信子
ônamako mizu hakidashite sabakarenu – tanabe fûshinko? (1997)
(large-seaslug water spew-outing, handled/tackled/disposed-of)　#311

a large sea slug
spews out water
as it's carved

This handful of modern and contemporary poems note what Sôseki did, without hinting at any metaphysical significance of the fact. They are remarkably similar, as the glosses, more than my translations, indicate.

蜆 子 に も 逢 は で 漂 ふ 生 海 鼠 か な　蓼 太

(2X) shijimi ni mo awa de tadayô namako kana – ryôta (1717-1787)

[#283,again]   (*corbicula*[a tiny shellfish]-even-to meet-not-because drifting sea-slug tis!/?/ó/the/˙tis)

homeless

finding n'er
a *corbicula*, sea slug
wanders on

ぬ け て 出 た 貝 も あ る べ き な ま こ 哉　路 尹

nuketedeta kai mo arubeki namako kana – roi (1770)

#312   (shed-left shell-even is-ought[to be] sea slug tis!/?/ó/the)

the sea slug
there should be a shell
it left behind

These poems pick up on a sea slug feature missed by the *Kojiki* just-so story. The second influenced my reading of the first. A *corbicula* is far too small to house a sea slug, but as hyperbole for a tiny shell house, it might do well. If a bluesman's possessions can fit in a match-box a sea slug can theoretically live in a *shijimi*. The sea slug does not look like it belongs out there unprotected. So, these poets muse, there ought to be or have been a shell somewhere. As one lame old poem put it,

浮 歩 く 生 海 鼠 に 家 は な か り け り　完 来

ukiaruku namako ni ie wa nakarikeri – kanrai (1733-1817)

#313   (floating/drifting-walk seaslug-to/with house-as-for not [having+finality])

poor² sea slug
just wandering about
a homeless!

1. *Watery Slugs* The dramatically large amount of water probably means that the sea slugs were in fresh water for a while and involuntarily sucked it up, as explained elsewhere, or that they were frozen with water filling the gutless cavity. Still, holothurians *do* have a circulatory fluid, so there *is* bleeding. No doubt, Sôseki assumed blood would be red. While most holothurians do not have enough haemoglobin to make their blood look like blood, there are exceptions:

> I'll never forget when cutting open my first high latitude molpadiian cuke. I sliced into it as I'd done 100's of times with tropical spp, the poor specimen contracted violently and BAM, bright red arterial-like BLOOD shot all over me and lab. I knew that this species had haemoglobin-based blood, but I'd never read that its spacious coelomic cavity was full of the stuff, about 1/2 litre! The psychological effect was such that standing there dripping with blood, a fresh scalpel in hand, and being the only

vertebrate in sight (this happened late at night), i fought to convince myself that, of course, the blood was from the little blob of cuke at the bottom of the sink. Still, i relented and ended up checking my hands for deep cuts just to appease the less reasonable parts of my brain. (Alexander Kerr: corresp)

These bloody fellows, AK notes, are "always burrowing forms" living in hypoxic environs.

2. *Poor Sea Slug* The adjective "poor" is mine, but it reflects the "float" in the compound verb "float-walk" (*uki-aruku*), which suggests a tragic life, as opposed to the happy, enlightened wandering of a sage. I feel tempted to speak of the sea slug as having a home everywhere and nowhere, but it is a fact that some places have few crevices and some crevices beat others. While the sea slug probably has no homing sense, it can sense light/dark and this should help it find crevices or stones. That would also be a reason for their being nocturnal rather than diurnal, for in the latter case slow pokes would be forced to find shelter in total darkness.

Let's take up a collection, make a home for our naked brother in the sea!   Actually, we are already doing it. An entire chapter (three pages) of Arakawa's *Sea Cucumber Reader* (ndh) explores various methods of *"Namako* Apartment Building."[1] Though sea slugs, unlike hermit crabs don't care to lug their homes around, they do take shelter in crevices (Think of them as pueblos in their cliff dwellings or Chinese in their donut-shaped underground homes!) and welcome our assistance.

水 底 に 平 家 ほ ろ び て 海 鼠 か な　寥 松

minasoko ni heike horobite namako kana – ryôshô (1762-1832)

(sea-bed-on heikei[clan] wiped-out sea slug/s!/?/ổ/the/'behold)   [#139, again]

the heike clan
wiped out to a man
now sea slugs

～

holothurians!
hiding on the sea floor
heike is no more

This may be as much if not more an explanation of the fate of the Heike than a sea slug just-so story, and it has a couple problems. First, if *namako* already got its mouth rent in Ancient Time, they can't have *originated* from the drowned warriors of Heike. Second, it is insulting to the warriors who went down fighting to turn them into a creature identified with spinelessness and limblessness, with its sinful karmic connotations. (As we have already seen, another poet replied that the Heike crab with its ferocious warrior-like expression on its back was the more befitting metamorphosis for the Heike.)

釣 鐘 の 海 へ 砕 け て 生 海 鼠 哉　希 固（因?）

tsurigane no umi e kudakete namako kana – kiko (kiin?) (early 18c)

(hanging-bell's ocean-to breaking/crumbling sea slug!/?/ổ/the/behold)   #314

the temple bell
crumbled into the sea:
loh, sea slugs!

～

namako, are you
bits of bells that once rang
on the sea floor

The *tsurigane* is a large-size bronze bell that hangs at Buddhist temples and has bumps along its shoulder that resemble those on the typical Japanese sea slug.[2] Some ended up in the sea – no doubt after being struck by lightning and fragmented – and sailors did not like to ship them because female sea dragons had a legendary desire for large bells. If that is not enough, there is a plant called *tsurigane-ninjin,* or, "hang-bell-ginseng," the root of which Chinese medicine in Japan (*kanpoyaku*) called *shajin* (sand-offering), which happens to be one name for the dried sea slug exported to China! So, then, do bells fragments on mountains make this plant and, under the sea, our creature?

#315

1. *Holothurian Housing* The traditional method, documented back to 1894 and further developed in the 1930's (ndh), was throwing in rocks (*tôseki*); the pictured method was an incredibly ugly barge-sized rusty metal grid resembling the bottom of a spring mattress filled with concrete and head-sized split rock. Bundles of brushwood worked best for juvenal sea slugs.

2. *Bell Bumps* The resemblance of the bumps found on Japanese cast bells to those on sea slugs has been haiku'ed, "the bumps on / the alarm bell frozen / a sea slug! (*hanshô no iboibo kôru namako kana* – tatsuoka tsutomu (contemp) 半鐘 の い ぼ い ぼ 凍 る 海 鼠 か な　龍 岡 普). Unless the bell is so hard frozen that it loses its voice, I think this metaphor belies itself.

なまこもし柳の露のかたまるか 大江丸?

namako moshi yanagi no tsuyu no katamaru ka – ôemaru? (1790)

#316

(sea slug: if willow's dew's hardening?)

just-so
(a haiku reading)

the sea slug
could it be coagulated
willow dew?

It is possible that this haiku belongs in the last chapter, for one reading is more than plausibly dirty. The willow was a well known symbol for a nubile woman and you can imagine what its dew meant – there is even a salacious senryu selection called *Yanagi-no-tsuyu,* or "willow-dew," taken from the *Haifu Suetsumuhana* volumes published (vol.1=1776, vol.3=1791) about the time the book (*Haizange*) in which this haiku appears. This allusion, then, might be that women are responsible for creating sea slugs – spineless dandies, or limbless sinners, you choose – a bizarre opposite image to the pure lotus that grows up from rank mud. At the same time, however, the idea of the sea slug as an overgrown pussy-willow calyx led me to imagine it as a *vagina* (sheath) at large [1] rather than a protuberance for the first time. You might say, this puts the *hole* back into the *holothurian.* A second interpretation, grammatically very iffy, restores the phallus:

just-so
(a senryu reading)

the sea slug
i'll bet willow dew
hardens it!

This scans well. Still, I think my first reading matches the poet's intent, because it fits a genre of Japanese folklore called *setsuwa,* or "explanatory-talk;" and, because *Haizange* poems are not pornographic * If the Europeans had geese growing from barnacles and swallows hibernating deep under the mud, Japanese had their sparrows turning clam and quails turning mole (and vice versa). There are hundreds, if not thousands of haiku about such supernatural facts, which, after all, are properly seasonal and easily located in the haiku almanac. If any more proof is needed that haiku can deal with surreality as well as reality, we need go no further than Shiki. Here is what may well be his

1. *Vaginas at Large* In native American mythology, one sometimes encounters vagina that rove far from their mistresses and behave like succubae or, when teethed, carnivores. Some crept and some, like classic penis sculpture, were winged. I fear the only reading of the sea-slug-as-sheath I have encountered is not vaginal but, judging from the general tenor of the website (which may, however, belie the quote) may well be anal or even oral: "You know, they can turn themselves inside out. I bet that would generate some impressive suction." – Ben Herman, theorizing about having sex with a sea cucumber (www.nmt.edu/~schlake/quotes.html). (The quote after it: "Like a snake is a penis, a mouse is a vagina?" – Eric Heatwole. I know Swedes talk about *mus* rather than pussy, but . . .?)
2. *Just-so Stories As a Genre* The term "creation myths" is not quite right because we tend to use it for explanations of the Big Questions (where our species came from and why we must die, when it should cover everything), and because the word "myth" has the connotation of being a pernicious fiction as opposed to the Christian *setsuwa* which is, by many, considered Gospel. It is strange but understandable that before Kipling – who borrowed most of his stories from the people (plural) of India) – the English language world had no useful term for stories of how things came to be, for "God made it so" being the only acceptable explanation for everything, the genre itself was caput. Christian children were short-changed for centuries. Perhaps, however, the starvation for reasons *why things are as they are* that resulted from this is what, more than anything else, fueled the birth of modern science, which had to invent new reasons from scratch. This note, of course, is *my* just-so story!

best just-so related effort. It has nothing to do with *namako*, but it surely belongs next to Shôha's *sea-slug-talking-to-the-jellyfish* as one of the, literally, most fabulous haiku ever written!

稲 雀 案 山 子 に 打 ら ん 海 に 入 子 規

ina-suzume kakashi-ni utsu ran umi ni iri – shiki ( )

(rice-sparrow/s scarecrow/s-by shot sea-into enter)

just so

harvest sparrow
shot down by scarecrow
sinks in the sea

time to clam up

harvest sparrows,
scarecrow will shoot you
you'd best dive in.

Speaking of sparrows and alluding to clams can make us hungry, for these two both end up barbecued in Japan: the former on a spit of pine and the latter spitting over a fire fueled with pine cones, also called "balls" (*fuguri,* or, gonads). [1] But just-so haiku need not be as spectacular as dew congealing into sea slugs or scarecrows shooting sparrows.

土 龍 化 し て 海 鼠 ぞ あ さ ひ じ ま 冨 慶

moguramochi kashite namako zo asahijima – fukei? (1682)

(mole metamorphicized seaslug! morning-sun-island)   #317

asahi island
a mole has become
a sea slug

~

asahi island
where a molehill grew
into a sea slug

~

sunrise island
where all the moles
are sea slugs

This is the one of a dozen or so haiku marrying sea slugs and places mentioned at the head of the chapter. Moles in the Sinosphere were known to turn into quail and vice versa; this is the only instance I know where mole turns sea slug. Could the shape of this island evoke some Japanese folklore (CZ vaguely recalls) that explains mole exorcism by sea slug as the cause of moles changing into sea slugs, instead? Is their mutual blindness considered? If mole can mean mole hill, the island sprouted up from the sea and grew to resemble a sea slug, or if it is so tiny its only garden is the surrounding reefs, the second or third readings might be possible. The probable reading is the first explaining the island's being shaped like a sea slug, but more information is needed to pin this down.

1. Clams and Sparrows Buson or Yayu has a fine rhyming verse about clams and sparrows, but I am afraid I have misplaced it.　第二版までに、蕪村あるいは他有の脚韻踏み蛤＋雀＋松かさ句を、誰か！

女 波 男 波 よ り う み 出 す な ま こ 　哉 政 俊

menami ônami yori umidasu namako kana – masatoshi? (1674)

#318

(female/gentle-wave/s male/rough-wave/s-from born[=sea]-out sea slug!/?/ó/the/'loh)

the sea slug:
born of male and
female waves

I reversed the order of the sexes [1] for sound, not philosophical, reasons. Had this haiku found long after the chapter was ostensibly finished, been in hand from the start, it would have been the lead haiku, for if it is hard to read it as a just-so story for the sea slug, without reading it as a just-so story for the whole world. The soothing ground swells are female, while the raging broken white-tops are male. From this *yin-yang*, the sea slug, the Taoist black-bag of the beginning was born, not on land, but in the sea.   Perhaps, I am overdoing it with my cosmic explanations, but even if the sea slug, as a naked being, is particularly like a newborn baby, it is hard to imagine the poet coming up with this poem in any other way.

沖 の 石 の ひ そ か に 産 み し 海 鼠 か な 　喜 舟

oki no ishi no hisoka ni umishi namako kana – kishû (1934)

#319

(offing's rock's/stone's quietly/steathily bear[give-birth-to] sea-slug/s!/?/ó/the)

just off shore
the stones steathily
bear sea slugs

石 こ ろ に な り き つ て い る 海 鼠 か な 　粟 谷 昭 二

ishikoro ni narikitteiru namako kana – kuritani shôji (contemp)

#320

(rocks/pebbles-into be/become-completely seaslug!/?/ó/these/'loh)

wow, sea slugs
manage to completely
pass for stones

∼

a sea slug
has managed
to become a stone

If the nursery for "baby" *namako* (larvae) is the open sea, recently settled juveniles do indeed tend to hide in rock crevices and Japanese mariculturists have long known that the protection of stone cover will increase the sea slug population.   The Japanese *namako* are a bit on the short-side and resemble rocks more than many other sea cucumber, Nomura Kishû's charming fantasy is strengthened by this apparent resemblance – that Kuritani's haiku independently confirms, unless it only describes a piece of sea slug in vinegar or dehydrated trepang, I am reminded of the ancient Japanese conceit of tiny pebbles growing into boulders. [2]

1. *Order of Sexes*   While most modern expressions put the "male" first, old Japanese expressions using *me* for "female" and *o* for "male" (prime example: *meoto*, a (married) couple/pair), have the female first, as in the case of the "bride and groom" in English.   I would have preferred to keep the order.

2. *Living Stones*   The most well-known phrase in what might be called the Japanese national anthem has pebbles *growing* into hoary boulders, a concept that some argue might lead back to coral and prove Japanese culture owes much to Southern (maritime) culture (see IPOOH, ny2: *kagami-mochi*).

汐 吹 き の 鯨 の 糞 の 海 鼠 か な 神 櫻

shiobuki no kujira no fun no namako kana – shinô (pre-1927)

(brine/spume-spouting whale-shit's sea-slug!/?/ó/these/ˈloh)   #321

the poop of
a brine-spouting whale:
these sea slugs

The sea slug is identified with the spume of the sea because it is often seen in shallow water where waves break, where the whale is associated with the same by his spout. Still, it is a weak connection and I wish this poet were alive so I could ask him how to account for the discrepancy in size between the whale and his poop to make things *just-so!* Would he call to my attention the compressive forces of the deep? Or would he point to a folk tale?[1]

天 橋 の 海 に 星 降 り 海 鼠 か な 佛 丈

amanohashi no umi ni hoshi furi namako kana – butsujô (1927)

(heaven's bridge's ocean-into stars fall: seaslugs!/?/ó/the/ˈthese/behold)   #322

fallen stars?
sea slugs in the sea by
heaven's bridge!

amanohashidate

stars have fallen
beneath heaven's bridge!
look, sea slugs!

This Heaven's Bridge (full name: *ama-no-hashidate*) is a real bridge in Kyoto prefecture on the West side of a bay. The view from it was known as one of the best three views in Japan. Thanks to the name of the bridge, you might say the ugly duckling sea slugs were upgraded to star-children. My first thought was of Pascal (the boy in the cartoon *"Rose is Rose"*) wondering if it would not be dangerous to survey the stars, what with their pointed edges. I.e., the many pointed star turned into the prickle-like sea slug. But, this was a very science-conscious age in Japan, and so, instead, I imagine the sea slugs – dark blobs on the seabed seen at a distance – were thought to resemble meteorites. I wonder if the poet remembered Shiki's poem "the coldness of / a night where falling stars / turn to stone" (*hoshi ochite ishi to naru yo no samusa* kana (m27)) . . . or, *namako*? Then, again, there is at least a hint of a *namako*-star connection in Japanese folklore for a folk tale from Iwate prefecture explains the practice of sea slug dragging as follows:

A cruel stepmother mistreats two sweet sisters, Moon and Star. God mercifully takes them up to heaven, putting them in the firmament while turning the cruel stepmother into a mole who cannot even see the sun, and lets their lonely father see them on the day of the first full moon of the New Year, when they descend to the shore of the sea. The sea cucumber serves to keep the hated step-mother at bay that day because she hated them. (Shortened from a googled story, *Furusato Iwate no Mukashibanashi* by Kagawa + Kimm(?))

1. ***Whale and Sea Slug*** There is a Yamaguchi Prefecture fable about the whale and the sea slug, which improves upon Aesop's – which in creative Japanese translation was a favorite during the long Isolation (1633-1853) – hare and tortoise, for the whale racing around the archipelago is told to look for the sea slug to be ahead of him at every harbor, and sure enough he was (for who could tell one from another?). If this story is older than the haiku, we could say the whale lost a race with his own shit.

The folk tale does not say *namako* was a star, but the relationship is close enough that a child might imagine it that way.

涅 槃 會 に 參 ら で 眼 な き 海 鼠 か な 　太 郎
nehane ni maira de menaki namako kana – tarô [1] (1927)

#323   (nirvana/buddha'sdeath-day-meeting attend-not eye-less/not sea-slug!/?/ó/the/behold)

why they see not

failing to show
the day buddha died,
eyeless sea slugs

If the sea slug failed to speak up before the native deities – or newly native colonial deities, if you prefer – and lost its voice when its mouth was mutilated, it likewise didn't show for Buddha's death and thereby failed to gain *the third eye of enlightenment* – or lost what sight it once had.[2] Buddha Death-day is synonymous with Enlightenment, or nirvana, and paintings of the scene show a paradise full of happy animals. Since this takes place in the middle (i.e. full moon day) of the second month of the Spring, it is not surprising that the sea slug is not around. It is officially out-of-season.

海 鼠 め く 雲 横 た は り 涅 槃 の 日 　高 沢 良 一
namakomeku kumo yokotawari nehan no hi – takasawa yoshikazu (2001)

#324   (seaslug-like cloud/s side/sideways-lie nehan[buddha-death=enlightenment=day])

clouds like
sea slugs low in the sky
on buddha day

No creature is more suitable for Buddhist Enlightenment than the sea slug, so it is not surprising if, contrary to Tarô's just-so-story and regardless of the date, it does appear. At any rate, Takasawa saw it and that is good enough for me.

二 夜 居 て 音 を 持 つ 桶 の 生 海 鼠 哉 　三 津 人
futaya ite oto o motsu oke no namako kana – mitsundo (d 1822)

#325   (two-nights be/stay sound/noise make/s tub/tray's seaslug/s!/?/ó/the)

for two nights
the tray made noise
ah, sea slugs

1. *A Poet called Tarô?* This poet's *nome de plume* is remarkable for being the most common – the quintessent – male name, Tarô, whereas poets usually have obviously poetic names. I'll bet no one previously thought to use it! Lafcadio Hearn wrote a fifty page essay+analysis of "Japanese Female Names" in *Shadowings* (Little Brown, 1900), but I have yet to read haiku poet names given similar treatment, though they are much more interesting.   In haiku, we have Banana Bashô, Turnip-village Buson, One-tea Issa, Cuckoo Shiki, Empty-element Kyoshi,   Rat-bones Sokotsu, etcetera – and many if not most names have a good story or a haiku (by which the poet became so famous, his name was changed to fit) behind them.
2. *Failure to Show* One could collect a whole book of *"failure to show"* stories.   Dispensations generally came at two times, the Creation and the death of a Divinity.   The African-Americans created witty Creation stories to explain their own slavery, poverty, powerlessness and skin-color as deriving from their own failure to show. (See Zora Neale Hurston's *Of Mules and Men* and/or *Every Tongue Got to Confess* for the best tellings).

This is a bare-bone realistic haiku of the type championed by Shiki shortly before he died and Kyoshi for another half century. Yet the poet is a contemporary of Issa's. There is no just-so story in the poem. I introduce it here as testimony to the noise that the next haiku can *just-so*.

海 を 恋 ひ 鼠 鳴 き す る 海 鼠 か な　村 山 清 愛

umi o koi nezuminaki suru namako kana – murayama seiai (2001)
(sea(obj) loving/longing-for mouse-cry[prostitutes-whistle etc.]-does sea-slug=mouse!/?/ó/the)　　　#326

> loving the sea
> it cries like a mouse:
> the sea slug

Namako, as explained in the introduction, is generally written with two Chinese characters, "sea-mouse," that bear no relationship with the way the word is pronounced. Since the mouse does not resemble the sea slug *that* closely, we wonder how it happened to be chosen. Does the noise sea slugs make, [1] attested to by Mitsundo's old haiku, resemble the cheeping of mice? (Here, it is too bad "cry" and "peep" are different in English, for it prevents clearly mousy metaphor and emotion from coexisting.). [2] Do we have a new folk etymology for the name here? *Probably not.* KS convinced me that my first reading is *wrong.* This is right:

> ***pssst, sea, over here!***
>
> wanting the brine,
> they mouse-call for it:
> the sea-mice

This is an idiomatic "mouse-call," i.e., the strange noises made by street-walkers trying to stop men – these are not limited to whistles, as my all-too-limited (though it is the largest!) English-Japanese dictionary thinks, but includes sweet chirpy sounds like those one might make to a parakeet, with a word or two (*ni-san, oide,* (["brother," "come in/over", etc.) included – and that means the sea slug/s=mouse/mice are not so much crying out of longing for the sea, as calling it in a secretive, seductive manner for which English lacks a verb. The poem is far more original than I had imagined. A paraverse:

> *conversation*
>
> hear them whisper
> back and forth! the sea
> and the sea slugs

1. Sea Slug "Mouse-Calls" I had imagined a slight release of air from the oral or aboral end of a sea slug, but KZ argues that they are probably rubbing together in their tub. Even if the sound were barely audible from a few feet away, it might qualify as psychological mimesis such *kyukkyu* – made when buttocks grind when walking – and suggest the *chucchu* or *chicchi* of mice and women of the street. Incredibly, he found a passage from literature where the *obi* belt – let's say "girdle" for the proper effect! – of such a woman disrobing makes mouse-calls on its own (*shanse to ureshiku tokeba obi mo sasshite nezuminaki*) for circumstantial evidence! OM adds that in a scene from Kurosawa's Ran, where the revengeful wife of the oldest son seduces the younger brother, the "untying of the silk obi makes these swishing sounds--which are not unlike the chirping of a mouse."

2. Crying, Peeping and Poetry One might think having different verbs for "cry" and "peep" would be a plus for poetry, but such diversity destroys metaphor. Japanese can "peep" when it wants to by crying+ onomatopoeia, yet enjoy the poetic advantages of the more inclusive *naku.*

please write your own just-so story
for the sea cucumber
and illustrate
this page.

13
<u>the tasty sea slug</u>

"The sea slug, from its grotesque shape[1] is called sea-mouse. But sea slug has a beautiful flavor unimaginable from its appearance. By all means, try some sea slug!" (Copy from an advertisement for an 80 gram bottle of sea slug guts (*konowata*) priced at Y 4,000 (~$50) netted)

"They might be the least appealing form of food found in the ocean, but they are edible and even prized by Chinese and Japanese." (United States Search and Rescue Task Force Survival At Sea: netted)

海 鼠 喰ふこの世可笑しきことばかり 角川春樹
namako kuu kono yo okashiki koto bakari – kadokawa haruki (contemp)
(seaslug[obj] eat/ing this world funny/strange things only)   #327

eating sea slug
the world is just full
of funny things

truth is stranger
than fiction: this world
eats sea slugs

eating sea slug
what about this world
is not strange?

this slug-eating
world of ours: one funny thing
after another

I had expected the culinary *namako* to be the least palatable sea slugs in this book, for, as a rule – contrary to what good haiku are supposed to be – I prefer metaphysical to physical poetry. I was wrong. Most slug-eating haiku are a challenge to describe taste beyond taste, a struggle to cut, then pinch and pick up slipperiness itself, or a head-trip occasioned by chewing or watching someone chew this chewiest of foods. Indeed, because of the large number of poems fitting one of these three categories (mostly modern haiku found after the first draft of what was to have been a book of old haiku alone), the culinary sea slug has been carved up into tasty, slippery and chewy chapters. Ecological concerns aside, some readers may feel regret that the sea slug, who has supplied us with so much poetic joy must end up in our belly; but the sad truth is that if sea slugs were not eaten, they would rarely if ever make it into haiku. After all, one sees as many if not more starfish – called *hitode*, or "people-hands" in Japanese – on the beaches in Japan as sea slugs, yet, I can't recall a single one in the 100,000 or so old haiku I have perused.   "Starfish"[2] → was not even one of 17,000 *kigo*

1. ***What Repulses Us*** Where the word *gurotesku* is *de rigor* for the sea cucumber in Japan and expresses the bumpy, far from sleek nature of the Japanese *namako,* an article by Catherine Malaval entitled "The Sea Cucumber Should Stay Under" published in *Liberation* (25/1/94) and excerpted in the SPC *Beche-de-mer Information Bulletin* #6 (April 1994) writes, "Unfortunately, this creature, whose soft body makes it at first glance quite repulsive, is today the target of a booming trade." I think she refers to a variety of sea cucumber eaten in South-east Asia because they look softer than the *namako.* Still, one wonders, since *when* has a "soft body" become something "repulsive," rather than attractive?   Latin radio still sings the praise of *suave de abajo, suave de arriba,* and I, for one am *de acuerdo.* What could be more unattractive than the "six-pack bellies" and "buns of steel" videos offer to women? Because muscles require more calories than fat, they are the equivalent of the gas-guzzling car and generally (mis)used in the same wasteful manner.

(seasonal words) – since there are usually several words for one thing, about 5,000 seasonal themes – found in Kodansha's large *saijiki* (haiku almanac).

風 味 に は 寒 さ を こ ふ る な ま こ 哉　作 者 不 知

fumi ni wa samusa o kouru namako kana – anon. (1672)

#328　　(flavor/bouquette/seasoning/taste/style-as-for, coldness[obj] loves/desires sea-slug[subj]!/?/ó/the/a)

for flavor sea slug wants the cold

trans cz

This is the oldest haiku I have found directly touching upon sea slug as cuisine – the only older ones concern it's relationship to regional economies. It is exceptionally hard to read.[1] Presumably, the poet is the one licking his chops, but the rhetoric has the sea slug *itself* loving the cold that improves its flavor, as if to say: *I love the cold because it makes me taste better!*

cool guys

sea slugs
the cold is what suits
their taste

Fumi means taste in both senses of the word (flavor and discriminatory "taste"), as it does in English, and additionally implies a touch of something we might call "character." So the original also seems to hint at a sage who seeks out cold mountains.   But I might be imagining things.

a sea slug
good taste longs
for the cold

Recently, scientists have been talking about adding a new basic flavor to salty, sour, sweet and hot (peppery): *umami,* which in ordinary Japanese means simply "deliciousness" and stands for whatever *msg* does to make food taste good. I think all this is ridiculous, for no food scientist can mix the essences of each of these basic flavors and come up with any food's flavor, as is the case with basic colors. But, to play along with their game, why don't we add another flavor, cold?[2] Instead of calling it *tsumetasa* (*samusa,* the word in the poem, generally refers to temperature in the narrower sense of temperature), we could name it after the food that embodies it: *namako!*

←**2. Starfish Haiku**   Perhaps starfish are not as seasonal a phenomenon as sea slug; but, if they were edible, they would find a season, i.e., would be placed in the time they tasted best. Doubtless, a handful of starfish lie quietly inside of haiku on "ebb-tide-day" or "low-tide-hunting" (i.e. shell-collecting – traditionally a spring event, although I dare say it is done more in the summer), but lacking *kigo* status, they do not make the index, so there is no way to look them up until more haiku are subjectable to a "find" search for vocabulary. (Large haiku data banks are very scarce on the web. The largest on-line collection, as explained in the *Fie! Fie!* (after the *Acknowledgments*), is restricted to academics, despite being the site of a supposedly public national research institute.

1. Hard to Read   Unsatisfied with such a reading, I am tempted to posit an improbability, namely, that the *kofuru* was a mistaken transcription by an editor who didn't know the verb *kouru,* an obscure packing term for cinching things up in bundles, such as sea slug. In that case, the poem reads "*bundled up / cold is their flavor: / sea slugs*" and may be thought of as either a poem accompanying a winter gift or one about the exports of a certain region. CZ, KS and LC all pooh-pooh this, so don't quote me!

2. Cold Flavor   I joke about the sea slug, but what about peppermint? It doesn't fit into the sweet, salty, sour, hot (*picante*) schema, does it?

海 鼠 畳 の ひ び き よ り 待 つ 小 雪 哉 角 枝

kodatami no hibiki yori matsu koyuki kana – kakushi? (1701)

(slug-chopping's echo-from waiting[for] small/light/beautiful snow!/?/ô/this/'tis)   #329

dicing out winter

a light snow
coming soon: the sound
of sea slugs

If the reader feels that English, too, can abbreviate an animal's name, the title can be dropped and the last line, more informatively speak "of *dicing* slugs." The dish *kodatami* (*ko* written with the Chinese characters for sea slug usually pronounced *namako*) requires some hard chopping on the cutting board. This is the *only* truly beautiful poem about preparing sea slug I know of and I couldn't ruin the poetry with a more direct translation. I am not certain why the sound of chopping and the first snow flurries associate but for some reason, it feels just right.

海 鼠 だ た み や 有 し 形 を 忘 れ 顔 太 祇

kodatami ya arishi katachi[sugata?] o wasuregao – taigi

(slug-diced: ancient/customary form (+contradictory "o") forgetting-face [i.e., who, me?])   #330

make-over

diced sea slug
enters the dining room
incognito

麗 し く 玉 堂 佳 器 に こ た ゝ み ぬ 召 波

uruwashiku gyokudôkaki ni kodataminu – shôha (1726-1771)

(gorgeous/beautiful precious utensil-into slug-dice/ing)   #331

inner beauty revealed

how elegantly
sea slug is diced into
a precious dish

The sea slug, as ugliness embodied, could never have conjured up beautiful flurries of snow nor been welcome on the best of tables without a great makeover, and that alone ensured it was a gourmet food. Somaru, who shares with Taigi and Shiki the distinction of having written five or more *namako* haiku, has found a more endearing way to put this:

料 ら れ て 利 口 に 成 し 生 海 鼠 哉 素 丸

ryôrarete[hakararete] rikô ni narishi namako kana – somaru (1712-95)

(prepared/cooked, smart becomes [the] sea slug!/?/ô/the/behold)   #332

cooking school

well prepared
the sea slug looks
smart enough

borrowed brains

given thought,
the sea slug becomes
quite clever

The method of preparation suggested by the verb in the last and more interesting haiku is the culinary equivalent of "cut-and-fill" in architecture. The raw sea slug is diced up and arranged so neatly – as indeed, is the case in Japan for its namesake, the land cucumber – that the result looks far more promising than the original. [1] Thank goodness, the English "smart" makes the same metaphorical leap between appearance and intelligence found in the Japanese. Such leaps are all too often lost when translating between exotic tongues. The "borrowed brains" (meaning the sage sea slug described in haiku and essay) interpretation is a long shot – the original only hints at it as a possible (but dubious) second reading – for *hakarete* can mean "considered." That this dish was considered a supreme delicacy is clear by the following, very old haiku with untranslateable puns about tatami matting: "nothing / can beat *kodatami* [2] / what food!" (*kodatami ni shiku mono wa naki ryôri kana* – shimogawa? __?(1672) 鼠だゝみにしく物はなき料理哉　下河邊晒[&M030894;＝艸/有]).

海鼠たたみもむつかしき世や独住み　嵐雪
kodatami mo muzukashiki yo ya hitorizumi – ransetsu (1653-1707)
(seaslug-slicing even difficult world! single-living)

#333(上), #334

living alone
even sliced sea slug
is too much

#335, #336 下

1. The Usefulness of Good Looks Human appearance stymied the Greek philosophers because they wanted to keep beauty, usefulness and good together, when they knew damn well the association was tenuous at best. In the case of food, however, an international team of researchers have done a multicultural experiment apparently proving that beauty is good for us (Lost Reference). People who ate beautifully displayed food not only thought it tasted better than the same food that went through a blender, but absorbed it better (as proven by blood tests)! Not marginally better, but in the case of some minerals, over twice as well! (This is from memory and might be a bit off) We may laugh at the degree to which Japanese arrange their food to satisfy the visual sense, even making cleverly molded and decorated food for their children's lunch-boxes, but that is actually a good way to get the most out of food nutrition-wise! Perhaps the marginally low nutrition available on the crowded isle favored the survival of family traditions of culinary aesthetics. Besides, as Confucius wrote long ago, people shouldn't eat ugly things.

2. Kodatami The raw sea slug is cut into thin slices and soaked in *sake*. It is generally dipped into a sauce with *mirin* (an almost alcohol-free *sake* which is very sweet yet has a tiny touch of vinegar) and grated horse-radish. The sauce is evidently whipped up; an old haiku puts it like this: "diced sea slug / bubbles like the spume of / his wavy home" (*kodatami ya ono ga sumika no nami no awa* – anshô (1679) 海鼠だゝみやをのが栖の浪の淡　安昌), or rhymed by CZ, "bubble on the *kodatami* / looks like his home, in the sea, in the *nami*." T[d]atami is homophonic for woven straw flooring (Can we say "mat" for something inches thick?). The characters for the cuisine *tatami* are hard to remember so poets often used the character for the matting, making it hard to be certain what the poems are about, especially when you know sea slugs can stand for *tatami* in certain cases. Eg. "a sea slug, / so you sneak it out: / on the thirteenth" (*sotto mochidase namako da to jûsan nichi* – YT-11 (1776) そっと持出せ海鼠だと十三日　柳多留 11). Here, the *namako* is said to mean the old *tatami* mats that have lost their stiffness. This thirteenth is almost certainly the soot-dusting (*susobarai* = 12/13 on the lunar calendar) when Japanese cities must have looked like the dust-bowl (see IPOOH-winter-bk 1). I do not know if the old *tatami* is handled so gently one seems to *sneak* because it would otherwise drop dirt or if the owner is embarrassed not to have a replaced it with a sweet-smelling new one. A less likely reading makes it 9/13 when courtesans tried to attract patrons to a second moon-viewing,: "quietly broach it! / he is a real sea slug / on the thirteenth" The combined verb *mochi-dase* can mean either "carry out[side]" or "bring up [an idea]." I imagine a spineless husband telling his wife he must be off.

This dish is not particularly complex to make; but most bachelor poets probably did not tackle sea slug, for it is not one those dishes one can easily make in minutes. A single man with time for poetry can not indulge in such little luxuries. But, *must* sea slug be so damn fancy?

輪切りにす海鼠土管のごとき腸　高沢良一

wagiri ni su namako dokan no gotoki chô – takasawa yoshikazu (2003)

(ring-cut-as-do seaslug-earth-pipe-like intestine/s)

#337

making sea slug rings

like a colon
made of plastic piping
this *namako*

cutting board thoughts

sea slug rings
somewhere between a colon
and pvc pipe

Japanese has a verb for cutting bodies latitudinally. English does not. The idea of the sea slug as a pipe and as guts is found in the nineteenth century German nomenclature, but the Japanese sea slug is relatively fat, so it takes the action of cutting out rings to make this image really sink in. PVC is what, I am told, plastic piping is called, so I used it. Takasawa's poem moves from the wit of the ugly-slug/pretty-food paradox to a straightforward reality. Or is it? Modern art might hold such ugliness as beautiful as anything else. I don't.

ぶつ切りは無邪気が良い赤海鼠　宙虫

bukkiri wa mujaki ga yoi akanamako – soran (contemp)

(rough-cut-as-for, artless is good: red-seaslug)

#338

chunky cubes
an artless knife for
red sea slug

primitive cuisine

the innocence
of roughly hewn chunks
of red sea slug

manly food

chopped large
befitting a red sea slug
artless chunks

The red sea slug, with meat that has more bite than the blue sea slug popular in the Tokyo area, is favored by the Kobe-Osaka-Kyoto food culture. Reputably tastier, it does not need looks. Or, the crude chunks might reflect a different approach toward ugliness. Rather than turning sea slug into a sophisticate, it becomes an exemplar for primitive-is-beautiful and, as such, is strangely attractive in its own way. Surprisingly, this is the only haiku I know of taking advantage of the nature of the red sea slug. This poem and the last attract me, for if I prepared sea slug, that is how I would do it, but artlessness in cooking is, I fear rare, especially with respect to sea slug. Here is the more common situation, uncommonly well put:

酢海鼠の酢加減母の舌借りぬ　永方裕子

sunamako no su kagen haha no shita karinu -- nagakata yûko (2000)

(vinegared-seaslug's add/subtract(flavor/seasoning): mom's tongue [i] borrow)

#339

dressing sea slug
i borrow mom's tongue to get
the vinegar right

pickling sea slug
mom's tongue helps me
taste the vinegar

I was tempted to translate: "*pickling sea slug / i borrow mom's tongue / for the vinegar*," but had to drop it, for the original has not a drop of sarcasm. The original has one word that defies translation: *kagen*. Literally, "add/increase-subtract/decrease," it means the process or the extent of adjustment of something that we can perceive (color, flavor, aroma, sound, touch) using one's natural intuition. Not a few pop-Japanologists have used this word – its presence in Japanese and absence in English – to help demonstrate the way foreigners=Occidentals lack true taste (though they don't state it quite that baldly). So I couldn't *trans-late* (carry across) so much as *peri-late* (carry around) this haiku. So what is it about? I netted it together with a page-long essay, most of which I translate below:

> In the busy kitchen, facing a grotesque sea slug. If ever there was a food where she needs the 'confident tongue' of her mother, this is it. There are plenty of idioms for lending a hand, head, breast [in Japanese] and other body parts, but this haiku is probably the first usage ever of *lending a tongue* . . . Is the amount of vinegar just right? How about the salt? Sugar? Only 'mother's tongue' knows for sure . . . A piece of pickled slug passes from the chopsticks of the daughter to those of the mother and are approached by her lips, then placed on the tongue, slowly rolled about the mouth, then there is a pause as she finishes fully tasting it and judges it fit or unfit by shaking the head, nodding or by the look of her eyes alone... Sea slug. Though its very appearance is ancient and it was popular from old, it was generally not indulged in more than two or three times per winter. A far cry from the food the young generation is familiar with, it is also not one of those gourmet foods that may be bought in the proper season. Mother and daughter work together in the kitchen, silently. Each knows her own and the other's task and respects her niche. Women in all families have their paltry conflicts and competition. A delicious table of food is a collaboration of feeling and skill of these women during a successful truce in this warfare. . . . a kitchen is a woman's castle, and through this castle comes a whiff of strong [white rice] vinegar. Vinegar brings food alive; it also kills germs. A food substance with logical underpinning, it is used matter-of-factly. The "taste/flavor of mother" is found in the crisp succulence of sea slug firmed up with vinegar. And this flavor,   the   mother's   taste,   is   handed   down   to   her   daughter.
> http://members.jcom.home.ne.jp/ohta.kahori/hk/hk1205.htm 俳句展望 1205

Such an explanation may seem excessive to one who feels that a haiku should be left to fend for itself. But I don't think I really grasped the extent to which sea slug, at least in vinegar-dressed form, was a mother food (like apple pie) until I read it. Vague hints about the flavor of home, of mother, did not really get through to me. But let us return to old haiku, before the sea slug was prepared by mothers.

海 鼠 た た み や 香 の 目 出 度 き に 今 一 椀　嘯 山
kodatami ya ka no medetaki ni ima hitowan – shôzan (1717-1801)

#340   (seaslug-diced! scent/bouquette's joyous/celebratory-to/for now/another one-bowl)

diced sea-slug	diced sea slug
a scent to celebrate	the scent of a saint
another bowl!	another bowl!

So, now the ugly slug not only looks good but possesses something rare among animals, a scent rather than a smell. *What* scent? I am embarrassed to admit that I have yet to try sea slug – the closest I have come is its relative, the *hoya,* or sea-squirt, a knobby creature resembling a miniature naval mine, that made me so explosively sick I can't even remember how it tasted. Many tastes can not be described, but only approached through simile and it would seem that all poetry – even haiku with its ample cross-sense metaphors – boasts more visual than gustatory simile. The closest we come to tasting the sea slug is a paragraph by Kyoroku (1655-1715), who wrote and edited haiku with what might be called an ethnographer's eye.

The smell of sea slug. There is no apt comparison. Interestingly, it bears some resemblance to the smell of *gobô* or the pungent smell of *matsutake* softened with *yuzu* [a small citrus that tastes midway between a tangerine and a lime and is used with sea slug, too]. (fuzoku bunsen [date?])[1]

Even here, the closest we come to a taste is a smell [2] and scent of the burdock is a subtle one. Most Westerners find the sea slug tasteless. As a food critic put it, "There is little flavor, just a gelatinous texture somewhere between *calamari* [squid] and a rubber-band." Though the Chinese always serve it with other things and a sauce so it is "very good," he snickers, "the chef needn't be so generous with the [expensive] sea cucumber." (Jeff Buetner reviewing the Yen Ching restuarant, somewhere out in internetland). Perhaps, we need a professional wine-taster to try sea slug. Or, failing that, whoever it is that comes up with the cigars, chocolate, violet and so forth found on wine labels!

月 雪 の 身 を 香 に 匂 ふ 海 鼠 哉 士 巧

tsuki yuki no mi o ka ni niou namako kana – shikô (1776)
(moon-snow's body[+contradictory "o"] scent-with smell seaslug!/?/ó/the)   #341

poetic slug	calliodorific
it has the scent	its beauty is
of moonshine and snow	in its moon-snow scent
the sea cucumber	the sea slug

If there ever was a *Lyrical Sea Slug,* this is it! The *ka/kô* is scent, but the *niofu,* or *niou,* is not only "to smell" but "to shine" – as in "shines in splendor" – or "to glow" as only beauty can. With respect to one of the senses, anyway, the conventionally ugly *namako* is a beauty. The poet Meiseki (1848-1926) took this scent quite literally:

> This is a bit hard to figure out, but the poem would seem to be playfully pointing out that because the sea slug has a nondescript shape and is chaotic, it has long been stylish to wonder about what it is *of,* so we should have it pertain to the moon, or the

The Smell of [raw] Sea Slug. KS had to correct me on the translation. I first translated the middle of the passage as: "Strangely, it bears resemblance to the smell of *gobô* (burdock), where you'd think it would be pungent like a *matsutake* (pine-mushroom)." The pine mushroom is identified with the broad-glans male member found in *ukiyoe* whereas the burdock, a thin root, is identified with a less overwhelming manhood – the stereotypical young man engaging a widow with many children is said to be *"washing a burdock in the sea!"* As far as the burdock root goes, all I can say is that it has a delicate flavor (suitable for gourmet cooking) compared to which carrots are crude and should be left for baby food and Bugs Bunny! Unfortunately, most Japanese restaurants in the USA neglect to offer it and, for that matter, most of the other vegetables unfamiliar to Occidentals (*udo, myôga, seri, mitsuba, etc.*). While I mistranslated, I'd bet my *shirikodama* Kyoroku was intentionally risque.

2. *Sea Slug Smell Out of Haiku but in Japanese* Miyazawa Kenji (1896-1933) came close to describing the smell of sea slug in his prose-poem "vacuum-culture" (*shinku-yôbo?*) in *Haru to Shura* when he wrote that the smell of ozone was just like that of a fresh sky/empty [or typo for tiger?] sea slug (*shinsen-na sora-no namako-no nioi*). A 1999 report (a netted "action diary") on an exhibition featuring experiments allowing visitors to experience the scientific phenomena Kenji wove into his poetry at the Miyazawa Kenji Memorial Museum in Tohoku, confirmed that "for sure, ozone's stink" resembled sea slug. Assuming A=B so B=A, sea slug smells like ozone (Compare this too another gourmet item, sea urchin row, that smells like iodine!). More important, if sea slugs really do emit ozone, we need to work on increasing their numbers to plug up that growing hole up there!

EXTRA *Sea Slug Smell in English* All I have found is this: "Meanwhile Shack was eying the ocean-scented soap, and I threw that onto my bill as well since I owed him money for one of the cab rides. Plus, I like to bribe people to be my friends. He later reported that after using it, he smelled like a sea cucumber. I'm not entirely sure what sea cucumbers smell like, or if that's a good thing, but I'm going to choose to believe it was a positive experience."(Dkk41ZplOZcC:www.glumpish. com/ maxpages/Toronto2)

snow, but, no, it is nothing unless we think of it as a flower [the moon and snow
suggest flower/blossoms to a haiku poet] for it does indeed have a slight scent . . . . .
I beg the advice of anyone knows of any literature casting light on this poem. (msbs)

But I think the scent is of a more symbolic nature and read the emotive particle *"o"* as a sign of
contradiction, rather than a lament for what is not, as Meiseki apparently did. The moon and snow are,
with blossoms and birds, half of the poetic foursome used to symbolize the nature-loving life of a poet,
hence the title on my first reading.

> born of the moon
> and the snow, the sea slug
> still boasts a scent

To have a scent is good. But I must say I agree with Meisetsu that something is missing in our
interpretations. The smelling (being sexy/beautiful/desirable) *from* scent is strange and suggests an
alusion, yet undiscovered. A similar poem, albeit scentless:

花 紅 葉 生 海 鼠 に も 物 の 心 哉　士 郎 or 仝
hanamomiji namako ni mo mono no kokoro kana – shirô (1741-1812) or dô

#342　　([spring]blossoms-red[fall]leaves)、 seaslug-with, too, thing-heart [aesthetic sensibilities]!/?/ó/the)

> spring bloom
> fall leaves: sea slug, too
> a poet's gold

It took some doing to save this poem, whose original wit lies largely in the word "thing" (*mono*) so
appropriate for describing a sea slug yet seamless here as part of an idiom. Okay, the sea slug has
some sort of *class*. It is something that a man of good taste – and all poets, of course, presume to have
that, though they may have nothing else – will not turn up his nose at. But weasels do not know this:

怪 し け に 鼬 の あ く む 海 鼠 哉　一 声
ayashige ni itachi no agumu namako kana – issei (1775)

#343　　　　　(suspiciousness-by weasel's stymied: sea slug!/?/ó/a)

> it's suspicious:
> the weasel is at a loss
> with a sea slug

At first, I thought to put this haiku with *The Featureless Sea Slug*, but then, realizing that the smell
would confuse the weasel more than the shape, decided to slip it in here, instead.

海 知 ら ぬ 山 賎 や 海 鼠 焼 く 夕 嵐 蘭
umi shiranu yamagatsu ya namako yaku yûbe – ranran (1646-93)

#344　　　　(ocean know-not mountain-poor/mountain-hut: roast sea slug evening)

sunset pastoral	*a hermit's luxury*
these hillbillies	my mountain hut
who never saw the sea	so far from the sea! at dusk
roasting sea slug!	roasting sea slug

"Mountain" and "ocean" are formal antonyms in Japan, where one may still be asked whether one
plans to vacation in the former or the latter. My first reading is the usual explanation for the poem.

One imagines the wood-chopper, coal-maker and other mountain folk marveling at "the large leech" and what might be the equivalent of caviar in the Ozarks. But the term *yamagatsu* can also mean a mountain hut, and *that* reading, I think is richer: what melancholic luxury! A fine marine product with metaphysical qualities suitable for the poet enjoyed in the place where such qualities are most at home!

め づ ら し と 海 鼠 を 焼 や 小 野 の 奥 俊 似

mezurashi to namako o yaku ya ono no oku – shunni? (1689)

(rare/precious/novelty so/and seaslug roast/burn! small-field's inner-reaches[i.e., farming back-country])   #345

a rare treat, so sea slug's roasted! deep in the hills	up in the hills sea slug gets burned because it's rare

This similar poem suggests either poetic borrowing or that roasting=burning (*yaku* is a crude way of cooking) was standard for sea slug that found its way into the hill-country. This might have something to do with its not being fresh, or it might be a dig at country cuisine[1] (While haikai poets were great ones for traveling and spoke more for the country than any other form of poetry, as urbanites, they did have their prejudices). Regardless, sea slug would not be common in the back-country and it is pleasant to imagine possible ways it got there. At this time in Japan, most boiled and dried sea slug was supposed to be exported, so this might be considered black-market[2] – or, at the least, grey-market (?) – food. Perhaps, too, restrictions on domestic sea cucumber sales helped make what managed to reach the market, in any form, a *chinbutsu* ("rare-thing" – now the term is *chinmi* = "rare-flavor"), i.e., a real delicacy, or gourmet novelty item.[3]

1. *Country Cuisine* My father, a fish lover, stayed in Japan a half year and never tired of complaining over the way his tiny country hotel insisted on "burning" whatever fish they served.   Fish was never put in a skillet, but always grilled over flames.

2. *Sea Slug Restrictions* If farming villages were forced to cough up a large portion of their rice, sesame oil. etc., to the central authorities, fishing villages were hard pressed for marine products of which sea slug as the leading export item was most desired. It is enough to google in an old date and *namako* to find examples. Eg. Among a list of ten rules posted in the village of Nanao (seven tails!) in April, 1596, magistrates are forbidden to borrow houses year round where villagers are required to give them temporary lodging, the mountainside forests were not to be cut and the villagers had "to catch [and presumably prepare] the same number of skewer sea slug (*kushiko/ketako*) as every year." (nanao machi sadamegaki?).   For Shinshu's? Shimane-ken (1774),   it was "forbidden for wholesalers in Nagasaki to retail any sea slug before finishing all their bundles for export." Nagasaki was long famous for being the only official port for trade with the world – mostly China, some Dutch – over the long period of isolation.

3. *Novelty Lovers/Haters* Depending on the manner of eating it, sea cuke in Japan is many things. Some parts of Japan think of lightly pickled *su-namako* as standard New Year fare. Most think of it as an occasional winter treat. The expensive gonads and guts, generally sold in tiny bottles are pretty much reserved for drinking on an expense account and are true gourmet novelty items, or *chinmi*. As is true for most things that taste so good people rave about them, sea slug is also one of the most *hated* foods. Many personal introductions on the net include *namako* among "things I hate," such as *natto* (slimy fermented soy beans), "warm beer," *enka* music and "my old man!" (My weirdest find was "cockroaches, celery and sea slug.") I dare say that sea cuke is so little known in the USA, that no one would think to include it on their hate list, but one American who made it to Seoul, Korea might: "The food takes a little getting used to and there are certain food-like substances that I avoid, but for the most part the Korean people have a rational and healthy diet. . . . I personally exclude the horrendous sea cucumber, which appears to be a large and recently living wart." (*"American view of Seoul"* Michael S. Fenton, Googled) He may be talking about the sea-squirt rather than the sea cucumber.   Paradoxically, the notoriety of the *namako* as a disgusting looking food – perhaps combined with other recent information (E.g., *"Namako, the world will devour you. Yes the world will devour you, so you better be tasty."* from *Namako: Sea Cucumber* by Linda Watanabe McFerrin) – has furthered the idea of sea cucumber-as-food to the extent that a faculty member of emc.maricopa.edu felt obliged to warn: "The class Holothuroidea has 1,500 species. Sorry, these are NOT good eating as a general rule!" Such a warning would probably be wasted in Minnesota.

をかしさや生海鼠の好か名に立ちし葛三

okashisa ya namako no suki ga na ni tachishi – katsusan (1751-1818)

#346

([the] funnyness [of it]!/: seaslug-lover name stands)

my name

what a joke!
to gain a reputation as
a sea slug lover

My guess is that Katsusan wrote one or more poems – which I have not yet found – about sea slug cuisine and was immediately nick-named "sea-slug lover." The sea slug may have a classy scent, be served up smartly dressed and boast a high *hakai* reputation, but the name still conjures up the warty "gurotesuku" image, which superimposed upon the poet is risible.

黄粉つけて丸ものとよぶなまこ哉 虚桐庵句会

kinako tsukete marumono to yobu namako kana – kyoshi *et al* (1894)

#347

(gold-dust [toasted soybean powder] put, round-thing/coin called sea slug/s!/?/ó/the)

kinako-coated

you may call them coin
sea slug

If money has class, the sea slug is a class act. In this poem, Kyoshi and friends come up with cuisine as coin. Japanese have coins that look like diced sea slug, i.e. washers, and they are called "round-things" (*marumono*). Toasted soybean flower is a common kitchen condiment. The characters for it read "yellow-powder." Because "yellow" can mean "gold" in Japanese, there is a hint of gold in it. [1]

丁銀の握りごゝろや初生海鼠 越蘭

chôgin no nigirigokoro ya hatsunamako – etsuran? (?)

#348

(chôgin's[coin] gripping-feeling! first-seaslug)

gripping
the first sea slug
like chôgin

Oblong coins, the most famous of which was the large silver *chôgin* minted in 1601, had an outline similar to a sea slug. The first bonito (*hatsugatsuo*) [of the year] went for an astronomical price and was heavily haiku'ed, but this is the only *first sea-slug* I know of. I suppose that makes the haiku even more valuable than the tightly gripped *namako*. Money in Japan is said to *have wings*, but I think, like the sea slug, it is, rather, *slimy*. And, in a sense, the sea slug *was* money, for the reason the lion's share of the sea cucumber was prepared in large outdoor (seashore) processing factories for export to China was to block the loss of gold, silver and copper currency to preserve face for the hyper-mercantilist central government. One 18th century salt-dealer turned slug wholesaler (*iriko-donya*) favored by the Shogun had a 300 *koku* (1 *koku*=10 cubic feet) boat that proudly flew the Shogunate *goyô* (imperial-business) flag, forcing all boats large and small to still their oars and lower their sails when they came into harbor. Dead, the sea slug commanded great respect!

1. *Golden Sea Slugs* These haiku may concern the *Cucumaria japonica*, or *kinko* = "gold sea slug," taken offshore of a locality in Okushu (NE Japan) called Kinkazan, or "Gold Flower Mountain" where they reputedly sucked up run-off with gold dust. My dictionary prefers to translate this as a "three-striped sea slug" (though I have not seen stripes in photographs) since they were sometimes called *torako* (tiger-slugs) and, recognizing their communality with the international product, as *trepang,* the Malayan term preferred as far North as Vladivostock. It is also cut into about ten rings and cured upon two skewers. But it is more likely the slug coin poems are about normal *namako*.

齢 と は 食 わ ず 嫌 ひ の 海 鼠 な り　山 田 桃 晃
yowai to wa kuwazugirai no namako nari – yamada tôkô (1997)
(age-as-for, eat-not dislike/hater's seaslug is)

#349

aphorism

age is a sea slug
disliked without ever
having tasted it

experience

what's age?
a sea slug yucky
till you try it

While this poem was found in a selection of haiku on sea slug, it is really about old age. Yet, it does indirectly confirm two things about the slug-as-food. First, it does not look appealing to most who have not tasted it. Second, it turns out to be better than expected. More importantly, it attests to the strong presence of the sea slug without which it could not have been used as a metaphor like this!

酢 海 鼠 と な り 果 て し 身 を 箸 に 懸 け　高 沢 良 一
sunamako to narihateshi mi o hashi ni kake – takasawa yoshikazu (2003)
(vinegar/pickle seaslug-as become-end circumstances/body chopstick-by held)

#350

chopstick-held
this body that ended up
a pickled slug

holding a body
reduced to pickled sea slug
with chopsticks

The poet feels sorry for what became of the gentle sea slug. As chopsticks are used to pick out the bones from cremated remains, the "body" is mentioned and the poem hints that this act of eating is also a wake as is confirmed by the following:

硬 直 の 酢 の も の 海 鼠 勘 弁 な　高 沢 良 一
kôchoku no sunomono namako kanben na – takasawa yoshikazu (2003)
(rigid/stiff's pickled seaslug [i'm] sorry[+emphasis])

#351

my apologies
for turning you into a
stiff, sea slug

sea cucumber
forgive my putting you
into this pickle

At first, I thought this an apology for making the pickled sea slug too hard, but the adjective *kôchoku* is *the* word to express the *rigor mortis*. The poet kindly explained that the (live) sea slug is dressed with rough salt before it is cut. There is an association here. Heaps of salt are commonly placed outside the door of the deceased, for purification. Some might find the haiku artificial if not maudlin, but I read it as a poetic expression of appreciation for the sea-slug-as-food, i.e., the life we take to preserve our own.

手 当 つ れ ば 胃 の 辺 で 哭 け る 海 鼠 と も　高 沢 良 一
teatsureba i no hen de nakeru namako to mo – takasawa yoshikazu (2003)
(hand-placed/palpate/d-if belly's area-in/at howl/wail seaslug probably)

#352

dirge

putting my hand
on my belly: does sea slug
wail for himself?

dirge

putting my hand
on my belly, is that
sea slug wailing?

Takasawa's affection for the sea slug has given birth to what must be the most imaginative poem about a noisy stomach ever written.[1]   Anthropologists have a specific word for burying people by eating them in order to give them a warm rather than cold resting place, or to absorb their spirit.[2]   This haiku implies that the poet has a similar respectful/worshipful attitude about eating sea slug.

わ が 腸 の 一 部 に な れ る 海 鼠 と も　　高 沢 良 一

waga chô no ichibu ni nareru namako to mo – takasawa yoshikazu (2003)

#353   (my intestines' one-part-into becomes seaslug[subj] probably)

the sea slug	this sea slug
it might just serve for	will it become a part
part of my guts	of my bowels

~

the sea slug
is it becoming part
of my guts?

The sea slug has been called a living bowel.   Reading this poem, I could not help thinking, . . . *and the vermicelli becomes your hair and the apples your cheeks and . . .* But the poet is just taking his beloved food another step into his body; and the bowels in Japanese, as in English, are more than tubes.   They are the deep seat of being.   Incorporating sea slug in the manner Takasawa's haiku suggests, is to say

le namako c'est moi!

1. ***Loud Belly Poems***   Although I am not Christian, much less Catholic – or, because I am neither – I cannot help dreaming up this: *how the lions / in my belly roar / for the wafer.*
2. ***Good Cannibalism***   Being poor and homeless as a sea slug, I had to leave almost all of my library in Japan; so I do not have my big volume on types of cannibalism (a Cambridge book, perhaps?) with me. Googling brought me to "reverential funerary endo-cannibalism," but I recall there was a proper Latin term for the whole shebang!   True, Takasawa and the sea slug do not have an *endo* relationship by standard anthropological standards, but, psycholog-ically speaking, his haiku is about *eating one's own.* There are those who would falsely claim that all reports of cannibalism are Occidentalist fiction, but that sort of lying (white lies in both senses of the word!) for the reputation of the UnWest is misplaced, for eating one's own is something to be celebrated, rather than covered up.   The most recent (2003) discoveries of the oldest homo-sapiens carrying about polished craniums suggests that endocannibalism may well have been one of our first religious practices.   For those of us too squeamish – or afraid, when we bear in mind the risks of taking in prions! – to eat our relatives, may I suggest eating *namako* as a proxy, a sort of trans-subtantiation, if I may borrow the Christian term, for the "white, round and soft" bread and sweet red wine of the Eucharist.

14
<u>the slippery sea slug</u>

目 に は 見（え）て 手 に は と ら こ の ぬ め り 哉　成 之
me ni wa miete te ni wa torako (tora ko) no numeri kana – seishi (1670/72?)
(eyes-in-as-for see/n hand-in-as-for tiger=take-not slug=cub's slimyness!/?/ó/the/'hoh)   #354

easier to see
than to hold a tiger
sea slug

The slimy *numeri* in the original slipped away from my translation! The tiger (*tora*) in the tiger-sea-slug (*torako*) variety puns as "hold-not," whereas I must waste words spelling out what is going on. Even then, I couldn't keep the farcical allusion to tale #73 of the *Tales of Ise*, where a girl beyond the reach of a would-be lover is likewise described as "*in eye, but not in hand*, like the *katsura* tree on the moon," a fetching simile itself borrowed from *Manyôshû* song #623. I do not know if the poet had in mind a whole sea slug (in the wild or on a cutting board), or prepared pieces of sea slug, but this is the oldest example I know of the slipperiness that features highly in the preparation and eating of sea slug.

終 に 下 女 か 手 を の が れ た る な ま こ 哉　花 讃 女
tsui ni gejo ga te o nogaretaru namako kana – kasanjo (1807-30)
(finally maid's hands' escape seaslug!/?/ó/the)   #355

in the end
the sea slug evaded
the maid's hands

This haiku, irregular for being purely secondary – a haiku about haiku existing only in an essay about poem writing – refers to an essay where a master teaches a student how to boil haiku down to the essentials, which was also, he pointed out, what *kanshi,* Chinese poetry was all about.[1] Here are the three poems, minus the pedagogy, in the order (of improvement) they appear.

板 敷 に 下 女 取 り 落 と す 海 鼠 か な　廣 瀬 淡 窓 の 随 筆 より
itajiki ni gejo toriotosu namako kana – hirose tansô (1782-1856)
(plank/wood-floor-on, maid takes/holds-drops seaslug!/?/ó/the)   #356

the maid drops
the sea slug she picks up
upon the floor

1. *Chinese Poetry* While the overdone quality of much Chinese decoration and rock gardens lead us to oppose it to the more subdued, miraculously good taste of the Japanese, Chinese poetry retained its telegraphic quality. Of course, *kanshi* here may mean Chinese poems written by and for Japanese, but for all the bad things which have been said about its artificiality, I think we should at least note that its terse style may, in an indirect way, have been one of the strongest influences on the development of haikai=haiku. Japanese, generally speaking, takes much longer to express things than Chinese (or, for that matter, English). I think the Chinese formal contribution to haiku (and not just the idea of nature poems) deserves more attention and Japanese poets deserve great credit for creating a short form *despite* the natural tendency of Japanese to run on at length!

板敷 に 取 り 落 と し た る 海 鼠 か な 廣瀬淡窓 の 随筆 より
itajiki ni toriotoshitaru namako kana – hirose tansô (1782-1856)
(plank/wood-floor-on, take/grab-drop/ping seaslug!/?/ó/the)

#357

the sea slug
picked up and dropped
upon the floor

取 り 落 と す 取 り 落 と し た る 海 鼠 か な 廣瀬淡窓 の 随筆 より
toriotosu toriotoshitaru namako kana – hirose tansô (1782-1856)
(take/grab-drop/ped take/grab-drop/ped seaslug!/?/ó/the)

#358

picked up dropped
picked up dropped
the sea slug

Before I re-found the story in a chatroom letter from "ayame," all the details I remembered from having read the haikus in the essay before are exactly those found in Kasanjo's haiku, funny for seeming to turn the lesson from one in haiku composition into a moral(?): *in the end, sea slugs escape maids.*   The haiku in the Hirose's essay may have come from this *Haikaibukuro* (1801) poem:

錠 口 に と り 落 し た る な ま こ か な 其角?
jôguchi ni toriotoshitaru namako kana – kikaku? (1669-1706)
(door-mouth[lady-in-waiting]-by held/taken/grabbed-dropped seaslug!/?/ó/the/'loh)

#359

the sea slug
held and dropped by
a lady in waiting

This haiku in turn spoofs some line in the *Tales of Heike* where the bar locking a gate is dropped. The *jôguchi* is a classical lady-in-waiting who guards a noble's woman's quarters, which suggests to me that this sea slug might have been a crafty wooer of the mistress. The *gejo* is closer to what English called "wenches" and the sea slug without the floor specified may well allude to *her* absconding lover. Still, allusions, aside, the repeated drop in the final version of the haiku in the essay – hard to translate because English lacks different length versions of the same verb – is a very effective way to bring out the slipperiness of the sea slug, which is usually described in more specific, task-related ways:

ぬ め り と る ま で を 海 鼠 に 鳴 か れ け り 吉田紫乃
numeri toru made o namako ni nakarekeri – yoshida shino (1997)
(slime take/remove-until seaslug-by cry[passive+finality])

#360

mistranslation	*bird in a tub?*	*salt in its eyes?*
until i can	the sea slugs	it keeps crying
de-slime the sea slug	just keep chirping until	until the slime is gone
makes me cry	i de-slime them	the sea slug

Here is my explanation for what turned out to be a mistranslation (occasioned by cognitive dissonance: I so wanted the perfect haiku to fit right here.): "*An account of Kwakiutl sea slug preparation translated by George Hunt in 1913 indicates just how slippery sea slugs were, for when boiling them, "the man tries to take hold of one of them with the tongs; and when he succeeds in taking one, it is done." (bruce@hallman.org).Imagine a day when nothing goes right, followed by food that won't stay put. Still the Chinese character for "cry" suggests more crying out than teardrops, so we shouldn't imagine the poet hysterically chasing the sea-mouse with her carving knife. I doubt that the haiku is about preparing sea slugs for curing, as is done in Japan for the cucumaria variety, but all Japanese sea slugs are slippery."* Chances are that the poet refers to rubbing down the *namako* intended for pickled slug in course salt and that she intends both meanings of cry (the sound and the liquid) to come from the poor sea slug, as the grammar demands. There is also a slight possibility that she refers to noises coming from waiting slug in a tub, prior to its prepping.

まなばしに挟み付んと海鼠哉　魚日

manabashi ni hasamitsukan to namako kana – gyojitsu (d.1753)

(real-fish-[large cooking-use]chopsticks-by pincer(hold-between)-try: seaslug tis!/?/ó/the/'tis)   #361

trying to hold down
something on the cutting board:
it's a sea slug!

far from fish

trying to hold on
to something with big chopsticks
a sea cucumber

I do not know how many Japanese readers would recall the Chinese characters for the large wood or, sometimes, metal-tipped chopsticks used for handling fish and other large pieces of food undergoing preparation, to wit: "real-fish-chopsticks!" [1] Irony? *Maybe.*

俎に生海鼠ははねもせざりけり　嘯山

manaita ni namako wa hane mo sezarikeri – shôzan (1717-1801)

(cutting-board-on seaslug/s-as-for jump/flip/flap/flop-too does-not[+finality])   #362

the sea slug
doesn't even flap about
the cutting board

Is Shôzan's poem only pointing out what the slug does *not* do, or is it intended to make us think: *Yes, but how difficult it is, none-the-less!* Not only do sea slugs harden when they shrink up – little bits of calcium line up and lock in place – they grow proportionately rounder. A contemporary poet warns:

包丁を研がねば海鼠さばかれず　清水信香

hôchô o toganeba namako sabakarezu – shimizu nobuka (contemp)

(knife sharpen-not-if seaslug handle/dispatch/carve-cannot)   #363

don't sharpen
your knife and you won't
carve sea slug

～

you have to
sharpen your knife
for sea slug

1. ***Character Recall*** Unless Microsoft gets literate and deigns to include such Chinese character readings in its all too paltry choices for we who use Japanese, much of the fun of the written language will die. It is a pity, for properly designed software should make it easier to preserve such pleasures!

Japanese have a saying to the effect that a master calligrapher need not choose a brush, but I suspect that even a top chef would not want to use a butter knife on a sea slug.   And even with a sharp knife, the layman must be careful to pin the sea slug down well and cut just right lest it pop out from under the knife and land on the floor.

海 鼠 切 る こ と に 器 用 を 働 か せ 大 橋 敦 子
namako kiru koto ni kiyô o hatarakase – ôhashi atsuko (contemp)

#364
(sea slug cut thing-with deftness work-put-to)

cutting sea slug
good hands can be
put to work

∼

carving sea slug
a good chance to show off
my deftness

Since I have often been called *kiyô binbo,* or "deft but poor" – the closest Japanese comes to *"jack of all trades and master of none"* – I like to imagine the poet, like me, lives below the poverty level; but that is not likely.   More likely, she is married, exceptionally good with her hands but ordinarily doesn't like to show-up her husband.   But, now, preparing sea slug for his consumption, she can dazzle him without fear of being put down for it.

も 一 ぅ 海 鼠 ず た ず た に 切 り 裂 い て や る 義 郎 舞 仁
mô namako zutazuta ni kiri saite yaru – yoshirô (2002)

#365
(eergh seaslug jagged/ragged-in/as cut-tear/split do)

errgh! i hack
the sea slug up into
ugly pieces

frustration

errrgh! i hack
the damn sea slug
to hell and gone

People who write haiku tend to be so polite to everything, as they quietly – to borrow a phrase from an American nature writer – bear witness to the world.   How refreshing to see this violent response!   To see a haiku poet admit, no boast, about losing his cool, exploding instead of crying in the face of *namako,* terror of the cutting board.

ぬ り 箸 に 兵 法 つ か う 生 鼠 哉 慰 角
nuribashi ni heihô/hyohô tsukau namako kana – ikaku (mod?)

#366
(painted chopsticks-with military-method use sea slug!/?/ô/the)

slippery opponent

painted chopsticks:
one must practice martial arts
with the sea slug

mismatch

lacquer chopsticks:
picking up sea slug requires
a black belt

The fact chopsticks [1] are painted shows they are for eating, not cooking. Pardon my anachronism in the second translation: I doubt that they had black-belts back then!   This *Slippery Sea Slug* is probably the single most common *namako* sub-theme in old haiku.

実 平 の 手 を 辷 り た る 生 海 鼠 哉　鳥 酔

sanehira no te o suberitaru namako kana – chôsui (1700-69)
(sanehira's hand/s-from slip/ped [raw]sea-slug!/?/ǒ/the)   #367

it even gave
the slip to sanehiru
sea slug sashimi

信 玄 も 箸 に 工 夫 の 生 海 鼠 か な　素 丸

shingen mo hashi ni kufû no namako kana – sômaru (1712-1795)
(shingen's chopsticks-to/with improvization's [raw]sea-slug!/?/ǒ/the)   #368

even shingen
had to improvise
eating sea slug

Doi Sanehira was the greatest military mind of the twelfth century. He specialized in large-scale search and destroy – in Japanese, "chase-strike" and "chase-catch" – missions, i.e. *pacification.* Takeda Shingen (1521-73), a great warlord of the Era of Warring States and noted tactician himself, was bright enough to employ an even more brilliant "wall-eyed cripple."(Sato: *Legends of the Samurai*) In other words, sea slug sashimi [2] is so hard to pick up, it might even escape the grasp of the relentless regent and require the warlord to exercise his tactical wile (scaring the surface of his chop-sticks?). Furthermore, Shingen invented a stew (*hôtô-nabe*) for feeding his soldiers which included udon noodles, themselves almost as slippery as raw sea slug. This and the fact that he was famously land-locked [3] and perhaps not accustomed to raw sea slug help flavor the poem.

酢 に あ ふ て 骨 あ る や う な な ま こ 哉　竹 紫

su ni ôte [aede?]hone aru yô na namako kana – chikushi (1703)
(vinegar-with treat/marinate bone/s is/are aspect's seaslug!/?/ǒ/the/'tis)   #369

bonyfide

pickled
sea slug seems
osseous

1. Chopsticks There is a big difference between an honest-to-goodness word and a description. I hate the descriptive "chopsticks." Although the "chop" means food, it sounds rude. What if our forks were called "pokesticks" or "chow-stabs?" In 1965, Bernard Rudofsky protested this "inappropiate term" at length in *The Kimono Mind,* so I will forebear here, and add only that in the 1980's some Japanese claimed the use of said implements contributed to the high IQ's destined to take the Far East past the stagnating West (see FROIS).

2. Sashimi I wrote "sashimi" because the poem includes the "raw" character in the name "sea-slug." Actually, there was little sashimi as we think of it today at that time – fish was generally soaked in Chinese mustard or soy-sauce and left to ferment a day or so --- while the sea slug was probably lightly marianated, as it still is.

3.Famously Landlocked Shingen's lifelong adversary, Kenshin, provided him with salt because true warriors fought with bow and arrow not food and this quickly became a famous tale of chivalry.

su dressed
you'd think sea slug
bone hard

酢 に 逢 う て 石 と な り た る 海 鼠 か な 喜舟
su ni aute ishi to naritaru namako kana – nomura kishû (1934)
(vinegar-to/with meeting, rock-as/into becomes seaslug!/?/ó/the/`loh)

#370

running into
vinegar, a sea slug
turns to stone

~

meeting *su*
sea slugs become
solid rock

Though Japanese vinegar (*su*) is much milder than that what is used for pickling or marinating in the West (USA, at least), it evidently worked like magic to give backbone to sea slug.[1] The bone/stone hyperbole – most likely thought up independently – explains why the *slipperiness index* of the slug is higher than that of the equally slimy noodle or yet slimier little mushrooms found in Japanese soup. It is harder to grab something *hard* and slippery than something *soft* and slippery (assuming it is convex).

腹 た て る 人 に ぬ め く る な ま こ 哉 支考
haradateru hito ni numekuru namako kana – shikô (1703)
(belly-stand[angry] person-with slip sea-slug!/?/ó/the)

#371

the sea slug
slips away from
angry men

気 短 な 箸 に か か ら ぬ 生 海 鼠 哉 茂楓
kimijika na hashi ni kakaranu namako kana – mofû (1790)
(temper-short-chopsticks-by catch-not sea-slug!/?/ó/the)

#372

short-tempered
chopsticks keep losing
the sea slug

~

sea cucumber
only cool chopsticks
can pick it up

1. *Hardening   and   Softening   Sea   Slug*   "When chewed," writes MT, chopped sea cucumber stiffens at first, but later becomes quite soft." That this usually doesn't happen, he explains, is due to the vinegar. "The low pH makes the dermis quite stiff."   Sea cucumber tissue tends to soften when near death, so chefs who want springy pickles – Americans with their chewing gum have nothing to laugh about here! – dice them up when they are still quick. Softening sea slug, likewise, is a special science. Marine scientist Arakawa Kohji notes the way straw mats have long been used to soften – and occasionally by mistake, dissolve! – sea slug products and that it is believed a chemical in straw does this, which, found, would make soft sea slug a cinch (some dishes, such as tempura and stews, call for soft sea slug, even in Japan). Indeed, he whispers "I hear that some experienced chefs have a secret method to do this and use it to create special highly reputed sea slug dishes." (ndh:1990)

The metaphysical message of these two haiku: one must be like a sea slug to successfully pick up and eat the sea slug.

はさむ時こころ尽しの海鼠哉 五鳳

hasamu toki kokorozukushi no namako kana – gohô (1916)

(squeeze/pinch/ing[between chopsticks] time/when heart/mind's-exhaust/care/-ing seaslug!/?/ó/the)   #373

careful chopsticks

pinching it
we're all solicitude:
the sea slug!

Sea slug is arguably good for you: it forces one to calm down, breath deeply and concentrate on eating! The verb with no suitable translation, *hasamu,* makes it unnecessary to mention "chopsticks" in the original. The "time/when" in the gloss (but not the translation) may suggest a contrast between the care taken when eating sea slugs and the happy-go-lucky slovenly image of the sea slugs.

海鼠喰ふひとり相撲の日なりけり 宮沢映子

namako kuu hitorizumo no hi narikeri – miyazawa eiko (contemp)

(seaslug eat alone/lone-sumo[wrestling] day becomes[+finality])   #374

eating sea slug
one-woman fighting
with herself

I think the fine untranslatable idiom: "*one-man-sumo,*" meaning something like "battling windmills," refers not only to the physical difficulty of holding slug with chopsticks, but to chewing it and, perhaps, even the poet's mental struggle to eat a man's dish, perhaps after becoming widowed.

心萎えしとき箸逃ぐる海鼠かな 石田波郷

kokoro naeshi toki hashi niguru namako kana – hakyô (1913-69)

(heart shrinks/droops time chopstick flees sea-slug tis!/?/ó/the)   #375

psyched-out

when my heart
wavers, sea slugs flee
my chopsticks

when your heart   a pickled slug
is weak, sea slug escapes   will flee your service the
the chopstick   instant you doubt

Here, I was sorely tempted to title the poem "Freudian slip." While there was little Freud could have added to traditional Japanese dream analysis, I do feel his theories encouraged this type of haiku, for he validated the subconscious as something *objective.* "Service" means the "chopsticks," of course.

酢海鼠や思案の箸のありどころ 松尾良久

sunamako ya shian no hashi no aridokoro – matsuo yoshihisa (contemp)

(pickled sea-slug!/: contemplation-chopsticks[=bridge]-place)   #376

pickled sea slug
the place chopsticks stop
and take stock

pickled sea slug
here, chopsticks look
before they eat

~

pickled sea slug
where people are absorbed
in their chopsticks

~

pinching my
pickled slug i pause
to ponder

The pun does not translate. *Chopsticks* are homophonic with *bridge* and the Bridge of Contemplation (*shianbashi*) is 1), a figure of speech for a place where a momentous decision is made (fortune-tellers used to work on top of bridges); 2), a real place next to the Yoshiwara Pleasure Quarters, where men once decided whether or not they dared enter and waste money, risk disease and incur their wife's wrath; and, 3) a pause to ponder what to do next. There may also be a hint at *shian-dokoro*, a pause for thought, typically equated with taking a smoke. We do not know if the haiku is pure observation or whether the poet is himself thinking about going to a contemporary cathouse.*

酢 海 鼠 の 逃 ぐ る を 箸 の 追 ひ に け り 小 島 飽 石
sunamako no niguru o hashi no oinikeri – kojima hôseki (1997)
(vinegar-seaslug's fleeing[+objective, i.e., after] chopsticks' chase [+finality])

#377

pickled sea slug
on the lambe, and chopsticks
chasing after

This is lighter, to be sure, but the "chasing" picture was charming enough to inspire a dramatic loose translation. Older haiku suggest the difficulty begins within the bowl or bottle:

料 理 に も か く る 数 千 里 の と ら こ 哉 保 友
ryôri ni mo kakuru sûsen ri no torako kana – hoyû (1670)
(food-for-even, move/run/dash several[=vinegar] thousand leagues' tiger-slug!/?/ó/the)

#378

vinegar seas

the tiger slug
even food can dash about
a thousand leagues

酢 の 中 を け た 逃 歩 く 海 鼠 か な 吐 月
su no naka o ketanigearuku namako kana – togetsu (1726-80)
(vinegar-inside uncompromisingly [?] fleeing-go/walk seaslug!/?/ó/the/my)

#379

in the vinegar
furiously fleeing about
my sea slug

1. *Contemporary Cathouse* Japanese no longer have formal houses and districts of prostitution such as we find today in Nevada and Amsterdam. But there are a great number of small establishments officially offering massages or shows, etc., where men illegally, but with little danger of arrest, buy various services. They are plentiful in districts where men might drink and chew their slug.

The older poem may well be the oldest sea slug haiku, for the poet flourished ~1645. It probably puns at the movement within the vinegar of pieces of a tiger sea slug. That reading (so convoluted I leave it for a footnote [1]) is supported by Togetsu's simpler poem about bits of cold sea slug with chopsticks in hot pursuit. The compound verb in the original gives a tough quality at odds with the action of fleeing. "Furiously" is not right, but neither is the word in the gloss. Oddity is hard to match.

I came across a proverb,
namako no aburage o kuu
(to eat a fried namako)
which means (one)
"talks a mile a minute,"
seemingly emphasizing
namako's slipperiness
made even slipperier
by frying it in oil!
(om:corresp)

I had never heard of deep-fried sea slug and seriously doubt that it would be any slipperier than sea slug in its raw or pickled state, but my correspondent's point is that the sea slug has indeed become synonymous with slippery. To continue,

酢 海 鼠 を 食 み て 生 死 の こ と 言 は ず 　 嶋 西 う た た
sunamako o hamite seishi no koto iwazu – shimanishi utata (2001)
(vinegar-seaslug chewing life-death's thing say-not)

                                                             #380

alive and dead
make no sense eating
pickled sea slug

dead or alive

who can talk
of life and death with
pickled slug

I remember how my father, a professor of thermodynamics and an engineer, was fooled by onion-skin-thin bonito shavings dancing on hot Japanese-style pancakes (*okonomiyaki*): "They're alive!" he shouted in horror. Pickled slug is hardly so remarkable as hot bonito flakes, but when its performance is contrasted with its live state, it is impressive: how many creatures are there livelier dead than alive?

口 の 中 な す す べ も な き 海 鼠 か な 　 平 方 文 雄
kuchi no naka nasu sube mo naki namako kana – hirakata fumiô (contemp)
(mouth's inside do-method-even not [ie. nothing that can be done] seaslug!/?/ó/the)

                                                             #381

in my mouth
the sea slug has run
out of tricks

1. Tiger Run The wit of the poem in question is untranslatable *as poetry*. The tiger-slug runs/travels several thousand leagues – it is exported to China. This plays on two sayings about gossip (how it gets around and what it takes to "make" a tiger a fact). The "running/dashing" (*kakuru*) also means "stirring" or "moving about" in the vinegar, *su*, which is suggested in the *sû*. And, finally, "tiger" or *tora*, is a homophone for "grab/hold-not." So, the poet would seem to be saying that the tiger slug really gets around – in the world, and in my dish – I sure have trouble catching it.

caught	***no free lunch***
in my mouth	in the mouth
too late to escape	sea slug is still hard
from the slug	to finish off!

The grammar of the original allows all of the above readings. The first follows the actively fleeing sea slug motif. The second reverses it, suggesting the poet has no choice but swallowing the sea slug once it is in his mouth. The plainspoken haiku that follows is a vote for the last reading, which itself is a cross between the *Slippery Sea Slug* and the *Chewy* one we will encounter in the next chapter.

海 鼠 噛 む 舌 一 枚 に た ら ざ あ る を 愿 山 紫 乃

namako kamu shita ichimai ni tarazaru o – genyama shino? (1978)

#382   (seaslug chew tongue one suffice-not [+regret/contradiction])

chewing slug
alas, one tongue
isn't enough

酢 海 鼠 の あ ち こ ち 動 く 口 の 中 未 知

sunamako no achikochi ugoku kuchi no naka – unknown (2000)

#383   (vinegar-seaslug's there-here moves/moving mouth's inside)

hyperactive

pickled sea-slug
moving here and there
in my mouth

海 鼠 畳 は 咽 通 る 間 の 手 ぎ は 哉 止 水

kodatami wa nodo tôru ma no tegiwa kana – shisui? (1707)

#384   (sea-slug-diced-as-for, throat-passes-while/pause's juggling!/?/ó/the/what)

diced sea slug:	diced sea slug
what juggling goes on	the juggling between gulps
between each gulp!	is what it is

The *kodatami* sauce is just a light dressing than the so the sea slug would not be as hard as *sunamako*, or vinegared-sea-slug, but it would be a slimier, so the slipperiness index would remain about the same.   Grammar first told me to translate *"sliced sea slug /as it goes down my throat / i keep juggling,"* but that would not be interesting, so I ditched the "while" reading of *ma* for the "between/pause," and the result, I think, is one of the best haiku in the book.

While slipperiness and swallowing are associated, I put the most dramatic slug-down-the-throat poems and writing in the *Lubricious Sea Slug*. This was because the swallowing brought to mind the "oral stage" of Freud, though, if I am not mistaken, that is lip, tongue and gum-centered and neglects the act of swallowing. So the last word in the *Slippery Sea Slug* is simply this: remember ***throat-feel***. [1]

1. *Throat-feel* Those calcium tablets, slightly squared off, no doubt to give an eye-feel of solidity (swallow us and your skeleton will be as strong as the proverbial outhouse?), choke up a large portion of would-be users (perhaps, those of us who should not try swallowing sea slug?). Is the idea to make us feel sicker? Or, is it just that drug companies pay no attention to throat-feel?

15
the chewy sea slug

見るだけに歯応えまでも海鼠かな 敬愚
miru dake ni hagotae made mo namako kana – keigu
(see-only-with tooth-reply-until-even seaslug!/?/ǿ/the/'tis)   #385

> just looking
> my teeth know how
> sea slug feels

the mind's mouth

> just to see
> the sea slug is
> to chew it

The eye is not the only sense with imagination, though it is through the eye that all but the blind will grasp the bumpy sea slug and imagine it must be knotty, if it were, in places and a challenge to chew up. Japanese has an everyday word encompassing the sound and feel of food, *ha-gotae,* or "tooth-reply"[1] and that is what Keigu's eye anticipates.

すきものの歯のきこきこと海鼠たぶ 飯田蛇笏
sukimono no ha no kikokiko[gikogiko?] to namako tabu – iida dakotsu (1885-1962)
(like-guys[people of taste]' teeths' *kikokiko*[mimesis]-with seaslug eat)   #386

the sound of gourmet

> men of taste
> their teeth noisy
> eating sea slug

aesthetics of chewing

> gourmet teeth
> go *kikokiko to*
> sea cucumber

crude delicacy

> eating sea slug
> just listen to the teeth
> of the aesthete

gikogiko

> the gourmet
> grinds his teeth by day
> pickled slug

Since the "muddy marks" indicating that the "k" sound becomes a "g" need not be written in the case of haiku, which tends to preserve the traditional style of leaving the choice up to the reader, we may read the *kikokiko* as *gikogiko* – the noise made by hard things rubbing on hard things such as the sound of a saw cutting hard wood or an oar on an oar-peg – though the more subtle *kikokiko* is favored by my Japanese readers, one of whose interpretation suggested the "crude" idea might be only in my head.

1. **Tooth-reply**   While *ha-gotae,* or "tooth-reply/response" can sometimes be Englished as "texture," it hardly addresses the resistance(?) of the food. Hopefully, *mouthfeel* (see next note) will become a common word, like "tooth-reply" is in Japanese. English-speakers may, however, lack the sensibility toward texture-as-sound possessed by Japanese speakers, due to the differing nature of our mimetics: both physiological and psychological onomatopoeia in English is obscure – it tends to hide in our verbs, whereas Japanese uses an adverb-like "goes *cockledoodledoo*" construction (viz EKN and OAO). It would be interesting to check the vocabulary of languages with our respective types of mimesis to see if there is a parallel dis/interest in the texture of food as represented in the vocabulary.

The "noisy" "listen" and "grinding" reflect the absence of an equivalent in English for *kikokiko, grind* being too fine-grained and *squeak* too high. Luckily, metaphor can work where mimesis fails:

なまこ喰ふ歯音や雪の高木履　素丸

namako kuu haoto ya yuki no takabokuri – somaru (1712-95)

(sea-slug-eating tooth-sound: snow's tall-wood-shoes)

#387

bokuri bokuri

eating sea slug
the sound of high-stilt clogs
in old snow

If taste and, to a large degree, smell, evaded sea slug haiku – except in the abstract sense of the "scent" – this old haiku proves that one important part of the slug eating experience, *sound*, did not. Somaru's simple expression "tooth-sound" (*ha-oto*) echoes the standard "tooth-reply," while playing on the fact that chappin (clog) stilts are called "teeth" in Japanese. *Bokuri* are usually lacquered and the name itself happens to be a perfect mimetic approximation of the sound the long rectangular stilts make crunching through somewhat old snow. Somaru's haiku often make such "sound sense." I believe that Issa, who is known as Mr. Onomatopoeia, learned a lot from this ignored poet, whom he studied under.

傘も海鼠も顕つる骨の音　高沢良一

karakasa mo namako mo tatsuru hone no oto – takasawa yoshikazu (2001)

(chinese-style-parasol/umbrella too, seaslug too raise/articulate bone's sound)

#388

the sound of bone
made by chinese parasols
made by sea slugs

The sound made folding up a Chinese parasol/umbrella and that made by chewing pickled slug is equally *korokori* or *parapara,* to use the mimesis offered by the poet (corresp). If Somaru's poem played with the name of the *geta* (*bokuri*) as mimesis, this poem plays on the polysemy of the "bone/s," *i.e.,* the ribs of an umbrella, something the sea slug lacks, and his own jawbone.

酢海鼠やきしきし均らす半世紀　菊池久子

sunamako ya kishikishi narasu hanseiki – kikuchi hisako (1997)

(vinegar/pickled-seaslug!/: squeakily/grindingly levels half-century)

#389

pickled slug
leveling *kishi-kishi*
a half century

I think the poem refers both to someone's teeth and the body politic. Japan, thanks to the McArthur's socialist land reform and the less avaricious nature of their CEO's has managed to become and stay far more equal than the increasingly plutocratic USA. The onomatopoeia was hopeless – English has nothing between a squeak and grind or grate – so I really *trans-lated*, i.e., *carried it over*, into English.

しこしこと歯ごたえうれし酢の海鼠　伸茶

shikoshiko to hagotae ureshi su no namako – nobucha? (contemp)

(*shikoshiko* [psychological mimesis] tooth-reply delighted vinegar-seaslug)

#390

the joy of feeling
spring against my teeth
pickled sea slug

shikoshiko

how delightful
your reply to my teeth,
pickled sea slug

happy teeth

how delightful
this insubordination
chewing slug

At first reading, I assumed *shikoshiko* was a squeaky sound, but checking my dictionary, found the second definition was "a word representing the nature of a food with elastic-power [resilience] that gives a tooth-reply when chewed." This is a psychological mimesis. When you think about it, silent onomatopoeia is a good match for our subject.

海 鼠 か む ひ か り の 粒 を 噛 む ご と く 小 檜 山 繁

namako kamu hikari no tsubu o kamu gotoku – kobiyama shigeru (mod)
(sea-slug-chew/ing light-bits/grains/granules/drops chew/ing-like)　　　　　#391

chewing sea slug
is just like chewing on
granules of light

Wow! This trans-sensory haiku from Ôno Zasôko's *Flavor Almanac* (Mikaku Saijiki) takes the whole idea of *mouthfeel* up a notch.[1] I suppose light reflects from shiny surfaces which tend to be more breakable, hence crunchier than dull ones. Or, that eating ossicle-filled globs of muscle suggests what it might feel like to chew up the tiny bulbs one finds on Christmas trees. KS writes "the *korikori*, *kokikoki* and *shikoshiko* feelings are expressed by 'chewing light-granules.'" Yes. But *what* makes this "crunchy," "crisp" and "squeaky" (a far from perfect translation for mimetic expressions that would do for chewing ice, blubber and undercooked green-beans, respectively) food feel like *particles of light*? And, why do I feel it might look nice to paint "$E=MC^2$" the side of a sea cucumber?

1. *Mouthfeel, the Whole Idea* Googling revealed that *mouthfeel* is a relatively recent term invented for the sake of food technologists, but quickly adopted if not dominated by wine-tasters ("young in *mouthfeel*," "toasty *mouthfeel* and finish;" "*mouthfeel* a bit too big;". "rich, round *mouthfeel*;" "fat *mouthfeel*', good "backbone; etc.) and beer-meisters [?] ("*mouthfeel* is very creamy and well-rounded" "full yeasty *mouthfeel*;" "*mouthfeel*: feel the beer swirl over your tongue and around your mouth"; "a warm or prickly *mouthfeel*;" "luminescent pale-gold body and succulent *mouthfeel*;" "very soft, thick, foamy head. ....". "a balancing, complementary *mouthfeel*;" etc.) I think the Japanese term "food/eat-feel/sense" (*shokkaku*) is better, for it includes the bite-feel(?) element more easily. Still, *mouthfeel* is remarkably transparent for a specialized term, so it should find its way into popular English before long. The best introduction on the web is "Texture and *Mouthfeel*: Making Rheology Real" August 1993 – QA/QC By: Ray Marsilli www.foodproductdesign.com/archive/ 1993/0893QA.html - 28k   1993 weeks publishing company). After an overall introduction to the concept including information such as "Cucumber pickles, for example, are evaluated for quality by the consumer primarily on the basis of texture. In a survey conducted jointly by Continental Can Co. and Nowland Co., 400 housewives were asked, 'What should a good pickle be like?' Almost 90% answered they should be crisp, firm and hard." He notes "Although it may be one of the most important organoleptic properties, a food's mouthfeel is probably the least understood and most neglected by food developers." Yet, it is not completely ignored for "The Universal TA-XT2 Texture Analyzer (from Texture Technologies Corp., Scarsdale, NY), which can perform a complete TPA calculation, comes with 25 standard probes, including various sizes of needles, cones, cylinders, punches, knives and balls. It can determine adhesion, bloom strength, breaking point, cohesion, creep, crispiness, density, extrudability, film strength, hardness, lumpiness, rubberiness, slipperiness, smoothness, softness, spreadability, springback, tackiness, tensile strength and nearly every other known rheological property of foods." For example (Text accompanying 0893QAtpa.jpg): Texture Profile Analysis of Cucumbers – Typical force-distance curve for TPA of 1 cm. cucumber slice: brittleness (kg) is the height of the first peak on "first bite" curve; hardness (kg) is the height of the second peak; cohesiveness is the ratio Area 2:Area 1; elasticity (mm) is the distance over which the sample was under compression in the "second bite"; gumminess (kg) is hardness (x) cohesiveness; chewiness (kg mm) is gumminess (x) elasticity; total work is Area 1. (Instrument: Instron Universal Testing Machine) Source: "Journal of Food Science." "Examples of Texture Terms Used in Sensory Texture Profiling" are given with definitions which may be found on the web. Here are the terms only: Adhesiveness, Bounce, Chewiness, Coarseness, Cohesiveness, Denseness, Dryness,, →

喰 ま ま に 我 を わ す る る な ま こ 哉 嵐 外

kuu mama ni ware o wasureru namako kana – rangai (d.1845)

(eat-as/like self[obj] forget/ting seaslug!/?/ŏ/the/'tis)

#392

eating
sea slug i forget
myself

Does eating something amorphous disolve the poet's form-based ego? Or is the poet lost in the revelry of chewing?[1] Has the sound carried him off?

海 鼠 食 べ 縄 文 人 の 夢 を 見 し 栗 谷 昭 二

namako tabe jômonjin no yume o mishi – kuritani shôji (2000)[2]

(seaslug eat/ate, *Jômon* [an era from ~10,000-2,200 bp] person's dream see)

#393

jômon-jin	*back to the mud-age*
ate sea slug	ate sea slug
and dreamed i was	fell asleep and became
in the stone-age	a *jômon-jin!*

All Japanese have images of their prehistoric ancestors, the *Jômon-jin,* or, "Jomon man," but the word isn't even in my 10 set OJD, which only admits the *Jômon* as a style of pottery or an era covering part (8,000 BC (or earlier) – 200 BC) of the Japanese stone-age. In contrast to the other prehistoric *Yayoi-jin* (200 or 300 BC – AD 300), the *Jômon-jin* is, to use OM's words, "more robust and rugged, more dynamic and masculine." (To put this into Occidental terms, could we say we are talking about cave-man food, something suitable for the Flintstones?) Had the poet seen a picture of the hunter-gatherers that included sea slug or of the stippled muddy-colored rococoesque Jômon figurines? Did this, perhaps, combine with Shiki's 18,0000 (18-*man*) year old sea slug to inspire this dream which, to better fit this chapter, might be described as an after-effect of the chewing, or a flashback?

→ Fracturability, Graininess, Gumminess, Hardness, Heaviness, Moisture absorption, Moisture release, Mouth-coating, Roughness, Slipperiness, Smoothness, Springiness, Uniformity, Uniformity of Chew, Uniformity of bite, Viscosity, Wetness." There are both definitions and "Sensory Techniques for Evaluating Mechanical Texture Characteristics" given. For the former, "hardness" is "Force required to deform the product to given distance, i.e., force to compress between molars, bite through with incisors, compress between tongue and palate;" while for the latter it is: "Place sample between molar teeth and bite down evenly, evaluating the force required to compress the food." Lacking the sea cucumber as the exemplar of chewy mouthfeel, our Occidental food folk must use gum drops for calibration: "Chewiness: Place sample in the mouth and masticate at one chew per second at a force equal to that required to penetrate a gum drop in 0.5 seconds, evaluating the number of chews required to reduce the sample to a state ready for swallowing."

1. *Lost in Chewing* Most readers have probably lost themselves in shaving or brushing their teeth. It would seem that chewing a food like sea slug has the same effect. The fact that we also tend to come up with great ideas while repeating certain motor-movements might explain why there are so many good *namako* haiku! The chewing itself inspires it. If chewing gum does not quite have the same effect, it is because the chewers do it for so long it becomes 100% automatic, whereas creative leaps require a touch of consciousness, i.e., *distraction.*

2. *Jômon-jin Haiku Source* Not only the content – which reverses and, to my mind, beats Seisei's famous Dreaming Sea Slugs haiku – but *the place* I found this poem is marvelous! It was among a score of poems selected in a haiku contest for the general public by a huge bakery of Japanese-style cakes called POÈME – its name sounds out with three Chinese characters, "mother+blessing+dream." They offer something called "Mother's Day Pucci? [Poochie?] Poems" which *may* – I clicked on it for more information to no avail – use the winners of the contest. Almost every other poem was about "mother" and, as might be expected, cloyingly sweet. This "dream" category sea slug was a breath of fresh air.

こきこきと海鼠を食めば海の底　守屋光雅

kokikoki to namako o hameba umi no soko – moriya koga [1] (2000)

(*kokikoki*-with [physio/psychological mimesis],seaslug devour-if, sea-bottom)

    #394

munching slug
i found myself
on the sea-floor

If the sea slug in the last haiku is a time-machine, this gold-prize winning [2] millennial haiku's sea slug is a space-machine. The entire middle line is added, for that is what the Japanese means. I couldn't help wondering what might be between the two lines and wrote the site on the off chance the poet might be a diver who saw a fish munching a sea slug on the sea floor, or did so himself (unlikely in the winter, but just thought I'd ask). The answer was "no" of course. I also wondered what exactly caused the transport of the eater, if, perhaps, the chewing sound, usually described as *korikori,* might resemble underwater sounds (scuba tank bubbles, etc). The editor of *Suien* replied that *kokikoki* was more a psychological mimesis. [3] The poet was, as it were, lost in chewing. In an explanation published in the magazine, she wrote that the poem had "an impact that can otherwise only be felt from a painting of the sea-floor." In a letter to me, she mentioned seeing dazzling blue.

.

海鼠噛む六〇〇〇〇ᵏ₀を汽笛きて　天気

namako kamu rokuman kiro o kiteki kite – tenki (2002)

(seaslug chew/ing sixtythousand kilometers steam-whistle coming)

    #395

chewing sea slug
a steam whistle comes
60,000 miles

ss trepang

a steam whistle
travels 60,000 miles
chewing sea slug

1. Koga? or Mitsumasa? This is one of many names which await confirmation. (Please visit www paraverse.org to make or read the *Errata*!) お名前の確認のために等、website の正誤表に来て下さい。
2. Gold Prize The gold prize is for a Spring 2000 internet haiku contest run by the haiku magazine *Suien* ("water-smoke") of the Bashô Memorial Museum. As I have never thought of art or literature as being contest-driven, I was as surprised to discover the extent to which Japanese poetry right up to the present day is contest-oriented as I was to read about the intensity of competition between Balinese Gamelan orchestras decades ago. In the mid-late Edo era (18th-19th century), poets were listed in charts resembling those made for ranking for Sumo wrestlers!
3. My Koki-koki Investigation My 6" thick Japanese-English dictionary didn't include *kokikoki*. My OJD defines it as a synonym with *dokidoki,* meaning excitement. But an internet search showed that almost every instance of it was primarily physiological, even if psychological excitement may have been included. About 70% of instances describe neck-cracking (Japanese, do this a lot for they tend to suffer from stiff necks, or, perhaps, doing it, get stiff necks?), 10% shoulder-cracking, 5% neck and shoulder-cracking, 5% jacking off (at last, the excitement!) and 10% a single famous haiku I had never heard of where someone opens a can (or cans) *koki-koki-koki* as migrating birds fly over. This modern haiku would seem to occupy the mind of half the school teachers in Japan and I particularly enjoyed learning that one student could vividly imagine a sad woman in a canning factory, another, a happy male poet on a picnic outing. The sea slug poem was the only reflective *kokikoki* I found, though I did find reflective *kokokiko* sea slug haiku. In Japan, there are any number of mimesis dictionaries. After this note and the earlier one on *gishigishi,* perhaps you (I assume a majority of readers don't read Japanese) will understand why!

Most English speakers associate a steam whistle with a train. In Japan, a boat is as likely an association. The large ships and their steam whistles – not only the fog horn we grant boats – evoke nostalgic distance, far-off places (a railroad can't go too far in Japan). The poet writes that when he ate sea slug by the Pacific Ocean on the East coast of Japan, he heard the part of Japan's soul that came from South East Asia and is still found in the South Sea. [1] He added that there is something about the sea slug that connects the seabed at his feet with the vast unseen ocean. Reading this, I start imagining the sea slug as a piece of intercontinental cable and fantasize them as relays for the low decibel calls of whales (which really do make it thousands of miles) . . .

海 鼠 食 ひ 故 郷 の 海 見 た く な る 　湯 田 洲 弘
namako kui kôkyô/furusato no umi mitaku naru – yuda kunihiro (1997)

#396   (seaslug-eating hometown/area's ocean see-want become)

> eating sea slug
> i start to miss the sea
> back home

The sea slug does not obviously transport this poet nor does the haiku mention any visions, but simply the desire to see something (as close as the Japanese can come to the verb "to miss"). Ah, but to desire to see *is* to see. In the mind's eye, the poet must already imagine the hometown sea. Compared to the stone-age, sea-floor and South Pacific, this is plain stuff, but the poet's feelings may be deeper.

ふつ切りの 海 鼠 ひたすら食むちちの夢醒めてなほ河岸のさざめき 　加藤 満智子
bukkiri no namako hitasura hamu chichi no yume samete nao kishi no sazameki – katô michiko (1999)
(chunk-cut seaslug intently chewing father's dream[from] waking, still [rocky]sea-shore's whispering[from a fine chop])
#397

> ***sea-side inn***
>
> when i wake
> from a dream of father
> intently chewing
> chunk sea slug: the still
> whispering waves

I added the title, for that is where I imagine it happened. The poet may have eaten sea slug, but we can't know for sure. In Japanese, there are different words for "shore" depending upon whether it is sand or rock. The one used here suggest the slapping of litttle waves against the stones. But, I fear that even if English had a word, the waves would still have to be specified because of our collective lack of what might be called sea-consciousness. Loving this poem, I hate my translation! As a rule, I think little of *tanka,* but this one is exceptional, for it contains far more than can possibly fit in a haiku [2] and it would take a chapter to explain everything. So I won't. Instead, I will only add parenthetically that Japanese scientists have recently (?) named a deep sea holothurian *yume-namako* or "dream sea slug" because this wine-red sea slug's "swimming form is dreamily beautiful" (*yume-no yô-ni utsukushii*).

1. *Southern Hypothesis* The Japanese have long debated their origins. The general opinion today is that they are a mixture of North and South and Equestrian and Farming and Fishing folk. Whenever the Japan's economy soars, various parts of this (including all=mongrel) are used to explain that success, but at all times, the diverse possibilities are convenient, for the variety allows one to wax nostalgic in just about any direction!

The research of Tsurumi Yoshiyuki (NNM) suggests that the practice of eating sea slug and producing trepang began in the North, a direction usually associated with horseback culture rather than fishing; but this does not at all invalidate the feelings of the poet whose ear opens to the South.
2. *Why I Prefer Haiku to Tanka* Most *tanka*, nine out of ten, in my opinion, can be boiled down to haiku length with no great loss to the content.

海鼠噛む時恍惚と成る海月噛む時朦朧となる　森崎和夫
namako kamu toki kôktsu to naru kurage kamu toki môrô to naru – morisaki kazuo (contemp)
(seaslug chew-time entranced/rapture/esctatic become // jellyfish chew time dopey/stuporous become)   #398

high-low, low-high

when i chew sea slug
i sink enraptured
when i chew jellyfish
i float in a stupor

This 7-7+7-7 poem is by a restaurant owner and web-aesthete "Morris" who includes both the sea slug and the jellyfish among the things he would like to be reborn as. [1] The poem would seem to combine the image of the thing eaten with the mouthfeel, for jellyfish has a pleasantly elastic *al dente* snap to it.. But the good trips, the manic reveries, the pleasant nostalgia evoked by chewing sea slug are not reported so often as the loneliness and melancholy that will later require a whole chapter.

海鼠買ふ夫在るごとく振舞ひて　坪井芳江
namako kau otto aru gotoku furumaite – tsuboi yoshie (contemp)
(seaslug buy/ing, husband is like/as-if acting/behaving)   #399

behaving as if
my husband's alive
i buy sea slug

海鼠食べさびしき夜と真向ひぬ　永井二三江
namako tabe sabishiki yoru to mamukainu – nagai fumie (contemp)
(seaslug eat, lonely night-to face directly)   #400

the sound of silence

face to face
with the lonely night
eating sea slug

The first poem is not a *Chewing Sea Slug*, but I thought it might go well with the second, where I imagine the sound made when chewing sea slug alone amplifies the silence of the room where her husband had eaten sea slug in a more cheerful atmosphere. A long winter night. Could *namako's* proverbial lack of a face bring out the fact the poetess no longer has a face to face across the table?

海鼠噛む真顔のときのすさまじき　加藤楸邨
namako kamu magao no toki no susamajiki – shûson (1905-93)
(sea-slug chew true-face-time's ferocity/dreadfulness)   #401

terrifying!
the unaffected face of
a slug-eater

1. *Reborn Wishes* "Morris" is not the only Japanese with such a desire. A young Japanese woman's internet diary reveals that if she were to be reborn, it would be as, "1. Jellyfish, 2. Trepang, 3.Indian 4.Italian, 5.Thai or Asiatic except Japanese." Her explanation for the first was *"To have only a mouth hole and a butt hole! I'd like to become such an animal! Wow!"* The Italians have short work hours, while the other Asians don't run about like crazy (that is to say, they follow the sea slug). I think it would be a good idea to make an international poll of our reborn preferences.

I do not think this is about the menacing animality of strained sinews on the jaw of a person chewing something hard, but that tension would magnify the chewer's intense expression. It might well be a self-portrait, caught in one of those unexpected double mirror side-views occasionally found in bars. [1.]

海 鼠 噛 む そ れ よ り 昏 き 眼 し て 中 村 苑 子

namako kamu sore yori umaki manako shite – nakamura sonoko (1996)

#402
(seaslug chew from-then delicious/good eyes-make/show/have)

after chewing
sea slug his eyes
look delicious

full of mettle

chewing
sea slug his eyes
look good

Perhaps his (I assume a man, for the poet is a woman) eyes show how contented he becomes with the flavor and texture of the sea slug, or a sort of chewing induced catharsis, where the sea slug takes away all his troubles so to speak. But he may still be chewing and this may be a haiku of love, where she spies on his expression from the side, and finds the intensity not frightening as she might were he a stranger, or beastly as she might were they estranged, but wonderfully alive.

海 鼠 噛 む そ の 眼 返 事 を 保 留 し て 高 沢 良 一

namako kamu sono me henji o hôryu shite – takasawa yoshikazu (2002)

#403
(seaslug chew/ing that/those eye/s answer[obj] hold/reserve)

chewing sea slug
eyes that say a reply
must wait a bit

chewing sea slug
with eyes that say your
reply is on hold

chewing sea slug
she holds her tongue
in her eyes

The upbeat nature of Nakamura Sonoko's poem and the cool observation of Takasawa Yoshikazu – or, is he saying, sea slug chewing time is sacred, *hsssh!* – is rare among chewing haiku. With the next poem, we return to the common hurtin' song chewers.

人 嫌 ひ 人 恋 ひ て お り 海 鼠 噛 む 藤 木 倶 子

hitogirai hito koiteori namako kamu – fujiki tomoko (1997)

#404
(person-hate[misanthrope] person/man-loving-am sea-slug [i] chew)

a man-hater
in love with a man
chews sea slug

～

a misanthrope
falling in love i chew
pickled sea slug

1. *The Turned Off Face* My *kids-say-the-darndest-things* age nephew-in-law was asked if he was OK by his grandmother, who spying his face in the back-mirror during a car trip, worried because he looked a bit glum. "No, I'm fine," he replied, "that was just how I keep my face when I am not using it." Could we say that Shûson's poem expresses the adult version of the same?

As KS explains, "a quite old woman who always prided herself at making it alone and having no need for a man, suddenly finds she is in love and has no idea what to do, how to approach him, so she sits in the bar chewing sea slug, drinking in despair." I cannot improve upon that. Next poem:

海 鼠 噛 む 汝 や 恋 を 失 ひ て 　西 東 三 鬼
namako kamu nanji ya koi o ushinaite – sanki (1899-1962)
(sea-slug chew you:/! love losing/lost)   #405

you chew	the way you	chewing slug?
sea slug: your love	chew that sea slug!	i see you must have
is gone	you lost her	been jilted

The first reading imagines a poet who hears his lover, wife or mistress chewing sea slug and realizes she doesn't care any more (for women of the old school knew that toilet and eating sounds can turn off the delicate sex, males). No, says KS, a friend of the poet's has lost his love and is drowning his sorrow in drink. [1]

酢 海 鼠 を 背 中 さ び し く 食 ひ に け り 　野 中 亮 介
sunamako o senaka sabishiku kuinikeri – nonaka ryôsuke (2001)
(vinegar-seaslug[obj] back lonely eat[+finality])   #406

the lonely back	a man with
of a man masticating	a lonely back eats
pickled sea slug	pickled slug

Forgetting oneself, facing the night, drinking in bars . . . this is when, with none of the drama of the usual out-of-body-experience, we can sometimes get a glimpse of our own lonely, hunched over form, seen from behind, diagonally from the side, and even, perhaps, from a height near the ceiling. *Right?* Or, the poet could be describing his father? By this time, the reader might note that pickled sea slug figures in many of the loneliest poems. Is it only because of its being the toughest to chew? Or is it possible that the vinegar in the pickled sea slug, though far weaker than the case with any pickles in the West,[2] might unconsciously work to pucker up and turn the chewer inward? Or, is it because it is a cheaper dish – served at home or honkytonks (*viz* the *Run-Down Sea Slug* in Sundry SS) – and, therefore, more depressing than the fancy diced *kodatami* served up with style for the old time poets? Or, is it because most of the poets are now washing it down with beer and the chemistry is different?

1. *Lost Love and Drinking Away Sorrow* This sounds corny in English, for English lacks the right vocabulary. *Shitsuren* "lose-love" with just two characters means a hopeless or failed love affair. *Yake-zake* "burnt-sake" means getting drunk to forget someone or some thing or to punish oneself. English can only match these words --- they are single words in Japanese – with long idioms like "getting shot down" or "drowning one's troubles."

2. *Pickled Sea Slugs* I have never had the opportunity to eat them. Here is testimony from someone who has: "This chapter brought back pleasant memories of a period of my life during my geisha days when I ate *namako* several times a week during the winter. I lived next to an *ippin-ryouriya* [lit: single-dish-restaurant] where I had dinner practically every night. The *namako* was always in the form of a *su-no-mono* – as in the haiku above. Besides its *kori-kori* chewy crunchiness (a texture unlike anything else I have ever eaten) its color was an incredible sky-blue. As you know, truly-blue foods are rather rare, and the blueness of this namako was amazing. I think the outer skin may have been removed somehow, as it seemed quite different from its living form. The vinegar brought out a sea-freshness of taste that I'm not sure the word "pickled" implies. (personal correspondence from Liza Dalby who apprenticed as a geisha and wrote about it) Later, I found this modern haiku: "put in vinegar / sea slug turns the color / of a japanese lamp" (*su ni otosu namako nihon no hi no iro ni* – ishida fûta? (1997) 酢 に 落 す 海 鼠 日 本 の 灯 の い ろ に 　石 田 風 太). My Japanese advisor KS thinks this may mean it reflects the lighting (be it candle or electric with a lamp-cover making it look like a lantern) in antiquated bar, but I, rightly or wrongly, imagine fox-fire blue . . .   **#407** (上) .

なだらかに老いるは難し海鼠噛む　小泉千代子

nadaraka ni oiru wa katashi namako kamu – koizumi chiyoko (2001)

#408   (gently/smoothly/mellowly age/aging-as-for [it's]difficult: sea-slug chew/ing)

chewing sea slug:
how hard it is, i think
to grow old gently

I was tempted to translate "it's so hard / to age gracefully: / chewing slug," but the poem is more than a contrast of gentle and rough and eating slug is not in itself a bar to gentle old age. While sea slug may be hard on the jaws of the elderly, something about the nature of chewing reminds us of a tendency for older people to be impatient and ornery. The poet feels her grace slipping away despite herself.

海鼠噛み残年測りゐたりけり　高瀬白洋

namako kami zannen hakari itarikeri – takase hakuyô (2001)

#409   (sea-slug chewing remaining-years measuring am[vague+finality])

chewing slug   chewing slug
i think about how long   i measure the time
i have to live   left in me

This man is neither lost in revelry, nor chewing away his troubles. For him, the effect of chewing is to bring to consciousness something he may not care to think about, the short time he has left. This haiku is so good, I had a hard time not doing a dozen translations!

行方なく海鼠食うべて欠けたる歯　皆吉爽雨

yukue naku namako taubete kaketaru ha – minakichi sou? (mod)

#410   (destination-not, seaslug eating/ate missing/lacking teeth)

where oh where   missing teeth
did my teeth all go   i eat sea slug like there
eating sea slug   is no tomorrow

I am not sure I get this poem, though it seems to make some sense in the second reading with the syntax of the original turned neatly on its head.

なまこ噛み老若といふ蟠り　伊丹さち子

namako kami rôjaku to iu wadakamari – itan sachiko (2001)

#411   (sea-slug chewing, age-youth[what's] called: vexations/grudge/bad-blood)

chewing slug
resentfulness builds:
age-difference

A young person is out-chewing an old one. The biggest question here is the poet's perspective. Is the poet resentful of how old her husband is? (Of having married an older man?) Is she observing that eating sea slug makes him act grumpy towards her and thinks this is why? Or is it mother and daughter?   A few more unhappy chews (and swallows) are found in the *Melancholy Sea Slug*, and all have one thing in common with those in this chapter. All are post World War II. Before then, there were plenty of sad sea slugs, but no poets sadly eating. Or none that I have found, at any rate. It would seem the sad image of the sea slug pioneered in the Edo era became conflated with the eater in more recent times! That is why I wish the more hopeful haiku that follows were better known.

かみきれぬ処味有る海鼠哉 伏せ名 虚桐庵句会
kamikirenu tokoro aji aru namako kana – kyoshi et al (1894)
(chew-up-can't place-in taste is: sea slug!/?/ǒ/the)   #412

sea cucumber
the unchewable part
is best of all

life lesson	*imagination*
eating sea slug the flavor is in the part you can't chew up	eating sea slug the part you can't chew up tastes best

The slipperiness of sea slug that gave rise to the sub-theme we might call the martial art of chopsticks was enhanced by the chewiness that so effects contemporary poets. This chewiness in turn includes, indeed, depends upon *an unchewable core* all too seldom haiku'ed. Would this be lumps of calcareous grissle, places chock full of ossicles? Or, would it be the calcareous plates around the mouth?[1] Whatever it is, it suggests a wonderful complex metaphor of desire, of longing most for what one can't quite attain, though one can swallow it. Such a metaphor lends itself to philosophy, doesn't it? [2] Perhaps because of that (haikus are not *supposed to be* philosophical) the haiku didn't make the cut at Kyoshi and his acquaintances *kukai* [3] and even today remains unknown. I was delighted to google this 2001 New Year's haiku from an internet forum called, in translation, Right Brain Haiku:

酢海鼠の噛み切れなくて年始酒　桃流
sunamako no kamikirenakute nenshizake – toryû (2001)
(vinegar-seaslug chew-cut/complete-not, year-first/start sake/drink)   #413

new year swallow

my first drink:
couldn't quite chew up
the pickled slug

Knowing the older poem about the best part being that you can't chew up, the newer poem seems more cheerful – downright auspicious – whether its author knew it or not!   #414

1. Eating Ossicles Rumors have it that sea slug, with those ossicles, might be bad for the teeth or guts, though I have not found confirmation. Even if it were shown to be particularly abrasive, the question would be whether the calcium eaten would make up for the wear to the surface of the teeth. Be that as it may, the ability to eat sea slug is the acid test of dental health: "eating sea slug / my wife notes aging / in my teeth" (*namako kuu ha no otoroe o tsuma mo iu* – bakunan (mod) 海鼠喰ふ歯のおとろへを妻も言ふ　麦南).

2. Philosophy of Chewing and Swallowing While chewing has metaphorical connotations in both Japanese and English, there are more, I think in Japanese. Some have become idiomatic. A young Japanese friend once wrote that getting to know me was "like eating dried squid" (*surume-no-gotoki*). I was dismayed at first, but soon discovered it stood for something that effort improved, i.e., the longer chewed the softer and the better the flavor! This idiom represents a mature philosophy of consumption opposed to the immature one of instant gratification. In the case of the sea slug, not only is much chewing called for, but the goal of total mastication/knowing is never reached.

3. Kukai A *kukai* is a haiku get-together. Seven people participated including Kyoshi, Hekigoto and Hyôtei who judged the poems and only gave the name of the poet for haiku selected as superior poems. I think they damn well should have picked the above poem. Poems from the Kyotohyô Kukai are found in Kyoshi Zenshu.

承知してやれば目のなき海鼠かな　加藤郁乎

shôchi shite yareba me no naki namako – katô ikuya (contemp)

(knowing/agreed-upon doing/did, eyes-not[crazy about] seaslug!/?/ő/the)

#415

> knew i was getting
> into a pickle but how
> i love my sea slug!

If you embark upon something difficult knowing what you are getting into, you will experience the hard-won satisfaction of chewing pickled sea slug. Of chewing haiku? (actually, I had some help from AQ) The poem might also be read to mean the poet is a sea slug, eyeless, yet unfazed as he goes about doing that hard thing he started (perhaps his fine haiku almanac (kkhk)?

酢海鼠食ぶ残る歯全て動員し　高沢良一

sunamako tabu nokoru ha subete dôinshi – takasawa yoshikazu (2003)

(vinegared-seaslug eat/ing remaining teeth all enlist/ing)

#416

> pickled sea slug
> i call up all of my
> dental reserves

酢海鼠に錆つく顎を使ひけり　高沢良一

sunamako ni sabitsuku ago o tsukaikeri – takasawa yoshikazu (2003)

(vinegared-seaslug-by/from/on rusty jaw[obj] use/ing)

#417

> pickled sea slug
> i put my rusty jaw
> back to work

The rusty jaw may be a result of a long hospitalization where sea slug would not be on the menu. But the particulars are less important than the fact that for all the fancy mimesis, there is a dearth of haiku concerning *the difficulty of chewing*, and Takasawa fills a gap in sea slug haiku by thoroughly developing this theme.

海鼠噛む歯がまだありてあほる酒　高沢良一

namako kamu ha ga mada arite aoru sake – takasawa yoshikazu (2003)

(seaslug chew/ing teeth still are/have, rouse sake[subj])

#418

> chewing sea slug　　　　　　chewing sea slug
> with jaw power to spare　　i've still got my teeth
> thanks to sake　　　　　　and sake for fuel

Alcohol would help – though *sake* would not do as much good as red wine because it does not contain salicylic acid (the active ingredient of aspirin) – to take the edge off. In the original, the *sake* eggs the poet on in an energetic way I just can't translate. OM comments re. the second reading, "I like this translation better, since the jaw power may not have anything to do with sake. He is probably drinking sake in glee that he still has some jaw-power left." OK, I can raise that, and I can paraverse *this:*

> *chewing sea slug*
> *i raise my drink to toast*
> *my good teeth*

酢 海 鼠 に 顎 の 運 動 い ち に っ さ ん　高 沢 良 一
sunamako ni ago no undô ichi ni san – takasawa yoshikazu (2003)
(vinegared-seaslug's jaw's exercise one-two-three)   #419

one! two! three!
pickled sea slug helps me
exercise my jaw

pickled sea slug
one! two! three! phys ed
for your jaw

one, two, three!
one, two, three! . . pickled slug's
good exercise!

This emphasis on the sheer physicality of chewing is welcome balance for the mystical identification with the sea slug found elsewhere in Takasawa's *namako* haiku. I suspect the mother of the outrageous *one, two three!* invention is the *sake* mentioned in the last poem.

酢 海 鼠 の こ れ は い け な い こ の 硬 さ　高 沢 良 一
sunamako no kore wa ikenai kono katasa – takasawa yoshikazu (2003)
(vinegared-seaslug's this-as-for won't do: this hardness)   #420

in a pickle
for my sea slug is
just too hard

i'm in a pickle
as my pickled sea slug is
too damn hard

pickled sea slug
you'd need the jawbone of
an ass for this!

こ ん な に も 硬 き 酢 海 鼠 閉 口 す　高 沢 良 一
konna ni mo kataki sunamako heikôsu – takasawa yoshikazu (2003)
(this[+intensifier]-even hard vinegared-seaslug, close-mouth-do/am)   #421

flabbergasted

pickled slug
so damn hard it
shuts *me* up

Yet, for all the benefits of that exercise, there was such a thing as *too* much. The wit of the second poem does not English, for in Japanese, to be "closed-mouth" is to be flabbergasted by something, to be so shocked and disgusted there is nothing to be said: an idiom that evokes the original close-mouthed sea slug. Now the table is turned and the non-sea-slug is mum.

海 鼠 嚙 む 顔 を 四 角 に 三 角 に　高 沢 良 一
namako kamu kao o shikaku ni sankaku ni – takasawa yoshikazu (2003)
(seaslug chew/ing face/s[obj] rectangular, triangular-to)   #422

faces chewing
sea slug turn square and
even triangular

One of those cross-cultural themes commonly discussed in Japan but never heard in the Occident concerns the basic shape of a powerful body. In the West, it is a triangle standing on its tip, with a thin waist, narrow hips and legs that taper off below a puffed-out chest framed with broad shoulders, whereas the Japanese paradigm of power, the sumo wrestler rests securely on his powerful haunches and belly. Atlas *vs* the Globe. Here, we are only talking faces, but it is true that Mongolian jaws – as measured by tooth surface – tend to be relatively thicker than Caucasian jaws. This is generally ascribed to the diet in the Far East being more heavily dependent on grain and the West on meat. Reading about what generations of chewing sea slug can do to the Japanese (and Korean, for I hear they also eat pickled sea slug) face in this imaginative haiku, I could not help but think of such things, and I suspect that many Japanese would too. If associations are part of reading poetry . . .

なまこ食ひなまこなまことなまけもの　高橋比呂子

namakogui namako namako to namakemono – takahashi hiroko (p2001)

#423   (seaslug "eater/ing seaslug! seaslug!" [say] lazy person/people)

eating sea slug	eating sea slug
sea slug! sea slug! cry	a chewer, a chewer and
the lazybones	a lazy bones

The *to* may indicate a statement, as per the first reading, or just be "and" as per the second. Either reading suggests that people who don't eat sea slug are too lazy to chew, true, perhaps, and a fine disassociation of laziness with sea slug (and, by extension, the sea slug-lover). This leads into a question: why would people seek out food that is practically unchewable? These sentences from two googled articles (one, no doubt plagiarizing the other [1]) advising people to be aware of what *feeling* they want when they eat, suggest we not only desire flavors but textures:

> If you want something crunchy and eat yogurt, you'll be looking for more food after your meal is over, even if you're physically full.

> If it is crunch you want, eating something smooth and creamy won't satisfy you, even it is healthy. In the long run, if you choose food textures you don't crave, you will likely end up consuming more calories because you will eat the food you didn't want—and then the food of the texture you craved!

I do not know if this has been, or can be proven, but the psychological implications on a cross-cultural level are particularly interesting. Is it possible that Japanese (not all Japanese to be sure) seek out this hard-to-chew food because their large consumption of white rice and soft noodles – as opposed to bread, which is usually harder – means they crave hardness? [2] Or is it a deeper need, where the wishy-washiness of communication in Japan, including fear to be clear and inability to put strong emotions into words, leaves a crying need for something concrete to chomp down on? If it is the latter, we have a creature cruelly silenced for being silent, serving the mental health of the people whose gods did the dastardly deed. Hardly justice, but very poetic.

1. *Credit for Texture Crave* If anyone knows who deserves credit for first putting this concept into words, please visit paraverse.org and tell me what's what, unless someone else has already done so (check the *Errata*). I know this craving very well, for when I was in grade school, I put potato chips into baloney sandwiches in order to satisfy it.

2. *Food Cravings and Physiology* Pop-Japanology in the 1970's and 80's claimed restrictions on beef imports were necessary because Japanese had proportionally smaller stomachs (needed to digest meat) and longer intestines than Westerners. The tariff link is a *non sequitur* but for all I know, there might be something to the physiological difference. In the case of chewing, Asians on the whole, have broader jaws and teeth. So it is possible that the increased chewing surface might be reflected in a slightly greater unconscious need, i.e., instinctive need, to grind up hard food. Since Japanese don't chew betel like Malays or fish-bones like Koreans – I suppose culture can overcome genes, but when I lived in Korea (1972 and 1980), I was amazed to see the way Koreans masticated small fish-bones – so, *namako* might be more important to Japanese than they realize. Chewing sea slug might be the only way they can satisfy their latent jaw power!

16
<u>drinking sea slugs</u>

海鼠くうて海鼠のごとく酔ひにけり 冬葉
namako kûte namako no gotoku yoinikeri – tôyô (1926)
(seaslug eating seaslug-like/resemble drunken[+finality])
           #424

eating sea slug
i end up as drunk
as a sea slug

This modifies "you are what you eat" to "you are *what you think* what you eat *is*." The poet thinks sea slugs act as if they are drunk (if the ocean was *sake*?) and, sure enough, he proves it. Seriously, for some Japanese missing the enzyme needed to digest alcohol, even vinegar can turn them pink and drowsy. This poet could be one such and by putting it this way puts a funny face on a real problem. The "drunk as a sea slug" has a good ring to it, but it never caught on.

酔いどれは生海鼠ににたり松の内　無名
yoidore wa namako ni nitari matsunouchi – anon (1900)
(drunken-as-for, seaslug-to resembles pine-within[new years week])
           #425

plastered callers
resembling sea slugs
on the new year

The title of this chapter is misleading for this is the only poem in it where the sea slug drinks and even here it drinks no more than the proverbial fish who drinks like a fish only when it is a man. "Inside the pines" refers to the seven-day period where pine decorations stand by the gates of each house at the start of the year. When we consider that *piss-drunk* in Japanese is "mud-drunk" and someone in that condition *does* resemble a sea slug – as illustrated by Buson's haiku of a Snoring Sea Slug and this "crazy haiku" [1] – it is surprising we do not find more such poems. *Enter Keigu* –

呑めば呑むとどのつまりは大海鼠 敬愚
nomeba nomu todo no tsumari wa ônamako – keigu
(drinking drink, in-the-end-as-for, big seaslug)
           #426

kuroda bushi blues

macho drinkers
mullet gullet ends up
a big sea slug

The most common etymology for *todo-no-tsumari,* an idiom for someone ending up something after passing through a lot, is a fish story: a fish called a *bora* (mullet), after passing through many schools

---

1. *Crazy Haiku* The haiku in question was published in a newspaper as a "crazy-body/style-haiku (*kyôtai haiku*). I have long wished for such haiku to be called *kyôku,* in the same way that unconventional 5-7-5-7-7 *tanka* are called *kyôka*.

The haiku may allude to a tiger sea-slug courtesan (see *Stone Sea Slugs* in "Sundry S.S.") for a kabuki play by the name of Matsunouchi takes place in the Ôiso (literally, "large reef") pleasure quarters the name of which she is associated.

of growth, each with a different name, becomes a big *todo,* something my Japanese-English dictionary neglects to translate (only giving its homophone, the walrus!). The *nomeba nomu todo* puns on the words (*nomeba nomu hodo*) of a glorious male drinking song,[1] which means "the more you drink" (the more manly patriotic warriors, you become) and parodies it. To return to authentic haiku:

やや あり て 酒 を もて 来る 海 鼠 哉　牧童

yaya arite sake o motekuru namako kana – bokudô (1703)

(awhile being/passing, *sake*[obj] bringing-comes, seaslug!/?/ó/the/hoh)

#427

after a while
the sea slug comes
with our *sake*

one calls for another

after a while
he brings over *sake*
for sea slug

This brings us to the real subject of the chapter: sea slug and drinking. My first reading is wrong, except in so far that it points out a possible identification of the person bringing the drink with the slow-moving sea slug. The question remaining at the end of the twelfth syllabet of the second, correct translation is: "What, more than anything else, would *sake* follow? I thought the sake's being *late* fits the slow mood(?) of the food, but KS opines matter-of-factly that *because it's winter,* sake *would take a while to heat.* I cannot help wondering if anything else might be substituted for sea slug in this poem and whether it would work. Strangely enough, I can find very few old haiku mentioning drink together with sea slug. This may well be because it is taken for granted. Still, it is puzzling to me not to have encountered poems like, say,

海 鼠 食ふ 酒 先 ず あり し 後 が 楽　敬愚

namako kuu sake mazu arishi ato ga raku – keigu

(seaslug:/hoh/!/? sake first is/exists/have, after-as-for, easy)

#428

sea slug
easy enough
after *sake*

That is to say, if men were drinking, it would not have required great bravery to try sea slug for the first time or anytime. Or, say,

海 鼠 腸 や 寒 酒 を の みて 談 話 あり　敬愚

konowata ya kanshu o nomite danwa ari – keigu

(seaslug-guts: cold*sake* drinking-even warm conversation is)

#429

sea slug guts   cold *sake*
cold *sake* warm   warm conversation
conversation   slug guts

Cold drinking usually means very cheap blue-collar *sake* or very good gourmet *sake.* In the latter case, the silent appreciation of the drink would be stretched out and include conversation thanks to the delicacy with the gross name – particularly in English – which shall be described in more detail soon. In the former case, I fear the result may be *fin de sicle* naturalism:

海鼠 かな 犬 が 噛む 生酔いがへど　敬愚
namako kana inu ga kamu namayoi ga hedo – keigu
(dog chews raw-[plastered] drunk's vomit: seaslug!/?/ó/the/'tis)   #430

a dog chews
on a drunk's puke:
pickled slug

Drunken men do not chew much. This is especially true in Japan, where audible slurping down of some solid foods is accepted. Because many Japanese have low tolerance for alcohol, yet drunkenness is not taboo, puking is all too frequent and dishes of noodles regurgitated without a single broken strand are a common sight. Since no drunk would take more than a perfunctory chew at each bite of sea slug, Keigu's sick imagination fills in the rest of the story.

切 に 誡 む 海 鼠 に 酒 を の む 勿 れ　子 規
setsu ni i[sa]mu namako ni sake o nomu nakare – shiki (1897)
(fervently/earnestly caution/forbid/abhor seaslug-with *sake* drink not!)   #431

entreating me   doc's order:
not to drink *sake*   don't eat sea slug
with sea slug   and drink!

beware the blues   ***double depressant?***

listen well!   seriously
never drink on top   don't drink with
of sea slug!   sea slug!

The grammar would as easily permit the first person (I earnestly caution ~). But, I guess that since Shiki was largely bed-ridden, he was advised not to mix alcohol with hard-to-digest food. The last two readings assume something completely different, that, Shiki was the first person to associate a consumer of sea slug, especially when drinking, with melancholy. But his next poem does not appear to support this:

海 鼠 喰 ひ 海 鼠 の やうな 人 ならし　子 規
namakogui namako no yôna hito naraji – shiki (1896)
(sea-slug-eater sea-slug-like person is/becomes not)   #432

men who eat   those people
sea slugs are not at all   who eat sea slug are
sea-slug-like   far from sluggish

Who says *we are what we eat*! If I am not mistaken, Shiki observes that most sea-slug-lovers are people with the good digestion that allows them to live exceptionally active lives, while eating and drinking *hard*.

海 鼠 酒 呑 む 婚 礼 の それでよし　萩 原 麦 草
namakozake nomu konrei no sore de yoshi – hagiwara bakusô (1935)
(seaslug-sake drink/ing wedding-celebration/reception's that-by okay)   #433

sea slug sake
at a wedding party
well, why not

While I am told this only shows the joy of a wedding reception not dampened by simple fare, I feel like pointing out an element in the aesthetics of Japanese celebration which might be summed up as *crude-ain't-rude*.   Either the habit of the Imperial Family of using simple plates and cups and throwing them away after one use, or appreciation for the natural texture felt in unpainted wood and unglazed clay led to the practice of using elemental material for celebrations.[1] Needless to say, the sea slug is richly "unfinished." I also cannot help but imagine a robust bride, groom and party. No dyspeptic urbanites would dare serve sea slug at such an occasion.

雪 の 日々 海 鼠 を と り て 海 に 生 く あ か が ね 色 に 酔 へ る 父 君　御 供 平 佶
yuki no hibi namako o torite umi ni iku akaganeiro ni yoeru chichikimi (t) – mitomo heikichi (1935)
(snow-days, seaslug[obj] catch/ing sea-at/in/by live redmetal[copper]color intoxicates/ed father-lord[term of affection])
#434

our dear dad
who heads out to sea
on snowy days
to catch sea slugs and
turns red when drunk

Anyone who has spent even a short time in rural Japan can immediately envision this guy. People who turn beet red – in this case "copper-red" – when they drink, yet still drink, tend to be very robust.

酢 海 鼠 を し ず め て 朝 を 迎 へ を り　清 水 昶
sunamako o shizumete asa o mukaeori – shimizu akira (contemp)
#435   (vinegar seaslug[obj] morning[obj] greet/ing-am)

sinking sea slug
into vinegar as i
greet the dawn

This may seem a bit out of place among the drinking=eating=consuming poems, but, to me, it is the supreme expression of a drinker in good health. Imagine the poet drinking all night and still having the energy to prepare sea slug for the following night! I *used to be* that way. Now, I must admit to reading the poem and feeling jealous!

酢 海 鼠 や 父 を あ や し む 子 ら の 顔　堀 口 星 眠
sunamako ya chichi o ayashimu kora no kao – horiguchi shômin (1936)
#436   (vinegar/pickled-seaslug:/! father[obj] suspect/doubt/marvel/ing-children's faces)

pickled sea slug:
the faces of the children
watching father!

Father, doubtless with with an open liter bottle of beer on the table, may only be innocently attacking his nibblies (an Aussie term for the French one so hard to spell); on the other hand, he may be hamming it up, proud of his bravery, eating something so *gurotesuku* (Japanese never fail to describe

1. **Crude as Fine** The Jesuits were surprised to find that the Japanese nobility brought out unfinished wood and unglazed clay on the occasions when the Europeans would bring out their finest precious metal and bejeweled service. The first serious essay about this fundamental difference in aesthetic value is found in the account of the Japanese envoys to Europe (late 16th century), scribed by de Sande, but mostly composed by the Far East Visitador, A. Valignano (see FROIS)

the *namako* as "grotesque"). Sôseki may have written, "we must respect the guts of the person who first ate a sea slug," [1] but the children were more likely feeling pure "!" and "?" One can not imagine such surprise from Chinese children, who grow up seeing people eating any number of things matter-of-factly (only the Chinese know that *food is food*.) The omnivorous Chinese are, not surprisingly, the world's greatest consumers of *namako*. But, as Arakawa Kohji points out, neither volume nor generalities on national behavior tells the whole story, for

> you can look the wide world over for another people who eat not just the meat (jacket or shell), but the guts (*konowata*) and gonads [2] (*konoko* or *kuchiko*), and these raw, salt-fermented, boiled and cured . . . . . thus using every part of the sea cucumber. Only the Japanese do this. (ndh)

So despite the tendency for Japanese to look askance at the sea slug, it is in a sense, still more *their* food than that of the Chinese!

海 鼠 腸 や 重 ね う け た る 小 盃　流 水

konowata ya kasaneuketaru kosakazuki – ryûsui (mod)
(slug-guts: compounding-receive small-*sake*-cup)

#437

chasing it down
(a little at a time)

sea slug guts
drinking one small cup
after another

海 鼠 腸 や 亡 父 の 好 み の 小 盃　二 階 堂 英 子

konowata ya nakichichi no konomi no kosakazuki – nikaidô eiko (contemp)
(slug-guts: dead-father's favorite small-sake-cup)

#438

cherishing

sea slug guts
i use the small sake cup
my dad loved

1. Sea Slugs as Normal or Strange Food Chinese generally eat boiled and dried sea slug that has been painstakingly restored – if this is the proper word for soaking dried food to regain its good humour. Depending upon how dry the trepang is, it may take up to five days to regain its original size! Stewed with other meats and flavoring or turned into a gelatin-like material, this, rather than the slippery or even slimy, pickled or raw sea cucumber relished by the Japanese might (with a little luck that was apparently not forthcoming) have achieved a degree of currency in Europe. According to Saville-Kent, who wrote about The Great Barrier Reef of Australia in 1883, sea cucumber soup was as good as turtle soup and *with a good Chinese name* might sweep Europe. Oshima Hiroki whose *Sea Cucumber and Sea Urchin* (NTU) is where I found Saville-Kent, notes that a type of sea cucumber called *Holothuria tubulosa* was popular among the lower classes in South Italy, especially Sicily (I've yet to find an Italian who will admit to this). But, the soup didn't catch on. Perhaps no one came up with the right name. According to Arakawa Kohman's *Sea Cucumber Reader:* (NDH), in World War II, a factory in Peugeot Sound, Washington, began canning the softest part of sea cucumber, the muscle fibers, which, "sautéed in butter are tender and resemble fancy bivalves," but the restaurants pretend they are "shellfish." "This," he continues, "is a good indication of the unfounded prejudice the white race feels toward *namako* as food."

2. Gonads? I do not really know if "roe" is better or "gonads," but either beats the expression found on a Japanese website: *kuchiko wa namako no taiji*, or, "*Kuchiko* is the fetus of sea slugs." Perhaps, the owner of the website had heard the title of Satie's composition (in *Sundry S.S.*) With abalone, I find the whitish male production (milt?) better than the orange female one, but unfortunately, I do not know what is what with the *namako* yet.

Sea slug guts are included with dried mullet roe and sea urchin as one of the three great delicacies of the sea. Ten to twenty percent salt, it demands that you drink like a fish and is far more effective than, say, potato chips, for also being very rank. [1] Yet, as these haiku make clear, neither the guts nor the *sake* are wolfed down. The guts – and the accompanying *sake* – are appreciated as brandy is, a bit at a time, though the sake cup used is as tiny as the brandy glass is large.

はらわたがありて海鼠の言ふことなし 橋間石

harawata ga arite namako no iu koto nashi – hashi kanseki (d.1992)

#439   (belly-guts/entrails having sea-slug's say thing not)

with these guts	guts and all!
sea slug leaves me	this sea slug leaves me
nothing to say	-- speechless –

I do not know if a sea slug bought to prepare has been found to have its guts intact or if the poet is served both the meat and the guts, but the point is that he is delighted – having nothing to say idiomatically implies that everything is perfect – *and,* in pun, that the sea slug has/had nothing to say because it is/was gutsy. Marine scientist Arakawa may exaggerate the cultural divide when he claims that this "pure Japanese style gourmet item enjoys tremendous popularity as a nibbly among Japanese, while Euro-Americans put it right on top of the list of foul and disgusting foods" – neither people eat with a single mouth and not one in a million Westerners have tasted it, so how could they judge to put it on such a list? – but one cannot overstate the love some Japanese hold for these guts. Like the more common and much cheaper squid tripe (*shiokara*), its preparation includes fermentation in a cool dark place.   The rankest of the rank, it is, in Arakawa's choice phrase, "the far right of foul food" (*akushoku-no saiuha*) and, as such, is beloved as only one's own stink can be. A taste not easily acquired, it never fails to excite. Arakawa's "foul" is facetious, for the word "right-wing" rings of patriotic love for *Things* thought to be especially *Japanese*.

酒 が 好 き 海 鼠 腸 が 好 き 愛 妻 家 無 名

sake ga suki konowata ga suki aisaika – anon (2000)

#440   (*sake* like/liking, slug-gut like/liking love-wife/husband)

uxurious taste	***fermentation***
loving my *sake*	mr uxorious
and sea slug gut, this	he loves warm *sake* and
one-woman man	cold slug gut

#441

1. Sea Slug Tripe While Liza Dalby liked the pickled sea slug, she added that "*konowata* [the guts], on the other hand, I find quite nasty." This is delicately put.   And it is *exact*.   According to someone's internet diary, novelist Nagai Kafu (best known for his controversial novel *The Pornographers*),   once compared the taste of *namako* guts to human excrement. I do not know if he meant he disliked it or if he was a coprophiliac! A master potter turned gourmet researcher-writer, Hokudaiji Rosanjin, who serves as the model for a best-selling *manga* (cartoon book series) *KUISHINBO* (the gourmet/glutton), clearly fell for *konowata*, and wrote that "while it was not like a beautiful woman one falls in love with at first sight" after "setting a long slimy string of it on your tongue, you get high on the supreme taste and the muscles of your face reflect the ecstasy of your heart, after which they begin to relax . . ." (I dare not try translating more. This was found on a site using the long passage as an example of sloppy reader-*un*friendly writing. And that is for Japanese readers!) If Lamb's paean to juicy suckling pig is erotic, this is downright pornographic!   Like tea leaves or wine, even the time of "harvest" mattered: "you can find / first and second vats / of sea slug guts" [or] "picky drinkers / with their first and second rank / sea slug guts" (*eriwakuru konowata ichiban niban ari* – sugihara takejo (mod): 撰 り 分 くるこのわた一番二番あり 杉原竹女).

I recall being surprised to read that insecure men go for women with big rumps while aggressive go-getters go for big boobs, where one might as easily have guessed the opposite – the survey was, however, not cross-cultural and may only reflect the psyche of the WASP.   What correlations might be found between our food tastes and our marital situation? Because *sake* requires more attention – it must be heated carefully – than beer, a wife is of more use to a *sake* drinker. And, I might add that a *senryu* once defined someone who qualified as a true tippler as one who "licked" slug gut.[1] Because slug gut is for many, if not most, a learned taste, might slug gut lovers not be more likely candidates for sticking it out with one woman and slowly learning to savor what she has to offer?

かけつけのこのわたざけはすこし無理　万太郎
kaketsuke no konowatazake wa sukoshi muri – mantarô (1888-1963)
(catch-add? slug-gut-sake-as-for, a bit impossible/unadvisable)   #442

a no-brainer round after round of slug-gut-sake	slug-gut-sake johny-come-latelys are too late	slug-gut-sake the usual penalty is pushing it

Japanese, like German, is free to create neologisms by simply sticking words together while beveling their edges. This is the first and only "slug-gut-sake" or *konowatazake* I've come across. The first reading assumes *kaketsuke* means a continuous round of drinking, the second that it means "to come running to join something in progress;" and, the third guesses it is an abbreviation for *kaketsukesanbai,* or, the three drinks a late-comer to a party had to chug one after another, ostensibly as punishment, but to ensure he catch up to the general level of inebriation and fit in. Regardless, the nature of "slug-gut-sake" (the guts are mixed in, so it is a bit salty) would seem to be at odds with chugalugging.

このわたに一壺の酒を啜るかな　柳川春葉
konowata ni hitotsubo no sake o susuru kana – shunyô (mod)
(slug-guts-with one-crock's/jug's *sake*[obj] sip/slurp/suck!/?/ỏ/huh)   #443

with slug guts
i sip down a whole
crock of sake

The crock is what the slug guts come in. We wonder if he is not finishing off his precious guts by filling the crock with sake and drinking that so not a bit of the essence is lost.[2] The "sip" is not quite right, for the Japanese *susuru* includes the possibility of noise, of a slurp, without sounding vulgar.

海鼠腸に一念の切れなかりけり　中原道夫
konowata ni ichinen no kire nakarikeri – nakahara michio (1998)
(slug-guts-with/by one-thought's cut/break not-at-all)   #444

with slug guts
there is no break
in your thought

1. *Licked Sea Slug Guts* The senryu, *konowata o namete shugô no retsu ni iru,* is just called "a senryu" in the fish talk site where I found it. It is common in Japan to cite senryu in the manner of a proverb, giving neither author (who is usually anonymous, anyway) nor source.

2. *Drinking from Crocks* Drinking *sake* from a crock that had slug guts is not *that* unusual, for Japanese drink *sake* – or, for that matter, tea! – from crab shells with bits of the eggs and whatnot still in it. They put various things in their drinks and vice-versa.

So the metaphorical nature of sea slug guts is pure continuation. You cannot stop nibbling it, drinking with it, nor even *thinking* as you do so!

父 の せ し ご と く 鋏 で 海 鼠 腸 を　福 島 万 沙 塔
chichi no seshi gotoku hasami de konowata o – fukushima masato (mod)

#445
([my]father's doing/did-like, scizzors-with slug-guts[obj])

<table>
<tr><td align="center">***family tradition***</td><td align="center">***inheritance***</td></tr>
<tr><td align="center">as father did
using a scissors for
sea slug guts</td><td align="center">like dad
i use scissors on
slug guts</td></tr>
</table>

One reason that the nibbling never ceased was the difficulty of breaking the thread of guts. Sucking in a bit more than intended, in turn, leads to drinking more to compensate and that leads to another thread . . . . This is a brilliant solution and the poet deserves some sort of award for reporting it!

海 鼠 腸 に ま た 呑 み 過 る 阿 呆 か な　田 畑 益 弘
konowata ni mata nomisugiru ahô* kana – tabata masuhiro (contemp)

#446
(slug-guts-by again drink-over[overdrink] fool!/?/ó/the/'hoh)

sea slug tripe
gets this fool drunk
once again!

海 鼠 腸 で 呑 ま む 死 ぬ に は 未 だ 早 き　田 畑 益 弘
konowata de nomamu shinu ni wa imada hayaki – tabata masuhiro (2000)

#447
(seaslug-guts-with/for drink-not die-as-for, still early)

i'm not ready
to die for not drinking
with slug guts

Before I found the second haiku – which means, I think, that the powerful stuff must be washed down with *sake* or else! – and more by the same poet, I wrote "this poet's youth reeks." As it turns out, he is not so young, so I lose my link to the next sentence which I will keep nonetheless, for lack of time to make a better one: Still, it's a fact that *konowata* has a long and noble pedigree in Japan. It was mentioned in the *Enkishi*, 50 volumes of law books written between 905-927 AD, as "person-red-plum,"[1.] a favorite of the court and records of tributes (*shinjô*) from Hatayama Yoshimune the ruler of Noto (if that's what it was called at the time) to the *bakufu* (central rulership of the time) in Kyoto, show 1680 tubs of *konowata* presented in 1481-3.[2] If the Japanese economy had kept growing in the

1. *Person Red Plum* The popularity of *konowata* is implicit in the splendid name given to it, but I would like to find mention of this person-red-plum in literature. 「人赤梅」の入っている和歌とか連歌は、ありそう！何か見つけたら、わが website, paraverse.org へどうぞ！

2. *Hatayama Tribute*   To grasp the overall importance/popularity of   *konowata* among the ruling elite, compare the 1680 tubs of slug guts to 70 tubs of sea slug roe (*konoko*), and 90 bundles of dried slug (*iriko*), 320 tubs of mackerel roe, 430 tubs of mackerel-dorsal-guts (?), and 50 salmon. I googled across these records published as part of the historical records of a city whose name translates as "seven-tails." (Nanao, we have seen it once already)   The onerously large tribute was necessary for Hatayama was on the wrong side of an uprising not long before. This was smack in the middle of the Warring Era. You might say the sea cucumber lost *its* guts so men could keep *theirs*!

1990's as it had in the 1980's, this venerable rank nibbly would probably be a world food by now, at least among gourmets.[1]

鱗 な き 烏 賊 章 魚 海 鼠 に 酒 か た む け よ　原 満 三 寿

urokonaki ika tako namako ni sake katamukeyo – hara masaji (1989)
(scales-not squid octopus sea-slug-to sake tilt-let's)

#448

hey, let's toast
the scale-less ones: squid
octopus, sea slug!

Still, it doesn't seem right to pay too much attention to the guts alone, nor to the sea slug alone. This promiscuous celebration is a relief. I do not buy octopus because I feel they are, like the dolphin, too close to us; but I appreciate the fact that eating things, like hunting them, can draw us closer to them, or, conversely, those who do not eat scaleless denizens of the sea because their god happened to be a finicky eater, do not necessarily love them more.

呑 み す ぎ て 哀 し く な り ぬ 酢 海 鼠 よ　田 畑 益 弘

nomisugitte kanashiku narinu sunamako yo – tabata masuhiro (contemp)
(drinking-too-much, sad/pitiful/beautiful become/ing, vinegar/pickled-seaslug!)

#449

in vino sentitas

over-drinking
i suddenly feel for
the pickled slug

pickled twosome

poor sea slug!
i know just how
you feel!

It is wonderful how alcohol can make us (all good people, at any rate) feel warmth for all creation, even that which we are chewing on. The poet ties one on and starts talking to – the exclamation *yo* suggests direct address – pickled sea slug. The character used for sadness is a particularly poetic one which puts a classical patina of beauty upon the sadness.

なまこなどつつきて酔ひのまた 楽し不意に傍を子らの立ちゆく　千代国一

namako nado tsutsukite yoi no mata tanoshi fui ni katawara o kora no tachiyuku – chiyo kunikazu(cont)
(seaslug etcetera, poking-away inebriation's also pleasurable inattentiveness-in, side-from children up and leave)

#450

happy household

playing with
sea slug and jellyfish
papa enjoys
his drinking: oops!
where are the kids?

That was, of course, not a haiku, but a *tanka,* a modern 5-7-5-7-7 poem. We are not going to let the sea slug slip away so easily. In Japan, a meal is finished as it is begun, by a single word grace.[1] → The four-chapter feast – the tasty, slippery, chewy, drinking sea slug – deserves a final thought.

1. *Economic Cuisine* As ridiculous as my linkage of slug guts with the economy may seem, the fact is that the cultural idiosyncrasies of the successful are copied. There are many items in Japanese cuisine not even found in the Japanese restaurants in the United States – especially, the vegetables *udoh, seri, myôga* and in many parts, even *gobo* are sorely missed, for they make most of the Occidental vegetables seem crude by comparison – and I fear they never will be unless Japan takes off again.

残すべき骨さへ持たぬ海鼠かな 東佳代子

nokosubeki hone sae motanu namako kana – azuma kayoko (1997)

#451   (leave-can/ought bone/s even has-not sea slug!/?/ó/the/loh)

gone for good

not one bone
left to the world:
a sea slug

wandering soul

loh, the poor
sea slug! not one bone
left to bury.

i knew him well

alas, not a bone
left behind to bemoan
my sea slug!

Excuse my Pope and Shakespeare! They, too, would roll in their graves at this. Whether the contemporary poet knows it or not, her haiku plays on a food theme long developed with respect to the Anglerfish (*ankô*), which is consumed, soft bones and all, leaving only, according to my favorite Anglerfish senryu (*ankô-wa kuchbiru bakari nokorunari*), its lips undevoured (I imagine this is how a self-consuming flip-book might end!). Were the intent of Higashi's poem merely formal, I would have put it with the *Featureless* or *Protean Sea Slugs*, but I think it something far more exalted. The lady is writing not so much of, as *for* a sea slug that has been consumed. In that sense, her poem itself serves as a *memento mori* for this thing with nothing else to remember it by. On a lower level, I associate it with an idiom for someone who is a *nobody*: "horse-bones from who knows where" (*doko no uma no hone da ka wakaranai hito*), often shortened to simply "horse-bones" (*uma-no-hone*).[2]

Alas, poor sea slug. Lacking bones to prove he existed, he is less than nobody![3]

1. Grace in a Word   The Japanese say *itadakimasu!* on beginning a meal and *gochisosama-deshita!* when they finish. I say them in America, for I like to be appreciative without having to specify anthropomorphic gods (mythological entities) in the Judeo-Christian manner. (see*: Orientalism & Occidentalism* (paraverse press))

2. Even Lower Level   As the above haiku is by a modern poet who may well still be alive, I hesitate to give a bawdy reading. Japanese keep some of the shards of their deceased relations, primary of which is the "throat-buddha" (*nodobotoke*) or "Adam's Apple." If the Japanese folk-song conceit of men swearing to "break their [most *namako*-like] bone" for a woman were only true, the widow might be left with a more touching memento!

3. Lacking Bones   Even scientists have long bemoaned the lack of holothurian remains. Taxonomy is difficult without good fossils. ("There are only about 20 body fossils of cukes known, though from my travels, I'd say many more probably lie on museum shelves waiting identification" A. Kerr) Only the Actinopygia, the "star-butt" left anything sizeable, its butt teeth. In recent years, the situation has changed 180 degrees, for it was discovered that holothurians had better tags than many other creatures. I refer to the beautiful bits (average span: 0.1 mm) of calcium carbonate called ossicles embedded in the creature's tissue. "The intricate and beautiful designs of these miniscule crystals [actually micro-crystals arranged on a protein scaffold: A.K]" (P. Lambert) is, if not unique to each species – "sometimes identical ossicles are found in different, though usually closely related species"(A.K.) – characteristic, and serve more or less in the capacity of a bone as an identification aid. With DNA analysis, this method of identification might seem to be rendered moot, but because not every lab has the facilities for such analysis, whereas ossicles can even be seen on a child's microscope, this aesthetically pleasing practice will continue. To my mind, these crystals are almost as interesting as snowflakes! ["For me, they are more so, since their construction and origin of form are far more mysterious. For example, there are anchor-shaped ossicles [see pic] whose tines protrude from the body wall and help pull certain apodan (without-feet) species along as the animal does full body peristalsis. Incredibly, practically identical anchor ossicles support the enlarged tubefeet of the sea urchin *Micropyga* AND occur in the stomach wall of another urchin *Chondrocidaris*. In these urchins the tines do not protrude and hence cant serve in locomotion or passing food along. Moreover, other identically shaped ossicles are found in both echinoderms and sponges. Why have identically shaped ossicles independently evolved to serve in such different roles? The intriguing possibility is that for all their diversity, cell-based systems for making ossicles not much bigger than themselves can only vary shape in a limited number of ways. The molecular genetics of such systems is a topic of intense research among tissue bioengineers" A.K.]

17
<u>the silent sea slug</u>

海鼠ひとり黙りこくって何に耐ふ　高沢良一
namako hitori damari-kokutte nani ni tau – takasawa yoshikazu (2003)
(seaslug alone/single silent/mum[in a unbending way] what-to/against resists/bears)　　#452

a sea slug
alone and silent bearing
what cross?

The idea of the *silent sea slug* goes back to the mythical encounter in the *Report of Ancient Things,* as we have seen. In this chapter, we see how it has grown into a multifaceted metaphor. I hope most readers do not mind my use of an idiom that is not only clearly foreign to Japanese, but comes from an anthropocentric religion contrary to the heart of haiku in so far that it (haiku) is animistic, in translating Takasawa's haiku. An alternative: *A sea slug / alone and silent: what / does it bear?*

海鼠腸をすゝる音のみ一人酒　田畑益弘
konowata o susuru oto nomi hitorizake – tabata masuhiro (2002)
(seaslug-guts slurp/ing sound only: one-person-*sake*)　　#453

one-man sake
only the sound of slurping
sea slug gut

only the sound
of slurping slug guts
i drink alone

The sound of slurping is as fine a foil for silence as any. Like a whistle, the fact it comes from a small hole adds something to the size of what remains. About the only complaint that might be made about this haiku is that it is too perfectly made, *tsukurisugi,* to use the critical vocabulary of haiku.[1] The words and the concept express the *Silent Sea Slug* to a T.

海鼠突竿おきし音舟にたて　八木林之助
namakotsuki sao okishi oto fune ni tate – yagi rinnosuke (mod)
(seaslug-gigger/ing pole put-down/store sound boat-on/from make)　　#454

the sound
of stowing the gig on
a slug-boat

sound aboard
when slugging poles
are laid down

I am not sure if the pole/gig is being stowed or just momentarily put down. The latter is more likely, for the proverbial silence of slugging is brought out through the occasional sound a pole makes in much the same way the old pond was served by Basho's frog/s and the room in which the solitary drinker of the last poem was by the slurping. Some fish do listen in on us and require silence, yet who would write of the noise of a fishing pole without the foil of silence offered by the sea slug?

1. *Tsukurisugi* Have you ever heard a Western critic complain that a sonnet is too perfectly crafted? Since the haiku is at its best supposed to be a sketch that leaves something to the imagination, it is desirable to leave something left undone, a thread to grasp.

口 重 き 店 主 の 包 む 海 鼠 か な   ユ リ

kuchi omoki tenshu no tsutsumu namako kana – yuri (contemp)

#455   (mouth-heavy/taciturn store-owner's wrap/ping seaslug!/?/ó/the)

>   a close-mouthed
>   fish shop owner wraps
>   my sea slug

The poet probably bought snapper and flounder and whatnot from the same man and left the shop without a haiku. But, like Jung with his synchronicity – could he *not* have mentioned that cicada? – no good haiku poet can just let so fine a metaphysical coincidence be. As she walked out of that shop, I bet she was already composing that haiku. After centuries of silent sea slugs, one might say the idea is a bit too obvious. But, again, I would reply that there is comfort in familiar associations wrapped in new words, and the details of the haiku are exceptionally fresh.

我 形 に 蓋 を し て い る 海 鼠 哉   可 幸

waganari ni futa o shiteiru namako kana – kakô (1773)

#456   (my/its-own form-on lid-putting[keep secret] seaslug/s!/?/ó/the)

>   ***the sight of silence***
>
>   it clams up
>   its very appearance:
>   the sea slug

undercover	*camouflage*
putting a lid	the sea slug
upon the way we are	its form well hidden
sea slugs!	by its form

The sea slug with its *just-so* lacerated mouth can no longer speak up even if it wants to. Ah, but it's body, too, without limbs cannot or dares not express itself imagines this poet. Or is he, perhaps describing his own conventional, don't-rock-the-boat nature? This haiku may as well have been placed with the *Meek Sea Slug* or the *Featureless Sea Slug*.[1] Hiding one's true self by giving up self-expression is the most common form of meekness. At the same time, as the third reading would show, the idea of formless form hiding form is quite witty by itself.

牡 蠣 よ り も 海 鼠 の 黙 ぞ 深 か ら む   相 生 垣 瓜 人

kaki yori mo namako no moku zo fukakaramu – aioigaki kajin (1898-1985)

#457   (oyster-more-than, seaslug's silence!/hey! deep-is)

>   the silence of
>   the sea slugs is deeper
>   than the oyster's

1. Featureless Meekness Expressiveness such as that needed for self-assertion is thought to depend on moving parts, primarily facial features, limbs, appendages etc.. Japanese of both sexes hid their hands in their sleeves, sartorial restrictions at times kept color on the inside rather than outside of silk jackets (the sea slug has some colorful innards) and women even shaved off their eyebrows, so one might argue some resemblance to the meek sea slug here. But the live sea slug is actually very expressive when it comes to expressing what seems like relaxation, tension, dread, and so forth. It would seem that much can be expressed by the trunk – which sea slug examples – alone.

One translation will do, but this is a hard poem to crack because there is no tradition of quiet shellfish in Japanese. Does the poet mean that the tightly compressed hard lips of the oyster shell are less poignant than the silent presence of the sea slug? Is he thinking about the respective psychological effect of eating these two sea foods that happen to share credit for being food hard to eat for the first time? Or is he expanding upon the *Melancholy Sea Slug* who cannot speak his mind, invented by Buson, and introduced in the next chapter?

黙 り ゐ る 事 の か し こ き 海 鼠 か な 　青 々
damariiru koto no kashikoki namako kana – seisei (1869-1937)
(shutting-up thing's smart/clever seaslug!/?/ó/the/'that's)　　　　#458

pragmatism

bright enough
to hold its peace:
the sea slug

sublimation

when it's smart
to hold your peace
eat sea slug!

advice for radicals

intelligence
remains mum: the word
is sea slug

quiet types

the sea slug:
does it look bright
clammed up?

question from a talker

sea slug, think
your silence makes
you look deep?

Hindsight does not allow us to call the sea slug's choice to remain quiet in the face of the gods a good one, nor did fish get caught because of excessive blabbering until recently – ultra-sound devices let fishermen listen in – so Seisei would appear to be describing a human sea slug who is 1), not necessarily resigned but bright enough not to get involved in the heated politics of the age [年付けは?] or argue with his or her spouse, or 2), sits and eats the food which best allows him to work off his frustration or anger. However, the vague grammar does not rule out further readings. Seisei's first *nom de plume,* Mushin=no-heart (*artlessness* in the Taoist sense), suggests he would appreciate silence, but he was also from Osaka, which has the most argumentative culture in Japan, so it is possible, though not probable, he was chiding smug silence.

沈 黙 は 金 な り 海 鼠 頑 に 　佐 々 木 正 男
chinmoku wa kin nari namako katakuna ni – sasaki masao (1999)
(silence-as-for, gold/en is, seaslug strictly/obdurately/absolutely)　　#459

silence may
be golden but sea slug's
a bonehead

stubborn

silence is
golden: sea slug
absolutely

kinko

silence is
golden ossified
sea slug

etiquette

silence is golden
one doesn't talk when
eating sea slug

what i eat

silence is golden
i'm a sea slug man
confirmed

(^ - ^)

silence *is*
golden: sea slug
my mantra

soul food

sea slug:
chewed in golden
silence

credo

silence
is golden: my food
sea slug

The original haiku was truncated even by haiku standards. The infinite possibilities of silence provoked half a dozen readings. I would bet on the slug=poet readings, mostly because contemporary haiku have taken the old theme of the *Silent Sea Slug* and turned it into the silent sea slug *eater*. Indeed, *silence* comes right after *slipperiness* and *chewiness* as a major sub-theme of the culinary sea slug. I was tempted to fuse it with the *Drinking Sea Slug* – not quite a metaphor – but it that would not have been fair to the *Chewy Sea Slug*, also involved with silence, so I gave it this chapter. If the reader rereads chewy and drinking sea slugs, the unmentioned silence will be felt more strongly for seeing these clear-cut silent sea slugs.

口 答 へ せ ぬ こ と に し て 海 鼠 食 ふ 大 西 素 之
kuchigotae senu koto ni shite namako kuu – ônishi motoyuki (contemp)
(mouth-reply/respond do thing-as doing, seaslug eat)

#460

making up my mind
not to respond
i eat sea slug

holding my peace

talk, talk
i let it go and eat
sea slug

Is the other party the stereotypical noisy wife? An overly enthusiastic young man? A rude drunken older one? This haiku echoes beautifully with the *Just-so Sea Slug* of the *Record*. Let us hope the other party does not get upset like that goddess with the dagger!

海 鼠 嚙 む 答 え ら れ な き こ と 問 は れ 水 内 慶 太
namako kamu kotaerarenaki koto toware – mizuuchi keita (contemp)
(seaslug chew/ing answer-cannot-thing asked)

#461

having no reply
for what i am asked i
chew sea slug

Here the poet admits to using sea slug as an accomplice to his silence, but we feel sympathetic for he admits to doing so because he has no answer.

いっこくの無口は海鼠にもありし　林翔

ikkoku no mukuchi wa namako ni mo arishi – hayashi shô (1996)
(stubborn/obstinate no-mouth/taciturn-as-for seaslug-in-also is)   #462

this sea slug:
something taciturn and
stubborn as me!

酢海鼠が好きで無口で意固地者　築城百々平

sunamako ga suki de mukuchi de ikojimono – tsuzuki momohei (2001)
(vinegar/pickled-seaslug [i/he/she]like and/because silent and/because stubborn-guy)   #463

taciturn and
obdurate: a pickled
sea slug-lover

Sometimes it takes a bit of identification to bring respect. Here, the poets probably do not think silence a mark of oppression or meekness, but of *strength*. Japanese action heroes often do no more then grunt a few times over the entire course of the movie (They make Clint Eastwood seem garrulous!) I think of the advertisement for Japan's best beer: "A *man* is silent, [drinking] Sapporo!" (*otoko-wa damatte, sapporo!*) [1] There really should have been a *namako* next to the bottle in that ad!

反骨をつらぬく余生海鼠噛む　大井車一路

hankotsu o tsuranuku yosei namako kamu – ôi toichiro (2001)
(defiant/unyielding/ornery penetrate/carrythrough remaining-life seaslug [i] chew)   #464

chewing sea slug:	chewing sea slug	chewing sea slug
for the rest of my life	for the rest of my days	from now on i'll be
no compromise	*my life, my way*	as tough as one

This one "chewy sea slug" is, to me, more silent than any of the poems mentioning *silence*. I imagine the poet has just retired from a job where he was not allowed to do as he wished and had to play the *yes*-man. Drinking and chewing sea slug, he pledges to himself that he will live the rest of his life with backbone. He sits alone and his eyes stare out at nothing. But, OM writes that it is more likely the poet always bucked the tide and that the attitude was lifelong, which *tsuranuku* does seem to imply.

chewing thoughts	*retirement resolution*
defiant from	chewing sea slug
birth to death, i love	i'll be a monkey wrench
my sea slug	til the day i die

1. *Silence in Japanese* If I were to do the Sapporo ad in English, I would include a few empty bottles on the table and let "many bottles, few words!" stand for manliness. "Silence" and "silent" are elegant, feminine(?) words equivalent to the Japanese *shizukesa* and *shizuka*. Neither of these are used with *namako*. It is always *damaru*, a true one-word verb with "shut up" power, or the noun *chinmoku*, a silence more deliberate and deep than "quiet" or "silence." There are many other words for *silence*. The one used by Emperor Shôwa (Hirohito) that included the character for "kill," meaning to ignore something, was mistranslated during World War II, making it easier for Truman to drop those bombs.

If OM is correct, which she, as a native-speaker and brilliant translator, probably is, my first three readings are wrong. But I left them because in my experience (asking poets for interpretations), one never *knows*.

海鼠提げ誰に逢ひても口きかず　加藤楸邨
namako sage dare-ni aite mo kuchi kikazu – katô shûson (contemp)
(sea-slug dangling/carrying whomever-to/with meet-even/though mouth work-not)

#465

with sea slug
in hand, i find that i
hold my tongue

carrying home
sea slug, i find myself
silent en route

it's a sea slug

i keep mum
when asked about what
i carry home

I guess the poet – or some one he observes – has bought a sea slug to take home for some serious drinking/thinking and is not in the mood for small talk. Here, as in most of the poems in this chapter, silence seems to indicate *more* rather than *less* backbone in the man, and perhaps his food. For some reason – perhaps only the unique combination of *carrying* (rather than *chewing* or *drinking*) the sea slug and silence – I find Katô Shûson's haiku my favorite of all the *Silent Sea Slug* haiku.

相居りて相知ること遅き海鼠かな　高田蝶衣
ai orite ai shiru koto osoki namako kana – chôi (1895-1930)
(together/mutually living/being, together/mutually knowing-thing late seaslug/s!/?/ó/the/'[we]are)

#466

cohabitation
sin communication
two sea slugs

living together
too late to know each other
sea slug lovers

in the same tub
slow to know each other
sea slugs

The last part of the original is vague. I see a couple, each chewing in silence, *eating* sea slug and *being* sea slug. KS thinks I think too much, and the poem concerns the real asocial sea slug, slow to comprehend the existence of other beings when put into the same tub,[1] as per the third (bottom right) reading. OM feels the slowness is "more figurative than literal" and seconds him. Regardless, the exorbitant length of the English "each other" or "one another" makes good translation impossible.

海鼠噛む終始寡黙の父老いて　立石勢津子
namako kamu shûshi kamoku no chichi oite – tachiishi seitsuko (contemp)
(seaslug eat/ing end-start[start-to-finish] taciturn father aged)

#467

chewing sea slug
silent the whole time
dad's grown old

1. Slow Recognition?   Though sea slugs may not jump up and lick each other like puppies, they can react quickly to each other's smell/chemicals, so the poet may be misreading the slow movement. Moreover, as MT has pointed out, the sea cucumber has a very slow metabolism, so it would be hard to say whether its "reaction" to a tub-mate was – in *namako* time – slower or faster than ours. (See his speeches on the web and book on the relativity of time in the animal kingdom, all in Japanese only).

Compared to the romanticized silence of the male poet, this is brutally real. Here was a man who might never have been a talker, but in his middle age did speak a few words now and then as he ate, even if it were sea slug. But now, he has turned inside and begun to resorb himself like a sea slug preparing for estivation or hibernation. His body armor has grown as thick as the shell on a hermit-crab.   I think his daughter understands that is a mark of weakness, not strength.

ち ぢ こ ま り 黙 の 重 さ の 海 鼠 か な 川 崎 展 宏

chijikomari moku no omosa no namako kana – kawasaki nobuhiro (contemp)

(shrink-up silence's heaviness's seaslug!/?/ó/the/'behold)   #468

the sea slug
how heavy is silence
shrunken up

0   海鼠

what heavy   the weight
silence in a hard ball   of congealed silence
the sea slug   sea slugs

"Shrunken" things rarely seem weighty, especially in English, where the verb lacks the connotations found in *chijikomaru* that required three readings to cover.   The poem may well allude to the slug eater – the poet or, perhaps, a man like the one described in the previous poem – because one doubts that the silence of the sea slug weighs that heavily upon the poet's mind.

黙 り を 決 め こ む や う に 寒 海 鼠　無 名

dannmari o kimekomu yô ni kannamako – anon. (contemp?)

(silence/taciturnity[+obj] presume/impersonate-like/as-if cold[season]-seaslug)   #469

cold sea slug   in mid-winter
seems to say silence   sea slug stands for all
c'est moi!   *taciturnity*

...
. . .

as if to say
i am the *mum*
mid-winter sea slug

The one character for "cold" expressing both the time of year and the coldness of the sea slug cannot be Englished in a word.   "Mid-winter" works well, but took up a big chunk of the poem.

海 鼠 に 髯 あ ら ば 弁 士 に う っ て つ け 高 沢 良 一

namako ni hige araba benshi ni uttetsuke – takasawa yoshikazu (2003)

(seaslug-on moustache was-if, [silent movie] talker-as tailormade)   #470

the silence of the sea slugs   ***the sound of silence?***

put a moustache   if the sea slug
on sea slug and it could   had whiskers it would look like
be its own talkie   its own talkie

I hope my additional explanation ("its *own* talkie"), makes it clear that the slug is being simultaneously viewed as a silent movie and fantasized as a narrator of the same.   At least, that's how I read the original, which I like as a *meta*-haiku, a *dada* take on the *Silent Sea Slug*.

触 れ て 硬 き 海 鼠 の い の ち 碓 む る 徳 永 れ つ 子

furete kataki namako no inochi tashikamuru – tokunaga retsuko (1973)

#471
(touching [it is] hard, seaslug's life confirm/check)

hard to the touch	a sea slug
confirming there is life	that feels so hard
in a sea slug	is it alive?

The silent is not uncommonly taken for dead. At first reading, I thought the haiku an erotic confirmation of "life" in hardness; but, the second reading – the sea slug's hardness made it seem dead (to the mind of someone who doesn't know that they soften when they die) – is so much better it must be correct.   No, maybe *not*.   For we have this, too:

突 っ つ い て 海 鼠 の 固 さ 碓 め る　こ う か い

tsuttsuite namako no katasa tashikameru – kôkai (contemp)

#472
(poke/ing, seaslug's hardness[obj] confirm/check)

poking, poking
confirming the hardness
of a sea slug

There is something about this "poke" – also meaning to "peck" or "pick" – that suggests repetition and the surprising cornstarch-like response delights the sense of touch enough to invite it.   I suppose this is the equivalent of squeezing fruit and just as disgraceful.   But to return to the theme at hand, *silence*:

海 鼠 と も 語 れ ぬ 今 や 友 と 酒　遊 凪

namako to mo katarenu ima ya tomo to sake – yûshi? (contemp)

#473
(seaslug-with-even speak-not now:/! friend/s and sake)

drinking with friends	too blue to talk
nowadays a man cannot	with a sea slug i drink
converse with slugs	with a friend

This is guesswork.   The original was tough for two of three Japanese who read and commented on it. One thought the poet was lamenting/missing an absent friend and, perhaps, finding the loneliness sweet.   Another, likewise, failed to imagine the poet drinking with friends. The third wrote that by suggesting a conversation between man and sea slug the poem seems surreal, but it means that "in the old days, men could drink alone with sea slug, but . . ."(Over-read at www.nifty.ne.jp/ forum/fhaiku/v58_03.htm). Today, the good old-fashioned lone-wolf samurai has become an other-directed wimp who cannot drink alone like a man.   Or, a more personal interpretation is possible.   Or?

言 ひ に く き こ と を す る り と 海 鼠 か な 大 石 悦 子

iinikuki koto o sururi to namako kana – ôishi etsuko (contemporary)

#474
(say-difficult-thing smoothly/easily said/and seaslug!/?/ó/the)

hard things
to say slip right out
with sea slug

If my reading is correct, this is a very impressive haiku, the only one to clearly contradict the old saw of the sea slug as silence-evoking food. We may find logical underpinning in the fact of the sea slug's slipperiness: *what slips in can slip out.* Furthermore, if chewing encourages creative free association, in the presence of another party, it could free the ego to divulge things normally held in. I hate to confess that my Japanese advisors think the poem means one of the following instead:

how embarrassing
to say this, but, for me,
sea slug's a breeze!

an ugly word
but it goes down smooth
oh, sea slug!

Though probably right – one can't argue with native speakers – such readings are trite, so I prefer to keep my probably wrong translation.

静けさや標本瓶に浮くナマコ　敬愚
shizukesa ya hyôhonbin ni uku namako – keigu
(silence:/!/behold: specimen-bottle-in float/ing seaslug)　　　　　　　#475

metaphorical taxonomy

my specimen
of silence, a sea slug
in alcohol

This haiku (or haikus, if you note the difference between the Japanese and the English readings) was inspired by a fine paragraph in a book by a Japanese-American. Here is most of that passage:

> Sitting cross-legged on my bed, I studied the specimen. I turned it around and around. The sea cucumber bobbed sadly in its mordant bath. I imagined it must have floated somewhere at the bottom of the sea like that, passive and silent, like something asleep. . . . It didn't seem right for living things to pass silently from existence with their secrets still locked up inside them. (Linda Watanabe McFerrin: NAMAKO sea cucumber (nsc))

Aseasonal or not, this is by far the most haiku-like *namako* found in English prose. Watanabe McFerrin's protagonist is a ten year-old Japanese-American, sitting in a manner we all have, but reading this set me to wondering: Could the *Silent Sea Slug* have been born had Japanese not sat cross-legged, limbs reflectively tucked in? And how then, the Finns and the Swedes? Could it be the way the cold made them sit (and tuck in their hands), rather than the cold itself, made them taciturn?

活舌の悪いわたしは海鼠かな　無名
katsuzetsu no warui watashi wa namako kana – anon (contemp)
(active-tongue[articulation]'s bad me-as-for, seaslug!/?/ô/a)　　　　　　#476

am i with
my poor articulation
a sea slug

As we have seen, people who identify with the silent sea slug usually think of themselves as stubborn. I mentioned that $E=MC^2$ might look good written on a sea cucumber. Well, *"My Way"* might look good, too. But, this haiku is different. It seems to be a *Victimized Sea Slug.*

海 鼠 突 き 声 使 は ぬ に 声 嗄 れ て 廣 波 青

namakotsuki koe tsukawanu ni koe shigarete – obasei? (contemp)
(seaslug-gigger, voice use-not-though, voice roughened/hoarse)

#477

little used but
the slug gigger's voice
sounds hoarse

∿

the voice
the slugger doesn't use
is hoarse

There is a haiku lesson here. Again, I would ask: Could the same haiku be written about someone engaged in any other solitary form of work? I think it highly unlikely. The *Silent Sea Slug* metaphor is behind the haiku. It is not all of it. The hoarse voice also suggests the idea of a roughly hewn, hyper-male sea slug. But let's end the chapter with something smoother, a poem of silence, unspoken:

海 照 り て 人 を 消 し ぬ る 海 鼠 舟 八 木 林 之 介

umi terite hito o keshinuru namakobune – yagi rinnosuke (mod)
(ocean shining, person/s [make]dissappear/vanish/erase seaslugboat)

#478

the sea shines   sea slug boats
and wipes the men off   the ocean gleams and all
the slug boats   the men are gone

after wang wei

reflecting sunlight
erases the man and leaves
a sea slug boat

∿

18
the melancholy sea slug

わ だ つ み の 底 に 物 あ る 海 鼠 か な 楽 南
wadatsumi no soko ni mono aru namako kana – rakunam (p1927)
(seabed/depths-bottom/floor-on/at thing is: seaslug!/?/ó/the/'lo)   #479

below the sea
a brooding presence
black namako

The sea has many names in Japanese. *Wadatsumi* has the strongest associations with myth, the Time of the Gods. With such profundity, the sea slug could not be put in, say, Davy Jone's Locker even if this folk expression were more catholic. But the lack of an equivalent "sea" in English is a small loss compared to the problem of translating the most important word in the original: *mono,* for "thing" in English is something inconsequential, [1] whereas in Japanese, it is of great consequence and may signify the presence of deep feelings (grudge or love) or even supernatural power, especially of the terrible – more precisely, awe-full – sort that once protected pristine Nature from human inroads and is subsumed in another fine Japanese word, *tatari.* [2] Had I simply translated "on the seabed / there is this thing / the sea slug," the reader would not feel the power of the Japanese *mono.* So, we have this "brooding presence," which the reader who can take words in their old sense may redo as "awful presence." Since the sea slugs traditionally taken in deep water are black, I colored the sea slug the better to bring out its melancholy, which is developed further in the following, well-known haiku.

思 ふ こ と い は ぬ さ ま な る 生 海 鼠 か な 蕪 村
omou koto iwanu sama naru namako kana – buson (1770)
(thinking/longing-thing says-not aspect is: sea slug!/?/ó/the)   #480

it looks like
it cannot speak its mind
the sea slug

the sea slug
like a man who keeps
it all within

anatomy of melancholy

the sea slug

all choked up
like a man with a real
troubled mind

&

my
sea slug's
a worried man
who holds his tongue

words for a picture

this sea slug
the picture of a man
holding it in

The eternal silencing of the sea slug recorded in the RECORD OF ANCIENT MATTERS adds a certain allegorical validity to the metaphor of mental anguish suggested by the creature's slow squirming and quivering. With haiku, the text often does not reveal which side is metaphor: whether sea slug is man *or* vice versa. In this case, it is surely the latter, though my translations do not all share that vector. A contemporary annotation for Buson's poem in his *Complete Work* (bzs) supplies the likely literary precedent, a passage in Kenko's *Essays in Idleness* (*tsurezuregusa* c.1330) about thoughts unvoiced

1. *Thing in English* Samuel Johnson has almost nothing good to say for out "thing," but the OED shows he forgot one usage where "thing" is popular if not powerful. I.e., "the thing" was already *the thing* in Johnson's day. If only "thing" and "think" were cognate, English could not only translate but improve upon the sea-slug-as-thing, for thought could be etymologically reified and vice versa!

2. *Tatari* A contingent natural curse. E.g., a mountain would jinx anyone who cut trees on it.

swelling the belly (idiomatic for discontent, anger or holding a grudge) and depicts the sea slug as a sullen burly male: "that guy called sea slug, rudely parking his body, swollen up like he is stuffed with discontent when something is rotten as hell." When this sea slug "twitches, it is the very picture of a swollen belly" (*namako to iu yatsu . . . nanika fute-kusarete-iru . . . piku-piku ugoku to . . .*). Since the *Essays in Idleness* passage seems to deal more with aesthetic melancholy than everyday life, Buson's sea slug may have not been *that* vernacular. And there is also a possibility he was thinking of something more classic:

apparently,
choked up with love
a sea slug!

In Japanese, love is equated with longing, and longing was generally called *mono-omoi,* or "thing-thinking."[1] This may seem strange if one thinks the heart lacks mind; but anyone who has experienced unrequited love knows that *one thought after another flows past at a bewildering rate*, so that mental overload, rather than lack of thought, is what knocks you out. The *omou koto,* or "think-things" in this poem does not specifically mean "longing" but such an interpretation is poetically fitting when you recall that the deity responsible for lacerating *Namako's* mouth was none other than the most erotic god/dess in the Shinto pantheon, the teaser Ame-no-Uzume. *Lovers speak up, or forever hold your peace!(?)*

憂 き 人 の 心 に も 似 し 生 海 鼠 哉　青 蘿
ukihito no kokoro ni mo nishi namako kana – seira (1739-1791)
(floating/troubled/ascetic=aesthete-person's mind/heart-even-as resembles/ing sea-slug!/?/ó/the/loh)

#481

ah, sea slug!
how you resemble
a lovesick heart

don't i know you?   ***for hank williams***

a resemblance   there it is
to my lovesick heart!   *your cold, cold heart!*
this sea slug   a sea slug

Unless I can get a precise date on Seira's poem, we cannot tell if it predates or postdates Buson's far more famous poem. Though very different, I think it equally good. A sea slug is a remarkable reification of the mind and metaphor for the mind/heart – in this case, perhaps, a pictorial mimesis for the state of mind called *longing* – though we should remember that premodern Japanese probably did not visualize the heart as a modern poet might, so the resemblance may be more abstract in Seira's poem than in contemporary *tanka* and haiku. As my English gloss should indicate, the word *ukihito* is
#482（下）

1. *Thing Thinking* An Australian jellyfishologist living in Okinawa who had just begun reading my manuscript (when the 1,000 haiku were but 200), signed off in Japanese: "In the freezing night / i chew on sea cucumber / and think thoughts – Dhugal J. Lindsay (*iteru yo no namako o kamite mono omou* – Dougaru 凍てる夜の海鼠を噛みてもの思ふ ドゥーグル). Aside from the redefinition of *mono-omou* in translation (no love-thoughts, we are both straight male) – and a possible reality problem (How cold does it get in Okinawa?) – this is a *very* Japanese haiku. There is something about chewing chewy things that encourages one to "think thoughts." Considering the *Cold Sea Slug* metaphor, Keigu should have replied, yes, "chewing sea-slug / warms the heart when / things are thought" (*namako kamu kokoro-zo atamaru mono omo[h]i* – see pg __ re *hi=fire* puns). It is indeed heart-warming to encounter other non-Japanese who enjoy old metaphor. Note, his "think thoughts," rather than "think things" in the English. Chewing is primary; thinking is secondary. Still. the sea slug as the quintessential *thing* is a fine fit for thing-thinking.

a challenge. In the oldest usages, the person with the lovesick blues is the *ukihito*, but toward the end of the Edo era, it came to mean the *other* person, the one who made the poet blue – the third reading is based on this, though I feel it is almost certainly wrong because haiku poets rarely attack others.

ukihito

behold the heart
of a suffering aesthete
in the sea slug

how sea slug
resembles the heart
of us melancholy poets

it looks like
a troubled mind:
the sea slug

This final reading follows the connotation of *ukihito* that dictionaries place last: an aesthete who is a melancholy ascetic,[1] such as the haiku saint Bashô was, or thought himself to be. This reading may have been first in the mind of the poet, but who is to say? (Buson experts, speak up!)

手 も 足 も 出 せ ぬ 想 い 海 鼠 か な 舞姫

te mo ashi mo idasenu omoi namako kana – maihime? (contemp)
(hand-even leg-even stick-out-not thought/feeling seaslug!/?/ó/the/loh)

#483

the sea slug
feelings that must stay
in the closet

the sea slug
feelings you must keep
to yourself

the sea slug
a thought doomed to
remain within

poor sea slugs
thoughts that never get outside
of themselves

sea slugs
ideas you would develop
but can't

While we are talking about how the poet feels, it is fun to visualize the sea slug as an expression of this. This is a paraverse of Buson's poem. Since English body language must throw up its hands at "ideas that cannot stick out their hands and feet," the poet's possible play upon the classic haiku by Roga, which has the sea slug appear in a likewise described season – limbless because of the cold – is lost in translation.

父 に し て 海 鼠 ほ ど に は 悩 ん で お り 等

chichi ni shite namako hodo ni wa nayandeori – hitoshi (contemp)
(father-as, seaslug degree-as-for suffering/troubled)

#484

as a father
i find i worry as much
as a sea slug

as a father
i'm as troubled as
a sea slug

1. *Aesthete=Asthetic* While Japan has its great carousers (Saikaku, Hokusai …) in art, there was a strong tradition that identified true beauty with something we might call cutting down to the bone of life. Genuine aesthetics was identified with sincerity and that was born of voluntary poverty and the accompanying suffering. "Ye, flies of Kiso / learn from the travels of / an *ukihito!*" haiku's Bashô. Yes, the *ukihito* wings it alone and doesn't fly after food. *Like*, Seira may be thinking, *namako!*

I guessed that Hitoshi had a teenage daughter, asked, and that was indeed the case. A minor poem, but it is nice, I think, to find someone worrying in poetry about something other than love or a lover!

海 底 が こ ひ し こ ひ し と 海 鼠 か な　藤 原 愛

unazoko/kaitei ga koishi koishi to namako kana – fujiwara ai (2001)

(sea-bottom-the dear dear [says/indicates/expresses] seaslug!/?/ó/the/loh)

#485

body/mind-language

this sea slug
seems to say *how i miss*
my sea bed

homesick holothurians

the sea slugs
a picture of yearning for
their sea bed

This haiku is not much at a glance. I must confess I was distracted by the cute (?) *koishi koishi* (how i long/miss x2) and missed its real significance, i.e., that it reinterprets *namako's* apparent agony in terms of the sea slug, itself. True, we have seen poems which describe the shrinking of the sea slug itself in freezing weather or at the point of a knife. But this is the only haiku I can think of that suggests that sea slugs look the way they do *because they are out of place*.[1] The *to* (after the *koishi*) may anthropomorphize the sea slug in so far that it is generally used to indicate deliberate expression, but *what* is expressed is far less anthropocentric than the usual metaphors to which we shall return after one more *possibly* slug-centric haiku.

海 鼠 に は 海 の 思 ひ 出 海 の 恋　八 木 忠 栄

namako ni wa umi no omoide umi no koi – yagi chûei (contemp)

(seaslug-to-as-for[even] ocean-memory/ies, ocean-love)

#486

sea slugs
recall the sea recall
their loves

a sea slug
has its sea memories
and sea love

we sea slugs
remember the sea and
our sea loves

with sea slug
i recall the sea and
its romance

If this is really about sea slugs, it suggests something of what the previous haiku does. The sea slug/s may simply be a metaphor for a bed-ridden sailor or, more likely, only mean/s that the poet eats *namako* and thinks of the sea and his other loves, or, perhaps, the sea that he loves. But my preferred readings take the point of view of the sea slug and, in a word, they say: *even a sea slug has a life.*

1. *Out-of-Place Appearance*   If sea slugs were observed working or mating on the sea floor at night, an entirely different *namako* would appear. While Fujiwara did not depict *that*, her re-interpretation of their body-language is a good start. I think of Merlin Tuttle, who changed the face, which is to say, the image of the bat in our eyes by becoming familiar if not friend to the bats he photographed – *National Geographic* showed him holed up in a hotel room with his subjects long enough to gain their trust -- so that they looked sweet rather than scary (previously, they were caught in defensive or frightened postures) and *proved* they deserved our kindness for their good character as well as because they ate millions of mosquitoes. Since Fujiwara's poem appeared in a minor newspaper, and is, as far as haiku go (by conventional standards), not much, and she herself may have no idea of its significance, my comments may astound Japanese readers.

砂を食む海鼠なるもの思ふときぬらりとこころ混沌を出づ　矢野千恵子

suna o hamu namako naru monoomou toki nurari to kokoro konton o izu (t) – yano chieko (2000))

(sand-eating sea-slug become thing-thinking[loving/having a crush] time slippery heart chaos outs[generates])

#487

confession

thinking of you
my heart is a sand
sucking sea slug
that turned to slime
breeds chaos

心臓と同じくらゐの海鼠かな　石原八束

shinzô to onaji kurai no namako kana – ishihara yatsuka (mod)

(heart-as same-amount/size's sea-slug/s!/?/ó/the/'this/loh)

#488

this sea slug:
about the same size
as the heart

In the *tanka*, eating sand is made a poetic preface (in Japanese called a "pillow-phrase") for a sea slug that further description suggests not only the squirming of Buson's slug, but the same mindset as that of the un-named American personality who declared she could tell when she was in love because it gave her diarrhea or, worse, the pitiful "low-down" condition of unrequited love or illicit love.[1] The haiku, with less baggage, comes right out with it: *sea-slug=heart*. The rest is left to us. But note that the word used for "heart," in his haiku, *shinzô,* ostensibly refers only to the anatomical or physical "heart"[2] so the poet might disclaim the metaphysics that are the subject of this chapter!

わが内に海鼠のごときものの住む　八木忠栄

waga uchi ni namako no gotoki mono no sumu – yagi chûei (contemp)

(my insides-in, seaslug/s-like thing's dwells/ing)

#489

inside of me
a sea-slug-like thing
is dwelling

1. Love-sick Sea Slug Tanka I think of *Manyoshû* song#2693, where a man claims he'd rather be the sand his love treads than endure his (hopeless) longing; or song #3400, where the lover says he/she would pick up gravel treaded by the beloved and keep it as gem-stones. As we say, we do *fall* in love and what is lower down than a sea slug!

2. Heart Problems In old Japanese poetry the anatomical term *shinzô* (heart-organ) doesn't appear; but the problem of whether and how to relate the organ to the metaphorical heart, which is also the mind, is nonetheless there. While the belly as a place of resolution and the head as a place of mentation (eyelids for dreaming!) also have their part of the mind, the breast was definitely identified with longing. Reading *Kokinwakashû waka* ,about how fires of longing singed the breast of the lover's robe (unless tears dampened the fire), one might view the heart-organ as the furnace, but other poems show that is too simple. For example, this by the most famous ancient love-poet of Japan: "we don't meet / and my longing in the dark / of the moon / sets fire to my breast / badly burning my heart" (*hito-ni awamu tsuki-no naki-ni-wa omohi-okite mune hashiribi-ni kokoro yake-ori* – onono komachi KKS #1030). My rough translation fails to do justice to the metaphorical fire started to gain some light that has exploded into a wildfire ("running fire" in the original) and the absent-moon=missed-opportunity punning, and so forth; no matter, my point, that the heart is but part of a breast-full of passion, is made. Had Onono Komachi written of a sea-slug heart, she could have roasted it from without.

in me
a seaslug-like
thing

Perhaps this poet [1] knows Saigyô's *waka* "inside my heart / that longs for you / an infant cries / but i fear i am / the one the tears besot" (*kimi shitau kokoro no uchi wa chigomekite namida moro ni mo naru waga mi kana*)! Instead of this crying baby, he gives us something much quieter but equally troubled, the sea slug, those his pent up feelings would not necessarily concern love.

雑 念 は 失 せ ぬ な ま こ の ご と く 居 る 鷹 女
zatsunen wa usenu namako no gotoku iru – takajo (d.1972)

#490
(sundry-thoughts-as-for lose-not sea-slug-like am/being/sitting)

i'm a sea slug
who can't escape my own
idle thoughts

This famous modern poet's name, hawk-woman, suggests the clarity of the high fall sky, but here she confesses to being bogged down in a morass of thought. Unlike Buson and Seira's sea slug, *mono-omoi* and *uki* is not all of it. She might be worrying about almost anything (the "sundry" of "sundred-thought" here is the same character used for the "omni" of *omnivorous*), children, money, health, etcetera, but the result, inaction – sea-sluggishness – is the same.

し ん と し て ゐ て も 海 鼠 の 水 濁 る 穴 井 節 子
shin to shite ite mo namako no mizu nigoru – anai setsuko (2001)

#491
(quiet/still doing-being[keeping] even, seaslug's water clouds/muddies)

though it's still	though sea slugs
the sea slug's water	keep still, their water
grows murky	turns cloudy

The sea slug is hardly the only sea life to foul its water – and, in the wild, at least, it is known to clean it! -- but it is the only where it is worth mentioning. This is because the idea fits the metaphorical image. Melancholy is dark in Japanese, as it is in English.

海 鼠 切 っ て 海 の 暗 さ の 手 に 残 る 宇 都 宮 伝
namako kitte umi no kurasa no te ni nokoru – utsunomiya den (contemp)

#492
(seaslug cut/ting, sea/ocean's darkness's hand/s-on remains)

cutting *namako*	sea slug cut
the darkness of the sea	the sea's darkness stays
stains my hand	on my hands

1. *Yagi Chûei* I ran into this contemporary poet's work in a review on the net. and was most impressed with: "thin clothing / the streets full of tits / for other men" (*usumono ya machi ni tanin no chichi bakari* (Yuki Yamazu).   The original's "other people's tits" means there are none for the poet. This is no *senryu*, no stereotype of city life, but an accurate portrayal of how it feels to be involuntarily celibate – in my case, because I cannot take time off from my work – in the summer, when the whole, literally fucking, world rubs itself in your face and says "bite!" When one is poor and lacks money to buy time, poetry and other creative work demands the sacrifice of what others call *life*. (I spout off from *my* experience. For all I know, Yagi is not poor like me, but ugly. Or, maybe he married early and thinks bachelors are enjoying the sights he saw. Regardless, it's a hell of a haiku!)

The poet seems to say the sea slug concentrates the darkness of the sea in much the same way oysters do radiation and sharks do mercury. What is this *darkness*? See this haiku not mentioning sea slugs:

海 の 月 魚 は く は れ て 成 仏 か 傘 下
umi no tsuki sakana wa kuwarete jôbutsu ka – sanka (18c?)
(sea's moon: fish-as-for eaten become-buddha/s[to die]?)   #493

the moonlit sea
are the fish now eaten
enlightened?

The Buddhist moon is a merciful one. Dying in its "Light of the Law," might help one achieve Buddhahood or get to Nirvana – depending whether you see grace as a state or a place, either reading will do. At first reading, this poem reminds us of Issa's request to a sea slug to become a buddha/die; but a second reading reveals the poet shuddering: *below the placid moonlit surface of the sea, there is wholesale slaughter going on.* And the sea slug lies at the bottom of all that, sucking in the detritus of the war of life and turning it into sand pure enough for an hourglass.

た れ こ め て 沖 の 暗 さ や 海 鼠 舟 杉 原 竹 女
tarekomete oki no kurasa ya namakobune – sugihara chikujo (contemp)
(drop-in/droop-down offshore[water's?] darkness!/& seaslug-boat)   #494

filled with all
the darkness of the sea
sea slug boats

〜

the darkness
from offshore comes in
sea slug boats

I think the poem means "low in the water, this darkness from offshore: slugging boats." But I am not sure. I couldn't fake it by just translating as-is, for English has no verb for a boat "low in the water." "Lying low" requires a boat to be still, which is not necessarily the case, and lacks the full-bodied feeling of the Japanese *tarekomeru*. The verb also is used for defecating into something, so I feel tempted to think of the boat as a sort of honey-wagon, but that is not the style of this particular poet, so let us just say that a large catch of sea slug might contribute to the darkness.

鉛 な す 海 よ り 重 き 海 鼠 か な せ い ち
namari nasu umi yori omoki namako kana – seichi (2002)
(lead/grey-being-sea more-than heavy seaslug/s!/?/ó/the/witness)   #495

heavier still
than the leaden sea
the sea slug

〜

heavier still
than the leaden sea
holothurians

The second "sea" is tedious so, for the second translation, the rare appearance of a single two-beat, five-syllable word which alliterates with the first word in the poem: *holothurians*.

冬 海 の 暗 さ 世 界 の つ ま ら な さ 灰 色 に し て な ま こ の 眠 り　馬 場 あ き 子
fuyu umi no kurasa sekai no tsumaranasa haiiro ni shite namako no nemuri – baba akiko (contemp)
(winter sea's darkness world's worthlessness/dullness, grey-color-as do, seaslug's sleep/drowsiness/slumber)

#496

the darkness
of the winter sea and
worthlessness
of the world in heavy
grey sea slug slumber

~

the dark sea
and worthless world,
of winter
paint it grey
a sea slug, asleep

~

sleeping
sea slug, the grey
worthless
world and dark
winter sea

If the world is a sleeping beauty, she seems terribly depressed! Winter will do that. This tanka, as so many poems, depends on how you read the poet's heart. Is *nemuri* sleep, sleepiness, drowsyness, slumber . . . ? I think the spare last reading, with the word order roughly reversed, works best.

寒 海 鼠 日 が な 割 く 手 の 汚 れ か な　清 家 信 博
kannamako higana saku te no yogore kana – seike nobuhiro (2001)
#497   (cold[coldest part of winter] seaslug day-in-day-out slit-open hands' dirtiness!/?/ó/the/behold)

what dirty hands
cutting mid-winter sea slugs
day in day out

mid-winter still life

stained hands
from opening sea slugs
day in and out

Though this would seem to be mere fact, *can there be mere fact* about something so pregnant with metaphor? What a pity English lacks a verb including the connotations of "to cut/slit/open-up."

海 鼠 腸 の 海 の 暗 さ を 綴 り け り　菅 村 あ さ 香
konowata no umi no kurasa o tsuzurikeri – sugemura asaka (1997)
#498   (sea-slug-guts' ocean's darkness[obj] slurping-down)

slurping down
the darkness of the sea:
namako guts

Usually chewing makes us reflect, but here we have identification: the eater finds herself in the original location of the sea slug – a dark place.   The guts themselves dark within the dark slug on the dark bottom of the sea are in the darkest place of all. I remember the literal meaning of *melancholy*.

海 鼠 腸 や 壺 中 の 雲 の 入 日 影 白 豚
konowata ya tsubo naka no kumo no iruhi kage – hakuton? (1680)
(slug-guts! crock/pot/bottle-within's cloud's entered-sun shadow [1]/image/shine)   #499

sea slug guts
the sun shines through
bottled clouds

sea slug guts!   slug guts:
a jar full of grey clouds   sun hidden in clouds
with silver linings   in bottles

sea slug guts
a sun-lit cloud reflects
within the jar

I thought the old poem described the semi-translucent cloudy color of the fermented guts, which were much more highly treasured than the meat of the sea slug, whereas OM favors an actual reflection, my final, added reading. I can't help wondering what the old poet would have thought of the more direct *swallowing darkness* poem by the contemporary woman or this next contradiction:

一 刀 に 断 ち て 海 鼠 の 腹 白 し 野 中 ち よ こ
ittô ni tachite namako no hara shiroshi --- nonaka chiyoko (contemp)
(one-sword cut/severed/ing seaslug's belly/guts-white=innocent)   #500

white inside!

cut through
with one chop, sea slug
proves clean

My Japanese advisor put this poem with a group having "no deep significance," which it doesn't, *by itself*. But, placed after all these melancholy poems, it has a contrary charm. Familiar with the dark image which so many other poets have reproduced, the poet was surprised to find the sea slug she was preparing had such light-colored or clean innards – a fact with metaphorical significance, for "white" means innocent,[2] and, remembering the Myth, may have thought – *Aha! the sea slug is exonerated!*

1. *"Shadow" in English* Only a hundred years ago, the connotation of "shadow" in English* included reflections and even bright things within a larger dark background. The Japanese *kage* is, similarly ambiguous. This *shadow* could have preserved the light melancholy of the original better. But it is obsolete. Aesop's dog has long since exchanged his "shadow" for his "reflection" in the pond where he dropped the meat by growling at himself. The New England theologian Jonathon Edwards wrote of *Shadows* rather than *Reflections* of *Divine Things*, etc.. (See IPOOH fall-moon)
2. *Whiteness in Japanese* The equation of *whiteness* and *innocence* comes from two dove-tailing sources. One is the idea of whiteness as *nothing*, in the same sense as the "blank" of *blanco* in Western language. I.e., there is nothing there. The other is from a homophonic pun that was so broadly used that it became idiomatic. "White" and "not-knowing," at least in poetic forms of the words, are both the same *shira*. This equation is steeped in "white-dew," perhaps the leading metaphor for innocence. But not-knowing, if knowingly engaged in, can be less than innocent. One recent metaphorical sea slug haiku, puts it like this: "just how far is / sea slug going to claim / he knows *naught*? (*doko made mo shira o kiru ki no namako kana* – ___? どこまでも 白 を 切 る 気 の 海 鼠 か な   未 知). The literal translation of "claim to know naught" is "cut white" (!).   #501

憂きことを海月に語る（生）海鼠かな（哉）召波

ukigoto o kurage ni kataru namako kana – shôha (1726-71)

#502   (lovesick/blue[=floating]-things to [the] jellyfish=moon=dark, speaking sea slug!/?/ó/the)

the sea-slug
saying sad things
to the jelly-fish

trans. Blyth (hh1)

~

sad stories
whispered to the jellyfish
by the seaslug

trans. Addiss+Yamamoto (hm)

love-sick	*escape-valve*
talking to	the sea slug
the moon-jellyfish	spills out his guts
a sea slug	to the jellyfish

Considering the bias in favor of the concrete in modern haiku, this fantastical poem is surprisingly well known.[1] It is the single example chosen for a paragraph-long explanation after the selection of the otherwise un-annotated *namako* haiku in Kodansha's large saijiki (nhds). The Addiss+Yamamoto translation is beautiful.   Far better than mine. With all those sibilants, you can hear the soft swishing of the sea.   But without explanation – and, *as is usual for haiku today,* there was none – no reader not in the know could possibly guess what the poem is about, much less understand how the original manages to justify such a fantastic menagerie of metaphor.

First, we should know that "jelly-fish" (*kurage*) is written with two Chinese characters: sea+moon, while it is a perfect homophone for "darkness".[2] This was not missed by the *waka* poets whom the haiku poets superceded. We need not, however, retrogress so far. The most relevant predecessor is a haiku by a Teimon school poet written about a hundred years earlier: "on the sea-bed / the fish, too, watch the moon-jellyfish[=in-the -dark]" (*minasoko-no sakana mo tsuki miru kurage kana* – josei (kzs) 海底の魚も月見るくらげ哉　助清 (kzs貞門１)). The fantastical mood is already there.   And we see that the haikai poets still paid attention to the nominal moon in the jellyfish.[3] But, benthic or not, the poem is shallow, for it is purely fabulous, *i.e.* has no metaphor which concerns us.

1. *Fantastical Ku* There are many haiku fantastical enough to merit a children's nonsense book. As a rule, however, such drollery is considered beneath haiku and ignored. The only one as famous as Shôha's would be Buson's vision of a red peony as the tongue of a demon. If the sea slug seems unsuitable for fantasy – precisely why some try to put it there – the luminous, floating jellyfish seems perfect for it. Shiki wrote: "a doll gallery / why not parasols / of jellyfish?" (*hinadan ni kurage no kasa wo mairasen* – (szs) 雛殿に海月の笠を参らせん 子規). Jellyfishologist haijin, LD, why not?

2. *Sea-Moon Significance* Some anthologies use the Chinese characters for "sea"+ "mother" rather than "sea"+"moon" for Shôha's jellyfish. While *kurage* can be written either way, I feel this is wrong, for I believe Shôha was thinking of the moon metaphor and that it is appropriate, given the close relationship of Buson and Shôha, and their evident familiarity with *waka* metaphor. While there is far more looking at the moon than talking to it in *waka*, in SANKASHU (mountain-home-collection), Saigyô talks to the moon about things of old (#1505: *tsuki ni ika de mukashi no koto o katarasete ...*) and finds the moon good medicine for the same *uki* feelings the sea slug has (#1506: *uki-yo to shi omowa de mo . . .*).

3. *Haiku Jellyfish* A better, but less relevant, early jellyfish haiku: "a sea of fog / the moon lies below: / a jellyfish" (*kiri no umi no soko naru tsuki wa kurage kana* – chikashige or ryûho (1595-1669) (霧の海の底なる月はくらげ哉　親重 (俳諧発句帳) or 立圃?). I am not certain if any psychological metaphor was intended.

Second, we should know that the *uki,* while written with the Chinese character for feeling tormented (classically by longing, but later by more general troubles in life) and melancholy is a homophone for "floating." Theoretically speaking, the "floating" pun may allude to the fact that sea slugs do actually float up a little during the full moon – they rise up to spawn at any rate, presumably "to better thrust their seed into the water column" (AK), but it is unlikely Shôha knew that. While a storm-tide may lift a mating *namako* up, up and away, I can't imagine any genuine floating, unless it is in the surf preliminary to being thrown up on the beach! [1] Only the tiny larvae (and some Benthic (deep sea) species that don't count in this context) – which have no more resemblance to the adult form than a caterpillar to a butterfly – not only float up, but make it as far as a modern haiku claims:

千 百 里 漂 ひ 来 る 海 鼠 か な 碧 梧 桐
senhyaku ri tadayoikitaru namako kana – hekigoto (1872-1937)
(thousand-hundred miles drifting-come sea-slug/s!/?/ó/the/loh)   #503

these sea slugs
here, after drifting
a thousand miles

Because of the uneasy connotations of "floating" to people in Shôha's time, I do not think, as some contemporary Japanese imagine, that the sea slug is discussing the joys of floating [2] – the equivalent of people wishing to fly – with the happy-go-lucky jellyfish, nor, considering the fact that jellyfish are eaten, is the sea slug disgruntled because the buoyant jellyfish is free of danger, while he might be caught at any time, as others claim.

Third, we should know that Shôha was a close friend of Buson's. Not a few of their poems seem to have been written in a spirit of playful one-upmanship and are best read together. [3] The chapter-head poem about the sea slug who can't get anything off its chest was clearly not one of Buson's better haiku. Even with words borrowed from an old poem, it was far too simple. Shôha must have said to himself *"Humph, I can do better than that!"* And, as you now can see, he certainly did, for his haiku beautifully combines elements of a fairyland fantasy, fine wordplay and Buson's metaphor.

1. The Extent Sea Cucumber Move The larvae and juveniles of many species do float, some for hundreds of miles, before settling down. One might think of these as old hippies who hitchhiked about when young and learned to appreciate swallowing the anchor later. It is the opposite of the caterpillar and butterfly, where the young stay put and the adult wanders. There are also "cukes that as adults of at least several cm in length float about their whole lives. They are truly pelagic, as pelagic as an open ocean jellyfish. There's even one . . . that lives attached to a mesopelagic fish, which surely gets around. (AK). Note: A National Geographic Warner documentary *Ocean Drifters: An Extraordinary Odyssey on the Incredible Superhighways of Marine Life* features the sea cucumber with the loggerhead turtle and the Portuguese man-of-war as a sea creature that spends its entire life adrift.
2. Floating Sensation. I used to float up in my dreams, so it is natural for me to equate floating with pleasant sensation, even the joy of flying, as did one Japanese correspondent who gave what I

thought to be a naive interpretation of Shôha's haiku. But, traditionally, "floating" was sad. One floated in one's tears and rootlessness was synonymous with a life of woe. The "floating world" or, *uki-yo,* was the illusion we all live in, and according to Buddhist catechism, hope to leave. In the Edo era, it also meant the world populated by the unhappy prostitutes, pimps, gamblers, conmen and artists depicted in *ukiyo-e.* The extent to which "floating" was synonymous with misfortune is apparent in Issa's poem: "young-water / even when straw floats / it's called 'lucky'" (*waka-mizu ya wara-ga uite-mo fuku to iu* – see IPOOH NY1: "young-water") Not surprisingly, *the* mark of a Japanese ghost is *leglessness.* This was true pre-Edo, Edo and, still, today. It would be curious how much this metaphorical *fear of floating* has effected Japanese dreams of flying over the centuries
3. One Upmanship This is my observation. Japanese scholars tend to be so overawed with Buson that they only think of Shôha as his "disciple" and have failed to pay close enough attention to their mutual influence.

うかうかと海月に交る生海鼠哉　車庸

ukauka to kurage ni majiru namako kana – shayô (1698)

#504

(nervously/carelessly jellyfish/s-with mix seaslug!/?/ô/the)

a sea slug
out of his element
with jellyfish

sea slugs   how carelessly
mixing nervously   these sea slugs float
with jellyfish   with jellyfish

There are two weak points in Shôha's complex metaphor. First, the jellyfish was a summer theme, so one of the creatures is out of time=place. [1] Nevertheless, I add this earlier poem with the same combination to show that things may be more complex than we know.   If the sea slug stayed put, the jellyfish with its floating life would hardly be a good influence. The psychological mimesis (*ukauka*) has two meanings. My "out-of-element" translation avoids choosing which.   The poem may be based on a sea-side scene, but it is strange to have the slower moving sea slugs do the mixing. It makes me think Shayô's haiku is a metaphor for a hermit-like poet getting in with the fast crowd.

浮出てゝ憂きともなかぬ生海鼠哉　士朗

ukidetete uki to mo nakanu namako kana – shirô (1741-1812)

#505

(float-appearing sad[float]-even cry-not sea-slug!/?/ô/the/loh)

though it floats up
full of love-sick anguish
the sea-slug doesn't cry

A more fundamental problem with Shôha's metaphor was that the sea slug was not supposed to talk at all.   Everyone knew its mouth was ruined by that goddess for good.   As Shirô's poem notes, it has a double *uki* of anguish and unease/floating, yet remains mum.   But, we must not think all sea cucumbers are so lonely as our *namako*.

> Others that live in the deep sea are apparently pair forming. It is very difficult to find a mate in the vast, sparsely populated and inky depths. E.g., the tiny male of the angler fish lives attached to his outsized consort his whole life, merging his tissues with hers (immunologists would love to figure out how they suppress tissue rejection) and becoming essentially a sperm receptacle. Some deep-sea cukes appear to have solved the problem of finding a mate by forming long-lasting pairs, crawling alongside one another for extending periods. (A. Kerr)

I find this very heart-warming to think about. A pair of sea cucumbers sticking as close as Mandarin Ducks. [2]   One wonders what these brainless and heartless creatures feel for one another: how, for example, would the death of one influence the health of the other?

1. Winter and Summer Blyth writes that "this verse belongs to summer, as sea-slugs and certain jellyfish are eaten in that season." (hh 1) Needless, to say, he is confused about haiku convention. As already noted, all Japanese anthologies I have seen place sea slug in the winter. Either sea slug or jellyfish is out of season. Questioned about this, I wonder if Shôha might not laugh and say, *That is precisely why the sea slug is feeling blue; he has woken up in the wrong season and doesn't fit in!* Otherwise, I would bet there is some winter jellyfish he could point out.

2. Duck Sea Slugs In the Sinosphere, Mandarin Ducks symbolize happy monogamy. →

むかし男なまこのやうにおはしけむ 大江丸

mukashi otoko namako no yô ni owashikemu – ôemaru (1721-1805)

(olden-day=once[upon a time] man/men: sea-slug/s liketh-on-to is[formal-style])   #506

once upon a time

there was
a lady's man liketh to
a sea slug

behold

the men of old:
dandies with the spine
of a sea slug!

the lady's man

a man of old!
forsooth, yonder sea slug
is his original

This well-known sea-slug-as-lover poem dating to about the same time as Buson's poem is metaphorically a different kettle of fish. Rather than being choked up with feeling, the sea slug is a spineless lady's man, a reference to a character (*mukashi otoko*) in the *Tales of Ise*. He was supposedly soft on women because he was so handsome. Ôemaru has pulled a fast one by equating a good-looking man with something ugly, a sea slug! The Japanese think that since a handsome man[1] has a good chance of succeeding in his love affairs, he just plays along with whatever women dish out to him – whereas the ugly man, who must save face by pretending he is a man's man and doesn't give a damn what women think, develops real character;[2] but choked-up or spineless, ugly or handsome, men devoted to wooing inevitably end up victims of what Burton aptly called *love-melancholy*.

なまこ が 腹 を 立 て ば 笑 は れ 武玉川

namako ga hara o tateba waraware – *mutamagawa* 11 (__?)

(seaslug/s belly[obj] stand/rise[get angry]-if/when laugh[laughed at])   #507

if a sea slug
were to get angry he would
be laughed at

→ **Mandarin Duck Sea Slugs** I found a website with a photo of two holothurians (not *namako,* but white with orange spots and latitudinally segmented) curled up together, with these words: "Sea cucumbers typically limit themselves to a single individual throughout their lives and together they form a commensal relationship." I suspected this statement reflected the psychological need of its author to envision warm relationships on the cold sea bed, but the big word in the sentence (commensal) had a link and it went straight to the pearl-fish (that lives inside the holothurian without doing it any real harm), which lead me to suspect that the author *lost a paragraph* without noticing it, dovetailed the two subjects, then, rewrote, inadvertently polishing his own fantasy!

1. A Good-looking Man   In her poetic *LA Times* review of the latest English translation of *The Tale of Genji*, Liza Dalby explained to her muscle-worshipping American readers that the protagonist, Genji, the "shining" prince all the women found irresistibly handsome, was, according to all Japanese illustrations: flabby, pale, and pudgy-faced (Oct __2001). In a word, he was an exemplar of the *soft-is-beautiful* school of beauty. About a month later, when THE T.O.G. finally made the *NY Times*, a less creative but good (unlike most worthless NYT reviews, it included comparison with previous editions) review by Janice P. Nimura was betrayed by a ridiculous illustration: a hard-faced samurai with two-swords, five-hundred or so years out of date! (Dec 2, 2001) Can you imagine a leading Japanese newspaper depicting Montaigne as Rambo? (Months later, the greatest wit of classic Japanese literature was described in the NYT as a "courtesan" – well, I guess Sei Shonagon *did* reside in the Imperial *court* . . .).

2. An Ugly Man Novelist playwright, Inoue Hisashi once wrote of the advantages of being a homely man. I can remember two. He wasn't encouraged to go out to the expensive bars and waste money because the women there did not lionize him; and his daughters would be able to find good husbands easily because, having become acclimatized (?) to him, they would not be burdened with an overly high standard of looks.

The idea of the sea slug lacking spine goes back at least as far as this *Mutamagawa* (bk11) short senryu (7-7) – or *zappai* – predating Buson and Ôemaru.   "Angry" in the Japanese idiom is "to raise one's belly" (Recognize that *hara*?   It is the same one found in *harakiri*.) Our closest etymological parallel is probably *contumacious*; but a sea slug "with tumor" would be a sorry sight, not a laughing stock..   I imagine the *senryu* is pure metaphor, but I can't help noting that because a *namako's* belly runs his enterity, he would balloon; and, since becoming round was synonymous for passivity/peace in the Sinosphere, ...   Regardless, the idea of the *Meek Sea Slug* comes through clearly.   In the same *Mutamagawa* (bk 11), it is the blowfish, rather than the sea slug that swells up to compensate for a lack of speech (*iwanu bakari ni fugu wa fukureru*).   This is probably the seed of Buson's haiku and it is a fine rationalization, but is it *just so*?   I could swear I once heard a blow-fish croak quite well, thank you.[1]   Be that as it may, it makes sense that the sea slug who can neither talk nor blow up in anger became the poet's body of melancholy.

独 酌 や よ べ も こ よ ひ も 酢 海 鼠 に　田 畑 益 弘

dokushaku ya yobe mo koyoi mo sunamako ni – tabata masuhiro (2002)

#508   (lone-pouring/drinking: last night-even tonight-even vinegared-seaslug-with/to)

> drinking alone
> with pickled slug last night
> and tonight

We have seen what chewing sea slug means emotionally already.   Not many people would want to eat it two nights in a row.   Unless this is a person who loves his privacy so much he prefers to drink alone – and I have yet to find any one like that, though I am sure they exist, for I myself would rather sit with pen in hand than with a nincompoop below a cherry tree – this is an expression of what Burton called "*nimia solitudo,* too much solitariness, by the testimony of all physicians, cause and symptom both" of melancholy.   Indeed, the *Melancholy Sea Slug* would seem to be a product of, and an encouragement for, just such a mindset, working independently of the Western tradition of melancholy summed up by Burton.   If, as George Wills once pointed out, the "endangered Right to be Unhappy" has been protected by Country and Western Music in the United States of America, in Japan, the equivalent tear-jerking genre of *enka* must share some credit with the sea slug.

#509, #510

1. *Blowfish Facts and Metaphors*   As a matter of fact, blowfish are known to be very noisy fish – that, together with their rounded faces, blinking eyes and regurgitation (of water), makes them seem human in many ways.   Perhaps the *Mutamagawa senryu* did not think of the noises a blowfish makes as speaking but as pure vituperative, accompanying the angry swelling.   We should not, however feel less sympathy for the noisy blowfish than we feel for the quiet sea slug.   Depending on the context, noise can reflect powerlessness as well as silence does.   When Shiki haiku's "a blowfish abusing a sea slug who won support on a public matter" (*kachikôji no namako o soshiru fukuto kana* – shiki (1898) 勝公事 の 海鼠 を 誹る 河豚哉　子規), I, at least, feel some sympathy for the overheated, or to use Burton's term, choleric, blowfish.   It would seem a case where the winning side has the luxury of remaining silent. [Had I time, I would move this to the *Silent Sea Slug* as a counter-example of silence reflecting power.] Another, more balanced and easily Englished haiku by Shiki, depicts the two fish as having adapted differing strategies to cope with life.   I think it is a haiku that deserves attention even if it is obviously pure allegory, i.e., a description of two types of personalities:

海 鼠 黙 し 河 豚 嘲 る 浮 世 か な　子規(1897)

namako modashi fugu fukururu ukiyo kana – shiki

> a floating world
> where sea slugs stay mum and
> blowfish snort!

The word/character translated as "snort" more precisely means to talk scornfully or vituperatively with spittle (in this case, spume?) flying from the mouth.   The "floating world" could be understood as our woeful world, or, more narrowly, as that of entertainment and play that we might translate as "in the bars." But I am not going to give away more blowfish haiku here (Look for a book, *Swellfish Soup,* before long!).

「 百 年 の 孤 独 」 の ボ ト ル 海 鼠 噛 む 白 山 羊

"hyakunen no kodoku" no botoru namako kamu – hakusanyô? (contemp)

("one hundred years of solitude" bottle sea-slug chew)   #511

shôchû

chewing sea slug
my bottle "a hundred
years of solitude"

High-brow readers (especially in Japan) may find this too clever to merit attention, but I think this contemporary haiku found on one of my favorite haiku sites, *Migi-Nô Haiku,* or "right-brain haiku," deserves inclusion in the sea slug section of every new haiku almanac, for little coincidences such as the one captured here, are what makes everyday life enjoyable.   Japanese beer, *sake* and even its "low-class distilled spirit" *shôchû* (cane sugar, potato or up-town wheat – this last with a designer label to attract yuppies and women – is honest-to-goodness rotgut) enjoy ridiculously creative names. If the content were half so original, Japan would have the best drinks in the world.[1]   This one was, of course, taken from the Gabriel Marquez novel.   How perfect a combination, that label and the sea slug! Someone should make a mezzotint of it.

海 鼠 噛 む 働 か ざ る に 疲 れ ゐ て 松 本 雨 生

namako kamu hatarakazaru ni tsukareite – matsumoto usei (contemp)

(seaslug chew/ing work-not-not-with/by/despite tired-of)   #512

chewing slug
how tired i am of
not working

海 鼠 洗 ひ つ つ い さ さ か を 世 に 倦 み し 能 村 登 四 郎

namako araitsutsu isasaka o yo ni umishi – nômura toshirô (contemp)

(seaslug washing-while somewhat[+emot] world-in/at tired/fed-up)   #513

melancholia vulgaris

rinsing sea slug
i feel a bit fed up
with the world

I had ended the chapter with *A Hundred Years of Solitude* – for some reason a large number like "hundred" is melancholy in a romantic way, whereas, say "ten years of solitude" would suggest the hard life of a castaway – but when I found these poems, knew they had to be pegged on. The specifics (not working and rinsing) bring us back to reality after the abstract darkness found in many of the earlier poems. This slight (*isasaka*) nausea – momentary grey lapses that rarely make their way into literature – may not be the most interesting type of melancholy, but they are the most common. Hence the title of the second poem.

1. *Japanese Drinks* If you have a belly for bourbon, some of this rot-gut is highly recommended. The wines are not.   The beer has some winners: Ebisu dark, full-bodied Sapporo draft and Suntory Moretsu (malt, which tastes almost identical to the green bottled Ballantine Ale of old). *Sake* is worth learning to like for it has diverse offerings. I recommend winter *sake* served in a square box (*masu-zake*) to all who like Greek retsina and Kiku-hime Oginzo for those who like a nutty flavor and the cheap 200 yen cup-*sake* in a green glass with two plums in it for the thin traveler who can use the sugar.   But I would ask the restaurant's advice for what to drink with your sea-slug!

生き難し海鼠を提げて立ちつくす 萩原麦草
ikigatashi namako o sagete tachitsukusu – bakusô (1935)
(living-difficult seaslug hanging/dangling stand-stay/keep/endure/ing)

#514

to live is hard
still standing there with
unsold sea slug

banishment

life is hard
to stand there watching with
your sea slugs

the vendor

life is no joke
to stand all day dangling
your sea slug

自らもたうべてありぬ海鼠売 軽部烏頭子
mizukara mo taubetearinu namakouri – karube utôshi (1932)
(self-from, too, eating-is/exists seaslug-vender)

#515

the slug vender
he, too
eats what he sells

Here we have a slug-specific melancholy. The original does not say *who* stands there, but we know from the "dangling" that whoever it is has a bucket or two of them. The first reading, suggested by KS, has a sea slug vendor standing there with his unsold merchandize. That is sad, especially if they are so old he will have to eat them himself); but my second (highly unlikely) reading is sadder yet. I allude to Shunkan (1143?-79), who was exiled to the Devil-world-cape islands and had to remain behind years later when the boat came to pick up the other men, who had been pardoned. (See my *FLY-KU!*). He is usually imagined as stamping his feet in chagrin, but he could be just standing there with his sea slugs – what more fitting fare for one so marooned? – gazing as the vessel disappears over the horizon. Sad or not, this is too romantic for a modern poem. Imagine, instead, standing out in the cold selling inexpensive perishable merchandize from dawn to dusk! And, eating the oldest of your merchandize so as not to waste it. But that is enough realism for this chapter. Let us end on a more abstract note, with a couple contemporary haiku.

死角にはかなしき色の海鼠いる 石部明
shikaku ni wa kanashiki iro no namako iru – ishibe akira (contemp)
(dead-ground/angle-in-as-for, sad-colored seaslug [there]is)

#516

in the dead zone
there is this sad-colored
sea cucumber

dead space

out of sight
a sea slug the color
of my sadness

This poem – compare it to the sea slug at the bottom of the sea at the start of the chapter – netted at the last moment, was preceded by a haiku about a spiteful mouth crammed with *inari-zushi* (a light brown-colored sack-like *sushi*) and followed by a sketch of a tattered, yellowing poster of human anatomy.   While there is nothing clearly first-person in the original Japanese, it seems to me a truly post-modern (?) poem along the lines of my second reading.

もう一つ呑み込めないでゐる海鼠　高沢良一

mô hitotsu nomikomenai de iru namako – takasawa yoshikazu (1999)

(still-one swallow-cannot[idiom for not understanding something]-as exists, seaslug[subj])   #517

the sea slug
an animal that just
doesn't get it

the sea slug
looks like it is still
thinking about it

looking like it
cannot digest its own thought
the sea slug

While this *could* be a satire (imagine if it were titled with the name of some slow-witted public figure), the poet assures me that this is his take on the thing itself, for the sea slug "looks like it always has something on its mind."   Presumably, this is what Buson thought, but Takasawa, by *not* using words for thought that suggest romance, keeps his poem, arguably, slug-centric.   Still, he does not mean to say the sea slug thinks – or does not think – as we do, but that its body evokes such an psychological image.   He does this without simile, so the "like" in readings two and three is a bit off.   I think the poem suggests that even the Goddess's unkind cut did not have much effect on *namako*.

~

Given this entire body of pensive if not downright troubled sea slugs, we can now appreciate the humor in Takasawa's meta-metaphorical musing:

頭掻く海鼠なんぞも見てみたし　高沢良一

atama kaku namako nanzo mo mitemitashi – takasawa yoshikazu (2003)

(head scratch sea slug [+emphatic] see-see-want)   #518

oh, how i'd
like to see a sea slug
scratch its head!

T his page is reserved
for the best illustration

of

the melancholy sea slug.

19
<u>the stuporous sea slug</u>

海 底 に 月 さ し 動 く 海 鼠 か な 竹 美
unazoko/kaitei ni tsuki sashi ugoku namako kana – takemi? (contemp)
(sea-bed-on moon shines moves seaslug/s!/?/ő/the/'loh)   #519

the moon shines
on the seabed: look!
moving sea slugs

The Japanese written name "sea-rat/mouse" is right on target. The sea slug is a nocturnal animal. So a sea slug *should* look like it is sleeping, because when we can see one, it generally *is*. We observe them behaving more like their English name, sea *cucumbers* than their Japanese one, sea *rats*. This is the only haiku I have seen which catches the *namako* at work, or possibly, breeding.[1] The (possible) pun in the poem, *tsuki sashi,* or, "moon shines," suggests the homophone *tsukisashi,* i.e., "stabs," which makes it seem like the moon is prodding the stuporous slug to move. Another modern poem:

わ が ま ま な 海 鼠 に 月 の 光 か な 功 刀 と も 子
wagamamana namako ni tsuki no hikari kana – kôtô tomoko (2001)
(self-as-is[capricious/wayward/self-indulgent] seaslug-on/in moon-light!/?/ő/the/loh)   #520

moonshine
on a free spirit
sea slug

I have no idea whether this capricious creature basking in the light of the moon is a self-indulgent homo sapiens sleeping it off – *the moon shines / on a selfish sea slug / sleeping it off* – a lazy sea slug imagined to sleep whenever it likes by a sleep-loving poet, or a *bona fide* holothurian working at "mai pehsu" (my pace), as Japanese call it when one does something as slowly as one likes!

人 起 す や う に し て 見 る 沙 セ ン (口片+巽) 哉 青 藍
hito okosu yô ni shitemiru sasen kana – seiran (1765)
(man/person/someone wake-up like-as do-try sea-slug tis!/?/ő/the)   #521

the sea slug

trying to
wake it as you would
a human

The word used for "sea slug" here is *sasen,* literally "sand-sifter."[1] → It is the only poem I have read with the term.   It also may be the oldest *Sleeping Sea Slug.*   I imagine someone shaking, poking,

1. *Moonshine and Sea Slugs* If fish are more active in the full moon, one might wonder why they would breed then. Apparently, simultaneous and obvious broadcast makes sense, not only for the reasons I have already hypothesized, but because the spawn is "chemically protected" (AK). That is to say, a fish that swallows some, won't want to swallow more.

pinching and splashing water on it as they might to wake a heavy sleeper.   When we consider the fact that sea slugs *do* sleep during the day, the haiku has it just right. A.K. points out, however, that asleep they react to a strong poke identically to the way they respond when awake (which makes me wonder if we could think of their time awake as sleep-walking). A Japanese friend thinks the poem more likely to refer to someone who is comatose. Possibly. Keigu could not resist paraversing –

見 る 度 に 起 し た く な る 海 鼠 子 か な 敬 愚
miru tabi ni okoshitakunaru namako kana – keigu
(see/ing-time/instance-at, wake-up-want-become seaslug/?/ó/the/loh)

#522

sea slugs

every time
i see one i want
to awaken it!

~

seeing a slug
we can't help wanting
to wake it up

寝 濃 そ の 胸 に な ま こ ぞ 置 ひ て 行 く 敬 愚
negoi [2] *sono mune ni namako zo oite yuku* – keigu
(sleep-heavy[sleepyhead/lazybones] that chest-on seaslug [+exclam] placing-go)

#523

returning home
after putting a sea slug
on sleepyhead's chest

lazybone

he sleeps in
i leave a sea slug
on his chest

It is fine to justify multiple translations where I cannot read the mind of the poet. But Keigu is me and I still can't read his mind. He/I imagine/s an early rising poet bringing home a sea slug early in the morning and leaving it on the chest of a buddy with a hang-over and he also imagines himself doing it.

濤 聴 い て 桶 の 眠 り の 海 鼠 た ち 高 野 寒 甫
nami kiite oke no nemuri no namakotachi – takano kanpo (1973)
(waves/sea/ocean hearing tub's/s' sleepy/ing seaslugs)

#524

sleepy slugs
in a tub listening
to the surf

← **1. Sand-Sifter** This term not in the 20 volume OJD dates back at least to a book called "*Rain-Channel Jottings*" (雨 航 雑 録) written between 1716-1735, according to an index of terms gathered by Arakawa (ndh).   With a 1679 haiku where *no dust/dirt is allowed on a sea slug* and a 1759 haiku where *sea slugs are sucked up by debris*, it would seem that the idea of the sea slug as a sand-eater (something obvious to whoever prepares the guts.) may well have been present in the popular culture.
2. Negoi. This old term common in *senryu* (usually describing maids who sleep so soundly they have no idea how many men played with them as they slept) is now obsolete. Keigu thinks it is wonderful to have a term for people who have trouble waking from sleep and would like to revive it.

This modern haiku is delightful in the original and unsatisfactory, I fear, in any translation. The use of a plural indicator *tachi,* usually reserved for humans or pets, for sea slugs endears them and the scene to us and I think of the satisfaction embodied by the animal appearing in the next, old haiku:

似 た 物 と 猫 も 見 て 居 る 海 鼠 か な 柳 居
nita mono to neko mo miteiru namako kana – ryûkyo (1694-1748)
(similar-things/ones-as cat-too looking sea slug!/?/ó/the/loh)   #525

two of a kind	***zzzzzzzz***
my old cat	the sea slug:
seems to recognize	it would seem our cat
the sea slug	is of its ilk

Although I had taken thousands of photos of sleeping cats and made hundreds of drawings, I might have failed to catch the meaning of this poem without the help of KS. I was thinking more of the name of the sea-slug: *"sea-mouse"* and imagining a cat stalking one in the kitchen. But the secret lay more with the cat, for one popular etymology of *neko,* is "sleep-ling." Imagine an old cat that spends most of its time motionless. The grammar permits one to read the seeming/seeing either way.

鈍 り て は 海 鼠 の ご と く 日 向 ぼ こ 高 沢 良 一
niburite wa namako no gotoku hinataboko – takasawa yoshikazu (2002)
(blunted/weakened-as-for, seaslug-like sun-bathing)   #526

out of form
i lie about sunbathing
a sea slug

Unless one belongs to the Occident where writing haiku, playing *go* and other intelligent forms of leisure have been replaced by body-centric activities such as working-out and sun-bathing (people who do one, generally do they other, for it is part of the same brainlessness syndrome), no one wastes their time sunbathing, unless they have been incapacitated for more interesting activity. The poet (see *"Sick Sea Slugs"* in the *Sundry* chapter) has undergone operations on his heart, so his lying about like a sea slug is nothing to be ashamed of. Since, he likes sea slugs, the identification was, no doubt a boost for his morale.

大 鼾 そ し れ ば う ご く 生 海 鼠 哉 蕪 村
ôibiki soshireba ugoku namako kana – buson (1750)
(big snore, cuss [out him] if, moves: sea slug!/?/ó/the/this/loh)   #527

the drunken guest	***midnight experiment***
loud snores	mr. snoreloud:
cuss him and he twitches	cuss out a sea slug
like a sea slug	and he squirms!

I have never heard a sea slug snore. Buson has the first sleeping sea slug that is human beyond doubt. Perhaps this person is drunken, but he might just be a very heavy sleeper. The vernacular detail – cussing and getting a movement from it – is masterful and this haiku (not *senryu,* for it does aim at a *type* of person (bachelor/maid/husband/wife/doctor/etc.)) deserves more attention than it has received.

山 妻 の 海 鼠 食 う た る 高 い び き 高沢良一
sansai no namako kuutaru takaibiki – takasawa yoshikazu (2003)

#528

(mountain-wife[self-depreciative term] seaslug eats/ate loud-snores)

how loudly
my wife snores after
eating sea slug

the loud snores
of my slug-eating
old lady

We encountered Japanese-style self(family-included)-depreciation with Sôseki's sea slug baby. The *mountain* in "mountain wife" means "country" – a nuance something like the American *hillbilly* – and is a more polite expression than the once usual, now increasingly old-fashioned, "foolish-wife" (*gusai*). Before looking up the term in the dictionary, I made a (wrong) guess translation: *the loud snoring of a mountain witch who ate up a sea cucumber.* The *old wife + sea slug* haiku is common, for *namako,* like drinking, was traditionally indulged in by women only after they lost their bloom. We may guess that the drink and aging are more responsible than the food for the loud snoring, but Takasawa's poem wittily makes it seem as though his wife caught the sleepy nature of the sea slug. Since Takasawa loves sea slugs, I think this juxtaposition is more loving than it otherwise might seem!

眠 た い や 吾 が 出 直 せ ば 大 海 鼠 敬愚
nemutai ya a ga denaoseba ônamako – keigu

#529

(sleepy! i reborn-if/when: big sea slug)

always sleepy
in my next life, let me be
a sea slug!

Real sleeping sea slugs do not look uncomfortable. They just lie there. And people who are tired presumably identify their deepest desires with them. But, I really think there must be an old poem out there something like Keigu's. There is one that goes: "what i thought / part of a tree branch: / a sea slug!" (*ki no hashi no yô ni omoeba namako kana* – otsuyû (1670-1739) 木 の は し の や う に 思 へ は 海 鼠 哉 乙 由). But Japanese didn't "sleep like logs;" they slept "like mud." The most positive old sleeping sea slug haiku I know of was written, most appropriately by a poet named "big+dream":

#530（上）

着 せ 合 て 余 念 な く 寝 し 海 鼠 哉 大 夢
kiseotte yonen naku ineshi namako kana – taimu (1793-1874)

#531

(wearing-meet/together extra-thought-not [engrossed in] sleeping sea slug!/?/ó/the/loh)

counterpane

covering each other
totally engrossed in sleep
sea cucumbers

sleeper and slept-in

each the other's quilt
sea slugs give undivided
attention to sleep

sea slug still-life

each the other's
cover, lying in the arms
of morpheus

sea slugs
lost in undivided
sleep

"Wearing" suggests *futon*. When the sleeping sea slug flattens out a little it can resemble *futon* or *dotera,* thick clothing-as-quilt. If a single sea slug is a lonely sight, a cluster looks comfortable. On first reading – not included in the translations – I failed to appreciate this as a straight sea slug poem.[1]

市 へ 出 て 未 た 目 の 覚 め ぬ 生 海 鼠 哉　春 波

ichi e dete mada me no samenu namako kana – shunpa (1774)

(market-to going/appear, still eyes awake-not sea slug!/?/ǒ)   #523

sleeping in

off to market
with eyes yet to open
sea slugs

god, is it early!

the fish-market
still too sleepy to see
sea slug me!

two of a kind

at the market
the sea slugs and i
still asleep

I couldn't fit the delightful ambiguity of the original into a single translation without making it too obvious (my third version). Old-fashioned fish markets are the same everywhere in the world: they open before dawn. The poet has also incorporated the structure and, by suggestion, some of the meaning, of an earlier poem by Kitô about one of the first signs of spring: "leaving the *kotatsu* / my eyes still half-asleep / (spring) mist (bleariness)!" (*kotatsu dete mada me-no samenu kasumi kana*). A *kotatsu* is a skirted table over a heater where indoor people snooze through the winter.[2]

糶 声 に 何 か 呟 く 海 鼠 か な　大 橋 敦 子

serigoe ni nani ka tsubuyaku namako kana – ôhashi atsuko (contemp)

(auction-voice-in, something mumbling: namako!/?/ǒ/the/it's/they're)   #533

the discovery

an auctioneer
what is he mumbling?
"sea slugs!"

海 鼠 舟 ら し ゆ る や か に 漕 ぎ う つ り　魚 井 苔 石

namakobunerashi yuruyaka ni kogiutsuri – gyoi taiseki? (contemp)

(seaslug-boat/s-like[resembling/~ish] slowly/loosely paddle/rowing-move/drift)   #534

something like
a sea slug boat slowly
rowing around

1. *On First Reading* With haiku so much is left unsaid that one can go back time again and find something new. This is especially true for a foreigner with imperfect knowledge of Japanese, but it also holds for most Japanese, to whom their own past is a foreign country. KS's explanation taught me I misread the meaning of "extra/ remaining-thought-not" (*yonen-naku*), when I read it as "abandoned [to sleep]" and assumed an allusion to a certain mid-winter group-sleep with what we would now call "free-sex." Now, *another* Japanese reader, less expert to be sure, advises me to remember that the sea slug could be a metaphor for sleeping people . . . .

2. *Kotatsu Wisdom* If I may build upon Watts, central heating is wasteful, for it is like carpeting the ground rather than making sandals to cover the sole of the foot alone. Moreover, it encourages movement within a house, while the *kotatsu* encourages one to sit still, thus conserving one's own energy – like a sea slug – as well as fossil fuel. More *kotatsu* thoughts in IPOOH-winter-1-*kotatsu*.

The first haiku doesn't actually mention sleepiness, but we know that fish auctions take place at dawn, so the author is probably only half awake. Although the haiku is modern in specifying an auctioneer,[1] the poet's achievement is traditional: she has found a new sense, *sound*, to fit the stuporous/nebulous nature of the slug. Before finding the two haiku that follow below, I wrote that *"if you can see that this is no sheer coincidence and comprehend why the sea slug could not be replaced by, say, sea bream in this poem, you have grasped what old-style haiku is all about."* Likewise, for the second haiku, above. If you understand why the vaguely perceived slow-moving boat can only be a slugger – where something like a tuna trawler would be meaningless – you have got it.

糶 声 に 目 醒 め て 桶 の 海 鼠 か な 橋 本 鶏 二
serigoe ni mesamete oke no namako kana – hashimoto keiji (1988)
(auction-voice-by, awakened tub's/s' seaslug/s!/?/ó/the/loh)

#535

awakened
by the auction: a tub
of sea slugs

海 鼠 に は 大 き す ぎ た る 糶 の 声 長 束 澄 江
namako ni wa ôkisugitaru seri no koe – nagatsuka sumie (1993)
(seaslug/s-as-for, large-excessive auction-voice)

#536

the voice of
the auctioneer's too loud
for sea slugs!

Or, rather, too loud for the *metaphorical sea slug* of haiku. Unless one is to assume that the poets were inspired by each other's work, which I think highly unlikely,[2] the similarity of the three auction poems was born of an identical aim to combine symbolic rightness with reality.

静 か さ の き の ふ に 同 じ 海 鼠 哉 成 美
shizukasa no kinô ni onaji namako kana – seibi (1748-1816)
(quietness/calmness' yesterday-as same sea-slug/s!/?/ó/hoh)

#537

soothing sight	*still-life*	*day two*
a calm bay the sea slugs today, just like yesterday	dawn calm the same sea slug as yesterday	morning calm sea slugs where they were yesterday

1. *Auctioneering in Japan*_ There are a half a dozen types of traditional auctions in Japan. The loudest, which was apparently learned from the West, is popularly called "banana-rapping" (*banana-tataki*) and is done for fun at street festivals, where ordinary people bid for the comically auctioned fruit. Another is the silent auction, where men strike bargains two-by-two using hand-signals invisible to onlookers because their hands do their talking within a specially tailored black sleeve! Unfortunately for haiku, this mode of auction most befitting the silent sea slug is almost obsolete and only remains in a single market for . . . blowfish!
2. *Plagarism in Haiku* Poets, unlike historians or novelists, rarely plagiarize. That may not have been true when poets were the lions of society, but if it happens today, I have not heard of it. Old haiku are often misattributed because sources can be wrong or mistakes made when they are copied – the manner in which poems are attributed may be confusing, and I, for one, have made many mistakes – so even when identical poems are found attributed to two poets, plagiarizing is seldom considered. Moreover, as I have already written, the practice of taking large parts of other's poems and building on them was once considered laudable. This is not true today, so I assume the above poems were independently conceived.

This elegantly simple haiku by Issa's patron and teacher Seibi describes something I have seen or think I have seen. I believe it is dawn and the sea slug, or sea slugs – number them as you will – dimly seen from the shore embody the still drowsy world (even if, in reality, the sandman has just transferred the sand from our eyes to the sea slugs'!).   The "same" (*onaji*) is problematic, for it applies both to the setting and the sea slug/s. For lack of similar grammar – or, perhaps, because of my lack of skill – I had to split the ambiguity into multiple clear translations. There is also a slight possibility that Seibi not talking about sea slugs at all, but was only describing nebulous *Sea Slug Weather* (next chapter)

ほ の ぼ の と 明 石 が 浦 の な ま こ 哉 　一 茶

honobono to akashigaura no namako kana – issa (1758-1823)

(dimly akashi=bright=visible-bay's[=behind] sea slug!/?/ŏ/the/loh)   #538

the bay at dawn

off akashi
a dim constellation
of sea slugs

a misty morning

dimly resting
in the bay of akashi
sea slugs

I worked to recreate poetry where none could be translated – the psychological mimesis, *honobono* is particularly unmatchable – because Issa's original is very interesting *given that the reader can catch the allusions*. But, today, I fear that not even most Japanese can do that. [1] Many will know that the first 12 syllabets come from the famous KOKINSHU *waka* #409, officially by Anonymous but often credited to Kakinomoto Hitomaro, Japan's most revered ancient poet.   In this *waka*, a boat is watched with longing as it rows away through the mist, disappearing from sight behind the islands of Akashino[ga]ura, literally "bright=visible-rock-bay" (*honobono-to akashi-no-ura-no-asa-giri-ni shima-gakure-yuku fune oshi-zo omou*). [2]   They may associate the place with the exile of Shining (Hikaru) Prince Genji of the TALES OF GENJI, which was written shortly after the poem was published in the KOKINSHU. Akashigaura is associated with *sleepy rural life,* as depicted by the following poems by Buson and Shiki, respectively, about the neighboring town of Suma: "a urine-stained quilt / drying on the line [3] – / suma village" (trans. Hass:HE (*ibari seshi futon hoshitari suma no sato* – bzs); "glimpses of men / taking noon-time naps / country suma" (*hirune suru hito mo mietari suma no sato* – szs, meiji 31).

1. *Many Japanese* Since writing those words, I have found out that very few Japanese under fifty recognize the allusion. Even Starfield had not picked up on it. After I told him, he checked in a library and found only one of eight books containing the *honobono* poem had a note about the once universally known *waka* in it. I presume that the last generation felt no note necessary and that editors from the new one don't know what they miss.

2. *The Honobono Waka* According to the earliest glosses, the boat carried the body of an Imperial Prince who died at age nineteen. LC writes that because the image and the language of the poem are so beautiful, it was destined to became very popular and, for that reason, a later note claims it was freed from the taboos associated with being a "mourning poem," by being placed in the "travel" section of the *Kokinshû* anthology (kks).

3. *Drying on the Line* Hass has the right beat and wording in most of his translations, but far more notes are needed. Japanese did not and usually still do not dry clothing, much less ten or twenty pound *futon* on lines. They use poles, once bamboo, now usually aluminum. Someone's haiku has cats in heat tight-roping upon them.

What contemporary Japanese rarely know is that, in Issa's day, the poem attributed to Hitomaro, his name corrupted to Hitomaru,[1] was used as *an alarm clock!* The first half of the poem was recited aloud (3 times, according to netted information) before falling asleep – presumably, all that dimness would hypnotize the reader and work as a sleeping pill, too! – with the intention of properly finishing the poem (3 times, again) when it woke the sleeper at the crack of dawn. This was useful on New Year's Eve when one wanted to see the Sun rise or, for getting up early to claim a good place at a blossom-viewing or catch the start of an all-day play. An early *senryu*: "shaming / mister hitomaru / a heavy sleeper" (*hitomaru-ni haji-o kakaseru negoi koto* – goraku (五楽). Other *senryu*, which I have misplaced, joke about men taking Hitomaru along as an alarum (lit. *makura-dokei*, "pillow-clock") when surreptitiously sleeping with the lord's ladies, or of poor temples – temples were usually in charge of time-keeping for the town – unable to afford anything better than the help of Hitomaru, etc.

With this background, can you see how marvelous Issa's largely borrowed poem is? How it depicts sea slugs seen hazily through the smooth morning sea surface simply by adding "sea slug/s 'tis (*kana*)" to the unchanged opening words (the "ga" vs "no" difference is only a matter of style) of an old poem, simultaneously evoking the sleepy sea slug and a hint of longing? The "visible=bright" name of the place (Akashi) is also a perfect foil for the dark and sightless sea slugs. A *kyôka,* or "crazy-verse" written by a poet only identified as "a blind man," dated not long after Issa's poem, and supposedly composed/read after thrice reciting the famous *honobono* poem at a memorial service on Hitomaro's deathday at the Hitomaro shrine, shows how important pun was in an age when they were not only "appreciated" but *taken seriously*:   "If the god of *akashi*=visibility is even dimly true to his name, then show it to me, too: the grave of hitomaru!" (*honobono to makoto akashi no kami naraba ware ni mo miseyo hitomaru no zuka.*)

仄 々 と 明 石 ち じ み の 小 傾 城　武 玉 川

honobono to akashi chijimi-no ko-keisei – mutamagawa 18
(dimly akashi/showing/glowing corbicula=crepe's small prostitute/beauty)

dimly seen
akashi corbicula:
young tarts!

1. *Hitomaro to Hitomaru: What's in a Name?* The poems of Kakinomoto Hitomaro are generally considered the most beautiful in the MANYOSHU. By the start of the Heian era, he was revered as a *sei,* a guardian saint of poetry. This is most famously reflected by the introduction to the KOKINSHÛ, yet the same anthology does not give him credit for the *honobono* poem. According to a Kamakura (1185-1333) source (the *jikkinsho setsuwashû*), in the early 12th century, Hitomaro appeared in the dream of Fujiwara Kanefusa, who hired a painter to depict what he saw. Kanefusa's poetry miraculously improved and soon Hitomaro's picture, with the *honobono* poem added to it, was enshrined and the guardian saint of poetry apotheosized (Presumably, things like this regained the poem for Hitomaro). Though he shared the shrine with two other gods of divine origin, the folk tradition soon turned him into the singular mighty deity Hitomaru-daimyôjin. With his name corrupted to "Hitomaru," meaning "man/person" or "man-boat," it punned as *hi-tomaru* or "fire-stop" and *hito-umaru* or "person-birth," so that his poetic

power expanded to fire-protection and easy-childbirth in the Edo era (Googled sources).

2. *Poetic Charm Alarm Senryu* Here are half of the senryu found on a web site: "ole hitomaru / flowers as the waking-watch / for our plays" (*hitomaru wa hana ya shibai no okishiban* – Y-121-22 – Perhaps he was also used to wake up people to leave plays?); "vaguely seen / the hitomaru shrine / like an arrow" (*honobono to hitomarudô o ya no gotoshi* ---Y(留拾 遺 9-1 – Time flew like an arrow in Japan, too, but I am not sure what the poem means); "waking up / by akashiura until / the end of the world" (*masse made akashiura de mezamashi* – Y 13-16) – the "end of the world" meaning the corrupt age in which the poet lived. Scholars suppose the *honobono* poem was originally a poem sending off a dead three year-old emperor, but none of the senryu care about that. The idea of a poem as an alarm clock and the sheer popularity of the old poem (eg. "the boat vanishes / but the old song sure / stays around!" (*kakureyuku fune kakurenaki mi uta nari* – Y 留 54-31 (From a googled "Komazawa_u ac:jp" site：ほのぼのと明石＋川柳 in Japanese)

Again, we meet these tiny shells called *shijimi* (*chijimi* is a variant) identified with the female privates, here doubling for crepe,[1] imported Chinese cloth associated with seduction, partially hiding to better reveal a woman's charms. *Keisei* literally reads "tip[-over]-castle," and means a beautiful prostitute with the power of Joshua (they are sometimes even called *keikoku*, or "tip-country!"). Being a *senryu*, the shells metaphor the girls, rather than vice-versa, as would be more likely for haiku.   Rereading this *senryu*, it suddenly occurred to me that Issa's poem could also suggest the opposite of this pretty sight: the dark-skinned men whom Sei Shonagon desired not to see through thin garments and the ugly men she thought should not be seen lying down, period.[2]

Despite the plentiful association I concoct (?), Issa's poem is so simple that it is amazing no one wrote the poem earlier. Of course, that is precisely the mark of a masterpiece. Done, it looks easy. The poem, however, does not even make the standard selection of his work (*Issa Kushû*: Iwanami). That may be because twentieth-century editors fail to recognize that incorporating large chunks of old poems does not *lessen* the worth of the haiku, but *increases* it, by virtue of the allusions gained thereby. True, there is humor in sea slugs replacing boats. Yet, does that change the aptness of every single word in Issa's haiku?   It is a big mistake to deep-six this sort of poem as parody (a word synonymous with worthless).[3]   Adaptation is *not* parody.   It only *looks like* parody.

And this was where the story ended until I found another *waka* (*Fugakushû* #923) by a losing general on the run, where the brightness of the name Akashigaura notwithstanding, his thoughts would not brighten.   If Issa knew that story, he may well have embodied these feelings in his sea slugs, but I am going to let it sleep![4]

うすずみに寒の海鼠の深ねむり　治司

usuzumi ni kan no namako no fukunemuri – haruji? (contemp)
(thin-ink[colored-water]-in, cold[season]'s seaslug/s deep-sleep)   #539

in thin ink
a cold-spell sea slug
fast asleep

#540

1. *Crepe and Sea Slugs* There is another connection here perhaps irrelevant to reading the poem; to wit: foreign exchange earned by exporting ugly sea slug=male-part paid for the titillating diaphanous fabrics imported from China and here identified with pretty little shellfish=female-part.

2. *Ugly Dark Bodies* In *The Pillow Book of Sei Shônagon,* under "Things That are Unpleasant to See" we find "a dark-skinned person looks very ugly in an unlined robe of stiff silk" and "ugly men should sleep only at night, for they cannnot be seen in the dark and, besides most people are in bed themselves. But they should get up at the crack of dawn, so that no one has to see them lying down."(Ivan Morris trans).   Speaking of Sei Shônagon, I cannot help but haiku: "how i'd love / to send sei shônagon / a sea slug!"(少納言に海鼠送りたい心あり ── そう、かの海苔のお伝えに腹立たしくなった男に代わって、「海苔ならば返事に目がない海鼠でも」仕返し（？）たかった。「この口の責任取れと海鼠かな」と女神の責任を負わしてみたら面白い。

3. *Parody and Honka-dori*   In an article (*Nagano*:219:2001) where Maruyama replied to some questions of mine on Issa's sea slug poems,

he actually used the word "parody" to describe the *honobono* poem. Since Japanese tend to overuse the term "parody" (as a Western term, they fancy it can mean whatever they want it to), I doubt he meant it precisely, but it still hints at why the poem was not included in his selection. There *are* haikai parody of the *honobono waka.*. One, of anonymous authorship (Teitoku, perhaps?), puns on Hitomaru as *hitomarumi* or, seeing people completely (i.e., their nakedness) dimly glowing in the moonlight (*honobono to tsukiya akashi no hito marumi* in Konzanshû:1651)). Issa's is *not* such. Maruyama pointed out one thing I missed. Since the slugs sub for the boat that disappears from sight, the intent might be to how hidden, how out-of-the-way the slugs are. A final note (mine): by modern standards, the poem (and Issa's other sea slug poems) might also be criticized for artificiality: Issa was nowhere near Akashigaura when the poem was written.

3. *If Issa* The scholar might ask if it is responsible to hazard such a guess without even checking to see whether Issa may have read the *Fugakushû*.   I would reply that *a guess is a guess, why not?* If the scholar cares to check further fine. The author can live with not knowing.

While sea slugs off the central seashores of Japan do not hibernate, they do in the North; but, in the absence of a place, we may assume the poem is a naïve image of something seen in real life, a painting – thin *sumi* can mean either a grey wash or water looking like it – or a product of the poet's imagination.

薄 濁 る 底 に な ま こ は 眠 る ご と　高 井 去 私
usunigoru soko ni namako wa nemuru goto – takai kyoshi (1997)
(thin-clouded bottom-on sea-slug-as-for sleeping-like/resembling)

#541

> on the slightly
> murky seabed, slugs
> seem asleep

The "like/resembling" was, no doubt intended for objectivity's sake: *they look like they are sleeping because they are so slow.* But, unless it was night, they really *were* asleep. Regardless, the "thinly clouded" is a touch of detail that makes the poem a good one.   Sea slugs do more sleeping in modern and contemporary haiku than in old haiku. I would guess that the long work-hours in twentieth-century Japan have something to do with this. If you worked 70-80 hrs per week (the case with the small companies I worked with (international comparisons of official company hours fail to catch the real situation), the sea-slug-as-sleep would seem like heaven incarnated. But there is also something about the atmosphere of the sea floor that makes us think "bed" and *sleep.* Modern Japanese do more diving than Edo era poets, and notice this.

海 鼠 突 く 銛 に 海 底 歪 ん だ り　有 風
namako tsuku mori ni kaitei yugandari – yûfû (mod)
(seaslug stab/bing gig-by seafloor distorts[sort-of])

#542

> the sea bed
> gets distorted by
> my slug gig

the ocean floor	the sea bottom
distorted by sea slug	a slug gig distorts it
stabbing gigs	now and then

海 鼠 な り 青 潮 の 底 揺 す れ る は　杉 田 智 栄 子
namako nari aoshio no soko yusureru wa – sugita chieko (contemp)
(sea-slug becomes: blue-tide's bottom sway/distort-as-for)

#543

blue-tide	*blue-tide*
that distortion	it's a sea-slug:
on the sea-floor?	the apparent wavering
a sea slug	on the sea-floor

The first haiku is sharp. As a gig reaches down it does seem to bring distortion with it; but the second haiku is truly remarkable. Had nothing – no clear mark – been down there, the mysterious motion of the water would not have been visible. (I imagine a difference in viscosity caused by a warmer current running over a still bottom layer, though I do not know why we can see it!) I think the slight distortion suggested by the "swaying" sea bottom suggests the dreamy state invented by Issa in the Akashigaura poem even better than murkiness.

ものぐさな雨に海鼠のかがやけり 穴井太

monogusana ame ni namako no kagayakeri – anai futoshi(contemp)
(idle/sluggish/indolent-rain-in seaslug's/s/s' shine/radiance/glitter/glow)   #544

the sea slug
looks radiant in this
drowsy rain

winter lullaby

in this *"old man*
is snoring!" rain how good
sea slug looks!

The poet, his metabolism stupefied by the cold drizzle, notes how it seems to improve the sea slug set outside in a tub. *Namako,* metaphysically the heart of this numbing chill, this winter somnolence, is in splendid form. (Actually, the rain would not feel good to the sea slug unless the salt water in its tub had evaporated enough to raise the salinity, but who cares about such details!) The second, admittedly ridiculous translation, points in the direction the chapter is heading.

大海鼠ひとを睡たくさせてゐる 牟田口吾鬼生

ônamako hito o nemutaku saseteiru – mutaguchi akio (2001)
(large-seaslug, people[obj] sleepy make/ing)   #545

a large sea slug
making us people
feel sleepy

Simply "a sea slug" might make one remonstrate, *of course. What else!* The "*large* sea slug"[1] → makes the haiku. There is something less obviously sleepy about largeness, as if we unconsciously pick up on the slower body-clock of large as opposed to small beasts. Large means low and the hypnotist always has a low voice. Keigu's reincarnation poem (written before reading Mutaguchi's) also specifies a large sea slug, although I did not English it. Here is an earlier *ônamako*:

大海鼠とろりと桶にうつしけり 白井冬青

ônamako torori to oke ni utsushikeri – shirai tôsei (mod)
(big-seaslug: ponderously/drowsily/gloppily? tub-in/to transfer[+finality])   #546

a large sea slug   a large slug
slides ponderously   slips heavily from
into the tub   tub to tub

torori to

drowsiness slides
from a bucket to a tub
a large sea slug

If this were a still-life, I would call it *Michelangelo's Dawn.* But it is not. The largeness translates from one language tub to another, but the mimesis – the molasses-in-movement of an adverb, *torori* – does *not*.

［催 眠 法 東 西 考］羊より一茶の海鼠いかがせん 敬愚

hitsuji yori issa no namako ikaga sen – keigu

#547

(sheep-rather-than, issa's seaslug/s how-about doing?)

soporifics east and west

forget sheep! [1]
how about counting
issa's sea-slugs?

眠られぬ夜には海鼠の数かぞふ 敬天

nemurarenu yo ni wa namako no kazu kazou – keiten

#548

(sleep-cannot night-on-as-for, seaslug's number count/ing)

<table>
<tr><td>a sleepless night
i count the number
of sea slugs</td><td>on those nights
when you can't sleep
count sea slugs</td></tr>
</table>

Awake or asleep, the sea slug seems unmoving to us. Our intellect tells us that all is relative and that to the slug, we must seem to fly about as fast as bullets. But it is almost impossible to *feel* this. We do not see ourselves as fast. We see them as slow. Some people, however, have become so sympathetic, so close to their charges, that I think it is clear they do understand from the heart. The happy creatures depicted below come from the pen of a man who has spent over a decade on "Taxing Problems," that is to say correctly identifying holothurians for the Royal BC Museum.

> They sprout from beneath rocks like orange carnations, ooze along the bottom at the speed of an hour hand, or slurp their way through rich organic mud. They are everywhere from the intertidal zone to the deepest parts of the ocean. Like a miniature herd of gnus trundling across the abyssal plains, they graze on the rich organic snow that has drifted down from above. (See Philip Lambert's article at http://rbcm.gov.bc.ca/nh_papers/taxing.html!)

Sublime is the only possible word for this magnificent moving image, this sea slug Shangri-La! I imagine it accompanied by loud classical music, whatever Captain Nemo – or was it Professor Beebe – listened to when he went down into the deep. *Hold your tears for the sea slug: the sea slug, thank you, has a life!*

#549

← **1.** *How Large is "Large"?* Most sea cucumbers that we notice from the shore or looking into the water from a boat are of cucumber dimension, though occasionally we see young ones that are only *gherkin*. Those who study sea cucumbers say they come in *all* lengths. The 1400-plus species of holothuroids measure in from 1 cm to 5m (A. Kerr). But measuring the length of a particular animal – something needed for ascertaining their growth rate – is not easy. "Frankly, measuring a holothurian is like trying to measure an accordion claims Conand [editor of *Beche de Mere Newsletter]*." (Catherine Malaval: *The Sea Cucumber Should Stay Under* (*"Liberation"* 25/1/94)) I would say harder than an accordion, because they only expand when they are relaxed or weak, not when you would measure them. A nineteenth century poet put it like this: "though you pull / it won't stretch a single inch: / the sea cucumber" (ひっぱれど一分も延び（ば？）ぬ海鼠哉　鳳朗 *hipparedo ichi-bu-mo nobanu namako kana* --- hôrô (1761-1845).   But the *namako* is not *all* sea cucumber, and I think that for *Apostichopus japonicus,* we could say anything larger than a large dill pickle is a large one.

2. *Counting Sheep in Japan.*   One of the 400+ channels on Japan's incredible cable radio (*yûsen*) has nothing but a monotonous voice counting sheep in Japanese, all day long!   I never learned how high the count goes because I could not endure more than a few sheep at a time! Other channels include *bug calls* all day, *steam locomotives* all day, *Elvis* all day, and . . . you name it!

20
<u>the nebulous sea slug</u>

生 海 鼠 哉 夜 か 明 け た や ら 暮 れ た や ら 露 川
namako kana yo ga aketa yara kureta yara – rosen (1660-1743)
(seaslug/s!/?/ó/the/a/i'm/: night has brightened [just dawned]perhaps? [or, day] darkened perhaps?)   #550

the witching hour

hoh, sea slugs!
are you creatures of dusk
or early dawn?

the vector of grey

sea slug time:
is it the dawning
or the dusk?

coming to

sea slug me
i cannot tell if it is
dusk or dawn!

edo identity

a sea slug world:
are we in our dawn,
or in our dusk?

dusk/dawn

these sea slugs!
are they half-asleep
or half-awake?

ambiguity

are sea slugs
drowsily stirring or
starting to nod?

mukashi otoko

dawn or dusk?
he don't know: the gallant
sea slug man!

Because English lacks a verb for the dusk, a straight translation – *sea slug/s! has it dawned or dusked?* – is hopeless. I hope at least one of my readings (two of which fit the last chapter better and one, the last, which describes the spineless lover of *The Tale of Ise* described elsewhere) matches the intent of the poet whose pen name translates "dew-river." This may be the first text to suggest the sea slug might have a nominal role in meteorology. Later, Seibi and Issa's sleepy sea slug poems indirectly link the *namako* to a calm or misty atmosphere, but the first person to come right out and say that a gentle nebulous day was *sea slug weather* was the most prolific author of haiku on *namako*, Shiki.

晴 れ も せ ず 雪 に も な ら ず 海 鼠 か な 子 規
hare mo sezu yuki ni mo narazu namako kana – shiki (1867-1902)
(clear does-not, snow-too become-not seaslug!/?/ó/the)   #551

nebulous

won't clear
won't snow: call it
"sea slug!"

weather-right food

it won't clear
yet won't snow, so let's
eat sea slug!

I have no idea whether my second reading is the reality-link one expects with haiku, but the next haiku, also by Shiki, suggests that the first reading may be all of it.

風 も な し 海 鼠 日 和 の 薄 曇 り 子 規

kaze mo nashi namakobiyori no usugumori – shiki

#552   (wind too not, seaslug calm's light-cloudiness)

weather report

a windless
and lightly overcast
sea slug calm

overcast

windless
balmy sea slug
weather

The *hiyori* (*biyori*) is hard to translate. It is written with the Chinese characters for "peace" and "day" and usually denotes a magically calm and clear fall or early winter day. In such weather, the sky is blue. Here, Shiki is trying to expand the word's usage. In this, he had a predecessor. Riyu (KKM), a poet of Basho's era, called a Spring-time *hiyori* – usually called simply a "spring-day" (*harubi*) – a "dumpling-*biyori*," i.e., : "on a steaming / dumpling-calm day: / mountain cherries!" (*mushi tatsuru manju-biyori ya yamazakura*).   I doubt if my English captures the steam wafting up – a sultry, shimmering haze – from the soft Chinese bun with a heart of meat, nor the fact that merely saying "mountain cherries" means (to the Japanese reader) that the trees are in blossom. The mountain cherries bloom relatively late, well into the Spring. Since there were food concessions in the blossom-viewing areas, the dumplings may have been for real. But, even so, they embody the entire scene, which in paraverse becomes: *cherries in bloom / haze wafts gently up from / a dumpling hill.* (This poem and Shiki's improve one another and should be back-to-back on a set of haiku cards.[1]) I doubt, however, that the polymath Shiki was looking back. He probably knew some of the strange English expressions used for clouds: mackerel, herring, and perhaps, unless it was already obsolete, calico. He may have asked himself, *Hell, how about a formless sky? A sea slug sky!*

---

1. Haiku Cards   There is a set of cards with a famous selection of 100 *waka* poems (each with a painting of the poet) called the *Hyakunin Isshû* . It has the first syllabet of each poem on the back from which players attempt to recite the poem. The game was traditionally played on New Year's day, girls prefer it and there are countless *senryu* pointing out the trivia such as how many women are in it, how many blind poets and so forth. That is all I know. (If an earlier generation could sometimes complete a song from one syllabet, today it is different, for OM writes: "The caller would recite the first two paragraphs (5-7), but the fast takers were able to pick the card up at first 5 syllables.") But *I have never heard of a haiku set of cards.* As far as I know, it is my idea. I would suggest placing two thematically complementary poems on the reverse side of a card, so that one could try to guess one from the other; or, chose a haiku for each phenomenon, where the play would involve arranging the cards in the correct seasonal order. There could also be droll sets matching a light haiku with a senryu, an elegant set of good haiku, and, for some poets, even one-wo/man sets.

肩 の 荷 を お ろ し て 海 鼠 日 和 か な　や ん ま

kata no ni o oroshite namakobiyori kana – yanma (contemp)

shoulder/s load/burden put/ting down, seaslug-clearday!/?/ó/'tis)

#553

a fine grey day

with the weight
off my shoulders, gentle
sea slug weather

一 段 落 つ き し 海 鼠 の 日 和 か な　黒 坂 晴 生

ichidanraku tsukishi namakobiyori kana – kurozaka haruo? (2002)

(one-rung[an episode of life]calms-setles, seaslug-clearday!/?/ó/a)

#554

fine weather

after things
finally calm down
a sea slug day

Shiki's expression failed to make the dictionary, but there is still hope, for I found these two recent haiku. Both were accompanied by comment. About the first, "I, too, am in a recently retired soft-bodied animal [translates as "mollusk," which is technically wrong but matches "sea slug!"] condition and share the poet's feelings." In the second, the poet himself says the net haiku party/contest/jam has ended without major foul-up, his spouse has recovered and is out of the hospital and the sky suggests snow – that strictly speaking it is not balmy spring-in-winter weather, but that he *feels* like it is. Shiki's sea slug weather has given birth to the concept of peaceful but cloudy rather than clear bliss.

を り を り に こ ぼ す 霰 や 海 鼠 売　黙 斗

oriori ni kobosu arare ya namakouri – mokuto (1932)

(time-time falls hail[subj]: seaslug-seller)

#555

cold chaos

now and then
hail falls on the vendor
of sea slugs

The bits of hail someway suggest the little nuggets of hardness found in the sea slug. But, perhaps more important they fall from an unsettled sky, a chaos of the sort identified with this most primordial of foods. The poem does not English well for "scattered" will only work in front of showers, not hail.

夕 さ れ ば 海 は し ぐ れ ぬ 海 鼠 売　富 岡 掬 池 路

yû sareba umi wa shigurenu namako uri – tomioka kikuchiro (1989)

(dusk becoming sea-as-for *shigure* [winter rain] falls, seaslug-seller)

#556

as dusk falls
it rains out at sea
a slug vendor

Like the hail, before, and Shiki's cloudiness, this, too, is *sea slug weather,* for the *shigure,* a winter drizzle (shower/squall depending on context) is, as mentioned before, cold and gloomy – just what the ascetic poet demanded.

ひろごりて 時 雨 ご こ ろ の 海 鼠 か な 永 田 耕 衣

hirogorite shiguregokoro no namako kana – nagata koi (mod)

#557   (spreading/sprawling, *shigure*[winter rain]heart/mind/soul/essence's seaslug!/?/ǒ/the/that/behold)

the sea slug
sprawling out the heart
of winter rain

the sea slug
sprawling out, at home
in the *shigure*

for alan watts

sprawled out
that sea slug is *it*
the cold rain

Until modernity marginalized the asceticism that was at the heart of Bashô school haikai – inherited from older Buddhist poetry – the cold rain was one of a dozen most haiku'ed themes. [1] There are 1,400 *shigure* haiku in Shiki's Categorical (brhz) alone! It reminds us that life, in the words of Saigyô (1118-1190), is but *a temporary shelter from the cold rain,* itself, the essence of temporality [2] when it chills the poet, ideally a recluse in a leaky hut, to the bone and tests his or her very soul.   Nagata's poem does great honor to the sea slug.

寒 な ま こ わ れ の こ の め は 市 場 よ り 時 雨 に ぬ れ て 妻 の 買 ひ 来 ぬ 吉 富 正 名

kannamako ware no konomeba ichiba yori shigure ni nurete tsuma no kaikonu – yoshitomi shômei (mod)

(cold[season]-seaslug, my wishing-if/when market/town-from *shigure*[winter rain]-in wet, wife/mate's buying-come)

#558

if i desire
cold season sea slug
my woman
will go to town for it
getting wet in the rain

The warm-hearted wife of this poet will get as wet and as cold as a sea slug to buy one. [3] The "cold season" is my Englishing of *kan,* the coldest two weeks of the year (according to the calendar). Needless to say, this is the same poetic "time-rain," or, *shigure,* and the whole poem is painted in what we might call a *namako* wash.

1. *A Dozen Haiku Themes* If I may hazard a guess, the other eleven themes that drew the largest number of poems in old haiku are: cherry-blossoms, the (fall) moon, plum blossoms, the cuckoo (*hototogisu*), the snow, the star-lovers, chrysanthemum, oppressive heat, cool evenings, colored leaves and the coming of spring.

2. *The Time-Rain* The *shigure* is generally writen with Chinese characters meaning "time+rain." Whether that means it stays a long time or is in and out in a jiffy, I do not know. With so much written about this rain, it has gathered may interesting

metaphors, some of micturation, the best of which is by Bashô – it has us imagine a dog wandering about the sky lifting its leg here and there, sometimes showering heavily and sometimes hardly squeezing out a drop – and inspired Santôka to write one of the shortest haiku ever written: is this sound / the time-rain? = おとはしぐれか (其中庵便り) (See IPOOH-Winter-shigure for more) Alan Watts once asked "What *is* this 'it' that rains?" *Indeed.*

3. *Working the Wife* Cruel? No, it makes sense, for a man is worse in bed for exercise, a woman, better.

ひ と し ぐ れ 過 ぎ た る 海 鼠 噛 み に け り 鷲 谷 七 菜 子
hito shigure sugitaru namako kaminikeri – washitani nanako (1978)
(one *shigure*[cold winter rain] passes, seaslug chewing-up [finality or tenacity])   #559

i keep chewing
sea slug as a cold rain
comes and goes

The heart of the poem is the simple equation of sea slug and *shigure*. It is possible the sound of the shower, the same cold time-rain falling on the dead leaves or tiles suggests the sound of chewing, but we cannot *know* that. I am not sure if the finality implied by the ~*keri* ending means that the sea slug is completely chewed up in the space of the rain's passage, if the idea of the is more to bring out the tenacity of the chewer (how engrossed she is in her activity or her thoughts the whole while), or if it means she chewed right through the *shigure,* as my translation suggests.

海 鼠 噛 む 遠 き 暮 天 の 波 を 見 て 飯 田 龍 太
namako kamu tôki bôten no nami o mite – iida ryûta (mod)
(sea slug chew, far dusk sky's waves seeing)   #560

chewing sea slug   chewing slug
i see the white-caps   i see waves far off
distant at dusk   in the dusk

Perhaps the most commonly anthologized of all post-WWII sea slug haiku, this, like some of the others we have seen, might fit as well if not better with the *Chewy Sea Slugs* ; but I put it here, because it is *also* the best depiction of the dim dusky sea slug atmosphere I know of.

酢 海 鼠 や 母 の 忌 の 海 遠 く 鳴 り 伊 達 雅 和
sunamako ya haha no ki no umi tôku nari – date masakazu (1997)
(vinegar/pickled-seaslug: mother's anniversary/deathday's ocean distantly sounds)   #561

pickled sea slug   mom's deathday
the distant sound of the sea   eating pickled slug the sound
on mom's deathday   of the sea far off

Was it Issa who haiku'ed that every time he heard the sea he thought of his mother? Though MSWord doesn't recognize it, "deathday" is *bona fide* English, from the OE *deothdaege*. Like birthdays, they are meant for observing. The nebulous quality here is audio rather than visual.

う ろ く づ の 宵 の う ご め く 海 鼠 か な 晈 友
urokuzu no yoi no [ni?] ugomeku namako kana – kôyû (1932)
(scales/fish-evening's move/squirm/wriggle seaslug!/?/ó/the/loh)   #562

squirming
in the scales of dusk
sea slugs

scale slag   squirming
starts to move at dusk   in the squamous dusk
sea slugs   sea slugs

Sea slugs do start working as it grows dark. The verb *ugomeku* suggests maggots – which, in a sense, sea slugs are, for they, too, eat organic waste – and an obscure movement which brings out the nebulous hour. Since English does not happen to have a single word meaning either/both "fish scales" or "fish," such as *urokuzu,* the ambiguity of the original is hard to preserve. The first reading allows the possibility of a sea slug mixed with fish in a market. The second has the sea slug on the sea floor near a fish-processing plant literally among waste including scales – the image is close to the toad of Juan Tablada (1871-1945)[1] haiku'ed in Spanish at about the same time. The third reads the scales as a light chop on the water reflecting the twilight or the rising moon.

階 段 が 無 く て 海 鼠 の 日 暮 か な 橋 閒 石

kaidan ga[no] nakute namako no higure kana – hashi kanseki (mod)

(stairs/tiers-not, seaslug's/s' dusk!/?/ó/the/loh/alas)

#563

no stairs . . .
a sea-slug
in the dusk

(trans anon[2])

〜

the seawall
lacks stairs – a sea slug
at nightfall

〜

tierless
this sea slug
twilight

味 は う て 閒 石 翁 の 海 鼠 の 句   高 沢 良 一

ajiwaute kanseki okina no namako no ku – takasawa yoshikazu (2000)

(taste/savoring kanseki-master[senor with class]'s seaslug [hai]ku)

#564

a taste to savor
the sea slug haiku by
master stone

Kanseki's poem is the most commonly seen twentieth century sea cucumber haiku. It is also the sketchiest. I don't get what it means and, unlike Takasawa, whose *meta*-haiku shows he got *something* of worth from it, I'm not even sure I appreciate it. Part of the *Matsuyama Declaration*[2] (found on the Ehime Prefecture's Culture Foundation website) introduces it as one of a number of examples of poems with "words that are cut for surrealistic effect" in "fixed form" (i.e., traditional haiku) using "techniques and rhetoric that are . . . innately Japanese" and "difficult for a non-Japanese to understand." For a non-Japanese, the first difficulty here would have more to do with unfamiliarity with the landscape; namely, Japanese seawalls tend to be tiered, therefore "tierless" suggests a seawall.

1. *Tablada's Toad* Instant translation: "chunks of mud / from the shade of the path / hop toads" (*trozos de barro / por la senda de penumbra / salatan los sapos*). Thinking of creation *ex nihilo,* I would title it *ex-humas*, but, in fact, it is titled simply "Los Sapos." Tablada, a Mexican who had a big influence on concrete poetry in Europe, is widely credited with being the first Western haiku writer.

2. *The Matsuyama Declaration* Matsuyama City is the birthplace of Shiki and Kyoshi, and this Declaration might be called a wish-in-words to create a sort of haiku evangelism to spread the (correct) Haiku Gospel around the world.

Further interpretation is difficult. What is the relationship between tierlessness and the sea slug? I thought the lack of tiers might suggest a completely smooth gradation, a grey slide into the dark – with sea slug in the original apparently modifying the dusk, but the Japanese man I contacted at the Foundation website [1] sees *steplessness* as a total separation or gulf between the human and the sea slug in Nature, while KS does not see the ocean in the poem at all, but thinks the sea slug a symbol for being *at ones wits end* (in Japanese *tohô-ni kureru,* or literally "route dusking/darkens") with the lack of stairs, up or down, indicating the utter despair of escape from the situation. Whatever,[2] one can hardly dare to be conclusive, what with the poet's professed philosophy being that "the true province of poetry is found in multi-layered ambiguity" (*shi no honryô wa jûsô no aimaisa ni aru*)! Rightly or wrongly, I took one of the two characters in Kanseki's name and translated it ("stone") for effect.

掬ひ売る海鼠日ぐれの色にかな　有働亨

sukuiuru namako higure no iro ni kana – udô tôru (1997)

(scooping-sell/selling/sold seaslug dusk's color-to/as/with!/?/ô/the/loh/ah)　　　　　#565

selling grey	*for sale*
live sea slugs	dripping brine
turning color with	sea slugs the color
the twilight	of the dusk

A colorful object loses its color as it grows dark, so that much of what we see in the moonlight is in our imagination. The sea slug is not a clear color to begin with.   How, then, does the dusk treat it? This poem was easy to read but impossible to translate accurately for there is no phrase to communicate that something is *sold while being scooped out from a tray or tank with water* in English.

海　鼠　漁　の　手　応　え　銀　の　日　暮　れ　の　な　か　伊　丹　公　子

namakoryo no tegotae gin no higure no naka – itami kimiko (contemp)

(seaslug-fishing's hand-reply[worthwhile/get results], silver-dusk-within)　　　　　#566

this is the time	sea slugging
for good sea slugging	paradise in the silver
the silver dusk	of the evening

in the dusk,
silver lining of the night
sea sluggers
make out like bandits

Gilt comes down on the side of light, and grey, though midway between black and white is more allied to the night to come than the day, but silver seems genuinely neutral. Not just sea slugs, but slug-related activities adapt liminal colors, i.e., the hues of the margin of night and day.

1. *Haiku Interpretation by Internet* As difficult as it is to grasp many Japanese haiku --- not true for most written in English! – the conventional (surprisingly contradictory) belief that a haiku explains itself on the one hand and depends on the reader to read between the lines on the other hand discourages sufficient questioning.   I am delighted when Japanese dare to give me their reading of a particular haiku, for all too often, I am told simply that "you are supposed to read it plainly (*sunao ni*), without thinking too much," which is fine if one is just reading, but poor advice for a translator. Inoue Hiromi was very kind to respond to my questions and come up with Kanseki's quote, as well!

2. *Interpreting Kanseki* Anyone who would like to try to enlighten me about the significance of Kanseki's poem is *welcome to try*. I can't promise I will understand, but I will try. And if what you write is interesting, it will be in the next edition.

.海 峡 の 日 の や は ら か し 海 鼠 突 く　角 雄 三

kaikyô no hi no yawarakashi namako tsuku – sumi yûzô (1998)

#567

(channel's sun's weakness/softness: sea slug gig)

enka dawn

in the channel's
soft northern sunlight
gigging slugs

Why dawn? Because that is when it is calmest and the sluggers are out. *Kaikyô* – "channel" or "strait" or "passage" – opens up a world of emotion to the Japanese reader. It is – or, in the last half of the twentieth century, *was* – a keyword in the vocabulary of the Japanese equivalent of country music* *enka*. Lovers parted across these straits, so they were associated with tears and sadness. Since, the strait between Hokkaido and *hondo* (the mainland) was the most commonly sung, straits were further associated with bitter cold, made colder by loneliness. While *enka*-haters see the genre as so much maudlin platitude, *enka* fans see it as the expression of a delicate sensitivity far beyond anything foreigners can imagine.[1] The modern haiku above may well be no more than an objective description of something experienced. But, hey, the *karaoke* singer in me is tempted to write an *enka* about it.

客 船 の ま ぶ し く 過 ぎ ぬ 海 鼠 突　川 崎 俊 子

kyakusen no mabushiku suginu namakotsuki – kawasaki toshiko (contemp)

#568

(passenger-boat's brilliant/dazzling-passes sea-slug-sticker/gigger)

a passenger ship,
passes by dazzling
the slug giggers

ss crystal palace

a cruise ship
bright enough to blind:
slug-giggers

Here, I imagine the sea slug giggers on barely painted boats in the shade of a rocky island while sunlight hits the the high white hull of the ship, or the sea sluggers barely visible at dawn or dusk, while the boats electric lights pass by as bright as a city. Dullness is brought out by the ship-as-back-glow.

1. Country and Enka Both genre can boast many excellent songs. The biggest difference may be that for all the hate some modern-minded Japanese feel for *enka*, far more Japanese intellectuals rose to defend *enka* than did American intellectuals *country*. The intellectual establishment in the USA still knows more about opera than their own country's music! Look, I have studied the lyrics of Opera – and the handful of New York song writers who are still given far too much prominence today – and the words from C&W numbers and tell you, the best songs of the latter are far more complex, wittier and in the best meaning of the word, sophisticated. I happen to think they sound better, too, but will admit that much is a matter of taste.
2. Far Beyond Foreigners The *enka* sensibility was generally held to be "moist," "sad" and emotionally complex, while American country was considered to be "dry," "happy" and moronically simple (I confirmed these stereotypes with a survey). A speaker at a pop-music conference once claimed that an *enka* about a woman separating from a man "for his good" would be beyond the comprehension of foreigners (Occidentals) with their black and white, clear-cut feelings of love or hate and nothing in between. He did not know about Dolly Parton's "I'll Always Love You," which happened to be the top country song for two years in a row! (For my part, I must admit surprise to see it revived with such success by Witney Huston (sp?) in a time when self-pride and conceit was *obligatory* in pop-America, black or white! Since she dropped the piteous recitation, I would guess many listeners didn't hear the humility at its humblest.)

海鼠食ふ夕白雲のかがやきに 中拓夫

namako kuu yû shiragumo no kagayaki ni – chûtakuo? (mod)
(seaslug eat/ing evening white-clouds' shine/brilliance/glow/ing-in)   #569

<table>
<tr><td>

eating sea slug
in the glow of white
evening clouds
</td><td>

eating slug
in early evening
cloudshine
</td></tr>
</table>

Not many people have noticed the way some well-placed white clouds, like photographer's assistants with their reflective umbrellas can assist with lighting in the evening. This is too light to be called sea slug weather, but the slug is darkened in contrast and evokes the falling dusk.

返照の一点ゆらぐ海鼠突 前田鶴子

hanshô no itten yuragu namako tsuki – maeda tsuruko (contemp)
(reflection-light's[sunset-glow?] one-spot flickers seaslug-gigger)   #570

a flicker
in the seashine
slugboat

a mote on
the glowing sea
slug boat

the sea glare
broken in one spot
by a slugger

sea slugger

a dimple
on the shiny face
of the sea

Translating "one spot in the light reflection (of the type we see in the morning or evening)" is not easy. I am sure the poet is looking down on the sea from a high vantage point but imagine two contrary possibilities: a painfully bright glare and the beautiful glow just before sunset. Chances are it is the latter, for if the sea slug is nebulous, there is something soft, even gentle in the dim work of the sluggers (elaborated later). The following *tanka* brings out the calm atmosphere of the poetic sea slug depicted in this chapter and leaves us with a circle of ripples expanding and . . .

海鼠つく船より起ちし水の輪のほのりほのりといつか消えにき 吉植庄亮

namako tsuku fune yori tachishi mizu no wa no honorihonori to itsuka kie ni ki – yoshiue shôryô (1884-1958)
(seaslug gig/ging boat-from occurs water-ring's gently, gently some-time[eventually] dissappear/vanish comes-to)#571

f
rom
the boat
of the slug–gigger
rings of ripples
gently expand and
eventually
vanish

[うんころもち]

Note the intense expression on the face of the little child dragging the *namako*. Is he concerned for the *namako*? Imagining the moles tunneling rapidly away below? Imagining some scary tiger-like spirit emanating from the *namako*? Admonished to be careful lest the *namako* slip its cord? I do not know what book this came from. It was found on a site with a modern version of an Ambrose Beirce-like dictionary, the same that had the sea slug proper leery of being conflated with the *namako* and being eaten. I have not yet managed to get through to the host. 誰か。原文？

21
the cold sea slug

活 て 居 る も の に て 寒 き 海 鼠 哉 几 董
ikiteiru mono nite samuki namako kana – kitô (1740-89)
(live thing for, [it's] cold: sea-slug/s!/?/ó/the)   #572

for something alive
how cold
the sea cucumber!
～
the sea slug
how can life be
so damn cold?

寒 天 に 海 鼠 な ら ざ る 雲 は な し 高 沢 良 一
kanten ni namako narazaru kumo wa nashi – takasawa yoshikazu (2001)
(cold-heaven/sky-in, seaslug is/become-not cloud-as-for not [1])   #573

not a cloud
not a sea slug in the cold
winter sky
～
every cloud
a sea slug in this
freezing cold

It was not easy to split off these *Cold Sea Slugs* from Bashô's frozen clump, but by putting them in the last chapter, I tell myself they come round to the beginning. So, in a sense, they are still together. There are tepid water slugs, but to the Japanese mind – or at least, mainland Japanese mind – everything connected with the creature was cold. This went back to the start, for the oldest sea slug haiku found so far identify it with a part of Japan known for its cold, even forbidding, climate and, if you recall, a pre-Basho haiku in the *Tasty Sea Slug* even makes *cold* the essence of its flavor.

生 海 鼠 干 す 袖 の 寒 さ よ 啼 ち ど り 士 郎
namako hosu sode no samusa yo naku chidori – shirô (1742-1813)
(sea slug drying's sleeves' coldness! cry/ing plover)   #574

seaside scene

plovers cry out
how cold the sleeves of men
drying sea slugs!

1. *Double negative in translation* The double negative without "that is" between "not a cloud" and "not a sea slug" may confuse some readers. Today (but not in the 19th c.), *no+no=yes* is not common in English. The translator is forced to choose between preserving the original syntax and losing readers.

Shirô's poem has *three* seasonal signs: *sea slug, cold* and *plover*.   While this is rare – the catechism has it that one seasonal indicator is sufficient, two is pushing it and three is too much – it still has a natural classic haiku feeling. I imagine *women* rather than *men* doing this work, but the middle line is too damn long for the two syllable sex. Note that the sleeve can stand for the clothing and the person wearing it.   A tear-drenched sleeve is standard trope for sad love poems.   Even today, Japanese comics wring out their sleeves [1] rather than their handkerchiefs. People exiled on islands or simply working by the water were conveniently (for the poet, that is) wet-sleeved and therefore romantically suffering all day long.   Haiku poets kept romantic trope alive, mainly to poke fun at it.   For if one is a true lover of nature writ large, it is hard to feel too serious about your own petty love affairs.   This is not to say whether the above poem was meant to imply anything more than what it says.

厚着して舟を寄せ合ふ海鼠突　斉藤夏風

atsugi shite fune o yoseau namakotsuki – saitô kafû (mod)

(thick-clothing doing/wearing boats nearing-meet seaslug-stabbers)

#575

> bringing together
> their boats: thickly bundled
> sea slug giggers

When I lived in a bamboo grove, not a few people who visited me when the baby bamboo were sprouting expressed amazement to find that the big bamboo was big from the start. This amazement was itself amazing because all of these people were Japanese and had bought bamboo shoots of various sizes at the grocers for years and therefore should have known about this. Well, I knew that slugging was done in the dead of winter and that it was freezing cold then, but all my images were those of bathing-suited South Pacific trepang giggers (which Japanese emigrants and seasonal workers used to do, too) or of the proverbial *ama,* the diving woman in her sexy white linen. Until I read this poem, I never *clearly* saw the reality, *winter clothing*.

天冴えて海鼠かゝれり網雫　師竹

ama saete namako kakareri ami shizuku – shichiku (1861-1919)

(heaven/sky chills seaslug/s caught net drops[of water])

#576

> it grows chilly
> as brine drips from a net
> with sea slugs

This poem makes me shiver. Psychologically speaking, drops of water are colder than ice. The original "heaven/sky;" is pretty close to *weather*, but seems more encompassing.   Hence, *it.*

#577, #578 (下記)

1. *Wet sleeved Sea Slug* The prototypical wet sleeve does something the handkerchief does not.   It reflects – or invites to *dwell* -- the moon, which itself may reflect the face of the beloved. Since the jellyfish is a sea-*moon*, this provides another way to couple it with the sea-slug-as-weak-spine-lover. Eg.: "sea slug me! / a moon jellyfish now rents / my briny sleeve! (*nuresode no kurage mo yadoru namako kana* (濡れ袖の海月も宿る海鼠かな 敬愚). Or, in reverse, "briny sleeved / sea slug, can you see /   the moon-jellyfish?" (*nuresode no namako o sasuga ni kurage kana* (ぬれ袖の海鼠をさすかに海月哉　敬愚). There is an old poem by Chora (樗良) to the effect that sea-moon shining up one's sleeve is cooling (*suzushisa ya sode ni sashiiruru uminotsuki*), that may hint of jellyfish, but it is likely he is only talking about the actual moon reflected from the sea up his sleeve. Doubtless, there are more jellyfish-on-the-sleeve out there, but even so, the chance of the same + *namako* are very slim considering the fact mentioned in our discussion of Shôha's fantasy of the sea slug talking to the moon jellyfish: *they belong to different seasons*

寒 凪 や タ ブ の 影 お く 海 鼠 の 江 　 前 田 普 羅
kannagi ya tabu no kage oku namako no e – fura (1934)
(cold[coldest-season]calm: tub's/s' shadow puts/sits [on] seaslug-inlet/bay)　　#579

a cold calm　　　　　　　winter doldrums
vat shadows fall on　　　the shadow of a tub
sea slug bay　　　　　　on seaslug bay

A boiling plant was generally by the sea and had many tubs or vats to boil slugs before curing them. Something about the poem suggests another coldness, the absence of man, a scene of desolation, the bones of a plant that died from over-fishing or competition from Korea (at this time a colony of Japan).

魚 市 の と ぼ り て 寒 き 海 鼠 か な 　 村 上 鬼 城
uoichi no toborite samuki namako kana – murakami kijô (1864-1938)
(fish-market's lighting-up cold seaslug/s!/?/ô/the)　　#580

when the lights　　　　　with the bare lights
turn on, the fish market　the cold: sea slugs are out
grows cold: sea slugs　　in the fish market

the first lights brighten
the cold fish market, call it
the sea slug hour

The slug season opens as the nights begin to overwhelm the day. One doesn't generally associate lights with cold, but the outdoor lights [1] would be seen a lot more in the cold season and they would turn on as the evening turns to night and the temperatures drop. *Namako* stand out because they last longer than fish, most of which were sold in the morning and this light, for some reason, accents their proverbial coldness. It is a great haiku in the original. These next two are, to my mind, mediocre:

海 鼠 売 る 桶 重 ね た り 橋 の 雪 　 長 谷 川 か な 女
namako uru oke kasanetari hashi no yuki – kanajo? ((1927)
(seaslug selling tubs piled[one on top of another] bridge's snow)　　#581

a bridge with snow　　　tub upon tub
and sea slug sold from　of sea slug for sale
stacked up tubs　　　　a snowy bridge

.A bridge is cold's fort, a place even light snow can feel safe. It certainly seems a perfect match for *Namako* as Mr Cold, but let us hope that customers do not slip and take a roll with their slugs!

1. Bare, outdoor lights Whether the market is truly outdoor or, more likely, an open-ended mall-like structure, light bulbs in Japan have ever tended to be bare, i.e. unshielded. This is even true indoors where, bare light bulbs (*hadaka-denkyû*), together with the toilet paper rolls used for tissue and clothing hung around the room rather than in closets, was one of my three hardest-to-get-used-to elements of ordinary Japanese life. till, in my room, working late at night on my books, I discovered one merit of such ugly bare lights. Working in freezing weather without a heater, I found the hat I had to wear any way shaded the light and whenever my pencil fell from my frozen fingers, I could simply cup the light bulb in my hands and it would restore the heat needed to keep writing. I do not think the coldness of my fingers was the only reason I could grasp the bulb. The light bulb itself was not so hot on the outside as is usually the case. You might say that I warmed it up, too.

海鼠売向ひ吹雪を行きにけり 大橋櫻坡子

namakouri mukaifubuki o yukinikeri – ôhashi ôhashi (1932)

(seaslug-seller facing-blizzard-into goes[+finality])

#582

> the slug vender
> goes straight into the face
> of a blizzard

This is too true to be good. Since the action is more metaphorically apt for a vendor of blowfish, (known to have warming qualities bringing it into high demand at such times, symbol of possible oblivion, etc.) we may assume this is a simple observation and no more.

ころ～と生海鼠もちゞむさむさ哉 紫道

korokoro to namako mo chijimu samusa kana – shidô (d.1741)

(rolling-round[psychological mimesis] sea-slug-even/also shrink cold!/?/ó/the/hoh/how)

#583

> oh, this cold!   cold enough
> even sea slugs are   to turn sea slugs
> round as balls   into balls!
>
> how cold it is!
> even sea slugs shrink
> like my balls!

This is not so much a sea slug poem as a "so cold that such-and-such happens" type *coldness* poem. It is impossible to tell whether the "too/even" suggests the poet's own balls or the fact that, it must really be freezing if the stereotypical coldest being is cold itself. I think the latter reading is the more likely.

石鉢に寒さをすくむ海鼠哉 老鼠

ishibachi ni samusa o sukumu namako kana – rôsô (1759)

(stone-bowl-in, coldness[obj] shrinks seaslug[subj]!/?/ó/the/a/behold)

#584

> in the crock
> cold is congealing:
> a sea slug
>
> in the crock   the stone pot
> a sea slug congeals   a sea slug congeals
> pure coldness   its coldness
>
> in the mortar
> cold makes a tight fist
> one sea slug

The verb *sukumu* usually is used with the indirect object and means to shrink up with fear. In this old poem, "cold/ness" is used as its direct object. I can only guess what the poet is driving at.

砂の中に海鼠の氷る小さゝよ 碧梧桐

suna no naka ni namako no kôru chiisasa yo – hekigotô (1894)

(sand-inside-of, seaslug's freeze/ing smallness!)

#585

> how small
> this sea slug freezing
> in the sand!

Finally, a plain poem! All I might add is that if the sea slug observed by Hekigoto is stressed out – probable if it were found "in the sand" – it would not only be shrunken up to its full shortness (note, we have no antonym for "full *length*!") but would have already jettisoned its innards.

目 鼻 なき な まこ を 見 れば 海 底 にひそめる もの のつめたく 思 ほ ゆ 大 坪 晶 一
mehananaki namako o mireba unazoko ni hisomeru mono no tsumetaku omohoyu – ôtsubo shôichi (cont)
(eye-nose[features]-not, seaslug/s see-when, seafloor-on/at hide/dwell ones/things' coldly think) #586

vis sea slug
eyeless & noseless:
think just how
cold life on the floor
of the sea must be!

~

when i see
sea slug, no nose
no face
i think the sea floor
is a cold, cold place

This modern *tanka*, that could as well have been placed with the *Featureless Sea Slugs* as with the *Cold* ones, makes me think of Eskimos and, more broadly, the Mongoloid race/s. Their narrow eye slits and small noses likewise suggest a cold origin.   [oops, no #587,#588!]

海 鼠 哉 人 も 手 足 は 出 さ ぬ 頃 露 牙
namako kana hito mo teashi wa dasanu koro – roga? (1759)
(sea slug!/?/ó/the/behold, people, too, hands-feet expose-not time)   #589

brrrrrr!

the sea slug
in a season we too
hide our limbs

Japanese dress resembles a turtle shell. In the winter, Japanese didn't only stick their hands into the opposing sleeves, as Chinese are often depicted doing, but used to *retract* their arms all the way into the body of their kimonos, leaving the sleeves to hang empty. *I.e.*, they applied the thermodynamic advantages of the mitten to their dress. As a 17th century haiku translated by Blyth puts it, "the winter moon / every shadow [-figure] / is handless" (*fuyu no tsuki minna te no nai kagebôshi*). Since Japanese walls were thin – houses were made with the sultry summer in mind – and used little heating, people stayed covered inside as well as out. They even had a *futon,* or quilt bed-cover, with sleeves so one could take one's warmth around the house, rather than abandoning it upon rising

海 鼠 か な 汝 元 来 痰 気 の 時 哲 阿 彌
namako kana nanji ganrai tanki no toki – tetsuami (1798)
(sea slug!/?/the/ó/behold you originally/afterall phlegmatic time)   #590

the fourth humor

ah, sea slug!
you are your season:
phlegmatic

By providing seasonal reasons why the sea slug is limbless and holds watery slime, these haiku share subject matter with the *Just-so Sea Slugs* and the *Seasonal Sea Slugs* (with the *Sundry S.S.*). My translation of Tetsuami's snotty sea cucumber poem takes advantage of an old-fashioned adjective (=phlegmatic) to play with a traditional Western concept of body-humor not found in Japan. The direct address of the sea slug – a formal *nanji* second-person, no less! – is refreshing and the first I have seen in a poem, though it had already been used in prose (*viz* "The Sea Slug Maxim," in the Appendum)

あたまからふとんかぶればなまこかな 蕪 村

atama kara futon kabureba namako kana – buson (1715-83)

#591   (head-from quilt wear-if: sea slug!/?/ó/the/behold/it's a/you're a/)

with the quilt
over your head: voila
a sea slug!

A modern annotation: "Pulling the quilt up over your head, it is hard to tell which side is your head and which your feet. A veritable sea slug, your body and heart are *gunyagunya*." (BUSON-ZENSHÛ 1(bzs)) The psychological mimesis *gunyagunya* is an unpleasant picture which translates as "pulpy/flabby/limp/flaccid/mushy/weak-kneed/squashy." As my translation shows, I have a quite different sense of the experience than the annotator! But I must admit the fact that the original was written *entirely in hiragana* (phonetic syllabary)[1] might suggest the *gunyagunya* picture was in the poet's mind. Or *was* it? ("I don't think *gunyagunya* conveys the image Buson is depicting. Even deep in a futon, one is still cold and his body must be taut." = MO (corresp). I agree, for houses were not heated back then.) Might it not, rather, mean that the poem was by someone else and only heard by Buson, who wrote it down? After all, someone else *did* write what is – aside from a different conjugation on the verb (*kaburishi* vs *kabureba*) – the same poem earlier.[2]

天 窓 か ら 蒲 団 被 り し 生 海 鼠 哉　 清 泉

atama kara futon kaburishi namako kana – seisen (1763)

#592   (head-from quilt wearing/worn: sea slug !/?/ó/the/behold/it's a/you're a)

on a day as cold as the bottom of the sea

wearing a quilt
over my head, call
me sea slug

a cold life

the sea slug:
its head always under
the blanket

1. *All Hiragana Haiku* Only one other haiku of the 3000 odd haiku attributed to Buson is written without a single Chinese character: It is about a slender/reeling dew-covered "male" flower (*otokoeshi*)) and contains a mimetic expression that shares the weakness of the expression in the sea slug poem. See IPOOH fall 1 (the two gendered yellow flower / ominaeshi to otokoeshi) for a translation of *hyoro-hyoro to nao tsuyukeshi ya otokoeshi* in context.

2. *Dating Haiku* The earliest book known to have Buson's poem is dated 1800, but it does not indicate when it was written. Chances are it was written after Seisen's poem published in 1763. Since the poem was published after Buson's death, he cannot be held responsible for the mistaken attribution. Perhaps it was just recorded for memory's sake by Buson because he liked it.

Mountains, especially Fuji, were also haiku'ed as wearing futons of snow.   Thicker than the Occidental "blanket" or any quilts I have seen, the plump *futon* is a fine embodiment of the cold. My dual translations attempt to resurrect the convenient ambiguity of Japanese, where one can't rightly say what side of the metaphor we are on.   The next two early modern haikus are clearer in this respect:

海 鼠 な り に 自 足 し て い る 闇 夜 か な 懸 圃

namako nari ni jisoku shiteiru yamiyo kana – kenpo (19c)
(seaslug form/becoming-like own-feet[self-sufficient]-doing/am dark[no-moon] night!/ǿ/the)   #593

moonless

a dark night:
like the sea slug i am
self-sufficient

self-sufficiency

hunkering down
in the dark of the moon
my own sea slug

A truly remarkable poem from a period (between Issa and Shiki) believed bereft of good poetry in Japan. The *yamiyo* may refer to the *ôyamiyo,* or "big-dark-night," i.e., New Year's Eve, or to any monthly absence of the moon.   At this time, nocturnal mobility was reduced to sea slug levels, seconding the isolation of winter life. A religious poet would feel the loss of 'the light of (Buddhist) law,' while a recluse would lose his only companion.   The term used for self-sufficient, literally "own-legs" is witty, for sea slugs were thought to be legless and the wintering poet has no use for his.

人 間 の 海 鼠 と な り 冬 篭 る 寺 田 虎 彦

ningen no namako to nari fuyugomori – terada torahiko (1878-1935)
(people sea slug into become wintering in)   #594

metamorphosis

wintering in
when human-beings
turn sea slug

Quail turn mole, sparrow turn clam, and *we* turn sea slug. As Shiki observes, "we shrink our hands / and shrink up our legs / wintering in" (*te o chijime ashi o chijimete fuyugomori*). There is, in the light of science, irony in using the sea slug to symbolize hibernation.   As we have seen, it is true with respect to the sea slug's low-energy life-style; but it is wrong, too, for the Japanese sea slug does not hibernate in the winter. Rather *it is most active* – that is to say, moves about 200 centimeters per hour – in cold water, with one peak around 23-4 degrees celsius and another at 16 or less degrees. (This double spike of activity intriguing scientists) and *estivates* when the water temperature rises.   A Japanese web site called this "taking a summer vacation."   I prefer to call it a long *siesta*, though a long *fast* would be as accurate. But movement of centimeters per hour are hard to notice especially when such activity takes place in the dark! Keigu feels obliged to fill in the gap, though it means putting the chapter theme (cold) on the back-burner for a couple pages:

1. *Why Estivate?* For a start, tepid sea-beds are not good places to breath. This not only means it is a good time to take a siesta from work, but that any work, i.e. feeding done would be less productive because most life absconds (floats up or drifts away) and the sands grow relatively barren in the heat. As a googled Chinese article put it, *the sea slug would starve if it didn't economize by estivating*

寝 る 海 鼠 夜 番 の 後 の 冬 景 色   敬 愚

neru namako yoban no ato no fuyugeshiki – keigu

(sleeping seaslug, night-shift-after's winter scene)

#595

scientific haiku

winter still-life:
sea slugs sleeping
after a hard night's work:

As the reader may have noticed, the made-to-order haiku is generally a bit on the shallow side, but this does have some depth to it, for once one is strongly conscious of what these creatures do at night, we can no longer view them as vegetables that spend their lives just lying there.

夜 は 稼 ぎ 昼 は 昼 寝 の 海 鼠 哉   敬 愚

yo wa kasegi hiru wa hirune no namako kana – keigu

(night earn/work, day-as-for day-sleep[nap]'s seaslug!/ó/the)

#596

they work all night
and sleep all day, so when
can sea slugs play?

や よ な ま こ 夜 稼 ぐ は 昼 寝 の 種 か   敬 愚

yayo namako yoru kasegu wa hirune no tane ka – keigu

(hoh, seaslug! night-earning-as-for, day-sleep[nap]'s seed[cause]?)

#597

hey, sea slugs!
is night-work behind
your lazy bones?

why sea slugs sleep

moonlighting
makes no hay while
the sun shines

よ く 寝 る も 働 く 報 い か 海 鼠 か な   敬 愚

yoku neru mo hataraku mukui namako kana – keigu

(well sleep even work-reward seaslug/s!/?/ó/the)

#598

the sea slug
sleeping well is its reward
for hard work

よ く 寝 る も 働 く 報 い か 海 鼠 達   敬 愚

yoku neru mo hataraku mukui ka namakotachi – keigu

(well sleep even work-reward? seaslugs)

#599

just reward

hey, sea slugs!
do you sleep so well
because you work?

So, why do sea slugs work at night rather than during the day? Let me transliterate a googled Chinese passage: "Sea water heats, small organisms float up, with nightfall, water temperature drops, small organisms again settle on sea-floor." (it parallels the seasonal change described in a note) So, to put it into the Namako's perspective, *sand would taste better (have more nutrition) at night.*

闇 寒 を ば か り 働 く 海 鼠 太 き   敬 愚
yamisamu o bakari hataraku namako futoki – keigu
(utterdark-cold only works seaslug [is] tough/awesome)   #600

working in the cold
working in the dark
sea slug is a brute!

冬 の 夜 ば か り 働 く 海 鼠 太 き   敬 愚
fuyu no yoru bakari hataraku namako futoki [1] – keigu
(winter-night/s only works seaslug [is] tough/awesome)   #601

winter

he only works
on the longest nights
slug's got balls

∼

working at night
in the winter: sea slug's
just awesome

Keigu has his tongue in cheek. Haiku poets – and Terada was a well known physicist, so we cannot just talk of unscientific poets – can be forgiven their mistaken metaphor. We *need* the day-time sea slug, a perfect do-nothing, a *Lilly of the Valley* that can even flourish in the inhospitable house of Old Man Winter. Who wants to talk about working animals? [2] As Shiki wrote in a hard-to-translate poem:

1. *Futoki or Kana* If the reader thinks that interpreting the sea slug's night work in terms of its character is ridiculous, the *futoki* may always be replaced by the meaningless *kana* and the poem retranslated accordingly.

2. *Working Animals* As I argue at length in *Han-Nihonjinron* (=anti-japanology:1984), in the Sinosphere, working rather than doing nothing was the traditional default: the easiest thing to do. Life was identified with work in a way rarely encountered in the West. In the West poverty is associated with lying about doing nothing, and this is often the case. In the Far East, there is a saying to the effect that "a poor man has no free time." Haiku poet Issa belonged to a Buddhist sect that held that it was enough simply to *trust* in the Buddha, yet even so, his haiku show he was fixated on work. He felt guilty as hell for not doing enough real labor and saw work everywhere he looked. The particulars of animal life he put into haiku were often explained as what they did to *kasegu,* or "earn a living." At the time I first read such poems, I thought, *my god, even the poets were economic animals!* But, in retrospect, I see that this was Issa's way to express sympathy: the animals are fellow-sufferers. They, *too,* must work. Be that as it may, the sea slug's work is not bad. It basically comprises one thing: *eating.* The same Chinese article mentioned in the main text, above, puts this in a way that only the food-centered Chinese culture could put it: In fact, . . . a sea cucumber stands a life as plankton is as pleasant as the thing which greatly receive and greatly drinks and to live." (a chinese→japanese→english machine translation of the cornucopia enjoyed by our charge in the winter) Looking at the Chinese original, I see this means that "when these plankton are plentiful, the sea cucumber eats and drinks abundantly and life is joyful." Neither the Western writer nor the Japanese could possibly write *that.*

世 の 中 を か し こ く く ら す 海 鼠 哉　子 規
yononaka o kashikoku kurasu namako kana – shiki (1893)

#602

(world-in smartly live sea slug!/?/ő/the/behold)

kashikoku

snug as a bug
in a rug: the sea slug
in our world

ugly is beautiful

the sea slug
sits right pretty
in this world

the exemplar

the sea slug
studies to be good
in this life

The adverb *kashikoku* is exceedingly meaning-full. It alludes to the cold without, for over two hundred years earlier, Teitoku wrote that even bugs politely settled in for the winter (*fuyugomori mushikera made mo ana-kashiko*). His *anakashiko* translates "hole-smart" (the *ana* really means "very" but puns as "hole") and may suggest monks, sometimes *mushikera*, or "bugs" in a sense close to "vermin," who chanted sutra which ended with the "hole-smart" expression while "wintering-in" (*fuyugomori*), or more strictly, in their winter-retreat (*tôango* lit. "winter-ease-dwell,"). Closer to Shiki's time, Issa, also wrote a couple haiku of dogs and cats behaving *kashikoku* in the winter. By this, he meant they were bright enough to settle down and behave well because they didn't want to be kicked out into the cold (a true observation, unlike Teitoku's allegorical generalization). I should add, parenthetically, that Shiki's snug sea slug poem followed directly after what may be the cleverest poem ever written on paper kimonos, called *kamiko*: "haikai's stomach-wadding=guts shows paper-kimono!/?/ő/the/a/behold" (*haikai no harawata miseru kamiko kana*). In Blyth's fine translation:

a *kamiko*
shows the bowels
of haikai

Explaining paper kimonos would take an entire chapter, so developing this poem is beyond the ken of this book. Suffice it to say that Shiki apparently – perhaps, unconsciously – associated the "bowels of *haikai*" (old paper with writing on it in this case) worn on his kimono with the sea slug.

大 い な る 海 鼠 火 鉢 に 畏 ま る　川 崎 展 宏
ôinaru namako hibachi ni kashikomaru – kawasaki nobuhiro (contemp)

#603

(old seaslug-hibachi/brazier-by [snuggily/smartly]humbling)

just thankful
to be sitting by my old
seaslug brazier

~

sitting snug
as a bug by her old
seaslug brazier

The *kashikomaru* in the original is the verb form of the *kashiko* explained already. I might add only that while *humble* and *smug* seem contradictory, if you sit still – smug as a bug – then you are acting humbly, while if you go zipping about wasting all of our energy, you are not behaving humbly though you may bow your head off or call yourself a conservationist a progressive or an ecologist. While the *namako* glaze brazier is no sea slug, for sure, the person acts like one.

海鼠汝れも身をちゞめたる寒さかな　島田青峰

namako nare mo mi o chijimetaru samusa kana – seihô (pre-1926) nez
(seaslug, thou, too, body[obj] shrinking cold!/?/ô/the)

#604

my sea slug	mr sea slug
is this cold enough to shrink	so you, too, shrink
thy body, too	in this cold!

how cold it is!
i see even you shrinking
right, namako?

If limblessness is one cold trait, compactness is another. This haiku plays off the idea of the *Cold Sea Slug* and the fact of shrinking. The poet knows the sea slug shrinks for many reasons, but his logic is that, the sea slug, as an animal at home in the cold, would not be expected to shrink. So, if even the sea slug shrinks, it must be cold indeed. Though the archaic *nare* used to address our charge suggests the respect in which he was and still is held by Japanese haiku poets (Without knowing more about this poet and where he wrote the poem, I cannot, however, rule out the slight possibility that the he is really addressing his private part.), the poem's subject is the cold.

腹中へ冷たさ落つる海鼠かな　田中拾夢

fukuchû e hietasa otsuru namako kana – tanaka hiromu (1993)
(belly-inside/mid coldness falls seaslug!/?/ô/the/some)

#605

descending	coldness
into my belly, cold	drops to my gut
cold sea slug	sea slug

That is one fine haiku! Chilled *sunamako* (pickled slug) and the beer or cold *sake* chasing it may provide the physical priming for this sensation, but the reader by now should know the psychology that makes the feeling significant.

海鼠腸の壺埋めたき氷室哉　利重

konowata no tsubo umetaki himuro kana – richô?(toshishige?(1689)
(sea-slugs' guts' urn/s bury-want to, ice-room!/?/ô/an)

#606

a nice idea	*home to the cold*
sea slug's urn	it would be nice
the sea-floor is far – perhaps	to bury the sea slug's guts
an ice room?	in an ice-cavern

R.I.P.

yes! an ice-room:
what better place to entomb
sea slug remains!

(Note: *the above translations and following explanation is wrong, but I like them better than what is right, so they stay. Please bear with me for a page or two. After that, I will set things straight!*)

With Shiki having so high an appreciation for this extraordinarily low form of life, it is hardly surprising to find this poem the first listed in a sub-category of "vessels" in the "sea slug" theme haiku in the Shiki ed. *Categorical* anthology (brbhz). Animistic cultures tend to treat the remains of what they eat with respect. Japanese religions split up their responsibilities. Confucianism for interpersonal and corporate relationship. Shinto for birth, birthdays, marriage and national celebration. Buddhism for death, funerals and memorial services for the repose of the soul. In other words, since Buddhism only had death to concern itself with – I am joking, for most of the primary schools were run by monks – the types of services proliferated to no end. In Japan, as the international press was often informed during the whaling war, we find mounds with plaques erected to console whales where Buddhist priests hold periodic ceremonies. Every year in the sweet old capital of Kyoto, they collect and console the souls of old needles, put to rest in soft slabs of tofu. And, with my own eyes, I have seen a mound for the repose of *rakugo* (Japanese traditional comic) monologues that were not allowed to be used in war-time because they touched upon alcohol (which the soldiers had little of) and adultery (which the soldiers feared [1]). So why, indeed, not something for the sea slug?[2]

My translations of the ice-room poem, hinted at some of the message between the lines. Eg., the Japanese have a great desire to be buried or scattered in their native element, so the sea slug's soul seeks the cold depths: failing that, the closer ice-room will have to do. Salted slug guts (*konowata*) were a delicacy, but, not all types are suitable for consumption and the guts can comprise up to 40% of the total body weight. The guts of the black sea slug, which was boiled and dried for export to China, were generally not eaten. Since it was metaphysically crueler to dispatch the sea slugs to a foreign land, there was indeed good reason to properly console their souls by preserving part of their bodies!

metaphysical consolation

a warm act, indeed
burying sea slug remains
in an ice room!

As poetic as this may be, I fear *all* my readings probably reflect the secondary meaning – which the term "bury" suggests was intended, for a *tsubo* is a crock as well as an urn – and entirely neglect the primary one, the one suggested by this poem:

このわたの壺を抱いて啜りけり　島田五空
konowata no tsubo o idaite susurikeri – gokû (1874-1928)

#607   (slug-guts' crock/pot/bottle hugging slurping-up)

hugging
a jar of slug guts
as i slurp

1. *War-time Adultery* The official line in Japan was that adultery would devastate Westerners (always depicted as lascivious beasts with no self-control) and Tokyo Rose and others played up the possibility of adultery back home in their propaganda intended to discourage Allied soldiers. But, it would seem they themselves worried the most!
2. *Sea Slug Mound* I have not yet heard of a mound for consoling sea-slugs. Whales were favored, perhaps because Japanese touched by the way mother whales gave up their lives for their calves by not fleeing. But, there is at least one mound for sluggers, the victims of a ship-wreck off the Great Barrier Reef. As Tsurumi Yoshiyuki explains, the broad range covered by the divers (owing to the quick exhaustion of any particular location – unlike the case with mobile fish or oysters with high density cultivation – makes them particularly liable to ship-wreck by typhoon, and the lack of protective gear and breathing devices (allowing one to sit tight) makes them a target of sharks. A more poetic reason for the shark attacks may be found in the Kiribati tongue, where the sea slug is called *uninga-ni-bakoa* or, the "shark's pillow!"

That is to say, *konowata* lovers are crazy for their favorite nibbly [1] and would keep it on hand as long as they could. The strength of their feelings are felt in gourmet haiku, of which one will do:

しる人そしる服部煙草（たばこ）伊勢海鼠腸 常矩
shiru hito zo shiru hattori tabako ise konowata – jôku?(18c?)).
(know/ing person/s[+emphatic] know/s: hattori[place] tobacco, ise[place] slug-guts)　　#608

> those who know
> know! hattori tobacco
> ise slug guts

So the primary and only valid reading of that Ice-room Haiku by Richô – if that, and not Toshishige, was his chosen pronunciation for 利 重 – *is as follows:*

perfect konowata

> how i'd like
> an ice room to keep
> my slug guts!

So, Richô was not performing a rite, but looking for a refrigerator – I joke, these were caverns or cellars full of ice enough to last from spring to fall [2] – to keep his perfectly fermented *konowata*. [3] Since *sake* sellers literally buried their kegs, leaving only part peeking out, the use of "bury" – the verb in the original that misled me – is valid, too. But, a total negation of the ritual association would be wrong, for there is no "*only*" in old haiku, where ambiguity is far too common to be accidental. It was often intended; and it is why any single translation of an old haiku must be taken with a grain of salt. And now that we have brought the world of the sea slug to close, we are ready for the *Summa Holothuridea,* the grand summation.

暗 き よ り 暗 き に 歸 る 生 海 鼠 哉　曉 臺
kuraki yori kuraki ni kaeru namako kana – gyôtai (1732-93)
(darkness-from, darkness-to returns [the] sea slug [cold-prayers?]!/?/ó/the/alas)　　#609

life cycle

> from darkness
> to darkness – the life
> of a sea slug

1. *Nibbly* I use what I imagine to be the Aussie term, for I cannot spell the French one and my MS Word spell-check gives me no help whether I start *hors* or *ors,* and only amuses me by claiming the intended word is *ordure,* which, as we have read already is exactly what some claim *konowata* tastes like!
2. *Ice Rooms* While refrigeration at home largely awaited electricity, the lack of air-condition made shaved ice treats and cold water a more important commodity in the pre-electrical age than it is today. Edo was full of ice. It was stored in something called an ice room/house (*himuro*) , which, without a sea slug in it, would be a summer theme, as was the more heavily haiku'ed ice-seller (*kôri-uri*). See IPOOH-summer-ice. Even ordinary people could afford an occasional shaved-ice or ice-water (sold on the street) in the summer; but the only people who could afford private ice rooms were nobles and imperial relations.
3. *Keeping Konowata* I do not know how long bottles of fermented gut would last, but imagine it would depend upon the percent of salt used as well as the temperature and amount of air in the bottle. I do know that no one would ship it to me in Miami, because, they claimed, it would not survive the trip.

Gyôtai's poem may allude to monks who walk about mumbling prayers in the night in the coldest part of the year, or it may allude to misguided souls reborn as sea slugs (both of these previously exampled).   More likely it metaphors the ordinary life-history of the unenlightened,[1] which is to say the poet himself, and, I would guess, all of us.   But, whatever the message (if there is a message), the poem accurately describes the life of a creature fished up from the sea and shortly thereafter swallowed down a human gullet.   Or, possibly, the *namako* is shorthand for its vendor.   To wit,

暗 き よ り 暗 き に 生 海 鼠 売 ら れ け り   仙 風
kuraki yori kuraki ni namako urarekeri – senpû (1793)

#610   (darkness-from darkness-to seaslug sold-is(+finality))

and sea slugs
are sold from one darkness
to another

from darkness   from dark
to darkness – a man   to dark live sea slugs
sells sea slugs   are for sale

The second, slightly later poem is, I guess, about a sea slug vendor walking about hawking his ware from dawn to dusk (sea slugs, sea slugs, alive, alive o![2]) The Japanese idiom is "from hole to hole," rather than "from womb to tomb."   But the ocean is a little too big to be called a hole (even if some have unfairly called it a mass grave) and the human gullet too warm for "cold to cold;" so, the sea slug has no choice but to slip dimly from dark to dark.[3]

1. *Unenlightened Sea Slug*   I had not realized how neatly this poem dovetails with the earlier ones on Buddhism until TALE OF MURASAKI author Liza Dalby asked, *What about Izumi Shikibu's famous "From dark to dark" waka?*   I checked and found out that Shikibu asks for light from the far-off moon, while setting forth *from the dark upon a dark road* (*kuraki yori kuraki michi ni zo irinubeki haruka ni terase yamanoha no tsuki*.)   The poem is interpreted to be a request to the man to whom the poem was addressed ("quality+ empty+above +person") for guidance on the path toward enlightenment, as the moon was a symbol of the light of the Buddhist Law and the "from dark to dark" (*kuraki yori kuraki*) in the *waka*'s first line comes from part of the Lotus Sutra, which reads verbatim: "dark-from dark-into enter, long=forever buddha-name hear-not." (*kuraki yori kuraki ni iri nagaku butsumyô o kikazu)* We cannot tell whether Gyôtai copied Shikibu or, like Shikibu, copied the catechism. Gyôtai has another poem that proves he was deeply into the metaphors of the dim and dark: "new year's day / out of darkness humans / appear" (*ganjitsu ya kuraki yori hito arawaruru*). This also suggests that his sea slugs are, if not us, *proto* us. And, by contrast, the pessimistic Buddhist version of damnation that the dark-to-dark evokes makes us better appreciate the joyous tone of Issa's   *uke namako,* or *Rise, Ye Sea Slugs!* poem. Yes, as I am write, I am humming an old Hank Williams tune *"Praise the Lord, I've seen the Light!* (No more darkness! No more night!)."   That Issa himself knew the "from dark to dark" metaphor directly

from the catechism is obvious from his use of more of it (10 syllabets to 8) than either Kyôtai or Shikibu: "from the dark / to the dark they go / cats in heat" (*kuraki yori kuraki ni iru ya neko no koi*). What are we, then? *Candles on a stage? Travelers beneath the moon? Sea slugs between dark and dark?* Or, *floating* – for cats in heat were said to float (*ukare*) – cats? Had LD commented a month earlier, when the cement was softer, I might have carved out a whole chapter for this quickly exploding dark stuff!

2. *Sea Slugs, Sea Slugs, Alive, Alive O!*   The first person to find me a bona fide *namako* vendor's song gets a hundred dollars and a mention in the next edition!

3. *How Dark the Dark?*   The poet who wrote the old haiku would be astounded to learn just how deep and dark a place sea slugs can thrive in! Thanks to their low metabolism and uniquely stiff yet elastic layers of smart chain-mail, *Holothurians* "account for 50% of the life forms at 4,000 m and 90% at 8000m." (Woodward: ibid) These deep-sea species tend to be flat and "are able to sail by undulating special 'veils' attached at the front and rear of the body."   (netted, lost credit: sorry!) These are obviously not the same species as those eaten by the Japanese, but it supports the idea of *namako* as *creatures from the deep* (and not just the shore). The deep sea cukes are generally members of the order Elasipodida, the only taxonomic order of animals entirely restricted to the deep sea.   "The veiled elasipodans are often a lovely purple or orangish pink." (H. Kerr)

闇 の 夜 の 沢 山 に な る 生 海 鼠 哉 祥 禾

yami no yo no takusan ni naru namako kana – shôka (1820?)
(dark[pitch-black/moonless]-night/s many/difficult become: sea slug!/?/ó/the)

#611

darkling

moonless nights
add up until we get
the sea slug

solace

when dark nights
grow too hard to bear!
the sea slugs

The first reading of this recent find is even more poetic than the mistranslated version of Gyôtai's Ice-room haiku I had sincerely intended to end the book with. The second reading might be hard to catch. It will make sense after you read the final final poem, below, which says that while the *namako* may be a creature of the cold and dark in *its* life, there is no question that it brings cheer to *our* lives. By an obscure poet, and found (so far) in only one recently published book of "droll haiku" (KKHK), this deserves to be as well known as any sea slug haiku:

寒 い 日 に 笑 の た え ぬ 海 鼠 哉 里 夕

samui hi ni warai no taenu namako kana – riyû (1751)
(cold day-on, laughter ceases/stops-not sea-slug!/?/ó/the/a)

#612

snowed in
laugh after laugh
a sea slug!

cold weather
a sea slug entertains us
all day long

a cold day
one sea slug provides
endless fun

wintering in
laughter without end
a sea slug

winter at home
laughter never ceases
with a sea slug

on a cold day
the sea slug has humor
enough for all

amen

〜

the
sea
.slug

is

no
thing
at
all

Sundry Sea Slugs

The Poem-bag Sea Slug

海 鼠 と い ふ 詩 嚢 の 深 さ は か ら れ ず 圓 水

namako to iu shinô no fukasa hakararezu – ensui (2002)
#613 (seaslug called poem-sack/bag's depth measure-able-not)

> this *sea slug*:
> a poem bag too deep
> for measuring

> ***benthic***

> who could plum
> this sack of poetry
> called sea slug

A *shinô* is a Chinese-derived term for a container into which one drops the drafts of poems. I recall Hank Williams with his cardboard boxes full of unfinished songs and I have myself used a variety of strange containers, but none of that is of any help translating, when a word demands a word and not a description. I looked up *shinô* in my Japanese-English dictionary just in case there *were* a word, perhaps of Latinate derivation, that I might enlist. Not only did it fail to give me one, but it did not so much as hint at the literal meaning. It only defined the figurative one: "poetic(al) sentiment; poetic sensibility" which, used in conjunction with a verb (*koyasu* = manure/enrich/fatten) means "to foster one's poetical sentiment." The original poem plays upon both the figurative meaning of the sea slug as good food for poets *and* the literal meaning for, in Japan where poems were written in one or two lines on strips of paper, the bag was probably oblong and bore some resemblance to a sea slug. [1] To me, it also evokes the deepest of all sea slugs, the unfathomable image we saw in the *Protean* and *Taoist Sea Slugs*, for the example usage (given in the OJD) has a Chinese monk-poet who visited Japan in 1329 speaking of the bottomless nature of such a poem bag. [2]

生 き て ゐ る ら し き 袋 の 海 鼠 か な 香 (金 沢 市)

ikiteiru rashiki fukuro no namako kana – kaori (contemp)
#614(alive-like/seeming pouch/sack/pocket-seaslug tis!/?/ǒ/the/a)

> the sea slug
> in my bag seems
> to be alive

1. *Japanese Shinô* Considering the single line of haiku poetry, I would expect a long and thin haiku/senryu/waka/tanka poem bag existed in Japan. I imagine it bound to the central post, the *hashira* of the house. But, to tell the truth, I have no idea whether such has ever existed. Readers who know are invited to write! Regardless, the Japanese sea slug is not *that* long and thin, so any old bag validates the poem.

2. *Chinese Poem Bag* The sentence with the poem-bag:「詩嚢無底未易空。」According to KS, this means it will never empty and has unlimited ideas for poems, yet to be written. The words 何氏書堂 found next to the example suggests to me that the sentence is the poetic name for someone's personal study/library, for it was common to paint (or tile in) a poetic line of poetry above the window of such a place and call it that.

Despite the holothurian plasticity of this book, I did not manage to squeeze all the squirming sea slugs into the 21 chapters – poem bags – comprising the main text.   Rather than throwing them overboard, I kept them, for what doesn't fit in is often instructive and always interesting. And, perhaps, I should add that some of these didn't fit because, as you will see, they were not poems.

~

The Laughing Sea Slug

老 人 の 呵 呵 大 笑 の 海 鼠 か な 美 保 子
rôjin no kaka taishô no namako kana – mihoko (contemp.)
#615 (old-people's ha-ha/hoh-hoh big-laugh's seaslug!/?/ó/the)

> hearty laughs
> old folk get a kick
> out of sea slug

> *eavesdroppable*

> loud laughter
> from an old couple
> with a sea slug

The last haiku of the last chapter mentions the winter cheer brought by a sea slug.   I wanted to add this charming example to it, but how could I with my last translation ending with *amen*? While this haiku also does not specify what was so funny, by specifying *old folk*, we cannot help but imagine their conversation.   Are they incapable of picking up pieces of pickled slug? Are they finding *every* piece too hard to chew? Or is it a whole one in a tub that provides outrageous body metaphors which the elderly (at least in Japan) are not shy about? I hope the Japanese Candid Camera (*dokkiri kamera*) tries this, if they haven't already!

~

The Molten Sea Slug

海 底 の 火 の 山 ね む る 海 鼠 か な 龍 岡 晋
unazoko no hi no yama nemuru namako kana – tatsuoka tsutomu (contemp)
#616 (sea-bottom's fire-mountain/s sleep[ing] sea slug/s!/?/ó/the/a/behold)

acala	*acala*
the volcano sleeps on the ocean floor a sea slug!	the sea slug sleeps on the ocean floor a volcano!

Earthquakes are said to be caused by the convulsions of a gigantic catfish. The Chinese, or, rather Japanese character [1] → for the catfish (*namazu*) is "fish+thought." Of the many characters signifying thought of one quality or another, this "thought" (*nen*) is the one associated with what we might call brooding and terrifying fixation. I find this poetically pleasing, as I do the fact that the surname of the modern poet who wrote the above haiku is, coincidentally, perfect: "dragon-hill!" I do not really know if the poet means for the *namako* to be for the volcanic eruption what the *namazu* is for the earthquake. The way a sea cucumber can spew things out its anus and mouth, not to mention, in the case of some species, instantly split open and squirt out its guts from the side [1] certainly makes it an appropriate god of the volcano!

I added the title *Acala*, for this Hindhi/Buddhist god of fire associated with mountains (and mountain mysticism) has the wonderful name of *Fudomyou,* or "not-move-mystery/holy," in Japanese. The idea of unmoving power, the strength to stay still moves me and provides a good offset to the weaker image of the sea slug in this book; but it is hard to tell what the poem means to the poet. One of my favorite MANYOSHU (c 900 ad) poems, *waka #3033* laments the author's own mountain burning up. After a preliminary line which can be roughly translated as "How the hell can you know [*my* suffering]!" she concludes, "I'd rather be the one watching the smoke from the outside!" (*nakanaka ni nanika shirikemu   waga yama ni moyuru keburi no yoso ni mimashi o*).   I have a dozen paraverses of this, but all are only shots in the dark. The poem can be read in many ways and I do not yet know which is more likely to be correct, but here is my best shot:

losing my cool

see the mountain blow its top
i wish that it weren't me!
and if we hadn't met, dear
it wouldn't be!

In other words, is it possible the sleeping volcano in Dragonhill's haiku is *inside* the sea slug poet's heart? [2]   In that case, the poem may belong with Buson's and Shôha's *Melancholy Romantic Sea Slug* rather than back here in the *Sundry* section. If so, it also supplies an element missed in the older poems. Namely, classical lovesickness *mono-omoi* ("thing-thinking,") often played on the single syllabet homophone, fire (*hi*) at the end of *omoi,* which was written *omohi.* Thanks to this fiction, lovers burnt holes in the chest of their kimonos and had to turn their tears into firefighters.* But the sea slug, as we have seen, was depicted as the coldest of creatures. Dragonhill has, then, resolved this contradiction by bringing in a sleeping, ie., inactive "fire-mountain."

←1. *Chinese and Japanese Characters* While most Chinese characters come from Chinese, the Japanese made hundreds, dozens of which are for fish. The catfish (namazu) is one of these. This will be elaborated upon in *Swellfish Soup,*
1. *Varieties of Disenbowlment* "Sea cucumbers generally do not have a choice of where they eviscerate. The most surprising split or, instant goo-ification of the 'side', only occurs in those autotomising the tentacle crown and never occurs in the forms that eviscerate through the anus." (A. Kerr*) In that case, what I wrote in chapter 3, the Protean Sea Slug may be partially wrong.*
2. *Fire Mountain Metaphor* I do not have my burning heart poems properly assembled for presentation, but as I write this, I happen to be rereading Saigyo's SANKA-SHŪ (Mountain Hut Collection) and poem 1307 reads: "when did it start? / this longing [omohi=love-thoughts=fire] that oozes out / like smoke from fûji / as i lie face down / my island bed afloat!" (*itsu to naki omohi-wa fûji-no kemuri-nite uchifusu toko ya uki-shima-ga-hara*). It would take many paraverses to catch all the puns. "Ukishima-ga-hara" is a swampy place South of Mt Fuji, which Englishes as "floating-island-field," where "field" is a

homophone for "belly." The original suggests the smoke from Fuji suggests is also the cause of what follows, namely, (the unmentioned, but understood) crying that brings forth tears enough to float the poet's bed! Whether Saigyô also knew that Fûji was once surrounded by more water or, simply pretends to see a reflection of his burning mountain self in his swamp of tears, in my opinion, the overall image would be a mountain of desire floating on a sea of its own tears! Saigyô, whom Bashô practically worshipped, was the boldest metaphor-maker – often by combining older metaphor – in the history of Japanese poetry.
3. *Tears as Firefighters* The best known of these and only one I can quickly get my hands on is Kokinshu *waka # 572,* to wit: "if not for / these tears of longing / for you, dear / the breast of my robe / would burn and love would out!" (*kimi kouru namida shi nakuba kara-goromo mune-no atari-wa iro moe-namashi* – ki-no tsurayuki). The poem is by no other than the editor of the anthology. As I reread, Erica Jong on the Diane Ream (sp?) Show speaks of Sapho's famous words: "You've torched my heart and set fire to my breast." This is not bad but crude compared to what the Japanese did with such metaphors.

the riddle

a volcano
sleeps on the sea floor
who is it?

namako

cold, lovesick
my heart is a volcano
sleeping in the sea

I have read haiku by Issa and others which turn both fireflies on the "back" of a river (*kawase*) and horse dung into *moxa* (burning blobs of mugwort applied to sensitive nodes on the body of men and beasts in the Far East, both as treatment for specific ailments and as a preventative medicine) and that, combined with the comic imagination translation stimulates, makes me imagine a new sort of *reverse moxacombustion,* where the poet's sea slug, or rather sea slugs, are big blobs of *anti-moxa,* cooling rather than heating the sea floor!   If it were not for these cool cukes, the sea-floor would be constantly exploding on us. Before Keigu got side-tracked on this fantastical train of thought, he wrote a more responsible envoi, which later acquired variations:

溶岩か海鼠と思ふ微動かな 敬愚
yôgan ka namako to omou bidô kana – keigu
(lava?/or seaslug think/wonder slight-movement!/?/ó/the/loh)

#617

sometimes
lava seems to move
sea slugs!

溶岩が動けば又も海鼠かな　敬愚
yôgan ga ugokeba mata mo namako kana – keigu
(lava-the move-if/when again-even seaslug/s!/?/ó/the/loh)

#618

abracadabra

the lava moves
and we have sea slugs
once again

溶岩や動き出したら海鼠にし 敬愚
yôgan ya ugokidashitara namako ni shi – keigu
(lava:/! move-start-if/when seaslug-as/into make)

#619

all that lava
it moves and i make out
the sea slugs

perception

lava moves
so i turn it into
a sea slug

∽

Seducing Sea Slug

In this poem by Hawaiian poet Lori Lei Hokyo Hunley, we find a sea slug who belongs neither to the Sinosphere nor to the West.. The poem is not complete [1] and the *italics* my doing.

Pahoehoe

Pele's hair streamed, ink dark
toward Kona bay, fire licking
at the strands.

We lay there after the flow
had hardened into hips,
thighs, shoulders.

Loli, Loli, charmer, charmer.

Between lips of solid smoke
we unmade each other. Breaking
waves all around us.

This kai turns flesh to stone.

Salt shone so bright on our bodies
we didn't know rock from water.

Hawaiian words defined:
Pahoehoe: thick, slow-moving lava that cools into smooth rippled fields.
Pele: the Hawaiian goddess of fire and volcanoes
Loli: *sea cucumber; in Hawaiian mythology a shape-changing demigod who in the guise of a handsome young man lured women into waters off shore and drowned them. The women's bodies were transfigured into stone formations that line the rocky coast.*
Kapu: [*a word from the missing part of the poem*] forbidden; places in the islands which people were forbidden to enter by the ali'i (royalty) or kahuna (priests); also places which were known to have special mana (power) or magic.
Kai: ocean

It is interesting that the male, rather than female seductor/ress, should be a sea slug. I cannot help but recall the Japanese tale [2] of a man who fell asleep outside one afternoon and had a wet dream with a beautiful girl and awakened to find a five-foot snake with semen oozing from its mouth lying dead next to him. In Japan, the snake, as a swallower, is female rather than phallic as in the West. In both Japan and the West, however, as we have seen, the sea slug is phallic. It would seem the same is the case for Hawaii, where its ugly apparent manhood apparently fused with "a handsome young man."

1. ***Incomplete Poem*** I exchanged letters with the poet who was in the Univ. of Minnesota master of creative writing program shortly before 9/11, but lost touch before obtaining the full poem. I hope to have it by the second ed.!
2. ***Japanese Tales*** The tale of a "snake// killed by semen" is from the *Konjaku Monogatari* (c1100). It is titled "The Pretty Woman," and is tale #109 in Royall Tyler's highly recommended anthology from many sources: *Japanese Tales* (Pantheon: 1987). As a rule, old Japanese tales are less corrupt (less de-sexed) than Western ones.

Dragon Palace Sea Slugs

龍 宮 の わ さ び お ろ し や 大 な ま こ　加 甲
ryûgu no wasabioroshi ya ônamako – kakô? (1680)
#620 (dragon-palace's horseradish-grater:/! big seaslug)

horseradish grater[1]
for the dragon palace?
a large sea slug

Sea slug prickles would be hard to spy on the floor of the sea, but Japanese never forget the prickles on sea slugs because their variety is on the prickly side. If you can only imagine the soft prickles are hard, a large sea slug can turn into a grater, but the poet neglects to say what will serve for the underwater horseradish.[2] The Dragon Palace is where the fisherman Urashima Taro fell out of time after he was carried there by a grateful turtle. I am not going to give away the story of this Japanese Rip Van Winkle, but will just say that this palace is the Sino-Japanese equivalent of Neptune's Palace.

龍 宮 の 天 井 裏 に 海 鼠 か な　化 羊
ryûgu no tenjôura ni namako kana – kayô (pre1927)
#621(dragon's ceiling-back-in/at/on seaslug!/?/ô/the/behold)

dragon palace:
behind the ceiling?
solid sea slug!

My "solid sea slug" was meant as hyperbole, but since writing it, I googled across Japanese tourist reports of *namako* "carpets" in parts of Guam. The reference in the poem is probably to a genuine building material, *namako-gawara*, or "sea slug tiles." *Tenjô-ura* (ceiling-back) is a strange way to say "roof," but if the Dragon Palace is under the seafloor, the ceiling inside would be a real structure, while there would be no roof *per se*. Another possibility, supported by readers, is that we are talking about a space between the ceiling and roof, where the sea slug coins (large oblong coins) are stashed, though I can't imagine having to hide money in a palace!

龍 宮 の 庭 に あ ま た の 海 鼠 か な　射 石
ryûgu no niwa ni amata no namako kana – shaseki?(pre1927)
#622 (dragon's garden-on, excessive seaslug/s!/?/ô/the/behold)

the grounds of
dragon palace overrun
by sea slugs

sea cucumber
to burn in the plots
of dragon palace

the garden plots
of dragon palace are full
of sea cucumber

dragon palace
in a pickle: too many
sea cucumber!

1, Horse-Radish Grater or Grated Horse-Radish In the case of *daikon,* the huge white radish, *daikon-oroshi* means the product, the grated radish, as well as the grater, so I assumed this was the case for *wasabi* and had the sea slug looking like a mound of grated *wasabi* until KK, a Japanese reader, caught my mistranslation. This was one of those cases where grammar is no guide, the reason why checks by native speakers are indispensable!

2. Horse-Radish & Dragons In case you wondered, *no!* Oriental dragons are not so fiery-breathed as their Occidental counterparts. They are associated with moisture more than fire and might be thought of as a meme that evolved to keep the snake in religion where it was before being thrown out by sky-god-worshipping, anti-earth Judeo-Christians.

I think the poet is thinking of *namako* as "sea-rat/mouse," of the seabed, but he might be thinking *mole,* for not only is the sea slug the mole's nemesis, but similarly blind. Then again, the 11th meaning of *namako* in my OJD is "a cucumber," (*kiuri*), argot for "thief." Since thieves in Japanese are called mouse-burglars (*nezumi-kozo*) rather than "cat-burglars" . . . There may well be dozens of Dragon Palace sea cucumber poems out there (perhaps in children's books), garden varieties would probably be rare, for so many sea plants and animals are eaten by Japanese that they tend to have their own names rather than echo those on land. [1]

~

The Cobbler Sea Slug

水 底 や わ ら ぢ の 如 き 大 海 鼠　耿 陽
minasoko ya waraji no gotoki ônamako – okada kôyô (mod)
#623 (seafloor: straw-sandal-like big seaslug)

on the sea floor
something like a sandal
a big sea slug

A *waraji* is a sandal made of twisted straw but it is also a proper word, so I did not wish to use the straw like an adjective, but that is the sandal you should imagine. It is the footwear of choice for pilgrimages, and for that matter, all serious travel, for they were cheap and expendable. Spares were often carried as we carry spare automobile tires (likewise for horses, who had straw horse-shoes!). The description is apt, yet magical: we can imagine the sandal of a human – for some reason, they always catch my eye on the beach – or, more magically, supernatural denizens of the sea. Keigu (influenced by the *Dragon Palace Sea Slugs*) is somewhere in between:

飛 び 絨 毯 羽 靴 も な く 海 鼠 か な　敬 愚
tobijutan hanegutsu mo naku namako kana – keigu
#624 (flying-carpet, feather/winged-shoes too not seaslug!/?/ô/the/it is)

oops!

no flying carpet
nor winged shoes, sea slug
underfoot

But to come down to earth, there is a more realistic old haiku by Rôka (trans. is "wave-flower=foam, possibly pron. Naniwa), which is remarkably modern in its objective depiction of a yucky incident:

#625

1. *Sea Slugs as Produce in Japanese* A googled line from a paragraph on fishing in a chapter ("Some Remarks On Gulls") from a nameless book written in English provides a perfect example of the garden context less likely in Japanese: "It may be any one of the grotesque products of Neptune's vegetable garden, a sea-cucumber, a sea-carrot, or a sea-cabbage." (www.kellscraft.com/ daysoffch10.html) The only poem I know in Japanese to treat a garden variety of holothurian is a strange *tanka* which puts the *namako* in a land-garden rather than in Neptune's (i.e., reverses the metaphor): "sea-slug-like / bitter-squash and lychee / their pimply butts / dingle-dangling / in the leafy shade" (*namako nasu reishi nigauri iboibo no shiri tarashitari hanyo(?)gakuri ni* – okamoto taimu (1877-1963) 海鼠なす荔枝苦瓜いぼいぼの尻垂らしたり繁(?)葉がくりに(t?k?) 岡本大無) A Japanese advisor informed me that lychee was the favorite food of the famous Chinese beauty Yôkihi (I've no idea how Chinese pronounce it!). The Okinawan "bitter-squash" is a favorite of mine, but I've no idea what to call it in English! It looks like a very warty cucumber.

網子むれて踏みつふしたる生海鼠哉　浪花? 作者不知?

amigo murete fumitsubusareshi namako kana – rôka (1670-1703)?
#626 (netters congregate step-on squashed sea slug!/?/ó/the)

good catch

a full net
sea slugs are trampled
in the rush

Perhaps, there was something rare caught that day.   As a matter of fact that is stranger than fiction, the trampled sea slug *does* shod at least one island people, and in a very unexpected way.

> The Palauan people use the sea cucumber to protect their feet when walking in the reef. They squeeze the sea cucumber until it squirts out sticky threads, which they put on their feet.[1] Even though this practice may seem harsh, the sea cucumber returns to the reef unharmed. These threads are normally used to trap its enemies. (http://pbs.org/edens/palau/p_sea_b_9.htm)

While there are countless accounts of less purposeful stepping on sea slugs by letter-writing and diary-keeping Japanese tourists, there are few haiku.

海鼠踏んだらトウキョウと音がした　倉本朝世

namako fundara tôkyô to oto ga shita – Kuramoto Asayo? (contemp)
#627 (seaslug step-on-when, "tokyo" sound made)

stepping on
a sea slug, i heard
to-u-ki-yo-u!

One site calls this a *senryu,* but I would call it a haiku, though I do not know if the poet means he is ready to return to the Big Toe, Tokyo, or that he felt Tokyo *is* a sea slug – perhaps in its urban sprawl? – or if, *that is just what his ears heard* (as mine heard a bird in Tokyo call *"beaver-creek!"* for years on end).   Maybe he needs to step on another slug to confirm his finding.

な ま こ 踏 む 感 触 の あ る 夜 道 な り 　玉 簾

namako fumu kanshoku no aru yomichi nari – tamasudare (2002)
#628 (seaslug tread/step-on feeling is/has night-road is/becomes)

a path at night
i feel like i'm walking
on sea slugs

It is spooky when hard ground turns springy on you.   I once felt something like this – The first time I smoked marijuana, the ground became alive – it pushed back and it gave way – like it did for those men camped out on a small island that happened to be a whale, or under Tamasudare's feet.

---

1. *Types of Stickiness* "Once i was spearfishing far from shore with a family on Guam and my finger was sliced open by a moray eel. The old lady took my finger and wrapped it up in these same sticky threads, the Cuvierian tubules. The tubules don't stick very well to hairless skin, so to make shoes from them, the Palauans would have to wrap some of the tubules completely around their feet, rather than just squirt them onto the soles. (A. Kerr) According to http://www.oceanicresearch.org/ echinoderm.html this "goo is so sticky that it absolutely cannot be removed from the skin without shaving off any hair with which it has come in contact." It would seem to be the perfect depilatory!

The Flying Sea Slug

While the sea slugs in the net, above, are the only ones trampled in old haiku, net-surfing reveals that inadvertently stepping on *namako* in the ocean constantly reported by Japanese tourists (Westerners step on them too, but don't think it worth special attention). The best report (2000/2/24) was by a woman working for a US software company in Japan, *title*: "iron-fist-cat-punch," *handle*: Michyorin.

> [Re. her Guam vacation:] for sure, the sea slugs are here [a common phrase in tourist reports being: "the sea is beautiful, but there are sea slugs" or the vice-versa, this qualifying phrase is understandable!], but once you've stepped on about ten [sense-translation=a dozen] of them, you get used to it. [And there are] Sea slugs washed up on the beach. We had the loser at *janken* [rock-scizzors-paper], pick them up and throw them out to sea. I lost one round after another. Me, holding them in my bare hand, throwing them out to sea! (OM=Thank goodness they weren't sea urchins!)

It is hard to say if the idea is to get the grossness off the beach or help save the sea slugs to eat them another day! (The "*me, holding ~*" is a difficult translation. It is interesting to find another woman (Chiaki) write about throwing sea slugs using identical cutesy female grammar which, Englishes awkwardly as: "sea-slug-throwing me" – actually, hers was past-tense (*namako-o-nagete-yatta watashi*), something English cannot handle (X=sea-slug-threw-me) at all. This second woman (site name lost) also wrote of poking and stretching sea slugs and ended her island (Gaohagan, S. Philippine) swim as follows: "We played for a while with sea slugs, and returned by the road we came." (*namako to shibaraku asobi, moto kita michi o modoru*) I find this line prose more poetic than 99% of poems on *any* subject I have read.

投 げ て 見 る 生 海 鼠 に 妹 が 笑 ひ 哉　嘯 山

nagetemiru namako ni imo ga warai kana – shôzan (1717-1801)

#629 (throw-see/try sea-slug-at little-sister/girlfriend laughs!/?/ỏ)

my girl laughs
as she tries her hand at
throwing sea slugs

my girl laughs
when i try tossing her
a sea slug

my girl laughing
at the sea slug as she
tries to throw it

my girl laughs
when i try to throw a = === ====>> > *seaslug*
back to sea

What a delightful haiku! My translations makes us imagine a father and daughter on a beach, but a man and his woman in the garden (the sea slug taken from a tub) is as likely, both because "little sister" means *sweetheart* and because sea slug suggests the winter and such a beach would be a cold place for play. Regardless, one should be careful not to overdo it with sea slugs, for their sake and ours:

> A.H. Banner, Professor of Zoology at the University of Hawaii, reported [to W.L.Orris]that "when my children were small they took delight in throwing apodous holothurian, *Opheodeosoma spectabilis,* at each other. I had finally to forbid it because it caused a skin rash; whether it was from the anchor-shaped spicules or from toxic compounds, I do not know." (Alexander A. Fisher: Atlas of AQUATIC DERMATOLOGY (Grune and Stratton: 1978))

Humans are not the only species known to play with sea slugs. [1] It goes without saying that dolphins play with sea cucumbers because they play with *everything*, but how about this 1995 report from Floreanna in "A Trip to the Galapagos" by Evan Bigall?

> Afternoon snorkeling at Champion Island with sea lions. Hordes of them. They played with us. One jumped over my back exactly the way they do with each other. A young male tried to get Roy to play catch with a sea cucumber. (world.std.com/~jegan/adventure.html - 23k)

~

Playing With Sea Slugs

Not all Sea Slug play is *squirting* or *throwing*. You will find something else, *sea-slug-as-fashion-accessory* in this report (found and lost on net) by a Japanese wind-surfing group representative:

> After treading on them by accident walking the beach, we played with the sea slugs for a while. We used them for *chonmage* (a clump of hair once bound tightly, cropped and placed in the center of the shaved part of a man's head), a moustache dance (*hige-dansu*) [*hige-dana* mistake?], and catch-ball, and found even sea slugs are quite cute. (*namako mo kekkô kawaii.*)

Amazingly, I was soon to not only encounter but *wear* that *chonmage,* myself.

As this book was nodding off and ready to be put to bed – a perfect description of the condition of your editor+author+proof-reader+deisgner+publisher at this moment – I was lampooned (in fun) at the haiku site where I had excused myself for not participating in the usual haiku games because I was being pursued by sea slugs (*namako ni owarete*). After thanking me for providing laughs enough to fortify her immune system, a relatively new participant haiku'ed,

太刀魚来海鼠に追はれる敬愚哉　　みよこ

tachiuo ki namako ni owareru keigu kana – miyoko (2003)

#630 (cutlassfish come, seaslugs-by pursued keigu!/?/ 'tis)

a cutlassfish	"cutlassfish come!
for keigu, now pursued	the sea slugs are after
by sea slugs!	poor respectfool!"

Said fish is the *Trichiurus lepturus,* (also called *ribbonfish, scabbardfish* and *snakefish*). This mayhem was capped (note that it begins with the last part of the previous poem) by another poet:

敬愚氏のちょんまげあれあれ海鼠かな　等

#631*keigu shi no chonmage areare namako kana* – hitoshi (2003)

(keigu-mr.'s chonmage[hair-clump] what,what/look-look! seaslug!/?/'tis)

mr respectfool
boasts a *chonmage,* what?
it's a sea slug!

This hairstyle, described above, is identified with the swordplay-loving Easterns (as I call the equivalent of the American Western). To think that my *nom de plume* would end up in a sea-floor drama! *Playing with sea slugs,* indeed! (念のため、前句は：天気雨からんころんと太刀魚来 振り子)

The Monster Sea Slug

怪 物 の 大 物 消 へ て 海 鼠 哉　敬 愚

#632 kaibutsu no ômono kiete namako kana – keigu
(monster-big-ones vanished/vanishing, seaslug!/?/ó/the/behold)

for sparky and tiny
(and Steinbeck and Ricketts who wrote of them)

the big monsters
all gone, all gone, only
sea slug remains

怪 物 が 絶 へ て 海 鼠 ぞ 有 り 難 き　敬 愚

#633 kaibutsu ga taete namako zo arigataki – keigu
(monsters vanished/extinct seaslug[emphatic]grateful)

with monsters   monsters gone
extinct, we're indebted   the sea slugs hold us
to sea slugs   in their debt

In the 1940's, when Steinbeck and Ricketts explored the Sea of Cortez, there were still people living in Monterey, California who believed in the Old Man of the Sea "who might well be a myth, except that to many people have seen him." (LSC) I doubt if that could be said today and that is a shame for as Steinbeck and Ricketts put it, "an ocean without its unnamed monsters would be like a completely dreamless sleep." One might think the sea slug too small to be a monster, much less inspire much terror, but one can never tell. Here is yet another Guam report.

> Guam is famous for its abundance of *namako*.   Picking up that information while still in Japan, Mama and Papa [that is to say, the authors are parents and are thinking from the perspective of their child/ren [1]] had *namako* on the tip of their tongue. "Just oodles of *namako* they say . . . . ," "Well, those *namako* . . ."   Yusuke heard this and developed a fear of this undefined and unknown creature, *namako*.   When [in Guam] we finally were able to go swimming, he adamantly refused, "No! No! There are *namako* here, I'm not getting in!" Even his response to the seaweed washing up on to the beach was "I'm afraid! I'm afraid! What's this, *namako*?" It didn't take long to clear up the misunderstanding about the seaweed, but he still wasn't about to enter the ocean.   Finally, we had to put a float on Yusuke and carry him out to join us. – from "The Tanaka Family's Foreign Travel Day by Day" (© Ayako and Minoru *tanaka ie no hizure kaigairyôkô* geocities.co.jp/ SilkRoad/ 3178/98guam/Guam-4th day.htm)

Keigu's poem is for Steinbeck and Ricketts because of their regret for the passing of the monsters of the deep expressed in *The Log of the Sea of Cortez.*

1. *Mama and Papa* The Japanese tend to be more flexible about names than English speakers. Sometimes this can make conversation easier. When I used the word "mama" to avoid the tedious description "your mom" (and a name won't do with a small child) – and, I suppose, to see if it would pass in English ---when addressing my three year-old nephew my sister immediately cut in, "I'm not *your* mother!" and Carter parroted in a slightly contemptuous tone, "She's not *your* mother!"

塩 振 って 海 鼠 おたけび 潮 吹ける 高沢 良一

#634 shio futte namako otakebi shio fukeru – takasawa yoshikazu (2003)
(salt shaking[as a dog shakes off water] seaslug male-bravado/battle-cry brine-blow)

a warrior never dies

scattering salt
sea slug yowls, squirting
brine and bowels!

shaking off salt   shaking off salt
sea slug let's out a whoop   a sea slug blows brine and
and blows brine   rises to the fray

halodeima

tossing off salt
sea slug lets loose a roar heard
o'er the ocean

塩ふって 海鼠の終を かがやかす   土田 河石

shio futte namako no oe o kagayakasu – tsuchida kaseki (contemp)
#635 (salt-shaking/shaked seaslug's end[obj.] shines)

tossing off salt   scattering salt
the sea slug enjoys   the sea slug goes down
a brilliant end   like a warrior

As mentioned in the introduction, there are holothurians called (or, that *used to be* called) *halodeima*, or "brine-monster," but this poem is about the Japanese *namako*.   Unfortunately, English has no specific word for male gallantry that is synonymous with a battle-cry – or, at least none that make my dictionary – so a smooth translation is impossible. Takasawa writes that the *namako* is roughly dressed with salt, after which it hardens and then is cut into rings and vinegared.   That only explains the salt. I am not certain where the rest of the poem comes from. Does the dying sea slug squirm more violently than at any other time? Do the poets play upon old poems about fighting – struggling with chopsticks – with pickled slugs? Do they imagine an SF-like scene of a rising monster? I could have asked Takasawa, but I didn't.   Steinbeck and Ricketts would have preferred not to know.

~

The Exorcist Sea Slug

The fact that Japanese have used sea slugs to combat moles was discussed in the main text and its notes. No haiku were given, for none were yet found when I wrote it.   After getting my own copy of the great Kaizosha *saijiki* (hksj) I found no less than twenty-one "mole-beating" (literally: "earth-dragon-beating") haiku! [1]   Generally, the sea slug is taken for granted and not mentioned.

1. *The Practice of Mole-exorcizing Sea Slugs*! My most broadly read Japanese reader had never heard of this practice and thought it must be restricted to a small part of Japan, namely Tohoku, the cold out-of-the-way place identified with sea slugs more than any other. The notes in the Kaizosha Saijiki make it clear that such was not the case, for they begin by mentioning Kinai, a term for the old capital of Kyoto, .and go on to mention Osaka, the merchant center of Japan and all of Saikoku (the "West Countries" meaning the area South-west of Edo extending to the China sea). We might also recall the ditty from Kyushu given earlier. According to *Wakan Sansai Zue*, cited by the Kaizosha s., in Kyoto, the skewer used for dried sea slug was driven into the ground in flower gardens.

蟄 虫 も 出 で よ と 土 龍 打 ち に け り　橡 面 坊
#636 chicchû mo ideyo to mogura uchinikeri – tochimenbô (mod)
(persevering/hibernating-bugs too come-out/leave mole-beating[+finality])

Out with all
the sleeping bugs too
mole-beating

If you ask me, Tochimenbô should have been content to single out the nemesis of any poet, the silverfish.   How about trying sea slug bookmarks?

打 ち 漏 ら す 土 龍 日 を 見 て 潜 み け り　橡 面 坊
uchimorasu mogura hi o mite hisomekeri – tochimenbô (mod)
#637(hit/beat-leak mole sun sees/seeing, dives/absconds/hides[+finality])

mole escapes
beating peeks out at the sun
and hides again
～
surviving moles
watch the sun set and
hunker down

I do not how hard the sea slug – except when it was a mallet? – beat the ground (the contemporary tendency to call the ceremony *namakohiki*, "seaslug-dragging" minimizes the violence). Perhaps the sound of the small drums and pots that were indeed beaten, rather than the smell of the mole's nemesis leaked through the "ceiling" of the mole's den waking him up and scaring him to abandon the field. It is still chilly – for the date, the 14th of January in much of Japan, was, at the time this poem was written, mid-winter (it was Spring by the old calendar).

夜 は 寺 の む ぐ ら 打 ち け り 桐 畠　青 々
yoru wa tera no mugura uchikeri kiribatake – seisei (1869-1937)
#638 (night-as-for temple's mole/s beat[+finality] pawlonia-garden)

the temple moles
are beaten in the night
a paulownia grove

This tree, or rather its individual falling leaves, is a symbol of mortality; but I think it is its usefulness for woodwork (especially making *geta*) that make it worth defending. I assume the Buddhists who are not supposed to need animistic protection and supposed to me equally merciful to all life are ashamed to do this in the day.

土 龍 打 お り お り 月 の 覗 き け り　山 県 瓜 青
mugurauchi oriori tsuki no nozokikeri – kasei (mod)
#639 (mole-beating time-time moon's peeking[+finality])

mole-beating
now and then the moon
peeks through

The Buddhist moon, the light of the merciful Law that even put ferocious boars to sleep, contrasts with this vulgar pandemonium.

土龍打とらごどうんとこけにけり 梨葉
#640 mogurauchi torago dôn to kokenikeri – riyô (mod.)
(mole/earth-dragon-beating tiger-master=thud-with collapse[+finality])

ole don tiger
beating earth-dragons
suddenly folds

Strangely – or, perhaps not so if we think of it as taboo=charmed – the sea slug is rarely named in theses poems.   When it is named, the talismanic name (as above) is more common than *namako*.   The sea slug dolls dragged behind each participant in the mole-beating look quite fat, almost like footballs in the photographs I've seen.   While the hardest beating was done on fertilizer buckets, pots, and drums, in some areas, the master-tiger dolls were themselves whacked against the ground.   I like to imagine a sea slug dragged over a large field, popping out somewhere along the way to chase the moles on its own, or more horrifically dragged to his death.   The mimetic *dôn* puns as the title *don*.

海 鼠 い つ 縄 抜 け け ら し 土 竜 打   楽 堂
namako itsu nawa nukekerashi mogurauchi – rakutô (mod)
#641(seaslug some-time cord slipped-off earth-dragon=mole-beating)

the mole-beat
when did sea slug manage
to slip its cord?

Perhaps, the slippery escape suggested a mention of the sea slug would be appropriate.   Seeing "sea slugs" dragged behind the participants as a child on a sled might be, one is first led to believe that the moles get the bad end of the deal, but after reading more, we find it is the sea-slugs that deserve our pity.   Thank goodness, they are usually used in name alone!   One haiku had the spike (or, ear of grain, rather than sea slug) fly off out of the straw covering:

ぬ け て 飛 ぶ 藁 の 穂 し べ や 土 龍 打 石 堂
nukete tobu wara no hoshibe[?] ya mogurauchi – sekidô (mod)
#642 (slip-off-fly/ies hay's head/spike:/! earth-dragon=mole/s-beating)

mole beating
out pops a flying
sheaf of hay

It is all too clear that the sea slug or its embodiment was mercilessly beaten and/or swung. With the "flying," I feel tempted to resurrect the flying sea slug guts described earlier.

土 竜 打 つ て コ ツ と 捨 て た る 海 鼠 か な 菅 原 師 竹
#643 mogura utte kotto sutetaru namako kana – shichiku (1868-1926)
(earth-dragon=mole-beating/en completely/cleanly abandoned seaslug!/?/ô/a)

beating moles	moles beaten
a sea slug abandoned	he's left to the dogs
just like that	tiger sea slug

As far as I can tell, all 21 poems in the Kaizosha *saijiki,* and the last poem from a different source, are from the Meiji era or later, so it would seem that this secondary sea slug *kidai* had to await the discovery of folk on the part of the haiku poets.[1]

土 龍 打 つ く り ぬ 男 の 子 の 数 を 草 駄

#644mugurauchi tsukurinu otoko no ko no kazu o – sôda (mod)
(earth-dragon=mole-hit/beat[ing device] make man-child's number[obj])

> mole beaters
> we make one for each
> male child

I doubt girls were excluded from the ritual, but I can well imagine boys fighting over the drums and "sea slugs." I was happy to find the handful of slug-dragging haiku in a more recent saijiki include this:

女 わ ら べ の こ と に 執 念 も ぐ ら 打 岡 入 万 寿 子

mewarabe no koto ni shûnen mogurauchi – okairi masuko (contemp?)
#645(girl-[small]child's especially vindictive/tenacious/intense: mole-beating/er/s)

> my little girls   my little girl
> particularly tenacious   makes a very thorough
> mole-beaters   mole-beater!

The reader might wonder what could make a girl – all little girls are, after all, sweet to the core – so ferocious. I suspect the apparent anomaly here is due, not to a certain Freudian concept, but to the little girls' greater sensitivity to the suffering moles cause their gardening parents, which makes them, for once, *appear* to be crueler than little boys. For this reason, I first wrote "vindictive" rather than "tenacious." The "my" is a matter of style and might be dropped for a generic statement about the nature of girls. The poet's name "hill-enter-myriad-longevity-child" made me think. If the ruckus – not to mention *namakophobia* – drives the moles down further, keeping them from popping out prematurely and catching cold, it might just be their best friend!

赤 海 鼠 蔑 ん で ゐ る 土 龍 か な 香 燿 子

akanamako sagesundeiru mogura kana – kayoko (contemp)
#646 (red-seaslug despises/ing earthdragon=mole!/?/ó/the)

> red sea slug
> completely disrespected
> by our moles

> *chuckling moles*
>
> the earth-dragon
> is not at all impressed with
> the red sea slug

1. ***Folk Practice and Haiku Themes*** While all seasonal folk events are, theoretically fit for haiku --- more so than aseasonal natural phenomena, we might note! – in old haiku practice, certain festivals and customs might be picked up while others would be missed. One example of a practice far more geographically restricted than this slug-dragging, which can, nonetheless, boast hundreds if not thousands of Edo era haiku, is the festival of Tsukuba, where women paraded with as many pots on their heads as men they slept with during the year. Today, this festival and its haiku are extinct.

Among *namako,* the red sea slug is *haute cuisine.* Harder than the blue sea slug, it would hold up to dragging better, but I suspect the reference may be, rather, to the dragged *representative* sea slug being red (something wrapped in red cloth), because red is the traditional color for charms against evil things. I recall Issa's little girl,[1] wearing a red bib, merrily bidding "bye, bye!" to bad-luck scapegoats (dolls and perhaps fleas!) set adrift in a river (I see I have conflated two poems here: *katashiro ni akabebe kiseru musume kana* and *katashiro ni saraba saraba o suru kodomo*). Here, too – as shown in the illustration on the back cover of this book – a little child does the dragging. *"Oh come on!"* says the mole. *"You aren't scaring me!"*

~

The Sea Slug that was a Catfish

Q= The sardine is probably representative of a fish easily injured in shipping. Many die during long distance transport resulting in serious monetary loss. But if a certain thing is put in the tank with the sardines, it is said they remain well for a long time. What is that "certain thing?"

A= A sea slug. I heard this from a restaurateur, so it is probably accurate. Sardines dislike sea slugs. Fleeing from fear, they keep swimming and stay well. Isn't there something deep in this juxtaposition of detested, rather than desired, things to keep one vigorous! I shouldn't lump together people and sardines, but there is something like this in human motivation . . . (*Ganbare Shacho! Kyo-no Pointo* 01/9/21 = on-line *keiei-komon "e-comon"* Takezawa Nobuyuki)

This was published in an internet magazine for company presidents (*shacho*) with 10,408 subscribers. A fish-dealer named Kumai from Kumamoto wrote in to correct one detail. The "certain thing" was not a *namako* (sea slug), but a *namazu* (cat-fish[2] !) In Japanese, we are talking about a one syllabet mistake.[3] Perhaps, the idea of sea slug-fearing moles and the tendency of Japanese to count sea slugs among the things they think most yucky (the high visibility of the slug breeds those who do *not* like it as no one would hate spinach if many did not eat it) may help explain the error.

~

Spam Sea Slugs

I asked Floridian SV for comments on RISE. "Nothing in particular. But as I read here and there, I keep coming back to the same question: Do we have anything like the sea slug? Do we have any food

1. *Issa's Little Girl* These poems were written a few years after Satojo died, so we do not really know it is about her. But when I read them, my eyes cloud, for what Issa has told us about Satojo has made her as real as life to me. Had she not died, I think Issa would have pioneered a new world of haiku, introducing an extraordinary number of fine observations of Satojo. So I also mourn for the missed possibilities.
Catfish There are salt-water catfish and those that live in brackish water last a while in salt water. They have one or two spines which they can raise. The sardines might smell the poison in them.

Catfish+Sea Slug The one-syllabet difference* is but one of the close approaches between these two. A mighty catfish was considered to be at the root of earthquakes, and there is the sea slug messing around on the bed of the sea. A New Year's dish eaten on the second day of the year in Nagasaki combines catfish and diced sea slug. There are no doubt more ways these two bottom dwellers come to mix in Japanese culture.
(* My final check of the 1000-odd *namako* poems in this book came up with two inadvertent *namazu*. So I would seem to turn 1 in 500 sea slugs into catfish. The switch was in my head not keyboard).

food that has received so much attention by poetry or philosophy?" *Good question.* If "we" means the entire Occident, who knows? But, the little I know suggests we do not.

海鼠哉アップルパイから程遠い　敬愚
namako kana appurupai kara hodo tôi – keigu
#647 (seaslug:/!/? apple pie-from very far)

sea slug
a far cry from
apple pie

Googling "apple pie philosophy" gets a respectable number of hits, mostly folksy, sometimes philosophical: *"'Mom...Apple Pie' is originated from the most Graceful Photons-String in the Cosmos.'"* (I skip the proof, for this is, in true Apple Pie (?) fashion, copyrighted!) A more pedagogical philosopher contrasts the *connotative* pie you subjectively like/hate with the *denotative* pie that is objectively what it is. He left out the most interesting part of the pie, the metaphorical identity lying somewhere between these extremes of individual reality and ostensibly shared ideal, which is where we find the *namako*, and for that matter, most of the world of haiku.

［生活様式］海鼠ならともかくホットドッグの真似は　敬愚
[raifu-sutairu]namako nara tomokaku hottodogu no mane wa – keigu
#648 ([lifestyle] seaslug-if at any rate, hotdog's copy-as-for)

you can live
like a sea slug but not
like a hot dog

But even when metaphor is allowed – where Apple pie becomes Mom or America – those who use such expressions do not themselves identify with apples. Granted, the apple is no animal. But aside from the sexy porcines of the classic blues (and that is not so much self-identity as description of women by men), we don't find much identification with our animal food in the USA and, I would guess, in Europe (the exceptions, I would guess, would be sexual metaphor: snakes, vixens, fish and fruit (banana and papaya, etc.)). This, it seems to me, is the result of compounding the overwhelmingly homocentric Classical Culture (note the big "C") with the exclusionist monotheism of Christian Culture, where things other than Man and God get short shrift. Had Ponge written in Chinese, Japanese or Korean, his subject matter would not have been regarded as an anomaly requiring a new name. The "object poem" – horses taut with air, familiar door knobs, to mention a couple I remember – would just be poetry.

アンリーポンジュ描くべきだった海鼠哉 敬愚
anri ponji kaku beki datta namako kana – keigu
#649 (henri ponge write should-have seaslug!/?/ø/the)

the object's object

poor henri ponge
missed the sea cucumber
and *vice versa*

There is an exception: *spam-ku.* Judging from the number of poems at the website (19,695 as of 3/9/03), spam is the most popular subject in American poetry. It has, like no other, drawn Americans into the haiku format. Some are far better than that pink substance. Snappy and thoughtful, they are closer to old haiku (outrageous *haikai* at any rate) than all too many of our plodding nature poems.

Fed meat product to / Japanese warriors; got / Deadly SPAMurai. (Haiku#: 3405 / Brian Beakley / May 14, 1996 / Hits: 3)

Why make SPAM haiku / Of ancient Japanese art? / They bombed Pearl Harbor (Haiku#: 7702 / Eliezer S. Yudkowsky / September 25, 1997 / Hits: 6)

Japanese fish SPAM / For all our great kosher friends / Now quit your carping! / (Haiku#: 14597 / Manhattan Sushi / March 07, 2000 / Hits: 12)

Conquering Gi's / gave SPAM to Japanese then / watched them jump off cliffs. (Haiku#: 15001 / Junkyard God / May 05, 2000 / Hits: 6)

When you think about it, spam, bears a close resemblance to the subject of this book. Like the namako, it is formless (takes the form of its container) and metaphors the indefinable, the gross and the ugly. Like the *namako*, it is loved and hated as food. That gives me an idea:

the organic look

ground-up sea slug
in a can: grey not pink
what healthy spam

it's free-range, too

sea cucumber
turned to spam: almost
vegetarian

deconstructed food

reborn as spam
namako is now beyond
the myth of beauty

(No Japanese here! Since "spam" (the food) is not known in Japan/ese, Keigu had to throw up his hands for this one! [1]) Yes, if namako were turned to spam, it might be very popular in America so long as the grey is not thought to conceal bottlenose dolphin. Of course, there is another possible future for the American *namako*:

アーテイストの海鼠作品洋ピクルス　　敬愚
ahteisto no namako sakuhin yôpikurusu – keigu
#650 (artist's seaslug work western-style pickle/s)

ukiuki/turedur

some day an artist
will put sea cucumbers
into a pickle jar

1. *Spam in Japanese*   I was wrong in one sense. OM writes, "You probably know that spam has been a companion for Japanese Americans, especially in Hawaii and the west coast. I was shocked when I first saw 'spam *omusubi*' [a round ball of rice with something inside] and 'spam *norimaki*' [a laver-wrapped bar of rice] in Hawaii, but since then I see them everywhere where Japanese Americans gather for potluck. It has something to do with the poverty of the *issei* (first-generation Japanese Americans). . . It was and is the least expensive protein food that is American." When I wondered if it might not be corned beef hash, she assured me that both of the above-mentioned treats would be found in the booths at a California Nisei festival that would be held soon, and "They even sell T shirts with 'Spam' logo and design on them." (OM corresp)

It might be spiced up by some chili peppers, more a condiment than a food, but important to the identity of Mexicans: *Yo soy como el chile verde, llorona, picante pero sabroso!* Yes, the Japanese might reply, but *yo soy como el namako, llorona, feo pero gustozo!* The strange title is part of a website, for I wanted to acknowledge Keigu's inspiration, the following passage by a Japanese *namako*-lover – I don't know if he eats them but he highly appreciates the cleaning job they do at the beach – married to (or living with?) a Brazilian (or Portuguese?) woman who loves pickles but seemed so disturbed when he said her pickles resembled the creature she had stepped on when they visited Okinawa that he stopped saying the word in her presence:

> As I watch her eating her pickles [one of my sisters used to have a dill pickle for lunch, so I think he means the whole thing!], I start pondering the life of a *namako*. About what *namako* think about to pass the time. About how nice it must be to have no natural enemy and only worry about being stepped on. And, when they are stepped on, whether they feel "Ouch!" About what in the world their happiness might be. I hear the sound of waves deep inside my head and become happy myself and as I feel a smile beginning, work up the nerve to ask: "So what do you call *namako* in Portuguese?" For a few seconds, she kept her composure, then, she burst out laughing and replied:

> "*Pepino do mar*" (ocean's cucumber)

> So when I looked at pickles and thought of *namako*, my mind had managed to plumb the depths of Portuguese and, unconsciously, get it just right . . . . at any rate, this is good positive reinforcement for my study of Portuguese! (2001-5-4)

This snippet from an internet journal (homepage2.nifty. com/ukiuki/turedur2.html - 101k) reflects a sensitivity to small things all too uncommon in the West. True, the writer apparently does not know that the namako has no more brain than a pickle, but that does not matter, does it? And in a sense, he has it right, for thinking about things is greatly enhanced by staying still, remaining seated (or in bed, as Lamb essayed so well) and letting things dance about in your head. Maybe I was wrong to blame the Greco-Roman-Christian tradition for our poetic shortcomings. It might be the problem has more to do with our lifestyle.[1] If we lived more like sea slugs, we would not necessarily think about them but we would, I think, have our sea slug equivalents.

~

The Burped Sea Slug

海 鼠 食 べ ら れ て 曖 と な り 出 づ る 高 沢 良 一
#651   namako taberarete okubi to nari izuru – takasawa yoshikazu (2003)
(seaslug eating/ate[respectful form of verb] eructation-as/into becomes leaves/comes-out)

eating *namako*
indulgence that ends
in a fine burp

I think I called sea slug *namako*, because I realized that no amount of explanation can make the burp as sweet as it is in the original. The added "indulgence" is my way to recover the politeness of the conjugation of the verb (eat). While Japanese have traditionally been allowed to burp to show their

---

1. *Japanese Lifestyle* True, Japanese have a strong tradition of tourism going back to the Edo era. But they were astounded by the Western practice of walking around their own neighborhoods, as they relaxed and, to a greater degree than Western people, still relax by staying still.

show their appreciation for good food, I do not believe it was *de rigor* as (I have been told) in the Near East. Unlike the slurp that is heard every day, for it is the only logical way to eat noodles or soup hot, the burp is rarely heard in Japan today. So said, I had only known the vulgar sounding *geppu,* until reading this haiku, which uses a more formal word for "burp," namely *okubi,* which is written with a single Chinese character, also new to me, comprised of two parts, "mouth+love." In fact, one pronunciation of the word is *ai,* the same as "love." Takasawa wrote me that the burp arises because (he/slug?) ate mud-like stuff. So, is the burp on behalf of both of them, the poet and his food?

～

The Unfinished Sea Slug

初 五 文 字 の す わ ら で や み ぬ 海 鼠 の 句 子 規
hatsu go moji no suwara de yaminu namako no ku – shiki (1867-1902)
#652 (first five letters' sit/fit/relax-not-from/because stop seaslug-haiku)

having trouble
with the first five syllabets
i stop my slug-*ku*

Shiki's first five "letters" means the five "letters" that would be used if the first part of the poem were written completely in the phonetic syllabary. I thought it a good chance to use my word "syllabet." I also use the short Japanese term for haiku, *ku,* because "haiku" will not fit in the poem.

a sea slug *ku*
abandoned when my lead
fails to scan

While it is true that the three syllabet *na-ma-ko* is hard to use in the first part of a haiku, it is tailor-made for the last part, where it combines, in most cases, with the common closing: *kana.* Besides, Shiki wrote so many (at least a dozen) slug poems that he couldn't mean this as a rule. It is, then, about a single poem he had to give up. Maybe it was even about one where he had the final part, including *namako* but couldn't come up with a good start. Either way, a meta-poem about a poem that wasn't written is very *namako.* The poem is also a sub-theme of the *Featureless* and *Protean Sea Slugs* of chapters 2 and 3.   *How hard it is to whip a sea slug into shape!* And, finally, note that the first part of Shiki's poem (*hatsu go moji no*) actually has six syllabets.

～

the kept sea slug

朧 か な 一 と 夜 か ぎ り の 海 鼠 飼 う 神 蔵 器
oboro kana hitoya kagiri no namako kau – kamikura utsuwa (contemp)
#653 (hazymoon!/?/ó/the, one-night-limit/extent/only's seaslug keep/raise)

the moon's hazy
on this one night i keep
a live sea slug

I suppose it is possible the poet has picked up a sea slug on the beach and brought it home with him, planning to release it the following day, but the likely scenario is that he brought it home planning to eat it that night but was either too tired to prepare it or found his drinking plans changed, so he gave it a one-day reprieve. The sea slug, then, is as good as dead. At the same time, the hazy moon indicates it is late winter or early spring, the slug's time to take a curtain call. The poem is witty if not endearing for its use of a verb generally associated with keeping pets or livestock. It makes us more aware of the sea slug and the poet's feelings toward it. Many of the other sea slug poems mentioning a tub are about keeping sea slugs, but only this one makes it the point of the poem. Even the way the hazy moon is presented (with the mid-poem kana), emphasizes this; it seems to say: *I am aware of how the moon is on this special occasion.* I first titled this sea slug *"The Ephemeral Sea Slug,"* and I considered squeezing it into *"The Nebulous Sea Slug,"* but the focus of the poem was just too clear. Still, I cannot help noting that had it been written a century ago, it might have been thought allegorical, for the idiom "one-night only" (*hitoya kagiri*) is standard for what Englishes as *a one-night stand.* Of course, the "keep" verb is not right for such a reading, but it is a perfect homophone for a verb that is: *kau,* meaning "buy." I hope the poet won't mind one more slightly risqué reading:

> hazy the moon!
> i bring home a sea slug
> for just one night

~

The Stone Sea Slug

Among the essays of Rokuhien-no-Ritsuro, there is mention of a station near the Ôiso temple called Endaiji (fate-stage-temple), which has a small placard announcing the Torako [tiger sea-slug] Stone.   When he went to check it out, he found a big stone that looked like a tiger sea slug, inscribed with its weight and kept on a table in a small treasure-room. On the wall of the room, inscribed on scraps of paper were the names of people who lifted this stone. Asking whether it was a test of strength, the reply was "no, no, love comes true for people who lift this stone!" [1] Evidently, this is not the same as the stone statue of the courtesan Tora [Toragozen] a traveler might expect. – Yamazaki Bisei: Seji-Hyakudan(world-things-hundred-stories):1842-3)

I have not yet found a date for the essays mentioned by Yamazaki or the age of this *Stone Sea Slug*. I hoped to find a "longing" connection predating Buson and Seira's (possibly) lovesick *namako*, but CZ, who found this stone slug – and adds that other legends say a good person can lift the stone where a bad one cannot! – writes that the essayist is the only person documented to have thought the tiger *was* a sea slug. He also writes that such stones, a fairly common folk phenomenon, were generally seen/named as tigers or tiger-foxes – this, according to father of modern Japanese ethnology, Yanagita Kunio (1875-1962), derived from the tiger-like names (tôro, toran, etc.) of wandering mediums, or shamanesses – and that the oldest documented mention of the *torako* stone is 1686 at a different temple, with no Toragozen connection, either, but that shortly later, another appears in a Nichiren sect temple.   Then, it is moved to a different Nichiren temple in Edo, but failing to earn its way – too many men and too few women for stone-lifting to help a guy's chances and therefore few "thank you!" offerings? – ends up in a pawn shop! Later, in the Bunka era (1804-18, when Issa flourished) it, or another stone, resurfaces in another Nichiren temple situated in the Benten (goddess of wealth and beauty) Hall, which, a generation later, moves to the Demon-child's Mother Shrine, where it was said not only to have taken an arrow for 12th century warrior Soga (Toragozen's lover) but bears the sword scars of the would-be assassin.   Thanks to the Toragozen connection, the most well known stone today is in Ôiso, the land where the courtesan – or wandering shamaness? – harked from.   And, I am now trying to find out if anyone else thinks the stone is a tiger sea slug.

Meaningless Sea Slugs

A website called Impact Literature where "quantity matters more than quality" run by Maruyama Chikako sensei (ipb) asks readers to send in free verse that 1) must be meaningless, 2) have a strong impact (she means "snap") and 3), not contain obscenity or innuendo. Here is a sampling from the sixth theme, yes, *namako*. I remove the parsing reduce the print to better reflect the value of the work:

> *Swim Meet Swarms with Sea Slugs* / *Sea Slug Pukes Guts in a Pinch: Heroes Who Throw Up Draw Continued PTA Protests* / *Super Sea Slug Brothers* / *The World Sea Slug Discovered?* / *Natural Sea Slug Water* [Possible violation of 1), for they *do* clean water!] / *Intel Pentium Sea Slug* / *If this humble sea slug will do . . .* [If it's not a true idiom, it could be!] / *Ah, ah, so sorry, I seem to have mistaken you for a sea slug . . .* / *If you want your child back, ready a year's supply of sea slug!* / *The Gandhi Sea Slug Theory* [Violates 1), for there really are many similarities.] / *Skeleton Sea Slug* [Like the pc mouse skeleton I've seen?] / *No Standing Sea Slugs!* [A reverse violation of 3)?] / *Sea Slug Rally* [contrast with sea slug's reputation violates 1)] / *Bright Sea Slug Plan* [a waffle with potential?] / *Sea Slug Advisory* [beware of grey skies?] / *Sea Slug from a Far-off Sea* [how about "the sea slug who came in from the cold?"] / *Beautiful Blue Sea Slug* [there is one, unknowing violation of 2)] / *Sea Slug Samurai* [can a bona fide word, *namakobushi,* be meaningless?] / *Sea Slug Park* [sea slug gardens] / *Alley Sea Slug* (ipb)

While I did not comment on all of the above, I find meaning in every "verse;" but, if I didn't find any meaning, well, that, too, would be meaningful, for the *namako* stands for meaninglessness. I could not tell who wrote what and hope the contributors will not mind the anonymity they richly deserve.

～

The Dream Sea Slug

夢海鼠ひらひらと舞ふ深海に還らぬ兄も踊りてゐるや　竹下洋一
yumenamako hirahira to mau shinkai ni kaeranu ani mo odoriteiru ya – takeshita yôichi (contemp)
#654 (dream-seaslug fluttering dance death-world-from return-not brother even/too dancing-is! ó)

> *a dream sea slug*
> *passes in fluttering waltz*
> *my brother who*
> *ne'er came back from*
> *the deep, dances, too*

This would be a description of the wine-colored *yumenamako,* or "dream sea cucumber," named by a Japanese scientist.   Is the poet a deep-sea-diving scientist? Or did he see a video? Was his brother lost, perhaps, in World War II? I was not successful at reaching the poet to find the circumstances behind this remarkable *tanka*; but, I suppose it is enough to think of the gravityless purgatory of Davy Jones Locker as a ballroom full of light-finned dancers . . .

ゆらりゆら夢海鼠となる風邪の午後　美沙
yurariyura yumenamako to naru kaze no gogo – misa (contemp)
#655 (flutter-flutter dream seaslug-as/into become cold[sickness]'s afternoon)

> a fluttering
> dream sea slug home
> with a cold

home with a cold
i flutter, a dream sea slug
this afternoon

The mimesis in the first *Dream Sea Slug* poem, *hirahira*, is generally used for butterflies and leaves. The mimesis in the second *Dream Sea Slug* poem, *yurariyura*, has a somewhat heavier quality more appropriate for the poet at home, I would guess, in her bed.

~

The Sea Slug as a Witch's Tit

海 鼠 よ り 寒 き 来 世 か と 思 う 斉 田 仁
namako yori samuki raise ka to omou – saida jin (contemp)
#656 (seaslug more-than cold next-world? [I] think)

the next world
will be a hell of a lot colder
than a sea slug

after the sun

i think that life
after death may be colder
than a sea slug

carbon cycle

next time around
the world may be colder
than a sea slug

This is the only haiku I recall with an "[I] think" in it! Not knowing the poet, I do not know if his next world is a personal one or the real one. While the sea slug only serves as an impromptu metaphor, it is more than a *Witch's Tit*, for a sea slug has a meteorite-like quality which carries time with it.

~

The Canary Watch-Dog Sea Slug

観 念 し 海 鼠 の 吐 け る 泥 の 量 高 沢 良 一
kannen shi namako no hakeru doro no ryô – takasawa yoshikazu (2003)
#657 (idea/concept-do[wondering], seaslug's vomit/disgorge mud amount)

something to wonder
about how much mud does
a sea slug disgorge?

questions addressed to the poet:

1. – *Quantity of detritus per sea slug bm?*
2. – *Total lifetime quantity of detritus passed?*
3. – *If, 2) The quantity for a single sea slug?*
4. – *If 2), The quantity for all of Japan's sea slugs? The world's sea slugs?*

His answer: *It's up to the reader..*

Sea slugs pass enough sand and silt through their guts to collect a large quantity of pollutants –harmful micro-organisms, excessive concentrations of organic matter, heavy metals – in their tissue. For water quality, the oyster may be a better monitor, but water travels more than sludge. If it is the local pollution you would know, the sea slug might be perfect. Needless to say, this is not kind to the canary.

今 の 世 や あ わ れ 海 鼠 に 毒 見 役 　 敬 愚
imanoyo ya aware namako ni dokumiyaku (s) – keigu
(now-world[now-a-days]:/!sad/pitiful seaslug-to poison-taster)

#658

bio-watch

a fine world
this is! sea slugs turning
into canaries!

I suppose you wouldn't need to wait for the sea slugs to die.   You could cut off, or punch out pieces for analysis and the sea slug would just grow back the missing pieces, though I guess that would dilute its level of pollution and ruin subsequent tests.

~

The Sewage Engineer Sea Slug

Sea Slug as Canary lives only in my imagination, but the sea slug as *filter* or *cleaning device* is a common idea.[1] *Janitor of the Sea* (*umi no* sôjiya) is a most common phrase pegged on to the sea slug by (googled) Japanese. Their ability to clean is actually being tested (for things like type/amount of absorption and lifespan). The light blue *kuma-namako* (bear-sea-cucumber – *Holothuridea ursis* if I may do a direct=guessing translation)) is said to gather around places with plentiful bacteria and minerals – such as the remains of whales,[2] which they swarm, if such a word can apply to crowding accomplished in slow motion! (Size-wise, they are to whales what maggots are to us.) When people die in droves (end of WWII in New Guinea?), who can doubt that the sea slugs lend a hand in the clean-up.   Or, at least, the following poem – if such can be said for a *tanka* that, despite a couple poetic words, is more prosaic than prose – suggests that something like that has been recorded.

1. *Cleaning Metaphors* In the introductory taxonomy we saw Buchsbaum and Milne's metaphor of the finger-licking holothurian. Ron Shimek keeps the "licking," i.e.: "These animals typically walk over the world, licking the substrate with their mucus-covered oral tentacles." but adds a new janitorial twist: "In effect, they mop their way through the world." (Shimek ibid) The metaphor is good for including the holothurian's movement, but a mop neither processes what it picks up (except to the extent the cleansing fluid acts) nor retains as much residue as holothurians. They just move dirt from one place to another. Should we call our charge a robot mop with a built-in filter?

Believe it or not, long after I wrote this, I found a GIF (hypershort animation) of a *Namako Robo* (sea cucumber robot), comprising a spiked éclair-shaped body with a vacuum cleaner's head attachment and a hatch-like anus to dump out the cleaned sand. This "sea cucumber soil-improvement robot" (*namako dojô kairyô robo*) is an amusing animation, though the metaphor is wrong, for a vacuum cleaner doesn't clean what it sucks up, but only gathers it to be discarded elsewhere. The artist makes one very good point in the short explanation accompanying the GIF. Namely, if the environment is *too* mucky, this "cleaner of the sea" will itself die, so "there is a chicken-or-egg aspect here." (bochiboke.hp.infoseek.co.jp/r_namako.html - 4k)

2. *Cleaning Researchers* A netted outline for a project proposal by a three-man ecosystem engineering team of Murasaki, Kozuki and Kengo at Tokushima University are the source of most of my (very limited) information here. But I can't remember where I found those dead whales. Perhaps Arakawa (ndh) or Tsurumi (nnm).

海鼠とは人の死骸を食ぶと聞きおぞましくなり口にせずなる 佐藤房子

namako to wa hito no shitai o tabu to kiki ozomashikunari kuchi ni sezu naru – satô fusako (contemp)
#659 (seaslug-as-for, peoples' corpses eat hearing, adamant/frightened-become mouth-in[eat] do-not-become)

> having heard
> that sea slugs ate
> human corpses
> i put down my foot
> i will not eat them

Less dramatically, *aonamako* (blue sea slugs) clean-up under oyster-beds, as elsewhere mentioned, but can easily be overwhelmed. Seriously polluted seabed requires the tough sludge-loving *kuronamako* (black sea slug). Mariculture wastes involving various seaweeds used as food for shellfish or people are best handled by the seaweed eating and cleaning capabilities of the *akanamako* (red sea slug). The use of sea slugs for improving the seashore environment may be economic and certainly beats the use of man's fuelish machines. It is sad, however, to think of a free spirit conscripted to serve us.

今の世や海鼠までも働かせて 敬愚

imanoyo ya namako made mo hatarakasete (s) – keigu
#660 (now-world[now-a-days]:/! seaslug-even work-made-to)

he has a job to do

> what a world!
> when even the sea slug
> must work

「ウンコ美人」ゴミ入るも出ると限らぬ海鼠かな 敬愚

#661 gomi iru mo deru to kagiranu namako kana -- keigu
(garbage-enter-even/though leave limit-not seaslug!/?/ǒ/the)

bm beauty

> "garbage in
> garbage out?" not
> with sea slugs!

The quality of a sea slug's work is reflected in the purity of their poop, which is, of course, the opposite of our poop because it comes out clean rather than dirty – I cannot repeat this too often: to think that eating can be constructive rather than destructive! – and some even decorate as they clean:

> Balates even have interesting poop. It comes out of them in a coiled, sandy ribbon with crenulated edges, making a pretty rosette on the sea floor that you can pick up. People always pick it up because it looks so pretty and unusual, and ask, "What is this thing?" Then they drop it fast when they are told that it's poop. (from "Critters of Guam" by Brenna Lorenz http://www.heptune. com/galwall1.html)

In Guam, Balates are called sea cucumbers. How many sanitation engineers finish a job like that! I can vaguely remember seeing such artwork as a boy, but I cannot remember if I knew who made it. And what is the name for the tubes which squeeze out garnishes of icing? But this is not so funny a matter for the *namako,* for according to Arakawa, sluggers hunt down their prey by looking out for their poop. The *namako* poop he shows are less interesting than that of the decorator poopers of Guam and look more like a segmented tuber (one of scores of Peruvian potatoes) than a rosette.→

海鼠糞F・ベーコンが夢を見し 敬愚
namako fun efu behkon ga yume o mishi – keigu
#662 (seaslug shit f bacon's dream[+obj] see/ing)

utopian science reified

sea slug bms:
you know francis bacon
had a dream

海鼠即錬金術師穢無糞　敬愚
namako soku renkinjutsushi kenaki fun – keigu
#663   (seaslug title alchemist-master: filth/pollution-not shit)

pretty good shit!

if cleanliness
is good as gold sea slugs
are alchemists

Some readers may be interested in the use of sea slugs to keep their aquariums clean. It works. But if a sea cucumber dies on you and you don't move quickly, the poison will kill all the fish. This is good for the sea slug, for it guarantees you will pay close attention to its needs! I joke, but *be careful*. Aquarium sites speak of popular holothurians that "nuke" all the fish when shredded by a powerhead (?) or sucked up a filter.

見ただけで海鼠嫌いとキレイ好き 敬愚
mita dake de namako kirai to kireizuki – keigu
#664   (seen only-by seaslug[obj] [he]hates[says] neatnick)

mister neatnick
says he hates the very sight
of a *namako*

海鼠みて箒持ち出す清潔家　敬愚
#665 *namako mite hôki mochidasu seikketsuya* – keigu
(seaslug seeing broom pick-up-bring-out [ ] cleanliness-lover)

seeing a sea slug
the cleanliness addict grabs
for her broom

The sea slug, as described in the Featureless and Protean Sea Slug chapters, has a formless form that at best is informal and at worst sloppy to behold. This would, as also noted, disturb those who take comfort in a clean-cut formal world. The second poem is meant to reflect an unconscious association. Considering the "work" the sea slug is engaged upon, there is no little irony in this.

←1. *Holothurian Poop*   In calm water, most holothurian poop holds up for days and is distinctive. If someone could go around the world photographing it, I would be happy to add a page of illustrations to a future addition.   The reader who cannot wait is advised to visit Brenna Lorenz's site "The Scoop on Poop" where she has posted a photograph of: "a pretty, coiled, crenulated poop rosette." They are a work of art and could be fixed in resin or cast and sold with part of the proceeds going to the Save the Sea Cuke fund, if there is one. Perhaps someone might feed such a "balate" rose-colored sand then place it on clean white, brown or grey sand for a particularly dramatic shot.

人でないキレイ好きなら好きよ海鼠　敬愚
#666 hito de nai kireizuki nara suki yo namako – keigu
(person-not clean-lover/liker if love/like! seaslug)

look, sea slug
i like all neatniks that
are not human

Keigu was tempted to rhyme, say, "one neatnik / a beatnik can stomach: / the sea slug," but persevered until he came up with a real idea: he really likes obsessive behavior *so long as it is not found in his own species*. To think of the literally mindless sea slug as obsessed is, of course, nonsensical, but so is associating one who cleans for a living with one who lives to clean.

掃除屋の兄貴と呼びぬ海鼠哉　敬愚
#667 sôjiya no aniki to yobinu namako kana – keigu
(cleaner/nightsoil-man's [older]brother-as called but seaslug/s!/?/ổ/a)

the night soil man
says "brother" when he talks
to a sea slug

the janitors
for schools of fish
sea slugs

This word for brother has a *yakuza*-like ring, it makes it sound as if man and slug are partners in a cleaning conspiracy. While a well-known Japanese children's song sings of the killifish (*medaka*) in their schools, other fish in Japanese do not have "schools" – the English "school" was, after all, born of accident (misspelled "shoal") in a language with weird collective terms (*pride of lions, exaltation of larks*, etc.) – and, as the song points out, the killifish schools are in rivers. So the second reading or, rather, *paraverse,* does not work in Japanese.

ぴかぴかの世を夢見たる海鼠かな　敬愚
#668 pikapika no yo o yumemitaru namako kana – keigu
(sparkling world[obj] dreamsees seaslug/s[subj] /s!/?/ổ/the/loh)

the sea slug
it dreams of a pretty
clean world

The tiniest animal has its dream of the ideal habitat, what it would live in, or create. In *Night Country,* Loren Eiseley describes the ill-fated attempt of a displaced meadow mouse to turn a flowerpot into its paradise, and notes that these little bundles of dreams constantly pass by and even under us unnoticed as we blithely walk the earth. True, *namako* might find it hard to dream without a brain, but I think we could say that it – whatever "it" is – has aspirations of a sort; and Keigu, at least, doubts that even a sea slug lives for bread alone. *If sea slugs tidy up the sea floor, it is because they want to.*

己が身を諦めて美に尽くす海鼠　敬愚
#669 onoga mi o akiramete bi ni tsukusu namako – keigu
(own body[obj] give-up[as hopeless], beauty-for work/exhaust seaslug/s)

ugly neatnick

neglecting itself
it slaves away for beauty
the sea slug

In his 1970's best-seller *Entropy,* Jeremy Riftkin noted that while life is wonderful for increasing its own order – i.e., being anti-entropic in an otherwise entropic universe – it comes at a price, namely the increased disorder of that which it consumes to do so. Speaking of humans, that makes good sense, but what about a creature who gobbles up gunk and turns it back to pristine sand?

浜 の 美 に 尽 く す ほ ど 醜 き 海 鼠 　 敬 愚
#670 hama no bi ni tsukusu hodo minikuki namako – keigu
(sand-for beauty[obj] work/exhaust[oneself for]-extent ugly seaslug/s)

the cleaner the beach
the more the sea slug
is called an eyesore

beautification

the sea slugs
eyesores on the very
sand they clean

Thanks to the sea slug's hard work the bathing beach becomes clean. The subsequent increase of visitors and heightened visibility of the water, leads to an increase in complaints about a creature some tourists think a blemish on the seascape. So, the sea slugs in the vicinity of the hotel are gathered up and dumped somewhere else (or worse). Talk about the ingratitude of man!

～

The Sick Sea Slug

一 病 を 持 ち て 海 鼠 の 類 ひ な る 高 沢 良 一
ichibyô o mochite namako no tagui naru – takasawa yoshikazu (1998)
#671 (one-illness[obj] having, seaslug species/type/ilk become/am/turn into)

one disease   one disease but
and now i belong to   enough to turn me into
the sea slug ilk   a sea cucumber

If I understand the information found on the poet's website *waga-haiku-arakaruto* (my haiku ala carte). Takas[z]awa (the same Chinese character, but for business, *Takazawa,* for haiku, the euphonious *Takasawa*) had a valve in his heart that sent blood packing the wrong way and an operation for it:

「病床二句」寝 て 覚 め て 脈 を と ら る る 病 ミ な ま こ 　 高 沢 良 一
byôshô ni ku – nete   samete myaku o toraruru yaminamako – takasawa yoshikazu (contemp)
#672 (sick-bed two poems – sleep/ing-wake/ing pulse taken sick seaslug)

two sick-bed poems

sleep, wake
have your pulse taken:
a sick sea slug

ふ つ つ か な 海 鼠 物 云 ふ 患 者 食　高 沢 良 一

futsutsukana namako monoiu kanjashoku – takasawa yoshikazu (contemp)
#673 (ill-bred/uncool[?] seaslug thing-says[complains] patient-food)

im/patient

an ill-bred
sea slug speaks up
hospital food!

人 づ て に 聞 け り 海 鼠 の 不 料 簡　高 沢 良 一

#674 *hitozute ni kikeri namako no furyôken* – takasawa yoshikazu
(people-communicated-by hear seaslug's thoughtlessness/impoliteness)

the grape vine
has it that there is this
thoughtless sea slug

To my mind, Takasawa deserves special care, for he has done more to make old haiku accessible for everyone (who reads Japanese) than all the academies combined (see acknowledgments).

一 通 り 聞 き て 入 院 梅 雨 海 鼠　高 沢 良 一

#675 *hitotôri kikite nyûin tsuyunamako* – takasawa yoshikazu (1997)
(entire-passage hear/take-in enter-institution[hospitalized] monsoon-sesslug)

hearing what's what
i check into the hospital
a monsoon sea slug

The poet decides on an operation. On the one hand, the monsoon would be a good time to spend in an air-conditioned hospital, for one would just be sitting inside one's home, anyway; on the other hand, the grey outside the window and lack of any sunlight coming in might be depressing. I first mistranslated Takasawa's poem as,

in the hospital
a sea slug hears each drop
of monsoon rain

~

the monsoon rain
heard start to finish by
a sick sea slug

The ear works overtime when one is trapped in bed. The sea slug (and other lowly things) take in everything, even if they don't seem to show it. But that wasn't the poem.

入 院 海 鼠 ざ っ と 大 部 屋 見 渡 せ り　高 沢 良 一

nyuinnamako zatto ôbeya miwataseri – takasawa yoshikazu (1997)
#676 (institutionalized/hospitalized-seaslug roughly big-room looks-crosses)

hospitalized
sea slug slowly scans
the big room

術 後 十 日 重 湯 す す り て 病 ミ 海 鼠　高 沢 良 一
#677 jutsugo toka omoyu susurite yaminamako – takasawa yoshikazu (1997)
(op[eration]-post ten-days, heavy-warm-water[thin rice gruel, i.e. soup] sipping sick seaslug)

post-op 10 days
a sick sea slug still
sipping soup

I was not going to include the last two poems about our human sea slug, but something about the *scanning* and *sipping* (or, if you prefer, *slurpinp* for the noise Japanese make drinking hot liquids from the side of their bowls as is their wont) caught my eye every time I reviewed the *hmmm* haiku list.

病 み 臥 す 身 昼 は 海 月 に 夜 は 海 鼠　高 沢 良 一
#678 yami fusumi hiru wa kurage ni yo wa namako – takasawa yoshikazu (1997)
(diseased/sick-lying body, daytime-as-for, sea-moon=jellyfish, night-as-for, seaslug)

my sick body
a jellyfish by day and
sea slug by night

I think not only of the translucence of the jellyfish seen by day – is he being x-rayed? – but of the bleached bone moon of the blue sky. Does he drift all about the hospital like a jellyfish in an unsettled current, then feel wedged in his bed like a sea slug in a crevice? The sea slug suggest both the immobility and, perhaps, squirming at night.   Or does the season-mixing illustrate how a haiku poet shut up in a hospital room can turn the day into summer and the night into winter?

海 鼠 な り 風 邪 こ じ ら せ て 臥 せ る 身 は　高 沢 良 一
namako nari kaze kojirasete fuseru mi wa – takasawa yoshikazu (1997)
#679 (seaslug become, [a] cold neglecting/aggravating lying down body-as-for)

neglecting
my cold now i lie
a sea slug

The poem is a bit more paradoxical in English where a type of undefined bacteriological or viral illness is called "cold," rather than "wind," as is the case in Japanese.   This poem has a light touch, but is not nearly so light as I thought it was on my first (mis)reading of *kojirasete* as koujiru=devise. Indeed, I chuckle to see that I even called my mistranslation "one of the most charming *namako* poems ever written"(!).   Keigu, will send off the Sick Sea Slug by turning the mistake into a new haiku or, rather, two or three –

講 じ た る 風 邪 や 海 鼠 に 成 り た が り 敬愚	こ じ つ け る 風 邪 や 海 鼠 を 憧 れ て　敬愚
kôjitaru kaze ya namako ni naritagari – keigu	*kojitsukeru kaze ya namako o akogarete* – keigu
(devised/employed cold: seaslug-into become-wanted)	(strained/distorted cold: seaslug[obj] longed for)
#680, 681	
bed-wish	***amae***
this body	wanting to be
would be a sea slug:	a sea slug, i pretend
faking a cold	to catch cold

The title for the second poem, *amae* is a word for a mindset often argued to be more common in Japan than the Occident, where one allows and may even desire things to be taken care of by another (See *The Anatomy of Dependence* by T. Doi, translated by John Bester and comments in my *OAO*). The cold may only be fake in retrospect. Here is a better way to express that:

sea slug me!
my cold's an excuse
to lie in bed

#682 （下記英訳抜け）

Anyone fortunate enough to have had a kind parent can understand the pleasure of being a "sea slug" in bed, even if the care is not what it was when you sucked up tea through cinnamon sticks, built houses of graham cracker in apple-sauce and found your name in alphabet soup (if I may be permitted some of my good memories). 心から風邪ひく海鼠願望者　敬愚　（英訳の題のみ＝sea slug wannabe）

～

The Sea Slug as "It"

The following paragraph comes from a sweet-tempered site providing the practical philosophy=advice of "Sea Slug Laotse" (*namako rôshi*).

> When I was a child there were many empty lots nearby where children of all ages would gather together and play. The broad age span brought an equally large difference in physical prowess, so there was a rule for playing tag that when a tiny tyke was caught he or she would not become the "devil." In our part of the country, these tiny tagees were called "sea slugs." (© Youichi Kouno, 2001)

In Japanese children's games, the child who is caught or tagged is called "devil" (*oni*) rather than "it," as is the case with English – or at least American English. In the Japanese case, even if you wanted to, it would be impossible to call a tagged child "it," because *it has no "it."* In Japanese, *it* doesn't rain, nor snow, nor feel cold or heat, nor is *it* a shame, a revelation, or anything. The closest Japanese can come to "it" is the third word of the *kore/sore/are = this/that/that there* triumvirate of indicators that English can only partially match by recourse to the Ozarkian (?) and which, in Japanese, is often used as rude euphemism – pronouns themselves are rude in Japanese and this is one of the rudest – so it is not used for *it*. How marvelous that the vague entity called *namako* could serve in that capacity!

～

The Sea Slug as God and Vice Versa

何 も 彼 も 聞 し っ て ゐ る 海 鼠 か な　鬼 城

#683 nanimokamo kikishitteiru namako kana – kijô (1933)
(any-even-that-even [everything] hear/s-knowing seaslug/s!/?/ô/the/loh)

·

omniscience

the sea slug
it hears and knows
everything!

Like Issa's *Yuck Yuck Sea Slug (oni mo iya . . .),* only a deep study of the poet or the discovery of additional information can crack this poem. Does the poet describes the uncanny ears of a comatose friend or parent?   Is he a poor and politically powerless man who reads the paper a lot? Or, does he see the intelligence apparatus of the increasingly fascist and military government or the local version of it, the neighborhood organizations that many intellectuals began running afoul of about this time, as sea slug like in their formlessness. Lacking further information, we probably should assume the subject is a *bona fide* sea slug, which the poet has watched *very* carefully, but I cannot help but feel he is witnessing a vague embodiment of . . .

GOD

a sea slug
that hears and knows
everything?

Considering the lack of obvious action on the part of deity and the difficulty of defining the same, the stereotypical formless and nebulous Japanese sea slug does fit the role of God far better than Leonardo's body-builder.

~

The Abbreviated Artificial Pornographic Sea Cucumber

Some of my readers expressed concern lest the inclusion of *Pornographic Sea Slugs* spoil my otherwise tasteful tome.   I do not want to drop them entirely for they represent a fascinating phenomenon and this book is intended to be encyclopedic. My compromise is to reduce the sampling by 90%, drop the disgusting names of the sites altogether, relocate them between *God* and *The Moral Sea Slug,* and, finally, reduce the size of the print to size 9 font.

I was googling "sea cucumber" and "translation," when, I came across a pink passage about a woman "folding up her sea cucumber" among the hits. Determined to get to the bottom of this, I clicked on the porn site, but before the site fully appeared, another pounced on top of it and yet another on that! I pulled the phone connection and skedaddled. The next day, I set out to investigate again, adding the word "folded" to my search. After a number of honest hits, I found things like

> Peggy B. folded his bucket, as Rhonda scrambled his sea cucumber . . . / the person next door folded his platypus as Rita fiddled her sea cucumber . . . / as Jughead reamed his sea cucumber into her love-bucket, Big Daddy Zeus folded her chocolate starfish . . . / Turgid wiggled his sea cucumber into his love ... , as Ryoga folded his function.

Each snippet was part of a paragraph of purple prose accompanying each hit (one does not go to the porn site to see this). It pops up instantaneously, i.e. is *made* in less than a second. It would seem that the porno sites are using artificial language machines to incorporate whatever you look for into their site information so that the Biblical injunction "Seek and Thou shall find!" has acquired a new meaning. The ideas of surrealist poetry are now a reality. True, much does not make sense (at least to a straight), but the vocabulary is impressive and, to me, humorous: "fnord *impoonerated* her sea cucumber;" "Aunt Jemima *transvested* her sea cucumber into his Madonna [his *what1?*]; "Chicken *archived* her sea cucumber into his mammoth-hole [sic: Martial would have liked that], "postulated his sea cucumber[?]," "etc.. Some expressions are exquisite: "Hello Kitty rode her sea cucumber;" "Turtles switched on her sea cucumber;" "Spankworthy powered up her sea cucumber," and "daughter of an indiscreet sea cucumber!?" As so long as you don't click to actually go to these sites, you may safely play with this artificial intelligence they so thoughtfully provide. Once I realized how it worked, I substituted "fish" to try to conjure up more marine metaphor. While I did get some, including "Holey Flying Fish Fucks!! as Big Ben handcuffed her sea cucumber. ... and rammed his Gigantic Manta Ray" and "Spock extended his sea cucumber into her steaming clam," it did not net much. I did better with some other words and here, with apologies to friends who might not approve, some samples:

"I'm a little tea-pot, short and stout! THIS is my handle; THIS is my SPOUT!!", Meat Helmet climaxed, as Antioedipus diddled his sea cucumber / Spinner heaved, as A. M. encroached his sea cucumber into her fruitbasket . / O. marvelled, as M. D. cut and threw his sea cucumber into her chocolate highway. .... / The Pink Ranger shoved his sea cucumber into his magic hat. ... / Thar she blows!" slutty daughter of an indiscreet sea cucumber! / "Suck my chocolate ass POPS", two clans of Maori tribesmen twittered, as The President powered up his sea cucumber / Jaffo sheathed his sea cucumber into her sucking eye socket ... "Let me take the ribbons ... Karl Zero tittered, as Akuma packed her sea cucumber into her clown's pocket ...

Perhaps we should call this AI (artificial inanity), or googled hodge-podge the *beche-de-mer,* or, *bishomar* of the internet 2002.

~

The Japanese Pornographic Sea Slug

She advanced, both cheeks of her ass tightening with *pikupiku* quivers, rolling up her skirt as the forest of enlightenment appeared to sandwich the sea slug. *Fufun!* In the hands of fallen-leaf dusk, the sea slug slowly got harder and harder and appeared to glow . . . (a rough translation from something googled from a "freeweb" site called *majocom,* or, "witch-company").

Though rare, there are passages of Japanese electronic pornography which include the sea slug; and they are *much* better than the artificial English ones. Perhaps that is because the computer is given more time to work (or corrected by humans), for the above was not an instant product. Still, I wonder. Since Japanese language-related software is far ahead of that available for English OS – the grammar reading capability of Ichitaro in 1995 was already light-years ahead of Win XP's Japanese IME – I would not put real pornography (by definition, writing which makes the sea slug on most men rise) beyond their computers!

Sea slug and I both wish to touch the breath of the cherry-blossom-color shell [referring to the cherry-shell, a carpenter's tellin thought to be a dead ringer for the vulva] you possess! (from a site claiming inspiration from tanka (5-7-5-7-7 poetry) with the male lines in blue and female ones in pink!)

This was obviously home-made and ridiculously corny. Still, the phrase "sea slug and I," where the speaker refers to his person is genuinely touching.

~

The Moral Sea Slug

I web-searched second-hand book stores in Japan for books about *namako* and found a number of them. Since Japanese generally don't use credit cards, American banks charge about $50. to transfer money electronically (you can sell hundreds of thousands of dollars of stocks for less!) and the post office (at least the one on Key Biscayne) no longer has international postal money orders (what the Japanese most want), I couldn't buy any of those books. The fact that international finance for the little guy is worse than it was fifty years ago is a crying shame, but the silver lining in this cloud is the following letter from someone in a bookstore which had a copy of *Namako Mo Itsuka Tsuki o Miru* (even sea cucumbers see the moon some day, i.e., every sea slug has its day?) by Shiina Makoto.[1]

1. *Shiina Makoto and Shii-namako-to* Chinese character conversion by computers supplies continuous entertainment for all who write in Japanese. With Shiina Makoto it is not uncommon for a *namako* to pop up in his name! If John Cage decided to pursue *mushrooms* because they came right before *music* in his dictionary, Shiina Makoto may have been drawn to his title by his own name.

Mr. robin gill, hello.

Inquiry thank you.
It is very poor at English.
Various mistakes may be in English.
This book does not exist with the book currently written about "NAMAKO."
It is alive firmly in fact, lying to the seabed calmly like "NAMAKO."
That is, man also needs to make a living like "NAMAKO."
It says.
It is the book which wrote man's moral theory pleasantly simply.
Thank you.

secondhand bookseller daruma

Shiina is a well-known travel reporter, one of whose books turned into a movie on a Mongolian boy and his horse, which I happened to see. I was curious how he might have interpreted Shôha's haiku about the sea slug talking to the moon, which I assumed suggested the title. I still don't know. The fifth line in the letter means that I need not buy the book for it is not really about sea slugs at all.

∼

The Non/Cartesian Sea Slug

海鼠あり故にわれありかぼすもある　川崎展宏
namako ari yue ni ware ari kabosu mo aru – kawasaki nobuhiro (contemp)
#684 (seaslug is, ergo/therefor i am, citron also is)

table philosophy	***barstool epiphany***
sea slug is	sea slug *is*
therefore i am	so i'm here and so
citrons are	is this citron

The poem starts mimicking Descartes' words, which are always Japanesed in a peculiar manner, for it was necessary to settle on a particular "I" that now sounds rather dated and there is no perfect Japanese equivalent of the Occidental "to be." Moreover, unlike English, the verb is the same for all persons (*ari*), so that the three entities above all equally *ergo sum*. The *kabosu* is South Japanese dialect for a type of citron (*yûzu*) that makes a good garnish for sea slug. We imagine the poet with the ingredients for the poem, including himself, sitting at a table or bar, though it is hard to say exactly what the poem means other than that sea slug brought him to the bar where he felt with the force of an epiphany that all life is kin and that Descartes me-ism was a mistake and that we (including all fauna and fola) exist together or not at all? Or is the poet more specifically thinking of the farming and fishing that kept his ancestors alive long enough to produce him? (OM= "I don't think so. He is just happy sitting there with *namako* and *kabosu*, and probably *sake*.")

∼

The Assertive Sea Slug

Here is a googled review, written from the perspective of Kurokuro, a cat living with the reviewer, a Japanese, a mathematician (who espouses admirable simplicity) living in California with his wife, the (cat's) landlady:

"Eye of Sea Cucumber"   Yoshiyuki Tsurumi (Chikuma Gakugei Bunko)
Sea cucumbers and Homo sapiens

This is an astounding oceanic report that focuses on the relationship between sea cucumbers and humans. It extends to anthropology, history, geology, philology, biology, colonial studies, agriculture and ethnology in depicting the history of the men of the sea in the Pacific Ocean and South East Asia from the perspective of sea cucumbers. The author is not only one of the most cultured and well-read Japanese scholars of modern times, but also has an unusually free mind and a keen eye.

This 556-page book with 88-pages of index and reference is not recommended for easy and casual pass-time reading, but is truly worth the time and effort for those who face the challenge. Landlady has read another book by the author, a shocking report that explains how the production of bananas [1] for export to Japan has devastated the lives of Philippine farmers when she was at college. She says that "Eye" is easier to read because sea cucumber is a less familiar food than banana is to her.

Another famous professor in Japan had a unique TV lecture on oceanic biology, in which he joyfully tortured a poor sea cucumber until it melted into a blotch of tar. This strange behavior has extremely strong charm to some kind of intellectuals, I guess. [2]

I ordered the book as soon as I read this review and found that while Tsurumi supports the sea cucumber, noting re gut-milking that it was hardly so easy on the sea cucumber as on cows, instancing over-fishing, and so forth; his main concern is *human history*, about which he dwells upon the following three points:

1) The cured sea cucumber known as *iriko* in Japan, and *trepang* or *beche de mar* internationally, was an extremely time-consuming and resource-consuming (trees cut down to fuel the boiling pots wreaked environmental havoc on land as over-fishing did on the sea-coasts) luxury product [3] → made by poor people, many of whom have been indentured or enslaved for the tables, or medicine cabinets of wealthy Chinese. Tsurumi points out that if men were Shanghaied for whaling, men and women in large number were captured for sea-slugging (mostly for the time-consuming processing).

1. *Sea Cucumber, Bananas, and Shrimp, too!* I might add that Tsurumi is especially well known for his expose of the ecological damage caused by the rapid growth of shrimp/prawn farms in South East Asia. I can remember thinking it strange indeed for Americans to have so great awareness of whaling and so little for shrimping. The oldest report of devastating shrimping practices I know of is purse-seining by a Japanese trawler reported by John Steinbeck in *The Log of the Sea of Cortez*. What Tsurumi decried, however, was the wholesale destruction of mangrove and marshland to create ponds for aquaculture which profited some at the cost of destroying the ecology that supported traditional fisheries from time immemorial

2. *Torturing Cukes* The anecdote is not surprising. I have seen sumo-wrestler's scare babies for the traditional crying contest (a "barbaric practice" according to foreigners who complain to the *Japan Times* every year) and I have seen Japan's most popular animal-expert masturbate a dog to obtain samples to put under the microscope to show the enormous difference between the sperm of young and old dogs. To me, this sort of thing is both refreshing and revolting; but mostly the former: too many Americans (most of the letters to the editor were from my compatriots) are upset about the wrong thing (body parts, politically correct vocabulary) instead of what matters, namely, our inability to create a peaceful and ecologically gentle society. I think scaring babies (just once in a ritual, not as a daily practice!) and masturbating dogs on television are far more cultured acts than auctioning off a dinner with [*"and you can take him home, the mayor said I can say that"*] a muscle-bound fireman [*"now we have his shirt off"*] for $350. 00 at an anti-Cancer festival in the Village Green (Key Biscayne). [*I hear the loud-speaker as I write!*] Muscle requires far more energy to maintain than the oft (and wrongly) vilified fat, and symbolizes the high-consumption state which guarantees we will take far more than we give to the world community. Funny that most(?) of the same folk who would condemn beauty contests happily worship muscle! What a crying shame to see women becoming hulks, rather than decrying our cultural barbarism! (The 'not surprising' anecdote, turned out to be off (see text), but this note stays.)

黄 精 の 花 や き ん こ の 寄 所 桃 隣

ôsei no hana ya kinko no yoru tokoro [yoridokoro?] – tôrin (1638-1719)

#685

(gold-spirit-blossom[*naruko-lilly*]:/! *kinko*[type of seaslug] approaches/lands place/s)

blossoms with
the spirit of gold where
kinko land

The root of the lilly with the yellow/gold spirit for its name was used to make a tonic, so it shares a medicinal property with the sea slug. The pun here on the flower's name suggests the *kinko*, the Cucumaria cuke cured for *iriko*, brought some money to those who gathered and prepared it, but the next haiku seems, to me, a better depiction of the cruel truth:

金 に 咲 く 海 鼠 の つ る や 瓜 の 先   才 麿

kane/kin(?) ni saku namako no tsuru ya uri no saki – saimaro (1656-1738)*

#686 (gold/money-as bloom sea-slug-vine: melon's/cuke's tip/end[purchaser/market])

sea cucumbers
the tips are where you find
the gold blossoms

2) In Japan, too, the lumpen fishing community suffered. During the height of the Japanese trade with China in the Tokugawa era, the import of vast amounts of silk for luxury dress reduced the supply of precious metals too far for mercantilist minds to bear and the *iriko,* as a high added-value product easy to ship and reduced to 5% its original size, almost worth its weight in gold, was impressed as the star export, the main defender of the national purse, while poor fishing villages saddled with onerously high *iriko* quotas suffered every bit as much as the sea cucumber, itself.[1] → The old haiku above uses homophonic allusion to note that the money in the sea slug trade is made at the selling end (*uri-saki/uri-no-saki*), not at the production end and the more prosaic contemporary *tanka* below specifies the China connection (neither poem are in Tsurumi's book, I just use them for illustrations).

珊 瑚 礁 の 海 鼠 に は あ れ ど 捕 ら れ て は 広 東 市 場 の 絹 布 と 代 へ ら る   川 田 順

sangoshô no namako ni wa aredo torarete wa kôtô ichiba no kinu to kaeraru – kawada jun (contemp)

#687 (coral-reefs' seaslugs-for are but, caught-as-for, canton market's silk cloth-with exchange-can)

though sea slugs
hail from coral reefs
taken they are
ransomed in canton
for bolts of silk

1. *Luxury or Poverty Food* One of Tsurumi's many fine questions is if *iriko* is so difficult to make (the cooking must be just right, many days are needed for drying, etc), and offers less protein before it is cured than fish, how did it ever start to be made? He guesses it was first used mainly as fertilizer in poor areas, then dried for food in the hardest months of the winter, perhaps by people without boats to fish or gathered by women while the men were fishing and that someone wealthy visiting the provinces tried some and liked it, so . . . Or, it may have begun as a way around the salt tax, a legal way to get salt into the mountains . . . or, it was brought by other (non-Japanese) peoples who made it for whatever reasons, maybe even magical: who knows why the Chinese thought it was a medicine for long life . . . He makes many guesses, as I make many readings for some haiku.

2. *Source* I found the second haiku on an internet site run by an amateur who has kindly put some old literary work on-line. This work on *katte-ni-haikai saijiki* is not found on any other public site. Unfortunately, most old work is not on-line and available only to the wealthy or academic elite.

.3) And, finally, the trade itself, like the sea cucumber vaguely seen on the sea floor, is subliminal to the official stream of world history.   Some Australian historians have begun to come to terms with its role in their land's trading history, but there is insufficient acceptance of it as their first industry (it is usurped by a far less complex whale products) because the whites – while there was some involvement – never fully controlled, much less understood it.   For the same reason, Tsurumi thinks that Western historians are wrong to assume *beche de mar* trade did not exist until the late seventeenth century because *they* have no records of it.

Review Revisited: *To Torture or Not to Torture Sea Cucumbers*

As a matter of fact, the "torture" may have been exaggerated. Kuro writes that he got carried away in writing and feels horrible about the possibility he encouraged cultural misunderstanding by not giving *the rest of the story,* namely, that after the apparent "abuse" (not "torture"), Dr Motokawa Tatsuo – yes, it was the "Singing Biology" (*utau seibutsugaku*) show of the sea slugs' friend, whose words grace the title page! – put the *doro-doro-shita,* which, is to say, completely goopified sea slug into another tub of properly prepared water to show how it regained its shape after a while! "He wasn't just entertaining people at the expense of the subject but wanted to show us its wondrous ability to recoup."

Considering how Tsurumi crisscrossed the Pacific over the course of his research, I feel this next haiku, by a surgeon who founded the Kyushu Haiku Association in 1925, really should have been in his book:

空 港 に 着 け ば 酒 あ り 海 鼠 食 ふ 横 山 白 虹
kûkô ni tsukeba sake ari namako kû – yokoyama hakukô (1899-1983)
#688 (airport-to arriving-when sake is, seaslug eat)

arriving at
the airport, there's *sake*
i eat sea slug

A man, probably traveling alone flies from one place to another expending enormous resources doing the opposite of what the sea slug counsels. Yet what does he do as soon as he reaches his destination? He eats sea slug. I don't know what the poet was thinking other than feeling delight that an airport had sea slug – proving, perhaps, that modernization does not necessarily mean Westernization – but to me, it sums up the modern condition.

~

→1. *Quotas and Ecology* The government's demand for *iriko* was too high for many locality's seashore to support and some resorted to buying them from other sources. From this experience, they learned the importance of giving the sea cucumbers time to repopulate and necessity apparently drove them to discover that throwing in rocks to give the *namako* more secure homes helped. Today, as I mention elsewhere, there are a number of methods for creating ideal habitat for young *namako,* mostly using stones, concrete and wood. But what gives additional food for thought here is that if a village fished without outside government pressure they would naturally learn to restrict their catch and, for that reason, create seasons or other boundaries/limits; but, in that case, they would never deplete the resources to the extent they would have to come to a complete stop and probably not consider radical solutions such as adding to the housing. There is, it seems, good in every bad.

The Seeing Sea Slug

海 す こ し 焦 げ 臭 く な り 海 鼠 の 眼 天 気

umi sukoshi kogekusaku nari namako no me – tenki (contemp)
#689 (ocean slightly burnt-odor is/becomes seaslug/s' eyes)

the sea smells
slightly burnt and i feel
namako eyes

seashore revelry

a faint odor
of something burnt
namako eyes

A Japanese participant of the Ukimido haiku "pub" that Tenki moderates [1] wrote to say how much he liked this poem, which I must admit to finding totally incomprehensible. So I asked the author for an explanation. He wrote a page or more. The source of the odor was never ascertained. Indeed, he joked, maybe it was the smell of a synapse in his mind shorting out. In other words, it might have been a burnt *feeling*. I got it. (*namako no me mitai na kibun ga atta*). Tenki also wrote that despite the common knowledge that *namako* have no eyes, he feels that since they have a front and a rear they *do* have eyes. As we have already seen, common knowledge is wrong. Tenki's intuition is right. But I find it hard to understand when he continues "so, I/it was at/in sea. There was a *namako*-eye-like feeling." But, then again, he also writes that when he made this haiku he asked himself "What the hell does this mean?" So I will not push him any further, and you are free to read this however you want! What is it about a faint burnt odor that conjures up an image of seeing sea slugs? Does the odor extend to the water itself and does it burn the sea slugs' eyes? I must admit that, with me, the poem gave rise to a strange association, indeed: *Ulysses and the Cyclops!*

〜

Getting & Giving Sea Slugs

能 州 の 人 に 生 海 鼠 を 貰 ひ 鳬 ？ （金華伝）

#690 nôshû no hito ni namako o moraikeri – anon. (late 17c ?)
(nô-isle[the peninsula country of nôtokuni]'s person-from seaslug received/given/accepted)

given to me
by a nôshû man:
sea slugs

Nôtô peninsula, mostly rocks and mountains, is still known for its sea food in general and sea slugs in particular. I suppose it might be called the Ozarks of Japan and the people would be hillbillies.[1] Instead of turnips or pork rind, we get sea slug, which, however was more highly valued.[2] → KS found this haiku inside a book on Bashô's vocabulary. It is a refreshingly simple poem I'd like to know more about!

1. Notoites and Hillbillies   I once tried to convince a translator to use her Tohokuben (the dialect spoken on the Noto peninsula) for some of the old-timers quoted in a Foxfire book on Christmas. ***Contin.*** →

山へやる荷物にふつゝかななまこ哉 篤老

#691 yama e yaru nimotsu futsutsukana namako kana – tokurô (1777-1826)
(mountain-to give/send luggage unrefined/bumpkinlike/vulgar sea slug!/?/ǒ/hoh)

in my baggage
for the hills, some very
crude sea slugs

Grammar permits the luggage itself to resemble a sea slug, but the most probable meaning is that substandard dried sea slug is perfect for taking into the hills for gifts, both for the value of the salt and because the lack of refinement wouldn't matter. There is also a hint of the urbanite's prejudice here: this crude food is a perfect match for the crude uncultured country folk, who, as we have observed, will only roast it over fires, anyway. Parenthetically, I suppose the sea slug and country bumpkins would be kin in Japanese, for *bukotsu,* literally "boneless" is a common term for a rustic lout (that English would tend to call *big-boned!)* I expect to find an old sea slug haiku taking advantage of this.

~

Trepang in the New World: an Ad

WANTED TO BUY DRIED SEA CUCUMBER
Sea Cucumber must gut out,
without smell
and very clean
(white teak)
grade A and B
We advocate and believe
it is the responsibility
of commercial fisherman
and processors
to fully utilized shark
and take the fins
from dead shark only.

A.F.F.C. Dried Seafood
Jamaica, Queens New York 11435
Tel. 718-526-1717 Fax 718-526-1717
E-MAIL SharkFinFishMaw@aol.com

→ **2.** *Notoites and Hillbillies.* ~ I found a Japanese publisher for. She chickened out and used the standard (Kansai, i.e. Tokyo) dialect throughout. I once lectured on the lyrics of country music and *enka* (the closest Japanese equivalent, but a bit more urban) at Kanazawa Daigaku, Tohoku's leading university, and could kick myself for not eating *namako* on that occasion! Sure enough, on the day of the lecture there was a sudden blizzard – the gods showing off Tohoku weather to the visitor – so the attendance was not very high, but the professor(world's top expert on Jimmy Davis!) who invited me wrote up my lecture for a Popular Music Conference paper of some sort and it was later reprinted in a country music magazine, as well.

→ **3** *Turnips and Pork Rind* I joke about turnips and hillbillies, but, to tell the truth, the depiction of the mountain folk in *Tobacco Road* (by a producer who is supposed to be a progressive!) – where they gobble down raw turnips (actually, juicy turnips are good raw, but the movie viewers wouldn't know that) – or country music in *Blues Brothers* and the London – New York – Chicago – Miami intellectual's ignorance of the great wording of the best of country music (thinking opera worthwhile, they know nothing about the equally if not more intelligent cheating songs in country and laugh about country singers' "hiccups," while lauding the far more artificial operatic voice, and listening to totally lame blues called jazz) infuriates me!

Place-Punning Sea Slugs

In 1682, a collection of old-style haikai (*Matsushima Chôbô Shû*) edited by Michikaze (1638-1707)* used puns and historical coincidence to link sea-slugs – mostly *Cucumaria japonica* called *kinko* (gold-slug) or *torako* = (tiger-slug) – with a score of different localities. Some have been dropped as untranslatable and some have been sent to other chapters – to reinforce other metaphorical sea slugs – but I tried to keep as many as possible here, to enable them to be seen together and give a better idea of the nature of the place-punning game.

金華山　金海鼡海をはしるやみねに月浮かぶ　桂葉
#692 kinka-zan // kinko umi o hashiru ya mine ni tsuki ukabu – keiyô (1682)
(gold-blossom-mountain // gold-seaslug ocean runs: peak-by/from moon floats/rises)

mount kinka

as the moon rises
above its peak, gold sea slug
runs o'er the ocean

mt kinka

gold sea slug
flies o'er the ocean
at moon rise

How touching, the golden sea slug leaving as the moon peeks over the face of the "gold-blossom-mountain" considered its parent! We think sailing *slow*, but until the late nineteenth century, the sailboat was considered a prime example of something *fast*: "on the full moon / sailboat, what makes you / hurry so!" (*meigetsu ni nani o isogu zo hokakebune* – kaikin? (shinsen)), as one haiku put it. Overnight ship travel was not allowed in Japan at this time (see: FROIS) but the protector of the mercantile balance of payments, the sea slug, was doubtless given such a privilege! Since gold was identified with the sun (silver with the moon), and the golden sea slug was sometimes called "shining-offering" (*kosan*), there may be a hint of this pair of heavenly bodies, often depicted together (this, something auspicious) in paintings of Mt Fuji or the magical Mt. Merhu. MO adds*, "I can also see the waves reflecting the golden moonlight shine like running sea slugs"*.

餌袋は金海鼡問屋ぞつるがさき　正種
#693 ebukuro wa kinkodonya zo tsurugasaki – seishû/masatane? (1682)
(feed-bag/craw[profit/money-bags]-as-for gold-seaslug-wholesaler! tsurugasaki(crane-cape/peak[location]))

crane point

tsurugasaki:
where scratch comes from gold
sea slug dealers!

tsurugasaki

the cape of crane
its crop filled with gold
sea slug dealers

In the Sinosphere, the crane (*tsuru* in Japanese) is a symbol of longevity often combined with the equally auspicious gold, so the (idea for the?) island's business seems appropriate.. Once they were surprisingly plentiful for being so precious, and were sometimes fed; so it is hard to tell if the feed-bag refers to actual feed or the bird-island's craw, i.e., source of nutrition=money=gold-sea-slugs.

びくにのくひものあさぎ生海鼠や花田浦　次通
#694 bikuni no kuimono no asagi namako ya hanadaura --- jitsû (1682)
(nun-prostitutes' food/victims' pale-yellow[poor samurai] seaslug/s:/!/loh hamadaura)

blossom-field

hick sea slugs
keep the bikuni fat
in hanada bay

The *bikuni* are street-walkers who plied their trade in the garb of nuns, were usually daughters of the mountain wizards [1] and often did indeed pay a tithe to certain religious orders.   Some solicited favors from small boats, possibly the case here. This is the only instance where "hicks" are associated with sea slugs.   Perhaps, the *namako* of this area are the color *asagi* (pale green) identified with raw-boned peasants and poor samurai.[2] Hanada (blossom-field) was a female euphemism for sea slug. (ojd)

蚖がさきのにへに備ふや生海鼠姫　末丹
#695 hebigasaki no nie ni sonau ya namakohime --- suetan?(1682)
(hebigasaki(snake-point[place])'s sacrifice/present offered:/! seaslug princess/s)

hebigasaki

look, sacrifices!
offerings for snake-point:
sea slug princesses

Most Occidental readers know of maidens offered to the Minotaur. Japanese know legends of maidens offered to Gods and the most well known involves girls given to a Serpent (Orochi).   There are also folk tales of snake-women and there were women who did what might be called snake-teases in real life. I do not know if such were ever called "snake princesses," but, if they were . . . . "The poem might best be understood as a joking explanation for the sighting of many sea slugs at this island" CZ. A *nie* is not just a sacrifice, but a food offering and is even used with respect to food presented by a guest to a host or anyone to a noble. If Hebigasaki has an inn, I can also imagine the poet coming up with this poem upon being offered a very ugly "maiden" to sleep with.

網の雨に金海鼠さきけりかれ木島　独笑
#696 ami no ame ni kinko sakikeri karekijima – dokushô (1682)
(nets' rain-in gold-seaslug blooms[+finality] dead/withered winter-trees-island)

kareki-jima

gold sea slugs
blossom in the net rain:
dead-tree isle

The gold sea slugs (*C. japonica*) with frond-like feeding extensions tends to stand up more than the *ma-namako* (*S. japonica*) and was often collected by drag-net. It is hard to say whether the "net rain" is the water dripping off the drying nets, or the wet nets with their catch of sea slug, but they certainly

1. *Nun Streetwalkers and Mountain Wizards* See my FROIS for info on the *bikuni* and *yamabushi,* respectively. Or, if you cannot wait, see Cooper's *They Came to Japan,* or Kaempfer.

2. *Light Green* The "light-green" was a popular color for the lining of clothing worn by provincials and *asagi-ura* became synonymous with uncouth travelers.

allude to the mercy of Buddha (the net of Buddhist law) which made it possible that this miracle could happen, as was the case with the dead-tree-blossoms-again type of folk legend from which the theme is borrowed. If only the Irish ate sea cucumber, they could thank St. Patrick for creating them by cutting up all the snakes.

西 行 じ ま 猫 を な げ て や 金 海 鼡 術　三 千 風?

#697saigyôjima neko o nagete ya kinkojutsu – michikaze (1682)
(saigyô island: cat[obj] throws/thrown/ing gold-seaslug-technique/magic)

creation ab neko?	*new trick*
saigyo's island: a cat-casting gold sea-slug trick?	saigyô's island: from a silver cat to gold sea slugs?

(*Neko* being cat in Japanese). Saigyo was not only a great poet-monk, as we have seen, but a legend. A warrior of high-birth, he was called down from his mountain hermitage to teach etiquette to the ruling War Lord (a country-bumpkin) in order that he might entertain the Kyoto nobility without serious *faux pass*; and, as a reward for these services he was given an exquisitely worked large silver cat, which he gave to the first children he came across. Since magi in the Sinosphere were known to cast things into the air in order to make their spells, perhaps the cat is cast (in some other legend) to create this island and invent the industry of gold sea slugs. Or, considering another connotation of *nagete* (toss away), we might say he gave up the silver cat trick for the gold sea slug trick, for which the island was named after him.

(鳥 見 山?) う つ け 居 士 金 海 鼡 な げ て と み の 山　三 千 風 ?

#698 utsukekoji kinko nagete tomi no yama – michikaze (1682)
(empty/enlightened/worthless young-monk/sage gold-seaslug/s throw-out/up wealth/riches' mountain)

富

tomi-

no-yama

the crazy sage
cast gold sea slugs: behold
a mountain of wealth!

mountain of riches	*words of gold?*
the careless sage tosses out gold sea slugs *tomi-no-yama*	the useless monk calls his gilded sea slug *tomi-no-yama*

The top and left readings are based on the poem alone. I thought the *kinko* here might suggest throwing up the homophonic gold dust, but felt it more likely to be a spoof on the way great men had thrown things or shot arrows to settle upon locations for esoteric temples or what not. CZ, noting this poem was preceded by one to the effect that michikaze heard good catechism ("gold-words of the moon") at a temple he was sorry to leave (*kingon no tsuki ya*), and contrasts that to the temple he went to, so that the sea slug serves in effect the role of the turtle in the idiom "as different as the moon and a snapping turtle" (i.e., the exalted and the low) – as with the reading on the bottom right. If CZ is right – though I think I only got half of what he tried to explain to me -- this would be the oldest *sea-slug-as-incoherent-language* metaphor. Incoherent, indeed!

金 海 䖳 く ち ぬ 縁 の 下 な る ま い の し ま 不 丹
#699 kinko kuchinu ennoshitanaru mainojima – futan? (1682)
(gold-seaslug/s' rotting porch/overhang-under, mainojima[dancing-island])

mai-no-jima

dancing-island:
a gold sea slug lies rotting
under the porch

Gold doesn't rot. But why does this have to be Dancing Island? Is the island particularly prone to earthquakes, so that the drying sea slug danced right off the porch?

落 葉 は な ま こ の し ら ぼ し き ん く は ざ ん 秀門
rakuyô wa namako no shiraboshi kinkazan – shûmon (1682)
#700   (fallen-leaves seaslugs' white-dried[sun-cured] gold-blossom-mountain)

kinka-zan

the fallen leaves
are dried up sea slugs
mt gold-bloom

This, again, is the mountain considered the metaphysical parent of the gold sea slug. Sea slugs –these Japanese ones, anyway – like leaves, turn dark as they dry up, so there is a touch of wit in the phrase "white-drying" (*shiraboshi* really means dehydrating marine (and farm) products without salting them).

I am sure there are many things I missed or misinterpreted in trying to solve these place-name explanations which are all, in a sense, riddles, and hope I will be able to find more answers for a later edition.

～

Ridiculous Prose Sea Slugs

While the *Place Name Pun Sea Slugs haiku* barely belong to be called literature, even they look good compared to what follows. I have reduced the font a ½ point to punish this sorry Occidental sampling.

Suddenly, the sea cucumber reared its head which didn't exist and roared mightily: "AUGHHHHHHHHHHHHHHHHHHHHHHHHHHHHHHHHHHHHH!" cried the campers and newsies. Then, the sea cucumber sucked up Dan, Charlie, Vessey, and Frank. The world spun around the remaining kids, and suddenly it was 1999. "marie's camp parody": www.geocities.com/ Hollywood/ Makeup/ 9670/ fanfiction /marie3.html

After what seemed like an eternity, I picked myself off the ground and pulled the cheese from my hair like an octopus molesting a sea cucumber. I began to walk home. "The HauntedHookup" (www.yale.edu/je/activities/ temptations/archives /10_29_98.html)

You'd never see a sea cucumber hurting anyone. They wouldn't touch a banana if you handed it to them, and their bodily waste is conveniently secreted into the surrounding water. All in all, I think a sea slug poem should far outscore a monkey poem. That's all I have to say about that. (jon replying to <u>slammin' it up Earlham College</u> posted by Emi Jenkins on October 04, 2001 at 00:39:08)

You fools! Don't interfere! We'll kill you all!! / *Yogic Flyer #2* / Oooh, somebody has bad karma! / *Yogic Flyer #3* / You'll spend your next life as a sea cucumber with that attitude. / They grab him by the arms and fly him kicking and screaming out the window. (aix1.uottawa.ca/~jevan093/ hydrogenguy/ episode10.html)

"Clammy" ("I don't care that you're clammy") / "Giving the Sea Cucumber Back to Susan" ("she needs it more than I do") / "Living It Up in the Octopus' Garden" (sample titles from *Nields Clamography* by Bruce (12/15/2000 net)

Well, this led to a discussion of marketing cheap, simple salads as snacks for children ages 6-15 (we were eating the salad snack-like, using our fingers). Obviously, the health angle would be a detriment, not a selling point, but the gross-out factor of "Hoagie [sub sandwich] Guts" might just work. Kids seem to like any food that is the wrong color or disgusting in some other way, after all. Okay, so we had the name, now we needed a mascot. I suggested the sea cucumber, an animal that can eject its digestive system and associated organs when disturbed. We have a guy in a costume, a giant foam sea cucumber suit, and at the end of the commercial he makes a horrible BLEEEEAH! noise and violently vomits lettuce, tomato, and onions out onto an audience of shrieking children. Tell me that wouldn't work! (rayontheweb 9-30-2001 net)

Billy'd escaped, just barely, by clinging to an octopus-hide pillow from his vast octopus-byproduct stores. It was weeks before he was rescued, weeks spent under the mocking glassy eye of the octopus pillow. He'd killed it himself, long ago, killed it and grafted one of its rubbery tentacles onto the stump of his own left arm, lost years ago to the grinding jaws of a voracious sea cucumber. ("Beyond the End of the Era of the Sea-Pirates" / Trelane's Story, part II / Posted by Byydo 11/9/2002 / www.wcnews.com/ loaf/wwwboard/ messages/2651.html)

"Feast your eyes on Rolf's customary dress - sewn together from the membranes of the great sea cucumber! The fitting was excruciating - but that's another story - all for the honour of Rolf's great nanno! As part of our guilt-ridden traditions every year Rolf's family pays tribute to Rolf's great nanno and the mighty sea cucumber. Welcome my friends, do not be shy --- and feast from the box of food made from the respective sea creature!" (Scott "diggs" Underwood dueling eds? net)

Oh slutty sea monkey! You've stolen my sea cucumber! Damn you to sea-hell, you porous bastard! Die, monkey, die! But yet you are so cute. So luscious, so intriguing... (Note: sea monkeys are a type of brine shrimp. Matt Sebastian and Kris Scott on the Sea Monkey Worship site's page of "negative poetry" mypage.uniserve.ca/ ~sbarclay/negpoetarchive.htm)

Komrade and I present to you our tiny endeavors with the FruityLoops program: the GOOD, the BAD, and the UNSPEAKABLY UGLY. We give you... MUSICAL HAIKU. Feast your ears! Feast! / PART I: ASCENSION OF THE NANOCHICKENS / Grapestream DNA: Primordial engenderings of the musical haiku / PART II: SEA CUCUMBER GREENDREAMS / Syncopated Eggbirths in the Hatchery . . . Sharkplunderings for the Brainscream: Ethereal HaikuSlaughterhouse (http:// feeblesquare.undonet.com/musichaiku/mh.html.)

Montague the Wicked ordered the color shift. . . . If an octopus wants his garden more of a sea-green, then by God, I believe that is his undeniable right. Sure, that may just be the trend of the month among the cephalopods, and his concubine (Mistress Bippie) will be whining for him to kill a sea cucumber or two to add a little red to the decor, but that is the risk he is taking and I assume he is well aware of it. Besides, if they really get tired of it, in a year or two they can just sub-let the the space to a family of inbred urchins. (Mike Gregg (Mr Scrappy)) 2001-04-16 10) tiles.ice.org/ tile_info_surreal.php? quilt_id =3&tile_id=2200

"Do not be one with your anger child of a thousand tantrums. Rolf is here too make all worries fly away like the barnacles of the Great Sea Cucumber!" (Foxyroxy: Ed-tching to tickle #6 net)

Memento Mori Sea Slug

Tim really enjoyed every aspect of biology . . . He was so enthusiastic he used to bring specimens back from Invertebrates practicals. . . .I remember one evening when I came back from jazz orchestra to find that Tim had kindly placed a sea cucumber in my bed. He explained that as I had missed the practical he thought that I might like to see. ("Funeral Tribute" by Greg Payne :www.hc09.dial.pipex .com/ tim/gro-07.html)

~

Tanzanian Chinese Sea Slugs

Considering the role of Chinese "coolies" in constructing the railroad that spanned North America over a hundred years earlier and the later tragedy in Panama (unlike the case in the United States, the opium supply was cut off by some dumb clerk and hundreds of the Chinese, who had been outworking the Irish and keeping clean (nightly baths) as well, hung themselves or paid Malay workers to behead them, etc.) it is a matter of no little interest to find the Chinese heading out to work on railroads, this time in an official capacity between May, 1968 and July 1976, when fifty thousand Chinese went to Africa to build the Tanzania-Zambia Railroad. Since there were up to 16,000 working at the peak of the project, we know many were there for several years at a time.[1] Kirino Manjirô visited Tanzania toward the end of the project and met Chinese laborers on the beach gathering sea slug. Years later he put his memories into haiku and sent them to Suien (watersmoke), a top internet haiku site.

海鼠採るみんなで砂に叩き付け 霧野萬地郎
namako toru minna de suna ni tatakitsuke – kirino manjirô (2000)
#701 (seaslugs taken/caught all[together] sand-into hit-attach/put)

chinese style	*chinese style*
gathering sea slug	throwing sea slugs
altogether throwing them	down hard upon the sand
into the hot sand	working in unison

Are the Chinese are simply bringing up loads of sea slugs collectively and throwing them down on the sand to dry, or throwing them down repeatedly to soften them?

故郷の食材得んと海鼠干す 霧野萬地郎
furusato no shokuzai en to namako hosu – kirino manjirô (2000)
#702 (home-country's food-material get-try seaslug dry)

trying to obtain
the food of their homeland
drying sea slugs

1. *Chinese in Africa* The Ministry of Foreign Affairs of the People's Republic of China put it like this: "Nyerere . . . said that China's assistance in constructing the Tanzania-Zambia railway is a "great contribution to the African people." "In past history, construction of railways by foreigners in Africa was for the purpose of plundering the wealth of Africa, while the Chinese did it [for] just the opposite [reason], to help us in developing our national economy". (www.fmprc.gov.cn) 63 Chinese died to create this 320-bridge, 22-tunnel miracle (it is remarkable how quickly it was made considering the forbidding terrain!) that "smashed the blockade by the then racist regime of South Africa and provided Zambia with a new and reliable route to the sea." I say, hats off to China!

Reading this, I can't help wondering if the Africans ever ate sea slug, or whether these Chinese started a new custom in Tanzania. Though the Chinese generally kept to themselves,[1] it is impossible that their cuking went unnoticed by the locals. I also suspect that these Chinese were thinking of the medicinal value of the sea slug for their aching joints.

海鼠押せばわたを発して海汚す　霧野萬地郎

namako oseba wata o hasshite umi yogosu – kirino manjirô (2000)
#703 (seaslug press-if/when guts shooting, ocean[obj] dirties)

> when squeezed
> sea slugs shoot their guts:
> dirtying the sea

Gut-shooting is seldom remarked in haiku. I felt tempted to put this into *Protean Sea Slugs*, where such *harakiri* is mentioned, but, as Takahashi Masako of *Suien* pointed out, this haiku describes something else: the pristine beauty of the Indian Ocean. Nogiri added that the Indian community of Tanzania, dressed up and gathered on the white sand beach by the blue ocean every evening.

$\sim$

English Sea Slug Haiku

> Week 9 Haiku. "Urge and urge and urge,. Always the procreant urge. ... rise to the matrix. *Sea cucumber soup,. someone swears this is tasty. not the cuke*, I bet. ..."
> 192.211.16.13/curricular/SOL/haiku9 – (My *italics*)

This Google hit is the only English language "haiku" on sea cucumber I found. A protest against eating cuke because the poaching in the Galapagos aroused(?) the poets's pity? Why not, say, *clam chowder / someone swears this is tasty / not the clams!* After all, the clam, unlike the sea cucumber has a brain . . .   If anyone has a *decent* haiku on sea cucumber written in English, I'd like to see it!

$\sim$

TOEFL Sea Slugs

> Passage 12 – Certainly no creature in the sea is odder than the common sea cucumber. All living creatures, especially human beings, have their peculiarities, but everything about the little sea cucumber seems unusual. What else can be said about a bizarre animal that, among other eccentricities, eats mud, feeds almost continuously day and night but can live without eating for long periods, and can be poisonous but is considered supremely edible by gourmets? . . . Although they have voracious appetites . . . sea cucumbers have the capacity to become quiescent and live at a low metabolic rate, feeding sparingly or not at all for long periods . . . If it were not for this faculty, they would devour all the food available in a short time and would probably starve themselves out of existence. .

After the 300-word article, the question: "Compared with other sea creatures the sea cucumber is very (A) *dangerous* (B) *intelligent* (C) *strange* (D) *fat*." (from a TOEFL (Test of English as a Foreign Language) training exercise at bwxixi.myetang.com)

---

1. Solitary Chinese I found a long article by the poet (whose name, Kirino Manjiro, I assume is a pun on the magnificent Mt. Kilimanjaro) and learned that he crashed the Chinese camp because he was suffering horribly from a hip injury and hoped to avail himself of the skills of the Chinese doctors. They treated him for free every day for over three months. It is a very touching story.

<u>Cotton=Gut Sea Slugs</u>

#704 このわたをうるかと宗祇戻し 橋荻上紘一
(konowata[kono wata] o uru ka [uruka] to sôgi modoshibashi)

AQ found a haikuby Koichi Ogiue,[1] that is untranslatable, for it simultaneously means *"Will you sell me this cotton?* Sôgi asked at turned-back-bridge," *Will you sell this slug gut?* at the Sôgi-Turned-back Bridge," and, perhaps, even, *"Would you call me 'beautiful,'* she asked at Sôgi-Turned-back Bridge." The haiku is based on a *waka* with many legends. One says when the great *renga* master Sôgi visited Shirakawa for a *renga* fest in 1481, a woman gave him the sad news that the event was already over and astounded him with a clever *waka* in reply to his playful request to buy her cotton (cloth maybe?). Another has him asking a young maid about the cotton she carried on her back who so impressed him with her witty *waka* that he turned back from his trip – turn back on a good note? because he has nothing to teach to the province? – right then and there. Either way, he heard the poem

「この綿は売るか」と尋ねると、少女は

〈阿武隈の川瀬にすめる鮎にこそうるかといへるわたはありけれ〉

and turned back at what is now known as the Sôgi-Turned-back Bridge. The *waka* turns the "sell?" in Sôgi's question: "Will you sell me this cotton?" (kono wata wa uru ka) into "beautiful" (*uruka*) and the "cotton" (*wata*) into "guts" – or, I would guess "I/me" [2]) that belong to the sweet-fish (*ayu*) living in the river below. Presumably, she thought of the sweetfish guts because Sôgi's "this cotton" (*kono* wata) is homophonic with "slug guts" (*konowata*). And this, outside of the far older *Record of Ancient Matters*, is is the closest the sea slug comes to appearing in literature before the latter half of the seventeenth century.

～

<u>Parade Sea Slug</u>

"I said to the jellyfish and the sea cucumber carrying the rest of the banner to my left, 'get ready to ... Dave was right, the situation did have a surreal flavor. ..." Sustainable Seas Expeditions - Channel Islands, June 5, 1999 sustainableseas.noaa.gov/missions/ channel1/ dailylogs/ june5.html - 28k – Cached

～

1. **Koichi Ogiue** I violate my usual rules and give his name here family name last, for he uses it so at his website which lists sixty seven journal articles. Most recently, "67. (with T. Itoh) On 3-dimensional isotropic submanifolds of a space form, Turkish J. Math. 22(1998)461-473. And, to give a few more that would be pure *namako* to most of us, 66. (with H.-f. Sun) *Minimal hypersurfaces of unit sphere*, Tohoku Math. J. 49(1997)423-429. 61. (with N. Takeuchi) *A sphere can be characterized as an ovaloid which contains one circle through each* point, J. Geom. 49(1994)163-165. 59. (with N. Takeuchi) *Hulahoop surfaces*, J. Geom. 46(1993)127-132. 47. *Positively curved totally real minimal submanifolds immersed in a complex projective space*, Proc. Amer. Math. Soc. 56(1976)264-26636. (with G. Ludden)

2. **Wata as I/me** My OJD only gives a *watai* version of the first-person, but I would be willing to bet (but not a lot) that in some dialects it would sound like *wata*. Sôgi's words and the *waka,* for Japanese readers:

Ridiculous Poetic Sea Slugs

The internetted poems (and criticism of poems) about sea cucumber in Occidental languages are a bit better than the prose, but not enough to deserve large font. I have not actually read some of the poems, good ones may be seriously considered for the next edition.

> One poem is a meditation on a sea cucumber, which ranks higher than humanity on the author's evolutionary scale. "For a sea cucumber has never suffered any sort of shipwreck... never gotten lost in a fog," writes Millman. "Which makes you wonder who's savvy and who's not." ("A review of Lawrence Millman's Northern Latitudes" (New Rivers Press) by AARON SPITZER in the Nunatsiaq News (IQALUIT))

> "By the way, *namako* in Finnish is 'merimakkara', sea sausage. My friend and colleague, Finnish-born American poet Anselm Hollo, wrote in his early poem: "The sea sausage cannot be eaten, neither can be her eggs – beautiful women should not be beaten, neither should ugly be ... etc etc" – this all rhymes very cleverly in Finnish: *"merimakkaraa ei voi syödä / eikä sen muniakaan / kauniita naisia ei saisi lyödä / eikä rumiakaan..."* I don't know if Anselm has made an English translation of it." (Kai Nieminen, corresp.)

> *"'Old Enough to Stop Bearing Children'*// Lily walks, debauched/ by breezes that stir/ the summer-washed atmosphere / like a colored stick in a clear drink/ When she happens to look down,/ she sees a baby mouse, soft/ as a sea cucumber, clinging/ to the button on her work shirt./ . . ."(Elizabeth Kirschner *The Gettysburg Review* Volume 13, Number 4 Winter 2000)

> "I'm stuck on this boat for a century!", he cries into his drink. / The alcohol in his system causes his brain to shake. / He takes the wheel of his ark of oak and steers it into a wave! / The wave had the face of a demon and it smashed the boat to bits! / Noah sinks with his fists clenched tightly around a sea cucumber. / He inflates it with a deep breathe and rises to the surface through a mastery of physics! (From "An Ode to Moses" in(?) "God Loves Moses, God Loves Me," The Salvation Army Concept Album. Published by: Bongfish , On: Jan-14-2003 www.demolicious.org/ modules/nsections/ index. *Much of this will fly clear over the heads of our American readers, but then again what doesn't? Ahaha. Ha... anyway.*)

> But to assign the Messiah human nature any more than the nature of a sea cucumber is beyond reason. In this sense, then, McClure declares in these poems that "MATTER IS SPIRIT!" that the universe "IS DIVINE" ("Springs," 66), and that we are all "Pseudopods of Messiah" ("The Basic Particle,"). (From the Substrate: Notes on the Work of Michael McClure by Gregory Stephenson)

> The Last Words of Alice the Goon // . . . Once I swam / deep as hurt to the sand floor of the sea / . . . In that garden/ I took in my hands and barely held/ a shivering sea cucumber/ and watched without blinking/ as its side ruptured, spilling/ crude organs, a pharynx, a gut, all/ purple and eviscerated, streaming away./ Strange flower, it survived/ this way: with nothing left in it,/ nothing was left to devour/ or desire. In it there was an end/ to hunger. And rising up/ from the water, this was a comfort./ This was a flower/ and it occurred to me that I had no hair/ in which to keep it,/ . . . . . / O awkward spark set fat in the flesh,/ I am no woman, only a doll./ and dollop of tallow, bauble of bone, ingrown hair./ Enough, enough. Already I'm singing. (Copyright © 2002 Paul Guest All rights reserved from crab orchard review in VERSE DAILY)

I may be unfair to some of these poets. It is a safe bet that Paul Guest and, for that matter, most people who appreciate modern poetry would not find his poem (of which I excerpt less than half) ridiculous. The problem is mine. I find the wordiness of modern poetry too much to swallow.

海 鼠 裂 く 花 の す が た は 生 き 仏 敬 愚

#705namako saku hana no sugata wa ikibotoke – keigu
(seaslug splits=blooms living-buddha world [let's]flow-away)

letting go

sea slug splits
behold the flower of
non-attachment

海 鼠 裂 く な に も な く 益 々 な に も 　 敬 愚

#706 namako saku nani mo naku masumasu nani mo – keigu
(seaslug splits=blooms what=nothing even not more and more what=nothing)

freedom

sea slug splits
nothing much has
nothing more

Guest's sea cucumber flower is a fine symbol. It and other modern poems whose flowers are lost in excessive verbiage might blossom if they were pruned back and repotted in *tanka* and haiku! The Japanese pun on *saku* (bloom/split) unfortunately won't English.

腹 の 中 も す っ き り 吐 け ば 海 鼠 か な 　 敬 愚

hara no naka sukkiri hakeba namako kana – keigu
#707(belly-within clean/pure spew-if seaslug!/?/ǿ/the)

mizu ni nagasu

spilling its guts
the silence of the sea slug
is now pure

This veers off to incorporate the idea of the discontented squirming sea slugs of Buson, by relieving it of its grudges, which metaphorically belong to the gut in Japanese, though the pun in the first line of the translation is purely English.

～

Bislamic Sea Slugs

ア カ コ ア オ コ ク ロ コ 共 通 海 鼠 語 圏 　 な む

#708 namakogo akakoaokokuroko kyôtsû namakogoken – namu (2003)
(seasluglanguage // redseaslugblueseaslugblackseaslug common seaslug-languagesphere)

seabed bislama

redslugblueslugblackslugcommontongue

English has two problems approximating *goken,* a word for meaning a sphere or area within which a certain language or languages reign. First, the language: "tongue" or "lingua" are concrete to the extent of being ridiculous when describing an imaginary language of a creature without said anatomical part; "~talk" and "~speak" are too human ("*slug-speak*, might be good for, say, describing waffling politicos). Second, the only suitable suffix, "~ese" (i.e., *slugese*), cannot be fit to the sphere/area, as suggested by my "commontongue." So, if I cannot do the poem justice, I might as well play with it:

bislama beginnings

redblueblack
one tongue for all
of holothuria

Bislama, a corruption of the Portuguese *bicho do mar* via the French *beche de mar* via English(?) *beachlamar*, is the name for the pidgin of the Trepang-gathering sphere, but I applied it here to the language of the namako itself.

republic of bislama

akako aoko
kuroko sea slugs speak
a common tongue

This is the only one haiku I know to include all three *namako*. The mimetic effect of putting them one after another like that suggests a crisper pronunciation than I would have expected from a holothurian.

the mother tongue

sea slugs speak
akakoaokokuroko
no babel below

If the sea slug can talk, its language clearly predates Babel. But, let me stop playing and let the poet explain his own poem:

> *Seaslugese*: As the sea cucumber consume their detritus, their tube-feet broadcast minute decibels of sound picked up by other sea cucumber who react, from which we imagine conversation, mainly reminiscing about ancient times, but not in the high style of mythology for, judging from the "First Period: The Study Group of Things Placed (*A Study of Marine Ornaments/Objects*?) in the Sea" by Guy Eddouard Larousse *et al*, the sea cucumber would seem to be a natural grumbler – or are we stepping out of bounds? (*Namakogo*)

So *Namako*, silenced by the Japanese Gods is given back a voice, no, a language, which we shall call "feet" rather than "tongue," by a surrealist poet in Japan with some help, perhaps, from a dead French artist. For my part, I wonder if any one has ever created a poem with the right feet for tap-dancing out Morse Code? [1]

1. Bislama Dialog After I showed the author my translations and asked him for more information about the Frenchman and the original name of that French book, he apologized for leading me on, and I, then, apologized for making him believe I took his spoof seriously and . . Perhaps I should add that he is the curate of a Pure-Land (same sect as Issa) temple and has published many haiku including, "the milky way:/ only the door-knob remains/ in my hand" (佐山哲郎『東京ぱれおろがす』)。

Renku'ed Sea Slug

. . . .

harukoromo midareru rohrahkohsutah – a

her spring dress / dishevelled riding / a roller-coaster

tôgyûjo de agaru ubugoe – pi

in the bullfight arena / a newborn baby cries

#709 中空に腸ぶちまける赤海鼠　勝之

chûkû ni wata buchimakeru akanamako – katsuyuki

and guts blast / high up into the sky / red sea slug

shosûminzoku shôki ni modoru – jin

a minority people / returns to sanity

. . . .

(8408.teacup.com/namubow/bbs - 21k)

This is a segment I crudely chopped from a *renku* (5-7-5//7-7//5-7-5//7-7) sequence found googling the *akanamako* (red seaslug). I'm not sure of what it means but it does bring out the violent spirit of the spring. Tenki writes that he participated, Namu (of Bislama fame) was the "master of ceremonies" (?) and Shôno is a haiku poet who loves *sake* and *namako*.

∼

Beloved Sea Slug

The following letter from one Honkyo Tomoe was published by a leading newspaper, the YOMIURI SHINBUN on November 17, 1878. I translate all but a bit cut from the introduction.

The sea slug is a *nopperabô* [*"an egg-like face without a nose and a mouth," "a blank face without features," "monotonous ∼"* according to my Japanese-English dict.. How about a "blob"?]. I don't know if it has eyes, but it doesn't seem to make out things nor smell them; [1] but its mouth is bigger than normal for historical reasons. As you all know [*so do we, see Preface*] in Ancient Times . . . . . . so now, it just has this big mouth (though it can't even hum) and is healthy, so a *nopperabô* person is called a *namake* [*"lazy" and similar to sea slug = namako or a typo?*] and as I, for one, love this *nopperabô* sea slug, I have composed the following soliloquy.

Sea slug, slug, slug! What a fine fellow you are! You don't fall into one-sided love affairs like the abalone [*single shell, alone*]; you don't devastate yam fields like the octopus [*bonzes with shaven pates were infamous potato lovers*]; but, gently and temperate as wind on straw [*straw was thought to tenderize sea slug, but the figure of speech escapes me*], if you happen to be thwacked by huge radishes [*if daikon are part of diced sea slug=kodatami are they, then, dish-mates? Or, is this a case of competitive exclusion by one phallic symbol on another?*] by suspicious officials [*daikon were suitable swords for namako bushi or sea slug samurai, but I don't get the official connection*] and get angry, you only harden your body, and do not bite or thrash about. Becoming a companion for my evening drink, you turn into *konowata* [*slug-guts*] to console my *doronken* [*drunken, from the Dutch, but with a doro, or "muddy" feeling*] heart, or turning into the nutritious gold sea-slug [*kinko*] endure your duty as a domestic product for export to China; though you are also called tiger slug [*torago*], you don't go running through the thickets o'er a thousand leagues, but simply sit quietly packed in the hold; and you are valued and loved for taking after neither shell nor fish but keeping your independent taste and, for this, I hold you dear and don't you slack off on your job inside the three-sip vinegar [*sanbaizu is part vinegar, part sake and part soy-sauce or salt and what raw sea slug was briefly marinated in*]!

KS, who found this, wrote: "This Honkyo Tomoe-san seems like he might be Gill-san's grandfather. This might be called a type of *haibun.*"   Honkyo's writing is *berabô*, notoriously bad, but I am honored, nonetheless, I guess!

∼

R/Lace-lover's Sea Slug

見ただけで海鼠を厭うレース好き 玉愚
#710 mita dake de namako o kirau rehsuzuki – tamagu
(looked[at] only-by/from seaslug[obj] hate/hating r/lace-lover)

r/lace-lovers
hate all sea slugs
at first sight

too gross

the very sight
of sea slug overwhelms
a lace-lover

too slow

the race fan
will change channels on
all sea slugs

too ugly

for eugenists
to see the slug race
is to hate it

Keigu's *namako-phobic* neatnik haiku did not grab a Japanese poet because she thought most Japanese, because they eat or are familiar with eating sea slugs, do not think of them as the opposite of *clean*, namely *dirty*. For my part, the intended antithesis was not with dirtiness *per se*, but with a certain part of the clean/dirty connotative cluster, i.e., *fastidious* versus *sloppy*. Be that as it may, this poem is her suggested alternative to the neatnik.   Ironically, it does not pun well in the language from which *rehsu* comes from, English.   So this was a sea slug artificially born to help a foreigner, Keigu. The poet's name combines the do-gooder Tamasudare's *tama* with the *gu* of Keigu.

∼

Urban Myth Sea Slugs

A friend of my brother was sent to work in the East in a very nice location on the Malaysian coast. One evening he popped into the local supermarket and bought a refrigerated seafood salad all ready to eat on a paper plate. He left it on the kitchen table while he had a quick shower. When he went back into the kitchen he noticed the shellfish and other 'seafood' on his plate was moving about. Unable to stomach the thought of eating live seafood, he waded out to sea and released his seafood salad back into the wild. // The same guy, by now a confirmed veggie, ordered sea cucumber in a local restaurant. He was shocked that the sea cucumber appeared to move whenever he stabbed it with his fork and sliced a bit off the end. His companion, a local employee at the same firm, patiently explained that the sea cucumber is actually an animal and it's best to start eating them from the head end so they don't wriggle right off the plate. (URBAN MYTHS - FOOD, DRINK, SHOPPING AND LEISURE of http://www.shartwell.freeserve.co.uk/ humor-site/food-myths.html.)

~

Mistaken Sea Slugs

1

While this book is full of admitted misreadings, riddled with dead-end alleys, the following two haiku wandered so far from the theme of the chapter where they began (*Melancholy Sea Slugs*) that I finally bit the bullet and cut them out. But rather than throwing away my mistake as writers are advised to do, I saved it.

わ た つ み や 餌 た に ま か て 生 海 鼠 か く 白 雄

#711 watatsumi ya esa dani maka de namako kaku – shirao/hakuyû (1738-1791)
take one: (sea/neptune! bait/feed [that is given to pets or stock]not even thrown so sea slug [is] such)

look what you've done!

wretched sea slugs
neptune, why don't you try
feeding them?

I thought this poem was an alternate explanation for the squirming anguish of Buson's *namako*. But I wasn't certain and essayed a half dozen more interpretations.[1] But they were nothing compared to this next, perhaps the most touching mistranslation I have *ever* done – touching because the image in my head lives on – of the second mistaken poem that, as we shall see, holds the key for understanding the first.

浦 人 や 思 あ り 気 に 生 海 鼠 か く   保 吉

urabito ya omoiarige ni namako kaku – hokichi (18c)
(cove-people: feeling suggested-with seaslug scratch/stroke/draw)

the fishing folk
look concerned as they
stroke sea-slugs

There is that *kaku* [2] written in phonetic script in this poem, by a less well-known poet contemporary to Shirao. It clearly is different from what it was in Shirao's poem. ("such" vs "scratch/stroke/draw"). The *ura* or "cove" is not only a topological description, but suggests backwardness and even *urami*,

1. *Crazy Readings* The readings are not worthy of large font. One, remembering song # 1,301 of the MANYOSHU ("because it/you/she is/are a gem tightly carried in neptune's hand [i'll] have to dive in the rocky cove," i.e., "because you/she is/are hard-to-get, I must . . ."), dares to get personal: "neptune, damn! / she won't even bait me: am i / a f___ing sea slug?" Another, assuming the poem puns on something called a "sea-slug collar" (*namako maki*) , a collar stuffed with cotton or straw to serve as a built-in scarf, because *watatsumi* (sea god) is a homophone for *wata* or cotton, and *tsumi,* pick/stuff, is, I think much better: "***winter collars*** // the stuffing shop: / with no special feed, / such fat sea-slugs!" But it is also ridiculously bold, considering that there is no proof whatsoever that such a shop has ever existed. Has there ever been a translator as scatter-brained as me?

or vengefulness, something not far from the holding-it-all-in uncomfortable sea slug of Buson. But, *urabito* can just mean people who live by and from the sea.

con sordino

the old conch
affectionately scratches
a sea slug

A "conch" is a term used for old-timers familiar with the sea in South Florida, where I grew up. In this reading, sea slug squirminess is associated with having a physical rather than mental itch, but I fear the affection bends *omoiarige ni* too much, so these must be considered my paraverses rather than translations. Likewise for this:

sea-side dwellers
they draw sea slugs
looking pensive

Kaku can mean "draw" and this haiku would make sense if rural folk habitually drew wildlife, but there is no record of such.

cove dwellers
look so pensive as they
scoop sea slugs

Yanagisawa Toyoshige of the Aichi Fisheries Research Institute informed me that the verb *kaku* describes what fishermen do with a *kagi,* a cross between a hook and a rake, which they manipulate underwater while leaning from the ship to scoop up sea cucumbers. While Chinese characters usually settle the meaning, in this case, it would not have prevented my mistranslation, for the same character means "scratch/stroke/scooping/raking." Without knowing the specialized vocabulary for sea-cucumber harvesting, I would have missed it all the same. Only the "drawing" paraverse would not have been written. But the story continues. Not long after being set straight, I came across an old print of sea slug processing on the internet. In it, I saw some people using easily recognizable rakes (remarkably similar to Western garden rakes) to space out sea slugs drying on a mat. And they – one man in particular – look very pensive!

a cove man
rakes sea slug with something
on his mind

the fisher folk
seem deep in thought
raking sea slug

1. *Kaku* Meanings "Write" or "draw" is the most common usage for the dozen or so word/s pronounced *kaku*. Only context, *knowing what's what*, can choose among them for translation. This brings out an interesting contradiction in the position of those who argue in favor of the phoneticization – or de-characterization – of Japanese. Though purely phonetic syllabary might be faster to type (therefore, more suitable for the modern age: something I dispute in ORIENTALISM AND OCCIDENTALISM), it makes good machine translation (also part of modernity) much *more* difficult, for computers, like foreigners, understand little of context. In cases where homophones are generally used in a distinctive syntax (subject/ indirect object/verb etc), Japanese AI is quite good at guessing which is which, but it is helpless in a case such as this one.   **#713**

2. *Really Stroking Sea Slugs*   The sea slug is not collected like its relatives the starfish and sea-urchin. In Keigu's words: *sea slugs: / how many people / bring them home? (mochikaeru hito ga sukunai namako kana* 持ち帰る人が少ない海 鼠哉 敬愚) But this might change. I have seen little children petting a small sea cuke at a Biscayne Nature Center booth on Key Biscayne. It makes a fine petting animal ("Nervous systems have a saturation response to stimuli." A.K.) I wonder if the positive effect on the stroker would be as strong as that proven for furry and feathered pets.

I do not know if there is anyway to settle on a final version for the haiku, for I know for a fact that poets were influenced by pictures, [1] which gives me confidence in "rake," yet an expert is an expert. And, returning to the first mistranslated poem, Shirao's Japanese Neptune, we can see the *kaku* that I misread as "such" or "like that," (an abbreviated *kaku-no-gotoku*) should *probably* be the "scoop/catch" suggested by Yanagisawa. So, here the poem is again. Take Two:

わ た つ み や 餌 た に ま か て 生 海 鼠 か く 白 雄

#711x2watatsumi ya esa dani maka de namako kaku – shirao/hakuyû (1738-1791)
(sea/neptune! bait/feed [that is given to pets or stock]not even thrown so sea slug <u>catch/scoop</u>)

cheap fishing

wondrous sea!
all these slugs caught
without bait!

As you can see, the poem no longer exhibits any *melancholy* whatsoever. It would seem to be celebrate one of nature's few free lunches – I joke, for the difficulty of the processing makes up for the ease of the taking – the sea slug!

2

There were more mistakes, far too many to leave in the main text, and many too much fun to abandon. The next concerns sea slugs I first thought lascivious. Mistakes tend to be more complex than correct readings. This is only slightly less complex than the last.

こ そ り あ ふ 寒 さ も 桶 の 海 鼠 哉 萬 古

[take one] *kosori au samusa mo oke no namako kana* – banko (1777)
#714 (secretly/crowd meeting coldness also tub's seaslug/s!/?/ô/the/loh)

bundling	*forbidden love*
what a cold	we meet
tete-a-tete: sea slugs	like sea slugs in a tub
in a bucket	of cold water

Is the poet having problems with "night-creeping," an accepted practice involving more sex than colonial New England's "bundling?" Or, worse, committing adultery? The "also" (*mo*) in the original apparently equates two types of cold, that cast by the eye of the social body on illicit love and the more obvious coldness of the sequestered sea slugs. But, I might be wrong and the poet was merely astounded to find cold sea slugs apparently doing it in a tub.[1] Or, am I imagining things? Probably.

#715, 716, 717

1. More Promiscuous Sleepers? The parallel to this old haiku is this modern one: "in front of the shop, / sea slugs, so ungainly / in their wanton sleep" (*misesaki ni namako buyô ni fute[i?]neshite* – someno ozuki (1997) 店先に海鼠不様に不貞寝して 染野小月). *Futei* 不貞 means "unchaste." but it is unlikely that sea slugs making contact in tubs were really thought to be engaging in sex, so we must assume , the Chinese characters are shorthand (?) for *fute*: 1) discontented 2) disobedient 3)wayword/indulgent/egoistic/carefree [behave-as-you-please] and the poem means: "the shop-front: / seas slugs sprawled / in sullen sleep."

It is hard for me to see sea slugs as a picture of petulance, but if sulky people tend to sleep with their limbs in disarray . . . Combining the unchaste readings of the modern haiku with the old one, we get this: "a tub of sea slug / look cold even in their / promiscuous sleep!" (*zakoneshite nao mi no samuki namako kana* – keigu 雑魚寝してなほ身の寒き海鼠哉　敬愚). This is the "sundry fish sleep" associated with carnival orgies. One contemporary haiku uses the *fute-ne* clearly: "sulkily sleeping / sea slugs on sale at / a dusk market" (*kureichi ni uraruru namako futene shite* – takasawa yoshikazu 暮市に売らるる海鼠ふて寝して 高沢良一)

While *kosori* is a rare variant of the more common *kossori*, * or "secretly," it makes far more sense to assume it reads *kozori* (the " " marks changing "so" to "zo" are not given, a common practice until the mid 20th century) as, indeed, some versions have it.   In this case, the correct translation is:

こ そ り あ ふ 寒 さ も 桶 の 海 鼠 哉 萬 古
#714[take two] *kozoriau samusa mo oke no namako kana* – banko (1777)
(together-meeting [a large number of people caucus] coldness, too, tub's seaslug/s!/?/ó/loh)

lying together
en masse: still a tub
of cold sea slugs

packed like sardines
yet still cold: a tub full
of sea cucumber

"*Kozoriau*" is a verb meaning "to gather close enough to rub together" and implies large numbers of people or other animals, so, the image is something like a pajama party in a freezing room, which is pretty much how it was to sleep at a temple in the dead of winter.   One Japanese reader thought "*kosori*" might rather have been a mistaken transcription for "*kosuri*," in which case the idea would be:

rubbing together
as they sleep, sea slugs
are still cold

cold though
rubbing together! a tub
of sea slugs

This is fun, but the poem is in a number of anthologies and the syllabets "*so*" and "*su*" are not that close.   In conclusion, so long as the result looks good, mistakes can be every bit as productive as correct translations or even more so, for if another person should translate the same poem, they would be more likely to do so correctly than to come up with the same mistranslation.   Indeed, my mistranslations – most of which I hope were corrected – created dozens of new poems in this book alone!

3

女 に は い や だ と 言 へ ぬ 海 鼠 か な　齋 藤 洪 郎
onna ni wa iya da to ienu namako kana – saitô kyôrô (contemp)
#718 (woman/women-as-for yuck! say-cannot sea-slug!/?/ó)

a woman
can't say "yuck!"
to sea-slug

women
must put up with
sea slugs

I remember walking with a coed at Georgetown University 30 years ago and feeling her squeeze my hand when I straddled over a post and thinking, *hah! she may be Catholic but . . . !* By expressing distress at being offered sea-slug, a young woman would be as much as confessing to thinking about *it*. Heaven forbid! Another possible reading is that it expresses the lot of not a few old wives: "women / must put up with / sea slugs," (flaccid penises), but I think the first more subtle reading was intended, for it is better.

Needless to say, I included this haiku and the above explanation with the "*Lubricious Sea Slug*," until MO noted that "both translations seem to reverse the meaning." It should, instead be:

a sea slug
cannot say "no"
to women

mukashi otoko updated

the sea slug
cannot just say "no way!"
to a woman

In other words, this is a modern version of the haiku about the spineless old-fashioned lady's man haiku of the *Tales of Ise*.   Since a sea slug is by metaphorical nature inactive, he just goes along with whatever the energetic sex, i.e., women, want.   Perhaps there is also a hint of fear for what women might do coming from the *Record of Ancient Matters*.[1]

POSTSCRIPT: Then, again, maybe i did not make a mistake. OM, again: "Now that I reread the '*onna ni wa*' haiku, it can be read both ways! I.e., Sea slug cannot say 'no way!' to a woman, OR a woman cannot say 'yuck!' to *namako*. Sorry." (Sometimes I feel that the only way to translate a haiku is by vote!)

4

This is a much simpler mistake than the usual, one that arose from a combination of laziness and wistful thinking. In this case, I will give the correct translation first:

ペンだこというもの持たず海鼠裂く 鈴木真砂女
#719 pendako to iu mono motazu namako saku – suzuki masajo (1906-)
(callus [take one = pen-sized octopus!?] called thing having-not, seaslug split[prepare])

the amateur

you won't find
any pen callus here
splitting slugs

Let me add that "callus" and "octopus" are perfect homophones (*tako*) in Japanese. As there is a small octopus often eaten in bars, which is about pen-sized and the poet, who runs a restaurant bar, is known for straight-forward haiku, I had *assumed* she was simply saying she ran out of said octopae and grabbed a *namako* for a substitute:

all out of
pen-octopus i split
a sea slug

The only problem was that such a name for tiny octopae does not, in fact, exist. I am probably the only person to have been fooled by her light pun on the octopus, for Japanese would immediately catch the normal idiomatic meaning. The poem is a good descriptive haiku for the wartiness of the Japanese sea slug is evoked by the contrast with none-existent calluses, and it is a fine declaration by someone who writes haiku from life, a life that is not primarily a writer's life, but a *real life* life. That is why I titled the poem as I did rather than calling it, say, "My Hand."

5

酢 海 鼠 を 啜 りて 男 反 転 す 時
#720sunamako o susurite otoko hanten su – toki (2000)
(vinegar-seaslug[obj] slurping man/men flip-over/tumble-back)

the lives of men
flip over as they slurp
pickled sea slug

This translation is not so much mistaken as meaningless. As pickled slug is synonymous with chewing, the sipping/slurping did not make sense to me. The poet mentioned an *amu-amu* noise, like slurping noodles, so I assumed she meant that, like squid, there are sea slug noodles. OM gamely guessed it was about a man changing his mind about a woman.

a man can change
his mind about his love
slurping sea slug

hearing her slurp
pickled sea slug he has
a change of heart

Either reading (my guesses of OM's guess) is *boring*.   If the "reversal" were a momentary feeling of knowing what it would be to live as a woman, now *that* would be something:

a man slurping
down pickled sea slug
changes sex

But the poet is female and could not have experienced such a reversal. Something is wrong here. *I wrote*. Toki replied that she had in mind a *sarariman,* (typical white-collar worker) drinking on his way home, who has had a bit too much and, rather than fishing out a piece of pickled slug at a time with his chopsticks (*remember, they are slippery and might escape a drunk*), has picked up the serving bowl and is slurping them up/down (gross even by slurp-permissive Japanese standards). Ordinarily, he is a mild corporate yes-man, but now he is out-of-control, with nothing but bad words for his superiors. Since OM had trouble, too, I would guess that the way *slurping* is expressed in the original may not communicate the rude manner of eating clearly enough to assure the reader can properly read the poem. Regardless, I like the opposition of the passive sea slug and the newly aggressive man.

slurping down
pickled slug a mild man's
poison tongue

transformation

noisely slurping
pickled slug a clerk
turns mr hyde

6

This next haiku, with a slight change is in *Featureless Sea Slugs*. Before MO caught my mistake, I evaluated it as "the most positive treatment of the *namako's* lack of features I have found."

徹 頭 徹 尾 せ ぬ を 見 [sic] 上 海 鼠 か な　成 瀬 桜 桃 子
#721 tettôtetsubi senu o miage namako kana – naruse ôtôshi (1993)
(thorough-head-thorough-tail do/have-not look-up seaslug!/?/ó/the)

the dolls we love
both ends left undone
viz: the sea slug

?original model?

the sea slug
how we adore our plain
japanese dolls

imagination

sea slug, you
are such a doll a very
japanese doll

The typical Japanese doll is lucky to have a hint, a mere speck of paint for eyes. Many, if not most, do not even have that. They have featureless faces and no visible limbs and if ever it could be said that clothes make the man, it would be the case for these dolls, who without clothing would be mistaken for what they are, polished sticks of wood, smooth balls of clay or stretched cloth. This haiku puns on the expression *miage ningyô,* a doll that is meant for looking up at --- putting on a high shelf? – and figuratively means a beautiful girl who is idolized by lesser mortals. Since *S. japonicus* is not smooth nor beautiful nor white/light – the literally blank face of the doll – the parallel is disingenuous, but the haiku posits an excellent hypothesis: could the featurelessness of the sea slug, allowing for greater play of the mind's eye, be one reason why the Japanese (some Japanese, at any rate) find the sea slug cuter than anyone else?

The only problem is that when I typed the Japanese into my computer, I made a mistake. Either my tired eyes mistook the somewhat similar characters for "body" and "see" or my computer coughed up the change automatically and I failed to catch it. But what fun I had! This is a mistake I wouldn't have missed for the world. *But this was only the first mistake with this haiku.* The second was my assumption that the "*body*+above" was pronounced *miue* and meant "one's circumstances." That created the following translations+explanation that almost slipped into the final draft:

muddle	*paint it grey*	*fuzzy fate*
there's nothing	the picture	inconclusive
clear-cut about the life	of my sloppy life	from start to finish: life
of a sea slug	a sea slug	life as a sea slug

allogical animal

no clear head
no clear tail sea slug
is all middle

The last reading makes literal use of the head and tail found in the original idiom. It is interesting to compare this poem with Kyorai's haiku about the failure to tell *head* from *tail* and the even closer mouth and butt (*shiri kuchi*) haiku. By "allogical," I mean that the sea slug, being *all* middle, disobeys the "law of the excluded middle" and is thus, not illogical, but unfit for proper logic-chopping. *Middle is muddle.* Of course, such a reading wanders far enough from the original to be a different poem altogether.

Different, indeed! A wandering reading on top of a misreading bears more in common with surreal party games than translation in the common sense of it.

~

The Medicinal Sea Slug I

Not a single old haiku, nor, for that matter, any modern one I know, describes sea cucumber as physiologically good for the person who eats it. Considering the fact that in the Sinosphere food has *itself* been considered medicine, this is extraordinary. Four-legged meat, eaten in the late fall, was called "medicine-eating," (*kusurigui*) and both snake and raw eggs in *sake* appear in haiku and *senryu* as potency enhancers. Blowfish had warming properties which were haiku'ed and senryu'ed as medicine, whereas the sea slug's coldness was not.   Ok, I ended up finding *one* haiku that would *seem* to be about the *Medicinal Sea Slug*.

鼻 を 診 て 貰 ひ に 通 ふ 海 鼠 か な 宮坂静生
hana o mite morai ni kayou namako kana – miyazaki shizuo (contemp) nez
#722 (nose[obj] see/diagnosed, getting/buying-to/for go/commute seaslug!/?/ó/the)

nose diagnosed
i'm off to buy a dose
sea cucumber!

medicine for a boxer?

i break my nose
and the doc tells me
to eat sea slug

I would guess either nose-bleeding (common in Japan, and sea cucumber lowers blood pressure) or broken cartilage is the problem and apologize if the poet is not a boxer for my taking liberty with his poem. There really should be many health-related sea cucumber poems, for *the* most common sea cucumber *hit* on the internet today concerns its medical uses. "Modern research has confirmed" says one web page, probably selling food supplements,

> sea cucumber is beneficial for musculoskeletal inflammatory diseases, especially rheumatoid arthritis, osteoarthritis, and ankylosing spondylitis, a rheumatic disease that affects the spine. Researchers in the US believe that sea cucumbers improve the balance of prostaglandin's, which regulate the inflammatory process. They also contain substances known as mucopolysaccharides and chondroitins, which are often lacking in people with arthitis and connective tissue disorders., not to mention proteins, vitamins A & C, riboflavin, niacin, calcium, iron, magnesium, zinc, sodium, fat and carbohydrate. Chinese doctors prescribe it as a general health tonic and more specifically for people with chronic joint pain as well as tendinitis, sprains, ligament stresses and arthritis. . .

Indeed, the author of *The Supplement Bible,* a best-seller published by Simon & Schuster, wrote that sea cucumber not only contains cartilage-building glucosamine and chondroitin sulfate, but "an even more potent anti-inflammatory agent than hydrocortisone." *I, who have been crippled since bashing my knee with pole a couple years ago wish I could afford it!*

膝 壊 れ 気 づ く 海 鼠 の 高 値 か な   敬愚
hiza koware kizuku namako no takane kana – keigu
#723 (knee busted, [i] notice sea slug's/s' high-price!/?/ó/the)

poor man in america

cracking my knee
i find sea cucumber
beyond my reach

That looks like a lot of heavy claims for one type of sea creature, but here is more, from a Malaysian page: "Known to be free of cholesterol, sea cucumber is also good for blood purification, enhancing kidney performance, lowering blood pressure, etc."   We can fill in the etcetera with "potency enhancers" – in Malaysia an extract of the boiled skin is drunk as a tonic – something this bright, cheery website evidently did not want to mention. Another Malaysian research site expands the possibilities further yet to include

> kinetic properties of crude lactate dehydrogenase, sterol or lipids, anti-bacteria activity and anti-fungus [the saponin works on jock itch and athlete's foot according to one Japanese site] anti-anaphylactic agents, wound healing, nerve-muscle blocking agents and histamine contents, anti-hypertension, antimicrobic and cytotoxic studies . . .

Still, "their greatest asset to man is as a source of Mucopolysaccharides, and substances called GAGS (Glucosaminoglycans)," which would appear to be fuller scientific terminology for things mentioned above.   Subhuti Dharmananda, Ph.D., Director, Institute for Traditional Medicine, Portland, adds further, that "sulfated polysaccharides also inhibit viruses," and "there is a Japanese patent for sea cucumber chondroitin sulfate for HIV therapy."   *Keigu is getting dizzy!*

化 学 用 語 び っ し り 詰 ま る 海 鼠 哉　敬 愚
kagaku yôgo bisshiri tsumaru namako kana – keigu
#724 (chemical term closely-packed stuff seaslug!/?/ó/the)

simple sea slug
so full of chemistry so
po-ly-syl-la-bic

That *is* a mouthful. For relief, enjoy this testimonial from a web-page titled *"Animals Love Sea Jerky Treats,"* a product from NutriSea, which contains a patented *Sea Cucumber extract* and a bit of cooperation from crabs and kelp as well.

> After one month of using your Sea Jerky product, my 13 year-old Springer Spaniel seems to have found the fountain of youth – he has the spunk of a dog half his age. I'm thinking of getting a bag for myself. ~ Glen Salvador.

Ponce de Leon had no need to come ashore and trek to his death across Florida. All he had to do is reach down, pick up a sea cucumber and squirt it. *Voila, there's your Fountain of Youth!*

顔 も あ る 海 鼠 汝 は 世 の 薬　敬 愚
kao mo aru namako nanji wa yo no kusuri – keigu
(face/reputation-even has seaslug, you are world's medicine)   #725

¿the world's original medicine-bag?

PANACEA
at last, the sea slug
has a face

海 鼠 か な 万 能 薬 に 顔 が 出 来　敬 愚
#726namako kana bannôyaku ni kao ga deki – keigu
(seaslug!/ó/the all-potent-medicine[panacea]-on/for face got)

the sea slug
is this, then, the face
of panacea?

Panacea gets a face, but so does the hitherto largely ignored holothurian. I hope conservationists keep to their guns and the sea cucumber farms expand their operations, or *namako's*   newly found international popularity will be the death of it and, in the long run, us!

ああメデア汝も化けた海鼠かな　敬愚
aa medea nanja mo baketa namako kana --- keigu

#727
(oh, medea, you too/even morphed/bewitched seaslug!/?/ŏ)

oh, medea,
did you, then, turn into
a sea slug?

天地の面効くべし海鼠の薬也　敬愚
ametsuchi no kao kiku beshi namako no kusuri nari – keigu

#728
(heaven-earth's face works-ought-to, [sea]slug medicine is/becomes)

global medicine   *the original drug*

with the face   with the face
of creation sea slug   of dreamtime, sea slug
works miracles [1]   is a shaman

This, of course, alludes to the equation of the sea slug with the face of ancient creation on the part of Shiki and other nineteenth century poets.

~

The Medicinal Sea Slug II

Eric Chong's "Traditional Healer of Langkawi [Malaysia]" is so entertaining, I will not paraphrase a word of it but will only cut out parts to shorten it.

> What is long, soft, and tubular and when you cut it into two, it is able to reattach itself? Well, you know it's not Lorena Bobbit's ex-husband's...... It is an unsightly sea creature called the 'sea cucumber' or the local Malay name 'gamat' – *Gamat* is a species of sea cucumber. . . .
>
> Apparently, the incident that led to the discovery of the medicinal value of the *gamat* was when a fisherman stepped on one of the *gamat*s on his way to his camp on the beach. The *gamat* secreted a kind of sticky milk which glued his hairy legs so effectively that the only solution was to have a clean shave after that. He took revenge by hacking all the sea cucumbers around him with his rusty old axe. Having finished his massacre, he went about his business but imagine his amazement on returning to his scene of crime and discovering that all his victims were whole and happy again. All their wounds had healed and those parts that were cut right through joined back again, leaving no trace whatsoever. That gave him food for thought. If the sea cucumber could heal itself, then it should also be able to heal people's wounds. Thus, the *'minyak gamat'* industry began.

1. Cold Water on a Miracle? "The unregulated nutrition industry's shilling of cuke bits seems criminal at times as some of it defies even high-school biology: Taking pills of a certain protein doesn't work since all proteins are digested in the gut and there's no guarantee that the body will reassemble the protein in the amount ingested, just as applying proteins to the hair is useless since the follicle can't incorporate it into its structure despite the promise of structural change (leading to fuller, glossy hair)." AK (corresp) I would go further and say that Medicine in general pays far too little attention to absorption, so it is not surprising that the nutrition industry does what it does.

The processed sea cucumber or *gamat* is marketed in two bottles. The pure type or "ayer gamat" is to be consumed orally. It is used to cure all internal ailments such as peptic ulcer, duodenal ulcer, bleeding piles and stomach aches. The mixed kind or "minyak gamat" is for external application. It is used to quicken the healing process of toothaches, cuts or wounds.

Other than the medicinal values mentioned above, another species of the sea cucumber is also the traditional healer for yet another ailment. The Chinese call it "Hai Som". The Chinese believe that "Hai Som" is an aphrodisiac. It is also considered a delicacy for the Chinese. For those of you who are on your honeymoon here in Malaysia, you may want to try ordering "Hai Som" for your next meal to give you that extra …….

The next time you see this long unsightly creatures, think of what they have done to help our pharmaceutical cause. A lot of research have been conducted and they are proving that this traditional cure is not just baseless claims but have actual healing properties. Who knows, the humble sea cucumber may hold the key to helping people like Lorena Bobbit's ex-husband – no surgeons required.

Chong also describes two ways of processing the sea cucumber. In the second , coconut oil and secret plant ingredients are added over three days of cooking. "The amazing thing about the whole cooking process," he claims, "is that you can dip your hand inside the fluid or oil and not be burnt!"[1]

~

The Bitten Hot Water Bottle Sea Slug

About a hundred years ago, Shiki described an old hot water bottle – hot water *auntie* as it is written in Chinese characters – as a *namako*.   This recent poem was written without knowledge of Shiki's poem.

海鼠へと入れ歯噛みついた痕が湯たんぽ　なむ

namako e to ireba kamitsuita ato ga yutanpo – namu (2002)
#729(seaslug-to dentures bit mark/scar/s-the/is warmwater bottle)

two of a kind	*an honest mistake*
grampa's sea slug	oh, sea slug!
denture toothmarks scar	a hot-water bottle scarred
the hot-water bottle	by dentures!

Or, that is how I read the poem until I rethought hard-to- untranslatable particle *ga* (the/is) and got this:

hot water bottles
like sea slugs impressed
by denture bite

The poet, whom I contacted, agrees that my first translation was wrong (So are they my poems or his?). Japanese hot water bottles can be corrugated and are made of "a hard rubbery, but probably metal" material. So this poem is closer to Shiki's than I realized and proves that Japanese do not require *namako* to be so cucuform as Occidentals, with their sea "cucumbers," do.

1. *Hai Som Preparations!*   Chong describes the preparation of *Hai Som*: "Early the next morning, I had to visit the out-house at the back of the restaurant. There, I witnessed my host digging nearby. I thought he was collecting worms – I was right. But these were extremely large. They were *Hai Som*. He had buried them overnight. By morning, the worms were crawling all over the *Hai Som*. The worms had eaten out the intestines of the *Hai Som*! Now the *Hai Som* is ready to be served!

おじいさんおばあさんをまとめて海鼠　等

#730 ojiisan obaasan o matomete namako – hitoshi (2002)
(grandpa grandma[obj] gathered/summarized [as] seaslug/s)

to put gramps
and granny in a word
sea cucumber

One cause for my misreading the hot water bottle poem was that it followed directly after – i.e. capped – this haiku (the end of which began the hot water bottle haiku) and "hot water bottle," for its part, was the name of a cabaret in the previous poem.   I had this image of strange senility. Parenthetically, I might add that the *namako* is tailor-made for the loose associations of capped link-verse (*renku*).

～

Double-cold Analyzed Sea Slug

陽 が 射 し て 冬 の 海 鼠 は 冬 の 手 に 　 満 月

hi ga sashite fuyu no namako wa fuyu no te ni – mangetsu (contemp)
#731 (sun shining, winter's seaslug-as-for, winter's hand-in/on)

the sun is shining
on a winter sea slug
in a winter hand

pastoral

rays of sunshine
the sea slugs of winter
in winter's hand

This poem didn't quite make the cut for my Cold Sea Slugs, but had to be saved, for it was googled together with something rare, a whole handful of *comments* by members of the 30th Aoyama Haiku Workshop Improvement Haiku Meet and provides a perfect window upon amateur haikudom in Japan.

Yûzuki: Putting aside the fact the sea slug is a Winter *kigo* [so, mentioning the winter even once is generally considered a *no-no*], you can imagine it cold and stiffly soft (*kataku yawarakai*) with the sun shining on its wet skin.
Natsu: (the selector) I couldn't read "sea-rat" [couldn't guess it was pronounced *namako*] and had to look it up in my Kanwa [Chinese-Japanese=kanji] Dictionary, but I just sort of liked it [this, the haiku he selected for discussion].
Bôshi: The first 5 [syllabets] are weak, but the bottom 12 remind me of Katô Ikuya's "Winter waves / come and bounce off / the winter wharf (*fuyu no nami fuyu no hatoba ni kite kaesu*).
Minoru: The seasonal redundancy is, conversely, interesting. Even the deep seabed has managed to take on a wintry aspect.
Hitsuji: For the first time, I feel something endearing about sea slug, the only food I dislike too much to eat.
Mizukurage: Winter sea slug is delicious. A small sea slug in the cold-benumbed hand of a fisherman. The fisherman's breath is white. (If the guts split out, you could slurp them up just like that!) The "sun shining" is very effective and this is the most delicious looking sea slug I have ever encountered. The poet's intent may lie in a deeper pocket, but my appetite got the better of me. Sorry.

The Chinese Sea Slug I: Cuisine

I have yet to find sea cucumber in a Chinese poem, but I imagine if it were found, it might embody very different metaphor than Japanese poems because I *did* find the following sentence in the Chinese Historical and Cultural Project Virtual Museum / Virtual Library Chinese Wedding Foods:

Vegetables with Sea Cucumber. Serving sea cucumber with vegetables is a sign of selflessness because "sea cucumber" sounds like "good heart" [1] and this dish wishes the couple to think in a similar way – to avoid conflict. (L. K. Yee)

The sea cucumber is not alone. Chinese, like the Japanese, gain great solace from their prodigious number of homophones. Fish are included in the banquette "because 'fish' sounds like 'plentiful' in Chinese," fried chicken is appropriate because in Chinese "red chicken" sounds like "good life," 7-Up is included with the more traditional tea and alcohol because "the words for 'up' and 'happiness' are homophones" and so forth. [2]

Chinese do not eat sea cucumber as sashimi or pickled raw. Their recipes usually call for dried sea cucumber that may soak for days to rehydrate.[3] Though already high in protein (near 50%!), it may be served with pork or lamb because various combinations of meat has different medicinal effect. For all this pragmatism, the main mark of Chinese food is variety of design. We find a Yunnan Dish of molded *"Sea Cucumber Toads"* sitting on green spinach-dyed agar agar jelly lotus leaves around a flower made of cut tomato! (www.chinavista.com/culture/ cuisine/yunnan/ yunnan2-6.html)

シナ不変海鼠が蝦蟇に変える国　敬愚
shina fuhen namako ga gama ni kaeru kuni – keigu
(china not-change, seaslug/s toad-into change country)

#732

forever china!
where sea slugs turn
to jelly toads

Other netted dishes include *"Custard of Sea Cucumber and Bean Curd"* and *Braised Sea Cucumber with Minced Shrimp Stuffing*, but these sound humdrum next to the likes of Mustard Cabbage with Duck Blood, Drunken Chicken, Five Flavor Intestines, Marinated Duck Tongue, and Mini Buddha Jumps Soup .[4]

1. *Good Heart* Perhaps because of this auspicious name, we find "Sea Cucumber brand shirts" included among examples of culturally wrong Chinese marketing (White Elephant brand batteries, Maxipuke playing cards, Pansy brand men's underwear, etc.) in the USA .
2. *Charmed Food* Homophones were not the all of it. The auspiciously red colored lobster is written dragon shrimp" while chicken feet are called "phoenix feet," creatures respectively appropriate for the Yang and Yin sexes. Shark's fin soup is a charm for wealth because it is very expensive. Roast suckling pig, presented entire by the groom's family, is a symbol of virginity (why?).
3. *Rehydration* The art of rehydration can be every bit as ridiculous sounding as the art of making pie crust. The "method" of making "Fried Shredded Beef With Double Celery And Sea Cucumber," a dish that "strengthens the lung 'Qi,' lowers blood pressure, clears the internal heat, and cleans the digestive system" starts like this: "Wash the sea cucumber clean. Bring the water to a simmer and scald the sea cucumber until shrink. Drain and rinse under cold running water until it becomes swollen."
4. *Buddha Jumps* Later I found this: "How 'Buddha Jumps the Wall' got its unusual name is explained by a local fable. A Fuzhou scholar went picnicking with friends in the suburbs and he had put all the ingredients he had with him in a wine jar, which he heated over a charcoal flame. The tantalizing smell spread all the way to a nearby temple and was so inviting that the monks, who were supposed to practice vegetarianism, could not resist and jumped over the wall to partake in the hearty dish. One of the friends wrote a poem in praise of the delicious dish, in which one line read: "Even Buddha himself would jump over the wall to taste this dish". Thus the name, 'Buddha Jumps the Wall' (.http://www. google.com/searchwww.hoteltravel.com/china/guid es/dining_shopping.htm).

The Chinese Sea Slug II: Poetry

While most *things Japanese* were first *things Chinese,* the Japanese *namako* may well be *en su generis.* [sp?] Up to the seventeenth century, sea cucumber only appears in Chinese sources as medicine and, even then, very little. Records of the importation of trepang from Oceania only go back to the late seventeenth century, which, coincidentally, was the time, haiku about *kinko* and *namako* arose in Japan. Theoretically speaking, the Chinese have had time to poeticize the trepang, but lacking a poetry like haiku (with its uniquely broad subject matter), this apparently has not happened. I wrote a Chinese poet in Taiwan to see if I could find any sea cucumbers and he replied that he knew of none but might just write one.

I hope he has done so, and will be happy to include it, or any Chinese poems on the sea cucumber, in the second edition. *Likewise for Korean poems and Malaysian poems.*

~

The Gigged Sea Slug (and the giggers)

If my primary interest had been new haiku rather than old, I would have included a full chapter on slug-gigging, for together with slug-eating, it is *the* most common contemporary sub-theme where, for some reason, [1] I found only a few old haiku even coming close to the subject and two of three were philosophical (Namako not falling for baited hook, *namako* not needing bait/feed and *namako* scooped up pensively).   The 10 or so slug-gigging haiku slipped into various metaphorical sea slugs represents only a tiny fraction of the hundreds of these haiku written.

大海鼠引つかけて立ちし舳かな　島田青峰
ônamako hikkakete tachishi hesaki kana – seihô (1881-1944)
#733 (large-seaslug caught/gafted, standing bowsprit!/?/ô)

he pulls up this
large sea slug standing
on the bowsprit

Probably a description of a South Asian sea slugger, for Japanese did not generally stand on bowsprits. The sea slug may have been caught by a hoe-like scoop rather than a gig.

磯畑に火かけ漕ぎ出で海鼠突く　米沢我亦香
#734 *isohata ni hi kake kogi ide namako tsuku* – yonezawa _____? (mod?)
(shore/reef-field[agricultural plot]-in fire made/left/placed rowing out seaslug stick/gig)

leaving a fire
on the shore, rowing out
to gig sea slugs

Gigged sea slugs. This is Japan. The original specifies a shore-side farm plot, something too long for haiku in translation. The fire is needed to warm up the hands, and possibly for guidance in the predawn dark. This man is going to be in place at dawn.

---

1. *Gigging Slugs* Most of these gigged sea slugs are eaten raw or pickled. Most sea slugs in the days of old haiku were cured and exported. Because gigging damaged the all important appearance – and dead sea slug was very vain: *iriko*=trepang was shaped while drying and poor specimens were even reboiled for reshaping(!) – gigging was probably rare and may help explain the lack of such poems.

火をおとすしらせうけたる海鼠かな 大島四月草
hi o otosu shirase uketaru namako kana – ôshima _____? (mod?)
#735 (fire drop/kill notice receive/s seaslug!/?/ô/hoh)

getting the sign
to kill the fires
must be slug

I guess the poet sees someone on a boat signaling someone on land to put out the fire mentioned in the last haiku and notes that it must be a slugger.

海鼠突舟炉煙らせつゝ漁る　徳永玄子
namakotsukibune rô?kemurase tsutsu asaru – tokunaga genshi? (mod)
#736 (seaslug gigging boat heater/stove smoking-while, fishing/taking)

sea slug gigging
with smoke wafting up
from the stove

The gigger must bear up to the cold, solitude and strain of manipulating a long pole to catch a distant object seen through water, but because he tends to work in the calmest hours, a small stove for hand-warming and tea could be left on as he worked.   Some types of slugging permit rougher weather,

なまこ曳き舟が押す波かへす波　高岸まなぶ
namakohikibune ga osu nami kaesu nami – takagishi manabu (1978)
#737 (seaslug-drag[gaffing/hooking?]-boat pushing-wave returning-wave)

the slug dragger
its bow pushing waves
stern pulling them

mole garden

bow waves
and stern waves
slug-dragging

These boats drag large cage-like devices [1] behind them. It is a totally unromantic and (I'd guess) destructive modern method of slugging so rare to haiku that I first imagined gigging: "with each slug / waves the boat pushes / waves it draws," something a careful reading rules out, though it doesn't rule out the (faint) possibility of the poem's being a metaphorical description of dragging a sea slug over the furrows of a field as part of the mole exorcism explained elsewhere. To me, the pushing and pulling waves reflect the overwhelming power of the machine versus the meek creature it is catching.

礁壺覗き移りて海鼠突く 水見句丈
isobe?tsubo nozoki utsurite namako tsuku – mizumi kujô (mod)
#738 (reef-pot/spot peek/ing-go-around seasslug gig)

the slug gigger
peeking into reef pocket
after pocket

1. *Sea Cucumber Dragging* The cages and nets with hardened openings tend to be about a meter or two across at the mouth and about a foot high. Some boats drag two at once. (ndh)

The *tsubo* may mean small pot-like impressions, but I think it means the sand-bottomed pool-like depressions found here and there ensconced within vast coral reefs.

磯 笛 は 息 継 ぐ て だ て 海 鼠 採 る　前 田 白 露

isobue wa ikitsugu tedate namako toru – maeda hakuro (1978)

#739(reef-whistle/flute-as-for breath-relay assistance seaslug catch/take)

the reef flute
helps with syncopation
gaffing sea slug

I thought this meant the sound of water pouring through the narrow opening of a reef helps the gigger syncopate his movement with the rising and falling of the waves that continuously changes the depth of his target. But, it turns out that "reef-flute" is the sound made by the breath of a surfacing diver!

海 鼠 突 く 一 人 一 舟 傾 け て 稲 畑 汀 子

namako tsuku hitori isshû katamukete – inahata teiko (mod)

#740 (seaslug gig one-person one-boat tipping)

slug gigging	sea sluggers
a man and a boat	each man tipping with
tipping low	his own boat

海 鼠 突 く 舟 を 傾 け 傾 け て　岡 安 仁 義

namako tsuku fune o katamuke katamukete – okayasu jingi (1998)

#741 (sea slug gig/ging boat [+obj] tilt, tilting)

tipsy work

slug gigging
the boat is tipped and
still tipped

こ れ 以 上 傾 け ぬ 舟 海 鼠 突 く　内 山 芳 子

kore ijô katamukenu fune namako tsuku – uchiyama yoshiko (1998)

#742 (this-above tip-not boat sea slug gig)

on the edge

gigging slugs
from a boat which cannot
tip any more

The Japanese word for "tip" (*katamukeru*) is long. I had trouble fleshing out these poems about sea slugging boats that tip way over without actually tipping over. The sailing term "keeling over" won't work.

波 に 息 ぶ つ け て な ま こ 突 き 得 た り　高 橋 安 郎

nami ni iki butsukete namako tsuki etari – takahashi yasurô (contemp?)

#743 (wave/surface-to/on/against hit/ting, seaslug hit/stab-suceed/able/end)

a sea slug	my breath
gigged as breath bounces	against the surface as
off waves	i gig a slug

The "stab-succeed" (*tsuki-etari*) is homophonic with "reaching something at the end of a road" (*tsuki-atari,* sometimes translatable as a dead-end) and this makes a pleasant contrast of bouncing-off and reaching an object.   Because the sea slug is gigged in the winter, the breath is visible.

海鼠突束の間波に息あはす　石橋ひかる
namakotsuki tsuka no ma nami ni iki awasu – ishibashi hikaru (1998)
#744(sea slug gigger momentarily wave-to breath-meet/join)

the slug gigger
quickly catches the rhythm
of the waves

This haiku is similar to the "reef flute" haiku both in the focus on breath and in the choreography of man and nature.   The two poems are not together because my eyes, perhaps from eagerness to follow up with the previous poem, turned breath (息) into "nose" (鼻) – "gigging sea slugs / his nose and a wave / briefly meet;" "the sea-slugger / briefly leans his nose / against a wave" – and I was so pleased with my translations (especially the nose on wave) that it would have snuck through had OM not called me on it only weeks before I p.d.f.ed for p.o.d.   A glass-bottomed tub is often used:

海 鼠 突 き 波 の た ゆ た に 伏 眼 鏡　楠 目 橙 黄 子
namakotsuki nami no tayuta ni fusu megane – kusume tôkôshi (1932) nez
#745 (seaslug-gigger waves looseness/dip-with/in sink/prone glasses)

the slug-gigger
pushes his glass down
between waves

覗 き 桶 の ぞ き つ つ 漕 ぎ 海 鼠 突 く　青 砥 静 江
nozokioke nozokitsutsu kogi namako tsuku – aoto shizue (1993)
#746 (peeking-tub peeking-while, paddling, seaslug stab)

peeking through
the bucket while paddling
he stabs slugs

.
The modern haiku is too matter-of-fact and the contemporary, too busy for me.   The next two are, to my mind, just right:

波 い な す 櫂 は 左 手 に 海 鼠 つ き　清 田 根
#747nami inasu kogi wa yunde ni namako-tsuki – kiyota kon? (mod)
(wave[obj] parry oar-as-for, left-hand-in/with seaslug-gigger/gigging[subj])

in his left hand
an oar to parry waves
a slug gigger

Written like this, one might think this business is as dangerous as big-game hunting with nothing but an oar and gig for protection.   The pronunciation of the left hand chosen for the reading (*yunde* rather than *sashû*) evokes bow-hunting, for it derives from "bow[holding]-hand."

海 中 へ の め る 寸 前 海 鼠 突 く　衣 川 砂 生
#748watanaka e nomeru sunzen namako tsuku –kinukawa sunao (1997)
(ocean-middle/in-to drunken/swallowed[tips/pitches-over] just-before seaslug stab)

on the edge

an instant before
he's swallowed by the sea
he gigs a sea-slug

"Swallow/drink" in this context means "pitching over" or "spilling into" the sea. Hope my dramatization is not minded!

横 波 を く ら ひ ど ほ し の 海 鼠 突　松 崎 楽 中
#749yokonami o kuraidôshi no namakotsuki – matsuzaki rakuchû (mod)
(side-wave/s accept/get[something rough, like a punch]passing seaslug-gigger/s)

sideswiped	waves broadside
by wave after wave	the sea slug giggers
the slugman	and move on

We must imagine a fine long groundswell, for gigging would be impossible in a truly rough sea.

海 光 や 身 を さ か し ま に 海 鼠 突 く　萩 原 記 代
kaikô ya mi o sakashima ni namako tsuku – hagiwara kiyo (1990) ndh
#750 (sea-shine:/! body upside-down-with, seaslug stab/gig/ging)

in seashine
a body upside-down
stabbing slugs

べ た 凪 や 身 を さ か し ま に 海 鼠 突　喜 多 み き 子
betanagi ya mi o sakashima ni namako tsuku – kita mikiko (1998)
#751 (utter/thick-calm:/! body upside-down-with sea slug stab/gig/ing)

still life	*still lives*
in dead calm	a dead calm
a body face down	bodies upside down
stabbing slugs	stabbing slugs

Upside down suggests the gigger not only leans out from the boat but down. Still, it can just mean face down, so I include one such translation. Exclamation-lovers may read these poems, respectively, "what seashine!" and "what a calm!" Since reflection of the early morning sun is brightest in glassy calm, the poems describe the same thing. The body may be in the water, though it is likely it is still aboard a radically tipping boat. My reading is third-person , but self-portrait is possible:

this utter calm
my body upside-down
sticking a slug

All of this is in slow motion, mind you.   Like a sea slug. But even slowness can tire when one is constantly looking down:

海鼠突き空を仰いで休みおり　園部雨汀
namakotsuki sora o aoide yasumiori – sonobe utei (2001)
#752 (seaslug-gigger sky-facing[upwards] resting)

a sea-slugger
takes a break lying
on his back

He lies back looking in the direction Western ancients, forgetting the frog, thought only man was designed to look, and listens to the tiny waves lapping against the hull as his body recovers.

海鼠突死ぬまでしやくり止まらぬか　宮坂静生
namakotsuki shinu made shakuri tomaranu ka – miyazaki shizuo (contemp)
#753 (seaslug-gigger die-until hickups stop-not)

the sea slugger
won't stop hiccupping 'til
the day he dies

At first I thought this a mere echo of his sudden jibe with the gig, but it may well reflect his *modus operandi.* Namely, anyone who remains at the water's edge is bound to swallow water.

海清くあはれ海鼠の突かれけり　村田脩
umi kiyoku aware namako no tsukarekeri – murata shûn (contemp)
#754 (ocean clear/pure, alas/wretched sea slug/s speared [+finality])

clear water
i feel something tragic in
a gigged sea slug

poor sea slug
gigged in this water as
clear as crystal

water, pale blue,
how poignant: a sea slug
stabbed through

Namako is not always found in the dark depths. Here, we imagine a sunny sea floor, from one to seven feet down. A sea slug soundly sleeping under the magically clear film of water is speared. The reader, too, awakes with a start. (I wonder to myself, *what if that Chinese philosopher were a sea slug instead of a butterfly?*)

嶋の子は嶋を広しと海鼠突き章魚突き笑らぎ遊び廻れる　北原白秋
shima no ko wa shima o hiroshi to namako tsuki tako tsuki eragi asobimawareru – kitahara hakushû (mod)
#755 (island kids-as-for, island broad [act/think], seaslug gig, octopus gig laughing-play wander around)

innocence

the island kids
in a world with room
to laugh as they
gig the octopus and
gig the sea slug

The original is only marginally more poetic than the translation, but Hakushu[1] has achieved something none of the other gigging haiku do; he has resurrected the world I, an island boy, once knew, where we did those things as easily as we walked or talked. To me such memories are worth more than the self-conscious environmentalism of a modern *tanka* such as,

珊 瑚 礁 に 潜 み て 生 け る 海 鼠 さ へ 海 賊 ど も の 眼 よ り 遁 れ ず 　 川 田 順

sangoshô ni hisomite ikeru namako sae kaizokudomo no me yori nogarezu – kawada jun (contemp)
#756 (coral-reef/s-in hiding/hidden, living seaslug-even, pirates'eye/s-from escape cannot)

<blockquote>
even those
living hidden deep
in coral reefs
sea slugs can't escape
the eyes of the pirates
</blockquote>

I suspect the tanka is about the historical trepang industry which included divers, rather than small time giggers for the Japanese market. But, the poles used by the giggers were long enough to reach down pretty far:

舟 よ り も 長 き 棹 繰 り 海 鼠 突 　 野 村 能 邨

fune yori mo nagaki sao kuri namakotsuki – nomura ___(mod)
#757 (boat more-than long pole manipulate???? seaslug-gigger)

<blockquote>
the slug man
master of a pole longer
than his boat
</blockquote>

As anyone who has worked on cleaning swimming pools knows, operating a long pole under water is surprisingly hard. Let's poke and take sea slugs in the tide point until it grows dark

汐 先 の 昏 れ て 来 る ま で 海 鼠 突 　 剣 持 不 知 火

#758 *shiosaki no kurete kuru made namako tsuku* – kenmochi shiranui (mod)
(tide[esp. evening tide]-tip/point[water-side of tideline] dusks-becomes-until, seaslugs gig)

<blockquote>
gigging slugs
until dusk comes to
the seashore
</blockquote>

(let's poke and take seaslugs in the tidepoint until it grows dark – japanese acquaintance's trans.)

<blockquote>
next to shore
gigging slugs until
i couldn't see
</blockquote>

Though the English went around the world, they never managed to bring as much of the sea home as the Japanese. At least that is what our respective vocabulary seems to show. This word *shiosaki* is a problem. I think it means the part of the sea closest to the low waterline. Or, perhaps it is the edge of the sea at either high or low tide. I have not yet figured it out.

1. *Hakushu, the Island Poet* I have a fond spot for this poet because he took the names of the Bonins – now (since the Japanese took them over from the backward Caucasian and Polynesian settlers) the Ogasawara islands, namely Chichi-jima (father-island), Haha-jima (mother-island), Ani-jima (older-brother island) etc and combined them into a poem made to delight the islanders.

まっすぐに光と戻る海鼠舟　宇多喜代子
massugu ni hikari to modoru namakobune – uda kiyoko (mod)
#759 (directly light-with return seaslug-boat)

sea slug boats　　　　　　a slug boat
come back in a beeline　　back like an arrow
with the light　　　　　　with the light

slug boats
return directly
with the light

Straight may be straight, but *massugu,* being emphatic, feels straighter than straight and this is backed by the dictionary, which offers the *arrow, bee-lines, crows* and *dead* to help out.　I fear that makes the translation too meaningful but could not help myself in the first two readings.

夕焼の潮筋もどる海鼠舟　羽田岳水
yûyake no shiosuji modoru namakobune – hada gakusui (1978)
#760 (sunset's ocean/surf-strip/line returns/ing seaslug-boat)

a slug boat
returns on a ribbon
of the sunset

The direct return of the boats is in stark contrast to their meandering sea slug ways that most haiku depict. Keigu, remembering the nocturnal nature of sea slugs, kicks in several more:

海鼠起き戻る船路の真下也　敬愚
#761*namako oki modoru funaji no mashita nari* – keigu
(seaslug wakes, returning boat-road/course's straight-below is)

under the hulls
of returning giggers
sea slugs wake

海人帰り起つる海鼠とすれ違ふ　　敬愚
#762*ama kaeri tatsuru namako to surechigau* – keigu
(divers return(home) seaslug/s-with pass[in oppos. direction])

as the giggers
speed to port sea slugs
start to work

人去れば残る海鼠が目を覚ます　敬愚
#763*hito sareba nokoru namako ga me o samasu* – keigu
(people leaving/left, remaining/surviving seaslugs-the awake)

men leave
the remaining sea slugs
wake up

Slug Boats, No Slugs

海 鼠 舟 波 に も ま れ て 幾 世 経 し 鈴 鹿 野 風 呂

#764 namakobune nami ni momarete iku yo heshi – suzuka nobûro (1932)

(seaslug-boat, waves-by rubbed how-many worlds/generations/reigns passed?)

rubbed by waves	how many men	wave-worn for
how many owners old	has this old wave-worn	how many generations
is this slugboat?	slug boat known	this slug boat

The Slugboat shows its bowsprit in the *Meek Sea Slugs,* its weathered deck in *Imagist Sea Slugs,* and its *modus operandi* with the *Sea Slug Giggers*, above. But some boats fit under nothing but "*Boats.*" I could not find a good direct translation for this haiku, and can only hope the "how many men" works.

糶 り 了 へ て 小 波 止 に 洗 ふ 海 鼠 舟 壺 井 久 子

#765 seri oete kobato ni arau namakobune – tsuboi hisako (1993)

(auction/ing over, small-wave-breaker[quay/wharf]-by wash/ing seaslug-boat/s)

after the auction
the slug boats are washed
by the small quay

The sluggers were as busy as the slug is not until they got their catch to the market and disposed of it, alive. The morning calm over, their small boats need the protection of the quay. Not knowing if there is running water, I hesitate to use the more vivid "slug boats are hosed off" for the second line.

長 竿 を 一 本 納 め 海 鼠 舟 大 石 悦 子

nagasao o ippon osame namakobune – ôishi etsuko (contemp)

#765B [oops!]   (long-pole one-stick[counter] store/pack/equipped[with] seaslug-boat)

a one
pole sea slug
boat

~

a one-long-pole-packing slugboat

There seems to be a playful hint at the blankety-blank-gun description of a frigate, here; but I am not certain. The single pole *might* hint at *Melancholy Sea Slugs. Might.* There are no two-pole slugboats, for there are no two-man slugboats. However, there are others besides sluggers using long poles –

礁 の 間 に 棹 の あ が る は 海 鼠 舟 山 崎 一 之 助

shô no ma ni sao no agaru wa namakobune – yamazaki kazunosuke (mod)

#766 (reef-among pole/s raise-as-for, seaslug-boat/s)

sea slug boats:
the ones whose poles rise
over the coral

The gigs of those after crustaceans, fish or whatnot, would do the opposite, for coral holds many treasures. The sea slugs, though they may take sleep in holes in coral, are generally like the c/antelope: out on the sand or in the grass when taken. Or that is what I guess the poem is saying.

Measured Sea Slugs

海 鼠 突 き 大 凡 の 数 を 読 み け り 碧梧桐
namakotsuki ôyoso no kazu o yomikeri – hekigotô? (1872-1937)
#767 (seaslug-gigger rough/round numbers reads/shouts)

the sea-slugger
shouts out his catch
in round numbers

Today, the verb "read," *yomu,* and "shout," *yobu,* are not conflated (except in the head of haiku poets with an antique? style), but once they were the same, hence the name of Japan's (and the world's) largest newspaper, the *Yomiuri,* which is now read as "read-sell" but originated in hawkers reading=shouting out the headlines! The haiku does not say what rough/vague numbers are being "read," but we know what it is. Large fish would be precisely counted, where tiny fish would be announced by weight, but sea slugs are guestimated by round numbers as befits their *namako* nature.

手 掴 み に 海 鼠 秤 る も 磯 の 市 鷹 野 清 子
#768 tezukami ni namako hakaru mo iso no ichi – takano kiyoko (2001)
(hand-hold/gripping-by seaslug measure/weigh/calculate, too seashore/coast-market)

fisherman's market	*fisherman's market*
sea cucumbers	sea slugs
estimated by taking	are taken in hand
them in hand	to price them

Most adults find it hard to touch a sea slug. The familiarity of those who sell slugs with their product is grasped by this image.   I imagine a gnarled fisherman's hand picks up not one but several sea slugs at once, but I could be wrong. Translation is hard because English lacks a word of measurement as general as *hakaru.* The switch to "price" is what Japanese call an *iyaku,* a translation that follows the intention of the original, rather than attempting to be "accurate" and losing it.[1]

小 銭 入 れ 海 鼠 の お も さ 海 鼠 買 ふ 光 部 美 千 代
kozeniire namako no omosa namako kau – kobe michiyo (2001)
#769 (small-change-enter[purse] seaslug's weight, seaslug buy)

my pinch purse
a slug's weight of change
buys a sea slug

We all know the expression "worth its weight in gold;" this haiku coins a new one: *"worth its weight in small change!"* The volume of coins would be larger than persons familiar with USA coins might imagine, for the most common small change is aluminum one-yen coins and large ten-yen coins. They would be in a "small-change-purse," something a bit larger than a *pinch purse* (but the latter makes better poetry). The weight observation may *thingify* the sea slug more in Japanese than in English, because bartering in Japanese is "thing-thing-exchange" (*butsubutsu-kokan*).

1. Iyaku The fact that most Japanese who have graduated from high-school and all university graduates know a word for translation that follows *meaning* rather than *wording,* where English lacks even a specialized term suggests we have neglected to incorporate the wisdom of others for too long.

The Seasonal Sea Slug

水 底 も 秋 経 し 色 や 初 海 鼠 志 太 野 坂
minasoko mo aki heshi iro ya hatsunamako – shidano saka? (contemp)
#770 (sea-floor, too/even, fall passes color!/: first-seaslug)

the seabed too
shows the passage of fall
first sea slug

Traditional Japanese poetry debated about where various seasons came from (and where they went). Autumn was generally held to be sky-born, heard in the howling wind and seen in the crystal clear blue sky of the sharp-eyed hawk. There must have been less debate about winter, for I don't know what the standard lines are. At any rate, this sea slug on the sea floor is a refreshing change from the high and lonesome sound of Fall.

海 鼠 売 ほ い ほ い 冬 木 道 来 た る 片 山 光 代
#771 namakouri hoihoi fuyukimichi kitaru – katayama mitsuyo (contemp)
(seaslug-seller [with a sound like] *hoihoi* [made while exerting] winter-tree-road comes/coming)

winter life

sea slug man
comes *hoi hoi* up the road
of bare trees

A famous haiku by Buson has a man with a handful of winter scallions walking homeward on such a road. How different this proud vendor vigorously trotting his load of slugs into town! Since no one runs along shouting *hoihoi* today, nor has anyone for almost a century, this haiku found when googling for sea slug vendors (*namakouri*) would seem to come from the poet's imagination. I wanted to ask him where the image came from – for I have not succeeded in locating a single picture of a sea slug seller – but the website's homepage (presumably with a contact) was "*Temporally* [sic] *suspended*;" so all I know is that Katayama is the head of an organization promoting a revolution in the accounting of government and other public bodies to bring about at least as much transparency as found with private enterprise.

玄 海 ヘ スバルが 落 ち ね ば 夜 明 け ざ る 季 を 海 鼠 は 極 ま り て う ま し 逆 瀬 川 康
genkai e subaru ga ochineba yoakezaru ki o namako wa kiwamarite umashi – sakasegawa kô (mod)
(genkai[sea between korea and japan]-to pleiades fall-when night-brightens-season, seaslug-as-for, peaks, delicious)
#772

when the pleiades
sink below the genkai
as the day breaks
that is when sea slug
tastes just heavenly!

The Genkai is a sea with a poetic name.[1→] To the Japanese ear it sounds deep and mysterious. The constellation *subaru* (Pleiades) etymologically means only "to control" or "orchestrate," but it *sounds* more interesting and that, I think, is why a famous literary magazine and a car have borrowed it. This *tanka* in its plush way, does what haiku does less bluntly. It records a coordinate marking the crossing of *thing* and *time* in *space*. Depending on the theme/thing/phenomenon/event, seasonal change becomes a parade, a contest, a race, a relay, a stage, or metaphysical cause-and-effect . Blossoms are forced open by warm rain and colorful leaves dyed by cold rain. What, then, brings the sea slug?

吹 か れ 来 て 海 鼠 の 貌 に な つ て お り 柴 田 朱 美

fukarekite namako no kao ni natteori – shibata akemi (2001)

#733 (blown-comes sea-slug's face-becomes)

blown in
it becomes the face
of the sea slug

This poet seems to say *the wind*. But I am not sure. Paraphrasing Watts "What is this *it* that is blown in?" While there is no *it* in Japanese, for verbs that do not require stated subjects and objects need no pronoun, either, the question applies: Is the un-mentioned "it" here the weather-worn face of a slug gigger, or, perhaps, the poet who has been out in a gale? Or, is *it* the "face" of the sea slug that looks like it has been out in the wind but, more importantly, is now (being in season), formally the food that is the "face" of the moment. The poet plays upon the metaphor of the *Passive Sea Slug* at the mercy of the elements. In this next poem, the "it" is specified:

風 吹 い て 海 鼠 に 旬 の 至 り け り 岩 本 尚 毅

kaze fuite namako ni shun no itarikeri – iwamoto naoki (2001)

#774 (wind blows/ing sea-slug-to seasonality arrives[+finality])

a cold wind   the wind blows
the sea slug is now   and seasonality comes
in season   to the sea slug

winter is icumen in

the winds blow
and the sea slug, again
is where it's at

I failed to find a word that would allow the stamp of seasonality to come, if it were, to the sea slug. "the wind blows/ *au courancy* comes / to the sea slug" doesn't work. In short, English, even with the help of modified French, lacks an elegant noun to express being "in season" and to describe the way the passive sea slug just *is,* while the *shun* (seasonally appropriateness) *arrives*. All I can think of is the unpoetic "seasonality" and slang, but the original is not at all slangy, so my third reading is a paraverse rather than a translation. Also, the Japanese means it is *at its peak.*

→1 *The Character* 玄 This character is defined as 1) black, dark, unpolished[eg., rice], black with a touch of red in it; 2) sky color, heaven, sky-yellow; 3) north [being black in Chinese element theory]; 4) far-off, hazy; 5) deep, profound; 6) quiet; 7) excellent to a preternatural degree; 8) the quality of the absolute origin of heaven and earth 9) which is to say, the Way of Lao Tse (Taoism).   In combination with a second character it can modify/mean, with "gate," Buddhist gate, with "empty", a void, with "yellow," heaven and earth, pretty colors, an exhausted horse, or by extension person, with "*sake*" [alcohol], water; with "elephant," heavenly elephant, which is to say the heavenly bodies, or, firmament, with "saint," a superior saint; with "bird", a swallow or a crane, with "heaven," the natural way, with "warrior," the god of the north, the water god, a turtle-snake chimera . . . Indeed, someone could write a doctoral dissertation on the one character.

櫻 貝 の 春 に も あ は ぬ 海 鼠 か な 一 樹
#775 sakuragai no haru ni mo awanu namako kana – ichiju (1774-1827)
(cherry-shell [carpenter's tellin: Nitidotellina nitidula]'s spring-to-even meet-not seaslug!/?/ó/loh/the)

it never meets
the cherry-shell spring:
poor sea slug!

This poem makes it clear that the sea slug goes out with the same cold wind it came in with. The shiny pink-tinged "cherry shell" (carpenter's tellin) is tossed up on the beaches in the spring when cherry petals flow into the sea from the rivers and wave blossoms (spume) blows in the wind. Poems about the cherry shell antedate any found on slugs.[1] In that sense, too, the *namako* missed the spring . . . of Japanese poetry. I cannot help wondering if the poem is only about the sea slug or also is a lament by a poet aging without ever enjoying the spring all too many poor men in pre-modern civilizations died without having known.

海 鼠 だ ゝ み や 鰹 の 花 の 帰 咲 重 春
#776 kodatami ya katsuo no hana no kaerizaki – shigeharu[?] (1680)
(seaslug-diced:/! bonito blossoms' return[indian-summer/second] blooming)

diced sea slug
the flower of bonito
blossoms again

Bonito was launched across the nation at summer's start and any good Edoite would pawn his winter kimono to buy the first fish (see IPOOH-Summer-1-Bonito). The "return-blossom" is a phenomenon of early Winter, generally applying to cherry or plum blossoms. "Blossom" was a term often applied to the bonito, but not to the sea slug. The poet is praising the dish as he puts it in its proper season.

海 鼠 売 甕 を か づ き て 移 り け り 軽 部 烏 頭 子
namakouri kame o kazukite utsurikeri – karube utôshi? (1932)
#777(seaslug-vendor pot/vat/s shoulders migrates/moves-about[+finality])

the sea slug man
shoulders his pole
and moves on

Actually, the vendor shoulders/carries his pot/vat – a *kame* is larger than the usual *oke,* or "tub" – and only uses his pole to do so, but English has no verb to put that picture in a word, so I added the pole, subtracting the container to make room to do so. This might be a purely objective haiku, a mere description, but something – I think it is the slight give in the bamboo pole and the unavoidable bobbing of the suspended container (if only one, behind his back) or containers (if two, one on each side) – makes me feel that we are seeing the sea slug vendor as the season itself. When he leaves, winter is over.

1. *Cherry Shell Waka* An example from Saigyô's SANKASHÛ: "when the wind blows / and the blossoming waves / start breaking / the cherry-shells come to / the beaches of mishima" (*kaze fukeba hana saku nami-no* . . .). While these are an innocent shell, all shells have vulvic associations .

Spring Sea Slug

御代にふる生海鼠ながら花の春　普居

#778 miyo ni furu namako nagara mo hana no haru – fukyo (1829)
(honorable-era-in happen/age seaslug-while/although-even/still flowery spring)

though we're old	flowery spring	even the slug
sea slugs, spring bloom	and from the old regime	so long in the world
is spring bloom	a holothurian!	knows spring

In South Japan, *namako* spawn in the spring (*wintry slug/ i see you, too / have a spring!*). But, that was probably not known to the poet. Is this, then, about an aseasonal slug dish? Or, is/are the slug/s the poet and his old cronies? Or, is it, rather, about an old *namako wall? brazier? roof tiles?* or (according to a source I forget) an old *tatami* mat? The usual way *Namako* makes it into the Spring is through its guts, for the *konowata* season lags that of fresh slugs because of the fermentation time involved.

磯くさき匂ひさめけり梅の花　吟江

#779 isokusaki nioi samekeri ume no hana – ginkô (18c?)
(reef/shore-smell/stink comes-too[i come to from] plum blossoms)

plum blossoms
the reef smell brings me
to my senses

このわたの旬も杉田の梅咲や　敬之

#780 konowata no shun mo sugita no ume saku ya – keishi (18c)
(slug-guts' season/best too sugita [place name=is past] plum[trees] bloom!)

the time to eat	when sugita plums	it's time for
slug gut in sugita when	bloom, slug guts, too	slug guts and plums
plums blossom	are in their prime	bloom in sugita

Sugita was famous for plum blossoms. As the Ginkô haiku'ed, in reference to Japan's vaunted cherry blossom viewing place, "only yoshino? / plum-time sugita, too / is *wow! wow!*" (*yoshino nomi ka ume no sugita mo kore wa kore wa*). We cannot know if Ginkô's "reef smell" was the result of his beachcombing or eating slug guts or ovaries which also have that smell but we do know that Sugita slug guts were well known, for Keishi's poem is seconded by the Edo aesthete, Issa's teacher Seibi:

海鼠腸をなつかしみ梅かとも　成美

konowata o natsukashimi [sic] ume ga[ka?] to mo [tomo?] – seibi (1748-1816)
#781 (seaslugut familiarity/dearness* plum/s scent/the even/friend/accompaniment])

ah, slug guts	sweet memories	once again
how well they go with	slurping slug guts again:	enjoying slug guts with
plum blossoms	the scent of plum	plum mates

The original lacks a couple syllabets and uses phonetic syllabary where characters would be clearer. By "plum friends," *if* that is the purport of the poem, blossom-viewing is implied. After the change to the Western calendar, slug guts had to exit Spring entirely and rejoin their body in the Winter.

Natsukashimi I am not certain about the ending of this word in this poem, but I know there is no good English translation for it. What can we do with recognition, nostalgia, and joy to meet again compressed into a single verb that may be used as an exclamation!

Hokkaidô Sea Slugs

What can be done with parts of Japan which fall beyond the pale of the traditional *saijiki?* Not finding any Hokkaido Sea Slug haiku, Keigu concocted some in order to obtain the same:

[解 禁 日] 時 鳥 海 鼠 舟のる 海 鼠 取り　敬 愚

[kaikinbi] hototogisu namakobune noru namakotori – keigu

#782

(open-restrictions-day // cuckoo! slug-boat boards seaslug-catchers)

the first day

cuckoo calls
and sea slug men board
sea slug boats

The Japanese cuckoo isn't the English one but it, too, comes in with the summer. June on the mainland but, I would guess, July in Hokkaido, which is when the slugging season officially begins. CZ, who was bred on Hokkaido, laughs at this effort. First, he writes, they don't have such boats in Hokkaido, second, the *hototogisu* (above written, "small cuckoo") doesn't get that far North.[1] Better to make it another cuckoo called kakkô or a lark. But that would ruin the fun.

ホトトギス 海 鼠 腸 ぶいと 飛 ばしけり 敬 愚

hototogisu konowata bui to tobashikeri – keigu

#783 (cuckoo! slug-guts spurting[mimesis] fly-out)

cuckoo calls
and a sea slug's guts
overshoot

Keigu imagines a middle-aged female employee because he saw a photo of one in A. Kohman's *Sea Cucumber Reader* (ndh) but cannot decide whether she squeezed the sea slug at the sound of the cuckoo or whether it was just a coincidence. Because the guts (in the photo) are aimed more-or-less sideways and squirted sideways over the container they fall into, theoretically, they can "overshoot."

海 鼠 腸 をぶいと 飛 ばせて 不 如 帰[2→] 敬 愚

konowata o bui to tobasete hototogisu – keigu

#784 (slug-gut's spurting flying, cuckoo!)

sea slug
entrails flying out:
cuckoo!

---

1. *Guts Not Shot in Hokkaido* CZ again. I'll quote, for he made the mistake of writing me in English. It is so interesting that I shall kick the font back up to 10.5 to encourage you to read it:

I have not ever seen that [squirting sea slug guts into buckets] DOSANKO [native-born] fishermen or their wives were doing so in OTARU. 1st. KONOWATA [slug guts] were not selling in the market or shops in OTARU a well-known fishing port] (perhaps whole in HOKKAIDOU). 2nd. people who loves KONOWATA in OTARU didn't cut NAMAKOs [I didn't say they were *cut* out; they were squirted from the aboral end] for eating KONOWATA. They will kiss to the ass of NAMAKO and directly pull out KONOWATA into their mouth [like sucking eggs!]. So, we didn't think KONOWATA is the food for selling.

If the locals eat them raw as CZ suggests, the practice of fermenting the guts would seem to be a well kept secret!

Shiki, who has a cork[1] from a bottle hit the ceiling at the cuckoo's call (*ramuneh no sen tenjo o tsuite hototogisu* – Meiji 24), would have liked this. To even more closely approximate Shiki's poem, we could have the "guts hit the wall" in the middle line!

北 海 道 や 季 題 に 浮 か ぶ 「夏 海 鼠」 敬 愚
#785 hokkaidô ya kidai ni ukabu "natsunamako" – keigu
(hokkaidô!/: seasonal-theme-as float/rise/appears "summer seaslug")

summer sea slug

hokkaidô haiku:
a new theme floats up
natsunamako

Here, we have a problem. The scientific sea slug and perhaps even the activity of fisherman catching sea slug for export may not jibe with the practice of the common folk. In CZ's words, "even [in] HOKKAIDOU the season when people likes to eat NAMAKO is winter." So, not only the haiku almanac, but the diet would seem to have been nationalized and poor Keigu fights a losing battle.

北 海 道 海 鼠 の 昼 寝 わ か る 猫 敬 愚
hokkaidô namako no hirune wakaru neko – keigu
(hokkaidô seaslug's day/afternoon-nap understand/s cat/s)   #786

hokkaidô
cats understand sea slugs
taking a nap

The *nap* in haiku belongs to spring or summer rather than winter. If you recall, there is an Edo era haiku where the cat recognizes the sea slug as one of its ilk in *Sleeping Sea Slugs*. Keigu resituates it.

北 海 の 猫 が 海 鼠 を 笑 ふ 夏 敬 愚
hokkai no neko ga namako o warau natsu – keigu
(north[hokkaido's]-sea cats[gulls] seaslug[obj] laugh summer)   #787

hokkaidô

north sea gulls
laugh at sea slugs
in the summer

→**2. Hototogisu**   Readers who may not read Japanese but still compare it with the Romanization will observe that the bird's name=call is written differently in each. The *kanji* in the first translates as "time-bird," and is one of the most common combinations for the cuckoo. The second is written in phonetic syllabets. The third is a rare combination, suggests "not-like-return/ing" and is suggestive in a more subtle way than might be the case for the bird's neither common nor rare name of "mutable/transient-bird" There are scores of ways to write this bird's name of which dozens are pronounced exactly the same way!
1. Ramune Cork   My dictionary translates it as "lemon pop." But the most incredible thing is not the taste of the carbonated drink but the bottle, for it has indentions on both ends of the neck between which a marble is trapped for the purpose of holding in the carbonation and, I would guess, preventing one from drinking too quickly and minimizing spills. I do not know if the bottles were once sealed with corks rather than caps as today or if Shiki's *sen* means that marble, blasting from the neck! Hearing the rather weak call of said *hototogisu* – not at all like its supposedly mimetic name – it is hard to understand the explosive reaction or parallel unless it is born purely of the anticipation that built up during the long wait.

one hypothesis would be the combination of sea slug and bug, namely, flies and mosquitoes.

This last was the only one of Keigu's Hokkaido haiku that CZ fully approved of, though the "road," which suggests the land of the north, was cut at his suggestion, to clearly move the scene into the sea where the cat turned into a gull, "sea-cat," in Japanese.

北海道のなまこや蝿がついている 敬愚

hokkaidô no namako ya hae ga tsuiteiru – keigu
#788 (hokkaidô's seaslug/s!/: flies sticking/lucky-are)

hokkaidô
sea slugs: how lucky
for the flies!

"Stuck-on" is idiom for *lucky.* On the mainland, flies and sea slugs rarely – the occasional winter fly – if ever meet.

北海道や蝿に踏まれし大海鼠 敬愚

hokkaidô ya hae ni fumareshi ônamako – keigu
#789 (hokkaidô!/: flies-by trodden large seaslug)

hokkaidô life:
big sea slugs tickled
by house-flies!

It is a safe bet flies will like sea slugs (unless the slight poison repels them) but anyone's guess as to whether the slug will find the contact threatening or comforting. CZ writes that he thinks "no hanô [reaction/response] is suitable for a sea slug," but kindly offers a less controversial substitute in English and Japanese: *"mosq. are comin', flies are comin', big namako moving. in the summer night (hae ka kitari namako ugomeku natsu no yoru)."* Keigu is grateful, but either the time must be dusk or one of the bugs ditched:

［北海道］蚊も来たり海鼠うごめく夏の夜 星愚

hokkaidô // ka mo kitari namako ugomeku natsu no yoru – cz+keigu
#790   (hokkaidô// mosquito too/even come[and stuff] seaslug /s squirm/s summer night)

hokkkaido

a sea slug moves
in the night as mosquitoes
come and go.

Though the original verb, *ugomeku,* or "squirm" implies discomfort, it is objective, for it is the common way to describe the movement of a worm, maggot or sea slug. Moreover, the mosquitoes and this movement are not causally related, so one could argue that the sea slug does not feel them. Hokkaido had to be added as the title.

北海鼠や蚊に蝿にどうなるらん

hokunamako ya ka ni hae ni dô naruran – keigu
#791   (north-sea's slugs: mosquitoes-about, flies-about how is it?)

hokkaido slugs
how do you feel about
flies, mosquitoes

Actually, I wonder how the bugs might affect the sea slug they touch. Do the sea slugs find them too slight to notice? Do they find them irritating at first but grow tolerant? The "ko" is an acceptable ellipsis for our charge. CZ gives the thumbs down to this imagined encounter:

> You don't understand the summer time in HOKKAIDOU. Well, even there flies are flying. But I have not seen they were gathering to NAMAKO. Boo...it's only [a] "jelly-fish-story" [talk about jellyfish bones is idiomatic for entertaining thought about a fiction]. First, there were many HIMONO [food cured by drying *al fresco*] of various fishes in those season, on the beach and fish-stands in market. If flies will gathering, they go on those HIMONOs, for they were great smellier than NAMAKOs. Second, when NAMAKO selling, they put into the water. How flies can landing? Moreover, presently, NAMAKO are selling which have been cut and packed. So those verses couldn't make if [unless] the NAMAKOs have left on the beach or on the street, rotten.[1]

Okay, but I can still imagine a sea slug lying *partly* out of water in a tub by an open window and I *doubt* that all the flies in Hokkaido are otherwise occupied.

~

The Christian Sea Slugs

I couldn't find any explicitly Christian sea slugs. But I did find a mysterious sea slugger on the net. The haiku was written by a woman who was, herself, once Christian. This is rare in Japan, and she explains that when she sold rode about town on a red bicycle selling haberdashery, she was forced to drink with clients and found it best to become Christian so that her abstention (these were the days when Christianity pushed temperance as if *"Thou shalt not drink!"* was in the *Decalogue*) would be respected, and came to believe for a decade or so – came to work with haiku master Kyoshi and, at 84 remains at the helm of the haiku group (?) and magazine *Fuyuno* (winter-field).

海 鼠 突 き に 行 く 年 守 り て 隠 れ 耶 蘇　小 原 菁 菁 子
namako tsuki ni yuku toshi morite kakureyaso – ohara seiseishi (mod)
(sea-slug-gigging-to go=departing year witnessing/protecting hidden-christian)　　　#792

the year goes	out gigging slugs
as a christian in hiding	while the new year comes in
gigs sea slug	a secret christian

This is probably a work of historical imagination: Christians hiding out on an island so they will not be forced to recant or die during the Tokugawa (17-mid19c), unless it refers to Christians taking refuge in the boondocks during WWII, when any Western influence was looked at askance. "Year-protecting/witnessing" is a standard *saijiki* theme and means staying up all night to witness the Old Year leave and New Year come with the Rising of the Sun. Non-Christian Japanese *revere* and *pay their respects* to the first Sun – not "worship" in the Christian sense of the term – and never go out to work at this sacred time. In this poem, the Christian happens to witness the event while gigging slugs to keep his or her family and their tradition alive through the harsh winter months. The *yuku* (is a pivot-word that first attaches to the gigging, then to the year. Vacillating between the leaving year (fitting the *yuku*) and coming year (fitting the *morite*), I ended up with two readings. We can't help but juxtapose the Christians and the silenced *namako*. After all, the Christians, too, were silenced in Japan (even if they were hardly so meek as sea slugs wherever *they* held power!).

1. Funny English I leave CZ's funny English as it is a welcome break from my own. Readers should remind themselves that the Japanese written by most graduate students in the West is no better.

海 鼠 突 く 有 馬 王 子 の 碑 の 下 に　香 月 梅 邨
namako tsuku arima ôji no hi no shita ni – kazuki baison?(contemp)
#793 (seaslug stabbing, arima-prince's tombstone's below-at)

gigging sea slugs
below the tombstone of
the prince of arima

I do not know if this refers to the man the Jesuits called the King [1] of Arima who was baptized in 1579, his nephew who was one of the four young Japanese "ambassadors" sent to Europe in 1582, or the son of the King, as prince implies. Whoever it was, he doubtless had a tragic end, if martyrdom can be so called (back in New Spain (Manila), news of such deaths brought celebration). Though no mention of Christianity is made, this contemporary poem seems to me the best of the *Christian Sea Slug* haiku.

海 鼠 つ く 海 に ひ び け り 弥 撒 の 鐘　栗 田 せ つ 子
namako tsuku umi ni hibikeri misa no kane – kurita setsuko (1997)
#794 (seaslug stabbing sea-to/in echo mass' bell)

the matin rings
over the ocean where
slugs are gigged

I suspect this is in Hiroshima or Nagasaki, for both are good sea slug towns and have more than the usual proportion of Catholics (can't charge Truman *et al* with discrimination on *that* account!).

聖 母 像 見 た も ふ 海 鼠 突 き に け り　小 野 喬 樹
seibôzo mita mô [mitamau?] namako tsukinikeri – ôno kyôju (contemp?)
#795 (holy-mother(mary*)-statue/idol saw, now seaslug gigs[finality])

she who saw
the virgin mary, now
sticking sea slugs

～

does he see
the image of the virgin
sticking slugs?

Either reading assumes a Japanese Christian who either once looked up on the sweet face of the Virgin Mary [2] statues and paintings in church, now, in hiding, looking down for and gigging sea slugs.   The juxtaposition of visions of Mary and the sea slugs is effective.

1. *Kings in Japan* The Jesuit's "kings" are often translated as *daimyô* or criticized by modern scholars, but this was the time when the nation was still in the process of unification and, considering the freedom men such as Arima Harinobu had until they were forced to obey higher powers, "king" *(rey)* was not an inappropriate title. Perhaps they practiced nominal obedience to the Emperor. Well, didn't the European kings bow down to Rome? The Jesuit Frois, witnessing the "kings" lack of power in the newly established order, pointed out that the term was no longer appropriate at the end of the sixteenth century in a fine reflection on what we might now call the apples and oranges problem in translation in the introduction to his (otherwise) lost Summary of Japan (see FROIS).

2. *Virgin Mary* In China and Japan, and perhaps some other cultures as well, the image of a bloody, tortured Jesus was thought an eyesore, if not obscene and corrupting of public morals.   The sweet Virgin on the other hand had the calm presence expected in an object of adoration. Missionaries in the Far East quickly learned they had far too many crucifixes and too few Marias.

伴天連の島に泊て食ふ海鼠かな　田尻牧夫

bateren no shima ni tomete kuu namako kana – tajiri makio (1993)

#796 (padre's/s' island-on stay/visiting eat seaslug!/?/ő/it's)

staying over on the island, padres ate sea slugs	spending a night on the isle of the padres we eat sea slug

island

padres once
came here, did they
eat sea slug?

The Jesuit missionaries began their rapid Christianization of Southern Japan [1] from islands on the South coast of Kyushu and in the Japan Sea. With righteous pride, they encouraged Christian converts to vandalize the religious treasures of others and even searched for and destroyed "idols" hidden in caves on small islands, some of which they returned to in order to hide out when their pride took its fall. In between, there was a very short but happy time when the Buddhist persecution ceased and the Jesuits had an admirable policy of *Accommodation* to Japanese mores, including cuisine. The extent to which the possessive *no* extends in the above poem is not clear. I don't know which period is imagined by the poet, and it may even be the case that the poet himself is the one eating sea slug.

～

Ancestor Sea Slug

In an unsigned UNESCO article titled "Can we afford to lose biodiversity?" (www.unesco.org/bpi/science/content/press/anglo/11.htm) about the importance of conservation, preserving the genetic potential we are destroying "with over 80 percent of all species still undiscovered," a quirky out-of-place paragraph puts our holothurian right in the thick of things:

> When we look at species that are very close, says Lasserre, it is as though nature was wasteful. There is a superabundance of solutions. There is only a fractional difference between these species. But, genetically, there is a constant, despite the variations. So, *the sea cucumber is an ancestor of man.* It has a primitive backbone, with a mouth, a gut and an anus. It gave rise to vertebrates, which in turn produced mammals and man. (*italics* mine)

I like those words *"the sea cucumber is an ancestor of man,"* but fear the idea is far too simple. First, the sea cucumbers alive today are not our ancestors any more than other primates are. They only show a common ancestry, which in some ways is more similar to them then to us. We only share a common ancestry (but to the extent to which they share more with our common ancestry than we do, it could be argued they represent our ancestors). Second, the sea cucumber is but part of the Echinodermata the common ancestor of which may be at the bottom of our branch of life and not be-

---

2. *Christianization of Japan* Most Japanese assume that their gentle forest-born culture had some sort of intellectual immunity to Christianity, a religion "caught" by people living in dry places with unforgiving right-or-wrong mentality. They forget that Japan not only began to Christianize much *faster* than Europe had, but that the Jesuits found them particularly well-suited for the higher offices denied to other non-Europeans. Ironically, the high speed of the conversion, more than anything else, was probably the cause of the reaction that oppressed Christianity with equally unprecedented speed and thoroughness! When I hear Japanese spout off climatic reductionist theories of religion, I remind them of the population of Muslims in monsoon Indonesia. Yet, there is *something* to it.

-cause it had a mouth, gut, anus and backbone, but because it had an anus that developed before its mouth yet had no backbone to speak of, as explained in a the introduction.   What is, nonetheless, interesting here is the choice of the holothurian, rather than any other Echinoderm, to be our root. This is common.   Apparently, the sea slug, *with its meaty torso* is a *more believable* proto-human than a starfish, sea urchin or sand dollar, though all are equally well/poorly qualified for the honor.

$\sim$

Don Sea Slug

指 さ し て こ れ が 海 鼠 の 中 の 首 領 （ ド ン ）　高 沢 良 一
yubi sashite kore ga namako no naka no shûryô – takasawa yoshikazu (2003)
#797 (finger-pointing, this seaslug-among's boss (don[indicated in original])

i point to one
now that's the don
of sea slugs

I had imagined a nurse or doctor laughing and talking to one another. As they pass the patient, Takasawa, "a finger points / that man? he's the don / of sea slugs."   But, when I asked the poet for details, he wrote that the "don" was the largest sea slug in a tub of non-descript black sea slugs.   Still, the poem *was* indeed a hospital poem and if there was an inspiration, it was the memory of post-operative visits by pods of residents inevitably lead by a head-doctor who expected to be and was deferred to as if he were God.[1.]   This absolute power is reminiscent of a Mafia don and, perhaps (now, I'm guessing), the soft-spoken Marlon Brando image transferred itself to the silent sea slug.

$\sim$

The Charmed Sea Slug

Excluding the moments when one pop-up page after another is thrown upon you and you deftly shoot through them trying not to wipe out, the internet does not seem like *surfing* to me.   I think of it, rather, as *beachcombing*.   Here is one of my unexpected finds:

Kyu Kyum Spin

Also known as: *Sea Cucumber Spin*
Category: Shamanism / Water
(Note: Kyu-Kyum Spin is sometimes confused for Zelas-Gort, even in the official Slayers references.)

This spell summons sea cucumbers from any nearby body of water. Its usefulness is limited to humiliating your opponent and procuring food if you're hungry.

This was on a site of "Spells," the first of which instructs us how to make an "Aero Bomb," i.e., "a compact ball of air explode in the desired location" (lr)

---

1. *Doctors as God*   Not long after a renowned Japanese doctor flubbed an eye operation performed on *me* (a tiny piece of the pterigium nearest to the pupil was missed and the overly economical stitching left a cyst), I showed it to Japanese friends – a nurse and a doctor, if I recall correctly – and was *amazed* to discover they could not see the problems in my eye (which I had to have redone later in the US).   The Doctor's fame blinded them to the sorry reality.   Cognitive dissonance (perception unconsciously warped to fit expectation) lets our "gods" get away with murder.

The Imagist Sea Slug

This *Imagist Sea Slug* began with three poems, one very old and classic, one modern and known, and one very recently submitted by an unnamed guest at a resort hotel in Tohoku to complement a painting of a camellia. The first two might have been squeezed into the *Featureless Sea Slugs* and *Cold Sea Slugs*, respectively, but I found myself visualizing them over and over, so here they are, mixed in with a handful of later additions:

むくつけき海鼠そ動く朝渚 露沾

#798 mukutsukeki namako zo ugoku asanagisa – rosen (1654-1733)
(inelegant/gross/undefinable/weird/eerie sea slug/s [+emphatic] moving morning shore)

haikai find	***low tide***
something *gross*	an eerie sight
in the still dawn water	sea slugs are squirming
a sea slug moves	in the morning surf

My first reading of this poem was a misreading. I told myself *mukutsukeki* was the old version of *mukatsuki,* or "nauseous" and imagined a poet, suffering from winter depression, nauseated to see the moving – not ambulatory, but slow squirming, shrinking and expanding for whatever reason – dark deformity. Then, I thought of Buson's sea slug pent up with unvoiced longing and imagined its bilious humour condensed into a heart-sized blob, discovered by the very man to whom it belonged, the melancholy poet![1] Unfortunately, *mukutsukeki* was not only different from my *desired* reading, but full of more varied connotations than one can shake a stick at. The gross – inelegant and disgusting – slug *does* stand out against the crystalline water of the morning (a bit *after* dawn, but I had a beat to keep). Before concrete – there's your real BC (AD, being After Development) – the entire seashore was a magical place for finding beautiful gems – as shells, as well as pearls were called – and was featured as such in old poetry. Look, says Rosen, **this**, too! The second reading assumes a mass of sea cucumbers such as the "millions" seen by Steinbeck in the *Sea of Cortez*.

ころんと海鼠転がりをりし浜青天 高沢良一

koron to namako korogari orishi hamaseiten – takasawa yoshikazu (2003)
#799 (*koron*[mimesis] with, seaslug rolls-is[respectful verb]beach-blue-sky[fair-weather])

lulling about	sea slugs
the beach fair weather	lull about on a clear
sea slugs	beach day

This is a new one. The "beach-clear-sky/weather" in the original suggests, I think, the second reading. I imagine a beach is protected by raised ground in the lee of whatever (little) wind there might be, and a poet delighted to come upon a comfortable cove on a chilly day, and sure enough the sea slugs seemed to be enjoying themselves, too. This image stands in strong contrast with Rosen's, where the sea slug is a disconcerting rather than assuring presence. Now, the well-known haiku:

#800

1. ***Heart-sized*** A contemporary poet made the bile connection by writing two sea slug haiku following an operation to remove his gall-bladder: "getting to see / pickled sea slug / sliced up" (*su namako-no kiri-kizamareshi toki mitari* – honda hideto 酢海鼠 に切りきざまれしとき見たり 日出登) and "in the vinegar / a sea slug's spirit / still lingers" (*su*

#801

no naka ni kokoro urotsuku namako kana – ditto 酢 の中にこころうろつく海鼠かな 日出登). Note, the same word *kokoro*. Japanese vinegar is perfectly clear, so it resembles the fluid specimens are put into. (69.tcup.com/.hondah1 "haiku-no-hiroba") Honda loves pickled slug so much he writes it is all he needs with his *sake* (corresp).

雪 の 上 に 落 ち 沈 み た る 海 鼠 か な 田 元 北 史
yuki no ue ni ochi shizumitaru namako kana – tamoto hokushi (mod)
#802 (snow-upon fallen-sinks sea slug!/?/ó/behold)

a sea slug
dropped on the snow
is sinking in

a sea slug
dropped and sinking
into snow

in the snow
a fallen still sinking
sea cucumber

The slug didn't necessarily slip right in like a mole fleeing a cat, but, being dark, it heated up enough to melt its way down, but not far enough to disappear from sight.   This poem, found in many anthologies, has left an impression on me every bit as strong as Issa's likewise famous straight pee-hole made in the same winter medium.   For reference sake, another slug on the snow:

魚 市 や 海 鼠 の ち ぢ む 雪 の 上 利 居
uoichi ya namako no chijimu yuki no ue – rikyo (mod?)
#803 (fish-market:/! seaslug/s shrink/s/ing snow-above)

the fish market
sea slugs shrinking up
on the snow

Here, I do not so much *see* the sea slugs as *feel* their coldness. I reflect that they, like we humans, are naked. I feel that the poem might as well have been put into *"The Cold Sea Slug,"* as an example of a slug that is not cold in the sense of contrasting with us warm-blooded animals, but in the same way we are. And, here is the last of the original trio.

海 鼠 舟 艫 に 一 輪 島 椿 無 名 の 客
namakobune tomo ni ichirin shimatsubaki – anon. (contemp)
#804 (seaslug [fishing] boat, stern-on/in one-blossom island-camellia)

island red

a slug boat
in the weathered stern
one camellia

The camellia in the picture is red with a finger-thick tube-like stamen, as is typical for one of the two basic types of camellia (the more natural/wild variety).[1→] The modern poem given in the Introduction

1. *Camellias and a Camellia Coincidence* I imagine what the on-site phot showed, but my dictionary was no help. It didn't even list the island-camellia (*shimatsubaki*).   But it did teach me that the operatic name of the Swedish bulk freighter I once worked on, *La Traviata,* is "Princess Camellia" (*tsubaki-hime*) in Japanese! (Another reason to learn foreign languages: more little coincidences to relish!). KK writes that this is no coincidence. Most Japanese cultured enough to write haiku know not only of Verdi's opera (1853) – whose tragic heroine is called *Violetta* – but of the Princess's original *La Dame aux Camelias* from the 1848 (1852?) novel by Alexandre Dumot *fils* (the son) of that name. It would seem the Japanese title for the opera (unlike Verdi's original) – and the woman, who is called by her original name – gives credit to the novelist. One thing I should add: in the novel, this breath-taking Parisian prostitute wore the flower to indicate her sexual availability, white camellias 25 days per month and red ones 5 days per month!

to this Volume (as an example of simple Japanese hard to translate because of our mutually exotic grammar) depicts sea slugs on a weathered deck. *This* haiku doesn't say "weathered," but are slug boats *ever* new? A little red goes a long way to bring out drabness.   And the camellia, like *namako, thrives* in the cold. I imagine the person who wrote this haiku – a guest at the Tadaya onsen (hot-springs inn) in the slug country of North East Japan – imagined a romance to go with it. Since what never happened can not be undone – unlike the diamond by the same name – this romance *is* forever.

蝋 の 海 ナ マ コ の 列 は 粛 粛 と　柴 崎 昭 雄

rô no umi namako no retsu wa shukushuku to – shibasaki akio (contemp)
#805 (wax-ocean seaslugs' row/column/line/s-as-for solemn/austere/hushedly)

a solemn line	quiet rows
of sea slugs crosses	of sea slugs below
a waxen sea	a waxen sea

AQ, who netted this "study from life," says it describes *the quiet movement of a line of sea slugs.* I first put this poem with *The Panoramic Sea Slugs,* despite the it's being so abstract we cannot tell whether it describes sea slugs that, for some reason, are lined up on the seafloor, boats carrying slug cargo, or simply low-floating freighters that, from a distance, remind the poet of sea slugs. But, on second reading, I keep thinking about a certain Swedish movie director. Even without a certain image, this is an *Imagist* haiku, isn't it? (*That is a real question:* AQ ventures that he sees the sea of wax as Japan's recession, and the sea slugs as the Japanese who silently bear it!)

浜 辺 に は 群 雄 割 拠 の 海 鼠 か な　伸 茶

hamabe ni wa gunyûkakkyo no namako kana – shinsa (contemp)
(beach-side-as-for crowd-male-split-tactic[heroic battle]'s seaslug!/?/ó/the)

#806

winner take all	*heroic holothurians*
off the beach	off the beach
a heroic battle evoked	a nation's fate decided
by sea slugs	by sea slugs

敗 け い く さ 一 日 海 鼠 と な り に け り　無 名

makeikusa ichinichi namako to nari ni keri—anon
(losing-battle/rebellion one-day seaslug become(+finality))

#807

after the uprising

in one day
the losing side turns
sea slug

It may be true that men who win get all pumped up with testosterone and run around sowing babies, while the losers deflate, the better to hide their emotions and live to f___(whichever) another day. Still, the second poem is *mere* metaphor and barely qualifies as a *senryu,* much less a haiku. The first, however, is good. Perhaps, it describes the feelings evoked by a mass confusion of sea slugs in Guam or, perhaps by a smaller number seen in Japan (at a coast where a historic battle was fought) is a different matter all together. It might not seem *imagist* at first, until you recall those Massive Pitched Battle Scenes that are not so much battles as art in the movies of the imagist directors (AQ, noting the poet is young, thinks the inspiration might rather be a Warring Era scene from a computer game!). That big word "crowd-male-split" means "*a battle between all of the regional powers contesting for control of a nation.*"   Since English has no such word, I had to improvise and you will have to imagine.

The Wall

五 月 雨 や 雨 の 中 よ り 海 鼠 壁　　芥 川 龍 之 介
samidare ya ame no naka yori namakokabe – akutagawa ryûnosuke (mod)

#808　(fifth[mid-june by gregorian calen.]-month-rain[heavy rain]: rain within-from seaslug-wall)

> monsoon days
> coming through the rain
> a sea slug wall

As Namako Hakase, *aka,* Dr. Sea Slug, explained, the "sea slugs" are the rounded protrusions of grout. *Imagine, if you will, a wall where the spacing/glue stands out more than the bricks!* The original haiku, by the storyteller who is usually associated with the prize given in his name (the top fiction prize in Japan) and *kappa,* the legendary water imp he so loved, has no verb. The middle seven syllabets translate "from within the rain." The fifth-month rain is the mid-summer monsoon, the opposite season to the *namako* winter, but equally gloomy. Perhaps, then, it is metaphorically fitting weather. And, it is definitely becoming to the sea slug grout, which only shines when it is wet.

冬 日 向 海 鼠 の 壁 の 温 み も て 喜 久
fuyu hinata namako no kabe no nukumi mote – kikyû (contemp)
#809(winter sun-facing[sunlight/sunny-place] seaslug-wall's warmth holds)

> winter sunshine
> the sea slug wall
> holds warmth

What is in a name? If the Sea Slug Wall was not a *sea slug* wall, the warmth in this poem would be purely physical. As it is, thanks to the name, there is a pleasant contradiction and a touch of affection=affectation – not in the bad sense, but in the good – for the comfortably warm sea slugs, who, in a wall, come to share a human, at any rate, mammalian, quality.

～

The Panoramic Sea Slug

松 風 と 千 島 の 下 の 生 海 鼠 哉　　阿 波 普 鮮
matsukaze to chidori no shita no namako kana – anami fusen (1820?)
#810 (pine-wind and plovers' below's sea-slug/s!/?/ó/the/behold)

> pine breeze,　　　　　　　　sea cucumber:
> plovers and, further down,　　below the plovers and
> the sea slugs　　　　　　　　moaning pine

We have many *two*-level vertical panorama haiku. Bashô's Milky Way over a whit-capped sea and Buson's Moon over the dwellings of poor-town come to mind. But, I cannot think of any *three*-level scenes like this. One imagines a modern cut-away drawing, a slice of littoral sea and beachscape. The original haiku is in the Japanese-style most foreign to the English poetic sense, where the entire poem modifies the subject, which, coming last is where the mind's eye stops: on the sea slug/s (the *kana* is but a bowtie on the package, marking it as a poem. Popular etymology had the plover born of the froth/spume of the white-caps, so we might best imagine a choppy sea rather than the calm one – still-life? – we are used to. That is why I specify a cut-away. I think the *namako* are *imagined* below.

新藁のさむしろ敷きて海鼠干す清き浜辺の松古りにけり 橋本徳寿

shinwara no samushiro shikite namako hosu kiyoki hamabe no matsu furinikeri – hashimoto tokuju?(mod?)
#811 (new-fine-strawmat/s spread/ing seaslug dry/ing fresh/pristine beach/seashore's pine/s age[+finality])

pines grow old	those pine trees	sea slug drying
on a pristine seashore	on the shore where they	on new straw mats
where sea slugs	spread new mats	spread out by
are spread out to dry	to dry out the sea slugs	a beautiful seashore
on new straw mats	how they have aged!	with aging pines

This *tanka* provides a panorama of texture, with the rough old bark, crisp new weave and salty deformed sea slug – the dealers speak of beautiful products, but dried things are not beautiful in the smooth sense by which it is generally understood – in high contrast with the crystalline blue sky and sea. Until the last word, the verb "age," the entire poem, in the original, is a modification of the "pine/s." Again, the virtually unEnglishable "Japanese style." There is a haiku about the horns of a cow being piteous for aging, as opposed to those of the deer, which fall off every year to grow afresh. At first reading, we may be drawn toward the freshly dead *namako,* yet, it is the long life – the slow deterioration – of the pines that we end up feeling.

さむしろに海鼠干したる道すぎて潮みなぎらふ海を見おろす 大場寅郎

samushiro ni namako hoshitaru michi sugite ushio minagirau umi o miorosu – ôba toraô? (contemp/)
#812 ([fine-strawmat/s-on seaslug drying road passing brine/surf brimming? sea[obj] look/ing-down)

after crossing
a road with sea slugs
drying on mats
i see the ocean below
bulging at full tide

If the last *tanka* paints a broad *canvas*, this one, using more or less the same ingredients, seems like a video snippet. Sometimes the sea *does* look as if the water is bulging, but what that has to do with the other sights I do not know. Maybe a reader more sensitive than I am can enlighten me. The next, more modest picture is an often anthologized sea slug haiku:

生海鼠干す伊良古が崎の二日凪 暁台

namako hosu irakogasaki no futsuka nagi – gyôtai (1731-92)
#813 (seaslug drying irakogasaki's two-day calm)

a two-day calm
at sea slug drying
cape irako

The "two-day calm" is a good concrete observation and the name Irako chimes silently with dried sea slug (*iriko*), but I almost left this haiku (which I have seen in many *saijiki*) out of the book because, I think, its true appreciation requires a visual knowledge of the Cape that can fill in the landscape haiku has no room for! Since I do not have it, myself, I find it boring.

海 鼠 干 す 女 ば か り の 日 和 か な　水 沼 三 郎
namako hosu onna bakari no hiyori kana – mizunuma saburô (1978)
#814 (seaslug dry/ing women only's clear-weather!/?/ó/this/it's)

woman-only
sea slug drying calm
clear weather

In this weather, all the men are at sea catching fish or sea slugs. While the observation might be contemporary, I imagine women in *monpe,* the decorated trousers worn in the first half of the twentieth century and I would love to find an old picture to validate it! I have left the typical Japanese-style syntax – shared with the last poem – in place in this translation.

雪 ず り 落 ち い（？）店 頭 の 海 鼠 震 ふ　猿 橋 統 流 子
yuki zuriochite? tentô no namako furû – sarubashi tôryûshi (1973)
#815 (snow slip-falls storefront's seaslug shake/quiver)

snow slides off   snow falls off
and sea slugs in front   the fish-shop roof and
of the store shake   sea slugs quiver

雪 あ と か ら あ と か ら 海 鼠 桶 の な か　三 木 聆 古
yuki ato kara ato kara namako oke no naka – miko reiko (contemp)
#816 (snow after-from after-from seaslug-tub's inside)

snow falls
and falls into the tub
of sea slug

If the blue-sky panorama was about drying sea slug for export, these are about the domestic market. These poems might have been squeezed in with the *Cold Sea Slugs*, but the pictures they make are so powerful in their own right that there is little room for metaphor.   I find the second extraordinary!

昼 月 や 底 の 小 暗 き 海 鼠 桶　角 川 春 樹
hiruzuki ya soko no oguraki namako oke – kadokawa haruki (1998)
#817 (day/noon/afternoon-moon :/! bottom's small-dark seaslug tub)

daytime moon
somewhat dark within
the sea slug tub

A panorama is usually thought of as a broad view. That is why cameras take horizontally expanded "panoramic" shots. Here we have something above and something below. Even for someone used to reading Japanese, which is usually written vertically, it is a scene hard, if not impossible to take in at once. I imagine the poet looking at a moon in the blue sky, then looking back down. Things would look a bit dark, for his pupils will have shrunken. The starkness of the daytime moon – to me, at any rate, it is a porous dry bone – and the tub are breathtaking. I would have put it with the *Imagist Sea Slugs,* but found it hard to imagine the moon and the tub together in one snapshot, such as Pound's wet leaf on the subway window.   Remember Melville's musings on what it might be like to have eyes on separate sides of your head that take in completely different worlds of sight? Until now, I have imagined a whale looking straight right and straight left, perhaps toward shore or a whaling ship with one eye and a horizon with nothing on the other. But reading this poem, for the first time, I turn that whale on his side and have him watching the clouds above and the sea-bed below. Has anyone ever turned a panorama-camera on its side? Another thing, I do not know if I should mention. The poet, son and heir of the Kadokawa publishing empire (top traditional publisher for haiku) spent four years in the slammer for importing cocaine [1] from the USA, where personalities freely enjoy it, so the tub might well be his cell and the sea slug him. [2]

海 鼠 笊 に 在 り 下 女 つ ん つ る て ん 猫 へ つ つ ひ に あ り 虚 子
namako zaru ni ari gejo tsuntsuruten neko hettsui ni ari – kyoshi (1918)
#818 (seaslug/s [bamboo slat] tray-in is/are, maid short robe, cat hearth-in/on is)

a sea cucumber
in a tray, the maid's knee-shine,
a cat on the hearth

This may be the strangest poem Kyoshi ever wrote. The excessive syllabet count (8-8-9) is surprising, for Kyoshi is known for championing the survival of the traditionally fixed haiku form in the face of free-verse-influenced innovation. But, what a fine domestic panorama! This haiku, as I picture it – the word *tentsuruten* means a bald head as well as a short kimono and, to my mind, sounds *shiny,* so I focused on the bent knees not specified in the original – calls for Hogarth.

1. *Cocaine* Thinking about cocaine, makes me both angry and depressed. Because of my exceptionally poor absorption, I cannot have coffee or tea with or after dinner, as I am kept up all night while the caffeine slowly percolates into my blood. This means I must be drowsy all evening. A quarter century ago, a housemate gave me some cocaine (I sniffed a small line every hour for several hours) and found it helped me do good brainwork – I was memorizing Chinese characters – in the evening, yet fell asleep quickly that night and woke with a clear memory, that I tested on those characters. It was easy to understand why Freud took advantage of cocaine to be so prolific a writer in his old age. Yet, because people -- most people, I fear – never develop self-control, this fine drug, so much less harmful than its competitor caffeine to someone with faulty intestines like me, is illegal. I am too cowardly (and too poor) to risk using it. Wealthy people know that cocaine is not necessarily bad for them, and use it. Kadokawa's main sin was not *using* cocaine, but having an employee smuggle it in and not having the guts to tell the court that cocaine, used properly, is not bad. But he had a family, so it was, no doubt, necessary to be contrite and pretend that he had dealings with the devil itself. (I am guessing here, and beg his apology if I have it wrong)

2. *Sea Slug = Him* Does knowing about Kadokawa's imprisonment and possible identification with the sea slug in that tub improve or damage the haiku? South Korea's fine essayist Lee Oh Young (i o ryong), in a rare analytical study of haiku, written in Japanese titled (in English translation) "WHY DID THE FROG JUMP INTO THE OLD POND? *** "(gakuseisha: 1993) cites Issa's "cicadas cry / how intense the red / of the pinwheel" (*semi naku ya tsukuzuku akai kazeguruma*) – as an example of a poem where it is better *not* to know the circumstances, not to know that the toy was beloved by Issa's recently dead daughter, for absorbing such information would ruin the pure cross-sensual genius of the cicada cries and the red pinwheel. Perhaps a majority of Japanese heavily into haiku would agree with Lee, but this approach seems wrong to me. In my mind, at least, such extrinsic information can coexist with a poem's intrinsic value, but that may depend upon the individual reader's ability to disassociate memories while rereading.

*** The title of Lee's book refers to Bashô's famous poem where a frog jumps into an old pond making a water-sound and Bashô is as suddenly enlightened about the universe and haiku as Newton was with his proverbial apple. Well, Lee says, Bashô was very familiar with the use of a sudden noise as a foil to deep silence in Chinese poems, so the sound of water was hardly anything new.

What was fresh in Bashô's poem, Lee argues, was that the sound is *not* a one-time thing, but something that repeats at irregular intervals all day and night long. Needless to say, English, with its need to number the frog/s and its/their verb, does not allow for such possibilities of interpretation.. Of the 100 or so translations given in Sato's *One Hundred Frogs,* only 2 are plural and none can be

either. 古池や
蛙飛び込む
水 の 音

Bethlehemite Sea Slug

This sea slug really belongs with the *Surreal Sea Slugs* or *Christian Sea Slugs* but it was misplaced, lost in a separate document when I thought I had not only already written it but placed it in the text, until I woke up this morning and thought, *Now where is it?* and ran a "Find" and found nothing? *Perhaps I just dreamt I wrote it.* But I did find the Japanese original and correspondence with the author elsewhere and, since time runs out as I type, the done pages will stay done and the Bethlehem Sea Slug will be put right here:

ベツレヘム海鼠ほたりほたりかな 等（俳蔵）

#819betsurehemu namako hotari hotari kana – hitoshi (2003)
(bethlehem-seaslug lurching[=mimesis] !/?/ó/the/behold/loh)

twenty centuries of stony sleep

the lamb now
a slug slouches back
to bethlehem

what rough beast

lurching along
a bethlehem-bound
sea cucumber

their hour

sea slugs
bethlehem *hotari*
hotari to

spiritus mundi

loh, a sea slug
slouching towards
bethlehem

I thought the verb would be easier to come up with in English than it would be to understand the mimesis in Japanese, because *hotari hotari* is not in the dictionary and might suggest practically anything in the absence of that Bethlehem hint. I was mistaken, for in my case, I remembered Keat's *Second Coming* wrong, with "*lurches*" rather than "*slouches* toward Bethlehem." Perhaps it was because I had read Belloc more recently than Keats:

> There is a poem by Hillaire Belloc, I think, which speaks of the donkey carrying the pregnant Mary "lurching toward Bethlehem." What a fascinating word, lurching. It implies that one is stumbling; tired out, determined on only one thing, going home, getting to one's center, no matter how. (*In-Directions* by Avril Maklouf   ...On the labyrinth as devotion = netted)

The description of *hotari hotari* given to me by the poet makes it clear that his image is more like *lurching*, or *tottering* than *slouching*. [1] That gave me the freedom to choose between Keats and my own inclination towards "lurch." In Japanese, *Bethlehem* modifies the sea slug, but it is uncertain whether it does so as an adjective-noun or as a verb, for the *mu* sound on the end makes it seem like the latter in this context. The *bethlehem* in *Their Hour* is supposed to be a verb. On the other hand, I have no excuse for my clear introduction of "the lamb" – obviously, I take my translating license too far! I fear the diamond arrangement of the translations is not quite right. I really should add a fifth. I say this because I made a wonderful discovery when I looked up "Bethlehem" in my O.E.D. (I was hoping to find a longer version, such as "bethelehem" to stretch the sound in the last line of the *Spiritus Mundi* reading but only found a shorter one, *bedlam!*). It is: *Bethlehemite.* This 13th century order of monks wore the five-rayed Star of Bethlehem. *Voila!* Pentaradial! So, it is only natural for the holothurian to replace Keats' horrific beast.

1. If anyone knows how the "slouches" in Keat's poem is Japanesed, please tell me at paraverse.org.

The Run-down Sea Slug

魚 屋 の 昔 や 暗 き 海 鼠 桶 石 川 桂 郎
sakanaya no mukashi ya kuraki namako oke – keirô 1930
#820 (fishshops' old-days: dark seaslug tub/s)

the fish shop
of the olden days, dark
tubs of sea slug

~

dark tubs
of sea slug like
fish shops of old

生 き 残 り 公 設 市 場 海 鼠 売 る 高 沢 良 一
ikinokori kôsetsu ichiba namako uru – takasawa yoshikazu (2001-01)
#821 (surviving public market/s seaslug[obj] sell)

a public market
survives and is selling
sea cucumber

The *Melancholy* and *Cold Sea Slugs* missed some of the dark in *namako*.   These haiku bring out a *run-down* and *out-of-it* aspect we might call the *Marginal Sea Slug*. In the first, the slugs are either outside or half-outside the store (because Japanese store-fronts open *completely,* there is no clear division between inside and out when they are open). There is a bare light-bulb or two, largely wasted for lack of a proper reflective surface. This darkness evokes the darkness once common to the entire store and already in 1930, at odds with the bright and shiny modern world. I have seen one of those last public markets, a vast, dimly lit mall-sized building, with extensive yet booth-like shops crowded under a shared roof.   The poet expresses his affection for such an *endangered space* with his zoomorphism and, for the people of that time, who, he writes, "lived like *namako*."(corresp)

アメヤ 横 丁 海 鼠 の 棲 め る 銀 盥 渡 辺 二 三 雄
ameya yôkocho namako no sumeru gindarai – watanabe fumio (contemp)
(ameya yôkocho (a wholesale district inTokyo), seaslugs living [in] silver-tubs/trays)   #822

modern times

ameya yôkocho
here the sea slugs live
in silver trays

Sounds luxurious, but this is a back-street in a wholesale district, and the silver shorthand for the color of modernity: *aluminum*.   Such a district is cheerful in boom times but more depressing than the darkest slum when the economy is slack.

町 古 り て 沖 の 暗 さ の 海 鼠 噛 む 梶 山 千 鶴 子
machi furite oki no kurasa no namako kamu – kajiyama chizuko (1997)
#823 (town aged, offshore's darkness's seaslug chew)

a rundown town i chew sea slug dark as the offshore sea	my old town chewing sea slug dark as the sea we fish	my town rundown i chew our dark ocean in this sea slug

Before modern times, the sea slug – more because of the difficulty of proper preparation than because of the cost of the ingredient – was generally served as fancy fare for male drinkers in Japan. But, rising wages and imports (mostly from Korea) have turned it into blue-collar nibblies, a sort of Japanese version of pickled pigs-feet (which, by the way, one can find in most Japanese bars). As uptown goes global, the other side of the track has become the place where one can count on finding good old-fashioned Japanese food, such as *namako*. That is why the sub-theme of sea slug in the run-down part of town is a not found in old haiku, though it is common today. This haiku, offers something a bit different than "mouthfeel." Shall we call it *heartfeel*? Here, the *furite* translated as "weathered" for the *Imagist Sea Slug* becomes "run-down," and if the sea slug on the weathered deck concentrated the eye, the run-down town encourages it to look around. This slug is not literally dark. It is the dark dug of the ocean which has supported the town. In America, most people can envision a run-down farming town, a place the dustbowl swallowed up; but few minds hold the image of a poor fishing town. In Japan, this is not the case. Most people would see Kajiyama's haiku vividly.

海 鼠 食 ひ し 男 ま ぎ れ ぬ 街 の 燈 に 川 崎 展 宏

namako kuishi otoko magirenu machi no hi ni – kawasaki nobuhiro (1977)
#824 (seaslug-eating men mix/divert/lose town/quarters' light-in)

eating sea slug
in cheap light where men
lose themselves

I had a hell of a time with this popular poem because in modern America, there is no part of the urban scene that resembles what I felt tempted to translate as the honkytonk district of Japan. In America, there may similar places where men can go if they are of the right skin color or ethnicity, but there is nothing for all of us. [1] Japanese *have* such a common refuge and there is a sort of sweet nostalgia in the scene described, though the hard lives of those who drink there are nothing to romanticize – "lonesome drinking, lost in the lonely din of a town past its prime" as KS put it, in my poor translation. This poem tells us something of sea slugs, too. *Namako* no longer belongs to the nobles or the poets, but to the white-collar slave (clerks in Japan have the longest hours) and the blue-color lumpen. When Bashô wrote of "a man alone / drinking without the moon / and the blossoms" (*tsuki hana mo nakute sake nomu hitori kana*) – which is to say, with no pretensions to poetry – he could have been writing of many of these slug-eaters, unaware that the food they eat signifies their condition.

哀 歓 や 灯 と も し 頃 を 海 鼠 食 ぶ 無 名

#825 *aikan ya hi tomoshi koro o namako tabu* – anon (2002/07/21)
(sorrow/s-joy/s:/! lamp/lights lighting [vague]time seaslug eat)

sadness and joy
when the lights come on
eating sea slugs

Lights coming on suggest outdoor tables found in blocks of restaurants where sweaty men drink after work. So the atmosphere is the same as for the last poem. But, oh, what a fine poem about the way dim outdoor lights effect us!

---

1. *Barbaric America* In Japan, there are no areas too dangerous to walk through for fear of being robbed or worse. How shameful that such areas should be allowed to exist – for the United States does *allow* them to exist and *race* is no excuse – and that there are so many people angry and sick enough to hurt others in a land with the wealth found in North America. While poverty, too, is no excuse for violence, it is hard to reduce hate and prevent crime with GWB jr pushing Reverse-Robinhood-ism. If GWB jr is not a secret Marxist intent upon creating class warfare, he certainly acts like one!

海 鼠 喰 ひ 弁 財 天 の 島 暮 れ る 　 無 名

#826 namako kui benzaiten no shima kureru – anon (2002)
(seaslug eating benzaiten's island darkens[dusks?])

benzaiten's isle
grows dark as we
eat sea slug

Benzaiten is the Goddess of Good Fortune (mostly wealth but also talent).[1] The poet is exploiting the contrast between the dream of wealth and the humble sea slug, or the nitty-gritty grey matter between his or her teeth.

~

Good Old Boy Sea Slugs

独 断 と 偏 見 満 ち る 海 鼠 か な 　 清 水 昶

#827 dokudan to henken michiru namako kana – shimizu akira (2001)
(arbitrary-judgement/dogmatism and prejudice full/overflow seaslug!/?/ó/the)

namako-eaters	**namako-eaters**
packed with	dogmatism
bias and prejudice	and prejudice *love*
sea cucumber	the sea slug

Toward the end of the *Silent Sea Slug* chapter, I broached a topic that might be called "sick silence," i.e., the body-armor of the slug-eater. Somewhere in the recesses of my mind, I vaguely recall the generally *silent type,* who at a certain level of inebriation suddenly spouts off on Yamato *damashi,* or the old-fashioned Japanese soul, a martial and spiritual wisdom(?) no foreigner, they claim, can comprehend. Young Japanese, I suspect, get some of the same treatment, this same dribble as, I would guess, this poet has at one time or another. I cannot say whether my interpretation of the poem is correct, but let me add a piece of information about the poet. He published a book from a major high-brow publisher (Shichôsha) in 2001, entitled *The Solitude of Wagner* (*wagunah no kodoku*).

酒 酌 み て 海 鼠 子 と 仲 の 睦 ま じ き 　 清 水 昶

#828 sake kumite namako to naka no mutsumajiki – shimizu akira (2001)
(*sake* exchanging, seaslug-with together/group/relationship's warm/close)

drinking together
how warm the bonds of
sea slugs and men

1. Benzaiten Island Symbolism Shinobazu Pond, by Western style painter Odano Naotake (1749-80) is described as follows by a well-published art historian specializing in Japan: "Shinobazu Pond, in the middle of which lies an island with a shrine dedicated to Benzaiten, the goddess of good fortune, was a famous Edo landmark. In this view, *however*, the distant shadowy shrine is subordinated to the crisply delineated and brightly colored urn of peonies in the foreground." (my *italics*) The "*however*" shows she is oblivious to the symbolism. The peony was the Flower of Wealth and Good Fortune (further emphasized by the colors red and white). In old painting, as with old haiku, the charm is in the *layers of meaning*. It is not enough to describe the picture itself. One must *read* it. Since the metaphors come from a common bank, I would advise art experts to consult with literary critics. (I do not give the name of the book I criticize because I'd rather be nice than academic.)

I don't know if the sea slugs are really *that* appreciated by the drinkers. But the obvious comradery of the men who sit slowly drinking together – for sea slug chewing takes time – that the poet, who I imagine is on the outside, feels a bit jealous of the dogmatic, prejudiced good ole boys. Or, I misread and this poem has nothing to do with the one before it and only means:

> drinking partners
> me and my sea slug
> grow very close

While one can grow close to what one chews – as a cat may lick what it bites – this seems suspicious.

~

New Year's Eve and Day Sea Slugs

［二回目］闇 の 夜 の 沢 山 に な る 生 海 鼠 哉　祥 禾
[encore#611] *yaminoyo no takusan ni naru namako kana* – shôka (1821)
(dark[pitch-black/moonless]-night/s many/difficult become: sea slug!/?/ô/the/behold)

> dark upon dark
> sea slug is perfect for
> new year's eve

Yami or "pitch-black" refers to the nights when there is no moon, as explained in *Cold Sea Slugs*, where the poem gets two different readings. Since New Year's Eve is *the* representative *yami,* it is possible to make a third reading, as above. If we put this together with Shiki's poem about the sea slug being 1,8000 years old, we might even think of the New Year's Eve as embodied by a sea slug. Still, the reading is a bit forced. Perhaps, the translation should be considered a paraverse by Keigu.
.

歳 の 夜 や 水 は な し た る 海 鼠 哉　里 東
toshinoyo ya mizu hanashitaru namako kana – ritô (18c)
#829 (age/year's night: water leave/separate sea slug tis!/?/ô/a/the)

> new years eve:
> a sea slug
> out of water!

This poem is yet another example of how the *namako* seems to attract ambiguity. It *could* describe sea slugs in a salt-water holding-tub taken out to be hawked, because they make good holiday food as they are alive and can keep without being immediately prepared (women in Japan take a cooking holiday over the New Years holiday, so highly sugared and soy-sauced food was prepared ahead of time and fresh fish would not be sold.) This was, after all, before refrigerators, and even in the winter, there are some days that are too warm to keep dead meat. Or, this could be an imagined secret Christian, a slug gigger on vacation, . . . but I prefer to think it a metaphor. In *Essays in Idleness,* Kenko describes the busy Japanese New Year's Eve – *shiwasu,* a strange word, written with the characters for "teacher/gentleman" and "running" – with millions of people's feet hardly touching the ground as they ran about doing last minute errands. A humorous haiku by Fûkoku (d. 1701): "the year departs / kicked by the feet of / market goers" (*yukutoshi-o kechirakashikeri ichi no hito*). Thinking of this mass hysteria, of ungrounded feet, the poet may be asking, "Are they, am I, are we all sea slugs out of water on this evening?" (Or, are we hamsters turning the wheel of time with our frantic running!)

海 鼠 ま て 出 て ゆ ら め く 師 走 哉　成 美
#830 namako made idete yurameku shiwasu kana – seibi (1779)
(sea slug until/even appear shake/flap/move teacher-run[new year's eve]!/?/ǿ/hoh)

even sea slug
is out flapping about
the big busy!

shiwasu

the year's end:
even the sea slug
is hauling ass!

Here, the *shiwasu,* is specified. I feel tempted to improvise with something that conveys the day to English readers: *The Big Busy.* Seibi probably means at least two things, possibly three. First, even phlegmatic homebodies are out and quivering with excitement. Second, slugs are being vigorously hawked. Third, and most unlikely, he might have observed sea slugs close up and noticed them move.

ナ マ コ た ち 利 己 に み え た り 師 走 哉　敬 愚
namakotachi riko ni mietari shiwasu kana – keigu
(seaslug/s[+plural] smart/wise-as look[etcetera] year-end ǿ /the)   #831

a frentic reflection

them sea slugs
look mighty smart on
new year's eve

海 鼠 こ そ 羨 ま し く て 師 走 哉　敬 愚
namako koso urayamashikute shiwasu kana – keigu
(seaslug/s especially [i/we] envy/[are]enviable year-end!/ǿ/the)   #832

new year's eve
this is when we envy
the sea slug

I would be willing to bet that Keigu is not the first to have written these haiku as trite as they are true.

横 た は り 海 鼠 の 如 き 師 走 雲　高 沢 良 一
yokotawari namako no gotoki shiwasugumo – takasawa yoshikazu (1998)
#833 (side-stretch/lying seaslug-like shiwasu/year's-end[busiest time]-clouds)

the big busy
some clouds look a lot
like sea slugs

shiwasu

the year's end
sea slug clouds float
by busy men

This poem received at the last moment, implies the same thing Keigu wrote, much more subtley. While a clever Chinese poet once put down clouds for having devious shifty-minds, clouds are generally symbolic of guileless letting go, just drifting along … suitable stuff for our sea slug,

海 鼠 舟 大 つ ご も り を た だ よ へ る　八 木 林 之 介
namakobune ôtsugomori o tadayoeru – yagi rinnosuke? (mod)
#834 (seaslug-boat big-monthend[year's end] drifts)

the slug boat
drifts about the entire
end of the year

Since out-of-use slug boats were hauled up on the beach rather than anchored, this means the slug gigger is out working on the last day of the year, which, in the post-Gregorian calendar Japan, means mid-winter, when sea slug is in its prime. There is a *wee* possibility that the poet is punning on drifts=*tadayoeru* → *tada yoeru*=just get drunk (rather than do year's end business).

海 鼠 売 年 立 つ 市 に 押 さ れ け り 檜 南
namakouri toshi tatsu ichi ni osarekeri – hinoki minami (mod)
#835 (seaslug-seller/s year comes market-in pushed/confined[+finality])

slug vendors
held within the market
on the new year

As noted already, fresh fish would not keep, but sea slugs could last out the New Year. Still, the vendor cannot go around to homes late in the evening, and certainly would not be welcome on New Year's Day, so he ends/begins the year restricted to the formal market. Or, that is my guess.

活 き て ゐ る も の 海 鼠 の み 海 鼠 買 ふ 狗 塚 貞 子
ikiteiru mono namako nomi namako kau – inuzuka sadako (mod)
#836 (living/lively seaslug only seaslug/s[obj] buy)

the only thing　　　　　　　　　　　　i buy the only
alive are the sea slugs　　　　　　　lively thing in the shop
i buy a sea slug　　　　　　　　　　a sea cucumber

in the fish shop

i buy only
sea slugs for they alone
are *quick*

The first Chinese character in the poem means "lively" or "active," yet as a verb is "to live." The "lively" in the second reading probably should be "living," but I hate to lose the wit of the original, which plays off liveliness with the sluggish *namako*. The last reading takes advantage of the only English word allowing this. Unfortunately, the "live" meaning of the word quick is virtually dead.

売 れ の こ り 更 に 明 日 待 つ 海 鼠 か な　阿 波 野 青 畝
#837 urenokori sara ni asu matsu namako kana – seiho (1899-1992)
(sold-left[unsold items] again tomorrow waiting seaslug/s!/?/ó)

unsold sea slugs　　　　　　　　　　　　　　　　　unsold, again
once again waiting　　　　　　　　　　　　　　　awaiting a new day
for tomorrow　　　　　　　　　　　　　　　　　　we sea slugs

Did this longevity, then, make them a problem for New Years, a day when one was not supposed to work? The "we" in the second reading reflects the fact that "unsold items" (*urenokori*) may stand for older women on the marriage market, but it probably has nothing to do with the original. The poem might or might not be intended for the tomorrow of tomorrows, The New Year.

日 を 拝 む 腹 に 目 も な き 海 鼠 哉 舎 羅

hi o agamu hara ni me mo naki namako kana – shara (1747-1816)
#838 (sun[obj] revere/worship belly-on/in eye-even-not sea slug!/?/ø/a)

inside the belly
of this sun-worshipper
a blind sea slug

Sun-revering or worshipping [1] is what Japanese do at sunrise on New Year's, provided they succeed in waking up and the weather is cooperative (see IPOOH ny 1: *hinode*). The poet is watching the sun rise with the sea slug eaten on New Year's Eve in his belly. The sea slug, alive, couldn't have enjoyed seeing the sun rise, so it is in some magical way benefiting from the arrangement! *That, at any rate, is how I like to read the poem.* But my Japanese literary expert did not go for this mystical assimilation at all. *"Even if the sea cucumber was in the poet's belly, it would not be whole but all chopped up,"* he snorted. No, he writes, it is a cock-eyed depiction of a sea slug *in nature*, facing the New Year sunrise. To me, a sea slug on the beach or trapped in a tiny tidal pool, is a depressing sight, so I can't imagine *that* (but another Japanese reader, KK seconds it!). If someone happened to spy a sea slug slightly raised up at the moment a ray of sunlight peeked through morning clouds at an angle sufficient to pierce the water and illuminate the happy creature this would make sense. But this is not at all likely. If the *namako* is not in the poet's belly, I think it must be in an artificial habitat.

a tub in my garden

blind sea-slug
do you revere the sun
on your belly?

I think the sea slug/s was in a room near a paper window, or was placed outside in the morning, perhaps deliberately to let it "see" the Sun rise! [2]

海 鼠 く う 松 の 内 な る 闇 夜 か な 萩 原 麦 草

#839 namako kû matsunouchi naru yamiyo kana – bakusô (1935)
(seaslug eat pine/s-within[first week of ny] is dark/moonless night!/ø/a)

eating sea slug
in new year season
moonlessness

1. Revere/Worship/Agamu I feel bad whenever I must translate *agamu*. Yes, it *is* "worship/revere;" but it is not so absolute as the former, nor so strange (we rarely use "revere") as the former. One sea slug poet, Matsumoto Seichi, wrote this haiku in 1940: "a child held-out to pee from the porch *agamu's* the moon" (*yohan no en nyô sasu ko ga tsuki agamu (net)*). Does the child "worship?" "Revere?" Do we have a verb for the occasion?
2. Placed to see the Sun or Moon The poet Kyorai offers to show the first full moon of the year to his house's "mirror-rice-cake" (an edible New Year's ornament) in a poem (*shôgatsu o dashite miseuzo kagamimochi*) famous enough to be parodied by Issa who offers to show a frog his pee waterfall (*shôben no taki o miseuzo naku kaeru*). Further afield, I think of the Japanese prison guard sneaking spy K'tut Tantri out of her cell to see the full moon during World War II (Stupid, stupid Hollywood! Her *Revolt In Paradise* should have become a movie *long ago*!). That is why I imagine Shara may well have helped the sea slug to a view.

When Japan adopted the Gregorian – which is to say Christian – calendar in the Meiji Era, the *Moon* and the *months* divorced and the New Moon ceased to introduce the New Year except by occasional coincidence.   With Bakusô's haiku, the dark of the moon – metaphysically appropriate sea slug time – which traditionally came the night before the New Year, is, instead, smack in the middle of the New Year Holiday week.

墨 に じ む 体 に 海 鼠 を 描 き け り 山 田 み づ え

sumi nijimu karada ni namako o egakikeri – yamada mizue (contemp)
#840 ([black]ink smear/oozing body/ies-on seaslug[obj] paint/draw[+finality])

on a body
oozing ink, i paint
sea slugs

When children, often with their parents or relatives, play battledore on New Years (see IPOOH NY bk3 re special holiday games), misses are recorded by *sumi*, or black ink, marks brushed onto the face. A body oozing with ink would indicate a poor player.   While one might assume the sea slug is a mark of sluggishness attributing to the misses, it may also be a way to make a bad start to the New Year an auspicious one for the player in question.   Take this passage from an official Shimonoseki city (on the coast facing Korea) website explaining *namako mochi,* or sea slug sweet-rice-cake:

> On New Year's Morning, the sea slug sent by the fish-shop with the message "may the sacks [sacks of rice were measures of wealth] pile high!" was placed on the Godshelf [Shinto altar] or Artnook (*tokonoma* [1] →).   The shape of the sea slug resembles a sack, so this is a propitious omen for bags=rice=wealth to come rolling in early in the Spring.   And, it was said that eating this brought a long life.   In the mountains, it became the practice to make elongated ovoid rice-cake in the form of sea slugs for placing on the Godshelf. (www.city.shimonoseki.yamaguchi.jp)

The writer confuses dried slug that was identified with sacks for two reasons given elsewhere and the live sea slug that was the model for the rice-cake in question.   Be that as it may, there is remarkably little information about sea slugs and the New Year on the web, so I am grateful for the effort.

海 鼠 食 ひ し 顔 に て ひ と り 初 わ ら ひ 加 藤 楸 邨

namako kuishi kao nite hitori hatsuwarai – shûson (1905-93)
#841 (sea-slug eating, face-from/on alone/by-self first-smile/laugh)

<table>
<tr><td>eating sea slug
alone, my face cracks
its first smile</td><td>all by myself
first smile on my face
eating sea slug</td></tr>
</table>

new year's alone

eating sea slug
my face cracks a smile:
my first laugh!

<table>
<tr><td>my first smile
of the year as i sit alone
eating sea slug</td><td>eating sea slug
alone: a first-smile
upon his face</td></tr>
</table>

The *hatsu-warai,* or 'first smile' of the New Year,[2] → which is now in Sea-slug season: the winter. I like the action in crack/s (justifiable because *hatsu* ('first') homophonically suggests it), but feel a milder smile (or *grin*) more suitable for a lone eater. The laugh+smile follows KK who *insists* it must be a laugh and provided the proverb: "happiness enters the laughing gate." Since a laugh is not found on, and cannot grammatically come from, a face in English, I had to translate the connotations of *warai* in separate words to comply.

年 の 酒 海 鼠 と な り て 眠 り こ け 高 沢 良 一

toshi no sake namako to narite nemurikoke – takasawa yoshikazu (2000)
#842 ([new]year's *sake*, seaslug-into becoming sleep/conk-out)

new year's wine
i turn into a sea slug
and fall asleep

For Japanese who think of the New Year as a time where lofty images such as Mount Fuji or soaring hawks are desired, this poem would be an unbecoming confession, but for the poets and artists who hold Taoist ideals, this is a perfect representation of an ideal behavior: *gu ni kaeru*, i.e., the return to [original] foolishness represented by the New Year. Usually, the image is one of being reborn as a baby, but why not go back even further to the sea slug, the original sack? Takasawa inspired Keigu to take part of his personal name meaning "good," and combining it to his own "fool," to make three haiku by a "good-fool" (ryôgu):

年の酒客も主も赤海鼠　良愚

toshi no sake kyaku mo aruji mo akanamako – ryôgu
#843 (([new]year's *sake*: guest-too, host-too red-seaslug)

new year's sake
both guest and the host
red sea slugs

About half of the Japanese turn bright red when they drink.[1] They also grow sleepy from the same. (Eating a lot of sea slug implies Takasawa keeps awake when drinking, so I doubt *he* turns red.)

年 酒 の 客 は 神 な る 海 鼠 哉　良 愚

toshizake no kyaku wa kami naru namako kana – ryôgu
#844(year-*sake*'s guest-as-for god is/becomes seaslug!/the/loh/it's)

new year's sake
the guest is god, indeed
hoh, a sea slug!

年 酒 や 客 は 神 な る 赤 海 鼠　良 愚

toshizake ya kyaku wa kami naru akanamako – ryôgu
#845 (year-*sake*: guest-as-for god is/becomes red seaslug)

new year's *sake*
the guest is a god
red sea slug!

→ **1. Artnook, or Tokonoma** The existence of a space (cut-away in the wall) for nothing but the presenting art in the traditional Japanese home is a credit to the culture and something we should copy.
→ **2. First Smile and First This and That** Almost *anything* – from marital duties to airline trips – is game for celebrating as the first ____ of the year. I find it very refreshing for it makes many things we take for granted (although I must confess to having enjoyed neither *firsts* given for example at any time last year!) special and thus, in some sense I shall not try to explain, consecrates it. (IPOOH: ny, vol 4)
1. *Alcohol Intolerance.* Besides turning red and drowsy, some suffer headaches and uncomfortable heat, etc.. When my step-dad, an MD, visited the East, he carried enzyme pills to treat people to a more comfortable drinking experience. I cannot understand why such pills are not big business there.

The Guest – or, in business, *client* – is God, according to a commonly heard Japanese proverb. I am not sure what I want the first haiku to mean. I have no idea if I mean that the sea slug *is* the guest, or the guest who brought the sea slug. In the second version, the implication is that the guest, being a god deserves the very best, a red sea slug, with the redness having the double implication of a newborn ("red-ling" (*akachan*) in Japanese) and an auspicious color, suitable for the New Year.

揚げられて正月物の大金海鼠 高沢良一
agerarete shôgatsumono no ôkinko – takasawa yoshikazu (1998)
#846 (pulled/raised newyear-thing-big-kinko(cucumaria namako))

we pull up
a big gold sea slug
for new years

up it comes
a golden new year
cucumaria

The *kinko,* or Golden Sea Slug, was the star in the days when dried slug kept Japanese mercantilism in the black, or rather in the gold. But it rarely shows its face in today's fresh new world. This haiku, I take it, depicts one of those happy coincidences of life. The poet, visiting the cold-side of Japan in the dead of the winter to enjoy a traditional New Year, got his just reward.

～

Analyzed Sea Slugs

I found this contemporary haiku, partly inspired by Shôha's *Moon Talk Sea Slug*, at the *Gui-Gui* (gulp-gulp) web-site for poems by the extraordinary website host and restaurateur Morris:

玄 海 の 海 月 を 案 ず 海 鼠 哉 森 崎 和 夫
#847 genkai no kurage o anzu namako kana – Morisaki Kazuo (contemp)
(genkai[name of sea]'s jellyfish/s-about←worry/ies/ponder/s seaslug[subj]ó/this)

this sea slug
anxious for jellyfish
in the genkai

Genkai, as already noted, is the Japan/Korean Sea. "Anxious for" is off, but the best I can do. *Anzu* means "to ponder with some anxiety," but English must all out *worry* or simply *ponder*. So, I had to *unverb*. The fact this slug has mixed thoughts about floating is classic Japanese, but I thought to ask the poet what *else* the poem was about. M.K. told me that *he* is the slug and has pretty much stayed put, while the jelly fish is a long-time friend, a Korean, a globe-trotter engaged in risky endeavors. A stay-at-home by nature, M.K. feels some envy for his friend's freedom, but mostly worries at the ups and downs in his uncertain fortunes. But, he continues, "I wrote the poem intuitively, and managed to come up with the above-written analysis [which I loosely translated] only in retrospect."

1. Jellyfish Drifter Long after receiving Morisaki's explanation for his sea slug and jellyfish haiku, I found a poem by Akinobo (d.1718): "the year ends! / drifting with the current: / a jellyfish" (*yukutoshi ya nagare-shidai-no mizu-kurage*). The jellyfish, like the sea slug, does not choose where it goes: though it might move more, it is still in the hands of fate. The wit in this poem comes in the allusion to Bashô's writing about the Year, Month=moon and Days=sun as travelers. Not only is the "moon" character in jellyfish, but the unnecessary "water" (*mizu*) pegged on the "sea-moon" (the *mizu-kurage* as the most common *kurage* doesn't require specifying) – evokes the transience of "water-life" and the way time (our share of it) flows by and vanishes. Lest my readers get the mistaken impression Japanese are only hooked on slugs, let me add that while there are fewer haiku on jellyfish, they tend to be *very* interesting (in a fantastic way) and the jellyfish, today most commonly written "water-mother," has one thing the slug lacks, a song, the seven-stanza *Kurage no Uta* by 金子光晴.

I am fascinated by what MK admits (I write *admits* because if there is a haiku party-line, it says that significance is improper and one does not explain haiku).   It would seem that haiku – some haiku at any rate – are written in a dream-like manner that, for proper appreciation requires something like dream analysis, which includes questioning the dreamer!

海鼠見て牡蠣の羨むことしきり　太田康直
namako mite kaki no uramimu koto shikiri – ôta yasunao (contemp)
#848 (seaslug seeing oyster's envy/evying thing often/keenly)

oysters, how	seeing sea slugs
they envy the life of	the oysters stew in
the sea slugs	their jealousy

With all the talk about not talking about haiku, I was delighted to find this googled poem had not one but two analyses pegged onto it, the first of which was by the author.   Ôta began by juxtaposing his poem with Shôha's classic.   He supposes the virtually stationary slug must have been voicing his envy of the free-floating jellyfish – a common contemporary reading, as we have seen – and adds, gratuitously that Shôha's haiku was clearly on the light side, for the two animals, as we have also seen, belonged to opposite seasons.   "*My* playing, on the other hand," he notes, immodestly, "is *serious*, for both the sea slug and the oyster share a season.   So then, what are the oysters envious of?   They cling fast to the sides of the boulders unlike the carefree slugs who lull about defenseless on top of the roof.   Yet, for all that clinging, they are taken by humans, all the same."   The second essay, by a third-party, read the haiku as a sharp comment on contemporary society.   The carefree sea slug is envied, but our society is no rose garden and "the sea slug as a human, whether he/she/it knows it or not is bound by something: *our sad nature.* Confucius wrote that after 40, men are not confused, but that is only an ideal."   His review(?) ends with appreciation for the thought-provoking contrast of the two creatures. I presume that it was not necessary to point out that the oysters stood for the vast majority of Japanese who cling to their corporations.   *Corporate man as oyster, rather than sheep.*

白 昼 の 海 鼠 に 尋 ね ら れ て お り 五 島 高 資
hakuchû no namako ni tazunerareteori – gotô takashi (contemp)
#849 (white[high]-noon's sea-slug-by visited[honorific-style])

at high-noon
sea slug makes
a visitation

high-noon

a sea slug
with the force of
an epiphany

This haiku stumped me completely.   I was delighted with the word "white-afternoon," which somehow, I had never learned but it seemed an awfully affected way to confess to eating sea slug (i.e. drinking) at mid-day.   It was unlikely the sea-slug meant its vendor, because today, people go to fish-shops.   I wondered if the author, a man, was writing from a woman's perspective or was gay; even my most staid Japanese advisor thought it might be a *bareku,* or dirty ditty).   Having had so good an experience with Morisaki, I thought I'd contact the poet and settle the matter.   I got Gotô's reply less than a day after e-mailing him, prefaced with an apology for a late reply!

Actually, this poem is intuitive and doesn't have that much meaning to it. If I had to say (*shiite-ieba*) it would be [free association coming from?] the historical tale about the sea slug having its mouth lacerated for not replying and my feeling of scorn for our human shallowness/baseness (*asamashisa*) seeing sea slugs on the Taima shore, noting their composure in stark contrast with the glib garrulousness and mannerisms (*kuchi-hatchô-ashi-hatchô*) of humans.

This is *it,* though it seems more an explanation of the poet's feelings than the poem *itself.*   As my advisor (KS), who was "astounded" by this explanation, put it, "the shorter a poem, the harder to make the message intelligible to others."   *Indeed.*   Even *with* the explanation, I am guessing when I write that Gotô means that the sea slug, a superior being[1] the Gods had wronged, visited the poet in a moment of high-noon giddiness, or magic, and made him feel its presence.

∼

Unchewed Sea Slug

雪 と な る 海 鼠 噛 ま ず に 飲 み 下 す　勝之
yuki to naru namako kamazu ni nomikudasu – katsuyuki (1999)
#850 (snow becomes, seaslug chew-not-as drink-down)

snow starts falling
and i drink down sea slug
without chewing

∼

snow falls
i swallow my sea slug
unchewed

What links the snow fall and the poet's behavior? *That, too, will be left unchewed.*   Sometimes a masterpiece, such as this one, do not need to be perfectly understood to be read with pleasure.

∼

Female Sea Slugs

皿 に の る め な ま こ 失 意 の か た ち し て　鈴 木 妙 子
sara ni noru menamako shitsui no katachi shite – suzuki taeko (1978)
#851 (plate-on ride/get female/small-seaslug despair's shape making)

to hell with the keeper of the eddystone light?

a female sea slug
on a plate: the very
picture of despair

1. Sea Slug as a Superior Being Gotô is not the only one to describe *namako* as a deity. A netted essay titled "sea slug thoughts" (*namako-zuisô*, 2001/03/20), begins with a confession of the author's strange "urge to cut-up, chew and swallow this embodiment of passive resistance," deriving from "cowardice" that made him "seek out the weak" although he "can't recall ever having bullied anyone." Then, after noting *namako* purify nature and not even *trying* to flee, resemble the Ainu god that *chooses to offer itself to be eaten,* he concludes that the least he can do to console his god-victim is to express his willingness, even delight to become food for *namako* should he die at sea. (lr)

I was not aware that anyone paid attention to the sex of sea slugs, for I would not think it would matter except for the egg/sperm, which, of course, would taste different. Sometimes Japanese uses *me,* or female (especially as pertains to non-human animals) to mean *small* or *substandard* but, here, with the poet a woman, I think she is talking about the imagined sex of the sea slug which she may identify with. The question is whether the sea slug is shrunken up or falling apart (melting).

電話待つ海鼠のやうな私かな　未知
denwa matsu namako no yô na watashi kana – anon (contemp.)
#852 (telephone wait/ing seaslug-like me!/?/ó/a)

i who am
waiting by the phone
a sea slug

metaphor

me, the girl
a sea slug waiting
for your call

This reminds me of the *Salad Anniversary tanka* (about 20 million books sold) of Tawara Machi. It was found on a *kukai* (haiku meet) website in a section called *kigo chokuyu shibari,* or "bound by seasonal-word metaphor." The *namako* would seem to stand for passivity. The use of the archaic *yau-na* for *youna* (*yôna*) is a nice touch (waiting for a call being old-fashioned?) but not quite haiku. To differentiate it from both the seasonal, or at least natural, haiku and the impersonal black humor of *senryu,* I think such should be called *tanku.*   This next from a poet who has written a number of sea slug poems, is much more impressive:

男より逃げて月夜の海鼠かな　真里子
otoko yori nigete tsukiyo no namako kana – torii mariko (contemp)
#853 (man-from fleeing moon-night's seaslug!/?/ó/a)

fleeing men
a sea slug below
the full moon

once there was a hut

a sea slug
on a moonlit night
away from man

call of the wild

away from men
a sea slug in the light
of the full moon

holothurian woman

slipping man
a sea slug bathes
in moonlight

I believe this is a poem about menstruation. The Sino-japanese word for it translates as "moon-passage." Holothurians tend to let their eggs flow in the light of the full moon. It is not quite like the case with humans, for we let flow when the cycle of fertility ends and the egg/s is/are flushed. I suspect the poet feels cold and lonely and full and squirmy and ugly. But she might, rather, be reveling in her sea slug days, time where she can just lie around (few notice how hard the sea slug works) without a man's attention.

海 鼠 割 く 女 だ て ら に 隠 し 酒 中 山 天 剣

namako saku onnadatera ni kakushizake – nakayama tenken (mod)

#854   (seaslug-split/gut/carve-ing woman-despite/though[tomboy/butch] hidden-*sake*)

cutting slugs	that tom-boy	that butch
just like a man she	splitting sea slugs took	gutting slugs i saw her
sneaks a drink	a nip on the side	sneak a drink

This is the first of these gender-conscious poems written by a male poet. The term *onnadatera ni* is one of reproach, but depending upon the reading, it is not necessarily mean-spirited(the opposite, *otokodatera*=acting like a sissy would be). The first reading is the most likely one: the poet pleasantly amused at a slight change in mannerism on the part of his wife when she tackles sea slug. If so, he may have misread *her*. Maybe she snuck that drink because she needed an infusion of courage. . .

傷 心 の 海 鼠 と 私 愛 し 合 う 美 愚

shôshin no namako to watashi aishiau – bigu

#855 (hurt-heart-seaslug and i love-meet/together)

a heart-broken	slighted sea slugs
sea slug and i loving	slighted women, we should
one another	love one another

haiku neophytes

poor sea slug
poor me, so we love
one another

This poem was made by a Japanese woman Keigu never met who misread a miswritten poem of his. He has no idea what it means, but takes half the credit with the "gu." The first guess suggests she may be with a man in love with another woman not in love with him. The second suggests that even if the perpetrator of the actual unkind cut was a woman, the silence of the sea slug in the face of cultural pressure gives it something in common with her gender. On the other hand, could that sea slug be Keigu? Chances are *all* of my readings are wrong.

～

Objective Sea Slugs

能 登 島 に 即 か ず 離 れ ず 海 鼠 舟 徳 永 春 風

notoshima ni tsukazu hanarezu namakobune – tokunaga shunpû

#856 (noto-island-to touch-not, separate-not seaslug-boat)

neither touching
nor leaving noto island
sea slug boats

A simple description, about as objective as a haiku can get. Noto Peninsula is known for sea slugs, but I am not sure exactly where the island is. It doesn't matter. Because the drop-off is fairly rapid in this part of Japan, the boats would string out in a line parallel to the shore. Objective or not, it is hard not to create an image of this *ring around an island.*   Maybe international installation artist Cristo (sp?) should do something with those boats.

なまこ突く潮の暗き日明るき日　山中一士子

namako tsuku shio? no kuraki hi akaruki hi – yamanaka _____(mod)
#857 (seaslug gig/ging current/ocean's dark days light/bright days)

gigging sea slugs	dark days and
days when the water is dark	bright days in the sea slug
days when it's light	gigging ocean

Though all water is grey at dawn, with the light, it quickly shows its true colors and the day to day difference can be as clear as black and white.   Though the information in the above poem is minimal even for a haiku, I feel it is a fine objective poem by someone who peered into the sea morning after morning.   We might call it the objectivity of time as opposed to that of the snapshot.

海鼠舟潮暗しとて引返す安部三魚

namakobune shio kurashi tote hikkaesu – abe sangyo?sabuo?(mod)
#858 (seaslug-boat current/water dark[murky] saying return/ed)

the sea slugger
turns back saying the sea
is too murky

The sea, then, can be too dark even for that symbol of obscurity the sea slug, or, at least for the men who would take it.   Though the slightly paradoxical contradiction brings thought into the haiku, that does not change the fact that it is a fact.

海鼠突き漏電個所を発見す　和田幸司

namakotsuki rôden kasho o hakken su – wada kôji (contemp)
#859 (seaslug-gigging/gigger leak-electricity one-place discover/s)

i discover
an electrical leak
gigging slug

body electric	*holothurian heaven*
out gigging	slug giggers
sea slug i'm shocked	discover electric
to find a short	hot spots

All too much of Japan's shoreline is developed, so it is not surprising to find some of the electric current mixing with that of the ocean.   Perhaps the poet-diver gigged a cable lying just below the sand.   Or, per the third reading, is it possible that giggers have learned that slugs are attracted by the electricity?   Either way, this is something no one could think up – as opposed to the haiku of Keigu that are *all* thought up – so we know it is a fact.   I cannot help thinking of the monster-electricity connection (eg. Frankenstein) and imagining a *namako* housing a couple D-size batteries, but the original is simply shocking, though the poet does not claim to be shocked as my second reading might suggest.   We might also note that those corrugated conical ceramic things found where electric wires connect to telephone poles are often called *namako.* (So, to steal from a haiku read and lost somewhere, one wouldn't want to touch a *namako* with a wet hand!)

二 つ 程 拾 ひ 海 鼠 の 黒 奴　高 沢 良一
futatsu hodo hiroi namako no kuroi yatsu – takazawa yoshikazu (2003)
#860 (two amount pick up sea slug black guys)

i pick-up
two sea slugs on the beach
both black
∼　∼
i pick up
two sea slugs
black guys

In recent years, with the population of the red and blue *namako* diminishing relative to that of the black, this must be true for many people.   For the young it might not be worth noting, but for someone who knew at first hand a time when that wasn't true, it would be a fact with significance. I do not know if he means the beach or the store, but it doesn't really matter.

潮 水 に 海 鼠 生 か し て 風 鳴 る 日　高 沢 良 一
shiomizu ni namako ikashite kaze naru hi – takasawa yoshikazu (2003)
#861 (salt-water-in seaslug alive-keep wind hums/howls/sings day)

keeping sea slug
alive in brine on a day
the wind howled

I imagined the high lonesome sound of the pines providing a suitable backdrop for the silent slugs, or, hyperlogically, thought that the wind, by stirring up ripples in the tub, supplied the sea slug with oxygen, etc., but the poet informed me that he grew up 5 minutes from the beach and more *namako* were found washed up in stormy weather and that he once kept one alive in sea-water (presumably he brought a bucket to the beach) and brought it home for his father to eat.   So the poem is a memory, objectively depicted.

一 寸 の 水 に 運 ば る 海 鼠 か な　未 知
issun no mizu ni hakobaru namako kana – not given (contemp)
#862 (one-inch-water-in carried seaslug/s!/?/ó/the)

carried home
in one inch of water
the sea slug

This poem, selected by two people at a *kukai* [1] at one of Takasawa's sites does not carry quite so rich a memory, but it does capture a side of sea slugs not haiku'ed by anyone else.   Only a flounder can make do with less water on its final trip.

1. *Kukai* Forgive me if this is not the first time I have introduced the *kukai*.   The usual English translation is "haiku *contest*," but the mood is often one of a *game*. The fact that haiku are judged blind makes it an ideal way for foreigners to enjoy equality (of reaction) often denied to those who do not look Japanese (not from any nefarious prejudice, but for more complex reasons I describe in *Orientalism & Occidentalism.*)   In the ideal *kukai,* the selectors=judges participate themselves.

こき〜 〜と海鼠を洗ふ鰯雲　萩原麦草

#863 k[g]okik[g]oki to namako o arau iwashigumo – bakusô (1935)
(*gokigoki*[hard objects rubbing together, onom.] seaslug wash/ing sardine-clouds)

a buttermilk sky
as i vigorously scrub
sea slugs

scrubadubbing
sea slugs under a wide
a mackerel sky

a mackerel sky
i scrub sea cucumber
until it squeaks

Unless one assumes the sea slug stands for a new born baby (highly unlikely, for only Sôseki and Kingsley have made that connection) or go so far as to imagine these clouds as fish – different fish, but remarkable both languages have so similar a term! – bumping their bellies on sea slugs, this is about as objective as one can come with a haiku. All my 10-volume dictionary offers for *gokogoki* is "the sound made when hard objects are rubbed together." I would add these are hard objects not so hard as to rasp but, rather, making a refreshingly vigorous squeegee-clean sound. I think it goes very well with the sky in question, which is not the standard one for *namako*.

桶に日の射し赤なまこ青なまこ　服部翠生

oke ni hi no sashi akanamako aonamako – hattori suisei (mod)
#864 (tub-into sun shines/beams, red-seaslug, blue-seaslug)

sun illuminates
a tray of red sea slugs and
blue sea slugs

While neither variety is actually anywhere near to their namesake's primary colors, we cannot help viewing them so if ever so briefly in our imagination. Yet this is about as objective a poem as one can make. Unlike the other sea slug color haiku introduced in *The Protean Sea Slug,* it doesn't play upon any metaphorical saw although there is no denying that it serves as a foil to the stereotype, by showing that sea slugs are not all mouse/rat-grey as implied by their name. Seen in bright light, they exhibit difference.

なまこ買ふ人差指で押してみて　鈴木真砂女

namako kau hitosashiyubi de oshitemite – suzuki masajo (1906-)
#865 (seaslug buy/ing, index-finger-with pressing-seeing/checking-trying)

buying sea slugs
first checked out by
my finger tip

touch test

i buy sea slugs
after pressing them with
my index finger

The poet runs an inn and that, more than anything else, means keeping tight reins on the kitchen. This was published in her recent collection, *Miyakodori* (oyster catcher, plover, sea pie), so we imagine an old woman, dressed in a kimono, as befits her business, buying a number of *namako*.   The haiku gives minimal information.   We do not know whether she is feeling for a response, springiness, or a texture. She needs sea slugs that are well, for slug tissue softens as they die and will not have the right mouthfeel.

正 装 の を ん な の つ つ く 赤 海 鼠　鈴 木 仁

seisô no onna no tsutsuku akanamako – suzuki jin (2001)

#866   (proper-dress[kimonoed]' woman's tapping/poking red-seaslug)

the echinoderm and the kimono

a woman
in fine attire poking
a sea slug

I have a sneaking suspicion that this poet either saw the above poem or saw the older woman out shopping.   Her high-class inn would certainly tend to favor the more expensive red sea slug.   But chances are she saw a different woman.   Unlike Suzuki Masajo's minimalist haiku, this one makes it a bit easier for the reader to pick up on the high contrast of ugly *namako* vs. pretty kimono – a picture, which might go well side-by-side with one of a man in a tuxedo holding a banana.

牡 蠣 海 鼠 銭 吊 つ て 笊 ゆ れ や ま ず　石 川 桂 郎

kaki namako zeni tsutte[tsurete?] zaru yureyamazu – keirô (1930)

#867   (oysters seaslugs change(money) hanging basket swing/vibrate-stop/ping-not)

winter sales

sea slugs, oysters
the change basket never
stops vibrating

Presumably, the owner stays close to his change basket – usually dangling from the rafters about shoulder level – and these two items which tend to be placed toward the front of the store.   Change is almost continually being tossed into the baskets because such goods are big items in the dead of winter.   Unless we are to imagine some energy field between the female oysters and the male slugs, this too is a simple depiction.

海 鼠 今 松 葉 し ぐ れ て 桶 の 中　松 瀬 青 々

namako ima matsuba shigurete oke no naka – seisei (1869-1937)

#868 (seaslug now pine needles showering/drizzling, tub's inside)

sea slug now
pine needles fall on you
and your tub

winter daphnae

the sea slug
in its tub showered by
pine needles

If Japanese, like English, called pine leaves "needles," we might imagine an allusion to Buson's *Acupuncture Practice Sea Slug*.   As it is, we only have a still life, though the poem's strange "now" –

the grammatical glue is lacking – indicates it is not yet still. The original is not responsible in any way for my flippant "Daphnae" – for some reason, that painting of her showered with gold coins flashes through my mind whenever I imagine the sea slug showered with pine needles!

~

Classical Avant-garde Sea Slug?

Some Japanese academic institution's August, 2000 music festival (*ensôkai*) – sometimes sites forget to say who they are, so I cannot be more specific on the University – had the strangest list of performances I have ever seen.

> A piano sonata called "*hostile is all around me*" [the title was in English]; "*Yoogamiobjique*" ["Western God Object?"] Op 109; the *Rondon Deiri* (London Daily) *Song*; *Tico-Tico no Fuba* [chico chico-no?]; *Mendelssohn's Wedding March* [arranged by?) Risuto=Horobuitsu [? and Horovitz]; The first piece from Satei's *"The Dried Up Fetus:"* The Sea Slug Fetus. --

I will not give the whole program; let me just say the *Sea Slug Fetus* was merrily sent off with a Baha (Bache) fugue and I still have no idea what the music sounds like, though an internet search did reveal the fact that composer Erik Satie (d. 1915) and his sonata *Embryons Desseches* are very well known to aficionados of avant-garde piano music. [1] A website devoted to his work included an Englishing of an explanation and poem that went with the piece, of which the first Part is indeed about our charge:

Dried Embryos

I. Of the Holothurian

> Ignorant people call it the "sea cucumber". The Holothurian ordinarily climbs on stones or blocks of rock. Like the cat, this sea animal purrs [2], moreover, it spins a dripping thread. The effect of light seems to disturb him. I observed an Holothurian in the Saint-Malo Bay.

> Morning outing / It rains. / The sun is behind the clouds. / Rather cold / Good / Little purr / What a beautiful rock! / This is a good place to live. / Like a nightingale with a toothache.[3] / Evening return / It is raining. / The sun is gone. / Provided that it never comes back. / Rather cold / Good / Mocking little purr / It was a very beautiful rock! / Sticky! / Don't make me laugh, sprig of moss: / you are tickling me. / I haven't any tobacco. / Fortunately I don't smoke. / Grandiose / To your best. [transl. by ?] [I telescoped the parsing to save paper].

Satie's "II. Of the Edriophthalma" concerns "Crustaceans with fixed eyes, that is to say, without stalk and immobile" who are "Very sad by nature" and live "withdrawn from the world, in holes bored out of the cliff." This writing, for better or worse, makes Ponge's object poems seem very traditional by comparison! About "I. Of the Holothurian," Mike Topp in the magazine *Beet* wrote:

> Satie's composition about a sea cucumber is probably one of the most sensitive compositions of a sea cucumber ever written. –

1. *Satie's Music*. A piano player's description: "Satie's music was influenced by the church modes of the dark ages, in a historical sense. Old Gregorian chant stuff his uncle taught him. So the tonal feeling is kind of tweaked. His Music takes unexpected turns. Pleasantly. I call Satie's music timeless. The Music could have been composed tomorrow. Or today or yesterday. It is not bound to any era in History." (Robert Fields Jr. http://www. pianosolos.com/june 4 99 letter in a Satie post)

2. *Purring Holothurians!?* I suspect that the word for a cat's 'purring' in French is tactual rather than acoustic, so that the twitching or the vibration of the slug could be so called without being outlandish.

3. *Like a Nightingale with a tooth-ache?* Satie's way of requesting a musician play *dulce doloroso?*

The Nightmare Sea Slug

なまこ見てまた夢にみてうがいせる　田中久子
namako mite mata yume ni mite ugai seru – tanaka hisako (contemp)
#869 (seaslug seeing/saw, again dream-in seeing/saw, gargling do)

seeing a sea slug
i saw it again in a dream
so i gargled

a persistent namako

i see a slug
and dream of it again
so i gargle

The poet does not speak of a nightmare, but if she goes so far as to gargle to try to rid herself of an image, though she herself did not eat it, we may assume that its presence in her mind is not welcome. This is a remarkable one-of-a-kind haiku!

～

The Imaginary Sea Slug

にぎったとおもへばすべる仏哉　壺中
nigitta to omoeba suberu hotoke kana – kochû (c 1720)
(grasped-if/when thought, slip buddha/corpse/dead-soul!/?/ó/the)

"life is like a sea slug?"

you think
you have grasped it
then, *hotoke!*

Not only does the word *hotoke* mean Buddha, Buddha-statue, corpse, the departed and bliss, but it can be read as a homophonic pun for "Let it/me go!" This poem is found in the late fall collection of a poet whose name translates as "urn-within" (what cremated remains, or sea slug guts might be kept in) and I assume it is either a personal death-poem (it was standard to try to write a last moment send-off [1]) or about an acquaintance – there is such a tradition of lamentation even in haiku, where natural metaphor is usually enlisted (Eg., when Issa's friend dies just after receiving a post as head of a temple, Issa *crazy-versed* that he "opened his mouth for sweet dew and got bird shit." Or, maybe these should be called "crazy-verse" (*kyôku*).) The title of Kochû's poem reflects what someone with *sea-slug-on-the-brain* (such as *Yours Truly*) may find in a poem that is *not* about sea slug.

1. *The Death-Poem* While John Donne moaned "Language thou art too narrow, and too weake / To ease us now; great sorrow cannot speake;" Sorrow certainly could *write* and, when it comes to death poems *for others*, i.e., elegy, the English language is so full of it that it is a wonder that old books of poetry are not eaten by worms instead of silverfish. But, when it comes to poems for one's *own* death, our tradition is sadly lacking. True, there are some touching good-byes, humor and bravado, but most of it is mere juvenilia compared to the mature death-poem tradition of the Sinosphere. By all means, see Yoel Hoffman's *Japanese Death Poems, written by zen monks and haiku poets on the verge of death* (Tuttle: 1986 and I would assume reprinted in paperback by now!).

The Sea Slug as a Known Revelation

Confirming the expectations of Western diplomats, Mr. Shenin told Tass that Mr. Kim is expected to become supreme party chief on October 10th, the anniversary of the party's founding. The North Korean media have also reported that mysterious events – such as the blooming of fruit trees in autumn and fishermen catching *a rare white sea cucumber* – signify that the times are auspicious for Mr. Kim's selection as the country's official leader. Flowers may be blooming, but far too little food is growing . . . (Source: *Voice of America*, September 25, 1997, *italics*=mine)

"Kim Jong Il is indeed the greatest of great men produced by heaven." State media in atheist North Korea singing the praises of Kim Jong Il after *a rare white sea cucumber* was found in Rajin-Sonbong, a sign that "nature is congratulating the Korean people on their great pride . . . of being blessed with great leaders." (—From *Far East Economic Review* – I hope the prejudicial adjective "atheist" was added by the Christian zealot website where I found this! *italics*=mine) [1]

In the United States about a decade ago, native Americans in the Midwest celebrated an albino "snow-bison." [2] That is something most English-speakers find understandable. But excitement over a white sea cucumber? That is something else again. The word *outlandish* comes to mind. But the Koreans are not alone in this. When a 20 cm 300 gram white sea cucumber, "as white as the New Year's sweet-rice cake" (*maru de shôgatsu no kagamimochi*) was found near a fishing town in Nagasaki prefecture in early 2003, the head of the fishing coop declared:

A white snake is believed to be auspicious [albino snakes are traditionally regarded as messengers from the deities of the earth], so a white sea cucumber must also be a good omen. I hope as many of our town-folk as possible can see it at the Sunday morning market [seeing an auspicious omen is supposed to bring good luck]. (*Nagasaki Shinbun* Jan. 9, 2003).

And there are more. [3] These albinos are attributed to mutation. I fear that we will have all too much of this good luck in the future as our growing populations and unseaslug-like lifestyle fills the seabed with radiation and other things that, in excess quantities, pollute and cause genetic flukes.

1. **Kim Jong Il Bashing** *When Kim admitted N. Korea had been kidnapping Japanese, what happened? The USA attacked him rather than praising his confession, thus killing his first attempt at moderation and forcing him to revert to the hard line right wing Americans feel so comfortable with!*
2. *White Bison* For a deeper perspective, see the snow bison story=chapter in Barry Lopez's masterpiece WINTER COUNT, a finely crafted, simultaneously spare but dream-provoking work of fiction (When helping with the Japanese translation, I unsuccessfully tried to convince him to follow the practice of Melville (MOBY DICK) and add some fact between the chapters. Especially considering the fact that fewer Japanese readers than English-speaking readers would recognize the factual underpinnings of the fiction, I wanted newspaper clippings on the albino bison, for the mentioned chapter, some of Buffon's writing on the smallness of everything in America (even the genitals of the natives!), for a chapter that mentioned something Jefferson wrote in defense of the grandeur of American nature, and other such relevant nonfiction information pinned to the tail of each chapter, but Barry thought it would damage the magical atmosphere, so we couldn't do it. I respectfully disagreed, but the author's word is God. Our difference of opinion on this point bears some resemblance with the difference of opinion regarding whether or not it is good to know the circumstances behind a haiku.) I disclose this here, because I love the *fiction-nonfiction-fiction-nonfiction* format of MOBY DICK and want to see it widely adopted!
3. *A Red and White One, Too!* According to a 2002/4/6 story from the Shizuoka edition of *Mytown* (Asahi.com) in mid-February, fishermen found two red and white sea slugs just off Numatsu (?) bay and thinking them *omedetai* (lucky/auspicious/celebratory/delightful) – red and white are the traditional festive colors in Japan – brought them to the nearby Shi Paradaisu (Sea Paradise), where they draw huge crowds. In the Occident, a sea slug would require a likeness of Christ or the Virgin – or a natural tatoo saying "i am cool"? – to attract enough visitors to make the newspaper!

The Sea Slug as an Unknown Revelation

I can never figure out who is sending and who is responding in those internet chains of letters that go on and on.   Rather than confuse names – and not wishing to embarrass any one – I just copied the text of two letters.

> Q   A friend told me about a dream she had ten years ago. Since I have been teaching here the faith I hoped that the dream would have meaning to Baha'is.
> Two angels woke her vigorously from sleep and told her of the urgent need to remember a word. She was told repeatedly how important it was to remember the word but not why. She was not told exactly how to spell the word so her best guess was _namako_.
> She has been trying unsuccessfully to find the meaning for the dream and the word for the last ten years. Does anyone know if this word has any meaning in Persian or Arabic or otherwise any significance to the Baha'i faith?
>
> A   I don't know about religious meaning, but after reading your post I decided it would be interesting to see what I could find by looking around on the net. Here's what I found:
> 1. In Japanese, the word *namako* (spelled like you said) means 'sea cucumber'.
> 2. It's also a style of pottery, and a style of tiling, on walls and such.
> 3. In the Zoroastrian religion, I found the following passage from a book. Not being any kind of Zoroastrian scholar or anything, I have no idea what it means, but the passage is as follows:
> > *"And more like unto the ancient skeptics (vimanako) have become the disciples,*
> > *among whom disagreement and enmity are produced, as is written in the same*
> > *writing (khadu-gun NAMAKO); and, owing t [to these?]] admonishing words, these >become enviousness and malici[ousness?]*
> > *Chapter 88 of the Dadestan-i Denig ('Religious Decisions')*
> > *Translated by E. W. West, from "Sacred Books of the East", volume*
> > *24, Oxford University Press, 1880.*
>
> Perhaps it's part of a book title, or something? I couldn't quite tell.
> Anyway, I hope this helps :).

Imagine if this RISE, YE SEA SLUGS! had been netted by this kind investigator! Or, better yet, could my book be a fabrication of the woman's dreams?

~

The Reciped Sea Slug

海鼠腸をつくるてんがう［癲狂］してみたる　岡崎筍林
konowata o tsukuru tengô shite mitaru – okuzaki junrin (mod)
#870 (seaslug-guts make/ing sport/mania-do try)

old age sport	my horseplay
trying to make good	in old age is making
sea slug guts	sea slug guts

I like the above haiku. It talks about the spirit, or, rather, one of many spirits of food-making. It gives no details. We don't hear that he left the sea slug with no food/sand to eat in clean sea water changed a few times in order for all the sand to leave the gut, which was either coaxed or cut from the slug and that this would be thoroughly washed and . . . I forget the rest. *Sorry.* People expect recipes and I hate writing them.   In Japan, I had enough of a name that a publisher once asked me to write a cooking book. I had to refuse. What editor could accept such skimpy instructions as this (*below*)?

> *If you ever find decent crab and artichoke at the same time, buy them and have a party around a table spread with newspaper. Remember to throw the shells and shreds into two different mountains for it is more colorful that way.*
>
> *To relish cheap ground-turkey – my sister S feels less guilty about eating them because they are they are "the dumbest animal on earth" – mix in plenty of raisins, anise (or celery, if it is not available) and curry to turn a wretched gamey flavor into a delicious exotic one.*
>
> *The same will work for faux crab, but use much more curry and substitute jalapeno peppers for the celery. Barbecued faux crab is not bad, either.*
>
> *Put half-inch thick slices of green avocado into rice while you steam it for a cardamom-like flavor and add some black pepper kernels so the rice will stay fresh if it sits out for a long time.*
>
> *Try Japonica (fat) rice with paper-thin slices of raw jalapeno pepper, good anchovy and raw egg. No other spices are needed, for the anchovy has salt and simplicity is what makes the dish.*
>
> *To make tilapia taste like food rather than cardboard, cook the fillets in lots of oil as well as whatever spices you wish to.*

I fear I have not prepared sea cucumber and dislike *translating* recipes as much as I dislike writing them, so the reader who wants this food for thought will have to visit my website (where you will find machine translations of netted recipes as soon as I find them).   Here, I will only provide a useful piece of information for cleaning a sea cucumber googled from a Japanese site:

> *use a spoon to scoop out the oral and aboral orifices*

Like you would for the hair around the luscious heart of an artichoke, I guess.   For some reason, I think that is one detail other recipes will lack!

And, I will leave you with one recipe that didn't need translation, which I dare say will *astound* my Japanese readers (though the name of the inventor(?) is two-thirds Japanese). "Recipe courtesy of Daryle Ryo Nagata" broadcast in the Great Canadian Food Show's "*Sea Goo*" episode, hosted by Carlo Rota, and found at www.foodtv.ca/recipes/browse:

BC Candied Sea Cucumber *

1/2 cup sugar
1/4 cup water
8 piece fresh sea cucumber, diced 1" by 1"
2 piece fresh ginger, sliced

Directions:

1. Add all ingredients to a small pot and cook on medium heat for approximately 20 minutes or until mixture has a syrup consistency.
2. Pull out sea cucumber and reserve on parchment paper until needed for garnish on cobbler.
..

* I would love to sample this if it keeps! Anyone flying from BC to Miami (check my website to be certain I am still here,) is welcome to bring this candy cuke *wampum* to trade for paraverse press books.

The Global Sea Slug

I *love* fishing for unexpected poems, but *hate* running down information. Gathering facts about sea slug import, export, consumption, and so forth is not my forte. So, let me simply distill the essence of one paper, *Beche-de-Mer Bulletin* editor Chantal Conand's "Overview of sea cucumber fisheries over the last decade – What possibilities for a durable management?" from *Echinoderms 2000* (Barker ed. published Zeitlinger).

Fisheries are mostly based on about thirty of the thousand plus known species. Since the mid-1980's demand has increased, fisheries have extended their grounds, mariculture has developed rapidly as has the exchange of information, largely through the auspices of the Secretariat of the Pacific Community and its internationally oriented *Beche-de-Mer Bulletin.* Yet research and information, especially with respect to the population biology of species newly exploited, lags that of other living marine resources.

1996 figures combining the Beche-de-Mer (often called trepang) product and *Stichopus japonicus* catches shows Japan with 7,226 tons/year catch, Indonesia with 2,800, Philippines 2,123, Korea 1,979, Madagascar 1,800, Tanzania 1,644, Canada 1288, Fiji 850. Since most of the Japanese and Korean catch is not dried, their figures should probably be reduced by 80%-90% for parity. (That would put the Japanese figures somewhere between Tanzania and Canada.)

Some countries show great ups and downs reflecting overexploitation. Compare 4,000+ for the Philippines in 1990 with 1,497 in 1994, or the Maldives with 33 in 1987, 553 in 1988 and 66 in 1994, with the steady figures for the Japanese and Koreans (who have centuries of experience).

The beche-de-mer market (as opposed to catch) is volume-wise, 90% (value-wise 70%) controlled by Hong Kong traders, with the remainder almost entirely in the hands of Singapore and Taiwan. A third of the tonnage of the Taiwan market comes from temperate countries such as Canada and the USA, but that overstates their contribution because the product is fresh or frozen, whereas the larger Indonesian portion is dried.

Professor Conand sums up with a warning that "although sea cucumbers have been exploited for a thousand years, the resource is fragile" and lists 4 indicators of overexploitation, catching more species, further trips to get them, diminishment of average size and increased competition among collectors resulting in lowered quality. (And this, I would add, was written before the medicinal sea cucumber really began to take off in the West.) All we can do is increase our surveillance, beef up management and support sea cucumber mariculture, she concludes.

~

The Unsolved Sea Slugs

1

塵 を だ に す ゑ じ と ぞ 思 ふ な ま こ か な 山 夕

#871 chiri o dani sueji to zo omou namako kana – sanyû (1679)
(dust even place[=suck?]-not [emphasis] [i]think seaslug!/?/ô/the/hoh)

sorry, it's all mine!

a sand-sucking
sea slug for sure, but
i won't share it!

on being asked to share a dish of namako

i'm sorry,
not my immaculate
sea slug!

This is one of the oldest sea slug haiku I have found and one of the strangest. The first 12 syllabets are straight from waka #167 in the KOKINWAKASHÛ (905), where the poet refuses a neighbor's request for a *tokonatsunohana,* or Chinese (Indian, Rainbow) pink – *Dianthus Chinensis* vae. *semperflorens* – by saying he loved it so much he wouldn't even let a speck of dust/dirt get on it (much less give it away). I think the haiku is a similar refusal to share a sea slug and there is an allusive pun on dust-sucking to the effect that "I don't think my precious sea slug could possibly eat sand!" The poem has a slightly risqué air because the *waka* included the line "sleep with my girl" as a "pillow-phrase" for the flower because the *toko* in its name, meaning perennial, may be punned as "bed." And, who would want dirt in their bed?

I think that I *may* have solved this haiku but, so far, have found no one who will venture so much as a guess on its meaning. Until I get expert confirmation, it will remain officially unsolved.

2
罪 な く も 浮 て あ そ ぶ や 夏 生 海 鼠　露 川

tsuminaku mo uite asobu ya natsunamako – rosen (1660-1743)
#872 (sinless-even float/rise-up-play/deigns: summer-sea-slug)

floating up
without sin to play
summer sea slugs

This is the only "summer" sea slug in olde haiku, so I cannot let it go, though I am not sure what it means. The straight Japanese scholar's reading is "looking at the sea slug bobbing (floating *pukapuka*) in the sea, i am envious (i.e. admire) of its innocence and detachment (from this world)." I wonder if there is anything else in that sinlessness. Is the sea slug sinless for not tempting people to commit the sin of killing and eating it because of its being out of season? (Thirty years ago in Texas, a child wrote something like this: *"Lake Austin has saved the lives of many people by their not trying to swim across it."*). I also wonder if the one doing the floating is the sea slug or the poet:

real floating
is play without sin
summer sea slugs

Floating is usually associated with extramarital sex, gambling and other sinful activities. We may imagine someone in a boat seeing sea slugs (assuming the poet is well North and sea slugs might be seen at this time) or someone performing their purifying ablutions in a river stark naked *as* sea slugs, or perhaps actually floating on their backs:

summer sea slug
my part bobs in total
innocence

3
い か さ ま に 世 は 動 き を り 海 鼠 喰 ふ 石 原 八 束

ikasama ni yo wa ugokiori namako kufu – ishihara yatsuka (mod)
(swindling/fakery-in/by world-as-for, moves/moving-is[polite] seaslug eat/ing)   #873

i eat my slug
shenanigans
are what run the world

Do you recall the *Shirikuchi* haiku that drove me crazy, the one about a world where the oral and aboral ends were at odds?   This may well be a modern version of the same.   If the final verb was "chew" rather than "eat" in Ishihara's poem, I think it would be clearer: the old-fashioned, inner-directed poet chews his sea slug while reflecting on the world which has always been a shallow confidence game.

let the hustlers
run the world, i think while
chewing my slug

I could have plopped the haiku into *Chewy Sea Slugs.* But it is not "chew;" it is "eat." In that case, the opposition becomes more philosophical. Yet, the significance is not expressed in the original, so I can not be sure if the following readings apply.

bar-stool thoughts	*prescription*	*advice for the young*
the world's run	in this world	all this quackery
by hucksters, thank god	of wheelers and dealers:	out and about: slow down
for the sea slug	*eat sea slug*	and eat sea slug

And, finally, there is the matter of that polite *~ori* after "move." It would seem to indicate that he feels some affection for the corrupt world even as he sticks to his sea slugs. . .   Perhaps, as OM writes, Japanese readers do not demand to know the exact sense of the poem.   But this translator *does.*

4
信［誤字？］託を聞きて海鼠の動かざり　高尾育樹
shintaku o kikite namako no ugokazari – takao ikuki (contemp)

#874   (trust-bank[sic. probably a *medium/oracle*][obj] hearing seaslug moves-not)

the sea slug
hears the oracle and
does not move
~
the medium
speaks and the sea slug
isn't moved

Is this an attempt to get some reaction from a comatose person called a *sea slug* rather than a *vegetable*?   Or, did the poet think a sea slug might make a good Oiji (sp?) Board or something and put one down in front of some fortune-teller? The first character in the *shintaku* is written so as to mean a trust bank rather than a medium. I think it a typo. I read another haiku that is not specifically about an oracle, but suggests that the sea slug itself is one.   For lack of a better place for it, here:

をらぬ人想へば海鼠うごきけり　野本京
oranu hito omoeba namako ugokikeri – nomoto kyô (contemp)
#875 (is-not person think-if/when, seaslug move/ing[+definite])

a sea slug moved	when i thought
the moment i thought of	of someone not here
someone dead	the slug moved

Occidentals and Japanese alike are liable to think of butterflies, moths or fireflies as *souls*. But what about the larva-like sea slug? There is a good chance this is about Nomoto Kyô's dead husband. But it could be about an absent lover. I do not know. Neither this, nor the previous poem are unsolved in the sense that we cannot read them. But both, to my mind, require more background information to fully appreciate.

5

蜑老いぬ根つき海鼠を突きながら　島村元

ama oinu ne tsuki namako o tsukinagara – shimamura gen (1973)
#876 (*ama* ages root/bottom sticking, seaslug sticking-while)

the *ama* ages
sticking to the bottom
sticking sea slugs

The *ama,* as we have seen, is a woman who collects things diving. "Root-sticking" (*netsuki*) is slang for swimming close to the sea floor and the second *tsuki,* "sticking," (as, for once is true in English, too!) also means sticking with something (to the end). OM also called to mind an expression *sei mo kon mo tsuki-hateru*, where the same "root" is pronounced *kon* rather than *ne*. It means to "totally exhaust oneself," and suggests the *ama* has given her everything to her work. But I cannot help wondering if a lighter note – perhaps a contrast with the Urashima Taro, who did not age at all so long as he stayed in the Dragon King's Palace on the bottom of the sea – is also intended. Hence, I do not feel I have solved the poem yet.

6

と し を へ て 何 の 用 に か 生 海 鼠 桶　小 春

toshi o hete nan no yô ni ka namako oke – sôshun (1666-1740)
#877 (year/s passing/gaining, what use-for? seaslug tub)

a new year
what can we do with
the slug tub?

years pass
what can i do with
the slug tub?

The first reading assumes the year is singular. Under the lunar calendar, the New Year, which is to say the arrival of Spring, brought an end to the slug-eating season. But there is also a chance we are talking about years passing in which case the tub is a *memento mori* for a dead slug-loving husband or parent: the second reading. Either way, I love the image of that empty sea slug tub. Half of that appeal comes from the metaphorical aptness of the lack following the thing. The other half is personal. I had a well-worn oval tub a bit over a foot-long with edges about 8" high, with the slats bound together with two bands of copper. I liked to fancy it was used in a bath-house, on the woman's side . . . but, now, I think it might have held sea slugs. OM believes this is a poem about "an old (and probably retired) gigger." That may well be the answer, for poems about the retired are common.

7

二 三 盃 浪 を は づ れ る 海 鼠 哉　祇 丞

#878 *nisan bai nami o hazureru namako kana* – gijô (1741)
(two, three loads/cups waves/sea-water removed sea slug!/?/ô/the)

a few drinks
and i am a sea slug
out of water

If the verb *hazureru* were only past tense and I could be certain that it is the slug that has been removed/separated, this reading would be definite and the poem would begin the chapter on *Drinking Sea Slugs*.   But, as it is, there are equally plausible readings:

<table>
<tr><td>a tub or two
removed from the sea:
sea cucumber</td><td>a few scoops
of sea water removed
for sea slugs</td></tr>
</table>

The reading on the left makes these *Measured Sea Slugs,* where the sea slug is not counted individually or by weight, but by tub.   The reading on the right follows the fact that, unlike most other fish, the sea slug is kept in sea water while awaiting customers, who may themselves keep their purchase in brine.

8

料理てはひかりやはらかく金海鼠哉　江名口季堅

ryôri de wa hikari yawarakaku kinko kana – ___kiken?(1674)
#879 (cuisine/cooking-as-for, light gently gold-seaslug/s!/?/ó/the)

as a cuisine
soft and gentle light:
gold sea slug

This puzzling old haiku probably plays upon one name for the gold sea slug: "light (*hikari*, as in 'brightness')+offering."   Here is my guess at its *real* meaning:

light-offering

to my palate
it shines rather less
gold sea slug

That is to say, the poet judges this star of the export trade – and tribute item to Japanese nobility – this expensive dried *Cucumaria* sea slug that had to be rehydrated to eat, did not make as good a dish as the cheaper fresh *Apostichopus japonicus* sea slugs he was more familiar with.   Or is it, more simply, a comparison of the sea slug's fame as an export versus its true value as food?

<table>
<tr><td>gold sea slugs
shine far more as money
than cuisine</td><td>dull to ingest
but brilliant to export
gold sea slugs</td></tr>
</table>

9

花 に あ ら ば 海 鼠 に 歌 も あ る べ き に　長 翠

#880 hana ni araba namako ni uta mo arubeki ni – chôsui (d.1813)
(blossoms-in were[/there]-if, seaslug/s-for songs[waka]-too are-should-be-but)

<table>
<tr><td>were they floral
there would be songs for
sea slugs, too</td><td>were they here
for the blossoms, sea slugs
would be sung</td></tr>
</table>

KS writes "if only this sea slug were a flower, even if it were not very pretty, it would be sung (in *waka* and *tanka*) and cherished (as sea-life, it is not made into song [*uta*, or classical poetry such as waka and tanka]), but only becomes fodder for *haikai*." For my part, making sea slugs blossoms only works if we can assume Chôsui *saw*, or saw an illustration of, varieties of slug other than the one Japanese commonly ate *actually flowering* (with tentacles extended, eating) at night. Since this is dubious, I came up with the second reading. The only problem is that we must find a classic poem where an unlyrical animal is sung because it is visible during blossom viewing, as is the case for Bashô's catfish soup with the cherry petals, often cited as the start of his espousal of *karumi*, which is to say a light touch, in *haikai*.

10
なまこ食べ体いちまい裏返す　田辺香代子
namako tabe karada ichimai uragaesu – tanabe kayoko (1997)
#881 (seaslug eat/ate body one[body], outside-change-about[inside-out])

eating sea slug
the whole body turns
inside out

I once ate "old sea mouse," which is to say *sea-squirt*, and did, from both sides of my body simultaneously; but I haven't heard of *namako* having so dire an effect on anyone, so I think the poet either means that the focus on chewing and swallowing and, perhaps, digestion, brings the generally ignored alimentary tract into the open, or that her whole body turns radically inward – making her all back and no front – a sort of melancholy island.

11
包丁を海鼠の上に置きて行く　高嶋文清
hôchô o namako no ue ni okite yuku – takashima ____(contemp)
#882 (knife[obj] seaslug-on-top-of placed/placing goes/leaves)

leaving a knife
on top of the sea slug
i go to town

My guess is that this haiku concerns a frozen sea slug, or a pack of frozen sea slug. But I have not heard of such in Japan and am not confident of my image.

having placed
a knife upon the sea slug
she goes out

Because this was found among haiku, we dare not give it a *Corridor of the Senses* type of interpretation, but I cannot help playing with it:

parting message

she places
a knife on a sea slug
and leaves

This is one of those haiku where I would like to ask the poet about the real or imagined circumstances. Unfortunately, the only hit for his name comes with the puzzling haiku.

The Exploding Sea Slug

海 鼠 突 き 万 が 一 爆 発 し ち ゃ う   敬 愚
namako tsuki mangaichi bakuhatsu shichau – keigu
(seaslug gig/ging ten-thousand-to-one explode-does[+finality])

#883

odds

gigging a slug
a million to one chance
it will blow up

I imagine the peg-arm of an old mine could look like a sea slug, though it would not seem likely. Perhaps this would be more realistic:

即 死 哉 電 気 鰻 ヲ 海 鼠 哉   敬 愚
sokushi kana denkiunagi o namako kana – keigu
(instant-death!/?/ŏ electric eel[obj] seaslug !/?/ŏ/it's/hoh)

#884

gigger gets a gig

instant death
an electric eel taken
for a sea slug

But, realistic [1] or not, this is not half so interesting as *exploding* sea slugs, though the only exploding creatures to kill men are the gas-filled innards of beached whales that can explode with the force of truck tires (or so I recall reading).

爆 弾 と 考 え て み な あ の 海 鼠   敬 愚
bakudan to kangaetemina ano namako – keigu
#885 (bomb-as think-see[imperitive]! that seaslug)

think of it
as plastic explosive
that sea slug

あ の 海 鼠 火 薬 詰 ん で お る か も 知 れ ぬ 敬 愚
ano namako kayaku tsundeoru ka mo shirenu – keigu
#886 (that seaslug dynamite stuffed-is even know-not)

you never know

that sea slug
it could be tamped with
plastic explosives

心 よ り 海 鼠 の 浜 ヲ 地 雷 原   敬 愚
kokoro yori namako no hama o chiraigen – keigu
#887 (heart/mind-from seaslug-beach-as mine-field)

self-defense

imagine
sea slug beach
as a minefield

スヌーピが鰐ならおいら海鼠機雷だ　敬愚

sunuhpi ga wani nara oira namako kirai da – keigu

#888 (snoopy alligator if, i seaslug mine-creature)

don't tread on me!

(pace charlie brown)

snoopy a gator?
then i'll be a land mine!
sez sea cucumber

This would have stopped those Galapagos pepineros dead in their tracks! Unfortunately for the sea slug, the reality is usually the other way around. Surely, this has happened:

爆 竹 を 食 わ せ て 投 げ ぬ 海 鼠 哉　敬愚

#889 bakuchiku o kuwasete nagenu namako kana – keigu

(explode-bamboo[fire-cracker etc] feed [stuff in mouth] throw seaslug/s!/ø)

grenade

chucking sea slugs
stuffed with cherry bombs
boys at play

As a boy in the 1960's, Keigu confesses to having sent a fish swimming off into a lake with a cherry bomb. He also considered the possibility of sea slugs exploding from fresh water, but it took the explosive haiku of Matsuki Hide (discovered together with "The Waiting Sea Slug," below) to inspire the above series.

～

The Waiting Sea Slug

レミングをひたすらに待つ海鼠かな　マツキ・ヒデ

#899 remingu o hitasura ni matsu namako kana – matsuki hide (contemp)

(lemmings[obj] earnestly/intently/continuously waits/waiting sea slug/s behold/'tis!/?/ø/the)

those sea slugs
waiting, waiting for
the lemmings

I recall reading an article about sea slugs (and, perhaps, other echinoderms) on the floor of the artic sea as thick as bison once were on the plains of North America. There are two reasons why they can

---

1. ***Explosive Haiku*** Two of Matsuki Hide's explosive haiku: "winter carp / sometime one will surely / blow up!" or, "winter carp / they will all explode / before long" (*kankoi no izure bakuhatsu suru darau* (tskc)). I have no idea whether this means they may *literally* explode from the cold, or *figuratively* in a Spring frenzy. Either way, the haiku is dynamite. In respect to the anniversary (deathday) of Kyoshi, he writes – again in two translations – "let's blow up! / terrorists one and all for / kyoshi day!" or, "kyoshi day: / i'll be a terrorist / exploding words!" (*bakuhatsu seyo kyoshi no ki no terorisuto* (tskc)).   While I admire Kyoshi's haiku and the work he did to create the modern haiku tradition, I find his poetry, on the whole, a bit too staid for my puerile taste, and cannot help chuckling at the spirit of this outrageous haiku.

exist in such abundance up where we might assume life would be sparse: First, thanks to the cold, melting ice or whatever, the artic waters are actually rich in nutrient: plentiful plankton (hence, lots of whales).   And, second, because cold water means low metabolism and living slowly, it allows more life to coexist within a given space.   No doubt, Matsuki knows that the proverbial lemmings[1] → are but a small fraction of the mountain of organic matter trickling down to the end-user on the bottom of the sea.   And, he knows that sea slugs "wait" not only for the annual lemmings to plunge but for them to sink (or get eaten by creatures eaten by lower swimming creatures), a process that takes time, years of it.

> the lemmings
> sea slug calmly
> awaits them

The adverb *hitasura* is a favorite of modern *tanka* and *haiku* poets, for it is intense yet beautiful.   It makes the waiting pure; but "*purely* waiting" would only mean "*just* waiting" in English, so I used "*calmly*" instead.   By combining this elegant word, usually used to describe human effort, with sea slugs, the poet may be poking fun at the precious all-too feminine world of contemporary haiku, where this adverb is overused for pretty subjects, and suggesting a possible allegory: to wit, *a do-little guy waiting out the rat-race*.   Yes, our sluggish rat of the sea is, in a fundamental way, wiser than the rats of the land.

～

The Wondrous Sea Slug

不思議とふことの一身海鼠かな　萩月

fushigi tou koto no isshin namako kana – hagizuki (2002)

#891
(wonder/ous/mysterious called thing's one-body/life seaslug!/?/ó/the)

an exemplar
of this thing called wonder
the sea slug

slime or sublime?

the sea slug
a body that makes
you wonder

interrogative animal

the namako
its entire being
a question

nomination

wonder
thy name is
sea slug

namako teleology

sea slugs
have but one end
wonder

the esoteric animal

sea cucumber
everything about it
says "mystery"

fushigichi

do you know
the second wisdom?
namako is it

The *fushigichi* I put in the last translation=reading is the second of the Five Wisdoms belonging to the Buddha (Amitâbha Tathâgata). This Wisdom is the "wisdom whose best part is beyond mental comprehension." Needless to say, it is a perfect fit for the *namako* we have come to know.

<table>
<tr><td>

clapping with no hands

sea slug
its whole life
a *kôan*

</td><td>

c'est moi

and what is
this thing called wonder
asks sea slug

</td></tr>
</table>

......

sea cucumber
struck speechless by
its own wonder

I thought the *tou* of the original meant *tou,* or "ask," but the poet told me it was an archaic ellipsis of *to iu,* or "[as] called." But I left the translations made before the poet set me straight. The "second wisdom" is the second of wisdoms possessed by the Buddha. It cannot be *shigi*'ed, which is to say put into clear thought and a *koan* a question not answerable my ordinary logic. The last translation – which isn't really a translation – is my idea for a new just-so story challenging that in *Records of Ancient Things (Kojiki).* I dare say Hagizuki will be surprised to see so many readings of his simple poem summing up the essence of *namako* to himself and many other Japanese.

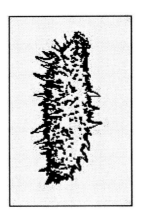

I forget where this was netted, but it is even spikier than the typical namako. Looking at it, you can appreciate the idea of the *daikon* (large radish) grater for the Dragon King's Palace encountered near the start of *Sundry Sea Slugs.*

1. *Proverbial Lemmings* I remember reading a fine tome by an Englishman about the supposed population explosions and suicidal behavior of lemmings. In a word, the myth was shown to be a myth. But I would hate to give up the proverbial lemming, for it is as useful a metaphor for the human population explosion that still continues as the dinosaur that went extinct from over-specialization in the form of gigantism is for criticizing the fuel-guzzling SUV, representative of our irresponsible civilization best described as a proverbial head-in-the-ground ostrich for the way "we" continue to live as if we didn't know we are destroying our world is not myopic but insane.

<u>**appendum**</u>
The Haiku Poet as Sea Slug, or Shikô's
sea cucumber maxim

After trying my best to find, select, understand, translate and explain *namako* haiku, I realized I had left out *the* premiere *haibun,* or haikai poet's essay on the subject. It is by one of Bashô's ten disciples, Shikô (1664-1731) and, written in 1727, comes little more than a decade after the first substantial prose introduction found so far appeared in Terashima Ryôan's *Wakansansaizue* (1712~) , a hundred-part (vol?) encyclopedia covering things of heaven, earth and people in Japan and China. Shikôs *Namako no Shin*, meaning either *"Sea Cucumber Maxim"* or *"Maxim For Sea Cucumbers,"* is much more difficult to follow than Terashima's natural history, despite the latter being written in Chinese characters (as English scholars once used Latin), because understanding not only depends on some knowledge of nature and history, but of between-the-line (or, *within-the-word*) details that must be sleuthed from a millennium of Japanese literature and several millennium of Chinese thought. So, rather than trying to squeeze or parse this *haibun* into the main text, I held back to present it here, in one piece, after we have gained some of the knowledge needed to grasp what we can of it.

> Some creatures protect their bodies with scales and plates, while others adorn themselves with feathers or hair, but no matter how they flourish, all are eventually overcome or decay. People, on their part, must scrimp with food and dress when young for fear of [not being prepared for] old age. Then, *there is the sea slug*. Completely defenseless, it roams the wide sea, apparently not seeking physical pleasure, just wandering about drunk on spring blossoms and high on the fall moon [=showing no concern whatsoever for making a living]. With man, those who retreat in the country are called Mountain-Hermits and those who retreat in the streets are called Town-Hermits, so shouldn't we, then, call the incomparable hermit-sage, the sea slug "Master Sea-Hermit" [*kai-in-sensei*]? [1] Indeed, our *haikai* already treat the sea slug like the hermit to beat all hermits – *"The sea slug / hides out though it has / the whole sea!"* (*daikai ni futoshi mo kakusu namako kana* – kyôryoku (1655-1715) 大海にふ としもかくすなまこ哉　許六) – but the Sea Hermit is known as many things. In the Northeast,[2] where the it is found in abundance offshore the treasure mountain where golden flowers [3] bloom, it bears the honorary title Gold Sea Slug; and . . [4] hails from Shimayama on the Noto Peninsula. In the capital, as skewer-slug (*kushiko*)

#892 (上)   (下) #893

1. Hermit types In the original, I added the phrase about *retreating in the country* because *mountains* in the Sinosphere mean the wilderness, the country, nature as opposed to civilization. "Mountain" could not, however, be ditched for, say, "wilderness" here, for it is *also* antonymic to the *Sea*. The word "hermit" is also far from adequate, for it ought to imply what might be called "a sage."
2. North-East   The North-East=Tohoku region combines the fishing economy of, say, Maine, and the cultural image of, say, the Ozarks. Should we call them *sea-billies?* The original uses a phrase identified with Tohoku, *michinoku,* an "out-of-the-way" place or, *the boondocks*.   This not only suggests Basho's *Oku no Hosomichi* trip, which is associated with ascetism – fleas, lice and horse-piss by his barn bed – but takes us to the oldest sea slug haiku to surface to date * (found by CZ): "you might say / the seabillies have something: / gold sea slugs!" (*michinoku ni ari to iunaru kinko kana   –*

fûrinken (1667) みちのくに有といふなる金 海鼠哉 風鈴軒). I was tempted to say "them sea-billies are rich!" for the second line, but the humor of the poem lies in the contrast between the existence of this valuable item for trade and the impoverished region, famous for having *nothing*, or at least nothing for the nobility who from time to time were ordered to go there. (* **Note**: the sea slug is listed as an 11th month *haikai* theme in a 1656 book, *Sewazukushi*, in a 1664 book, *Hanahigusa*, likewise, and as an early winter theme in an undated possibly earlier book *Hatsugakushô* if it is indeed edited by Tokugen (1558-1647).   There should be older poems out there. よろしく誰か！)
3. Golden Flowers This is an allusion to a Manyoshu poem. Indeed, there is an allusion every dozen or so words and, in translation, picking up on more than a small part of them would kill the *haibun*.
4. And . . Here, there's an allusion to *salt* my Japanese advisors can't comprehend. よろしく誰か！

and girder-slug (*ketako*), the Sea Hermit has made a name for itself to rival that of sea bream and sea bass. Availing itself of Chinese boats [1] it crossed the sea where it very smartly took the title of Sea Ginseng (*kaijin*) and, today, as a tonic, [2] has come to be valued as highly as its namesake. Basking in this medicinal reputation, here, it is served up finely sliced in a golden brocade-handled dish, dressed with warm *sake* and *wasabi*; and faced with a strand [3] of *konowata* (sea-slug guts). Facing this, even Ekiga [Chinese master chef of a hundred flavors] would be affected like a man overcome by musk. Knowing nothing about Shinno, the God of Medicine, [4] the Sea Hermit came to be sold for in three or five *sen* units for use as a fortifier for the liver [seat of wellness that may be sapped by sexual indulgence], like mountain potato (*yama-imo: Dioscorea japonica*), until eventually, it came to be the rage of the sensualists, so that even King Keiô [identified with a chapter of Mencius advising gentleman to remove themselves from the kitchen] couldn't stay out of the kitchen, and the likes of Lord Scent and Temple Smell [two rather lascivious characters in the TALE OF GENJI] just couldn't get enough of the delicate taste of pickled slug (*suko*) and cured slug (*iriko*). So, even if you hardly resemble the consummate sensualist, parting the dewy grass as he leaves his lover's house through the scent of plum blossoms in the misty light of the waning moon, [5] should you lubriciously wander [*numeri-aruki*] about sleeping with straw [a material thought antithetical to sea slugs and suggestive of the pallets belonging to cheap prostitutes], you will ruin your aimless self [*yukuei-naki mi*]. As someone once put it, "a straw bag [bribes/corruption] can topple a nation." Sensuality is a different bag, but for a sea slug, any straw can spell disaster, so let my squib wake you up, let it serve as a maxim for sea slugs! (wkbs)

This would seem to be an admonishment for popular poets lest they forget their *namako*-like beginnings and fail to set a good example for the nation. But it may have been meant for everyone. Since the poem quoted is by Kyôroku (1655-1715), he must be credited with the idea of the sea slug as a hermit-sage, unless an earlier reference can be found. Shikô does not tell where his information about sea slugs came from. The *namako* (*torago*) section of *Wakansansaizue* does not include much on lifestyle. Descriptions in/by(?) *Fukuyama Chinryô* (福山陳良 unfortunately, undated), [6] about live sea slugs (海参) in the East Sea mention they "lie low on the sea floor" and at certain times of the year took to "hugging rocks" in the depths or staying "holed up in the mud." As for the paradoxically opposite behavior of wandering, Terashima and others use the term *yûko*, literally "play-go," which has connotations of traveling without destination, something associated with sages and poets.

1. Chinese Boats and Japanese *Karabune* (Chinese boats) has an elegant ring our funny word "junk" belies! The best indication of how uppity the Sea Hermit had become was the fact that the major *iriko* wholesalers – a governmental monopoly – got to fly sails showing they were on Imperial business, so that when they came into a harbor lesser boats – meaning all other boats – had to heave to, lower their sails, and do all the other things a boat does to genuflect! (Netted on a site about an *iriko* trader who was apparently a well-known haiku poet. 海参問屋の 18 世紀俳人 (岩城司鱸))
2. Tonic. Sex was thought to exhaust the liver and cause wasting away (*jinbyô*), so tonics were (and still are) taken. "Tonics" is not quite the right word, for it implies instantly working medicine, such as "pep-pills" and "aphrodisiacs."
3. Strand of Guts   "Boar's mouth" in the original means a shriveled up bamboo sprout, not "strand." It was used because the name of the famous cook,

Ekiga includes "tusk" and because there are names for the sea slug including bamboo shoot (泥笋、土笋、塗笋、上塗笋、蒜塗笋). There is more word play in the *haibun* that I have chosen to overlook.
4. Shinno Passage The grammar beats me. Could it mean the Sea Hermit knows things the God doesn't?
5. Waning Moon No moon in the essay, but it was in the *Tsurezuregusa* passage alluded to. It was an *ariake*, or "have-light," i.e., a moon remaining at dawn. That means the *waning moon*. Because the plum blooms at the end of winter – around the traditional New Year – it and the *namako* can meet.
6. Fukuyama Chinryô I found it in Ôshima Hiroshi's Sea Cucumber and Sea Urchin (*namako to uni*= ntu). It could come from a different volume – products by geographic area? – of *Wakansanzue* then the one I have with the *namako/torago*. The passage speaks of 海参, the Chinese word for either *namako* or *iriko* (dried cucumaria), and mentions them floating up to the surface(!?) in Spring.誰か丶?

The fuzz is not in your eyes. I blew this picture up from a thumbnail-sized copy of a picture in the above-noted Terashima's *Wakansansaizue,* published in 1712. What intrigues me is the similarity between this picture and the one found in Kaempfer's *History of Japan* a decade earlier (below). Both show three *namako,* a smattering of sea grass, similar current marks, mountain-like boulders in the left foreground and smaller sharp-edged rock/s in the distance. Both are probably reproductions from an older original. Kaempfer's is nearly an exact reproduction of a 訓蒙図画 pictured in Arakawa's *Namako Dokuhon* (ndh) with no further attribution. I would *guess* it was published with the 本草項目(1596), for it is one of the earliest Japanese sources using the word "earth-meat" (the Chinese characters above *Namako* in Kaempfer's picture) and included plentiful illustrations. The Terashima picture is not so exact and enlarges the proportions of the sea cucumber. Theoretically, it is possible the similarity comes from Chinese laws of composition 誰か。海鼠図絵図画の小暦を、作くらせて頂けませんか？ but . . .

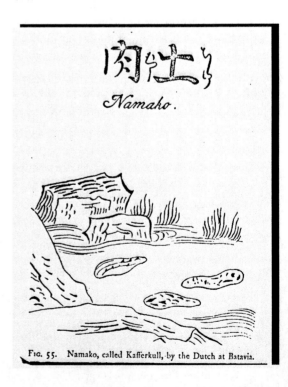

Fig. 55.   Namako, called Kafferkull, by the Dutch at Batavia.

The Serendipitous Sea Slug

Days before I gave a talk at the Key Biscayne Public Library on that sea slug who told "sad stories" to the jellyfish, and only seconds after I told someone about it while walking together on the beach, we came across a jellyfish, not just any jellyfish, mind you, but a *Moon* Jellyfish!

Then, months later, right as I was thinking of a *Postscript*, wouldn't you know, I came across the first sea cucumber I have seen in years! He or she – I haven't gotten around to sexing them yet and probably never will – lay on the sand a foot or two from the ocean right off the new Marjory Stoneman Douglas Biscayne Nature Center. [1]   The countless holothurians I saw and played with growing up by the beach on Key Biscayne in the 1950's were brownish, paint-it-green-and-it-would-pass-for-a-cucumber, textbook sea cucumbers.   This one seemed a cross between a foot-long 1" x 4" plank and buttermilk vomit.   I asked a jogger who happened to be going by whether he saw many of these, but he did not even reply.   He spit out something about how "nasty" it looked, and never glanced back.

I remembered then, that "the gay beach" was in the direction he ran, and that the father of English science, Francis Bacon, married but evidently gay, hated frogs for being slimy, while Yukio Mishima, also married and gay, hated even unclean *sounds*,[2] and I wondered to myself what would be the reaction had the sea cucumber been cast ashore on *that* beach, or if I had already heard it.

Well, the sea cucumber, if he really was a sea cucumber, was indeed an ugly sight, and I would have bet ten-to-one he was dead as a doornail, but the excitement of his being coincidental with writing this book (only a one month task,[3] because I have haiku on many subjects gathered over five years of unpaid work) gave me the courage to touch him and see what happened.

He moved! Reflexive action, I told myself, the sea cucumber might be dead, anyway. I gently placed him into the now calm water and rubbed the sand off his back. It took a little while, for the sand had begun drying and when he shrunk at my touch, the sand particles wedged in his folds. By the time I had him cleaned up, he was the shape of a small loaf of home-made bread. He was thickest in the middle, only half of his original length and reminded me of the back of one of those massive necks with folds that I had seen sitting in front of me at a football game decades earlier. He relaxed and I had to hold him with two hands again.   By this time, my nephew had come close and joined me in marveling at the plastic properties of this creature, who so resembled the new, stretchable toy frogs and gecko he had just got in his stocking the day before.

Merry Christmas, sea cucumber! Together, we walked him out into the sea grass. I hope he is still out there, and lives to be 1,8000 years old.

Notes for the Postscript

1. *Marjory Stoneman Douglas and the Biscayne Nature Center*

Douglas (1890-1998) was best known for her RIVER OF GRASS, a fine book on the Everglades predating Rachel Carson and later nature writers. In her nineties, she led the successful fight against the Everglades airport and in her second pre-teen (?) was still working on a biography of the world's most prolific and all-too-little-known nature writer, W.H.Hudson, when she died. This grand dame of Florida and my mother, author of a fine book on Key Biscayne, were close friends.'

2. *Bacon and Mishima's Fixation*

Bacon's disgust at frogs was unfortunate, for he was very fond of ponds. Mishima thought the onamotopoetic and mimetic words most Japanese are delighted with sullied the ears and insisted upon using what he considered higher and cleaner language. I hope the reader will forgive me for revealing my thoughts, hardly pc! I really have no idea whether this type of thing is related to homosexuality or not, and even if it was, it would not lessen my admiration for what may be the most creative – no, *alive!* – part of American culture.

3. *One Month Task?!*

Not quite! Thanks to the assistance (especially the additional information and haiku found by KS and CZ) and the demands (to add sources/citations to mollify – I could never satisfy – the academic) of others, and my own addiction to googling out strange information, and so forth, the book tripled in size while the time I have spent on it, increased by the square of that! At last check, it is 139,160 words, 44,913 minutes ("editing time") and 755 revisions-long. I am not joking, I just checked the Statistics in the Properties in the File in my MS-WORD. This translates into about 3 wds/min (which explains why secretaries make so much more money than I do) and proves (it is as good as a time clock!) that I have put in about 19 work-weeks by the 40 hour standard. Continued editing of difficult things left to last promise to reduce my productivity yet further before this is printed to about 2wds/min. That is about one inch of progress per minute and that, the reader will be delighted to know, makes me more sluggish than the Japanese sea cucumber, who zip by me going 3, 4, or even 5 inches per minute!

Oh My Gosh!

Now the book is 226,273 words long (and I have lost track of my time because "Properties" started counting all over again when the doc. was resaved and renamed either for a freeze or to put in the Japanese yet keep a separate version.) – well over *a million* characters! *What happened is* that because I could not afford XP or a high-end Mac when I started, the original Japanese had to be left out, and when I searched for it on the internet to save looking for the poems scattered through messy notes, books and, in some cases lost, and, then, typing it in (MS WORD is not good with some of the more difficult characters and I am not fast at typing in any language), I found a *handful of other* sea slug haiku for every *one* of the haiku I was looking for. That is to say, for every ten minutes or so I saved myself, I lost an hour or more in placing, annotating and translating the new ones! It got to the point where I realized that I might as well get *all* the good contemporary haiku as well as the old ones and, if that was not enough, Japanese who learned of my endeavor through this effort, kindly sent me their *namako* poems and even made some specially for me . . . . . I will admit that no plan *was* my plan of writing, but if I had known things would go this far, I think I would have not included any haiku newer than the 19th century!

ロビン・ギル氏海鼠枕に沈みけり　振り子

> *sinking for good*　　　　　　　#894
> *into his sea slug pillow*
> *mr robin gill*

Furiko's poem was posted in a "People Names 1000 Kukai" at a Namu-hosted site on July 8, 2003. I just found it now (Sept. 7) and must squeeze it in. Am I morbid to recall the *Moby Dick* recounting of the man who drowned in a whale's brain?

4. *The Strange Sea Cucumber.*

I dare not ask a specialist what type of sea cucumber he was, for it might turn out that he was not a sea cucumber, but a sea slug proper or, worse, a sea worm; and then what would I do for this *Postscript?*

See what happens when authors edit their own books!

Readers with *Specialized Knowledge or Anecdotes of Interest* are invited to help improve the Second Edition. **Please Visit www.Paraverse.org and Put Your 2-Bits into the Glossing!**

Key
<u>to</u>
Romanization and English Glossing

i
romanizing

Like most present day English speakers of Japanese, I try to transcribe Japanese into Roman letters in the manner most likely to allow people not familiar with the language to correctly pronounce it. Some people, mostly Japanese, *insist* on writing "ti" and "tu," rather than "chi" and "tsu," because the syllabet in question is part of the *ta, ti/chi, tu/tsu, te, to* row of syllabets. While appreciating the logic of this scheme, and admitting the fact that we do not change letters to ensure correct pronunciation in the case of Spanish, where the "j" is still "j" though pronounced as an "h," following logic is not advised because far fewer English-speakers know how to pronounce Japanese than, say, Spanish.

So saying, if the reader can only remember to pronounce *vowels* in the same manner as in any romance language – this happy coincidence among exotic tongues astounds me – Japanese will prove remarkably easy. For the reader who cannot easily do this, I suggest he or she learn to pronounce one proper name: *Buenos Aires,* for it contains all five of the vowel sounds. So, we need not write *nahmahkoh* to show the pronunciation to the reader but simply *namako,* which is exactly how Japanese "Romanize" the word.

The only real difficulty with Japanese vowels is that they are of *two lengths*. Discriminating between short and long "o" and "u" sounds is vital for recognizing many Japanese words. By convention, the extended vowel sound has been Romanized with a tiny line over the vowel – the same one English grammar uses to indicate a "hard" vowel – but computer hardware and software make this difficult to write. Luckily, the "^" sign remains on the keyboard and may, with little trouble, be used. So, *that* is what you see. At any rate, mastering the short and long vowel is as hard for English speakers (individual English vowels do not stretch out except in song) as "l" and "r" are for the Japanese. It is symptomatic of our Orientalism that we know and kid them for their inability in this respect, while most of us are completely ignorant of our larger hearing/pronunciation problem!

Consonants are also easy, except that the "f" followed by "u" should sound halfway to "h," and the "g" followed by "a" should be strongly nasalized. The double consonant indicates a slight pause before the consonant (or, rather, syllabet beginning with a consonant sound) where the speaker builds up what seems to be some sort of psychological tension before bursting out with the consonant. Thus, when we write "Nippon" – the most aggressive (or, energetic, at any rate) way to say "Japan," – written with the same two Chinese characters (sun+origin), yet read *Nihon, Nipon* or *Nippon* – it is meant to be pronounced "Ni [pause] Pon!" with that "p" sound coming out with a plosive pop. I'd prefer to use an apostrophe, but the convention is too well settled to buck. "N" is the only consonant that can officially end a word in Japanese. That is to say, it is the only syllabet without a vowel sound Some, however, argue that the way the sound is swallowed, it isn't really a consonant. *As you like.*

If unRomanized Japanese seems shorter than Romanized, it is because it is. Each consonant+vowel comprising two Roman=English (Japanese sometimes use the equal sign in their writing and I copy them, here) letters can be written with a single Japanese phonetic letter. As a result, Japanese will say that *"uni"* (sea urchin) – *u+ni* – pronounced backwards is *"niu"* (meaningless) rather than *"inu"* (dog).

ii
glossing

As a form of translation alone, verbatim Englishing is *not* recommended. While apparently "accurate," it is incomprehensible and crude to the point of insulting the original language. Retaining the order of the post-positions by pegging our pre-positions on the back of the words, where they were in the original makes for particularly dismal reading for all but patient anagram-lovers. However*, in conjunction with translations and explanations* which attempt to convey the intent of the original, such word-for-word ugliness is invaluable for showing the reader who cannot read the original just how much liberty has been taken by the translator in his re-creation and how much was left behind. Note, I have heavily relied upon the following signs:

!/?/Ø/behold/loh/'tis This (or something like it) strange compound standing for the expression "*kana*" is by no means the most common sign used in the glosses, but it is bound to be the most confusing, so let us start with it. Dictionaries usually define "*kana*" as "how ~ !" "what ~ !" or "alas ~ !" though a classicist will remind us that it has a touch of iffyness, a "?" quality, as well. In haiku, I feel that it is rarely felt to be particularly emphatic or quizzical because it is so common as to have become a convention, a way to say, *this is a haiku.* It gives a Japanese-style train of modification, such as described in the *Foreword*, a poetic presence it otherwise might lack, as well as serving to fill out a poem where the poet prefers not to add anything more specific. In other words, it may mean *nothing.* When it means something, it most commonly might be thought of as a way of indicating the subjecthood(?) of the word before it, as "the" does to the word after it in English, or, further, making what it modifies the equivalent of a *marked case* (When we write "*I* think it is ~" the "I" is marked case).   But, what is interesting is that one can never tell exactly what it means and that is why my gloss offers so many alternatives and why I often must do multiple translations.   Pre-twentieth century poems tend to use this *kana* much more than modern ones, partly because it is now thought to be manneristic (which, I guess, it is) and a waste of space better filled, and partly because modern poems, being less likely to have layers of allusion, need to fill that space to obtain a sufficient load of information.   The reader who compares my *FLY-KU!* (2004) with this book will notice the percent of poems with *kana* are far lower. That is because *namako*, with three syllabets becomes five syllabets with the addition of *kana*, while *hae* (fly) with two and *hae-uchi* (fly-swatter/ing), with four, are respectively too short and too long to use it!

:/! This combination usually means "*ya.*" Semantically similar to *kana,* and occasionally written with the same Chinese character, it usually concludes the first 5 syllabets rather than the last 5, so that it serves to cut off what comes before it from what comes after – though this can also create an equivalence – as a colon does (it is called a *kireji,* or "cutting letter" – so is *kana,* but I feel that is wrong if the poem does not continue and if it does continue it is not a haiku but a *tanka,* excluding the very rare poem that uses a *kana* within it). I gloss this "*ya*" as "!" or ":" or both (and, occasionally add a "the" or a "?") but often don't write *any* mark down in the translation where the change of line in English serves to separate the train of thought well enough.

/   A slash indicates alternative or ambiguous possibilities, found in the original but not translatable, in a single word. In most cases, this concerns *number*, for the singular/plural is indicated by neither noun nor verb in Japanese, whereas English usually must choose one or the other (For economy's sake, when the number is obvious, I do not show this grammatical ambiguity). The slash sign is also useful to let the reader see possibly relevant connotations present in the original, not usually found in a single translated word.

=   An equal sound indicates puns, something so common in Japanese poetry, that Japan has been called a "punning culture" as opposed to a "rhyming culture," such as found in China. Most of the puns are homophonic, where the use of phonetic syllabets allow more than one possible word (that would be written with different Chinese characters) to be imagined or where the primary meaning, given by the Chinese character, phonetically suggests a different word.   Not a few homophones also act as a pivot-word, where a word means one thing when first seen in the context of what has already been read, but changes meaning when further reading suggests its homophone.   Japanese has so many homophones that some of these puns may not be intended by the poet.   I suppose it is a sly thing to do, but by indicating the *possibilities*, I let you share with me some of the responsibility of guessing.

: The colon is used a lot despite not being found in Japanese – Japanese has more grammar that is phonetic than English, which relies heavily on tone in speech and must make up signs to indicate and/or compensate for it in writing – to show a break in the original that may or may not use a so-called *kireji*, or, cutting syllabet (e.g., *ya* below).

" ",   Quote marks indicate quotelike remarks, even though no marks are in the original. Japanese traditionally marked very few of their quotes, both because colloquial and written style differ more than in English (so it is obvious what is speech and what is not) and because of *spoken* markers such as 'tte or *tote,* or just *to,* which have no equivalent in English ("he said," "she said" and so forth seems *very* boring in comparison).

"?"   Likewise, spoken interrogatives, most notably the *"ka"* sound at the end of a sentence in Japanese require these written signs in English.   I do not always supply the "?" but leave it to you.

"!" The exclamatory ending *zo* and *yo* have nothing remotely similar in English, so the "!" mark is necessary in the gloss, though I sometimes make them "hey!" and use other words in the translation.

, Comma are not found in Japanese haiku, even though they are printed in one line.   The original may suggest a slight pause by the grammar, or just leave it up to the reader to figure out.

~[+conclusive] [+completion]   This sort of sign (I may have used different words at times) means ~*kiri* a suffix pegged on a verb to give an air of conclusiveness, or, to use a currently popular word, *closure* to the action.   On rare occasions, the English phrase "for good" works, on others, which happen to be haiku amendable to a vulgar translation, I can use the hillbilly "done," as in "done gone" or "done ate."   Often, the only thing to do is find the strongest English possible: eg. "gone" or "ate up" instead of "left" or "ate."

~even/too/also   These words are overused to indicate *"mo",* but, as you may notice from my translations, its real meaning is often much more difficult to grasp, for it often alludes to something not written in the poem which contains the key to the riddle I call olde haiku.   I have never found this *mo,* which is, on the face of it, an ordinary adverb, called a haiku expression, but I feel it is.

~as-for,   This pegged on the back of a word is ugliness itself, but serves to gloss "~*wa*", an article-like postposition indicating a subject that is about to be modified/discussed.

"( )" A parenthesis explains something. Because original haikus have no parenthesis, it is always mine.

"[ ]" A bracket serves to add something implicit but not explicit in the original. But I sometimes use it for other purposes.

The above examples by no means cover all the strange things I may have done, nor do they cover all of Japanese grammar that does not translate into English. I try to note problems as I go on a case-by-case basis. I have never read a book giving as much information as I do, and must admit to being very curious as to whether this is because no one wants it or because it is too much trouble to the author.

How much of this sort of information should I provide in future books? I would greatly appreciate feedback from readers about what you think is and is not helpful!

菊池真一、高沢良一、西原天気、小貫昌子を始めに、多くの方々の御助言に狂いなし。有難う。

acknowledgement
thank you!

海 鼠 の 句 大 い に う け て 羽 振 り よ き　高 沢 良 一
#895 namako no ku ôi ni ukete haburi yoki – takasawa yoshikazu (2002)
(seaslug [hai]ku greatly/enthusiastically received, feather-form-good[popular/dashing])

highly praised
for my sea slug poem i cut
a dashing figure

To literary scholar Kikuchi Shinichi of Konan Woman's College for finding hundreds of *namako* haiku and *tanka* I would have missed (as well as additional historical material) and fielding an equal number of questions about haiku meanings and name pronunciations=spellings with super-human patience and speed (If you read Japanese, visit his enormous e-text web-site: （菊池真一研究室）)

To web-host, editor and the world's most prolific composer of *namako* haiku (something I only discovered when he sent me about 60(!) of his *namako* haiku a week before the final deadline!), Takazawa (Takasawa) Yoshikazu, whose tremendous (700,000 haiku) free and searchable [1] e-databank of old and modern haiku allowed me to find dozens of poems I otherwise would have missed;

To *holothurian* expert and evolutionary biologist Alexander M. Kerr of James Cook University, for answering scores of questions, correcting equally numerous mistakes and introducing anecdote both relevant and entertaining on matters scientific;

To old friend Starfield (Hoshino Takashi, aka Charlie Zhang: if you read Japanese, enjoy his Chinese nursery rhyme resources web-site (google his *aka* and "nursery rhyme")), for helping with the *namako*-mole connection, finding the oldest batch of *namako* haiku and helping me interpret many of them, and for being a good sport about Keigu's Hokkaido haiku.

To Saibara Tenki, host of Ukimidô haiku pub(?) for help with improving Keigu's haiku and understanding many others I had problems with, as well as helping me get help from more members of Ukimidô who gave me important moral support in the home-stretch (and, AQ, special thanks for the dozen or two keepers!);

To the world's best translator,[2] Ohnuki Masako, who made time to read (sorry, KC, some must have come from time supposed to be spent on translating your book) a late draft and found scores of problems missed by the author and other readers. I am grateful, too, for her occasional comments ("musings") that help spice up my dull prose.

To Liza Dalby, David G. Lanoue, and Gary Warner for reading an early draft and providing enough praise to keep me from giving up, constructive criticism and more, as noted in the text (Please visit David's extensive Issa Site and Gary's comfortable Haiku World, and read Liza's enthralling meta-novel *TALE OF MURASAKI* (about the woman who wrote the world's oldest novel *and* an indirect reading of that novel) her account of being an apprentice geisha, or anything she writes.

To broad-minded biologist Ellen Thomas of Wesleyan for a third pair of eyes to add to Alexander's and mine, right when I needed them to finish (rather than deep-six) my unorthodox nesting/taxonomy.

To Lewis Cook of CUNY and Columbia, who reading a mid-period draft gave me my first support for "muchness" in a world intent upon shortening books, caught some errors obvious to his exacting classically trained eye and convinced me to give sources and the original Japanese to ensure that scholars have no excuse not to read *RISE* (I only pray he gains tenure *quickly*, so he will have time to read rather than write: I wished he could have read the entire draft, for I have met no one to match his

Japanese ability in the English-speaking world and want it reflected in the second edition!);

To Michael Watson, whose non-discriminatory – no university affiliations required – PMJS (Pre-modern Japan Studies) site allowed me to become acquainted with Lewis, Liza and other luminaries I would probably not have met otherwise;

To mathematician Tanaka Kuro, a prolific reader and reviewer (google "kurokuro" to find his reviews in English) who gave me many good leads and saved me from two or three major mistranslations and, come to think about it, it was his review that convinced me to buy Tsurumi Yoshiyuki's *Namako no Manako,* so I am doubly in his debt.

To echinoderm and connective tissue expert, best-selling author of basic biology (time and size,etc.), and NHK (Japanese public television) host, Motokawa Tatsuo of Tokyo Institute of Technology for answering some rather dumb questions on my part (early on), sending me his poem revealing the sea cucumber defense mechanism, and, later on, responding to my somewhat improved questions (We might have corresponded more had my damn XP + Outlook only allowed proper setting of types of plaintext (Hey, BG, not everyone uses html!). Our last letters had to be transferred via Tenki!);

To Mike Reich, Centre of Geosciences, U. of Gottinger, Germany for generosity re. the ossicle photo.

To holothurian experts Igor Dolmatov in Vladivostok, Sven Uthicke in Australia, Chantal Conand in France and Yanagisawa Toyoshige in Japan for generous responses to my questions;

To Maruyama Haruhiko and Yaba Katsuyoshi, the top two Issa experts in Japan, for giving me their interpretation of Issa's sea slug haiku (If you read Japanese, any books by these prolific writers and editors who are among Japan's leading experts on old haiku are worth acquiring);

To America's top haiku popularizer and international saijiki researcher/translator William J. Higginson for assistance with the haiku about sea slugs that don't seem Japanese;

To poet laureate Robert Hass for responding on the same;

To the Kyoshi Memorial Museum (kyoshi kinen bungakukan) for prompt help on several occasions;

To the world's top Swedish-Japanese translator and diver Jan Fornell for alerting me early to the sensitive nature of the name problem (sea cucumber vs sea slug);

To translators and friends Suzuki Tôyô, Moriyama Naomi who have helped me with some name pronunciations and ordering books;

To chef, restaurateur and tasteful web-host Morisaki Kazuo, *aka* Morris, for thoroughly explaining his *namako* poems to me;

To all poets kind enough to have answered my questions, or whose names I may have misspelled or, worse, failed to locate, and/or whose poems I have used without permission (this book is so long and haiku so short that I feel it is OK, but I wish I could find a way to thank you all personally!);

To editor and antiquarian Tsurugaya Shinichi for speeding my fall into haiku by introducing some good books;

To designer Charles King for introducing me to Lightningsource, the printer that allows me to give you this big book at a decent cost and for advising me to do more in MsWord before pdf'ing;

To R.H. Blyth and Hokuseido press for their example and Others living or dead I failed to squeeze in.

To my Mother, whose financial support allowed her penniless middle-aged son to finish this book (If you like my book and have an interest in American history, you may show your gratitude by buying *hers*: *KEY BISCAYNE – a History of Miami's Tropical Island and the Cape Florida Lighthouse (Pineapple Press: 1996).*)

I do not yet know if this book will gain me the praise that Takasawa's poem (*which* haiku, I do not know, but *that* is very namako) brought him; but, if it does, it is thanks to all of you! On my part, I have done my best, so please forgive me if I have screwed up anything you set me straight on. *r.d. gill*

notes to the acknowledgment

1. *Takasawa's Site*   Unfortunately, the huge site now needs a password. Apparently, there were some copyright issues. While I have had six books published, my position on copyrights in Japan *or* the USA is that only truly malicious uses of someone's material, or the unapproved reprinting and sale of whole chapters or books is worth complaining about. Ridiculous rules about the number of pages to be copied at the library only serve to penalize the researcher not wealthy enough to buy a huge library. I, for one, could not have done the research needed to write the books I have written under the strict conditions now operating and I shudder for future writers if this overzealous guarding of intellectual property continues! Authorities, listen up! Authors worth their salt don't need to be guarded.

2. *Best Translator in the World*
Masako (Onuki, or Ohnuki) must have translated dozens of top science books, including Richard Feynman's *Surely You Are Joking, Mr. Feynman* (and other books by and on him), James Gleick's *Chaos* and E. O. Wilson's *Biodiversity,* Ed Regis' *Who Got Einstein's Office,* etc.. Almost every one you can think of, she has put into Japanese. A couple of her translations were published by a publisher I worked for and of the scores of books I have checked, her translations both had fewer significant errors and better flow – this requires one to really comprehend the meaning of the original and do serious reconstruction of sentences and occasionally paragraphs because of the huge difference in syntax – than those by any other translator. Yet, googling her name in English brings a truly paltry number of hits and most are about a book she translated into English (Seiya Uyeda's *New View of Earth*). When you consider that in most cases it is far harder to translate a book between exotic tongues than to write the original, is it fair that excellence goes unrewarded? One would think that the Library of Congress or the National Academy of Science or someone out there would be keeping track of services rendered for English language books and doling out awards. Or, if the government doesn't know what's what, how about a McArthur Genius award? You guys, whoever you are, might not realize this, but it takes every bit as much creative genius to do a good job of translating between Japanese and English as it does to write one's "own" work. (Masako is a very humble soul who would never blow her own horn (she has no homepage boasting of all the books she's translated) and will be horrified to read the above, but I am fed up with the lack of recognition given to translators in the English language world.)

或る国立研究所*fie! fie!*三回登録申込拒否

To a certain national institute. *Thanks for nothing!* If only Japan's largest data bank of classic literature had allowed me the access they allow to any university student (though he or she care not a wit for literature and cannot even read the Chinese characters for *namako*) I would have found more haiku on my subject and saved my time, and that of others whom I was forced to ask to check things for me (but it is never the same as researching oneself (岩波古典大系をみたかったなぁ)). I tried three times to gain permission to use this data bank my taxes (I worked and paid taxes in Japan for 20 years) helped pay for and was summarily denied access. It is ludicrous for the Japanese government to claim concern for the image of Japanese culture around the world, while allowing such a closed-door policy to persist. The Japanese bureaucracy has much to learn from Kikuchi, Takasawa and Watson.

To Microsoft. Sure there are some good things to be said for XP and MS-Word. But there are bad things, too. If I were a lawyer I would sue you. When I bought XP I assumed you would make sure to have OCR capability for Asian languages if you were Asian-enabled. *Nope.* This has cost me months of work. I guess I should not expect a broad vocabulary ready to use with the Japanese, for it only follows the lead of your paltry dictionary in English. Since it is only normal for multilingual people to Romanize (express in the English alphabet) a foreign language sometimes, your spell-check *must* have a way to either supplement the dictionary with Romanized foreign language word-sets (which you should allow for literary English as well) or, at the very least, allow the spell-check to be turned off for all italicized words. Adjusting double column fake-notes (for your real notes do not allow columns) – not a luxury, but *necessity* with POD printers charging by the page, because a large page requires it – is as slow as a sea slug. There is so much crap (games and video and corporate-use this and thats) that can be done efficiently with your software, yet you have given almost no thought to *the needs of writers*. I will detail these complaints and requests for improvement at my website and invite other writers to unite in *demanding* our fair share of progress from the programmers! (Additional *fies* for other software makers who cover up user-unfriendly software by calling it "professional," and security like McAfee that sold me a defective product which stole 3GB of my space and made me miss the deadline on this book!)

annotated bibliography

海鼠切りもとの形に寄せてある 小原啄葉

namako kiri moto no katachi ni yosetearu – ohara takuyo (2001)
#896 (seaslug cut/ting, original shape-as/in collected/gathered[together])

cutting sea slug
and reassembling it in
its original form

~

a sea slug
cut and reassembled
perfectly!

One cannot tell whether to credit the poet Ohara [1] or someone else in his household for this play upon the cutting board. But a reconstructed sea slug is something fine to imagine, and I am grateful for the world wide web without which I would never have found it. Dozens of the modern haiku included in this book were netted. Not all had contactable addresses – they were simply out there, a dead end link to god knows what site – and, in dozens of cases, not only was it impossible to contact the poet for permission, it was impossible to check on the correct pronunciation of the his or her name. In a number of cases, there was no name, because haiku entered in contests are often shown anonymously in order not to bias judges and to prevent embarrassment for losers. In some other cases, more effort might have found the poet, but I am out of time for this edition. What information I have for each haiku, *senryu, kyôka,* and *tanka* and poet is in the Sea Slug *Poem Index* and accompanying Bibliographic Acronym List. In one sense, the latter list is misleading, for it treats all the sources equally, where the truth is that some were far more valuable for me than others. Here, I will try to put things in perspective to help haiku aficionados and prospective researchers.

ARUSU Vol. 11 and 12 of Arusu's (publishing house's) SHIKI ZENSHÛ (anthology of all of Shiki's work), containing haiku by about 150 poets(1 to 40 pages each) of the Edo era selected by Shiki. This, the best introduction to old haiku I know of, is virtually unknown. Most poems found here are also in BUNRUI and/or KAIZO, below. The book is undated, but a front-piece photograph is dated Taisho 12 (1924).

BRHKZ = Matsuyama Shiki ed. BUNRUI-HAIKU-ZENSHU (categorized haiku complete collection), in 12 volumes, Arusu, 1929-9. The 63 sea slug poems are in vol 10. Shiki died in 1902, so the editor Sokotsu probably deserves credit, too. The categories used to sub-divide seasonal themes are largely worthless, but the set is invaluable as a *saijiki,* or haiku-almanac source-book, for it is the largest there is. Still, many poets are not sufficiently represented. If modern haiku researchers sufficiently appreciated old haiku, we would already have a web-site with a hundred times more haiku than BRHZS, searchable by theme, author, words and, to the extent possible, in chronological order. This is by far my most valuable sourcebook.

HAIKU R.(Reginald) H. Blyth: HAIKU: The Hokuseido Press, vol 4 (autumn/winter) 1952/92. My most valuable sourcebook in the English language. The large number of poems on subjects dear to Blyth's heart (eg. Scarecrows and blowfish) makes the book a better read but detracts from its overall value, for many themes are short-changed.

1. *Ohara Takuyô* I have only read one other haiku by Ohara so far: "on takiji day / the waves bring in / a male *geta*" (*takiji-ki no nami no hakaberu otoko geta*). As the www article explains, Takiji, imprisoned for political reasons, was tortured to death in jail on August 2, 1933. Takiji Day means his deathday, when someone is remembered in the Sinosphere. In *A PILGRIM AT TINKER CREEK,* Annie Dillard, hyperbolizing the flood of melted ice-water overflowing her creek, exuberantly throws in pieces of the Erebus and Terror (ships of the Franklin Expedition that disappeared trying to find the Northwest Passage). Here, we have something far darker, the history of pre-World War Japan, even today washing ashore. If Ohara has written many like the reconstituted sea slug and this washed-in clog, I want to read them. 男下駄

HKDZ HAIKU DAIZEN: Imai Kashiura (Kindai Bungeisha: 1928). The 52 sea slug haiku in this make it the second largest collection after BRHKZ, above. It has more early modern poems and less old ones. Most themes are less fully covered than in the HKSJ, but some eccentric(?) themes such as sea slug or blowfish are exceptionally well-covered and include questionable but entertaining haiku not found in other saijiki.

HKSJ HAIKAI SAIJIKI: Kaizosha. My New Year's volume of the five-book collection is by Hirata Kiichiro et al (1933) and the Winter volume by Yokoseki? Aizo et al (1954). There are many other editions of this partly prewar haiku almanac, the best I have seen. It is my second most valuable sourcebook, after BRHKZ. Its editors think a lot like me, for the seasonal collections contain many -- in some cases, most – of what I think the most interesting haiku (After having gathered them, myself, from many sources, it was disappointing to see!). With 35 sea slug haiku, this is my fourth largest source.

KHKG = KIHON KIGO 500-SEN: Yamamoto Kenkichi (Kodansha Gakujutsu-bunko: 1989) With 47 sea slugs, this is the third largest collection, yet I did not depend much on it, for almost all of these are found in BRHKZ and HKDZ or Yamamoto's own NHDSJ. This is by far the best no-nonsense compact saijiki-in-a-book.

KSKK   Katô Ikuya: KINSE KOKKEI HAIKU DAIZEN (early modern droll haiku anthology), yomiuri shinbunsha, 1993). Over half of its 28 sea-slug were missed by my other sources, so this ranks up with BRHKZ and HKDZ as an invaluable source. And, most important of all, Katô includes biographical information (pronunciation+date) of his old sources! Without them, I would have been unable to date most of the poems given in Shiki's BRHKZ, which fails to give that information.

NEZ = Nezumi Komakura (mouse small pillow) is the name of Takazawa (Takasawa) Yoshikazu's site that was open to all and had the most old haiku outside of Shiki's BRHKZ. Unfortunately, the site is no longer public for copyright considerations (it has modern haiku, too). If you read Japanese well and research haiku, I will put you in contact with the new site and, hopefully, you will get a password to use it. Had the 60 or so *namako* haiku by Takasawa himself (e-mailed to me) been in a single book, they would have been the second largest source!

NHDSJ   Mizuhara et al ed. NIHON DAI-SAIJIKI, Kodansha, 1983.   The largest modern saijiki in my possession (with ample illustrations, definitely the most for the money). The main themes done by Yamamoto Kenkichi are particularly thorough, but there are few old haiku not found in BRHKZ and/or HKSJ. (Unfortunately, I did not have the money to buy other major contemporary saijiki to compare with this!)

OJD = My acronym for the NIHON-KOKUGO-DAI-JITEN published by Shogakukan that I call the Only Japanese Dictionary (I pun on the OED).   Most dictionaries are seldom of much assistance to the writer with antiquarian interests. This 20 vol. (or 10 vol. small-print) set is almost always helpful! If enlarged another ten or twenty percent – the dating and first-usages are particularly weak – copies of this dictionary could be sent around the world and Japan can then safely blow up and sink into the sea yet rest assured its culture will survive.   I am amazed at how many scholars in Japan and the USA do not have this *absolutely* essential source.

sea-cucumber-related

The books available in Japanese or Russian are mentioned in a note to the foreword. Here, I add two things. First, Arakawa Kohman's NAMAKO DOKUHON (("a handbook on the japanese sea cucumber, its biology, propogation and utilization"): Midori Shobo 1990) has enough illustrations to be worth buying, even if you do not read Japanese, if holothurians are your bag. Also, a Sea Cucumber Guidebook (*namako gaidobukku*) by Motokawa Tatsuo [Tatsuo Motokawa, in Western name order] *et al* is being published by Hankyu Communications as this book goes to bed. (I have not seen it). Though the text is in Japanese, it "contains photos of all shallow water Japanese species" with the Latin name identifying each, so it may be useful to non-Japanese, too. Finally, **if** you have an exceptionally literate Japanese friend with plenty of time on his or her hands, there is little about the human history of the trepang trade *not* in Tsurumi Yoshiyuki's huge *Namako no Manako* (Chikuma: 1993) Try Fuji.com or Amazon to order.

As mentioned in the body of the book, somewhere, the on-line *Beche-de-mere Bulletin* is fine, though not a source for much on the sea cucumber culture of Japan. And the *Virtual Echinoderm Newsletter* is a *beautiful* production, including a culture/literature corner.

appeal to potential sponsors

禁 欲 や 或 る 夜 海 鼠 に 星 の 色　蒲 田 陵 塢
kinyoku ya aru yoru namako ni hoshi no iro – futa shuno (contemp)
#897(prohibit-desire/continence/asceticism:/! one night seaslug-to/in star/s-color)

asceticism
one night the sea slugs
turn into stars

I have lived frugally for the thirty years since I graduated from college, publishing six books (from top Japanese publishers, RISE is my first POD book) of my own, while mid-husbanding hundreds of fine non-fiction books by authors including Evan Connell, Annie Dillard, Loren Eiseley, Bernard Le Bovier de Fontanelle, F. Gonzales-Crussi, Stephen J. Gould, Primo Levi, Barry Lopez, James Lovelock, James Hamilton-Patterson, Michael Prishvin, John Steinbeck and Henry David Thoreau into Japanese while serving two small publishers as acquisitions editor and translation checker. There are few people (dozens? hundreds?) in the world capable of doing the type of rapid checking+correcting I did for minimum wage and a handkerchief-sized parachute that amounted to about a thousand dollars per publisher (and there were only two) after twenty years with one and a few with the other. No, the publishers did *not* exploit me. They just happen to be, monetarily speaking, poor. Meanwhile, most of my own books are out of print. Four were reprinted and one became a pocket-book (20,000 copy first printing), but none became best-sellers. Since most of my time has been spent studying and writing for the past decade, today, I am penniless. Why does that matter? The painter Mengs told Casanova –

> Understand that there is not a picture in the world which is finished more than relatively. This Magdalene will never be finished until I stop working on it, but it will not really be so, for it is certain that if I worked on it another day it would be more finished . . . (*History of My Life*, trans. Willard R. Trask)

That is even truer for books; this one is not close to finished. I regret not pursuing a number of leads, not re-editing to create more large chapters incorporating many of the *Sundry Sea Slugs* (and reorganizing the rest!), not polishing each paragraph into an aphorism, not finding the right word for a translated poem that fails to excite . . . But make no mistake, if I had not had to waste most of my time (perhaps 80% of the time spent on this book) doing things part-time help could have done better, or deserting the book altogether to further the interests of others because I was not wealthy enough to say "No!" or caring for family members for lack of money to buy help, I could have taken the book to another level. To do as much (as little) as I have, I have had to forgo medicine for years (I got hospital insurance last year to protect my family, but I cannot afford the full insurance or fees required to actually see a doctor), cut down to one shower every three days and one shave per week, forgo all society – no dating, though single! – and so forth. The only exception are Saturday morning garage sales and some on-line participation in haiku activities.

Most writers would neither admit to such dissatisfaction with their book nor the poverty which limited them. They would hold on to their manuscript until they had the time to work it to their satisfaction. I cannot. Besides RISE, I have half a dozen books 50% done if my poverty continues and I must do it all myself, but 90% done if I can afford some help in filling in Japanese where I couldn't before because I couldn't afford a computer with Japanese capabilities when I wrote the books, chasing down names, investigating anecdotes, going to the library for articles not available on the net, getting permissions, helping me format, etc… And behind them, I have a *scores of books* in various stages of preparation – all nonfiction and most researched for decades – and books are but part of what I create, or would like to, if I only had the time which only money can buy.   (Please visit my website, PARAVERSE.org, and I think you will understand these claims that seem outlandish in this necessarily short outline) Over fifty, I can no longer play the sea slug. I *must* get going immediately to finish even a small part of what I began, naively assuming help would come when it was needed.

I am not ashamed to appeal for patrons. Just before the preface of Blyth's books on Haiku, we read "The publication of this volume was made possible through the kindness and patriotism of Naoto Ichimada, governor of the Bank of Japan."   Needless to say, the presence of a bank governor in no way cheapens Blyth's work. I would be happy to likewise credit my benefactors, who may chose from a list of books which to support and will get to read the book in manuscript if they so wish. And, I am so confident of the medium-term success of my writing that I even offer to payback whatever money I receive, with interest, or donate it to someone else within ten years of the time I receive it.

What about grants? Grants – at least those I am aware of – are made for people who 1) have the academic qualifications I lack, 2) don't mind wasting a good deal of their time writing proposals, 3) suck up to the accepted pc line or, 4), belong to a minority other than "poor." If we make the assumption – perhaps wrong – that grants influence as well as reflect our culture, look at the nonfiction best-seller list in the *New York Times*. How much is truly creative? Most of the non-fiction is little more than fancy journalism or how-I-overcame-this-or-that autobiography. My guess is that this reflects the fact that most funding goes for unreadable academic work on the one hand and its opposite on the other, and intelligent laymen and women are shut out.   Also, I fear it is generally the case that work good enough to last for centuries requires *decades* of preparation and the freedom to go where the work leads, whereas grants teach us to rush to prove ourselves worthy in the short-run. Seeing much of the work that has been done on grants, I almost feel we could apply to our entire arts culture the comments a reflective president of a certain South American republic (Bolivia, perhaps?) once made in respect to "American" foreign aid. "They gave us just enough rope to hang ourselves."

If RISE, YE SEA SLUGS! suggests to you that I may have something to offer English letters, please check out my website, take a look at the books and projects listed and, if you wish to, please help me get the show on the road!

～

にんげんは滅び海鼠は這ひをりぬ　奥坂まや
ningen wa horobi namako wa haiorinu – okuzaka maya (contemp)
#898 (humans-as-for perish/die-out, seaslug-as-for crawl/creep[+honorific])

deja vu

after Man
for *namako* it is
work as usual

matter over mind?

man is gone
behold the sea slug
still creeping

post-post-modern

after humanity
has perished, the sea slug
keeps crawling

the tortoise and the hare

man dies out
sea cucumbers creep on

～　～　～

英語読解力不足の読読者へ

本書の英訳俳句の読み方に一言

本書の俳句のかなりの数には、同じ句に多数の英訳もある．それが、重層なる意味が一つの英訳では尽くせない、あるいは尽くしてしまったら句がくどくなるのを防ぐための工夫ではあるが、場合によって、その数なる英訳は、むしろ私にとって最初に解けない謎だった俳句の解答への道筋ないし、経緯を、読者と分かち合うためでもある。手始めに間違ってしまった幾つかの句に限って、「正解」まで遂げるのが、丸一章（その間に別な俳句も出てくるが）かかってしまいますが。。

これを馬鹿馬鹿しく思う方もおられよが、読み物として、単なる句集より読み応えあるかと、確信しておる。ただし、その場合、最初に出てくる英訳は、とんでもない誤訳になりかねないから、英語読解力に恵まれていない方には、大変な注文でしょうが、早合点を避けるように、句の出た章を、完読したまで、ご判断を遠慮して下さい！（その後、びしばしと批判なさっても、構いません。）

誤訳句を残すこを、おかしく思われても仕方が無い。けれど、誤訳の方が、しばしば、正訳より優れた句になる。それを永遠に隠す必要があるでしょうか？『誤訳天国』という本も書いた小生だから、笑っちゃいますが、何回も、勝手な（間違った）読みから面白い英訳ができた経験があるから、今は、難句に出会えば、自分よりよく読める人と相談する前に、カナラズ当てずっぽうの英訳を何通りも作って置きます。一度ものが解ってしまったら、脳に害がなければ、二度と無知楽に戻れまい。だから、これは、わがポリシーとまでなっています。

一句多訳は、又、審美上あってもいい翻訳型だと思います。ステレオ効果だってある。（万葉第一歌の「みつくしもち」（み掘串持ち）が同時に「美夫君志持」となっているのが面白いとおもわない？）二つ以上の面白い翻訳できたら、読者にも見せては、何故いけないでしょうか？しかし、句意のとんでもない拡大や多様性という、でたらめな異訳、変わった title まで加えたりする姿勢　—　わが得意なる「似句」、ないし paraverse と呼ぶもの　—　は？！　それだけ行なったら、まったく無責任に違いありません。認めます。が、同時に、原文の逐訳（という不完全な道具）を、読者に明かして、一所懸命に句の内容を、解らせております。すべてが OPEN だからこそ、翻訳は自由自在に遊べるというわけです。言い換えれば、一句一句の英訳について、どこかが原文の本意、どこかが我が望みかと、ちゃんと指摘してあるから、一見したところほど法外的（？）な本では、ありません。［　校正なしの日本語を許して下さい。］

P.S.　本書のれっきとした俳句に入り交じてある敬愚（私）の駄句を、とりわけご笑納下さい！

ナマコ
句募集

誰でも、わが見逃してしまった面白いナマコ句に出会えば、是非 Site に送って下さい。何よりも、あまり見当たらない古い発句集からの、世の歳時記に見逃された珍物は、有り難い！例えば、

１）滑稽句　日本俳書大系には嘯山の「葎亭句集」はあるが、嘯山の「葎亭画賛集」（「画」は古字ですが）という滑稽句の多い方がどこにも見当たらばい。中には、笑ってしまうナマコ句もきっとあるかと思います。

２）業者句　あるいは、海参問屋の 18 世紀俳人（岩城司鱸）のような方もおられるが、その名前は Google できても、その句集はなかなか見当たらぬ。

３）女流句　花賛女の海鼠句が、ほんとうに良かったが、それより古い女によるナマコの句は本当にないでしょうか？

４）最古句　一番古い句。本書では、もっとも古いものは 1667. でも、ナマコそのものでなくとも、海鼠腸はあれだけ愛されていたかと思えば、その百年前にもぜったい、俳諧か落ちこぼれた連歌か、狂歌かどこかで顔を出しているかと思いますが。古い本、また一次的資料にアクセスある方おられるなら、*please keep your eyes open,* あるいは少し調べてみて頂けないでしょうか？

５）見逃句　私が読んでみても入れなかった句も数百ありますが、場合によって、それがわが不理解のためかもしれない。これも入れないとバチが当たるぞ、と思った句がご存知ならば、句と一緒にその良さの数行説明を送って下さい！再版に、と考慮します。

６）川柳は　あまり入れなかったのは、嫌いからではない。金がないからです。多くの川柳集は手元にないし買えない。「日本史伝川柳狂句」は七万円。「柳多留」だけでも、全集は３万円。そして、買っても、季節順になっていないし、５０音順の索引ですから、多くの読者に頼むしかない。（「柳多留」の場合、海鼠で始まる川柳すでに在日の頃コピーできたがその他の）海鼠に出会えば、掴んでは送って下さい！

..

只今、執筆中の２０冊古句歳時記もある。その関係の句の不可解読の場合、皆さんのご助言を頼むしかない。Paraverse.org の俳Ｑペイジへ、どうぞ。言うまでもなく、俳句中心ですが、普通の俳句歳時記と異なって、季題によって、連歌、短歌、それにも自由詩も適切に、紹介したいから、俳句・俳諧以外の方の協力も頼みたい。又、歳時記の場合、一季題に二、三十頁しか明けないから、そう深くは、突っ込まないが、海鼠の如く、spin-off（脱線作？）も、年々２，３冊も出したいから、ある季題に凝ってらっしゃる方の、そのマニアでしか出ない力を、借りたい。貸して欲しい。勝手なお願い事ばかり言うっては、失礼しましたが、俳句は好き同士だから、わかって下さるかと思ひます。メ

（paraverseのwebsiteより）　再版の本に加えたくなるナニかが、御座いませんか？

＜ｇｌｏｓｓ＞
欄外注

欄外注＝GLOSS とは何か
＜正誤表＞から頂く指摘によって、一般的な「直し」を版ごとに加えますが、
その他にも、なるほどと思われる、新しい情報が入ったら
それも本に加えたい。もともと、中世の西欧の本には、
著者でない人による書き加え文がまだ無ければ
本が未完成で読み甲斐がないという
考えがあったらしい。

今こそ GLOSS の時代が
今のソフトのおかげで、書き加えは早いし、ＰＯＤ印刷で再版が、楽に出来ます。
＄150. の新 Set-up 代に、$50. の新 ISBN#だけで、新版出し得るから、
他人から親切に頂いたコメント＝ＧＬＯＳＳ文＝欄外注を
加えない理由も全くないから、拙著の場合、それを
どんどん加えて、版を重ねる毎に、本を一割、
一割と、拡大してゆくも構いません。
だから、ご参加をよろしく
お願いします！

求めている GLOSS とは
何よりも聞きたい、本に入れたいなのは、句主あるいはその周りの方の御意見。
わが英訳や解釈に対する疑問や批判や感想を遠慮なく、教えて下さい！
それに、季題（最初の本は海鼠ですが、なんであれ）に対する
特別な知識のお持ち主からのクレームあるいは
ただ面白くて、「これもあるよ！」って
情報をわが方へと投げつけて下さい。
そして、俳句数寄の皆さま
「見逃してはいけない」
と思う句あれば
是非それを
教えて
くれ
！

欄外注投稿説明
・ご文章をそのまま引用してもいいかどうか、はっきりと書いて下さい。
・ご文章をサイトの欄外注欄で、公表できるか、再版を待つべきか、のいずれ。
・本の中でご氏名を使うか、頭文字だけでいい（後記にそのＫｅｙあるが）
・送ったものを当分預かって下さい。こちらにメイル問題あれば再送できるように。
・日本語か英語、どちらでもいいが、英語ならそのままの引用になりますよ！
・他人でも見つけるかもしれない事柄なら、既に投稿されたかどうかを見て下さい。

　　欄外注欄閲覧　　　（ここでＣｌｉｃｋ！）
　　欄外注の投稿　　　rangaichuu@paraverse.org

念のため、殊に古い句を探す場合、ナマコの書き方の多様性をあらかじめに知るべし.

ナマコ：　奈万古、奈麻古、奈末古、海鼠　生海鼠、海鼠子、生海鼠子、海鼠児、古（コ）、生子、なまこ、虎海鼠（とらこ）、虎子（とらこ）、とらご、とは正名と言えようか？また、俳諧に、土閦、沙口＋巽、沙蒜の例もこの本にあるし、土肉、泥蓋、泥笋、土笋、塗筍、上塗筍、蒜塗筍、海蛆など、俳句以外の文献に見られた、その他の名もあり得る。中国人のいう海参とか海男子も、現れてはおかしくない。老海鼠は、正確的にホヤであっても、俳家がそれを年寄りのナマコと見做せば、海鼠句の中に入るべし。

キンコ：　金海鼠、虎海鼠（とらこ）、虎子（とらこ）は、その多くの書き方からして、食べ方の異なる、別種であっても、海鼠句の中にも虎ある。

イリコ：　煎海鼠、止良古（いらこ）、海参、そして俵物として輸出して大繁栄中だから、初期俳諧には、このキンコが多いかと思います、

コノワタ：　海鼠腸。延喜式などでは「人紅梅」。この腸をはじめに、製品もある。クシコ：　串海鼠。ケタコ：　桁子。　コノコ：　海鼠の卵子、また、クチコ。

アオコ、アカコ：　これは、どういうわけか、まだ俳句に拝見していないが, ありそう。

死んでから来いと海鼠に言われけり　等
#899 shinde kara koi to namako ni iwarekeri – hitoshi (2003)
("die/dead-from/after come[imperative]" seaslug/s-by/from hear[+finality]

come back
after you die says
the sea slug

the wannabe

then, i was told
by the sea slug to drop in
when i was dead

brain-check

"once you're dead
come back!" – i was told
by the sea slugs

invitation

so come back
when you're good & dead!
says sea slug

The original does not mention coming *back,* but the imperative tone of the sea slug's voice suggests that the poet has been refused permission to join the ilk *at the time.* Compared to the frenzy of frogs that almost pulled Eiseley's professor into the pond with them, these *namako* are cool as cucumbers. I cannot determine whether the poet means they desire him to try a *sea-burial,* where instead of having his body chopped up for the condor – or buzzards – in the Tibetan *sky-burial* style, it might be reduced a bit further and, to be crude, fed to the sea slugs (Soaring in the heavens or lolling on the seabed: the contrast in choices is pleasant to contemplate, no?); or, if he means that they tell him to get up off his ass and not act like a sea slug until his next life, where he can reincarnate as one, if he so wishes. I am in contact with the poet, but I will not ask about this poem. Sometimes it is pleasant *not* to know.

本を言及する前に、必ず正誤表をご覧になって下さい。

（これは、paraverse.org の page です。）

＜ｅｒｒａｔａ＞
正誤表

白状あり。

一人で書く、一人で編集、一人で校正、一人で出版・販売する、
貧乏しかも PC や website 作りに弱い、吾が輩（は外人）ながら、満足のいくまで詳細を
調べ尽くすことをしたくても、まず出来ない。資料が高くて買えない。他人の時間を買
えない。だから、お名前を出せなかったり、間違ったりした方（きっとおられる）。
あるいは、出典すら乗せなかった句（Internet で見つけても、その元への道の見出さな
かった場合もある）、その他にも、深くお詫び
致しながらも、それを正すために皆さんの
ご協力を願いします。

ご苦労が重複しないように

すでに直している可能性もあるから、先ず必ず、＜正誤表＞の
句番号（拙著各句付き番号）を見て下さい。そして、直していない場合、未知の名前、
漢字かローマ字化が間違った名前、未知か、間違った、あるいは広過ぎる年付（下記参
照）、そして、句（あるいは歌）の誤植かローマ字化の示す
発音ミス等等を知らせて頂ければ、次版まで直します。
句の英訳・解釈などのご指摘は、＜欄外注＞へ。

＜正誤表＞をみる（ここでＣｌｉｃｋ！）
誤謬を知らす（seigohyou@paraverse.org）

年付けに関する一語

出典ですが、出典一つ、二つがあっても、
その句の作られた年付けとは必ずしも同じではない。もしも、それを
ご存知ならば、知りたいと思います。確実に解った場合、俳人の生（死）年とか、
「mod」（現代）とか「contemp」（現在＝戦後俳人）という大雑把の記、あるいは、そ
れを載せた選集とか歳時記の出版年の換わりに、各々句の現に
出来た年を使わせて頂きたい。ある季題のテーマの開発・発展
を考える上で、大事なことです。そう思いながらも、
小生は詳細苦手でご協力は不可欠。
よろしくお願いします！

Bibliography, or Source Acronyms

<u>ABC順の句引でその原典の頭文字を先ず見て、</u>
<u>そして,下記のABC順でもう少し詳しく知る。</u>

The English-speaking reader may wonder why so little is Romanized here.   The reason is simple. *I am fed up with second-hand bibliographies.* If you quote a poem in this book and you don't read Japanese, then you damn well better cite me.   I will sum up for you: Most of the old poems have properly cited sources, while many, if not most modern poems were netted on the web and some were never successfully traced to their source. I am asking the cooperation of Japanese readers (especially the poets themselves) to improve the bibliography. （さて、これはナニよりも日本人読者、とりわけ俳人のためのものです。その不完全性を、お詫びします。うまく追求できなくって、きちんとしたクレジットも取れなかったことも申し訳ないが、詳細な事にこれ以上に時間を割いたら、俳句の編集、英訳、解釈のための時間も無くなってしまい、この本も未然に終わったはず。金ないから、手伝手もいない。よろしく、ご了解を乞い、ご助けを願いします。）

ajy = 国士舘大学 （大学別） of http://www.city.tsuru.yamanashi.jp/haiku/oubo.htm.

AK = Alexander Kerr. See the Acknowledgments!

akgs = 「馬酔木季語集」水原春朗編 ふらんす堂 2001

akio = http://www.jomon.ne.jp/~ayumi/index.HTM

ayame = あやめが「ある本」に読んだ「江戸後期―明治初年のナマコの俳句」（そのchatroom に access できず、原典未知。）

bba = わが短歌・俳句入門＜女性歌人と海＞www.tssplaza.co.jp/sakuhinsha/book/ zui-bekan/tapin / 8501. htm

bnbs = 「蕪村七部集俳句評釈」内藤鳴雪 大学棺発行 1907

brhzs = 「分類俳句全集」（十二巻） 子規編 アルス 1929

bkk = 「蕪村句集講義・蕪村遺稿講義 縮刷合本」俳書堂発行 大正5

bsgi = 「芭蕉語彙」宇田零雨著 青土社 1984

bz = 「蕪村全集」尾形仂、森田蘭他校注 講談社 1992

corresp. (or pc) Correspondence, mostly e-mail.

cjco = 「鳥獣虫魚歳時記・秋冬の巻」朝日新聞社 2000

CZ = Hoshino Takashi. See the Acknowledgments.

ddk = 駄句だく会 平成13・12・12 net

dgc = 全句集『稽古』（2002年）より「ペン電子文藝館」のために自選

dhl = dhugal j. lindsay (corresp) この方は小生と違って真面目に句を詠むから、e-mail でのちょっとしたものを紹介しては申し訳ないが。。。

eh = the essential haiku: robert hass (ecco press: 1994)

eeks = 「江戸上方「艶句」の世界」鈴木勝忠 三樹書房 1996

eno = 「江ノ島古俳句」 net 高澤良一抄出; 杉田.金澤古俳句 杉田梅林(妙法寺 杉田海岸)

fjm = 『延年』富士見書房. 出版年月, 2002.07.http://www.jfast1.net/~takazawa /db3area/yajimaennen.pdf

fshsj = 「新装版風生編歳時記」富安風生編 東京美術 昭和46 1981

fuji = 佐賀新聞 読者文芸 2001/02/01

gdhks = 「現代俳句歳時記」中村汀女監修 実業乃日本社 昭和48 1973

gdhs = 「現代俳句 歳時記辞典」夏本一郎監修 北堂 1993

gdsj = 「現代歳時記」金子兜太、黒田杏子他編 たちばな出版 2001

gdtkb = 「現代短歌分類辞典 新装版39巻 同辞典発行所 平成六

ghgd = 「合本現代俳句歳時記」角川春樹編 角川春樹事務所 1998

ghhk = 「合本俳句歳時記 第三版 角川書店編 平成九、十一

gks = 「現代教育新聞」(GKS) 子育て川柳作品集の参考作品（食欲小学生の部 gyo = http://members.tripod.co.jp/kankan31/kigo_huyu.html 秋桜句会

he = 00/12/30 ハードエッジ 開発素句報抜 2000 770句 net; #656 ＝ハード エッジ (97) http://www.gendaihaiku.gr.jp/haikukai/result/11_happyou.htm.

hers = #2＝ ハード・エッジの落選俳句 640句 1995-2001, 1995/2/28 net

hh1 = history of haiku (vol 1): blyth (hokuseido:1963/84)

hh2 = history of haiku (vol 2): blyth (hokuseido: 1963/84)

hhdg = 「俳諧発句大業」冬中に(発句大業＝1820？)

hito = 「しゅわるつ 大畑等」(#484),

hkdz = 「俳句大全」今井柏浦編 近代文芸社 昭和三 1928 （初版白水社 1927）

hkb = 「俳諧袋」 nhhstk にて, はいかい袋 1801 (kkhk)

hkcl = #291=catwalk 俳句クリニック（ドクター　わたなべ　じゅんこ，#495 =(2002/2/11) 同じく 2002 年 2,3 月分（ドクター：塩見恵介）

hked = 俳諧江戸蛇之鮓

hkgr ＝ハイカグラって、灰神楽か、俳神楽？

hkkg ＝「必携季語秀句用字用例辞典」斉藤慎称（の右の古字で平＋雨、阿久根末忠編　柏書房 1997　net

hkkk ＝俳句航海日誌９５００句！清水昶（武蔵野）句♯414、415　（01・11）net

hkks ＝「俳諧古選」三宅嘯山編宝暦 13=1763

hkrs ＝「発句類聚」冬部十月に

hksj ＝「俳諧歳時記」虚子他編 改造社 昭和 29

hkss ＝「俳諧新選」嘯山編　安永二　1773

hkst ＝「俳句選択」頴原退蔵著日本文学社 sh10

hkzs ＝「俳家全集」子規編　アルス社の「子規全集」11、12 巻

hm = a haiku menagerie: addiss stephen, yamamoto F&A (weatherhill inc. 1992/98)

hrdg = http://www.gendaihaiku.gr.jp/haikukai/result/ 11_happyou.htm. 120

hrkt = （ホテル・ザー・サンクラ　平成 12/12/26 ） (Hoteru Za Sanraku (2000/12/26), www.gunma.med.or.jp/isesa/hobby/haiku/haiku_502.htm

htt ＝　ホトトギス歳時記__

hzg ＝「俳諧懺悔　あるいは？はいかい悔　又俳諧悔（1790）

ibg ＝ インパクト文学　丸山ちかこセンセイ（1998.1.18~）６回なまこ

ic = 2001. Copyright,haiku@maki-taro.net

ihks ＝「一茶俳句集」丸山一彦 岩波書店 1990

iids ＝「一茶一代集」の中の「一茶紀行・日記集」16 頁　1927 (in nhhstk12). See pg 32 of izs 2 on why this poem (with others appended to "hana mi no ki") is now attributed to chikua, not issa.)

idj ＝「一茶大辞典」矢羽勝幸大修館書店 1993

iku ＝細石俳句コンテスト（品川玲子先生選）

imy ＝時勢梱（粧?)＝いまやうすがた (kthb 2)

ino ＝ いのちの緒

izs1 ＝「一茶全集　第１巻」　信濃毎日新聞社一巻は、歳時記式全発句集です

izs2 ＝「一茶全集　第２巻」　信濃毎日新聞社「花見の記」解説に竹阿の事

izs3 ＝「一茶全集　第３巻」　信濃毎日新聞社

izs8 ＝「一茶全集　第８巻」　信濃毎日新聞社

izsb ＝「一茶全集別巻（資料補遺）信濃毎日””"

jin = 第９３回藍生砥会平成十三年 12 月 22 日

jskk = 自選五十句　kankoi: miki reikô? in e-literary magazine 7 umi[shio].

kaki = ww10.ocn.ne.jp/~ha283ma/kouryuubun ngei.htm

kami = 『木守』『心後』『幻』(net)

kao ＝伊吹嶺HP句会選句結果のページ 第４４回（１２月）HP俳句会選句経過

kata ＝公会計改革を進める会世話人代表 www.katayama.org/shunsho/2/common/sakuhin.b5.htm

kazu = http://members.tripod.co.jp/kankan31/kigo_huyu.html (秋桜句会)

kd = 虚桐庵句会 明治二六 12/26 「虚子全集」晦日新聞社版 第二巻 (kzs)

kdb 93, 97, 2001 = 「季題別現代俳句集」俳人協会版　平成 五,九,十三

kdkwhs = 第４８回角川俳句賞「百人力」2002 年 鷹 3 月号

kh = KOTO 風通信 vol 61 平成 12.1.20

kik = net Shirahige？一月選句結果

khkg =「基本季語五〇〇選」講談社学術文庫 1989

KK = KuroKuro=Tanaka Kuro. See Acknowledgts.

kkhk = 「滑稽俳句海鼠の舌」丘の蛙著　國華堂本店　大正六

kki = きふみ会? (net)

knkn ＝今日の句日記 2002/12/9

kobe = 2001 鷹 ４ 月号インターネット佳句抄 轍 郁摩　抄出

kobs ＝「河」応募作品 李花村 2002/07/21　net (geocities.co.jp/Bookend-Shikibu/8418/geodiary. html)

krt = http://www.pref.mie.jp/BUNKA/HP/HAIKU/

krzk = 2002/１２/１７　　今日の句日記 net

KS = Kikuchi Shinichi. 菊池真一. See Acknowled.

kskk = 「近世滑稽俳句大全」加藤郁乎編　読売新聞社発行 1993

ksks =「虚子句集」　植竹書院　大正四

kszs =「虚子全集」我が読んだのが書名知らないが、後で記念館で確認。kd 見て。

kthb2 = 古典俳文学大系　２ = 貞門俳諧集 集英社

kthb3 = 古典俳文学大系　３ = 談林俳諧集 集英社

kthb4 = 古典俳文学大系 4 = 談林俳諧集 2 集英社

net ktbgd = 「改訂版　現代俳句歳時記」金子兜太編　チクマ秀出？版 平成元年

ktm = (etu/1999 06/sakuhin-minadukishuu.html)水無月集

kts = （鷹）　昭和 28 年生まれの俳人たち www.sakai.zaq.ne.jp/syunsei/ syouwa28.html

kty = 俳句文芸２号冬の島二十句 shuntô bk?

ktzt = 現代俳句協会 www.gendaihaiku. gr.jp/haikukai/result/23_itiran.[htm] - 23k#578

kura = (ww3.tiki.ne.jp/~akuru/ mano-no 3-kuramoto.html), Mano 3-go

kyb = 「季寄せ」山本健吉編 文藝春秋 昭和 48

kym = 「季寄せ　新装版」大野林火、安住敦編　明治書院 平成九 1977

Lhe = Ludwig H. 1889-1892. *Echinodermen. Die Seewalzen*. In: Bronn HG (ed.) Bronn's *Klassen und Ordnungen des Their-Reichs*. Band II. Abteilung 3. Buch 1. Leipzig. Unpublished translation by Alexander M. Kerr.

Lr = Lost Reference

mang =第30回　青山俳句工場向上句会選句結果 www.linkclub.or.jp/~jibun/kojo /30.html

maya = www.alles.or.jp/~wadachi/haiku/h-maya.html インターネット佳句抄 轍 郁摩　抄出 鷹3月号より

mcj = Golownin Captain, R.N.: MEMOIRS OF A CAPTIVITY IN JAPAN 1811-13 (Oxford U. Press: 1973 (orig Henry Colburn: London:1824)) in 3 vol

mcng = 題13回お～いお茶新俳句大賞受賞作品 都道府県賞その2　www.itoen.co.jp/new-haiku/contents/13todou02.html

mhs = 「鳴雪俳句集」春秋社（246頁）大正 15

miho = http://homepage1.nifty.com/aoi-kinuta/jisen/jisen112.htm.[?]

misa = http://ginnews.hb-arts.co.jp/030601/020310kekka.[htm]

mksj = 「味覚歳時記」大野雑草子編博友社 1997

mmc = 「団団珍聞」狂体俳句欄　（1248 号）明治 33 年一月　1900

mmk = MUMONKAN (zen and zen classics v.4): R.H. Blyth; The Hokuseido Press 1966/78

mnh = 右脳俳句 (right brain haiku) という気持ちよく寛いだ on-line 俳句会

mmsk = 松 本 正 氣 http://www.geocities.co.jp/Hollywood-Kouen/3428/hairekia6.htm

mns = 日曜の毎日新聞より 2002 11月11日（月） SIRO の雑記帳

mrs = #398 歌集『嗜好朔語』morris (net); #770 = Morris にて岡田信「百人百句」より.

msbs = 「秋冬　蕪村七部集俳句評釈」内藤鳴雪　大学館発行　明治三十九

msc = 「松嶋眺望集」三千風　（1638－1707）1682 (in kthb4)

mts=www.netlaputa.ne.jp/~ntsuna/wk 200112.html or http://www.3ac.co.jp/ fri/kukai/27g3c001.html

nbc = 《お題の貯蔵庫》www.geocities. co.jp/Bookend-Shikibu/6419/odai.html

NDH = 「なまこ読本」荒川好満　緑書房 1990　NAMAKO DOKUHON (many illus)

ndjks = 「年代順虚子句集 (第三巻 大正六)

net = インターネットで見つけても、それ以上の糸口のない、幻の出典。

nez = ねずみ　こまくら　という、高沢良一の日本一の俳句 Data Bank ですが、只今、著作権などの配慮のため password が必要。そこに出ていた俳句の出典や俳人の名前の発音もありましたが、わがＰＣのＷＯＲＤには最初の内、日本語できなくて、などのいい訳もできますが、情報が不十分の場合、私が悪い。Nez ではなく。

ngt = www.aozora.gr.jp/cards/ nagatsuka/htmlfiles/NAGATU_1.html

nhdsj = 「日本大歳時記」水原秋桜子他監修（海鼠の題＝山本健吉）講談社 1983

nhhstk = 「日本俳書大系」

nhhstk12 = 「日本俳書大系　第 12 巻」

nhk = NHK の俳句テレビ番組らしきペイジだが、訊ねるべき email がなくて。

nhsj = 「俳句歳時記」永田義直編 金園社 1972

nhsk = 「日本詩歌 30 俳句集」中央文庫　1976

nkd = http://members.tripod.co.jp/kankan31/kigo_huyu.html のキャッシュ

nkhr = 句作銀化　花神社 98－7－7

nkk = 海鼠句会 2002/12/14 (ukmd)

nmb = 8421.teacup.com/namubow3/bbs そーくるなら、これでどーだバトル句会３１　投稿者：紫野　投稿日：2003 8月 11, #709=十一吟歌仙「初暦の巻」http://homepage3.nifty.com/gatten-haikunet/　8408.teacup.com/namubow/bbs; #894=人名千句句会１７ 同 8421

nmsj = 「入門歳時記」大野林火著 角川書店 1980

nmtk = #119 = インターネット佳句抄　轍 郁摩　抄出 1991 刊) 句集「わたしがゐてもゐなくても」；#875 = インターネット佳句抄 轍 郁摩　抄出 ２００２年

NNM = 「ナマコの眼」鶴見良行著　（1990）ちくま文芸文庫　2001

ntkhh = 懐かしい母の海鼠クレームする者いないか？ http://www.haiku.or.jp/ haikukai/kekka/ 199912_seiki.htm#104

ntkk = 七天句会の句

NTU = 「ナマコとウニ」大島廣著　（1962）内田老鶴圃　1995

oba =homepage2.nifty.com/banryoku-haiku/a08back

ogi = http://svrrd2.niad.ac.jp/faculty/ogiue/kyoka.[html],

ojd = Only Japanese Dictionary 日本国語大辞典　小学館　1979

okite = 第 41 回 全 国 俳 句 大 会 www2.famille.ne.jp/~haiku/sho-zen41-1

OM = O(h)nuki Masako 小貫昌子. See Acknowl.

oni = 句 集 『 舫 ひ 舟 』 t087177.ipgw.phs.yoyogi.mopera.ne.jp

onsen = 和倉温泉　多田屋（能登）俳句の部優秀作品

ouc = 『大団』(1688-1703) in 狂歌大観 (明治書院 vol 1: 1983)

phsj 「ポケット俳句歳時記」山口青邨、石塚友二監修　平凡社　1981

poe = POÉME 母恵夢　母の日のプチポエム

pp = ぽぷら 21 net

reiko =寒鯉 jskk netwww2s.biglobe.ne.jp/~hatak/emag/data/miki-reiko01.htm

reon = 玲音 http://www5e.biglobe.ne.jp/ ~reon_s/

rdhs = 「類題発句集」十月に 1774

rdks = 類題句集(=rdhs=類題発句集の略?),

rik = http://members.tripod.co.jp/kankan31/kigo_

huyu. html
rrs = 寥松(八朶園句)のものか、それとも嘯山の俳文によると涼菟の夢に見たか？ 赤間関で平家蟹を見たか、私が江戸時代の散文に弱いし、原典も色々ある。誰か整理をよろしく！
sai = 勝手に俳諧歳時記 = www.ne.jp/asahi/kareki/saiziki/shiryou/pdf/rotu.pdf
sato = 日本海読者文芸 歌壇４−９ 年？
sawa = 月間澤のところかな？ #718= www.sawahaiku.com/tokyokukai/tokyokukai.html
sgk = 珠玉抄 菅原章風選 [1998/3 号(www//kula wanka .ne.jp/~hamada/UGUISU/ shugyoku 98.html)]]
sgs = 秋顔子 1790 (izs8)
shhk = 「新版俳句歳時記」桂信子、金子兜太他監修 雄山閣出版版 2001
shin = 東京在住 http://www.geocities.co.jp/Bookend-Shikibu/6419/
shira = t081205.ipgw.phs.yoyogi.mopera.ne.jp
shks = 「食の俳句歳時記」岡田日郎 梅里書房 昭和２０〜５０の句？
sks = 「子規句集」 虚子編:1941岩波文庫 1993
skmks = 子規名句集 精文館書店大正八
sksj = 「作句歳時記」楠本憲吉編著 講談社 1989
sphk = 「新編俳句歳時記」野澤節子編 講談社 1978
smhs = 「素丸発句集」 （izsb にて）寛政八
snb = (www.haiku.or.jp/haikukai/kekka/200012_hikou.htm)
srdhs = 「新類題発句集」冬の部十月 1793
srsth = 「川柳末摘花輪講初篇」西原、鴨下、山口、八木共著太平書屋 平成 7
srsi = 川柳集「居場所がない」太田とねり （100句＋自注 8）net
srzps = 「川柳雑俳集」日本名著全集刊行会 1927
sshk = 「新装俳句歳時記 冬」平凡社（1959年初版）2000
ssjk = 「食の歳時記三六五日」毎日新聞社 1996
ssk = 早稲田大学の安藤文人氏は親切に漱石の海鼠全句を送ってくださったが古 pc の中じゃ。
sskm = age 60 糸魚川市・西頸城郡関係新聞 1999/07/15
sssj = 「新成歳時記」吉田冬葉編著 交蘭社 sh7
stb = shuntô bk?俳句文芸２号 冬の島二十句
suien = mry: shikokune.hiroko47haikucontest gold metal 2000 haru (suien)
szs = 「子規全集」講談社かアルスか。
tak = #646=www.jfast1.net/~takazawa/dfrontpage/KUKAI/ 0001/toukusyabetutouku 0001.htm ; #862= ~KUKAI/ 0302/saveSENJYABETUSENKU0302.htm -
taka = # 672 , 673, #675 句集 ぱらりとせ www.asahi-net.or.jp/ ~ec6y-;#679=句集 さざなみやっこ （同じ~ec6y-)
take = www4.ocn.ne.jp/~gekko/kashi/kashi 70/70

tanka.htm
takuyo = ohta kahori: haiku tenbô 1208 www に yoyo kushû？
tans = 淡窓詩話 （出典は『名文の秘訣及文例』大正九年)
tbt =(www.kyoto.zaq.ne.jp/masahiro/sinsaku 16.html)
tgks = 「太祇句集」 （頴原退蔵編大正１５）
TLA= R. Buchsbaum+ L. Milne: The Lower Animals; Doubleday & co (undated! 1950's or 60's)
tora = http://homepage3.nifty.com/tora-89wab~23/
tsc = the sea cucumber: martin johnston university of queensland press (1978)
tskc = 短詩型貯庫: matsuku hide (site: matsutanka; konton@plum.plala.or.jp)
tsr = KINSEIhaikusyuuKURIYAMAnado125.txt
trd = youtk.hp.infoseek.co.jp/bunjin/torahiko pdf
tsu= 新俳句人連盟会員 net
ty = 冬葉第一句集(明治〜大正) nez?
uet =句集「架橋」net
ukmd = 浮御堂 on-line#395:海鼠句会 2002/12/14 (これらの句で浮御堂の皆さんに出会った！)
ume = 優秀俳句集 www.lcv.ne.jp/~kens12/kukai/kukai03.htm
unk = 朝日新聞平成？12/12/17
unsj = 「海の歳時記」大野雑草子編 博友社 1998
uoko = 魚子は,難茶亭 銀柳のキャラクタ- http://www28.tok2.com/home/surusyoku/md_hike.htm
wgh = wagahaikuarakaruto yoshikazu takazawa 高沢良一のサイト （01 とか 03＝月付)
wkbs = 「和漢文操」支考撰 享保十二 1727
ya50 = 柳多留？？？全５０音
yagi = (#486) いちばん寒い場所２２号, (#489) ikkubak 日刊：この一句 sendan.kaisya.co.jp/ikkubak_1201.html
yanma =第 83 回桃李１２月定例句会選句一覧 www.freeml.com/message /torikadan@freeml.com/
yano = (www5.airnet.ne.jp/~ttsc/tankajin/reigetu/200012/sakuhin-kaiin1-1.html))
yatsu = 仮幻の詩 netwww.japanpen.or.jp/e-bungeikan/ charm/ishiharayatsuka.html
ymn = kukai.asahi-net.or.jp/cgi-bin/ kukai.
ymym 四方山 Namakogo Sender: Namu Date: 3/18/03 22h/43m/32s (ukmd の所)
ytri = 「俳風柳多留」山澤英雄校訂岩波文庫 1995
yuri = wbs.ne.ja/bt/0_keisan/mikuriya/mikuriya 1302.htm （十中五得点)
yuu = 第 58 回バーチャル句会録 03 www.nifty.ne.jp/forum/fhaiku/v58_03.htm
zhtt =続ホトトギス
zps = 雑俳瀬とり舟(ojd)
zpu = 雑俳鶯宿梅 (ojd)
zsks = 「続境海草」1670−2 in kthb3?
zssk = 「図説魚と貝の大辞典」望月賢二監修 柏書房 1997

464

haiku index

Haiku, Senryû (s), Tanka(t), Kyôka (k) and Folksongs (f) about Namako in this Book romanized, in alphabetic order. (外人も引ける和英辞典の方法で、長い母音は初字に従う)

----

aa medea keigu #727

abatanaru tsuma meimei (1750-1824) hkdz #245

agerarete takasawa yoshikazu (1998) wgh01sono1 #846

ahteisto no keigu #650

ai orite ai shiru chôi (1895-1930) nez #466

aikan ya hi anon (2002/07/21) kobs #825

ajiwaute kanseki takasawa yoshikazu (2000)wgh12 sono1 #564

akakoaokokuroko namu (contemp.) ymym #708

akanamako manukia hirade gashun? (contemp.) hrdg #292

akanamako nara. matsumoto seiki (1942)mmsk #6

akanamako sagesunde kayoko (contemp) tak #646

akitsushima bakeshi ensui (2000-12) mnh #230

akumu nite keigu #59

ama kaeri keigu #762

ama oinu shimamura gen (1973) kyb, gdhks #876

ama saete shichiku (1861-1919) hkdz, nez #576

ama ukabu shimomura umeko (contemp.) ndh #296

amagako wa getsukyo (1755-1824) hhdg #181

amanohashi butsujô (1927) hkdz #322

ametsuchi (see tenchi, too)

ametsuchi no kao keigu #728

ametsuchi no mukashi bakuran (pub1714-60) やまかづら kskk #100

ametsuchi o waga shiki (1867-1902) szs, sks #103

ameya yô. watanabe fumio (contemp) ghgd #822

ami no ame dokushô (1682) msc:kthb4 #696

amigo[ko?]murete rôka?(1670-1703)hzg,srdhs #626

ano namako keigu #886

anrih ponju keigu #649

ao to mireba tôyôjô (1929) 千句 nez #86

ashiato bakurô (d.1768) brhkz (潮干部に) #900

atama kaku takasawa yoshikazu (2003) wgh03-4 #518

atama kara futon kabureba buson? (1715-1783) 新五子稿 1800brhkz, hkdz, kskk, bzs #591

atama kara futon kaburishi seisen? (1763) 俳諧古選 brhkz, khkg, kskk #592

atsugi shite saitô kafû (modern) nez #575

awabitori (s) suetsumuhana (1776)初 33 srsth #280

ayashige ni issei (1775) brhkz #343

bakuchiku keigu #889

bakudan to keigu #885

banbutsu no roya (early19c) ayame #102

banshaku ni takasawa yoshikazu (2003) wgh03 sono3 #220

bashô no ku usami gyomoku (pre1936) 「秋収冬蔵」 nez, shks #13

bateren no tajiri makio (1993) kdb #796

betanagi no seto sekiyô (1997) kdb #177

betanagi ya kita mikiko (1998) uns #751

betsurehemu hitoshi (2003) (俳蔵) #819

bikuni no itsû (1682) msc:kthb4 #694

binnasa ya taigi (1709-72) tgks, brhkz, hkdz #50

bodai moto shiki (1897) szs #129

bukkiri no (t) katô michiko (contemp.) ktm #397

bukkiri wa soran (2002) nkk (ukd) #338

buttokute miyoko (2003) ukmd #278

chicchû mo tochimenbô (mod.) hksj, hkdz #636

chichi ni shite hitoshi (contemp) hito #484

chichi no seshi fukushima masato (mod) nhds #445

chijikomari kawasaki nobuhiro (contemp) nez #468

chinmoku wa kin sasaki masao (1999) sskm #459

chinpoko ja keigu #269

chiri o dani sanyû (1679) 俳諧坂東太郎 kthb4 #871

chôgin no etsuran (?) 正風彦根躰 kskk #348

chokusen o matsuku hide? (contemp) tskc #11

chôtei ni hôri takasawa yoshikazu (2001) wgh12 sono3 #155

chûkû ni wata (renku) katsuyuki (contemp) nmb#709

daiakunin kyoshi mizuuchi keita (mod) net #247

daijin no serifu fujii sankichi (2001) shhk #89

daikai ni futoshi kyoroku (1655-1715) 支考撰和漢 文藻 #892

damariiru koto seisei (1869-1937) hkdz #458

dannmari o kimekomu anon. (contemp?) nhk? #469

darumaki wa taigi+issa+shiki+keigu #140

darumaki ya nakimono tôgan (1790) sgs (izs8) #96

darumaki ya todana shiki (1892) szs #95

dashite okeba shakufu (1773) hkss, brhkz, kskk #72

denwa matsu anon (耕月 泡羽撰?) #852

dô nari to seikô? (1820) 発句題業 hhdg, kskk #163

dôgiri ni shi taigi (1709-72) tgks, hkdz #48

doko made mo anon (contemp) shira #501

dôkoku no ane miyoko (contemp) ukd #76

dokudan to henken shimizu akira (2001) hkkk #827

dokushaku ya tabata masuhiro (2002) lr #508

dotchimichi ikihaji nomoto kyô (1991) nmtk #119

ebukuro wa seishû/masatane (1682) msc:kthb4 #693

eriwakuru konowata sugihara takejo (mod) htt #441

fugu kûte nagusamu shiki+keigu #242

fugu kûte yume shiki+keigu+tenki #243

fukarekite shibata akemi (2001) shhk #773

fukuchû e hietasa tanaka hiromu (1993) kdb #605

fûmi ni wa anon. (1672) imy (kthb 2) #328

fundoshi mo (s) chiekai (1723) eeks #279

fune yori mo nomura nôton? (mod) htt #757

furete kataki tokunaga retsuko(1973) gdhks #471

furu tanpo shiki (1867-1902) szs #56

furubitaru sôjô (1901-1956) nhds, khkg, sksj #10

furusato no kirino manjirô (2000) suien #702

furutsuma mo kishû (1934) 小石川 nez #251

furutsuma ya seihô (1881-1944) nmsj, nez #300

fushigi hagizuki (2002) ukmd 海鼠句会 12/14 #891

futatsu hodo takasawa yoshikazu (2003) wgh03 sono3 #860

futaya ite oto mitsundo (d. 1822) hhdg #325

futsufutsu to ôishi etsuko (contemp) nez #84

futsutsukana takasawa yoshikazu (1997) taka #673

fuyu hinata kikyû? (contemp.) kik #809

fuyu no yoru keigu #601

fuyu umi[tôkai?]no (t) baba akiko (1928-) bba #496

gaiken yori anon (contemp) nhk #232

genkai e subaru (t) sakasegawa kô (mod.) gdtkb #772

genkai no morisaki kazuo (contemp.) mrs #847

gohyakushô ôemaru (-1805) 俳諧袋 nhhstk #144

gomi iru mo keigu #661

gunnya to keigu #287

hachi no namako rokuko? (1820?) hhdg #213

haikai no jôzu anon (1995) hers #2

hakuchû no gotô takashi (contemp) net #849

hama no bi keigu #670

hamabe ni wa   shinsa (contemp) shin #806
hana ni   chôsui (d.1813) nez? #880
hana o   miyazaki shizuo (contemp) nez? #722
hanamomiji   shirô? dô? hhd g #342
hankotsu   ôi toichiro (2001) ddk #464
hanshô no ibo. tatsuoka tsutomu (cont.) shks #315
hanshô no itten   maeda tsuruko (akgs) #570
hara no naka   keigu #707
hara tatete kobushi   keigan (keigu+tôgan) #198
hara tatete marou   tôgan (1790) sgs(izs8) #197
haradateru   shikô (1703) 草刈笛 nhds, sshksj #371
harawata ga hashi kanseki (contemp.) ktbgd #439
harawata no   chitsuka (1927), hkdz #192
hare mo sezu   shiki (1867-1902) szs skmks #551
hasamiage (t)   mitomo heikichi (1983) gdtkb #262
hasamu toki   gohô (pre 1916) lr #373
hatsu go moji   shiki (1867-1902) #652
hebigasaki   suetan? (1682) msc:kthb4 #695
heisei no tenshi   katô shizuo (contemp) kts #127
hekomu takasawa yoshikazu(2003)wgh03sono4 #210
hi ga sashite   mangetsu (contemp.) mang #731
hi o ogamu   shara (1747-1816) hkrs #838
hi o otosu   ôshima _____? (mod.?) 鶴 sshksj #735
hikishio ni   shiki (1895) szs #154
hikishio no wasurete yukishi namako kana   chômu
    (1731-95) khkg, cjco #151
hikishio no wasurete yukishi ônamako   kurita
    setsuko (2001) kdb #153
hipparedo   hôrô (1761-1845) nez? #549
hirogorite   nagata koi (mod) nez #557
hiruzuki ya   kadokawa haruki (1998) ghgd #817
hito de nai   keigu #666
hito nani o   yôsui (1683) brhkz #97
hito naraba   issa (1810) izs 1, 3 #235
hito no me   ôda toneri (c 2000) srsi #32
hito no te   keirô (1930) 高蘆 nez #248
hito okosu   seiran (1765) kskk #521
hito sareba   keigu #763
hito shigure   washitani nanako (1978) 花寂び sphk,
ghgd #559
hitofuyu   kadô (1790) sgs(izs8) #225
hitogirai   fujiki tomoko (1997) mksj #404
hitoguchi ni   yamazaki fusako (2001) kdb, shhk #88
hitokami ni   keigu #120
hitokokyû oite   kaneko kunirô (2002) #47
hitosuji no   okada kôyô (mod?) sshk, zssk #138
hitotôri kikite   takasawa yoshikazu (1997) wgh 0710
    #675
hitozute ni   takasawa yoshikazu (1997) taka #674
hitsuji yori   keigu #547
hiza koware   keigu #723
hôchô no ha atatete   anon. (contemp) nhk #204
hôchô no ha ni   rikyo? (contemp?) rik #203
hôchô no iredokoro   mori mitsuko (1998) sgk #49
hôchô no kireaji kawasaki nobuhiro (cont) nez #202
hôchô o namako takashima _? (contemp) okite #882
hôchô o toganeba shimizu nobuka (cont.) pp #363
hôen ni masuda harako (mod/contemp) ndh #79
hokkai no neko   keigu #787
hokkaidô namako   keigu #786
hokkaidô no   keigu #788
hokkaidô ya hae   keigu #789
hokkaidô ya kidai   keigu #785
hokunamako ya   keigu #791
hômatsu no   gesô (1729-85) hkrs #157
hone no naki   fusui? (1773) 新選 brhkz #193
honenashi mo   keigu #289
honobono to   issa (1758-1823) izs 2,3 #538

hototogisu namakobune   keigu #782
hototogisu konowata keigu #783
hyakunen no   hakusanyô? (contemp) mnh #511
ichi e dete   shunpa (1774) brhkz #532
ichibyô takasawa yoshikazu (1998)wgh12sono3 #671
ichidanraku   kurozaka haruo (contemp) krzk #554
ii ko ishi   shiki+keigu #241
iinikuki   ôishi etsuko (contemp.) nez #474
ikasama ni   ishihara yatsuka (mod.) yatsu #873
iki no mama   kodama koshû? (2001) akgs #20
ikigatashi   bakusô (1935) 麦嵐 nez #514
ikikata wa   icchi (contemp) ic #118
ikinagara   basho (1693) brhzs, hkdz, hksj, nhdsj,
    khkg, rdhs, bzs, etc.#12
ikinokori takasawa yoshikazu (2001) wgh01sono1
    #821
ikiteiru mono namako inuzuka sadako (mod) net #836
ikiteiru mono nite   kitô (1740-89) hksj, brhkz, hkdz,
    khkg, hkkg #572
ikiteiru namako   bakujin (1876-1965) hkdz #33
ikiteiru rashiki   kaori (contemp.)kao #614
ikkai no mama   tokuda chizuko (2001) akgs #18
ikkoku no   hayashi shô ( )ssjk (96) shks? #462
ikkyû no fun   shiki (1897) szs #142
ikkyû no kôte   kasanjo (1807-30) nez, kskk #147
ikkyû no uo   keigu #145
imanoyo ya aware (s)   keigu #658
imanoyo ya namako (s)   keigu #660
inishie no (s?)   anon. editor (contemp) gks #131
inochi mada   keigu #27
iremono no nari ni naritaru ranyû (1699) brhkz #69
iremono no nari[kata] ni neteiru sani? sanki? (1774)
    rdhs, brhkzs #71
ishibachi ni   rôsô (1759) 靭随筆 brhkz, khkg #584
ishikoro ni   kuritani (?) shôji (contemp) #320
isobe?tsubo   mizumi kujô (mod) htt #738
isobue wa   maeda hakuro? (1978) sphk #739
isogusa   dôji? (1790) sgs (izs 8) #136
isohata ni   yonezawa _____? (mod.?) sphk #734
isokusaki   ginkô (18th c?) eno #779
issun no mizu   anon (contemp) issun #862
itajiki ni gejo   hirose tansô (1782-1856) tans #356
itajiki ni tori   hirose tansô (1782-1856) tans #357
iteru yo   dhugal (2001) dhl #482
itsu mite mo bakô (1686-1751) brhkz, khkg #99,#259
ittô ni tachite nonaka chiyoko (contemp.) akgs #500
iyashikumo   seisei (1869-1937) lr #191
iza kireba   keigu #25
jutsugo toka takasawa yoshikazu (1997) wgh 0710
    #677
jôguchi ni   kikaku? (1669-1706) hkb #359
jûbako no   ôemaru? (1801) hkb, nhhstk #67
jûnigatsu yôka   harada akira (contemp) #135
ka mo kitari   cz+keigu #790
kabe no namako (s)   yanagidaru ( ) 122-26, 123-61,
    125-11 ya50 #229
kachikôji   shiki (1898) szs (m31) #509
kagaku yôgo   keigu #724
kaibutsu ga taete   keigu #633
kaibutsu no   keigu #632
kaichû →watanaka
kaidan ga[no]   hashi kanseki (mod.) nez (and here
    and there on the net!) #563
kaikyô no   sumi yûzo (1998) uns #567
kaikô ya   hagiwara kiyo (1990) ndh #750
kaitei →unazoko
kakaru yo   anon (1763) brhkz #98
kaketsuke no   mantarô (1888-1963) khkg #442

kaki namako   keirô (1930) 高蘆 nez #867
kaki yori aioigaki kajin (1898-1985) khkg, akgs #457
kamikirenu   kyoshi et al (1894) kd #412
kanashimi   shugyô (contemp.) net #16
kane ni saku   saimaro (1655-1738) sai #686
kani no ko   shôhaku (1649-1722) nez #231
kannagi ya   fura (1934) 能登蒼し nez #579
kannamako higana   seike nobuhiro (2001) kdb #497
kannamako ni mo   saotome ken (1997) kdb #31-B
kannamako ware (t)   yoshitomi shômei? gdtk #558
kannen shi takasawa yoshikazu (2003)wgh03s4 #657
kanten ni takasawa yoshikazu(2001) wgh02s2 #573
kao mo aru   keigu #725
karakasa mo   takasawa yoshikazu (2001) wgh06
                                              sono2 #388
karisome ni harawata   seisei+keigu #81
kata no ni o   yanma (contemp) yanma #553
katamarite iro   kishû (1934) 小石川 nez #87
katamatte aware   kijô (1864-1938) hkkg #15
katsuzetsu   anon (contemp) ktzt #476
kawaii zo   uoko-chan (contemp) uok #233
kawara to mo   raizan (1653-1716) hkdz (skms では、
              子規句として「かな」
              が「とも」と。 間違い? #7
kazamuki ga   takasawa yoshikazu (1999)
                                       wgh01sono1 #180
kaze fuite   iwamoto naoki (p2001) gdsj #774
kaze mo   shiki (1867-1902) szs #552
keigu shi   hitoshi (2003) ukmd #631
kenbutsu bunpô   seibi (1748-1816) arusu #226
kenmei ni   harada kyô? (modern) nez #305
ki no hashi no   otsuyû (1670-1739) brhkz, nez #530
kimi ni yori (fs) nagatsuka takashi (1879-1915)
                                         (1901) ngt #75
kimi shiru ya   kôroku (1873-1949) kkhk #4
kimijika   mofû (1790) 秋顔子 izs8 #372
kinako   kyoshi et al (1894) kd #347
kinko kuchinu   futan? (1682) msc: kthb4 #699
kinko umi o   keiyô (1682) msc:kthb4 #692
kintama no   matsumoto seiki (1940) mmsk #194
kinyoku   futa shuno?(contemp)sshk #897
kiseotte   taimu (1793-1874) brhkz #531
kita e muku   bantoku (d. 1792) kskk (in nhhstk,
                                      ôemaru) #38
kobitai o   uetami shin (contemp?) uet #122
kôbutsu ni   namu (2003) ukmd #113
kôchoku no takasawa yoshikazu (2003) wgh03sono4
                                                #351
kodatami ya arishi   taigi (1709-72) tgks #330
kodatami mo muzukashiki ransetsu (1653-1707)
                                      brhkz, hksj #334
kodatami ni shiku   shimokawa   ? (1672) imy
                                  (kthb 2) #333
kodatami no hibiki   kakushi? (1701) 焦尾琴 brhkzs
                                                #329
kodatami wa nodo shisui? (1707) 類柑子 brhkz #384
kodatami ya ka no shôzan (1717-1801) nez? #340
kodatami ya katsuo   shigeharu? (1680) 落陽集
                                            kthbg4 #776
kodatami ya ono anshô? (1679) hked(kthbg3) #335
kogarashi   rogetsu (1872-1928) nez #22
koishi ni mo   shiki (1867-1902) szs #8
kôjitaru kaze   keigu #680
kojitsukeru   keigu #681
kokikoki to. . . arau   bakusô (1935) 麦嵐 nez #863
kokikoki to . hameba moriya koga (2000) suien-mry
                                                #394
kokoro kara kaze hiku namako ganbôsha keigu #682

kokoro naeshi   hakyô (1913-69) nhdz, nmsj, khkg,
                                   sphk, sksj, #375
kokoro yori   keigu #887
kokyô nite   ajikawa yôyo? (contemp) ajy #254
komawari yagi rinnosuke(mod)青霞 nez, sphk #168
kômon no   yû (2003) nmb #148
kondate ni   yayû (1701-83) ありづか kskk #238
kônkôn to   hyakken (1878-1971) nhds, khkg #308
konna   takasawa yoshikazu (2003) wgh03-4#421
konnyaku no itoko hakusetsu (b 1660 - ?) nez #215
konnyaku no kado   saji (1774?) rdks (=rdhs?) brhkz,
                                   nez #211
konnyaku no suna   keigu #212
konnyaku ya namako   seisei (1869-1937) hkdz #214
kono kao ga   doi tamiko (2001) kdb #115
konowata de   tabata masuhiro (2000) lr #447
konowata ni hitotsubo   shunyô (mod) nhds #443
konowata ni ichinen   nakahara michio (1998) nkhr
                                                #444
konowata ni mata tabata masuhiro (cont.) tbt #446
konowata no shun   keishi (18th c?) eno #780
konowata no tsubo o   gokû (1874-1928) sshsj, nhds,
                                        fshj #607
konowata no tsubo umetaki   richô? toshishige? (1689)
                              阿羅野 brhkz, khkg #606
konowata no umi sugemura asaka (1997) kdb #498
konowata o bui   keigu #784
konowata o natsukashimi [sic]   seibi (1748-1816)
                                            eno #781
konowata o oyogaseteiru yajima nagisaô (contemp)
                                   (2000.01) fjm #83
konowata o susuri ni   chiko? senrai? (1699?) 小弓
                                         brhkz #302
konowata o susuru oto tabata masuhiro (2002) net
                                                #453
konowata o susuru ya   isobe shakusanshi? takusanko?
                                   (1973) gdhks, khkg #301
konowata o tsukuru okazaki junrin (cont.) web #870
konowata wa kodaru masajo (1937) 夕螢(nez) #82
konowata ya kanshu   keigu #429
konowata ya kasane   ryûsui (mod) ホトトギス hksj
                                                #437
konowata ya nakichichi nikaidô eiko (cont) nkd #438
konowata ya tsubo hakuton? (1680) 桃青門弟独吟
                                      nez? #499
konowata/kono wata ogiue koichi (contem.) ogi #704
konton o shiki d.1902) szs, sks, hksj, sphk, nez #107
konton to otsutô?   otsutaku? (1699) hksj, brhkz #74
kore ijô   uchiyama yoshiko (1998) uns #742
kôrioute seisei (1869-1937) hkdz, nmsj, ndh, nez #30
korishô no sakebitakunaru   keigu #60
korishô o ijimeru   keigu #61
korokoro to   shidô (d.1741) nez? #583
koron to takasawa yoshikazu (2003)wgh03son3 #799
kororin to takasawa yoshikazu (2003) wgh03s2 #161
kowagawa to yoshiwara mubô[?] (c 2000) ntkk #46
kowai to ya   kyoshi et al (1894) kd #295
kozeniire   kobe michiyo (2001) kobe #769
kozoriau   banko (1777)句鑑 brhkz, khkg #714
koôkonrai kitte   sôseki (1867-1916) nhsk #307
kuchi no naka   hirakata fumiô (contem.) hrkt #381
kuchi omoki   yuri (contemp)yuri #455
kuchi tsugumu   takasawa yoshikazu (2003)
                                   wgh03sono4 #303
kuchigotae ônishi motoyuki (contemp) oni #460
kûkô ni yokoyama hakukô (1899-1983) ktbgd #688
kumu shio   risetsu (1698) 続猿蓑 brhkz, hkdz, rdhs,
                                      khkg #282

kuraki yori kuraki ni kaeru   gyôtai (1732-93) hksj, hkdz #609

kuraki yori kuraki ni namako   senpû(1793)srdhs #610
kureichi   takasawa yoshikazu (2001) 01sono1 #717
kurushimi   seira (1739-1791) 新五子 brhkz #273
kuruwa   gôtô yahan? (1932) 翠黛 nez, sshksj, sksj, khkg #260
kuttaku   sugiyama nozomi (2001) kdb #206
kuu? mama ni ware o   rangai (d.1845) hkzs #392
kyakusen no   kawasaki toshiko (contemp) akgs #568
machi furite   kajiyama chizuko (1997) ghhk hs9 #823
majimesa   miyoko (contemp) hkgr #14
makeikusa   anon. net #807
manabashi ni   gyojitsu (d.1753) nez #361
manaita ni agureba   issô (1732-1820) hkdz, hhdg #29
manaita ni chijimi   arakawa yûki (1997) kdb #201
manaita ni hau   taigi (1709-72) tgks, hksj, hkdz #23
manaita ni mada   somaru (1712-95) smhs (iszb), kskk #94
manaita ni namako   shôzan (1717-1801) nez? #362
manaita no dochira   katsura nobuko (1993) gdhs #40
manaita no kokoro   sani? (1699) brhkz #39
manaita no kôri   taigi (1709-72) brhkz, tgks, hkdz, nhds, khkg #24
manaita no namako ni   keigu #44
manaita no namako wa   nagata suiko? (contemp.?) ndh #309
manaita no ue   takasawa yoshikazu (2003) #167
massugu ni   uda kiyoko (modern) nez #759
matsukaze   anami fusen (1820?) hhdg #810
me mo hana   fuseki (1679)談林功用群鑑 kthb 4 #237
me ni wa   seishi (1670/72?) zsks, kskk #354
mehananaki (t)   ôtsubo shôichi ( ) gdtkb #586
menaki koso   keigu #91
menami   masatoshi? (1674) 桜川 kskk #318
menbokubô   ôemaru?(1801) 俳諧袋 nhhstk #234
mewarabe   okairi mantoko? (contemp?) ghhk #645
mezurashi   shunni? (1689) あらの=brhkz, hkdz, khkg #345
mi o mamoru   taigi (1709-72) tgks #188
michinoku   fûrinken (1667) 続山井 kthb2 #893
michiteyuku   wakô (1759) brhkz #150
migaru   maihime (contemp) reon #80
minasoko mo   shidano saka (contemp) #770 mrs
minasoko ni heike   ryôshô (1831) rrs, hskk, nez? #139-C [[313~14,#139]]
minasoko no namako   baimei (1772) 其雪影 hksj, brhkz, hkdz #137
minasoko ya waraji   okada kôyô (mod.) hksj, nhsj, fshj #623
minisukahto   kazunaga fujiyo (1997) kdb #116
miru dake ni   keigu #385
miru tabi ni   keigu #522
misesaki ni namako   someno ozuki (1997) kdb #715
mita dake de namako kirai   keigu #664
mita dake de namako o   tamagu (tamasudare+keigu) ymym #710
mitsugyô   zankuro (2002) net #104
miyo ni   fukyo (1829) brhkz (花の春・動物) #778
mizu kireta   keigu+tenki #264
mizu kirete namako   keigu #265
mizu kirete umi   keigu #263
mizudeppô   keigu #268
mizukara   karube utôshi (1932) しどみの花 nez #515
mochikaeru   keigu #713
mogura utte   shichiku (mod.) nez #643

moguramochi kashite   fukei?(1682) msc (kthb 4) #317
mogurauchi toragodôn   riyô (mod.) hksj #640
mogurauchi tsukurinu   sôda (mod.) hksj #644
moji katachi   itô kitajo (1993) kdbgd #5
monogusana   anai futoshi (contemp.) nez #544
mou namako   yoshiro (2002)句会 12/14 ukmd #365
mugurauchi oriori   kasei (mod.) hksj, ghhk #639
mui ni   shiki (1867-1902) szs, skmks, hkdz, hksj, b:h(a), nhds, khkg, fshsj, nez #106
mukashi otoko   ôemaru (1721-1805) hkb, nhds, khkg, kskk #506
mukutsukeki   rosen (1690) arusu, hksj, brhkz, khkg #798
mô hitotsu   takasawa yoshikazu (1999) wgh 01s1 #517
naburarete   fukumoto geiyô (cont.) sphk, shks #200
nadaraka ni   koizumi chiyoko (2001) kdb #408
nagarekite   giki (1759) 靭随筆 brhkz #158
nagasao o   ôishi etsuko (contemp) nez #765-B
nagetemiru   shôzan (1717-1801) nez? #629
namako araitsutsu   nômura toshirô (cont.) hkkg #513
namako ari hôchû   hekigotô (1872-1937) hkdz, sssj #45
namako ari yue   kawasaki nobuhiro (cont) nez? #684
namako da to   keigu #43
namako e to   namu (2002) ukmd 句会 12/14 #729
namako ebi (t)   minami masatane (mod.) gdtkb #281
namako eri (see namakoeri)
namako fumu   tamasudare (2002) ukmd? #628
namako fun efu   keigu #662
namako fundara   kuramoto asayo (cont.) kura #627
namako ga hara (z)   mutamagawa 11(1771) #507
namako hitori   takasawa yoshikazu (2003) wgh03 sono4 #452
namako hosu irakogasaki   gyôtai (1731-92) khkg, cjco #813
namako hosu onna   mizunuma saburo (1978) sphk #814
namako hosu sode   shirô (1742-1813) hkzs nez? #574
namako ima   seisei (1869-1937) nez #868
namako iru oke   chôtsuki (1932) sssj #21
namako itsu   rakutô (mod.) hksj #641
namako kami rôjaku   itan sachiko (2001?) akgs #411
namako kami zannen   takase hakuyô (2001) kdb #409
namako kamu ha ga   takasawa yoshikazu (2003) wgh03sono4#418
namako kamu hatarakazaru   matsumoto usei (contemp) mksj #512
namako kamu hikari   kobiyama shigeru (modern) nez, mksj #391
namako kamu jiryû   sugahara sadao (2001) kdb #117
namako kamu kao   takasawa yoshikazu (2003) wgh03sono4#422
namako kamu kotaerarenaki   mizuuchi keita (contemp) 『月の匣』 lr #461
namako kamu magao   shûson (1905-93) nez? #401
namako kamu nanji   sanki (1899-1962) gdhks, nez? #405
namako kamu rokuman   tenki (2002) ukmd #395
namako kamu shita   genyama shino? (cont) sphk #382
namako kamu shûshi   tateishi seitsuko (contemp) akgs #467
namako kamu sono   takasawa yoshikazu (2002) wgh12sono1#403
namako kamu sore   nakamura sonoko (1996)花隠れ nez? #402

namako kamu toki kôkotsu (t)   morisaki kazuo (contemp.) mrs #398

namako kamu tôki bôten   iida ryûta (mod.?) ghhk, nhds, khkg, sksj, ghhk, nez, shks #560

namako kana appurupai   keigu #647

namako kana bannôyaku   keigu #726

namako kana hito   roga? (1759) 靭随筆 brhkz #589

namako kana inu   keigu #430

namako kana nanji   tetsuami (1798) 哲阿彌句藻? #590

namako kana toraeraretaru meisetsu (1848-1926) ` mhs #186

namako kana yo ga   rosen (1660-1743) hkzs, brhkz, rdhs, #550

namako kau hitosashiyubi suzuki masajo (1906-) 「句集都鳥」#865

namako kau otto   tsuboi yoshie (cont.) shks? #399

namako kiri inochi   keigu #277

namako kiri isogazuni   keigu #275

namako kiri moto   ohara takuyo (2001) kdb, takuyo #896

namako kiri tamashii   keigu #276

namako kiru doko   keigu #26

namako kiru kashirarashiki takasawa yoshikazu (2003) corresp #41

namako kiru koto   ôhashi atsuko (contemp?) 句玉 nhds, khkg, nez #364

namako kishi itamae k eigu #42

namako kitte   utsunomiya den (contemp) lr #492

namako koso   keigu #832

namako kui benzaiten anon (2002/07/21) kobs #826

namako kui furusato yuda kunihiro(1997) mksj #396

namako kuishi kao   shûson (1905-93) nez? #841

namako kuishi otoko kawasaki nobuhiro? (1977) kym, nhds, khkg, ndh, nez #824

namako kute   tôyô (mod.) ty #424

namako kuu ha no   bakunan (mod.) sphk, nmsj, shks #414

namako kuu haoto somaru (1712-95) smhs (isz b), kskk #387

namako kuu hitorizumo miyazawa eiko (contemp) shks? #374

namako kuu kono kadokawa haruki (cont.) net #327

namako kuu matsunouchi bakusô (1935) 麦嵐 nez #839

namako kuu mazu   keigu #428

namako kuu wa   ransetsu (1690) nhds, brhkz, hksj, hkdz, khkg, hkrs, etc #143

namako kuu watashi kasama keiko (2001) shhk #114

namako kuu yû   chûtakuo? (modern) nez #569

namako made   seibi (1779) brhkz #830

namako mata   kyoshi (1874-1959) nhds, khkg #218

namako menashi   shiki (1898) szs #239

namako mite hôki   keigu #665

namako mite kaki   ôta yasunao (contemp) kaki #848

namako mite mata tanaka hisako (contemp) net #869

namako modashi   shiki (1897) szs #510

namako moshi yanagi   ôemaru? (1790?) hzg #316

namako nado tsutsukite (t) chiyo kunikazu (contem.) gdtkb #450

namako nado uri.. michihiko (1746-1819) nez? #227

namako namako   seisetsu (1871-1917) b:hh(2) #1

namako nanji   gyokudô (1872-1957) fshsj #244

namako nara   keigu #648

namako nare mo   seihô (pre1926) nez #604

namako nari aoshio sugita chieko (cont.) akgs #543

namako nari kaze   takasawa yoshikazu (1997) taka#679

namako nari ni   kenpo? (19th c) ayame #593

namako nasu reishi(t) okamoto taimu (1877-1963) gdtkb #625

namako ni hige takasawa yoshikazu (2003) wgh03 sono4#470

namako ni mo hari buson (1715-1783) hksj, bz, hkdz, nhds #272

namako ni shôben   takasawa yoshikazu (2003) corresp #166

namako ni wa umi   yagi chûei (contemp) yagi #486

namako ni wa ôkisugiru nagatsuka sumie (1993) kdb #536

[nama]ko no jumyo deguchi kojô (2002) dgc #110

namako no ku aredo   ryûka (1927) hkdz #77n

namako no ku ôi   takasawa yoshikazu (2002) wgh07sono1 #895

namako no wa (s)   obanagasa? (c1720) 亭保中 eeks #294

namako oite   ôshi (mod.?) hkdz #141

namako oki modoru   keigu #761

namako oseba   kirino manjirô (2000) suien #703

namako sae nigeru baishitsu (1839) 梅室家集 hksj, hkzs #183

namako sage katô shûson (con) nysj, ndh, nmsj #465

namako saku hana   keigu #705

namako saku itamae   shinobugusa (2000) snb #304

namako saku nani   keigu #706

namako saku onna.. nakayama tenken (mod) htt #854

namako seru kobushi izaka tsukiko (2001) kdb #199

namako soku renkinjutsushi   keigu #663

namako su ni takasawa yoshikazu (2003) wgh03 sono4 #28

namako tabe jômonjin kuritani shôji (2000) poe #393

namako tabe karada tanabe kayoko (1997) hkkg #881

namako tabe sabishiki nagai fumie (cont) shks? #400

namako tabe tsutsu torii mariko (contemp.) (2002) mns #293

namako taberarete takasawa yoshikazu (2003) wgh 03sono4 #651

namako to iu   ensui (2002) mnh1-3 #613

namako to mo katarenu   yûshi? (contemp) yuu #473

namako to mo nara   ryôto (1658-1717) rrs, brhkz, khkg, hkks #139-A

namako to wa (t) satô fusako (contemp) sato #659

namako toru minna kirino manjirô (2000) suien #701

namako toru namako inoue hirô (2001) shhk #179

namako tsuki mangaichi   keigu #883

namako tsuku ama hayashi taima (cont.) nhds #169

namako tsuku arima   kazuki baison? (?) kazu #793

namako tsuku fune o okayasu jingi (1998) uns #741

namako tsuku fune yori (t)   yoshiue shôryô (1884-1958) gdtkb #571

namako tsuku hitori inahata teiko (mod) htt #740

namako tsuku mori   yûfû (mod.) zhtt, hksj #542

namako tsuku shio? yamanaka   (mod) htt #857

namako tsuku umi ni kurita setsuko (1997) kdb #794

namako uru   kanajo? (1927) 龍胆 nez #581

namako yori   saida jin (contemp) hers #656

namako zaru kyoshi (1918) ksks, ndjks, hksj #818

namakobiki yodachi   keigu #288

namakobune fuji kinukawa sunao (1990) ndh #176

namakobune fukururu noburo (1932) 浜木綿 sphk, nez, khkg #175

namakobune hesaki o   kuroda sakura no en [?] (pub 2001) akgs #174

namakobune hesakinaki yamamoto shunji (1998) uns #173

namakobune nami ni suzuka nobûro (1932) 浜木綿 nez #764

namakobune ôtsugomori yagi rinnosuke? (mod.) 青霞集 nez #834

namakobune shio kurashi abe sangyo?(mod) #858

namakobune tomo anon. (contemp.) onsen #804

namakobunerashi gyoi taiseki? (contemp?) gyo #534

namakoeri tokeru (s) yanagidaru 107-9 ya50 #228

namakoeri wara (s) yanagidaru 64, ygd50, ojd #271

namakogui namako namako takahashi hiroko (p 2001) gdsj #423

namakogui namako no shiki (1896) szs, skmks #432

namakohiki fune takagishi manabu (1978) sphk #737

namakomeku takasawa yoshikazu (2001) hka200103 sono1 #324

namakoryo itami kimiko (contemp) nez #566

namakotachi keigu #831

namakotsuki ashi ôuchi itsuzan (2001) kdb #178

namakotsuki koe obasei (contemp) oba #477

namakotsuki nami kusume tôkôshi (1932) nez #745

namakotsuki ni ohara seiseishi (mod.) net #792

namakotsuki ôyoso hekigotô? (1872-1937) lr (if mistaken, ippekiro) #767

namakotsuki rôden wada kôji (contemp.) gdsj #859

namakotsuki sao yagi rinnosuke (mod.) ndh #454

namakotsuki shinu miyazaki shizuo (cont) nez #753

namakotsuki shio no ôtake kinya? uns (1998) #170

namakotsuki sora sonobe utei (2001) kdb #752

namakotsuki tsuka.. ishibashi hikaru (1998) uns #456

namakotsukibune rô? tokunaga genshi? (mod) ntt #736

namakouri hoihoi katayama mitsuyo (con.) kata #771

namakouri kame karube utôshi? (1932) しどみの花 nez?#777

namakouri mukai.. ôhashi ôhashi (1932) 雨月 #582

namakouri toshi hinoki minami (mod.) 国民俳句 sshksj #835

namakouri tsumande (s) mutamagawa 13 (1759) srzps, ojd #261

namakozake hagiwara bakusô (1935) #433

namakusaku umeko (contemp) ume #149

namari nasu seichi (2002) hkcl #495

nami inasu kiyota kon? (mod) #747

nami kiite takano kanpo (1973) gdhks #524

nami ni iki takahashi yasurô (contemp?) ndh #743

nan no mi bifû? (1768) kskk # 9

nan no yue sôseki (1867-1916) ssk #209

nanimo nai keigu+tenki #256

nanimo naku keigu #255

nanimokamo kijô (1933) net? #683

natsukashiki anon. ntkhh #252

negoi sono keigu #523

nehane ni maira tarô (1927) hkdz #323

nemurarenu yo keiten (keigu+tenki) #548

nemutai ya keigu #529

nenbutsu wa namako shiki (1896) szs #130

neru namako keigu #595

nete samete takasawa yoshikazu (1997) taka #672

niburite takasawa yoshikazu (2002) wgh11-2 #526

ningen no terada torahiko (1878-1935) nnm #594

ningen wa okuzaka maya (contemp) maya #898

nisan bai gijô (1741) kskkhk #878

nisen nen katô shizuo (contemp.) kdkwhks #111

nita mono ryûkyo (1694-1748) kskk #525

nite yaite takasawa yoshikazu (1997) wgh0710 #164

nodo suguru taniguchi mitsuko (contem.) sawa #298

nokosubeki azuma kayoko (1997) kdb #451

nomeba nomu keigu #426

nomisugitte tabata masuhiro (contemp.) tbt #449

nôshû no hito anon (17c.?) （金華伝）bsgi #690

notoshima tokunaga shunpû #856

nozokioke aoto shizue (1993) kdb #746

nukete tobu sekidô (mod.) #642

nuketedeta roi (1770) 武埜談笑 kskk #312

numeri toru yoshida shino (1997) kdb #360

nuresode no kurage keigu #577

nuresode no namako keigu #578

nuribashi ni ikaku ( ) brhkz, kskk #366

nyuinnamako takasawa yoshikazu (1997) wgh 0710 #676

o mo hire mo motanu anon (contemp) nhk? #65

o mo hire mo naku(te?) kotani yukio (conte?) stb #64

obire furu bigo (1793) 古橘 srdhs #159

oboro kana kamikura utsuwa (contemp) kami #653

ôibiki buson (1750) hksj, bzs #527

ôinaru kawasaki nobuhiro (contemp.) nez #603

ojiisan hitoshi (2002)ukmdh 句会 12/14 #730

okamochi no tetsua (1798?) lr (if 哲阿, 1798?) #70

okashira no fumei keigu #63

okashira no kokoronaki kyorai (1689) 猿蓑 brhkz, hkdz, b:h(a), nhds, khkg, rdhs, ndh, etc #36

okashisa katsusan (1751-1818) hkzs, hhdg #346

oke ni hi hattori suisei (mod) #864

oke no namako gyosô (1927) hkdz #196

okezoko ni takasawa yoshikazu (2003) wgh03s3 #132

oki no ishi kishû (1934) 小石川 sshksj #319

omeikô waraie (s) yanagidaru (___) y-102 (ojd) #134

omomuro ni tsuru (mod.?) zhtt, hksj #189

omou koto buson (1770) 落日庵句集 bz, hdz, hksj,nhds, khkg #480

ônamako hikkakete seihô (1881-1944) sssj, nez #733

ônamako hito mutaguchi akio (2001) kdb #545

ônamako mizu tanabe fûshinko (1997) ghhk #311

ônamako torori shirai tôsei (mod) htt #546

ônamako tsukameba shimakura mitsuru (1993) kdb #310

ônamako tsutsukeba kotani yukio (contem.) kty #190

oni mo iya issa (1814) izs1,3 #123

onna ni wa saitô kyôrô? (contemp) sawa #718

ono ga mi ni fushitemo keigu #205

onoga mi ni tsuno keigu #216

onoga mi o akiramete keigu #669

oranu hito nomoto kyô (contemp) nmtk #875

oriori ni kobosu mokuto (1932) sssj #555

ôsei no hana tôrin (1638-1719) nez #685

oshi itadaku kawasaki nobuhiro (contem.) nez #250

ôsugiru takasawa yoshikazu (2003) hka03sono5 #66

otoko yori torii mariko (contemp)『鼬の姉妹』#853

pendako suzuki masajo (1906-) lr #719

pikapika no keigu #668

rainichi shi keigu #266

rakuyô shûmon (1682) msc: kthb4 #700

reitô de tora (contemp) tora #57

remingu matsuki hide (contemp) tskc #890

rô no umi shibasaki akio (contemp) akio #805

robin giru furiko (2003) nmb #894

rôhachi ya shiki ?(1867-1902) szs #133

rôjin no kaka mihoko (contemp) miho #615

rôshi kyomu terada toruhiko (1878-1935) #108

ryôrarete rikô somaru (1712-95) smhs(izs b) #332

ryôri de[hakarate?]wa hikari ??? (1674) 俳諧桜川 ojd #879

ryôri ni mo hoyû (1670) (fl.1645) zsks (kthb3) #378

ryôtei no nanchatte kurikintoki? (2000?) hkcl #291

ryûgu no niwa shaseki? (pre 1927) hkdz #622

ryûgu no tenjôura   kayô (pre 1927) hkdz #621
ryûgu no wasabioroshi   kakô? (1680) brhkzs #620
saigyôjima   michikaze? (1682) msc:kthb4 #697
sakana to wa   keigu #146
sakanaya   keirô (1930) 高蘆 nez? #820
sake ga suki   anon (2000) he #440
sake kumite   shimizu akira (2001) hkkk #828
sakuragai   ichiju (1774-1827) eno #775
samidare ya   akutagawa ryûnosuke (mod.) nez #808
samui hi ni   riyû (1751) kskk #612
samushiro ni (t)   ôba torao (contemp.?) gdtkb #812
sanehira   chôsui (1700-69) hhdg #367
sangoshô ni (t)   kawada jun (contemp.) gdtkb #756
sangoshô no (t)   kawada jun (contemp.) gdtk #687
sansai   takasawa yoshikazu (2003) wgh03sono5 #528
sara ni noru   suzuki taeko ( ) sphk (1978) #851
sasuga ni   ryôto(1658-1717) rrs, brhkz #139b
seibô zo   ôno kyôju (contemp?) ndh #795
seiippai   ebisudani hisayo (2001) kdb #208
seija no fu   fura (1883-1954) nez #221
seisô no onna   suzuki jin (2001) jin #866
senhyaku ri   hekigotô (1872-1937) nez #503
sensuigi   ôta aa (2001) shhk #171
seri oete   tsuboi hisako (1993) kdb #765
seridai   hayashi kunjo (contemp.) sphk 1978? #207
serigoe ni mesamete hashimoto keiji (con.) shks #535
serigoe ni nani ka ôhashi atsuko (contem) ghhk #533
setsu ni i[sa]mu   shiki (1897) szs? #431
shijimi   ryôta (1717-1787) khkg, nez #283
shikaku ishibe akira (contemp) 「あかんべ」 net #516
shikoshiko to   nobucha? (contemp). nbc #390
shima no ko (t) kitahara hakushû (mod.) gdtkb #755
shin to   anai setsuko (2001) kdb #491
shina fuhen   keigu #732
shinan koto   shikô (1793) srdhs #162
shinde kara   hitoshi (haikagura 2003) #899
shingen   somaru (1712-1795) smhs (isz b) #368
shinpai takasawa yoshikazu (1999) wgh02son3 #165
shintaku takao ikuki (contemp.) iku #874
shinwara no (t) hashimoto tokuju? (co?) gdtkb #811
shinzô ishihara yatsuka (modern) nez #488
shio futte namako no tsuchida kaseki (conte) tsu #635
shio futte namako otakebi   takasawa yoshikazu
         (2003)wgh03sono3 #634
shiobuki   shinô (1927) hkdz #321
shiomizu ni takasawa yoshikazu(2003)wgh03s3 #861
shiosaki no   kenmochi shiranui (mod) lr #758
shiranami   kakubei (?) hhdg (ks?) #53
shiranu kana shôritsu (1679) 談林功用群監 kthb 4
         #236
shirikuchi   sôya (1756) brhkz, kskk #51
shiru hito   jôku?(18th c?) 雑中brhz #608
shizukasa no   seibi (1748-1816) hkzs #537
shizukesa ya   keigu #475
shô no ma ni nagaki   kusume tôkôshi (1932) 橙圃,
         nez? zssk #172
shô no ma ni sao yamazaki kazunosuke (mod) ntt #766
shôchi shite   katô ikuya (contemp) net #415
shônagon ni   keigu #540
shôshin nite   keigu #62
shôshin no   bigu (miyoko+keigu) #855
shûbi o tatsu   hekigotô (1872-1937) hkdz #37
sôjiya   keigu #667
soko koko   taigi (1709-72) tgks, brhkz, hkdz #92
sokoiwa ni   shimamura hajime (1868-1926) nez #68
sokushi kana keigu #884
sotto fure   tanaka harue (2001) kdb #249
sotto mochidase (s) yanagidaru 11 (1776) srzps, ytri,

         ojd #336
su ni aute ishi nomura kishû (1934)小石川 ndh #370
su ni ôte[aede?] hone chikushi (1703) 草苅笛
         (kskkhk) #369
su ni otosu   ishida fûta (1997) zssk #407
su no naka ni kokoro hideto (conte) corresp, net #801
su no naka o ketanigearuku togetsu (1726-1780)
         hkrs #379
su o saseba ôemaru (1721-1805) hzg, hkdz #274
sube sube keigu #184
subin ikutsu tashiro shôi? (mod.?) tsr #306
sufinkusu keigu #90
sukimono no ha iida dakotsu (1885-1962) sshksj,
phksj, fshj #386
sukuiiru namako udô tôru(1997) ghhk #565
sumi nijimu yamada mizue (contemp) sphk #840
suna no naka hekigotô (1894) 虚桐庵句会 kzs, hksj,
         kyb, nez #585
suna o hamu (t) yano chieko (2000) yano #487
sunabara ni nyogyô (1692) 葛松原 brhkz, rdhs #152
sunamako ga tsuzuki momohei (2001) akgs #463
sunamako ni ago takasawa yoshikazu (2003)
         wgh03sono4 #419
sunamako ni sabitsuku takasawa yoshikazu (2003)
         wgh03sono4 #417
sunamako no achikochi unknown (2000) unk #383
sunamako no furuete iida kimiko (contemp.) mksj
         (1997) #185
sunamako no hito~ izawa masae (1978) sphk #299
sunamako no kamikire... toryû (2001 ny) mnh #413
sunamako no kirikizamareshi hideto (contemp.)
         correp., net #800
sunamako no kore takasawa yoshikazu (2003)
         wgh03 sono4#420
sunamako no niguru kojima hôseki (1997) kdb #377
sunamako no su kagen nagakata yûko (2000) #339
sunamako o hamite shimanishi utata (2001) kdb #380
sunamako o se~ nonaka ryôsuke (2001) akgs #406
sunamako o shizumete shimizu akira (cont.) #435
sunamako o susurite   toki (2000) via ymym #720
sunamako tabu takasawa yoshikazu (2003) wgh03
         sono4 #416
sunamako to takasawa y. (2003) wgh03 sono4 #350
sunamako ya chichi horiguchi shômin (1936) 営巣期
         shks, nez #436
sunamako ya gokuri   K.H. (2000) kh #297
sunamako ya haha date masakazu (1997) kdb #561
sunamako ya kishi kikuchi hisako (1997) kdb#389
sunamako ya natsukashiki   kadokawa haruki
         (contemp) ino #253
sunamako ya shian matsuo yoshihisa (con.) mts #376
sunuhpi   keigu #888
suribachi okada shajin (mod.?) 若葉 (sshk), fshsj
         #258
sutetearu   mino nampo? (1793) srdhs #54
tabuh   tazumi michio (1993) gdhs #3
tachiuo   miyoko (2003) ukmd #630
tako ni hone (f) anrai bushi (early modern?) ndh #35
takotsubo   yanagidaru (=ygd) 新編 31 #279-b
tanegashima   keigu #267
tarekomete sugihara chikujo (contem) fshsj #494
te mo ashi   maihime(contemp) reon #483
te ni toreba buchôhônaru kyoshi (1916) kzs, ksks,
         zssk #73
te ni toreba mada (s) mutama.16 (1771) srzps #270
te ni toreba sasuga ginkô (1775) 古姿 brhkz #182
teatsureba takasawa yoshikazu (2003)wgh03sono4
teijo   shiki (1894) szs #240   #352

tenchi (see ametsuchi, too)
tenchi imada sûya?shûkoku? (early 19c) ayame #101
tettôtetsubi … miage [my mistake] naruse ôtôshi (1993) kdb #721
tettôtetsubi... shinjô naruse ôtôshi (1993) kdb #58
tezukami takano kiyoko (2001) akgs #768
tobujutan keigu #624
toge hinoki kiyo (1996) ssjk #187
toke somaru (1712-95) smhs #17
tokiori keigu #156
tomogui keigu #285
tomokaku (t) yosano hiroshi (1873-1935) gdtkb #55
tomoshibi ishizuka masao (1973) gdhks #195
toriotosu hirose tansô (1782-1856) tans #358
toshi no sake kyaku ryôgu (takasawa+keigu) #843
toshi no sake namako takasawa yoshikazu (2000) wgh 01sono1 #842
toshi no yo ritô (18c) nez #829
toshi o hete sôshun (1666-1740) nez #877
toshiyori yamane (contemp) ymn #109
toshizake no ryôgu (takasawa+keigu) #844
toshizake ya ryôgu (takasawa+keigu) #845
tôsô ni akite masaki yûko (contemp) #217
tsui ni gejo kasanjo (1807-30) nez #355
tsukamarete (k) ogiue koichi (contemp) ogi #85
tsukamidasu okada hisae (2001) kdb #248-B
tsuki yuki shikô (1776) 続明烏=brhkz, khkg #341
tsumi naku rosen (1660-1743) nez? #872
tsuribari yayû (1701-83) 蕪葉集(1767) hksj, khkg #105
tsurigane no kiko(kiin?) (early 18th c) hkdz #314
tsuttsuite kôkai? (contemp) kki #472
uba wa nakatsuka ippekiro (1885-1946) nez #290
uchimorasu tochimenbô (mod.) hksj #637
uka shayô (1698) 続猿蓑 brhkz, hkdz, khkg#504
uke namako buppôrufu issa (1814) ihks, izs 1,3, hksj #219
uke namako iwanu keigu #222
uke namako mikami keigu #223
uke namako shigure keigu #224
ukiaruku kanrai (1733-1817) hhdg, hkrs #313
ukidetete shirô (1741-1812) hkzs, hhdg, arusu #505
ukigoto shôha (1726-1771) hksj, hkdz, hh1, nhds, khkg, sphk, etc #502
ukihito seira (1739-1791) hhdg #481
umi kiyoku murata shûn ghhk hs9 #754
umi ni aru kokusui?(1773) hkss, brhkzs #52
umi no soko anon (contemp) net #286
umi no tsuki [oops,no slug!] sanka (18c?) nez #493
umi o koi murayama seiai (2001) kdb #326
umi shiranu ranran (1646-93) 武蔵曲=brhkz #344
umi sukoshi tenki (2003) ukmd #689
umi terite yagi rinnosuke (mod) 青霞集 nez #478
umidanshi keigu #284
unazoko ni hito matsumoto seiki (1942) net #34
unazoko/kaitei ni tsuki takemi?(contemp?) sshk 国民俳句 #519
unazoko/kaitei ga fujiwara ai (2001) #485
unazoko/kaitei ni kôkogaku mochinaga mariko (contemp) mcng #112
unazoko ni manako torii mariko (2002) mns #93
unazoko/kaitei no hinoyama tatsuoka tsutomu (contemp.) nhds, khkg, ghgd #616
uoichi no murakami kijô (1864-1938) cjco #580
uoichi ya rikyo (mod.?) hkdz #803

urabito ya hokichi arusu 74, hhdg #712
urenokori seiho (1899-1992) hkkg #837
uri urite raiu? (1772) brhkz, hdz #19
urokonaki hara masaji (1989) ktbgd #448
urokuzu kôyû (1932) sssj #562
uruwashiku shôha (1726-1771) 春泥発句集 hkdz, hksj #331
usunigoru takai kyoshi (1997) kdb #541
usuzumi ni haruji? (contemp) khkg #539
utsukekoji michikaze (1682) msc:kthb4 #698
utsunami shayô (c1700) brhkz, nez #160
wadatsumi (also watatsumi)
wadatsumi no soko ni mono rakunan (mod.?) hkdz #257,479diff. meaning, two #'s)
waga chô no ichibu takasawa yoshikazu (2003) wgh 03sono4 #353
waga chô no mono issa (sic) [chikua] (d. 1790) iids, hh1, eh (eng. only) #124
waga nari kakô? (1773) 新選 brhkz #456
waga uchi yagi chûei (contemp) yagi #489
wagamamana kôtô tomoko (2001) shhk #520
wagiri takasawa yoshikazu (2003) wgh03-4 #337
wara mokugû (z) anon zps (ojd) #125
warazuto ni anon. zpu (ojd) #126
watanaka/kaichû e kinukawa sunao (1997) kdb, akgs #748
watatsumi ya esa shirao/hakuyû (1738-1791) arusu, hksj, hhdg, cjco #711
yama e yaru tokurô (1777-1826) kskk #691
yami fusumi takasawa yoshikazu (1997) #678
yami no yo shôka (1820?) hhdg #611
yami samu keigu #600
yasuyasu to sôseki (1899) ndh, net, all over! #246
yaya arite bokudô (1703) 草刈笛 sshksj, nez #427
yayo namako keigu #597
yo hisoka ni rogetsu (1872-1928) nez #121
yo wa kasegi keigu #596
yôgan ga keigu #618
yôgan ka keigu #617
yôgan ya keigu #619
yoidore wa anon. (1900) mmc #425
yokonami matsuzaki rakuchû (mod) htt #749
yokotawari takasawa yoshikazu (1998) wgh01 sono1#833
yoku mireba jinen (contemp) corresp #128
yoku neru . . keigu #599
yoku neru . . keigu #598
yone ni (k) kuroda getsudôkan (17c) ouc #78
yononaka shiki (1893) szs #602
yoru wa tera . . seisei (1869-1937) hksj, hkdz #638
yowai to wa yamada tôkô (1997) kdb #349
yû sareba tomioka kikuchiro (1989) khkg, akgs #556
yubi takasawa yoshikazu (2003) wgh03sono4 #797
yuki ato miki reiko (contemp.) reiko #816
yuki no hibi (t) mitomo heikichi (1935) gdtkb #434
yuki no ue tamoto hokushi (mod) nhds, ndh #802
yuki no yo takahashi mutsurô (conte). 稽古 nez #31
yuki to naru katsuyuki (1999) 『月天 1999 春』#850
yuki zuriochite sarubashi tôryûshi (1973) gdhks #815
yukue naku minakichi sou? (mod.) nez, sphk #410
yumenamako (t) takeshitsa yôichi (1955-) take #654
yurariyura misa (contemp) misa #655
yûyake hada gakusui (1978) sphk #760
zakoneshite keigu #716
zatsunen takajo (d.1972) khkg, cjco #490

poet index

さて限られている時間とenergyでこれは、第一版の限界です。不完全性をお詫び、又第二版の改良のために、皆さんのご協力を、よろしくお願いします。Please check the *errata* at paraverse.org!

abe sangyo? #858
aioigaki kajin #457
ajikawa yôyo? #254
akutagawa ryûnosuke #808
anai futoshi #544
anai setsuko #491
anami fusen #810
anon .#2 #65 #98 #125 #126 #131 #204 #232 #252 #286 #328 #383 #425 #440 #469 #476 #501 #690 #804 #807 #825 #826 #852 #862 #879(pronunciation? 江名 口季堅)
anrai bushi #35
anshô? #335
aoto shizue #746
arakawa yûki #201
azuma kayoko #451
baba akiko #496
baimei #137
baishitsu #183
bakô #99,#259
bakujin #33
bakunan #414
bakuran #100
bakurô #900
bakusô #514#863 #839
banko #714
bantoku #38
bashô #9
bigo #159
bigu (miyoko+keigu) #855
bokudô #427
buson #272 #480 #527 #591
butsujô #322
chiekai #279
chikua [not issa] #124
chiko? senrai? #302
chikushi #369
chitsuka #192
chiyo kunikazu #450
chôi #466
chômu #151
chôsui #367
chôsui #880
chôtsuki #21
chûtakuo? #569
cz+keigu #790
date masakazu #561
deguchi kojô #110
dhugal #482
doi tamiko #115
dôji? #136
dokushô #696
ebisudani hisayo #208
ensui #230#613
etsuran (?) #348
fujii sankichi #89
fujiki tomoko #404
fujiwara ai #485
fukei? #317

fukumoto geiyô #200
fukushima masato #445
fukyo #778
fura #221 #579
furiko #894
fûrinken #893
fuseki #237
fusui? #193
futa shuno? #897
futan? #699
genyama shino? #382
gesô #157
getsukyo #181
gijô #878
giki #158
ginkô #182 #779
gohô #373
gokû #607
gotô takashi #849
gôtô yahan? #260
gyoi taiseki? #534
gyojitsu #361
gyokudô #244
gyosô #196
gyôtai #609 #813
hada gakusui #760
hagiwara kiyo #750
hagiwara bakusô #433
hagizuki #891
hakusanyô? #511
hakusetsu #215
hakuton? #499
hakyô #375
hara masaji #448
harada akira #135
harada kyô? #305
haruji? #539
hashi kanseki #439 #563
hashimoto keiji #535
hashimoto tokuju? #811
hattori suisei #864
hayashi kunjo #207
hayashi shô #462
hayashi taima #169
hekigotô #37 #45 #503 #585 #767? (maybe, ippekiro?)
hideto #800 #801
hino sôjô #10
hinoki kiyo #187
hinoki minami #835
hirade gashun? #292
hirakata fumiô #381
hirose tansô #356 #357 #358
hitoshi #484 #631 #730 #819 #899
hokichi #712
horiguchi shômin #436
hôrô #549
hoyû #378
hyakken #308

icchi #118
ichiju #775
iida dakotsu #386
iida kimiko #185
iida ryûta #560
ikaku #366
inahata teiko #740
inoue hirô #179
inuzuka sadako #836
ippekiro #290
ishibashi hikaru #744
ishibe akira #516
ishida fûta #407
ishihara yatsuka #488 #873
ishizuka masao #195
isobe shakusanshi?takusanko? #301
issa #123#538#235#219 #124 [chikua]
issei #343
issô #29
itami kimiko #566
itan sachiko #411
itô kitajo #5
iwamoto naoki #774
izaka tsukiko #199
izawa masae #299
jinen #128
jitsû #694
jôku? #608
k.h. #297
kadô #225
kadokawa haruki #253#817#327
kajiyama chizuko #823
kakô? #620 #456
kakubei #53
kakushi? #329
kamikura utsuwa #653
kanajo #581
kaneko kunirô #47
kanrai #313
kaori #614
karube utôshi #515#777
kasama keiko #114
kasanjo #355#147
kasei #639
katayama mitsuyo #771
katô ikuya #415
katô michiko #397
katô shizuo #127#111
katô [see: shûson]
katsura nobuko #40
katsusan #346
katsuyuki #850
katsuyuki #709
kawada jun #687#756
kawasaki nobuhiro #250 #202 #468 #684 #603 #824
kawasaki toshiko #568
kayô #621
kayoko #646

kazuki baison? #793
kazunaga fujiyo #116
keigan (keigu+tôgan) #198
keigu #25 #26 #27 #42 #43 #59
#60 #61 #62 #63 #72 #90 #91 #120
#145 #146 #156 #184 #205 #212
#216 #222 #223 #224 #255 #263
#265 #266 #267 #268 #269 #275
#276 #277 #284 #285 #287 #289
#288 #385 #426 #428 #429 #430
#44 #475 #522 #523 #529 #540
#547 #577 #578 #595 #596 #597
#598 #599 #600 #601 #617 #618
#619 #624 #632 #633 #647 #648
#649 #650 #658 #660 #661 #662
#663 #665 #666 #667 #668 #669
#670 #680 #681 #682 #705 #706
#707 #713 #716 #723 #724 #726
#727 #728 #732 #761 #762 #763
#782 #783 #784 #785 #786 #787
#788 #789 #791 #831 #832 #883
#884 #885 #886 #887 #888 #889
[also see keiten, ryôgu, tamagu]
keirô #248 #820 #867
keishi #780
keiten=keigu+tenki #256 #264
#548
keiyô #692
kenmochi shiranui #758
kenpo? #593
kijô #15 #580 #683
kikaku? #359
kiko(kiin?) #314
kikuchi hisako #389
kikyû? #809
kinukawa sunao #176 #748
kirino manjirô #701 #702 #703
kishû #87 #251 #319 #370
kita mikiko #751
kitahara hakushû #755
kitô #572
kiyota kon? #747
kobe michiyo #769
kobiyama shigeru #391
kodama koshû? #20
koizumi chiyoko #408
kojima hôseki #377
kôkai? #472
kokusui? #52
kôroku #4
kotani yukio #190
kotani yukio #64
kôtô tomoko #520
kôyû #562
kuramoto asayo #627
kurita setsuko #153 #794
kuritani (?) shôji #320 #393
kuroda getsudôkan #78
kuroda sakura no en [?] #174
kurozaka haruo #554
kusume tôkôshi #172 #745
kyorai #36
kyoroku #892
kyoshi #73 #218 #818
kyoshi et al #295 #347 #412
maeda hakuro? #739
maeda tsuruko #570
maihime #80 #483

mangetsu #731
mantarô #442
masajo #82
masaki yûko #217
masatoshi? #318
masuda harako #79
matsuki hide #11 #890
matsumoto seiki #6 #34 #194
matsumoto usei #512
matsuo yoshihisa #376
matsuzaki rakuchû #749
meimei #245
meisetsu #186
michihiko #227
michikaze #697 #698
mihoko #615
miki reiko #816
minakichi sou? #410
minami masatane #281
mino nampo? #54
misa #655
mitomo heikichi #262 #434
mitsundo #325
miyazaki shizuo #722 #753
miyazawa eiko #374
miyoko #14 #76 #278 #630
mizumi kujô #738
mizunuma saburo #814
mizuuchi keita #247 #461
mochinaga mariko #112
mofû #372
mokuto #555
mori mitsuko #49
morisaki kazuo #398 #847
moriya koga #394
murakami kijô [see kijô]
murata shûn #754
murayama seiai #326
mutaguchi akio #545
mutamagawa #261 #270 #507
nagai fumie #400
nagakata yûko #339
nagata koi #557
nagata suiko? #309
nagatsuka sumie #536
nagatsuka takashi #75
nakahara michio #444
nakamura sonoko #402
nakayama tenken #854
namu #113 #729 #708
nanchatte kurikintoki? #291
naruse ôtôshi #58 #721
nikaidô eiko #438
nobucha? #390
noburo #175
nomoto kyô #119 #875
nomura kishû [see kishû]
nomura nôton? #757
nômura toshirô #513
nonaka chiyoko #500
nonaka ryôsuke #406
nyogyô #152
ôba torao #812
obanagasa? #294
obasei #477
ôda toneri #32
ôemaru #67? #144? #234? #274
#316? #506

ogiue koichi #85 #704
ohara seiseishi #792
ohara takuyo #896
ôhashi atsuko #364 #533
ôhashi ôhashi #582
ôi toichiro #464
ôishi etsuko #84 #474 #765-B
okada hisae #248-B
okada kôyô #623 #138
okada shajin #258
okairi mantoko? #645
okamoto taimu #625
okayasu jingi #741
okazaki junrin #870
okuzaka maya #898
ônishi motoyuki #460
ôno kyôju #795
ôshi #141
ôshima   ? #735
ôta aa #171
ôta yasunao #848
ôtake kinya? #170
ôtsubo shôichi #586
otsutô? otsutaku? #74
otsuyû #530
ôuchi itsuzan #178
raiu? #19
raizan #7?
rakunan   #257,479 (same one)
rakutô #641
rangai #392
ranran #344
ransetsu #334 #143
ranyû #69
richô? toshishige? #606
rikyo (mod.?) #803
rikyo? (contemp?) #203
risetsu #282
ritô #829
riyô #640
riyû #612
roga? #589
rogetsu #121 #22
roi #312
rôka? (naniwa?) #626
rokuko? #213
rosen #550 #798 #872
rôsô #584
roya #102
ryôgu   (takasawa+keigu)   #843
#844 #845
ryôshô [ryôto, too]#139-C
ryôta #283
ryôto [ryôshô, too] #139-A,B
ryûka #77
ryûkyo #525
ryûsui #437
saida jin #656
saimaro #686
saitô kafû #575
saitô kyôrô? #718
saji #211
sakasegawa kô #772
sani? #39 #71
sanka [oops! no namako!!!] #493
sanki #405
sanyû #871
saotome ken #31-B

sarubashi tôryûshi #815
sasaki masao #459
satô fusako #659
seibi #226 #537 #781 #830
seichi #495
seihô #300 #604 #733 #837
seike nobuhiro (2001) kdb #497
seikô? #163
seira #273 #481
seiran #521
seisei #214 #458 #30 #638 #191
#868
seisei+keigu #81
seisen? #592
seisetsu #1
seishi #354
seishû/masatane #693
sekidô #642
senpû #610
seto sekiyô #177
shakufu #72
shara #838
shaseki? #622
shayô #160 #504
shibasaki akio #805
shibata akemi #773
shichiku #576 #643
shidano saka #770
shidô #583
shigeharu? #776
shiki #8 #56 #95 #103 #106 #107
#129 #130 #133 #142 #154 #239
#240 #431 #432 #509 #510 #551
#552 #602 #652
shiki+keigu #241
shiki+keigu #242
shiki+keigu+tenki #243
shikô (1703) #371
shikô (later than above) #162 #341
shimakura mitsuru #310
shimamura gen #876
shimamura hajime #68
shimanishi utata #380
shimizu akira #435 #827 #828
shimizu nobuka #363
shimokawa ___? #333
shimomura umeko #296
shinô #321
shinobugusa #304
shinsa #806
shirai tôsei #546
shirao/hakuyû cjco #711
shirô #342? #505 #574
shisui? #384
shôha #331 #502
shôhaku #231
shôka #611
shôritsu #236
shôzan #629 #340 #362
shugyô #16
shûmon #700
shunni? #345
shunpa #532
shunyô #443
shûson #401 #465 #841
sôda #644
somaru #17 #94 #332 #368 #387

someno ozuki #715
sonobe utei #752
soran #338
sôseki #209 #307 #246 (he wrote 5
or 6, some wretched)
sôshun #877
sôya #51
suetan? #695
suetsumuhana #280
sugahara sadao #117
sugemura asaka #498
sugihara chikujo #494
sugihara takejo #441
sugita chieko #543
sugiyama nozomi #206
sumi yûzo #567
sôya? shûkoku? #101
suzuka nobûro #764
suzuki jin #866
suzuki masajo #719 #865
suzuki taeko #851
tabata masuhiro #446 #447 #449
#453 #508
taigi #23 #24 #48 #50 #92 #188
#330
taigi+issa+shiki+keigu #140
taimu #531
tajiri makio #796
takagishi manabu #737
takahashi hiroko #423
takahashi mutsurô #31
takahashi yasurô #743
takai kyoshi #541
takajo #490
takano kanpo #524
takano kiyoko #768
takao ikuki #874
takasawa yoshikazu #28 #41 #66
#132 #155 #161 #164 #165 #166
#167 #180 #210 #220 #303 #324
#337 #350 #351 #352 #353 #388
#403 #416 #417 #418 #419 #420
#421 #422 #452 #470 #517 #518
#526 #528 #564 #573 #634 #651
#657 #678 #671 #672 #673 #675
#679 #674 #676 #677 #717 #797
#799 #821 #833 #842 #846 #860
#861 #895
takase hakuyô #409
takashima ___? #882
takemi? #519
takeshitsa yôichi #654
tamagu (tamasudare+keigu) #710
tamasudare #628
tamoto hokushi #802
tanabe fûshinko #311
tanabe kayoko #881
tanaka harue #249
tanaka hiromu #605
tanaka hisako #869
taniguchi mitsuko #298
tarô #323
tashiro shôi? #306
tateishi seitsuko #467
tatsuoka tsutomu #315 #616
tazumi michio #3
tenki #395 #689

terada torahiko #108 #594
tetsua #70
tetsuami #590
tochimenbô #636 #637
tôgan #96 #197
togetsu #379
toki #720
tokuda chizuko #18
tokunaga genshi? #736
tokunaga retsuko #471
tokunaga shunpû #856
tokurô #691
tomioka kikuchiro #556
tora #57
torii mariko #93 #293 #853
tôrin #685
toryû #413
tôyô #424
tôyôjô #86
tsuboi hisako #765
tsuboi yoshie #399
tsuchida kaseki #635
tsuru #189
tsuzuki momohei #463
uchiyama yoshiko #742
uda kiyoko #759
udô tôru #565
uetami shin #122
umeko #149
uoko-chan #233
usami gyomoku #13
utsunomiya den #492
wada kôji #859
wakô #150
washitani nanako #559
watanabe fumio #822
yagi chûei #486 #489
yagi rinnosuke #168 #454 #478
#834
yajima nagisaô #83
yamada mizue #840
yamada tôkô #349
yamamoto shunji #173
yamanaka ___ #857
yamane #109
yamazaki fusako #88
yamazaki kazunosuke #766
yanagidaru (=ygd) #134, #228,
#229, #271, #279-b, #336
yanma #553
yano chieko #487
yayû #105 #238
yokoyama hakukô #688
yonezawa ___? #734
yosano hiroshi #55
yoshida shino #360
yoshiro #365
yoshitomi shômei? #558
yoshiue shôryô #571
yoshiwara mubôn[?] #46
yôsui #97
yû #148
yuda kunihiro #396
yûfû #542
yuri #455
yûshi? #473
zankuro #104

TOO MUCH MONKEY BUSINESS!

Your author did his best to accomplish more, but MS-WORD ate up too much of his time. For example, adjusting double and triple columns was so slow he had to double his ram! He also wasted hours trying without success to get the above Index to accept headers; but even though every heading-related setting in "page set-up" and in "insert" and in "view" was IDENTICAL to that in files where it *does* work, it was, and still is, as good as dead. The footer space shows but even when I hit the "switch between header and footer, only the page number highlites and no header space appears even when it is clicked upon. All your author can do is cuss enough to save himself from having a stroke! He tried copying the file to another where the headers *do* work, but these triple-column files do not copy well. But even if the headers did appear, they could not vary from page to page for lack of a change of "section." Worse, the mix of languages and columns slow down the operation so much (imagine taking a half-hour to load!!) that the big book had to be split into chapters, so the "searches" of the total book needed for quick index making became impossible. MSW should learn from Nissus Writer, which is much more efficient, and Ichitaro which is far more intelligent. . .

So, other indexes are not yet ready.

Please visit paraverse.org for print-outs as soon as they become available.

metaphor index

Many Poems fit under more than one Metaphorical Heading and there are far more metaphors than chapters. In other words, when poems are linearly arranged and not repeated (though exceptions were made for some), to chose one metaphor is to lose another. This index, when completed, should help show the true affiliations of the poems. I was unable to make it before publishing the first edition. *If any reader has time on his or her hands and would like to make such an index (and claim credit for it: Your Name came be appended to it in the next edition (you can advertise your editorial services, if you like indexing)). Or, if several people wish to try, we can make it a contest. Your respective indexes can be uploaded to the site for other readers to download and grade. At any rate, please go to Paraverse.org. Indexes will be posted as they are ready.*

science index

Though I wish to neither segregate science nor pretend to introduce more than some rudiments of it in this book, a specialized index would make it easier for busy scientists to peek at their areas of expertise and, I would hope, become interested enough to add their glosses to the next edition. *Again, any volunteer for indexing?*

people index

This would be for all the people who are in the book except the poets unless they also were significant in another way. People indexes are fun. One never knows who will pop up. A few names I recall offhand (limiting myself to the Holothurian Haiku H's) – Robert Hass, Lafcadio Hearn, Piet Hein, William Higginson, Douglas Hofstadter, Hogarth, Hoshino Takashi, Zora Neale Hurston . . . *Likewise, volunteers? This one is the easiest!*

idea index

The typical index today confuses words for subjects because that is the best a computer can do. I hope to do better by remembering that subjects are, basically, ideas. The only trouble here is that there will be some redundancy with the Metaphor Index and the Science Index. *I will work on this index and post it at paraverse.org. I was not able to do it in time for this edition because of the aforementioned (and more) technical difficulties. In the meantime, I apologize for any inconvenience the lack of an index might cause.*

見逃された海鼠

Any Sea Slugs Left Behind?

In one of my Japanese language pages, I appeal to readers to help me find more sea slug haiku. I suggested areas in which I was particularly interested: Very Old Poems (I lack the access to resources and the skill, for I am not good with the "grass(script)-style writing) of whatever type; Interesting "Bad" Poems (many old anthologies are never reprinted because they are held to be worthless for this or that sin against Bashô-style proper haiku, but they often include some very amusing poems); Poems by Women (not so much because they are by women as because the sea slug is particularly under-represented among pre-modern female poets); Any Good Poem I may have overlooked or failed to introduce because of my inability to comprehend its value (in this case, I asked for an explanation, too).

Though I had already placed a copy of a page from Shiki's Categorical Collection of Haiku here in order to show how each page included 23 *namako* haiku, at this last moment (2003/9/29), I have just now deleted it to add the above paragraph because another haiku, perfectly fitting to end the book with, popped up by accident last night as I skimmed through a Spring theme called "Low-tide" – meaning the social practice of going to the beach to collect pretty things – for another book, when the pdfing of this one was put on hold until I received a decision from the printer on what font to buy (that's right! I have to buy font for $100. from Adobe because the New Times Roman in my computer is not the right type for serious printing!) This fine haiku reminds me that there are sea slugs out there, invisible to a standard search because they are outside of the Winter *Namako* theme (Shiki's hot-water-bottle was such, but thanks to his fame, I found it anyway). That is another area where I could use the help of a multitude Japanese readers to find haiku for my second edition. （季語外の海鼠もよろしく！）

足跡になまこの遊ふ潮干哉　麦浪
ashiato ni namako no asobu shiohi kana – bakurô (d.1768)
#900 (footprint/s-in/on/by seaslug/s play/s/playing tide-dry!/?/loh)

ebb-tide day
when sea slugs play
in footprints

a sea slug lies
on the footprint of
a beachcomber

sea slugs lolling
among footprints left by
shell-collectors

The verb "play" (*asobu*) can mean simply lying about not working, which, we have seen, is exactly what the sea *cucumber* we have called sea *slug* – now that the book draws to a close, readers must take care to leave the "sea *slug*" behind – does all day long. My first two readings assume the parties of shell (and starfish, I would think) collecting may still be going on. Some people walk in the shallow water, or the tide has come up far enough that footprints, theoretically speaking, now lie on the sea floor. Though the original does not mention that the event is past, it may be that the tide has completely turned and "ebb-tide" stands for the entire day and its activities, which will be described in the first Spring volume of *In Praise of Olde Haiku*.

夫婦の
初海鼠
？

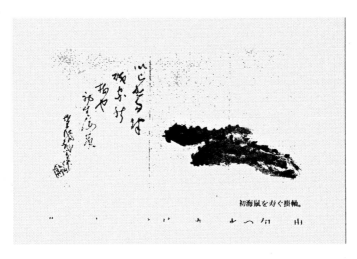

初海鼠を寿ぐ掛軸。

This is a photo of a fine hanging scroll of the first pair of *namako,* symbolizing the first sea cucumber of the year (of the two, three and of three all?) that is reproduced in a tiny 1x2" format in the preface of Tsurumi Yoshiyuki's *Namako no Manako* (the sea cucumber's eye=nnm). One email failed to find out more information about it　ー　鶴見良行の『ナマコの眼』の「はじめに」にあるこの掛軸に対する情報もちおられば、ご連絡下さい！メオトなまこみたいのを暖かく描くこの傑作、のいい複製を見たいし、その上に書いてある句（？）を読みたい！一度は、出版社に e-mail を送ったが。。。　　　　誰か、よろしくお願いします！

478

pre-publication comments for rise, ye sea slugs!

b l u r b

From Haiku: "*Keigu (the author's haiku name) is not interested in making yet another collection of masterpiece haiku. He would create an exhibition of sea cucumber [namako] and haiku or, to put it another way, a museum of poetic language.*" – Saibara Tenki, host of informal on-line haiku "pub" Ukimidô. (note: a full explanation of why "sea *cucumbers*" become "sea slugs" is within the book.)

From Literature: "*Uke Namako (the Japanese title) is the most touching, fun, erudite, and altogether enjoyable thing I have read in ages. It is also the most intelligent approach to Japanese poetry I think I have ever seen.* – Liza Dalby, anthropologist and author of *Tale of Murasaki* (and other fine Japan-related fiction and nonfiction, including *Kimono* and *Geisha*)

From Science: "*It's amazing; I absolutely love it. I've spent many years studying my little friends and have always felt that they have been unkindly maligned or forgotten. The contrast between Japanese and European literature on cukes [sea cucumbers] couldn't be greater . . . Alas, the divide between science and literature, even in terminology much less in theory, is quite vast at points and I admire your blending of the two in a deep and satisfying way.*" – Dr. Alexander Kerr, evolutionary biologist, James Cook University).

From Academia: *On some pristine level, the argument is you never thought sea slugs could be interesting and you already see (after 20, 30, 50 pages) you're wrong, right? To really nail this kind of argument you want (I think, even if you don't quite need) a heavy load. Maybe 400 going on 500 pages? I don't mean to sound demanding, but it just keeps getting better . . .*"– Japanese medieval poetry scholar and polymath Lewis Cook (CUNY and Columbia). RDG: L.C. should be happy to see this ended up over 1,100,000 characters! He also cautioned me to tone down a bit, but I fear I have not been very successful at that!.

From the Author: *How funny to think that with this one book not only will the number of haiku about sea cucumber (namako) translated into English multiply a hundred-fold, but the sea cucumber will become the most translated haiku theme in the English language, for it is unlikely that any of the most popular themes (cherry blossoms, summer heat, cicada, the fall moon, crickets, scarecrows, and snow?) enjoy an equal number of translations. I hope haiku powers on both sides of the Pacific forgive me and namako our gross distortion of their world!*

著者 About the Author – robin d. gill

Gill, who grew up on Key Biscayne, Florida, is a well-known author in Japan, where he had 7 books published by top Japanese presses, including Chikuma Shobo, Hakusuisha and Kousakusha. This is his first book in his native tongue. Visit Paraverse.org for reviews of previous books and information on a score of forthcoming books, some of which are mentioned in *RISE!* Because your infidel shares a first and last name with a frightfully prolific theologian writer, he would greatly appreciate it if all citations could include his middle initial and small letters, if possible – namely, "robin d. gill."

要約 A Simple Synopsis

The traditional **haiku** is a **seven-beat poem with a seasonal connection**. The *namako,* or **sea cucumber** – Englished as "*sea slug*" for brevity's sake, with apologies to biologists – is **a winter theme**, because that is when it is most active and eaten in the part of Japan where haiku came of age. With almost **1000 haiku**, of which less than a dozen have been previously translated, this book is **far and away the deepest study of a single haiku theme** (*kigo*) **ever published,** yet it is also a light-hearted romp through science, metaphysics and literature reminiscent of Borges, Burton, Carlyle, De La Mare, Montaigne, and Sterne. Each of the 21 chapters is devoted to a **metaphorical category** such as *Cold Sea Slugs, Featureless Sea Slugs, Lubricious Sea Slugs, Meek Sea Slugs, Melancholy Sea Slugs, Protean Sea Slugs* and *Sleepy Sea Slugs,* while scores of minor sub-themes, including such disparate categories as *analytical sea slugs, dream sea slugs, imagist sea slugs, medicinal sea slugs, [mole] exorcist sea slugs, lava sea slugs and waste-treatment engineer sea slugs*, are more lightly essayed in a 150-page *Sundry Sea Slugs* section. **Following Blyth, the original Japanese is provided for all of the poems.** The title comes from a challenging haiku by Issa (#219 in this book) expressing his (and the author's) affection for the lowly, meek and plain.

RISE, YE SEA SLUGS! will be an immediate classic,

for it proves that 500 pages (if printed with a normal-sized footprint, it would be 1,000 pages!) of **translated sea cucumber poetry can be as entertaining as a good novel. (Please feel free to disagree!** *The author asks critics not to pull any punches,* but to **be prepared for counter-punches, for** *he loves to argue.*)

句数 Actually, only **900-odd haiku** (and senryu/tanka/kyôka) are included in this edition, but *at least a 1000 haiku* will be in the final edition.

表紙 In case a library covers the cover, it has an old illustration of sea slug dragging on the back

and a tasteful photo of sea cucumber ossicles by Dr Mike Reich, Centre of Geosciences, University of Göttingen, Germany, in front. I apologize for changes I made to it for POD printing! The original is beautiful grey!

印刷 Printed by Lightningsource (distrib Ingram, Baker &Taylor, etc.), **ISBN# is 0-9742618-0-7**

and the recommended retail price is **only $25.** for the time being, but check at **paraverse org.**

This illustration found in Arakawa Kohman's *Namako Dokuhon* (ndh), or, "handbook on the japanese sea cucumber," goes back to a 1955 article in a Russian magazine. Igor Dolmatov emailed me that the (to me undecipherable) Japanese citation "domitorieba: 1955" meant what I have hand-written in the book, above. Do you agree with me that the way the spawn rises, one gets the impression that aerosol cans are reproducing themselves? Contrast this with the stuff dripping down the sea cucumbers' heads in the Palau photograph on the bottom of the first page of this book! I am not certain what to make of this spectacular difference.

Printed in the United States
23813LVS00002B/71